HANDBOOK
OF
College
Science
TEACHING

HANDBOOK OF College Science TEACHING

Joel J. Mintzes and William H. Leonard, Editors

NATIONAL SCIENCE TEACHERS ASSOCIATION

Arlington, Virginia

NATIONAL SCIENCE TEACHERS ASSOCIATION

Claire Reinburg, Director
Judy Cusick, Senior Editor
Andrew Cocke, Associate Editor
Betty Smith, Associate Editor
Robin Allan, Book Acquisitions Coordinator

Will Thomas, Jr., Art Director
Tracey Shipley, Assistant Art Director, Cover and Inside Design

PRINTING AND PRODUCTION Catherine Lorrain, Director
Nguyet Tran, Assistant Production Manager
Jack Parker, Electronic Prepress Technician

NATIONAL SCIENCE TEACHERS ASSOCIATION
Gerald F. Wheeler, Executive Director
David Beacom, Publisher

LIBRARY OF CONGRESS CATALOGING-IN-PUBLICATION DATA

Handbook of college science teaching / Joel J. Mintzes and William H. Leonard, editors.
    p. cm.
 Includes bibliographical references and index.
 ISBN-13: 978-0-87355-260-8
 1. Science--Study and teaching (Higher)--United States--Handbooks, manuals, etc. I. Mintzes, Joel J.
II. Leonard, William H., 1941-
Q183.3.A1H35 2006
507.1'1--dc22
                              2006015957

CONTENTS

UNIT I

UNIT II

UNIT III

Factors Affecting Learning   107

UNIT IV

UNIT V

UNIT VI

UNIT VII

UNIT VIII

Preface

Joel J. Mintzes and William H. Leonard

The *Handbook of College Science Teaching* was developed for college and university faculty who teach a wide range of natural science courses, including those offered in traditional departments of biology, chemistry, Earth and space sciences, and physics and also in the health sciences, engineering, and computer and information technology. The *Handbook* was conceived by the editors in early 2005 out of a recognition that, although most college and university science faculty have had extensive preparation in their subject discipline, they have had little or no theoretical preparation in teaching their subject other than their own teaching experiences. Generic handbooks for college teaching have been published (see, e.g., Prichard and Sawyer 1994), but none specifically for the teaching of natural sciences.

Nonetheless, we have found that college and university science faculty do seek resources and information to make their teaching more effective and the learning of their students more successful. Some of the traditional sources of ideas about teaching have been the science teaching journals: *American Biology Teacher, Journal of Chemical Education, Journal of Geoscience Education, The Physics Teacher,* and especially *Journal of College Science Teaching.* Although these journals remain useful sources, there is to date no single volume devoted exclusively to current ideas on teaching approaches for college and university faculty. Thus, this *Handbook* fills a unique niche in assisting science faculty who wish to make their courses more effective learning experiences for students.

A handbook such as this could be done in at least two ways. One way is to map out the content in advance by identifying desired chapters (such as laboratory teaching, field teaching, lecture instruction, meeting the needs of special students, and assessment) and then finding authors with special expertise in those specific areas. We chose instead a more eclectic approach, issuing a national call for proposals through the network of the National Science Teachers Association and its affiliate, the Society for College Science Teachers. A portion of this call for proposals is reprinted below:

The development of a new resource book for college science teachers has been launched by the National Science Teachers Association (NSTA). We invite proposals from the college science teaching community and from science educators for manuscripts on contemporary topics of college science teaching. Each manuscript will represent a chapter of the book. These can include quantitative or qualitative research studies; research summaries in specific subjects such as biology, chemistry, Earth and space sciences, or physics; or generalized studies about most or all of science learning. Well-documented position papers, descriptions of innovative teaching and learning methods, meta-analyses, and historical perspectives are also encouraged. Authors will receive a modest honorarium and full academic and intellectual credit for their published contributions. The areas for which we invite manuscripts are:

- Learning Theory and Study Strategies
- Learning Styles and Learning Preferences
- Improving Instruction in Large Classes

- Active Learning
- Small Group Learning
- Laboratory and Field Learning
- Uses of Computer Technology
- Science for Nonmajors
- Alternative Assessment and Evaluation Strategies
- Reading, Writing, and Literacy
- Nonformal Settings
- Case Studies

Over 80 chapter proposals were received by the deadline and several more proposals and inquiries thereafter. Of these, the editors selected 38 that they thought appropriate, very useful, and well articulated. These proposals also represented a diverse treatment of important and contemporary issues and strategies for teaching the sciences in colleges and universities. We then asked the 38 proposers to write their chapters. The resulting chapters were reviewed, and recommendations (usually minor) for revisions were communicated to the authors. The chapters were then assembled into the following topical units:

I. Attitudes and Motivation
II. Active Learning
III. Factors Affecting Learning
IV. Innovative Teaching Approaches
V. Use of Technology
VI. Meeting Special Challenges
VII. Pre-College Science Instruction
VIII. Improving Instruction

Although this eclectic approach produced something of a "hodgepodge" of topics, the editors feel that the volume is representative of a wide range of issues and questions about science teaching that are currently on the minds of many college and university science teachers. Indeed, some of the manuscripts represent passionate views, though nearly all chapters were grounded in research on teaching. Most chapters were written by scientists from a disciplinary perspective (e.g., biology, chemistry, or physics); however, most of the ideas are relatively generic and potentially transferable across disciplines.

The editors wish to thank the chapter authors for taking many days out of their academic lives to write the chapters. We wish also to thank them for their tremendous creativity and talents. Without the volunteer efforts of the authors, this *Handbook* would not have been possible. We wish also to thank NSTA Press for its willingness to publish the *Handbook*.

We welcome feedback from readers of the *Handbook* about the usefulness and interest level of the chapters they read. In anticipation of a possible Volume II of the *Handbook*, we invite your suggestions for potential new chapters.

Reference

Prichard, K. W., and R. M. Sawyer. 1994. *Handbook of college teaching: Theory and applications.* Westport, CT: Greenwood Press.

Endorsement of the Society for College Science Teachers

At the beginning of the 21st century, we are looking at the continued expansion of scientific knowledge and the increasing impact of science and technology in our daily lives. The previous century was a time of increased mechanization and educational methods that equipped people to be consumers of knowledge and followers of directions, but our students face a century where the major commodity is information and creating knowledge and problem solving are the skills that will be most important to them. One hundred years ago, the medium for transferring knowledge was print or face-to-face storytelling and therefore slow; memorizing information was a valuable skill. Now, information flows freely and rapidly, and students need the skills to interpret, analyze, judge, modify, add to, and communicate information.

Early in the last century, John Dewey provided great insight into how students learn and how we should teach; at the beginning of this century, the National Research Council summarized much of the current understanding of how students learn. Much has changed and much has stayed the same. Acceptance of constructivism has led to the use of collaborative learning groups, case-based and problem-based learning, and a variety of other techniques to encourage students' active participation in the classroom. Recognition that learning about the process of science is important has led to inquiry-based laboratories and service learning. Research on motivation, attitudes, and learning styles and the recognition of student diversity along many dimensions have resulted in a call for more student-centered teaching. Availability of new technologies offers great potential to increase access and student learning but requires adapting and developing teaching strategies to make these tools effective.

For every answer to questions about teaching and learning, another question emerges and some general questions remain. How can we take what research has shown us about teaching and learning and convert it to classroom practices at the college level? How can we adapt our teaching to our students' needs so that the outcome is students who are motivated to learn, are inquisitive, and are effective problem solvers? How can we do this in the face of the demands on our time and the constraints imposed by the graduate education that most of us received, which was primarily focused on our scientific research?

When Bill Leonard and Joel Mintzes approached the Executive Board of the Society for College Science Teachers with the idea for this book, we saw a plan for a great tool to help college science teachers increase their effectiveness in the classroom through an understanding of research-based pedagogy. The product clearly matched our expectations. The *Handbook of College Science Teaching* provides insight into what motivates students, what interferes with or facilitates their learning of science, what techniques and current technologies best serve students' needs, and what challenges students and teachers face. The members of the Executive Board are proud to have been associated with this project and hope you are as pleased with the result as we are.

Executive Board, Society for College Science Teachers
Donald P. French, President 2005–2007

About the Editors

Joel J. Mintzes has been a college biology teacher for 32 years, the last 27 of them as professor in the Department of Biology and Marine Biology at the University of North Carolina Wilmington. He earned BS and MS degrees in biology at the University of Illinois at Chicago and a PhD in biological science education at Northwestern University. His research focuses on conceptual development and cognitive processes in biology, and environmental education. He has served on editorial boards of the *Journal of Research in Science Teaching* and *Science Education,* as guest editor of the Special Issue on Learning of the *International Journal of Science and Mathematics Education,* and as co-editor (with James H. Wandersee and Joseph D. Novak) of two books, *Teaching Science for Understanding* and *Assessing Science Understanding: A Human Constructivist View* (Elsevier Academic Press 2005). In addition, Dr. Mintzes served as director of research of the Private Universe Project at the Harvard-Smithsonian Center for Astrophysics; lead fellow of the College Level One Team at the National Institute for Science Education, University of Wisconsin–Madison; visiting professor at the Homi Bhaba Centre for Science Education of the National Institute for Fundamental Research (Bombay, India); visiting scholar in the Ecology Department at Providence University in Taiwan; and Fulbright-Technion Fellow at the Israel Institute of Technology in Haifa. He teaches courses in general biology, cell biology, and zoology and a seminar on cognition, evolution, and behavior.

William "Bill" H. Leonard is professor of science education emeritus at Clemson University in South Carolina. He has bachelor's and master's degrees in biology from San Jose State University and a PhD in biology education from the University of California at Berkeley. Bill has also been on the faculty in both biology and education at Louisiana State University and the University of Nebraska-Lincoln, and was a high school biology teacher in San Jose, California. Among the courses he has taught in higher education have been General Biology, Evolutionary Biology, Conceptual Themes in Biology, Science Teaching Methods, Research in Science Teaching, Teaching Science Through Inquiry, and Directed Research. Dr. Leonard is the author of nearly 200 articles and chapters in science education journals, monographs, and resource books. He was a coauthor of several secondary science curricula, including Environmental Science; BSCS Biology: An Ecological Approach; and Biology: A Community Context and a general biology laboratory text, *Laboratory Investigations in Biology.* He was editor of the Teaching and Research Section of the *Journal of College Science Teaching* (JCST) from 1991 to 2005 and has served on the Publications Review Board for JCST, *American Biology Teacher,* and *The Science Teacher.* He has twice served as director-at-large for the National Association of Biology Teachers. He has received several university-wide awards for both research and teaching.

Dedication and Acknowledgments

The *Handbook of College Science Teaching* is dedicated to all teachers of the natural sciences and allied fields in higher education worldwide. These teachers work diligently to craft modern courses in their fields of expertise and with quality pedagogy—all at a time when it is clear that research and grant production often represent the largest share of how they are rewarded, especially at research universities. It is hoped that the *Handbook* will give college and university teachers research-based ideas to make the learning of their students more productive and effective.

The editors wish to thank the National Science Teachers Association for quickly and willingly accepting this project and for its efforts in the final production, publishing, and marketing of the *Handbook*.

Attitudes and Motivation

Science anxiety has been shown to seriously impede student learning. —Jeffry V. Mallow

Research indicates a positive correlation between achievement in science courses and attitude toward science. —Donald P. French and Connie Russell

All instructors have a stake in determining how students learn science best, what feelings characterize them during learning, and why some students become autonomous lifelong science learners while others do not. —Shawn M. Glynn and Thomas R. Koballa, Jr.

For most of us who spend years in and out of college science classrooms, the joy of encouraging meaningful and lasting learning is one of our most important professional rewards. In many cases we chose teaching because we experienced a particularly supportive teacher who stimulated our interest in science and motivated us to devote our lives to it. In some ways, college science teachers are the "success stories" of previous college science teachers. But what about those large numbers of students who need motivational assistance or suffer debilitating anxiety in the course of studying science? What if anything can we do to help?

We begin this book with a unit on attitudes and motivation, believing that all learning starts with feelings. Psychologists refer to the world of feelings and emotions as the *affective domain* (Krathwohl, Bloom, and Masia 1973), and most believe that establishing a "meaningful learning set" (Ausubel, Novak, and Hanesian 1978) or receptive mental state depends heavily on how we feel about the subject we intend to study.

In this unit, Jeffry Mallow describes his pioneering work on *science anxiety*. Working in the Physics Department at Loyola University Chicago, he tells of his own students' struggles with this debilitating condition, its causes and effects, its widespread occurrence in students, research he and others have conducted on it, and what college science teachers can do to counteract it. Included in the chapter is a copy of the Science Anxiety Questionnaire, which college science teachers can use to identify this condition in their own students.

Don French and Connie Russell, at Oklahoma State University and Angelo State University (Texas), respectively, describe their efforts to *improve student attitudes through a student-centered pedagogy* that focuses on generating and answering important biological questions. Using a combination of interesting scenarios, mini-lectures, and collaborative activities that employ animation and other multimedia presentations, students are guided to generate and answer questions through discussion, formative assessment, and laboratory investigation. Results of a study that evaluates the effects of the new format on student attitudes are presented.

Shawn Glynn and Tom Koballa of the University of Georgia review some of the basic constructs of *motivation*. The fundamental distinction between intrinsic and extrinsic motivation is described, and factors that affect students' motivation to learn science are explained. Included in the chapter is a copy of the Science Motivation Questionnaire, *which college instructors may use in their own classes.*

References

Ausubel, D. P., J. D. Novak, and H. Hanesian. 1978. *Educational psychology: A cognitive view.* 2nd ed. New York: Holt, Rinehart and Winston.

Krathwohl, D. R., B. S. Bloom, and B. B. Masia. 1964. *Taxonomy of educational objectives: The classification of educational goals. Handbook II. The affective domain.* New York: David McKay.

CHAPTER 1

Science Anxiety: Research and Action

Jeffry V. Mallow

Jeffry V. Mallow is professor of physics at Loyola University Chicago. He earned a PhD in astrophysics at Northwestern University and conducts research on quantum theory and on gender and science. He teaches liberal arts physics, modern physics, and quantum mechanics.

S cience anxiety has been shown to seriously impede student learning. This chapter will describe research done on science anxiety and will explain specific actions that college science teachers can take to build the confidence of their students.

In 1977, I identified the phenomenon for which I coined the term *science anxiety*. It usually manifests itself as a crippling panic on exams in science classes, but it is distinct from general test or performance anxiety. Students suffering from science anxiety are often calm and productive in their nonscience courses, including their mathematics courses.

The first Science Anxiety Clinic was founded at Loyola University Chicago (Mallow 1978). Techniques that we developed in the clinic reduce science anxiety by blending three separate approaches: (1) science skills learning, (2) changing of students' negative self-thoughts, and (3) desensitization, through muscle relaxation, to science anxiety–producing scenarios (Mallow 1986). Several studies were carried out with students at the Loyola University Science Anxiety Clinic (Alvaro 1978; Hermes 1985) to assess its effectiveness. A variety of instruments were used, including three questionnaires: the Mathematics Anxiety Rating Scale (Richardson and Suinn 1972), a general anxiety measure (Spielberger, Gorsuch, and Lushene 1970), and a general academic test anxiety measure (Alpert and Haber 1960). In addition, the students' muscle tension was measured by electromyography while they imagined science anxiety scenarios, such as taking a physics test. Alvaro (1978) developed a Science Anxiety Questionnaire. She, and subsequently Hermes (1985), demonstrated that significant decreases in anxiety, measured by this instrument, by electromyography, and by the questionnaires described above, occurred for students in clinic groups over those in control groups.

Causes of Science Anxiety

The causes of science anxiety are varied. Numerous anecdotal reports suggest that students receive negative messages about science throughout their school careers. Many, if not most, of the science teachers in the lower grades believe the same myth as much of the rest of society: that the talent necessary for doing science is given only to a select few. High school counselors often advise students to avoid more than the minimum science, especially physics, to keep their grade average high and thus improve their chances of getting into college.

Students frequently receive little or no training in analytical thinking in the early school years, and even through high school. Memorization is stressed to the detriment of other skills. Science courses in the lower grades are generally descriptive. Emphasis is often on the "gee-whiz" kinds of demonstrations that keep students interested without teaching them very much. The true nature of science as a puzzle to be solved is not made clear. Confronted with the reality of science, many students become anxious.

Teachers may also provoke anxiety. Who, for example, is teaching physics, the least populated of high school science courses? An American Institute of Physics (AIP) study at the beginning of this millennium (AIP 2001) yielded the startling statistic that only 47% of the people teaching physics in high school had either a minor or more in physics or physics education; only 33% had a bachelor's degree with a physics or physics education major. Who are the others, what are they teaching, and what view of science do they communicate? Are they themselves anxious?

Science anxiety is affected by role models, or the lack thereof. Despite marked decreases in some gender disparities in science study, males and females still follow traditional patterns (Mallow 1994, 1998), with physics the field with the fewest female students (Tobias, Urry, and Venkatesan 2002). The low numbers of female (and minority) physics teachers depresses the number of students who might see themselves as future physicists. For the 2000–2001 academic year, only 29% of high school physics teachers were women (AIP 2001); the percentage of female faculty in all university physics departments was 10% in 2002, up from 6% in 1994. Although these numbers have improved over the last few years, there is still sufficient disparity to discourage young women from considering physics as a career. In addition, high school counselors still selectively steer females away from math and science. This appears to be true for female as well as male counselors, and it is not restricted to the United States.

Last but not least in the science anxiety pantheon are the still-prevalent stereotypes of the scientist: male, geeky, intelligent but boring, hardly a role model (Rahm and Charbonneau 1997). Vedelsby (1991) documented these stereotypes in Denmark, even among science students. "They are little boys with round glasses, and they always look boring. We call them owls." was the comment of a female medical student about physics students. Universities are still divided into humanities and sciences—in different buildings and rarely interacting with each other. More than a few humanities professors still promulgate the stereotype of the warm artistic soul versus the cold scientific brain. (The Austrian modernist writer Robert Musil satirized this attitude in his novel *The Man Without Qualities*, in which he says, "What is a soul? It is easy to define negatively: it is simply that which sneaks off at the mention of algebraic series.")

Science Anxiety Research

Instrument and Analysis

The Science Anxiety Questionnaire (Alvaro 1978; Mallow 1986, 1994; Udo et al. 2001), used in all of our research studies, is a 44-item questionnaire that asks students to imagine themselves in certain situations and to rate their level of anxiety on a 5-degree scale: "not at all," "a little," "a fair amount," "much," or "very much." Items are evenly divided between science and nonscience content, with emphasis on analogous situations, such as studying for a science exam versus studying for a humanities exam. The questionnaire is provided at the end of this chapter as an appendix.

We analyzed the questionnaires in two ways: (1) by multiple regression analysis on all responses and (2) by chi-square analysis on "acute anxiety": the number of students who gave "much" or "very much" responses to one or more of the 44 items. This acute anxiety was characterized as "general anxiety" if there were "much" or "very much" responses to any item. Acute general anxiety was then subdivided into acute science anxiety: "much" or "very much" responses to any of the 22 science items, and acute nonscience anxiety: "much" or "very much" responses to any of the 22 nonscience items. Figure 1.1 summarizes the terminology of science anxiety.

The Role of Gender and Nationality

In U.S. science anxiety clinics, the majority of the clientele has been female. Chiarelott and Czerniak (1985, 1987) discovered that science anxiety starts as soon as children begin to learn science: age 8 or younger in the United States. Greater science anxiety among girls begins at the same time.

Contemporaneous with our activities, a group of female physics teachers was doing similar work in Denmark (Beyer et al. 1988). I undertook a study to investigate whether science anxiety was related to gender, and whether it varied across national lines, between American and Danish students (Mallow 1994). I found that in both groups, females scored higher on science anxiety than did males. Science anxiety proved also to be related to general anxiety and to field of study, with nonscience students (not surprisingly) having more anxiety. For those students who expressed acute science anxiety (giving "much" or "very much" responses to one or more of the science items), Danish females and males registered lower anxiety than their American counterparts of the same gender. Furthermore, Danish females registered slightly lower than American males (see Figure 1.2). These results suggest several conclusions. First, there is little likelihood of a "natural" female tendency toward science anxiety. Second, remediation attempts, both pedagogical and psychological, that are effective for one gender should be effective for both; the same is true for different nationalities. This has been shown to be the case in the American science anxiety clinic (Alvaro 1978; Hermes 1985) and in the Danish classroom (Beyer et al. 1988).

In a subsequent study (Mallow 1995), I considered the national differences in anxiety discussed above and examined whether the nature of science teaching plays a role. Do the Danish teachers make different choices in the classroom than their American counterparts? The American Association of Physics Teachers (AAPT) created a workshop, Developing Student Confidence in Physics (Fuller et al. 1985), to assess and modify teachers' styles. One of its features is a Personal Self-

Figure 1.1

Terminology of Science Anxiety

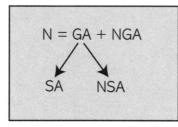

N = total sample; GA = generally anxious (number of students who gave at least one "much" or "very much" response to any science or nonscience question); NGA = not generally anxious (number of students who did not give any "much" or "very much" responses); SA = science anxious (number of students who gave at least one "much" or "very much" response to any science question); NSA = nonscience anxious (number of students who gave at least one "much" or "very much" response to any nonscience question, but not to any science question).

Figure 1.2

Percentage of Science-Anxious (SA) Students Among Generally Anxious (GA) Samples, From Science Anxiety Questionnaire

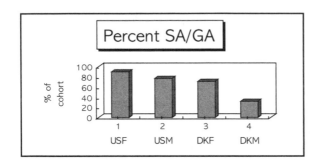

Ranking from most to least anxious: U.S. females (USF), U.S. males (USM), Danish females (DKF), Danish males (DKM). SA students answered "much" or "very much" to any of the 22 science questions. GA students answered "much" or "very much" to any of the 44 questions.

Inventory—a questionnaire describing various classroom scenarios and asking teachers to select their most likely responses. The inventory has been administered at national meetings of both the Danish Association of Physics Teachers (Fysiklærerforeningen) and the AAPT. Danish and American teaching practices sampled by the questionnaire do not seem to differ significantly and cannot therefore account for the lower Danish science anxiety. One possible explanation may simply be that constant exposure to science, from the early school years, makes Danish students more confident than American students. Another possibility is that Danish students keep the same teachers throughout primary school; this relationship itself might build confidence. Some U.S. elementary schools have begun experimenting with this method. Note, however, that neither greater exposure nor closer relationship to the teacher reduces the gender differences in science confidence. There is considerable evidence that even sensitive teachers exhibit different behaviors to male and female students in both Denmark and the United States (and probably many other countries).

Using our Science Anxiety Questionnaire, Brownlow and her co-workers studied science anxiety in a group of American university students (Brownlow, Jacobi, and Rogers 2000). For their cohort, gender turned out not to be a significant predictor of science anxiety. However, females who were science anxious assessed their ability to do science less positively than males and took fewer science courses. Beyer and colleagues (1988) observed similar gender differences in Danish students.

The Role of Science Courses

We have examined the effect of an introductory physics course on science anxiety. Our cohort consisted of Loyola University students enrolled in introductory physics courses for nonscience students, for pre-health and biology students, for chemistry students, and for physics and pre-engineering students. The Science Anxiety Questionnaire was administered unannounced on both the first day (pretest) and last day (posttest) of each class. This study (Udo et al. 2001) confirmed the results of the earlier study (Mallow 1994): The best predictor of science anxiety is nonscience anxiety; the next best is gender. Our pre- and posttest results showed that an introductory physics course tended to somewhat reduce acute science anxiety (see Figure 1.3). (We also found that nonscience anxiety decreased.) We found that different pedagogies, as well as gender role models, may correlate with anxiety reduction. Males taught by a man in an interactive physics course (lecture and demonstration plus group work) reaped some additional benefit, as did females in an interactive course taught by a woman. Finally, we discovered that anxious females tended to stay in their physics courses, whereas anxious males tended to drop out. This corroborates the findings of Seymour and Hewitt (2000) as to why students, male and female, choose to stay in or to leave science.

Figure 1.3

Changes in Acute Science Anxiety in a Semester of Physics

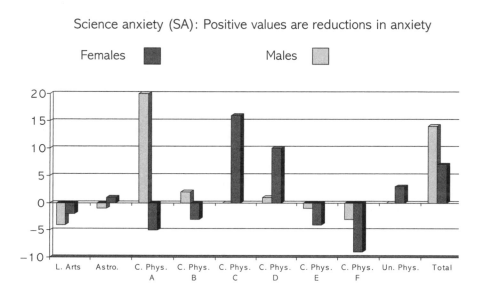

L. Arts = Liberal Arts Physics, algebra-geometry based, for nonscience majors; Astro = Astronomy, algebra-geometry based, for nonscience majors; C. Phys = College Physics, algebra-trigonometry based, for biology and pre-health students (there are six sections, labeled A–F); Un. Phys = University Physics, calculus based, primarily for chemistry majors.

We have also measured science anxiety among university students taking required science courses for nonscience majors (Udo et al. 2004). We administered the Science Anxiety Questionnaire to several hundred humanities, social science, mathematics, business, education, and nursing students who were taking courses in biology, chemistry, and physics. (A few science majors also turned up in these courses. We include them for completeness in our results [Figure 1.4], but their absolute numbers were not significant.)

Comparing the results shown in Figure 1.4 with our earlier studies of science students (Udo et al. 2001), we conclude that

- Nonscience students, both female and male, are very science anxious, with acute anxiety percentages ranging as high as 88% of a group. Among the most science anxious students are our education majors, still almost all female, the teachers of the next generation. We also found that nonscience students are not only more science anxious but also more generally anxious than science students.
- Gender differences in acute science anxiety are especially significant among nonscience students.

A summary of the work in gender and science anxiety, as well as discussion of related issues, can be found in *Gender Issues in Physics/Science Education (GIPSE)* (Mallow and Hake 2002), a continually updated online list of references dealing with gender and science.

Figure 1.4

Acute Science Anxiety (SA) in Students in Various Majors

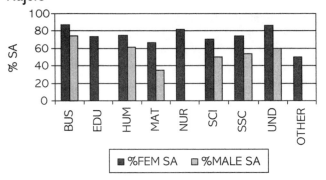

The percentage of students reporting acute science anxiety, in each course of study: BUS = business; EDU = education; HUM = humanities; MAT = mathematics; NUR = nursing; SCI = science; SSC = social science; UND = undeclared major.

But What Do We Do Monday Morning?

A variety of practices can help alleviate science anxiety. Nine recommended practices are discussed in this section.

1. *Explicit science skills teaching.* Frequently, students have been taught only the skill of memorization, which is not effective in understanding science. They must therefore be taught, for example, that one needs to read science differently from history or literature (Mallow 1991); that there are particular techniques for organizing and solving word problems; and that there are special ways to take notes in science classes, to perform effectively in science laboratories, and to take quizzes and examinations (Mallow 1986). Females in particular need to recognize that their learning depends on asking questions in and out of class and that they must have hands-on laboratory experiences.

2. *Group work.* This has been shown to enhance student performance and to improve retention in the major and at the university (Gautreau and Novemsky 1997; Hake 1998; Heller, Keith, and Anderson 1992; Mazur 1997; Meltzer and Manivannan 1996; Michaelsen et al. 1982; Treisman 1992). There is also an important gender component in group work. Females report that they prefer group projects to traditional lectures, because of the interactive, cooperative components and the control of individual competition (Beyer 1992; Legge 1997; Mallow 1993).

3. *Theme-based curricula.* Drawing students into science through themes is an effective way of providing them with a comfortable classroom environment. To do this in a whole course may be a fairly radical departure from the norm. It has, however, been successfully applied elsewhere (Beyer 1992). It can in any case be introduced as one element of a course (Mallow, Forthcoming).

4. *Attention to wait time and gender equity in calling on students.* When faculty pause frequently during lectures, students absorb significantly more information (Ruhl, Hughes, and Schloss 1987). Pauses for questions and discussion must be longer to invoke female responses (Didion 1997). In particular, when a teacher asks a question, he or she must wait at least 10 seconds for a reply (Fuller et al. 1985). The teacher must be especially vigilant about distributing the questions equally to both genders. Keeping a written record of which students have been called on is very helpful.

5. *"Catch students doing something right!"* (Fuller et al. 1985). The version of this approach that I have found effective is to stay with the student who has been questioned, work backward through Socratic dialogue until the student reaches the last concept that he or she understood, and then move forward to eliciting the right answer.

6. *Gender-equitable laboratory practice.* Most science teachers have observed male students' eagerness to play with (and break) equipment, contrasted with females' anxiety about doing the same. The remedy is careful monitoring of laboratory group practice, to make sure that groups are not divided into scientists and secretaries.

7. *Balancing content and relationship in teacher-student interactions.* The AAPT workshop (Fuller et al. 1985) focuses on four aspects of teaching:

   1. the classroom learning environment,
   2. information transfer between teacher and student,
   3. teacher-student interaction, and
   4. teachers' evaluations of student performance.

   The learning environment includes body language, tone of voice, word selection, and classroom organization by the teacher. Information transfer deals with all aspects of content, from course ground rules to teaching techniques, and how these can affect student confidence. Teacher-student interaction focuses primarily on the technique known as active listening, helping teachers modify their listening styles so that they hear the student's whole agenda, not simply the one he or she presents. Even such subtle but critical items as placement of chairs in the teacher's office are important. Finally, evaluation of student performance deals not only with fair and effective grading but also with the nature of comments on papers and tests and how these comments can diminish or enhance student confidence.

   The workshop also deals specifically with issues of females and underrepresented minorities in the science classroom. Workshop "graduates" are then expected to bring these techniques not only to their own classrooms but to their colleagues as well. As noted earlier, I have used the workshop materials for binational comparison studies of teachers' styles in the United States and Denmark (Mallow 1995). Several hundred teachers in at least two countries have benefited from training in science anxiety reduction. The workshop manual is available from AAPT.

8. *Explicit focus on metacognition.* Effective learning has been shown to be highly correlated with the use of metacognitive or self-regulatory skills (Beyer 1992). Monitoring "how we learn what we learn" can lower students' anxieties in the classroom, while providing a unique way for students to process the material they are learning. This "stepping back" helps demystify the learning of science and undercuts the myth that there is a special, rare, and unteachable talent needed for doing so.

9. *Response to the wide variety of student learning styles.* This practice encompasses many of the other recommendations. The more multimodal the classroom—lecture, demonstra-

tions, group work, brief writing exercises, Socratic dialogue—the more students will be engaged and the less estranged and fearful they will be.

Conclusion

It is clear that college science teachers have a daunting challenge. Despite the numerous exceptions, many of our students come to us with the baggage of poorly taught pre-college science, lack of appropriate role models, and societal prejudices. This baggage is both cognitive and emotional. Thus, our task is not only to teach, but to teach in a way that will overcome students' anxieties. In addition to including confidence building in our own pedagogy, we need to increase collaborations such as university-sponsored inservice training courses for K–12 science teachers. Science anxiety reduction should become an integral part of such programs. We must be especially aware of the high level of anxiety among education majors, our future teachers. If we can succeed with them, then we will have taken an important step toward improvement of science education for the coming generations.

Appendix
Science Anxiety Questionnaire

Date:_____   Name:_____

The items in the questionnaire refer to things and experiences that may cause fear or apprehension. For each item, place a check mark on the line under the column that describes how much YOU ARE FRIGHTENED BY IT NOWADAYS.

Not at all	A little	A fair amount	Much	Very much

1. Learning how to convert Celsius to Fahrenheit degrees as you travel in Canada.
   Not at all   A little   A fair amount   Much   Very much

2. In a Philosophy discussion group, reading a chapter on the Categorical Imperative and being asked to answer questions.
   Not at all   A little   A fair amount   Much   Very much

3. Asking a question in a science class.
   Not at all   A little   A fair amount   Much   Very much

4. Converting kilometers to miles.
   Not at all   A little   A fair amount   Much   Very much

5. Studying for a midterm exam in Chemistry, Physics, or Biology.
   Not at all   A little   A fair amount   Much   Very much

6. Planning a well balanced diet.
   Not at all   A little   A fair amount   Much   Very much

7. Converting American dollars to English pounds as you travel in the British Isles.
   Not at all   A little   A fair amount   Much   Very much

8. Cooling down a hot tub of water to an appropriate temperature for a bath.
   Not at all   A little   A fair amount   Much   Very much

9. Planning the electrical circuit or pathway for a simple "light bulb" experiment.
   Not at all   A little   A fair amount   Much   Very much

10. Replacing a bulb on a movie projector.

Not at all   A little   A fair amount   Much   Very much

11. Focusing the lens on your camera.

Not at all   A little   A fair amount   Much   Very much

12. Changing the eyepiece on a microscope.

Not at all   A little   A fair amount   Much   Very much

13. Using a thermometer in order to record the boiling point of a heating solution.

Not at all   A little   A fair amount   Much   Very much

14. You want to vote on an upcoming referendum on student activities fees, and you are reading about it so that you might make an informed choice.

Not at all   A little   A fair amount   Much   Very much

15. Having a fellow student watch you perform an experiment in the lab.

Not at all   A little   A fair amount   Much   Very much

16. Visiting the Museum of Science and Industry and being asked to explain atomic energy to a 12-year-old.

Not at all   A little   A fair amount   Much   Very much

17. Studying for a final exam in English, History, or Philosophy.

Not at all   A little   A fair amount   Much   Very much

18. Mixing the proper amount of baking soda and water to put on a bee sting.

Not at all   A little   A fair amount   Much   Very much

19. Igniting a Coleman stove in preparation for cooking outdoors.

Not at all   A little   A fair amount   Much   Very much

20. Tuning your guitar to a piano or some other musical instrument.

Not at all   A little   A fair amount   Much   Very much

21. Filling your bicycle tires with the right amount of air.

Not at all   A little   A fair amount   Much   Very much

22. Memorizing a chart of historical dates.

Not at all   A little   A fair amount   Much   Very much

23. In a Physics discussion group, reading a chapter on Quantum Systems and being asked to answer some questions.

Not at all   A little   A fair amount   Much   Very much

24. Having a fellow student listen to you read in a foreign language.

Not at all   A little   A fair amount   Much   Very much

25. Reading signs on buildings in a foreign country.

Not at all   A little   A fair amount   Much   Very much

26. Memorizing the names of elements in the periodic table.

Not at all   A little   A fair amount   Much   Very much

27. Having your music teacher listen to you as you play an instrument.

Not at all   A little   A fair amount   Much   Very much

28. Reading the Theater page of *Time* magazine and having one of your friends ask your opinion on what you have read.

Not at all   A little   A fair amount   Much   Very much

29. Adding minute quantities of acid to a base solution in order to neutralize it.

Not at all   A little   A fair amount   Much   Very much

30. Precisely inflating a balloon to be used as apparatus in a Physics experiment.

Not at all   A little   A fair amount   Much   Very much

31. Lighting a Bunsen burner in the preparation of an experiment.

Not at all   A little   A fair amount   Much   Very much

32. A vote is coming up on the issue of nuclear power plants, and you are reading background material in order to decide how to vote.

    Not at all   A little   A fair amount   Much   Very much

33. Using a tuning fork in an acoustical experiment.

    Not at all   A little   A fair amount   Much   Very much

34. Mixing boiling water and ice to get water at 70 degrees Fahrenheit.

    Not at all   A little   A fair amount   Much   Very much

35. Studying for a midterm in a History course.

    Not at all   A little   A fair amount   Much   Very much

36. Having your professor watch you perform an experiment in the lab.

    Not at all   A little   A fair amount   Much   Very much

37. Having a teaching assistant watch you perform an experiment in the lab.

    Not at all   A little   A fair amount   Much   Very much

38. Focusing a microscope.

    Not at all   A little   A fair amount   Much   Very much

39. Using a meat thermometer for the first time, and checking the temperature periodically till the meat reaches the desired "doneness."

    Not at all   A little   A fair amount   Much   Very much

40. Having a teaching assistant watch you draw in Art class.

    Not at all   A little   A fair amount   Much   Very much

41. Reading the Science page of *Time* magazine and having one of your friends ask your opinion on what you have read.

    Not at all   A little   A fair amount   Much   Very much

42. Studying for a final exam in Chemistry, Physics, or Biology.

    Not at all   A little   A fair amount   Much   Very much

43. Being asked to explain the artistic quality of pop art to a 7th grader on a visit to the Art Museum.

    Not at all   A little   A fair amount   Much   Very much

44. Asking a question in an English Literature class.

    Not at all   A little   A fair amount   Much   Very much

References

Alpert, R., and R. N. Haber. 1960. Anxiety in academic achievement situations. *Journal of Abnormal Psychology* 61: 207–215.

Alvaro, R. 1978. The effectiveness of a science-therapy program on science-anxious undergraduates. PhD diss., Loyola University Chicago.

American Institute of Physics (AIP). 2001. *AIP Statistical Research Center: 2000-01 high school physics survey. www.aip. org/statistics/trends/highlite/hs2001/figure7.htm; www.aip.org/statistics/trends/highlite/hs2001.table5.htm*

Beyer, K. 1992. Project organized university studies in science: Gender, metacognition and quality of learning. In *Contributions to the Gender and Science and Technology (GASAT) Conference*, Vol. II, 363–372. Eindhoven, The Netherlands: Eindhoven University of Technology.

Beyer, K., S. Blegaa, B. Olsen, J. Reich, and M. Vedelsby. 1988. *Piger og fysik* [Females and physics]. Roskilde, Denmark: IMFUFA Texts, Roskilde University Center.

Brownlow, S., T. Jacobi, and M. Rogers. 2000. Science anxiety as a function of gender and experience. *Sex Roles* 42: 119–131.

Chiarelott, L., and C. Czerniak. 1985. Science anxiety among elementary school students: An equity issue. *Journal of Educational Equity and Leadership* 5: 291–308.

Chiarelott, L., and C. Czerniak. 1987. Science anxiety: Implications for science curriculum and teaching. *The Clearing House* 60: 202–205.

Didion, C. J. 1997. A report card on gender equity on the twenty-fifth anniversary of Title IX. *Journal of College Science Teaching* 27: 97–98.

Fuller, R., S. Agruso, J. Mallow, D. Nichols, R. Sapp, A. Strassenburg, and G. Allen. 1985. *Developing student confidence in physics.* College Park, MD: American Association of Physics Teachers.

Gautreau, R., and L. Novemsky. 1997. Concepts first—a small group approach to physics learning. *American Journal of Physics* 65: 418–428.

Hake, R. 1998. Interactive engagement vs. traditional methods: A six-thousand-student survey of mechanics test data for introductory physics courses. *American Journal of Physics* 66: 64–74.

Heller, P., R. Keith, and S. Anderson. 1992. Teaching problem solving through cooperative grouping Part 1: Group versus individual problem solving. *American Journal of Physics* 60: 627–636; Teaching problem solving through cooperative grouping Part 2: Designing and structuring groups. *American Journal of Physics* 60: 637–644.

Hermes, J. 1985. The comparative effectiveness of a science anxiety group and a stress management program in the treatment of science-anxious college students. PhD diss., Loyola University Chicago.

Legge, K. 1997. *Problem-oriented group project work at Roskilde University.* Roskilde, Denmark: IMFUFA Texts, Roskilde University Center.

Mallow, J. V. 1978. A science anxiety program. *American Journal of Physics* 46: 862.

Mallow, J. V. 1986. *Science anxiety.* Clearwater, FL: H&H.

Mallow, J. V. 1991. Reading science. *Journal of Reading* 34: 324–338.

Mallow, J. V. 1993. The science learning climate: Danish female and male students' descriptions. In *Contributions to the Seventh Gender and Science and Technology (GASAT) Conference,* Vol. I, 75–87. Waterloo, ON, Canada: Ontario Women's Directorate.

Mallow, J. V. 1994. Gender-related science anxiety: A first binational study. *Journal of Science Education and Technology* 3: 227–238.

Mallow, J. V. 1995. Students' confidence and teachers' styles: A binational comparison. *American Journal of Physics* 63: 1007–1011.

Mallow, J. V. 1998. Student attitudes and enrolments in physics, with emphasis on gender, nationality, and science anxiety. In *Justification and enrolment problems in education involving mathematics or physics,* eds. J. H. Jensen, M. Niss, and T. Wedege, 237–258. Roskilde, Denmark: Roskilde University Press.

Mallow, J. V. Forthcoming. Science education for civic engagement: Energy for a sustainable future. In *Proceedings of the Triennial Congress of Nordic Teachers of Mathematics, Physics and Chemistry (LMFK).*

Mallow, J. V., and R. Hake. 2002. *Gender issues in physics/science education (GIPSE)—some annotated references. www. physics.luc.edu/people/faculty/jmallow/GIPSE-4b.pdf*

Mazur, E. 1997. *Peer Instruction: A user's manual.* Upper Saddle River, NJ: Prentice Hall.

Meltzer, D. E., and K. Manivannan. 1996. Promoting interactivity in physics lecture classes. *The Physics Teacher* 34: 72–76.

Michaelsen, L., W. Watson, J. Cragin, and L. Fink. 1982. Team learning: A potential solution to the problem of large classes. *Exchange: The Organizational Behavior Teaching Journal* 7: 13–22.

Rahm, I., and P. Charbonneau. 1997. Probing stereotypes through students' drawings of scientists. *American Journal of Physics* 65: 774–778.

Richardson, F. C., and R. M. Suinn. 1972. The Mathematics Anxiety Rating Scale: Psychometric data. *Journal of Counseling Psychology* 19: 551–554.

Ruhl, K. L., C. A. Hughes, and P. J. Schloss. 1987. Using the pause procedure to enhance lecture recall. *Teacher Education and Special Education* 10: 14–18.

Seymour, E., and N. Hewitt. 2000. *Talking about leaving: Why undergraduates leave the sciences.* Boulder, CO: Westview Press.

Spielberger, C. D., R. L. Gorsuch, and R. E. Lushene. 1970. *STAI manual for the State-Trait Anxiety Inventory*. Palo Alto, CA: Consulting Psychologist Press.

Tobias, S., M. Urry, and A. Venkatesan. 2002. Physics: For women, the last frontier. *Science* 296: 1201.

Treisman, U. 1992. Studying students studying calculus: A look at the lives of minority mathematics students in college. *College Mathematics Journal* 23: 362–372.

Udo, M. K., G. P. Ramsey, S. Reynolds-Alpert, and J. V. Mallow. 2001. Does physics teaching affect gender-based science anxiety? *Journal of Science Education and Technology* 10: 237–247.

Udo, M. K., G. P. Ramsey, S. Reynolds-Alpert, and J. V. Mallow. 2004. Science anxiety and gender in students taking general education science courses. *Journal of Science Education and Technology* 13: 435–446.

CHAPTER 2

Improving Student Attitudes Toward Biology

Donald P. French and Connie P. Russell

Donald P. French is professor of zoology at Oklahoma State University and president of the Society for College Science Teachers. He earned a PhD in zoology at Indiana University and conducts research in animal behavior and science education. He teaches courses in introductory biology and the teaching of zoology.

Connie P. Russell is associate professor of biology at Angelo State University in Texas. She earned a PhD in zoology at Oklahoma State University and conducts research in science education. She teaches principles of biology, general zoology, human anatomy, and advanced instructional methods in science education.

"Attitudes are enduring while knowledge often has an ephemeral quality." With this quote, Osborne, Simon, and Collins (2003, p. 1074) articulate what many introductory science teachers have long suspected—that students are much more likely to remember how we made them feel about science than any of the "facts" that we seem determined to try to pour into their heads.

As we design introductory science courses, whether or not our students like science may seem to be a trivial concern. We get caught up in making sure that content is "covered" using the same teaching strategy used to teach us successfully—primarily didactic lectures and verification laboratories. But, arguably, we were successful because we liked science and maybe even persevered in spite of the teaching (Tobias 1990). Now we are frustrated teaching introductory college science courses because many students, even science majors, don't like science and expect hard and boring courses that they see as a chore, not a challenge. Teaching students with such attitudes can be disheartening and unsuccessful. Research indicates a positive correlation between achievement in science courses and attitude toward science (Osborne, Simon, and Collins 2003; Russell and Hollander 1975; Shrigley, Koballa, and Simpson 1988). Poor or ambivalent attitudes toward science as it is taught may be a major contributing factor to the "swing away from science" experienced in many countries and the continued disparity between males and females in science (Osborne, Simon, and Collins 2003; Tobias 1990; see also Chapter 3 in this volume).

Can we improve student attitudes? Osborne, Simon, and Collins (2003) found positive correlations between attitude and certain characteristics of the classroom environment, including student-centered instructional designs, high levels of personal support, use of a variety of teaching strategies, and innovative learning activities. This parallels the National Research Council's (1996) recommendations at the K–12 level. While methods the NRC suggests have been used successfully at the pre-college level (see, e.g., Von Secker and Lissitz 1999), they are rare at the college level. In this chapter we describe our version of a student-centered, active-learning science classroom and present results that indicate that our efforts were successful in changing students' attitudes toward science.

Our Model

Originally, our institution offered three introductory courses: one nonmajors course with content emphasis on ecology, evolution, and genetics (OLD-NM1), one nonmajors course focused on subcellular, cellular, and organismal biology (OLD-NM2), and one majors course encompassing all the concepts of the two nonmajors courses (OLD-M). All three of these courses were taught using a traditional expository manner in lecture and verification-style laboratories (see Chapter 21 in this volume). Formal and informal surveys indicated that the students' attitudes toward biology, particularly among the life science majors, declined during these courses. The three courses were replaced with a mixed-majors course (SEM).

The new course introduces students to biological concepts integrated from the subcellular to the ecological through an investigative approach. In lecture, the instructors introduce students to concepts in the format of "scenarios"—stories that provide context including background material and observations leading to a general question for the students to answer. The instructors use multimedia presentations that include narrated stories illustrated by photographs, graphs, and animations (see Chapter 23 in this volume). These presentations set the stage for discussions during which students develop explanations or pose solutions collaboratively to be tested virtually in lecture and/or empirically in the accompanying lab (see Chapter 21). For example, we introduce cellular respiration during a scenario in which students take a virtual fishing trip with a group of Amazon natives who are using a chemical found in vines to "stun" fish that "gasp at the surface for air." This narrative, inspired by a description of the event in Mark Plotkin's *Tales of a Shaman's Apprentice* (1993), provides observations leading to the general question "What's happening to the fish?" We ask the students to propose as many hypotheses, "good" or "bad," as they can, then guide them as they reach an agreement as to the more likely ones. This approach allows the instructor to deal with misconceptions (e.g., fish breathe dissolved oxygen in the water, not the oxygen atom of a water molecule) before moving on to a discussion concerning how cells use oxygen.

Multimedia-enhanced mini-lectures and discussions are intermixed as the concepts of secondary metabolites, natural selection, mitochondria as organelles, the laws of thermodynamics, competition, energy flow through an ecosystem, and the mechanics of cellular respiration are introduced. Students engage in a variety of collaborative lecture activities as they work to explain each of these concepts in terms of their relation to the general question. We use animations to help students visualize abstract processes such as the movement of electrons through the electron transport chain and the way chemiosmosis produces adenosine triphosphate (ATP). Daily formative assessments using group activities (short essay answers written on index cards, graphs, concept maps, and annotated illustrations of processes) help keep students engaged in answering higher-level questions like those on summative exams.

In the old courses exams focused on basic recall; in the new course they require students to apply concepts to novel situations, although they are still multiple choice. In the new course, we evaluate students' laboratory performances based on the quality of their research (individual planning forms and group lab reports); in the old courses it was based on lab quizzes that were primarily factual.

Assessment of Student Attitudes

Timeline
Starting the semester before we launched the new course, we surveyed students in all three traditional courses to determine how their attitudes toward biology and content knowledge changed during the semester. We also observed students during lab. We continued this during the first two spring semesters the new course was offered (SEM1 and SEM2).

Subjects
We invited all students enrolled in all the courses to participate. The majority of students were in their first year. While there were different courses for majors and nonmajors prior to SEM1, neither majors nor nonmajors populated a course exclusively. We only included students that gave informed consent and completed all components of the survey in the study. We obtained complete data from 306 students from one nonmajors course (OLD-NM1), 311 students from the old course for majors (OLD-M), 406 students in the new course during the first spring (SEM1), and 662 during the second spring (SEM2). We did not obtain sufficient data from the other nonmajors course to include it in the analysis.

Survey Instrument
The survey instrument included 40 biology content questions from the National Association of Biology Teachers / National Science Teachers Association (NABT/NSTA) 1990 High School Biology Examination, a 14-item Biology Attitude Scale (Russell and Hollander 1975; the scale is reprinted in an appendix at the end of this chapter), and several questions about student characteristics, only three of which are used in our analysis (gender, major, and class standing). We used the NABT/NSTA examination and the Biology Attitude Scale because they had been well validated in previous studies. We administered the survey during one hour of the first and last weeks' laboratory of each semester.

The student's response to each item on the attitude survey was scored on a Likert-type scale (1–5). Following Russell and Hollander's method (1975), we generated overall attitude scores by summing the individual ratings. The resulting continuous scale ranged from 14 (poorest attitude) through 42 (ambivalent attitude) to 70 (most strongly favorable attitude). To evaluate change in each student's attitude over the course of the semester, we subtracted the initial attitude score from the final score to yield difference scores. A positive difference indicated an improvement in attitude toward biology, and a negative difference indicated a decline in attitude toward biology.

Statistical Analysis

We characterized students according to four factors: sex, major, class standing (as reported by Oklahoma State University's Office of Institutional Research for first-year or greater than first-year [nonfreshman] students), and ACT composite scores (provided by the Office of Institutional Research). Majors were self-reported and subdivided into life sciences (botany, biology, microbiology, physiology, zoology, wildlife, or the health sciences) or non–life sciences (all other majors).

We analyzed the attitude scores by analysis of covariance (ANCOVA). In each ANCOVA model, the main factors or treatments were course, major, class standing, and sex. We could not add an additional factor (year) to the design because of the complexity of our model; therefore, we compared scores for OLD-M and OLD-NM1 to SEM1 and SEM2, separately. We used the difference scores (change in attitude) as the dependent variable and ACT and initial attitude scores as covariates, after examining their fit ($R^2 = 0.6388$). We used the unequal slopes model and selected three values of ACT composite scores for our analysis of Course × Sex × Major × Class Standing: 21 (minimum required for normal admission at the time), 25 (average ACT for course), and 30 (highest value obtained by a sufficient number of subjects). We focused our analysis on the four-way interaction terms (e.g., Are there differences in the average change in attitude scores among male freshman life science majors in OLD-NM1, OLD-M, and SEM1?). We eliminated categories with insufficient sample sizes (e.g., nonfreshman majors in SEM1).

Results

Each subgroup exhibited a significant improvement in attitude toward biology in the new course when compared with the old courses. For freshman life science majors, the results were particularly dramatic (see Figure 2.1). There was a significant difference between OLD-M males and those in the new course at all ACT levels. There also appears to be continued improvement between SEM1 and SEM2. There was no statistically significant difference among students at different ACT levels. This group (male freshman life science majors) showed the most positive gain in change in attitude, and this is the only group that exhibited a positive change in attitude at all ACT levels by SEM2. In female freshman life science majors, there was a significant difference among courses at medium and high ACT levels. Again, attitude changes appeared to improve between SEM1 and SEM2. There appear to be differences among students with different ACT scores. Attitude did not improve as much for those with lower ACT scores (21) in the new course as for those with higher ACT scores and did not show a significant change in attitude score in the new course when compared with either of the OLD courses that we included in our analysis. Those with the highest ACT scores had the most negative change in attitude toward biology scores in OLD-M but exhibited a positive change in attitude toward biology in the new course.

Similar trends were seen in the nonmajors (male and female, first year and non–first year). Again, particularly for females, those with higher ACT scores (25, 30) had a more negative change in attitude toward biology in the old courses but exhibited a less negative change in attitude toward biology in the revised course, and this appeared to improve further in SEM2.

We found several associations between lab participation, attitude, and performance, as measured by changes in the NABT/NSTA exam scores (Russell and French 2001). In the revised inquiry labs the more successful students spent more time actively participating

($^2 = 9.254$, $df = 2$, $P = 0.01$) than students whose scores decreased; this was not the case in the traditional labs. Students in the inquiry labs with more positive change in attitude scores tended to write more ($^2 = 4.823$, $df = 1$, $P < 0.03$) and spent almost twice as much time performing experimental tasks ($^2 = 2.993$, $df = 1$, $P < 0.08$).

Figure 2.1

Change in Attitude Difference Scores for Freshman Life Science Majors

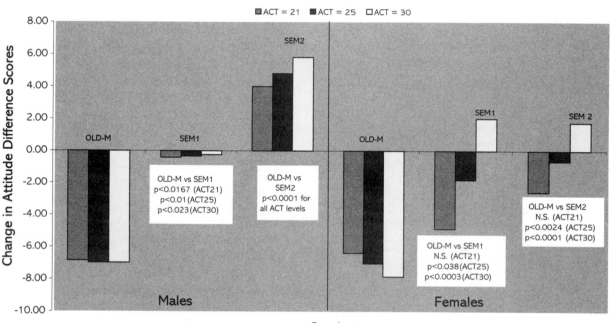

OLD-M = old course for majors; SEM1 = new course, first spring semester; SEM2 = new course, second spring semester.

Discussion

Our change to a more student-centered pedagogy clearly affected students' attitudes toward biology. While our traditionally taught courses were characterized by substantial declines in attitude, this attitude change was moderated in our revised course for almost all student groups, regardless of sex, class standing, starting attitude, or ACT score. There was a significant improvement for all males and for females who scored 25 or higher on the ACT composite exam. Females who earned low scores on the ACT showed nonsignificant improvements in their attitudes. Generally, it also appears that attitudes improved over time. This temporal aspect may reflect the importance of gaining experience with new teaching practices. All the instructors were experienced teachers but were novices at these techniques, and some were skeptical of them. Using techniques effectively takes time, so initial attempts may not produce positive responses (Orzechowski 1995; Sundberg and Moncada 1994). It may also take time for the course culture to change, for students to build a community of acceptance as former students inform new ones about a course.

Our results are quite consistent with those of other studies. Gogolin and Swartz (1992) found that science majors started with a more positive attitude toward science than did nonmajors and that while attitudes of nonscience majors improved at the end of their traditionally taught course, attitudes of science majors declined. In their case, the courses were separate majors and nonmajors biology courses taught using a traditional expository lecture format. The nonscience majors course included applications and material considered to be relevant to the students, and there were no prerequisite skills or knowledge required for enrollment. Gogolin and Swartz described the majors course as "less-stimulating" and more "subject-oriented"; the nonmajors course was more "student-oriented." Sundberg and Dini (1993) attributed the more positive attitudes toward science among students in their nonmajors course compared with those in their majors course to the reduced level of detail and greater emphasis on current application and social relevance in the nonmajors course. Many other studies comparing more student-centered approaches such as problem-based learning, investigative learning, and cooperative learning in nonmajors courses reported the same trend (Ebert-May, Brewer, and Allred 1997; Goodwin, Miller, and Cheetham 1991; Miller and Cheetham 1990). Rogers and Ford (1997), using the same attitude scale we did, also reported increases in attitude toward biology by students in nonmajors courses and declines in the attitudes toward biology by students in a majors course.

Thus it appears that restructuring a course to include introducing concepts within a relevant context, more cooperative learning, more inquiry, more problem-based learning, and more investigations in the laboratory is beneficial to both majors and nonmajors. Most notably, our biology majors, groups whose attitudes have been negatively affected by the traditional expository teaching approach at our institution and elsewhere, have been positively influenced by our revised approach. We agree with Sundberg and Dini's (1993) conclusion that majors and nonmajors both need to be taught differently than the traditional expository style, which emphasizes memorization of facts and terminology.

That certain groups are not as positively affected as others still presents a challenge to us as we seek to improve scientific literacy. In particular, we note that women with low ACT scores did not show a significant change in attitude. While we cannot be sure that this actually reflects the situation (they do show a positive trend, just not a significant one), it is consistent with findings of Von Secker and Lissitz (1999), which supported the conclusion that females who were low achievers did not benefit from student-centered practices, and those of Meece and Jones (1996), which supported the conclusion that only low-ability females were less motivated than males to learn. Both of these studies were at the pre-college level. Because we did not assess motivation, self-confidence, or learning styles, it is impossible to speculate how these influence attitudes among these students.

One of the most striking differences we saw between student- and teacher-centered instruction was among female life science majors whose ACT scores were high (30). This group showed the most dramatic improvement in attitudes toward biology with the change in teaching style. Many studies suggest that gender may be the biggest contributor to attitudes toward science. Various studies have indicated that males have a more positive attitude toward science (Simpson and Oliver 1985), perform better in science classes (Rafal 1996; Steinkamp and Maehr 1984), choose science fields more often (Mason and Kahle 1988; Seymour and Hewitt

1997), and are more likely to remain in the field (Seymour and Hewitt 1997). Other studies have indicated no difference between males and females in their attitude toward science (Morrell and Lederman 1998; Shaw and Doan 1990), particularly in studies of biology-related subjects (Osborne, Simon, and Collins 2003). Lack of a valid and reliable measurement of attitude and poor research methodology may contribute to the conflict among these findings (Germann 1988; Gogolin and Swartz 1992; Osborne, Simon, and Collins 2003). However, if, as Seymour and Hewitt (1997) and Tobias (1990) suggest, capable female students are more likely to leave the sciences as a major than their male counterparts because of the competitive nature of, poor teaching in, lack of opportunities to participate in, or the inability to see connections to their personal lives in many traditionally taught science courses, then the use of inquiry and collaboration may help to balance the gender gap as students progress into upper-division science courses. We found that moving to a student-centered teaching style in laboratories influenced participation, that women participated more equally with men in inquiry labs, and that participation was positively related to attitude and increase in improved achievement (Russell and French 2001).

Conclusions

Of all the ways that faculty can modify their teaching to improve student attitudes, three appear critical: providing a real-world context that sparks students' interest in science content, showing students that learning the material has concrete value, and linking the utility of science content to students' future personal and professional lives (Osborne, Simon, and Collins 2003). We conclude that courses like ours, using multimedia to provide context and visualization, collaborative learning, and inquiry-oriented instruction in lecture and laboratory, provide positive environments for learning and contribute to improving students attitudes toward biology. Although the link between student attitude toward science and many factors associated with success in a course has been difficult to establish, this model of instruction should help promote both general science literacy and the continued pursuit of science as a career.

Acknowledgment

This material is based on research partially supported by the National Science Foundation under Award No. DUE 9752402. Any opinions, findings, and conclusions or recommendations expressed in the publication are those of the authors and do not necessarily reflect the views of the National Science Foundation.

Appendix
Biology Attitude Scale

Each of the statements below expresses a feeling toward biology. Please rate each statement on the extent to which you agree. For each, you may:

Strongly Agree (A) Agree (B) Be Undecided (C) Disagree (D) Strongly Disagree (E)

1. Biology is very interesting to me.
2. I don't like biology, and it scares me to have to take it.
3. I am always under a terrible strain in a biology class.
4. Biology is fascinating and fun.
5. Biology makes me feel secure, and at the same time is stimulating.
6. Biology makes me feel uncomfortable, restless, irritable, and impatient.
7. In general, I have a good feeling toward biology.
8. When I hear the word "biology," I have a feeling of dislike.

9. I approach biology with a feeling of hesitation.
10. I really like biology.
11. I have always enjoyed studying biology in school.
12. It makes me nervous to even think about doing a biology experiment.
13. I feel at ease in biology and like it very much.
14. I feel a definite positive reaction to biology; it's enjoyable.

Source: Russell, J., and S. Hollander. 1975. A biology attitude scale. *American Biology Teacher* 37: 270–273. Reprinted by permission of the National Association of Biology Teachers.

References

Ebert-May, D., C. Brewer, and S. Allred. 1997. Innovation in large lectures—teaching for active learning. *BioScience* 47: 601–607.

Germann, P. J. 1988. Development of the attitude toward science in school assessment and its use to investigate the relationship between science achievement and attitude toward science in school. *Journal of Research in Science Teaching* 25: 689–703.

Gogolin, L., and F. Swartz. 1992. A quantitative and qualitative inquiry into the attitudes toward science of non-science college students. *Journal of Research in Science Teaching* 29: 487–504.

Goodwin, L., J. E. Miller, and R. D. Cheetham. 1991. Teaching freshmen to think—does active learning work? *BioScience* 41: 719–722.

Mason, C. L., and J. B. Kahle. 1989. Student attitudes toward science-related careers: A program designed to promote a stimulating gender-free learning environment. *Journal of Research in Science Teaching* 26: 25–39.

Meece, J. L., and M. G. Jones. 1996. Gender differences in motivation and strategy use in science: Are girls rote learners? *Journal of Research in Science Teaching* 33: 393–406.

Miller, J. E., and R. D. Cheetham. 1990. Teaching freshman to think—active learning in introductory biology. *BioScience* 40: 388–391.

Morrell, P. D., and N. G. Lederman. 1998. Students' attitudes toward school and classroom science: Are they independent phenomena? *School Science and Mathematics* 98: 76–83.

National Research Council (NRC). 1996. *National science education standards.* Washington, DC: National Academy Press.

Orzechowski, R. F. 1995. Factors to consider before introducing active learning into a large lecture-based course. *Journal of College Science Teaching* 24: 347–349.

Osborne, J., S. Simon, and S. Collins. 2003. Attitudes towards science: A review of the literature and its implications. *International Journal of Science Education* 25: 1049–1079.

Plotkin, M. J. 1993. *Tales of a shaman's apprentice.* New York: Penguin Books.

Rafal, C. T. 1996. From co-construction to takeovers: Science talk in a group of four girls. *Journal of the Learning Sciences* 5: 279–293.

Rogers, W. D., and R. Ford. 1997. Factors that affect student attitude toward biology. *Bioscene* 23 (2): 3–5. Also available online at *http://papa.indstate.edu/amcbt/volume_23*.

Russell, C. P., and D. P. French. 2001. Factors affecting participation in traditional and inquiry-based laboratories. *Journal of College Science Teaching* 31: 225–229.

Russell, J., and S. Hollander. 1975. A biology attitude scale. *American Biology Teacher* 37: 270–273.

Seymour, E., and N. M. Hewitt. 1997. *Talking about leaving: Why undergraduates leave the sciences.* Boulder, CO: Westview Press.

Shaw, E. L., and R. L. Doan. 1990. An investigation of the differences in attitude and achievement between male and female second and fifth grade students. Paper presented at the annual meeting of the National Association for the Research in Science Teaching, Atlanta, GA.

Shrigley, R. L., T. R. Koballa, and R. D. Simpson. 1988. Defining attitude for science educators. *Journal of Research in Science Teaching* 25: 659–678.

Simpson, R. D., and J. S. Oliver. 1985. Attitude toward science and achievement motivation profiles of male and female science students in grades six through ten. *Science Education* 69: 511–526.

Steinkamp, M. W., and M. L. Maehr. 1984. Gender differences in motivational orientations toward achievement in school science: A quantitative synthesis. *American Educational Research Journal* 21: 39–59.

Sundberg, M. D., and M. L. Dini. 1993. Science majors vs nonmajors: Is there a difference? *Journal of College Science Teaching* 22: 299–304.

Sundberg, M. D., and G. J. Moncada. 1994. Creating effective investigative laboratories for undergraduates. *BioScience* 44: 698–704.

Tobias, S. 1990. *They're not dumb, they're different: Stalking the second tier.* Tucson, AZ: Research Corporation.

Von Secker, C. E., and R. W. Lissitz. 1999. Estimating the impact of instructional practices on student achievement in science. *Journal of Research in Science Teaching* 36: 1110–1126.

CHAPTER 3

Motivation to Learn in College Science

Shawn M. Glynn and Thomas R. Koballa, Jr.

Shawn M. Glynn is Josiah Meigs Distinguished Teaching Professor of educational psychology and instructional technology at the University of Georgia. He earned a PhD in educational psychology at Pennsylvania State University and conducts research on psychology applied to learning science. He teaches courses in psychology of learning and instruction, and cognition for education.

Thomas R. Koballa, Jr., is professor of science education at the University of Georgia. He earned a PhD in science education at Pennsylvania State University and conducts research on the affective domain in science education and science teacher mentoring. He teaches courses in science methods and the affective domain in science education.

All college science teachers share the important goal of motivating college students to learn science. In this chapter, we discuss motivational theory and research in college science teaching and draw implications for effective practices. We also present a new questionnaire designed specifically to help college science teachers assess their students' motivation to learn science.

Definition of Motivation

Motivation is an internal state that arouses, directs, and sustains students' behavior. The study of motivation by science education researchers attempts to explain why students strive for particular goals when learning science, how intensively they strive, how long they strive, and what feelings and emotions characterize them in this process. As science education researchers respond to current national initiatives to foster students' science achievement, the emphasis placed on motivation has been increasing, as evidenced by recent articles with titles such as "Skill and Will: The Role of Motivation and Cognition in the Learning of College Chemistry" (Zusho and Pintrich 2003).

Today, more than ever, students' motivation to learn college science remains an area of discussion and debate—an area constantly in need of innovative approaches because the societal factors that play a role in learning science are constantly changing. According to a recent national report, "Of those students entering college with plans to major in science or engineering, less than 40 percent graduate with a degree in that field within six years" (Business-Higher Education Forum 2005, p. 6). This report, like many others, concludes that America is in danger of losing its international leadership in scientific creativity.

Motivation to Learn in College Science Courses

According to Brophy (1988), *motivation to learn* is "a student tendency to find academic activities meaningful and worthwhile and to try to derive the intended academic benefits from them" (pp. 205–206). What motivates students to learn in college science courses? The important motivational constructs being examined by researchers include *intrinsic* and *extrinsic motivation, goal orientation, self-determination, self-efficacy,* and *assessment anxiety*; the related attitudinal constructs are discussed by French and Russell in Chapter 2 of this volume.

Intrinsic and Extrinsic Motivation

Motivation to do something for its own sake is mainly intrinsic, whereas motivation to do it as a means to an end is mainly extrinsic (Mazlo et al. 2002; Pintrich and Schunk 2002). Intrinsic motivation taps into the natural human tendency to pursue interests and exercise capabilities (Ryan and Deci 2000; Singh, Granville, and Dika 2002). Students who are intrinsically motivated to learn often experience "flow," a feeling of enjoyment that occurs when they have developed a sense of mastery and are concentrating intensely on the task at hand, such as a lab activity (Csikszentmihalyi 2000).

Students often perform tasks for reasons that are both intrinsically and extrinsically motivated. For example, the student who carries out a science project may enjoy the process, particularly if the student can approach the project in different ways, but may also be motivated by the prospect of receiving an award if the project is entered in a competition.

A survey conducted by Smith, Gould, and Jones (2004) of more than 500 nonscience majors enrolled in college physics or biology courses indicated that the most popular reasons for taking the courses were to complete a general requirement, to fulfill a requirement for a major, to perform well in a job after college, to get ahead in a job, and to be hired for a job—these reasons appear to be extrinsically motivated. The less popular reasons included to better understand the natural world, to lead a better personal life, to satisfy curiosity about the natural world, and to be a better citizen—these appear to be intrinsically motivated. These findings are particularly noteworthy because scientific organizations such as the National Academy of Sciences and the American Association for the Advancement of Science stress intrinsically motivated reasons for learning science.

Goal Orientation

A distinction often is made between *learning goals* and *performance goals* (e.g., Cavallo, Rozman, and Potter 2004). College students with learning goals focus on the challenge and mastery of a science task. They are not concerned about how many mistakes they make or how they appear to others. They view mistakes as learning opportunities and do not hesitate to ask others for feedback and help. For example, in a study of science majors enrolled in either a biology or a physics course, Cavallo and colleagues (2003) found the following:

Motivation to learn for the sake of learning was most important for course achievement, followed by reasoning ability. Meaningful learning and a tentative view of science were positively related to learn-

ing goals, which means these may underlie the motivation to learn for the sake of learning. (p. 22)

Students with performance goals often are preoccupied with gaining social status, pleasing teachers, and avoiding "extra" work. These students frequently compare their grades with others and choose tasks that are easy for them so they can maximize their grade. They are often reluctant to help others achieve. Their self-esteem is based on the external evaluation of their performance, so their esteem can be as fleeting as their last grade on a biology test.

While it can be useful to distinguish among students in terms of their goal orientations in college science courses, it should be kept in mind that these categorizations are relative. Students often have a combination of learning and performance goals.

Self-Determination

Self-determination is the ability to have choices and some degree of control over what we do and how we do it (Reeve, Hamm, and Nix 2003). Most people strive to be in charge of their own behavior—to be captains of their own ships. Most people are unhappy when they feel they have lost control, either to another person or to the environment.

When college science students have the opportunity to help determine what their educational activities will be, they are more likely to benefit from them (Glynn and Koballa 2005). A good example of how to increase students' intrinsic motivation by increasing their self-determination was provided by Garcia and Pintrich (1996). They found that the intrinsic motivation of college biology students increased when the students had input into course policies, such as the selection of course readings and term paper topics, as well as the due dates for class assignments.

When students lack self-determination, it is difficult for them to feel intrinsically motivated. They may come to believe that their performance in a college science course is mostly uncontrollable, and, as a result, they expend less effort on learning. For example, Maria's comments below are typical of some biology majors we recently interviewed who feel they have little control of their learning:

Studying biology can be pretty boring sometimes. Like, it can drive me crazy. I wish I could find a course or an instructor that makes it really interesting. It would be really nice to be excited about something in biology—it just hasn't happened yet. I hope I get a good course next semester—if it's interesting and if I think it's relevant, I'll probably get motivated and maybe work harder. I want to go to med school and I want to be sure I can get in.

Self-Efficacy

Bandura (1997) defined self-efficacy as "beliefs in one's capabilities to organize and execute the courses of action required to produce given attainments" (p. 3). When science education researchers use the term, they refer to the confidence a student has about his or her ability to succeed in a field of science (Koballa and Glynn, Forthcoming).

Self-efficacy is specific. For example, a college student may have high self-efficacy with respect to knowledge and skills in biology, but low self-efficacy with respect to knowledge and skills in physics. Students' judgments of their self-efficacy in particular areas of science have been found to predict their performance in these areas. For example, Zusho and Pintrich (2003) found that students' self-efficacy was the best predictor of grades in an introductory college chemistry course, even after controlling for prior achievement.

Anxiety

All students experience anxiety from time to time, particularly in college science courses (Seymour 1992; see also Chapter 1 in this volume). A *moderate* level of anxiety is good, in fact, in that it helps motivate learning (Cassady and Johnson 2002).

To ensure that anxiety remains in a moderate range, it is important for instructors to determine how well prepared students are for the learning that will be required of them in college science courses. If students lack adequate preparation, their anxiety will be excessive. In addition, it is important for instructors to gauge individual differences in the students' personalities because some students, even prepared ones, might be threatened by assignments that other students would find enjoyable. For example, introverted students might be extremely nervous about reporting the results of a lab in front of a class, whereas extroverted students might be enthusiastic about it.

Assessing Motivation to Learn in College Science Courses

Guided by the research on the preceding motivational constructs and by individual and group interviews conducted with students learning science in college courses, we developed the Science Motivation Questionnaire (SMQ), which is reprinted in the appendix at the end of this chapter. The SMQ assesses six components of motivation: *intrinsically motivated science learning* (items 1, 16, 22, 27, and 30), *extrinsically motivated science learning* (items 3, 7, 10, 15, and 17), *relevance of learning science to personal goals* (items 2, 11, 19, 23, and 25), *responsibility (self-determination) for learning science* (items 5, 8, 9, 20, and 26), *confidence (self-efficacy) in learning science* (items 12, 21, 24, 28, and 29), and *anxiety about science assessment* (items 4, 6, 13, 14, and 18). Students respond to each of the 30 items on a 5-point Likert-type scale ranging from 1 (never) to 5 (always). The *anxiety about science assessment* items are reverse scored. The SMQ maximum total score is 150 and the minimum is 30. Preliminary findings indicate that the SMQ is reliable in its internal consistency ($\alpha = 0.93$) and correlates positively with students' interest in science careers, number of science courses taken, and science grades.

The SMQ provides instructors and researchers with a convenient means of assessing a student's overall motivation to learn science in college courses, as well as the student's specific motivation in terms of each of the six components. The SMQ can be administered prior to a course for purposes of advisement or on the first day of a course to gauge the motivation of a class and identify students who have particular needs. The SMQ also can be administered at both the beginning and end of a course to show changes that have occurred in students' motivation as a result of instruction. The 30-item SMQ, with its six components, provides information about a student's motivation that is not assessed in other science-motivation questionnaires, such as the 10-item Achievement Motivation Questionnaire (Cavallo et al. 2003). And, because the SMQ is specific to science, it is more relevant to college science instruction than general content-area questionnaires, such as the Motivated Strategies for Learning Questionnaire (Pintrich et al. 1991).

Implications for Practice

The constructs we have described have important implications for understanding and increasing students' motivation to learn in college science courses. These implications include the following:

1. Use inquiry and discovery activities that present college science students with ideas that are somewhat in conflict with their current knowledge and beliefs. These discrepancies between what students think they know and what they are being taught heighten motivation by stimulating interest and curiosity.

2. Encourage college science students to set and pursue goals for themselves. The students who do this will become self-determined learners. Also, help students see the relevance of what they are learning to their personal goals. This promotes intrinsic motivation that goes beyond obtaining an extrinsic reward such as a good grade.

3. Help college science students see that extrinsic and intrinsic motivation can be mutually supportive. In their future careers, students will be motivated by a combination of extrinsic factors (e.g., awards and salary) and intrinsic factors (e.g., confidence and a sense of accomplishment) that together lead to personal success. Questionnaires such as the SMQ can provide information on what motivates students to learn science.

4. Give college science students some degree of control over what they learn and how they learn it. This will foster self-confidence and responsibility for learning. At the same time, reduce anxiety about assessment by incorporating it into tasks that are authentic and performance based, such as laboratories, projects, journals, presentations, and projects.

5. Look for opportunities to model good learning behavior for college science students, because they often identify with their instructors. Also, look for opportunities to promote collaborative learning—the social ties that result will contribute to a positive learning environment.

6. Have high, yet reasonable, expectations of college science students and be sure to communicate these expectations clearly. Give students constructive feedback, but focus it on the students' performance. It is important that students realize that they are valued personally and that any criticism they receive is directed at specific behaviors. Finally, when providing feedback, remember to recognize both effort and outcomes.

Conclusion

All college science instructors share the important goal of fostering college students' motivation to learn science. All instructors have a stake in determining how students learn science best, what feelings characterize them during learning, and why some students become autonomous lifelong science learners while others do not. An evolving understanding of the constructs involved in the motivation to learn science is essential if college instructors are to meet the challenge of successfully preparing students who can preserve and extend America's international leadership in scientific creativity and innovation.

Appendix

Science Motivation Questionnaire (SMQ)
©2005 Shawn M. Glynn and Thomas R. Koballa, Jr.

In order to better understand what you think and feel about your college science courses, please respond to each of the following statements from the perspective of:
"When I am in a college science course..."

01. I enjoy learning the science.
    O Never   O Rarely   O Sometimes   O Usually   O Always

02. The science I learn relates to my personal goals.
    O Never   O Rarely   O Sometimes   O Usually   O Always

03. I like to do better than the other students on the science tests.
    O Never   O Rarely   O Sometimes   O Usually   O Always

04. I am nervous about how I will do on the science tests.
    O Never   O Rarely   O Sometimes   O Usually   O Always

05. If I am having trouble learning the science, I try to figure out why.
    O Never   O Rarely   O Sometimes   O Usually   O Always

06. I become anxious when it is time to take a science test.
    O Never   O Rarely   O Sometimes   O Usually   O Always

07. Earning a good science grade is important to me.
    O Never   O Rarely   O Sometimes   O Usually   O Always

08. I put enough effort into learning the science.
    O Never   O Rarely   O Sometimes   O Usually   O Always

09. I use strategies that ensure I learn the science well.
    O Never   O Rarely   O Sometimes   O Usually   O Always

10. I think about how learning the science can help me get a good job.
    O Never   O Rarely   O Sometimes   O Usually   O Always

11. I think about how the science I learn will be helpful to me.
    O Never   O Rarely   O Sometimes   O Usually   O Always

12. I expect to do as well as or better than other students in the science course.
    O Never   O Rarely   O Sometimes   O Usually   O Always

13. I worry about failing the science tests.
    O Never   O Rarely   O Sometimes   O Usually   O Always

14. I am concerned that the other students are better in science.
    O Never   O Rarely   O Sometimes   O Usually   O Always

15. I think about how my science grade will affect my overall grade point average.
    O Never   O Rarely   O Sometimes   O Usually   O Always

16. The science I learn is more important to me than the grade I receive.
    O Never   O Rarely   O Sometimes   O Usually   O Always

17. I think about how learning the science can help my career.
    O Never   O Rarely   O Sometimes   O Usually   O Always

18. I hate taking the science tests.
    O Never   O Rarely   O Sometimes   O Usually   O Always

19. I think about how I will use the science I learn.
    O Never   O Rarely   O Sometimes   O Usually   O Always

20. It is my fault if I do not understand the science.
    O Never   O Rarely   O Sometimes   O Usually   O Always

21. I am confident I will do well on the science labs and projects.
    O Never   O Rarely   O Sometimes   O Usually   O Always

22. I find learning the science interesting.
    O Never   O Rarely   O Sometimes   O Usually   O Always

23. The science I learn is relevant to my life.
    O Never   O Rarely   O Sometimes   O Usually   O Always

24. I believe I can master the knowledge and skills in the science course.
    O Never   O Rarely   O Sometimes   O Usually   O Always

25. The science I learn has practical value for me.
    O Never   O Rarely   O Sometimes   O Usually   O Always

26. I prepare well for the science tests and labs.
    O Never   O Rarely   O Sometimes   O Usually   O Always

27. I like science that challenges me.
    O Never   O Rarely   O Sometimes   O Usually   O Always

28. I am confident I will do well on the science tests.
    O Never   O Rarely   O Sometimes   O Usually   O Always

29. I believe I can earn a grade of "A" in the science course.
    O Never   O Rarely   O Sometimes   O Usually   O Always

30. Understanding the science gives me a sense of accomplishment.
    O Never   O Rarely   O Sometimes   O Usually   O Always

Note: College science teachers who wish to use the Science Motivation Questionnaire for teaching and research have permission to do so if they comply with the fair use of a copyrighted and registered work, acknowledge the authors, and cite this book and chapter.

References

Bandura, A. 1997. *Self-efficacy: The exercise of control.* New York: Freeman.

Brophy, J. E. 1988. On motivating students. In *Talks to teachers,* eds. D. Berliner and B. Rosenshine, 201–245. New York: Random House.

Business-Higher Education Forum (BHEF). January 2005. *A commitment to America's future: Responding to the crisis in mathematics & science education.* Washington, DC: BHEF. *www.bhef.com/MathEduReport-press.pdf*

Cassady, J. C., and R. E. Johnson. 2002. Cognitive test anxiety and academic performance. *Contemporary Educational Psychology* 27: 270–295.

Cavallo, A. M. L., M. Rozman, J. Blinkenstaff, and N. Walker. 2003. Students' learning approaches, reasoning abilities, motivational goals, and epistemological beliefs in differing college science courses. *Journal of College Science Teaching* 33 (3): 18–23.

Cavallo, A. M. L., M. Rozman, and W. H. Potter. 2004. Gender differences in learning constructs, shifts in learning constructs, and their relationship to course achievement in a structured inquiry, yearlong college physics course for life science majors. *School Science and Mathematics* 104: 288–300.

Csikszentmihalyi, M. 2000. *Flow: Beyond boredom and anxiety.* San Francisco: Jossey-Bass.

Garcia, T., and P. R. Pintrich. 1996. The effects of autonomy on motivation and performance in college classrooms.

Contemporary Educational Psychology 21: 477–486.

Glynn, S. M., and T. R. Koballa, Jr. 2005. The contextual teaching and learning instructional approach. In *Exemplary science: Best practices in professional development,* ed. R. E. Yager, 75–84. Arlington, VA: NSTA Press.

Koballa, T. R., Jr., and S. M. Glynn. Forthcoming. Attitudinal and motivational constructs in science education. In *Handbook for research in science education,* eds. S. K. Abell and N. Lederman. Mahwah, NJ: Erlbaum.

Mazlo, J., D. F. Dormedy, J. D. Neimoth-Anderson, T. Urlacher, G. A. Carson, and P. B. Kelter. 2002. Assessment of motivational methods in the general chemistry laboratory. *Journal of College Science Teaching* 36 (5): 318–321.

Pintrich, P. R., and D. H. Schunk. 2002. *Motivation in education: Theory, research, and applications.* 2nd ed. Columbus, OH: Merrill.

Pintrich, P. R., D. A. F. Smith, T. Garcia, and W. J. McKeachie. 1991. *A manual for the use of the Motivated Strategies for Learning Questionnaire (MSLQ).* Ann Arbor: University of Michigan, National Center for Research to Improve Postsecondary Teaching and Learning.

Reeve, J., D. Hamm, and G. Nix. 2003. Testing models of the experience of self-determination in intrinsic motivation and the conundrum of choice. *Journal of Educational Psychology* 95: 375–392.

Ryan, R. M., and E. L. Deci. 2000. Intrinsic and extrinsic motivations: Classic definitions and new directions. *Contemporary Educational Psychology* 25: 54–67.

Seymour, E. 1992. "The problem iceberg" in science, mathematics, and engineering education: Student explanations for high attrition rates. *Journal of College Science Teaching* 21 (4): 230–238.

Singh, K., M. Granville, and S. Dika. 2002. Mathematics and science achievement: Effects of motivation, interest, and academic engagement. *Journal of Educational Research* 95: 323–332.

Smith, W. S., S. M. Gould, and J. A. Jones. 2004. Starting the semester at odds. *Journal of College Science Teaching* 34 (3): 44–49.

Zusho, A., and P. R. Pintrich. 2003. Skill and will: The role of motivation and cognition in the learning of college chemistry. *International Journal of Science Education* 25: 1081–1094.

UNIT II
Active Learning

We learn from everything we do, and everything we do becomes part of what we are. The important teaching goal is not to have students just pass the exams, but to provide experiences that make a lasting impact on the students' lives. —Marvin Druger

Because we can't change the students' expectations and needs, we need to start in our own classrooms by making some revolutionary philosophical changes in the service of improving the quality and quantity of learning. The first step toward improvement is to recognize that students aren't simply younger versions of professors. —Timothy F. Slater, Edward E. Prather, and Michael Zeilik

[Undergraduate research] is a powerful experience for students, developing skills, knowledge, attitudes, and behaviors that have a profound impact on their emergent adult identity. —Sandra Laursen, Anne-Barrie Hunter, Elaine Seymour, Tracee DeAntoni, Kristine De Welde, and Heather Thiry

Many students have considerable difficulty assimilating and understanding fundamental concepts in the natural sciences. Sometimes problems associated with meaningful learning begin in the schools where memorization is rewarded at the expense of conceptual understanding. —Joel J. Mintzes

The traditional model for teaching assumes that all information presented to students is automatically learned. As a result, most students leave their introductory science courses frustrated and without a solid conceptual understanding. —Jessica L. Rosenberg, Mercedes Lorenzo, and Eric Mazur

Unlike the past when most students had education as their primary responsibility, an ever-increasing number of students now work full-time or part-time and have family obligations. Many students also commute rather than live on campus. The open lab system gives them more flexibility. —Susan Godbey, Tom Otieno, and Daniel Tofan

We believe that teachers and students need to incorporate active learning, hands-on activities, and visualizations in the teaching and learning of scientific phenomena and processes, especially when dealing with abstract concepts. —Robert J. Beichner, Yehudit Judy Dori, and John Belcher

33

Sooner or later, many of us who interact regularly with undergraduates come to the remarkable realization that students are not "little professors" (for better or worse)! In fact, many students enter college today with an entirely different set of assumptions, experiences, and expectations than we did even a decade ago. Asking them to sit passively for 50 minutes while a professor delivers an unadorned monologue may be a recipe for disaster, given a generation accustomed to laptops, cell phones, iPods, text messaging, and BlackBerry devices. Further, it seems that this kind of traditional learning experience is bound to produce just the kind of rote learning that many of us would like to discourage. What can we do to encourage active engagement and meaningful learning in college science? In this unit we present several ideas for accommodating our teaching to the demands of a new generation of science learners.

Marvin Druger of Syracuse University describes his efforts to develop an experiential learning environment for students enrolled in a large lecture course in introductory biology. A teaching veteran of many years, Marvin has introduced a wide range of innovative practices centered on an *individualized,* self-instructional teaching-learning laboratory. Most of the practices he describes (e.g., electronic communication channels, informal meals, undergraduate research projects, flexible assessment strategies, and teaching assistant training sessions) may be readily adapted to almost any undergraduate science course.

Tim Slater, Ed Prather, and Mike Zeilik, from the University of Arizona (Slater and Prather) and University of New Mexico (Zeilik), have introduced a wide range of classroom activities designed to actively engage students in their large-enrollment lecture courses in astronomy. Many of the strategies they use are equally applicable to courses in biology, chemistry, physics, and other science-related disciplines, including several *learner-centered* techniques such as interactive demonstrations and simulations, question-posing approaches, think-pair-share, creating products, and small collaborative group activities.

One strategy that has been tried at many institutions is the *undergraduate research* experience, discussed here by Sandra Laursen, Anne-Barrie Hunter, Elaine Seymour, and associates at the University of Colorado. Based on in-depth interviews with 76 "rising seniors" and their faculty advisors and program administrators, the authors describe the personal and professional gains experienced by undergraduate researchers at several universities. The interviews offer a revealing and valuable glimpse into the minds of those engaged in these experiences.

For those who want to engage students in an activity that encourages and supports meaningful learning in science, we offer a chapter by Joel Mintzes of the University of North Carolina Wilmington describing the *concept mapping* strategy. Concept maps are two-dimensional, hierarchical, node-link diagrams that have been used successfully in virtually every scientific and technical field and at every level from elementary schools through graduate programs. Techniques for teaching and scoring concept maps and a summary of research on their usefulness are included.

Peer Instruction (PI) has been successfully used for many years by Eric Mazur and associates (including Jessica Rosenberg and Mercedes Lorenzo) in the Department of Physics at Harvard University. Integrating features of preclass reading, mini-lectures, conceptual diagnostic testing, and discussion, the PI approach has been shown to boost conceptual understanding and problem-solving abilities and to provide instructors with valuable feedback on their teaching. An assessment of this approach is included in the chapter.

The *open laboratory* is a readily implemented strategy for accommodating instruction to a multitasking generation of students whose often-busy schedules demand flexibility in scheduling. Susan Godbey, Tom Otieno, and Daniel Tofan describe how the approach has been implemented in the Department of Chemistry at Eastern Kentucky University (EKU). In addition to the time flexibility it offers, the strategy promotes efficient use of space and saves costs. This chapter discusses EKU's current laboratory arrangement and their plans for further development.

Bob Beichner, Judy Dori, and John Belcher describe their efforts to implement *interactive learning* in physics courses at North Carolina State University (NCSU) and the Massachusetts Institute of Technology (MIT). The SCALE-UP (Student-Centered Activities for Large Enrollment Undergraduate Programs) effort at NCSU and the TEAL (Technology Enabled Active Learning) environment at MIT are designed to encourage understanding of physics concepts and to help students create cognitive links between the world of mathematics and physics. Results of assessment studies are presented.

CHAPTER 4

Experiential Learning in a Large Introductory Biology Course

Marvin Druger

Marvin Druger is professor of biology and science education, Laura J. and L. Douglas Meredith Professor for Teaching Excellence, and chairman of the Department of Science Teaching at Syracuse University. He earned a PhD in zoology at Columbia University and conducts research in science education and science literacy. He teaches general biology and a graduate course in science education. Dr. Druger is former president of the Society for College Science Teachers, the National Science Teachers Association, and the Association for Science Teacher Education.

The development and the teaching of large introductory college science courses is not an easy task. Such courses generally enroll first-year students with diverse backgrounds and abilities, and psychological as well as content components need to be considered. This chapter describes and discusses effective approaches to teaching a large, two-semester introductory college biology course (General Biology 121 and 123) at Syracuse University. I have taught introductory biology at Syracuse University since 1962, and the philosophy and teaching methods that have evolved for this course will be discussed. Elements that are transferable and generalizable for other introductory science courses will be emphasized.

The chapter emphasizes the significance of unusual, meaningful experiences, rather than acquisition of scientific content per se. The theme is "we learn from everything we do, and everything we do becomes part of what we are." The important teaching goal is not to have students just pass the exams, but to provide experiences that make a lasting impact on the students' lives.

Goals of the Course

Some major goals of the introductory biology course are described below.

- *Increase subject matter competency:* This means learning basic scientific vocabulary and how to use it to understand and communicate concepts. Some teachers argue that students should not have to memorize vocabulary but rather should learn how to think critically. Critical thinking is desirable, but students cannot think critically about nothing. They need a vocabulary base, and advanced biology courses can build on this base. I believe that vocabulary building is important. New terms are constantly being introduced in science as new discoveries are made (e.g., *genomics, proteomics, bioinformatics*). Scientists don't make up words for fun; they invent them as devices to explain concepts and facilitate communication.

- *Recognize science as a human activity:* Science is a process and a body of knowledge that is built by human beings who are trying to make logical sense out of nature. As such, there are uncertainties, mistakes, changing "truths," and even fraud. Students should recognize the logical processes of science and the fallible aspects of humans who try to work with these processes to reveal natural principles. Students often think they "know" the answers when they enter the course, and that these answers are unchanging. We need to convince students that they know *less* about biology when they complete the course than they *think* they knew when they started the course. Then they can approach science with an open, inquiring mind that can critically analyze our scientific knowledge and how it was obtained.

- *Recognize the relevance of science:* Whenever possible, we need to stress how biology is relevant to the student's everyday life. A key question the teacher should ask is, "If I were a student in this class, what would I want to know about the subject and why?" and teach accordingly. But we also need to inform students that not everything they will learn in the course is relevant to health, society, environmental issues, and other practical areas. Some of the content is simply relevant to their intellectual framework. It's just nice to know things, even if they aren't relevant in a practical sense. Informing students about these different interpretations of "relevance" enables them to view the course offerings in a broader context.

- *Think about problems in a scientific manner:* I believe this is a very difficult goal to achieve, but we should try to encourage it as much as possible. It's very difficult to turn students into critical thinkers in one or two semesters. This process needs to be started in childhood and sustained over many years, but we do the best we can.

- *Improve reading, writing, and speaking skills:* Students need such skills in every arena of life, and opportunities should be offered in the course to improve these skills.

- *Improve skills in use of technology:* The modern world certainly emphasizes technology, and students need to be proficient in its use.

- *Develop a positive attitude toward science and life:* In a class of mixed science majors and nonscience majors, there are some students who dislike science but must take a science course to fulfill a college requirement. Our challenge is to show them that science is interesting and relevant and that they can learn science.

- *Help students become motivated self-learners:* I believe this is the most important goal for an introductory college science course. We want students to enjoy science, recognize its role in the world, gain greater self-confidence about learning science, and want to learn more about science. One colleague commented, "Our job as teachers is to inform and motivate students, but, if we motivate them, they inform themselves." One of the most important goals in my biology course is to "teach students to want to learn."

The overall goal is to provide unusual, meaningful experiences that will enrich the students' lives and influence their thinking and attitude about themselves and about *life* many years after the course is over. We want to create a motivational learning environment concerning life, and many special features have been incorporated into the course to accomplish this mission.

Teaching Methods and Special Features

The core of the course is taught using audio CDs that integrate lecture and laboratory components. Students work in study carrels in an individualized, flexible fashion. Lab is open six days a week, including nights, and students attend on a flexible, individual schedule. This approach places the learning and time management in the students' hands, and they are obliged to acquire individualized study skills (see Chapter 9 in this volume for a description of the open laboratory strategy). I developed the laboratory manuals and the accompanying CDs. In addition to spending four to six hours a week in the lab/CD setting, students attend one recitation a week (taught by a graduate teaching assistant [TA]) and one lecture a week (taught by me). I also hold an optional session each week for discussions, questions, or showing relevant science films.

Special features in the course are listed below.

- *Helpful Hints:* This is a comprehensive course syllabus that explains everything students might want to know about the course, including course objectives, content outline, schedules, lab hours, books and materials, reading assignments, special assignments, special events, policies on attendance, policy on academic dishonesty, information about exams and grading procedures, and other helpful hints about how to be successful in the course. The importance of experiences is emphasized right at the start of the semester, and regular attendance is essential to benefit from the experiences.
- *Communication:* An integral part of a motivational learning environment involves having channels for frequent communication and interactions between the teacher and the students. I prepare a weekly newsletter that has many useful features, including "Content Updates" and a "What's Going On" column. By reading this newsletter, students always know exactly what's happening in the course. The newsletter is also posted on the course website each week. In addition, we use Blackboard as an electronic communication channel. Also, the Staff Locator List provides information about names, addresses, e-mail addresses, and availability of all the TAs. TA mailboxes are also available to students in the lab. I hold open office hours and make myself available for student interactions at *any* time of day or night, including weekends. Whenever students have a problem or question, they are encouraged to contact me in the office or at home. I also

have official office hours on Wednesday mornings from 8:30 to 10:30 a.m. Students do not abuse the concept of open office hours. When a student knocks on the office door and asks if I'm busy, it is tempting to scream and say, "Yes. Please don't bother me now." Instead, I remind myself that students are my business. I deal with the student's problem and soon realize that my "important" work could really wait. This approach builds good rapport and demonstrates to students that I care.

- *Bio-lunches:* Several students drop their names into a suggestion box along with the phone number of one student, who is the designated contact. I call the designated contact student and arrange a bio-lunch at the residence dining hall. The bio-lunches provide me with an opportunity to interact with students in a small group several times a week. Bio-lunches also provide me with feedback about the course. Complimentary meal tickets for me are provided by the Office of Residential Life.

- *Bio-creativity project:* In addition to optional laboratory projects, students are encouraged to develop a special project about life. The goal is to stimulate students to think creatively about life. Students have created poems, short stories, songs, posters, computer animations, models, and constructions of many designs. Students whose projects show creativity and effort are awarded points toward their final course grade.

- *Frontiers of Science lecture series:* Since 1988, I have been coordinating an evening lecture series of three lectures per semester that involve presentations by scientists in the local community. The series is designed to make people aware of some of the latest developments in science and to stimulate thought and discussion about the social, moral, and ethical implications of these advances. The audience includes students from my general biology course and other science courses, graduate students, faculty, staff, high school students, and people from the Syracuse community. Many units at the university contribute money to pay for brochures, advertising, refreshments, and a small gift for the speakers.

- *Pathways to Knowledge lecture series:* This series involves three lectures per semester by advanced PhD students in different disciplines. The audience consists of students from my general biology course and other courses, as well as graduate students. The goal is to provide students with insights about PhD-level research in different disciplines and to give the PhD student an opportunity to practice making a dissertation presentation to a nonthreatening audience.

- *Midnight Lectures:* This series of research presentations made by research scientists provides a subject-matter enrichment for the general biology students and gives them insights about scientific research. The lectures were originally scheduled for 11 p.m. to midnight, and door prizes (from the Dollar Store) were given out at midnight. In 2005, the Midnight Lectures were moved to 8:00–9:00 p.m., but they are still called Midnight Lectures.

- *Benefit-of-the-doubt credit:* I want to encourage all students in my general biology course to experience all the extra learning opportunities that are made available. If they do not attend, they miss the experience, and they'll never know what they missed. If they do attend, they may enrich their lives. An effective way of encouraging attendance is to offer benefit-of-the-doubt credit for attendance at these special events. Students obtain a ticket to the event in class, and, at the end of the event, they hand in the ticket with their name and section number on it. We keep a computerized record of attendance at these events. At the end of the semester, we check the attendance. If a student is on a grade borderline, attendance at the special events will boost the grade. Students have responded very well to this approach, and hundreds of students attend each special event.

- *Biofeast:* Near the end of the General Biology 121 course, I organize the Biofeast. This is designed as a celebration of the completion of the course. A dining hall manager sets up a special meal, complete with hors d'oeuvres, tablecloths, and a huge cake, and students get a ticket for this event. A review session for the last exam and door prizes are part of the festivities. TAs also attend, and the Biofeast serves as a memorable climax to the first semester of the course.

- *Cooperative plant research project:* I want every student in the course to have a firsthand research experience. At the start of the second semester, teams of two to four students are established. They are introduced to scientific methodology, and each team has to develop a well-designed plant research project. The TA critiques the plan and then approves the project. The teams do the research over the entire semester. A written research report is handed in, and a grade is assigned. Each member of the team has to contribute in some substantial way to the project, and the contributions are included in the report. Oral reports in recitation class are also encouraged.

- *Special sections:* Because of the large, diverse student enrollment, I want to provide a variety of optional learning opportunities, so that all students can be sufficiently challenged. Students who earn a B or better in the first semester can apply to take a special section concurrently with the second-semester (General Biology 123) course. The special sections focus on specific areas of biology (e.g., molecular biology, cancer biology, ecology), and they are taught by an experienced biology TA who has expertise in the special topic. Students thus learn the core subject matter in the second semester (earning 4 credits) and can delve into greater depth in Biology 200 (earning 2 credits). We also have a special section for students who worked hard but earned a C or lower in the first semester. This section is not for additional course credit, but students have two recitations a week, instead of one, and the section is taught by an experienced TA. Students are given the extra attention and help that they need, and grades usually improve for the second semester.

- *Pig interview:* Students do a pig dissection as part of the course. I encourage students to have this firsthand experience, but students who object strongly to dissection are given alternatives. Students who do the dissection can work with a partner, but each student must meet with a TA at the end of the semester for a 15-minute pig interview. The student's knowledge of anatomy and physiology are assessed, and, most important, the TA is told to have a conversation with each student about course performance and future career plans. I try to meet as many students as I can, but conversing individually with many hundreds of students is not feasible. So the pig interview was established to make sure that every student in the course has a one-on-one conversation with an instructor at least once during the year.

- *Review sessions:* I hold a review session before each major exam. Basically, I review an old exam, and many questions on the actual exam are modifications of questions asked on old exams. The rationale is that I know what I think is important for students to know, so why not tell them? Students should not have to guess what's important in the instructor's mind. For example, I want students to be able to analyze inheritance of ABO blood groups. So, I tell them that a question on the exam will be similar to the following question: "If the mother is type A and the father is not AB, which of the following could not be the blood type of the child?" The actual question on the exam will simply change the blood types in the question. Also, former exams are available on reserve in the libraries, so that students can review content and get a good idea of the style of the exams.

- *Biophone:* The night before major exams, I encourage students to call me at home (or a TA on duty at school) to get answers to last-minute questions or to get psychological reassurance.

- *Exam reforms:* I want to know how well students know the course content, not how fast they know it. So, three major exams are given in the evening, outside of class hours, and students are allowed two hours for a one-hour exam. More time is available if needed. Students keep the exam, and answer keys are distributed immediately after each exam so that students can check their answers when they are most interested in doing so. In fact, after each exam, I throw answer keys out of a second-floor window to a crowd of eager students below. This is an efficient and fun way to distribute the answer keys, and students respond well to this unusual approach.

- *Grading procedures:* A flexible grading scale is established at the start of the course. About 70% of the final grade comes from my major exams, and about 30% of the final grade comes from the recitations taught by TAs. My exams consist of multiple-choice questions, but the quizzes in recitation consist of essay questions. The grading components are set up as points. All students who earn 90% of the points or above will get an A, and so on. Students who get less than 50% of the course do not pass, unless there are special extenuating circumstances. Thus, students do not compete against each other for a grade. At the end of the semester, I meet individually with each TA for a grade interview. TAs have assembled grade records and are prepared to discuss special circumstances. Attendance is considered and appropriate adjustments are made. These procedures are thus fair and individualized.

- *Praise and rewards:* I want to recognize and praise students who earn an A or A− in the course. Each student who does excellent work is sent a letter of congratulations and encouragement at the end of the Biology 121 and 123 semesters; the letter invites them to drop in to talk about their future careers. If a student earns an A both semesters, he or she also receives a wallet-sized certificate of excellence. These tokens of recognition have been greatly appreciated and are motivating to students.

- *TA professional development:* I have instituted a program in the Biology Department to help TAs who assist in the general biology course be more effective teachers. All new TAs are required to participate in an all-university orientation session conducted by the graduate school. The training is continued in various departments. The TA training program in the Biology Department involves Teaching Notes with teaching tips and updates; resource notebooks containing materials from previous TAs; peer videotaping and critiques; written critiques of TA teaching by students enrolled in my course on the teaching of college science; formative and summative assessments by students; and a compilation of positive and negative student comments into a teaching profile for each TA.

- *Formative and summative course assessment:* A student assessment of all parts of the course is done a few weeks after the course starts. This early feedback allows for changes while the course is still in progress. An anonymous, open-ended student evaluation is done at the end of each semester, as well as a more specific, anonymous evaluation about the course components. More than 70% of the students consistently rate the overall course (including all aspects) from Good to Excellent. Considering the large size of the course and its heterogeneous composition, this rating seems very positive. There is room for improvement, but, after many years of student evaluations, I am convinced that it's not possible to please every student. With a large, heterogeneous class, there will always be students who love the course and those who dislike it. We have to accept this fact, and keep trying our best to do better.

To accomplish our goals, it is essential that students be encouraged to attend special events and to participate fully. Benefit-of-the-doubt credit does serve as an incentive. If students attend, they may well be "turned on" and motivated to attend even more special events in the future. If they don't attend, they'll never know what they missed. If they do experience the event, it may convey a new insight that they "never thought about that way before." I feel strongly about attendance, and the course policy is that students who don't attend and participate in lecture, lab, and recitation will not receive a passing grade in the course, even if they do well on major exams and earn a passing percentage of total points. If we are to achieve our objectives, experiential learning warrants mandatory attendance.

An important part of success in our approach is to provide the rationale for each component of the course. For example, rather than simply tell students that we hold the major exams at night, we explain the reasons, including room availability, allowing two hours to complete a one-hour exam, the intent to avoid stressing the student about time, and the intent to determine how well students know the content rather than how fast they know it. If we don't have a good rationale for each course component, then why include it?

Conclusion

Overall, the course seems to have a positive influence on students, as evidenced by course evaluations and by informal communications from former students. The course offers many unusual and creative experiences that enhance student learning and create a motivational learning environment that will influence the future lives of students in a positive manner. The experiences focus on personal growth, reflection, and a desire to learn, as well as scientific content. All of the course features described in this chapter are transferable to other introductory college science courses, and I hope that some of these features may prove useful for your course.

CHAPTER 5

Strategies for Interactive Engagement in Large Lecture Science Survey Classes

Timothy F. Slater, Edward E. Prather, and Michael Zeilik

Timothy F. Slater is associate professor of astronomy at the University of Arizona. He earned a PhD in astronomy education at the University of South Carolina and conducts research on the teaching and learning of astronomy. He teaches courses in introductory astronomy.

Edward E. Prather is assistant research scientist at the University of Arizona. He earned a PhD in physics education at the University of Maine and conducts research on the teaching and learning of astronomy. He teaches courses in introductory astronomy.

Michael Zeilik is professor emeritus of physics and astronomy at the University of New Mexico. He earned a PhD in astronomy at Harvard University and conducts research on the teaching and learning of astronomy. He teaches courses in introductory astronomy.

What is so hard about teaching large-enrollment introductory science courses anyway? It seems as if all the hard work should pay off, doesn't it? You can see the effort that goes into a class when you walk down the department hallways, peering into faculty offices. Faculty are feverishly preparing their lecture notes to carefully cover all the many ideas presented in their textbook. They are madly searching internet sites to find just the right image or animation to make complex ideas crystal clear to students. Moreover, faculty often allocate considerable time to organize as many of these resources as possible into projected PowerPoint presentations that can be shared electronically with students and build multilayered websites with countless hyperlinks to even more detailed information than faculty had time to

5

adequately describe during lecture. And then there are tests to create, and, if other time or resources are available, homework to design, assign, collect, grade, record, and return.

One has to wonder if all of this effort is really worth it. Faculty often report to us that, for the first time they teach a class, they allocate three to five hours for preparing each 50-minute lecture. Yet at the end of the semester, even for the most knowledgeable, enthusiastic, and dedicated lecturers, far too many nonscience major undergraduates report that their classes are boring, irrelevant, and just plain a waste of everyone's limited time (Tobias 1990). All the bases are covered, and yet no one is fully satisfied in the end. How could this be?

Who's to Blame?

The lore among many students is that college faculty have never been taught how to teach, are too busy with their "publish or perish" world, are unapproachable, or just don't care about teaching nonmajors. A quick stroll through the online site *www.ratemyprofessors.com* reveals a pretty dismal perspective on the experience of many college students. Such negative impressions about poor teaching are confirmed by systematic research studies, even when looking at students with high aptitudes (Goodstein 1993a, 1993b; Seymour and Hewitt 1997; Tobias 1992).

The fingers of blame point the other way, too. Hallway conversations among faculty often describe students as being lazy, ill prepared, unwilling or unable to read science texts, too busy with their social lives, working at their jobs for too many hours, taking too many classes, generally too unmotivated to see how science is relevant to their lives, and just not like students were when the faculty members were undergraduates. You might be surprised to know from our experience talking with hundreds of faculty that complaints about students are nearly identical across institutions, whether they are describing students at rural, commuter community colleges, open-enrollment state universities, or private Ivy League universities.

It is possible that as you read this you are saying to yourself, "Oh, no, not me, not my class. Everything is great in my class." That might well be true—there are some amazing teachers who are doing amazing things in their classes—but it is our position that every class can be improved. Sometimes it can appear that everything is going just fine, when it really isn't. This is because many professors and students have a sort of "hidden contract" with one another (see Slater 2003). The gist of this unwritten and unstated contract is that "the professor will tell the students what to memorize and will only ask students questions directly related to this list on the exams, and, in exchange, students will dutifully memorize the material given during lecture and, if they fail to adequately memorize the material, students will not complain too loudly if a poor grade is assigned." Designing a class that subconsciously and quietly takes advantage of the hidden contract isn't terrible; in fact, it is quite common. However, higher education research on faculty evaluations convincingly dispels the myth that faculty who have the easiest classes and give the largest percentage of A grades also achieve the highest course evaluation scores. In multiple institutions and various classes it is clear that students actually give the highest ratings to faculty when students perceive that they have been appropriately challenged and have grown intellectually from the experience (Gusthart et al. 2005; Harrison, Ryan, and Moore 1996; Ryan and Harrison 1995).

Rethinking Introductory Science Courses

How does one begin to bridge this gulf between expectations and needs of students and professors? Because we can't change the students' expectations and needs, we need to start in our own classrooms by making some revolutionary philosophical changes in the service of improving the quality and quantity of learning. The first step toward improvement is to recognize that students aren't simply younger versions of professors. Most students do not have the same motivations, interests, backgrounds, learning styles, or aptitudes as college professors. Many science faculty actually wanted to become practicing scientists and went through many years of training in science, adopting a scientific doctrine that is quite foreign to most students. The second step is to accept that much of the responsibility for student learning resides squarely with the students—not with the professor. Faculty can motivate, inspire, and build a series of experiences that make the discipline more accessible, but they cannot do the learning for students. In fact, this notion has encouraged us to adopt the perspective that "it's not what the instructor does that matters; rather, it is what the students do" (Slater and Adams 2002). If faculty can accept these two propositions, then the way is paved to make some remarkable changes to improve the large-enrollment Science 101 course.

A learner-centered course is one that is structured around what students are doing to learn the material instead of just what the professor happens to be lecturing about. Indeed, lecture is still an important part of a learner-centered course. However, the role of lecture in a learner-centered course is radically shifted from dispensing knowledge in a conventional course to a focus on guiding students through meaningful learning experiences.

The following subsections describe some things that faculty in large-enrollment introductory astronomy courses do to intellectually engage students in learning the material during class time. These strategies are easily transferable to other scientific disciplines; however, the effectiveness of these approaches has been particularly well documented from a research perspective in a large-enrollment introductory astronomy survey course for nonscience majors and is described in that context. The strategies are listed somewhat hierarchically, from most professor-centered and easiest to implement to most learner-centered and requiring more skill to implement. Although important, an in-depth discussion of out-of-class assignments or inquiry-based laboratory experiences is beyond the scope of this chapter.

Use Interactive Lecture Demonstrations and Simulations

Faculty in the physical sciences have the distinct advantage over faculty in other areas in that classroom demonstrations can be provocative, provide illustrative clarification, and, most importantly, excite the learner through direct experiences with unexpected physical phenomena. Similarly, computer-based simulations can be easily demonstrated to students in most classrooms. However, research on the effectiveness of classroom demonstrations shows that the most important part of the demonstration is asking students to predict what they will see and what will happen when particular variables are changed and then having the students commit to these predictions in writing. It is in the act of predicting and rationalizing these predictions where most of the learning occurs from demonstrations and simulations (Sokoloff and Thornton 1997).

Pose Meaningful Questions to Students

To suggest asking students some questions in class as another technique to improve learning using an learner-centered approach might seem a tad silly. However, the number of faculty who actually pose nonrhetorical questions to students is surprisingly small, especially in large lecture courses. Probably the biggest mistake that faculty make is to pose cognitively low-level questions that are too easily answered by students relying on preexisting declarative knowledge. Students responding quickly, and in unison, is often mistaken for meaningful dialogue between a professor and the class. Questions should be intellectually challenging and should be carefully crafted to lead the students to deeper levels of understanding or to illustrate the power of scientific ideas. In a similar way, questions such as "Does everyone understand?" and "Do you have any questions?" do not provide faculty with the desired insight into whether or not students actually comprehend the ideas being presented.

Particularly in the context of a large lecture hall, it is very easy for faculty to hold classroom discussion with only the students in the first few front rows (Perkins and Wieman 2005). In this situation, it doesn't take too many class sessions before students farther back in the classroom realize that questions posed by the professors don't actually need to be contemplated because only the first few rows are required to respond. Therefore, some system of accountability needs to be implemented. Some faculty draw names at random from a hat to ask specific students questions and award credit for their participation. One popular technique is to write names on flat wooden sticks using a color code that distinguishes male names from female names so that faculty can evenly alternate between males and females, even though the process appears random to students. Faculty also find value in repeating questions posed in class verbatim as a small portion of exams to emphasize the importance of the questions used in class.

Probably the easiest teaching skill to understand, yet the most difficult to implement, is to ask meaningful questions and then wait patiently. The most common error in leading classroom discussions is a lack of wait time. Researchers who carefully track classroom dynamics have found that faculty who too quickly provide clarifying information or respond to the first person who answers a question completely squash further discussion and divergent thinking (Rowe 1987; Tobin 1987). The common advice is to wait at least 10 seconds before saying anything after posing a question. If everyone in the class can answer your question in less than 10 seconds, then the question isn't conceptually challenging enough. When you pose a question, it is reasonable to ask students to think for a little while before raising their hands to offer answers. One particularly useful strategy to help fidgety faculty be certain that a full 10 seconds elapses before accepting a range of student responses is to fill the time by turning away from the class, taking a sip of coffee, or flipping through lecture notes without looking at the class. Moreover, it is important to ask students to explain the reasoning behind their answers and not reveal if the initial responses are correct before accepting several other answers.

Ask Students to Think-Pair-Share

Think-pair-share is a technique that capitalizes on the gregarious nature of many students. The teacher first poses a multiple-choice question and asks students to individually think about the question and then, without talking to anyone else, commit to and vote on an answer. It is crucial that students commit to an initial idea so that they can actively compare their initial thinking with any new understandings that might result after discussion with a peer. Next, students are asked to pair with another person in the class, usually the one sitting next to them, and to share their answer and articulate the reasoning behind their answer. In our application, we ask each student to convince his or her neighbor why the answer is correct. After a minute or two, at most, of collaborative discussion, students are then asked to respond to, or vote on, the question a second time. We ask students to vote anonymously by holding one, two, three, or four fingers close to their chests to indicate their answers. Colored or lettered index cards can also be used.

The hope of the teacher is that through social conversations with peers, students will develop a more complete understanding (Crouch et al. 2004; Crouch and Mazur 2001; Green 2003; Mazur 1997). The voting allows faculty to monitor the students' conceptual growth.

Inexpensive technology is now available to make this process of voting and collecting student responses more attractive to students. Wireless personal response systems (PRS), which usually look like TV remote controls and are sometimes known simply as "clickers," are becoming common across the country in many large lecture halls. Publishing companies, to increase textbook adoptions for large-enrollment courses, will often install all the needed receiving technology for colleges in exchange for the promise of textbook adoptions where students also buy (or rent). These systems allow faculty to quickly obtain a range of responses in think-pair-share settings. Although the direct impact of the technology on student learning is debatable, there is considerable evidence that students like using the clickers (Dokter et al. 2004; Duncan 2005).

Challenge Students to Create Products

Lecture has been sometimes described pejoratively as "the process by which what is written on the professor's notes gets transferred into students' notebooks without passing through the brains of either." In contrast, all learner-centered classrooms have at least one thing in common—students are actually creating products rather than just passively listening to a professor dispensing knowledge. Students in even the most basic of learner-centered classrooms do more than mindlessly recopy notes projected by the professor; they add notations and fill in missing pieces to partially completed forms distributed to students at the beginning of class. Providing students with fragmented notes to be completed during class gives students an expert framework to build their own understanding in a way that is much more effective than providing students with complete copies of faculty lecture notes (Cohn, Cohn, and Bradley 1995).

There is a long tradition in astronomy courses to ask students to select, read, and summarize articles from the popular press to support faculty goals aimed at building students' interest in lifelong learning (Bobrowsky 1999; Shipman 2000). Although these are important experiences, there are other approaches that would be considered to be more learner centered. One such approach, advocated by Talenquer and Morgan (2005) and others, has students organize their knowledge into their own media products by creating press releases, brochures, posters, board games, websites, newspaper stories, and point/counterpoint op-ed pieces. These can be turned in like any other assignment or, better yet, displayed for other students as part of a mini-symposium or collected in a science learning portfolio (Astwood and Slater 1997; Slater 1997).

One of us (MZ) has had considerable success in introductory astronomy using a strategy known as concept maps (Brissenden, Slater, and Mathieu 2002; Zeilik et al. 1997). A concept map is a diagram of nodes, each containing concept labels enclosed in a box or an oval, which are linked together with directional lines, also labeled. The concept nodes are arranged in hierarchical levels that move from general to specific concepts. The core element of a concept map is a proposition, which consists of two or more concepts connected by a labeled link. In a concept map, propositions are connected to form a branching structure that represents the organization of astronomy knowledge in long-term memory. The basic assumptions of the concept map are that interrelatedness is an essential property of knowledge and that understanding can be represented through a rich set of relations among important concepts in a discipline.

What underlies this approach is that meaningful human learning, as opposed to rote memorization, occurs when new knowledge is consciously and purposively linked to an existing framework of prior knowledge in a nonarbitrary, substantive fashion. In rote memorization, new concepts are added to the learner's framework in an arbitrary and verbatim way, producing a weak and unstable structure that quickly fades after the students have taken the exam. Concept maps can help students develop more robust conceptual structures.

Because of the creative nature of concept maps, student frustration levels can be very high when concept mapping is first introduced, especially in large classes. To mitigate some of this anxiety and to encourage students to reflect on their own thinking, groups of three or four students can work collaboratively on a concept map, which initially may or may not be related to astronomy. This approach can engender a rich learning experience as peers argue, debate, and cajole each other. The result is a genuine effort at negotiating the meaning of scientific concepts and attempting to reach consensus. As with most collaborative group learning activities, the power of the process resides in the social construction of knowledge.

Capitalize on Students' Tendency to Socialize With Learning Groups

Breaking students into small, collaborative learning groups to solve a meaningful task is one of the most successful and fully evaluated teaching techniques implemented over the last century. Many faculty initially express concern that if they stop lecturing and leave the students to talk among themselves, students will not naturally engage in a discussion of the subject at hand. Our experience is that students will readily talk to one another and stay on task for several minutes at a time if the questions are posed at the right conceptual level, not too easy or too hard, and if students see that struggling with the question has relevance to their class grade. Indeed, students speaking readily in the classroom as opposed to simply listening is a hallmark of learner-centered classrooms. As an example, we have had tremendous success in large lecture classes using brief small-group activities we call lecture-tutorials (Adams, Prather, and Slater 2005). Lecture-tutorials use carefully crafted question sequences based on Socratic dialogues that lead students to develop conceptual models that are then used to demonstrate the depth of the understanding in novel situations (Prather et al. 2004).

Another approach that often engages collaborative learning groups in meaningful conversations is providing students with dilemmas to be solved through case studies. Case study tasks ask students to synthesize several ideas or evaluate scenarios that have not been presented to them in class or in their texts. For example, if learning about small telescopes is an important component of a class, the following might be a corresponding case study:

You have been given $6,000 to spend on telescope equipment for a local outreach program at the community museum. Using the provided telescope and binocular catalog, explain exactly how you would allocate this money and justify each piece of equipment purchased.

This type of case study (adapted from Adams and Slater 2000), which might have the initial appearance of being simplistic, asks students to work at the higher levels of Bloom's taxonomy of educational objectives (Bloom et al. 1956) and asks students to use their knowledge to create and justify decisions as well as evaluate scenarios.

Implementing small collaborative learning groups in large lecture classes warrants some special considerations (Adams and Slater 2002). Although conventional logic suggests that faculty should intentionally form learning groups heterogeneously to mix gender, aptitude, interest, cultural background, and other factors (Adams et al. 2002), we have found that forcing group composition is impractical in large lecture halls. Rather, we ask students to stand up and form their own groups. Groups that are sitting four in a row never work as well as groups of four sitting in two rows face-to-face so they can interact more easily. Sitting on desks or on the backs of chairs is perfectly acceptable to us. Another suggestion is to ask students who arrive after the collaborative learning activity begins to come down to the front of the class and work with other students who have arrived late. This has the dual benefit of encouraging students to be on time and not allowing students to ride on the coattails of their peers.

Which Topics Should Be Taught?

Given the breadth of astronomy, a course that quite literally "covers the entire universe" is impractical. In fact, courses that attempt to cover too much material force students away from genuine efforts to actually understand the concepts and instead push them toward shallow, short-term memorization strategies and "survival" techniques. The most challenging part of designing an introductory astronomy course is not what to include, but rather what to leave out! Fortunately, there exists at least some consensus among people who teach astronomy. Faculty preregistered for a workshop on teaching introductory astronomy were asked to describe their three main goals for the course (Slater et al. 2001). For faculty course goals, this sample revealed that faculty most valued acquiring scientific knowledge (57% of respondents), followed by an appreciation of the nature of science (28%) and engendering a value for lifelong learning (15%). Second, we examined 37 course syllabi and compared the content to 67 topics extracted from the extended table of contents for popular introductory astronomy textbooks. Based on the frequency of topic coverage, the top five topics were (1) nature of light and the electromagnetic spectrum, (2) spectroscopic techniques in astronomy, (3) cosmology and the big bang, (4) tools and telescopes, and (5) the solar system.

Using a different approach, one of us (MZ) asked 42 participants in an American Association of Physics Teachers workshop on teaching astronomy to complete a conceptual ranking task on the topics they teach (Zeilik and Morris-Dueer 2005). Their top five were (1) electromagnetic spectrum, (2) Hertzsprung-Russell diagram, (3) Newton's law of gravitation, (4) distances, and (5) spectra.

From a totally different perspective, the American Astronomical Society (AAS) (Partridge and Greenstein 2003) convened two working groups of department chairs and other department instructional leaders from the largest PhD-granting research universities. The sessions involved three dozen participants from 30 institutions. Their consensus for what should be included in an introductory astronomy course is summarized as follows:

- A cosmic perspective: a broad understanding of the nature, scope, and evolution of the universe and where the Earth and solar system fit in
- An understanding of a limited number of crucial astronomical quantities together with some knowledge of appropriate physical laws
- The notion that physical laws and processes are universal
- The notions that the world is knowable and that we are coming to know it through observations, experiments, and theory (the nature of progress in science)
- An exposure to the types, roles, and degrees of uncertainty in science

When Lippert and Partridge (2004) adopted all the outcomes from the AAS list in a small ($N = 38$) introductory astronomy class at Haverford College, they found that the students ranked "a cosmic perspective" as having the highest interest.

Taken together, what we find is that faculty say they are most interested in having students learn the fundamental ideas underlying astrophysical concepts, and not simply the vocabulary defined by the bold-faced words in the textbooks. This also means it is most important to cover fewer topics but in more depth, with numerous examples and applications.

Final Thoughts

To paraphrase the theologian and philosopher Paul Tillich (1886–1965), the fatal pedagogical error is to throw answers, like stones, to students that do not have questions. This is particularly true in the large lecture classroom where having meaningful interactions with many students seems daunting. However, by converting from a professor-centered classroom where the lecturing professor is the fountain of all knowledge to a learner-centered classroom where students are actively engaged and metacognitively monitoring their learning, faculty can get out from behind the lectern and actually listen to and interact with students by walking around the room. For some faculty, there is a paradigm shift, or simply a sense of a leap of faith, that accompanies the recognition that students don't learn the same way that faculty did. For others, a motivation to move away from lectures is based on years of being unsatisfied with student achievement and attitudes, particularly in the large lecture classroom. Regardless, we rarely encounter a faculty member who was not sincerely pleased when he or she earnestly adopted a learner-centered classroom that changed the focus from the professor's lecture to a classroom centered on what students are actually doing. After all, are you really teaching if no one is learning?

References

Adams, J. P., E. E. Prather, and T. F. Slater. 2005. *Lecture-tutorials for introductory astronomy.* Upper Saddle River, NJ: Prentice Hall/Pearson Education.

Adams, J. P., and T. F. Slater. 2000. *Mysteries of the sky.* Dubuque, IA: Kendall/Hunt.

Adams, J. P., and T. F. Slater. 2002. Learning through sharing: Supplementing the astronomy lecture with collaborative learning group activities. *Journal of College Science Teaching* 31 (6): 384–387.

Adams, J. P., T. F. Slater, G. Brissenden, R. Lindell-Adrian, and J. Wallace. 2002. Observations of student behavior in collaborative learning groups. *Astronomy Education Review* 1 (1): 25–32.

Astwood, P. M., and T. F. Slater. 1997. The effectiveness and management of portfolio assessment in large-enrollment courses. *Journal of Geoscience Education* 45 (3): 238–242.

Bloom, B. S., M. B. Englehart, E. J. Furst, W. H. Hill, and D. R. Krathwohl. 1956. *Taxonomy of educational objectives: The classification of educational goals.* Handbook I: Cognitive domain. New York: Longmans, Green.

Bobrowsky, M. 1999. News clippings for introductory astronomy. *The Physics Teacher* 37 (6): 374–375.

Brissenden, G., T. F. Slater, and R. Mathieu. 2002. An assessment primer for Introductory Astronomy. *Astronomy Education Review* 1 (1): 1–24.

Cohn, E., S. Cohn, and J. Bradley. 1995. Notetaking, working memory, and learning in Principles of Economics. *Journal of Economic Education* 26 (4): 291–307.

Crouch, C. H., and E. Mazur. 2001. Peer Instruction: Ten years of experience and results. *American Journal of Physics* 69 (9): 970–977.

Crouch, C. H., A. P. Fagen, J. P. Callan, and E. Mazur. 2004. Classroom demonstrations: Learning tools or entertainment? *American Journal of Physics* 72 (6): 835–838.

Dokter, E. C., G. Brissenden, E. E. Prather, and T. F. Slater. 2004. The use and impact of personal responder devices in Astro 101. *Bulletin of the American Astronomical Society* 36 (2): [Abstract] 16.04.

Duncan, D. 2005. *Clickers in the classroom: How to enhance science teaching using classroom response systems.* San Francisco, CA: Pearson Education.

Goodstein, D. 1993a. Scientific elites and scientific illiterates. In *1993 Sigma Xi forum proceedings: Ethics, values, and the promise of science.* [Research Triangle Park, NC]: Sigma Xi, the Scientific Research Society.

Goodstein, D. 1993b. Scientific Ph.D problems. *American Scholar* 62 (2): 215–220.

Green, P. J. 2003. *Peer instruction for astronomy.* Upper Saddle River, NJ: Prentice Hall/Pearson Education.

Gusthart, L., P. Harrison, J. Ryan, and P. Moore. 2005. An examination of college students' insights into how they make overall evaluations of teaching effectiveness. *Journal of Excellence in College Teaching* 16 (1): 109–124.

Harrison, P. D., J. M. Ryan, and P. S. Moore. 1996. College students' self-insight and common implicit theories in rating of teaching effectiveness. *Journal of Educational Psychology* 88: 775–782.

Lippert, N., and B. Partridge. 2004. To hear ourselves as others hear us. *Astronomy Education Review* 3 (1): 31–50.

Mazur, E. 1997. *Peer Instruction: A user's manual.* Upper Saddle River, NJ: Prentice Hall.

Partridge, B., and G. Greenstein. 2003. Goals for "Astro 101": Report on workshops for department leaders. *Astronomy Education Review* 2 (2): 46–89.

Perkins, K. K., and C. E. Wieman. 2005. The surprising impact of seat location on student performance. *The Physics Teacher* 43 (1): 30–33.

Prather, E. E., T. F. Slater, J. P. Adams, J. M. Bailey, L. V. Jones, and J. A. Dostal. 2004. Research on a lecture-tutorial approach to teaching introductory astronomy for nonscience majors. *Astronomy Education Review* 3 (2): 122–136.

Rowe, M. B. 1987. Wait time: Slowing down may be a way of speeding up. *American Educator* 11: 38–43, 47.

Ryan, J. M., and P. D. Harrison. 1995. The relationship between individual instructional characteristics and the overall assessment of teaching effectiveness across different instructional contexts. *Research in Higher Education* 36 (5): 577–594.

Seymour, E., and N. M. Hewitt. 1997. *Talking about leaving: Why undergraduates leave the sciences.* Boulder, CO: Westview Press.

Shipman, H. 2000. Teaching astronomy through the news media. *The Physics Teacher* 38 (9): 541–542.

Slater, T. F. 1997. The effectiveness of portfolio assessments in science. *Journal of College Science Teaching* 26 (5): 315–318.

Slater, T. F. 2003. When is a good day teaching a bad thing? *The Physics Teacher* 41 (7): 437–438.

Slater, T. F., and J. P. Adams. 2002. *Learner-centered astronomy teaching: Strategies for Astro 101.* Upper Saddle River, NJ: Prentice Hall/Pearson Education.

Slater, T. F., J. P. Adams, G. Brissenden, and D. Duncan. 2001. What topics are taught in introductory astronomy courses? *The Physics Teacher* 39 (1): 52–55.

Sokoloff, D. R., and R. K. Thornton. 1997. Using interactive lecture demonstrations to create an active learning environment. *The Physics Teacher* 35 (6): 340.

Talenquer, V., and D. Morgan. 2005. Learning to teach: The role of evidence. *Journal of College Science Teaching* 34: 28.

Tobias, S. 1990. *They're not dumb, they're different: Stalking the second tier.* Tucson, AZ: Research Corporation.

Tobias, S. 1992. *Revitalizing undergraduate science: Why some things work and most don't.* Tucson, AZ: Research Corporation.

Tobin, K. 1987. The role of wait time in higher cognitive level learning. *Review of Educational Research* 57: 69–95.

Zeilik, M., and V. J. Morris-Dueer. 2005. What are essential concepts in "Astronomy 101"? A new approach to find consensus from two different samples of instructors. *Astronomy Education Review* 3 (2): 61–108.

Zeilik, M., C. Schau, N. Mattern, S. Hall, K. Teague, and W. Bisard. 1997. Conceptual astronomy: A novel model for teaching postsecondary science courses. *American Journal of Physics* 65 (10): 987–996.

CHAPTER 6

Undergraduate Research in Science:
Not Just for Scientists Anymore

Sandra Laursen, Anne-Barrie Hunter, Elaine Seymour, Tracee DeAntoni, Kristine De Welde, and Heather Thiry

Sandra Laursen is a research associate in Ethnography and Evaluation Research (E&ER) at the Center to Advance Research and Teaching in the Social Sciences (CARTSS), University of Colorado at Boulder. She earned a PhD in physical chemistry at the University of California at Berkeley and conducts research in K–20 science education, career paths of scientists, and inquiry-based learning and teaching. She has taught courses in introductory and physical chemistry, molecular spectroscopy, and Earth and space science.

Anne-Barrie Hunter is a senior professional research associate at CARTSS. She earned an MA in mass communication research at the University of Colorado and conducts research on undergraduate research, innovative pedagogy in college science, and career paths of scientists.

Elaine Seymour is a research associate in E&ER at CARTSS. She earned a PhD in sociology at the University of Colorado and conducts research on issues in undergraduate and graduate STEM (science, technology, engineering, and mathematics) education and careers. She has taught courses in medical sociology, sociology of deviance, and sociology of knowledge.

Tracee DeAntoni is an undergraduate academic advisor at the University of Colorado. She earned an MA in educational foundations, policy, and practice at the University of Colorado and conducts research in sociology of education, gender, and race issues.

Kristine De Welde is assistant professor of sociology at Flagler College in Florida. She earned a PhD in sociology at the University of Colorado and conducts research on women's agency and resistance, sociology of work and family, and embodiment. She teaches courses in introductory sociology; sex, gender, and society; marriage and family; and ethnography methods.

Heather Thiry is a research associate at CARTSS. She earned a PhD in educational policy at the University of Colorado and conducts research on gender and science, equity in education, and cooperative involvement in education. She has taught courses on school and society.

Undergraduate research (UR) is of great national interest, influenced both by the traditional role of the research apprenticeship in scientists' education and by growing interest in development of thinking skills important for science literacy. The number of UR students nationwide is unknown, but the Boyer Commission on Educating Undergraduates in the Research University (2002) estimates that one-fifth of science and engineering students at research universities engage in UR. UR programs sponsored by the National Science Foundation (NSF) may support some 14,000 students per year (Russell 2005a). Public and private foundations invest substantially in UR, supporting students through both targeted UR programs and grants to individual investigators. National organizations promote UR experiences through student fellowships, conferences, publications, expert advice, and other resources.

High rates of student and faculty participation and national investment in UR signify widespread belief in the value of UR for students' educational and career development. However, we as yet lack a thorough, research-based understanding of the character and range of benefits to students, faculty, or institutions that are generated by different types of UR experiences. Institutional measures, such as the fraction of UR students who later pursue a PhD in science, do not reflect the value of UR as an educational and personal growth experience for students; moreover, little data exist to justify any causal connection between UR and career outcomes.

Our research group has begun to address this lacuna through a five-year study of science, technology, engineering, and mathematics (STEM) undergraduates and faculty who participate in summer UR programs at four liberal arts institutions with a strong history of UR. The study is both comparative—with student and faculty groups of UR nonparticipants—and longitudinal, as we have followed both participating and nonparticipating students through their senior years and beyond graduation. We continue to analyze the resulting large and richly detailed body of data. The study is designed to explore

- the benefits to students of conducting UR—both immediate and longer term, as viewed by both students and their faculty advisors;
- the benefits and costs to faculty of their own engagement in UR;
- what, if anything, is lost by students who do not participate in UR; and
- the processes by which gains to students are generated.

In this chapter, we summarize our findings to date (Hunter, Laursen, and Seymour 2006; Seymour, Hunter, and Laursen 2006; Seymour et al. 2004) about the benefits to students of participating in UR. Participation in UR is widely believed to recruit, encourage, and prepare students for scientific careers, particularly among underrepresented groups. Such potential contributions of UR are important to investigate.

We emphasize here, however, the *transferability* of the benefits of UR to a wide variety of personal, education, and career experiences. We propose that the benefits of UR are profound and valuable not only for students who plan to continue in scientific research, but also for those who will use science in professions vital to society and in their daily lives. Although such arguments have been made before (Bunnett 1984), the transferable benefits of UR are most clearly articulated by the students themselves.

Methods

The *interview samples* included UR students studying three sciences offered at all four sites—physics, chemistry, and biology—plus additional STEM fields. The data set emphasized here is the interviews with 76 "rising seniors" engaged in UR in summer 2000. We re-interviewed them shortly before their graduation in spring 2001 and as graduates in 2003–2004. Their 55 faculty advisors were also interviewed, as were nine UR administrators.

We shall report elsewhere findings from second- and third-round interviews with UR students; from the comparative group of 62 students, interviewed as seniors and as graduates, who did not undertake summer UR for varying reasons; and from a faculty comparison group who did not conduct UR. Together, the data sets total 368 interviews.

Interview protocols addressed the nature, value, and career consequences of UR experiences, and how these were achieved. From the array of benefits claimed in the literature, we constructed a "gains" checklist to discuss with all participants "what faculty think students may gain from UR." We asked students to estimate their gains from UR or other sources, to identify any gains not on our list, to highlight gains significant to them, and to describe the sources of gains. With slight alterations, we invited comments on the same checklist from the comparison group and explored gains from other experiences.

Our *methods of data collection and analysis* are ethnographic, rooted in theoretical work and methodological traditions from sociology, anthropology, and social psychology. Classically, qualitative studies uncover and explore issues that shape informants' thinking and actions, thus generating hypotheses to test and survey questions to ask. Modern software allows ethnographers to disentangle patterns in very large text data sets and report them using descriptive statistics. The results from careful sampling and consistent coding of text data can be very powerful.

Our methods are detailed in Seymour et al. (2004). Briefly, interview transcripts are searched for information bearing on the research questions. Text segments referencing distinct ideas are tagged by code names. Codes are not preconceived, but empirical: each new code marks a discrete idea not previously raised. Codes and passages are linked via software, amassing a data set for each interview group. Groups of codes that cluster around particular themes are given domain names, and these clustered codes and domains define the themes of qualitative analysis.

In addition, the frequency of use can be counted for codes across the data set, using conservative counting conventions to avoid overestimating the weight of opinion. Together, these frequencies describe the relative weighting of issues in the participants' collective report. They hypothesize the strength of particular variables and their relationships that may later be tested by surveys or other means.

Findings

Students were overwhelmingly positive about their UR experiences: of 1,335 evaluative comments by students, 92% referenced gains made. Only 4% of responses reflected a particular gain not made, and 4% offered qualified, ambivalent, or mixed assessments. Likewise, faculty viewed UR as highly beneficial for their students. Of 2,495 evaluative observations by faculty on student gains, 90% were positive, 6% negative, and 5% qualified or uncertain.

Faculty and students described the same range and types of gains, providing important corroboration. Six major categories of gains emerged from our analysis. One category, "becoming a scientist," was not reported initially (Seymour et al. 2004). It emerged only after analyzing faculty views of students' gains, and its discovery enabled us to subsequently recognize it within the student data. The resulting reassessment of frequencies for student-reported gains is detailed by Hunter, Laursen, and Seymour (2006), whose final figures we cite here.

Lastly, faculty and students interpreted particular gains differently. Students' observations focused on their own experiences—their comments were "all about me." Interviewed just after their summer UR experience, entering their senior year, many were still uncertain about future plans. Thus the gains most salient to them were immediately useful and personally important—technical and thinking skills, growth in confidence, and identity as a scientist. In contrast, faculty offered observations from long experience with UR, reporting gains seen for student researchers collectively over time. They were more aware of students' progress in defining future education and career paths and of their adoption of the behaviors and attitudes of professional scientists. Thus faculty and student rankings of gains differ somewhat.

In the following sections we discuss each major category of student gain, in descending order of importance to students. We describe the gains primarily as seen by students, emphasizing their views of how these gains transfer to their future work and personal lives. Percentages cited are out of all (1,230) positive observations by students. For a detailed breakout of each gains category and comparison of student and faculty perceptions, see Hunter, Laursen, and Seymour (2006).

Personal/Professional Gains

This category (25%) includes personal gains that carry a perceived professional value—especially confidence. This is not a gain in general self-esteem, but gains specific to doing research: increased confidence in their ability "to do" science, to contribute meaningfully to scientific knowledge, and "to be" a scientist.

I've learned not to be so intimidated by the research because, before, when we would read these articles for class, it just seems a bit intimidating. But now that I'm actually doing what they're doing, I've realized that I could do this.

I really like the idea that I am doing science research and I feel like it's something that's new and exciting.... I get a lot of satisfaction out of the fact that I'm doing something new.

Growth in confidence was demonstrated by making decisions more independently of faculty, such as taking the next step in their project.

At the beginning, I asked a lot of questions to get a good basis and a good idea when I didn't really know what I was doing. But by the end of the summer, I didn't speak to my advisor much, because I would just do it.

This confidence was not limited to current projects. Having mastered new techniques and ideas for one project, they felt ready to tackle whatever new learning might be required in the future.

I now feel confident that I can walk into any room with any instrument and figure out how to make that instrument work.... When I look at somebody's list of 10–15 different methods of analysis they're using, I can look down that list and say, "I know how to do half of these, and another half of them I can figure out pretty easily."

As students undertook "real" science—managing a project, facing its challenges and technical setbacks, discovering and sharing new findings, being taken seriously by others—they felt more sure of their identity as a scientist. They often expressed this as "feeling like a scientist."

It's kinda scary, especially at the very beginning. I was like, "How can someone like me be doing this?" I'm coming up with valuable information for this project and it's great ... actually producing data and actually doing it. I felt like a scientist. But you really feel more like a scientist when you have something good!

This category also includes gains in collegiality. Students valued the chance to work with faculty one-on-one and recognized how this relationship differed from the classroom setting.

As a researcher, [faculty] are your peers; you're working with them. And you ask them questions, and they are just as excited to know what I'm doing as I am to know how they're doing, or what they could help me with.... You don't have to be intimidated by them any more.

Collegial working relationships with peers were also new and specific to the summer research community. Students took pleasure in discussing shared intellectual interests, gained ideas from others' different perspectives, and felt supported through their everyday challenges.

Thinking and Working Like a Scientist

These gains (24%) were broadly of two types: gains in knowledge or understanding of science and research, and gains in the ability to *apply* knowledge and skills to research.

Many students were able to apply their knowledge and skills to real research. Students often discussed application as a realization of the difference between authentic research on an unsolved problem and a "canned" laboratory assignment. They saw that a solution would rely on their own knowledge, thinking skills, reading, and hard work.

When you're faced with ... a novel problem, when there's no right answer yet, and you have to find the right answer, I think research does a good job at teaching those skills. Because you don't have anything to go back and rely on ... you're having to do it yourself.

I think there's only so much you can get from classroom learning.... You get into the lab and you say, "OK. This should work." No, it doesn't work! Because there are so many other considerations that you have to make. And that's the kind of thing you can only get from research.

Students' abilities to troubleshoot and detect errors in their logic improved.

It really does help you learn to detect your own dumb mistakes. Like, it's easy to think about something conceptually a little bit wrong, and go with that for about a week. But then you look at what you've got, and ... you realize what the problem is. You learn to recognize things like that quicker and quicker the more you do it.

Spontaneously, students often emphasized the transferability of these gains to other settings.

> *I think on a very basic level you can use these skills in any science field. Just learning how to plan, learning how to be careful, how to take care of mistakes, and recover from mistakes—I think that's something you can really apply to any field.*

While many students were able to use and hone their problem-solving skills, far fewer developed more generalized "higher-order thinking skills" (Kardash 2000)—the very skills that faculty most desire and seek to foster in their UR students. These skills include understanding how to identify, frame, and refine new research questions, and how to select or develop research methods. Even fewer students reached broader epistemological conclusions, describing a shift from understanding science as a body of received knowledge to seeing it as a set of methods for exploring and explaining natural phenomena—from science as facts to science as process.

> *As a student you're handed this as fact ... and you don't question that. But what you find out in research is that a lot of things that people have found out need to be questioned.... We can stand on the backs of people who have figured out ... but scientists have been wrong in the past.... You have to do experimental work and explain why it's going that way.*

> *I think a lot of people think science is truth, this all-encompassing certainty.... And what I found out is that often what research does is just to explain how something could happen, or probably happens, and not necessarily how it does happen.*

Our data suggest that active participation in UR offers the potential for students to move through this sequence of intellectual gains from application to design to abstraction—but also that this process is neither easy nor guaranteed. It may also be unrealistic to expect such gains during a typical 10-week summer program.

Students also made gains in knowledge and understanding. Some understood concepts more deeply, saw connections among ideas, and solidified existing knowledge through using it. Others developed more appreciation of their field, interest in their course work, and an ability to transfer knowledge between courses and research.

> *Certainly, I find that when I take classes that use chemistry that I've used in research, it seems more straightforward. And also in an interesting way, it reinforces things so that it makes it much easier.*

Students drew from their UR experiences an intellectual and affective appreciation of "real science" at work. They applied their problem-solving skills to a real problem and gained depth and breadth in understanding their discipline, its links to others, and the nature of research work. Deeper gains in understanding the nature of science were reported, but more rarely. Without prompting, students often anticipated how these intellectual gains would transfer to other contexts and serve them in the future.

Gains in Skills

The steep learning curve students encountered led to many skill gains (17%), especially in communication. Other gains included laboratory and field skills and computer, work organization, reading comprehension, information retrieval, and collaborative working skills.

Oral communication skills were strongly developed through discussion, argument, and presentations.

Public presentation is something ... I've definitely improved on.... I used to become very nervous doing a public presentation of any sort, and that's much less the case now.

Students initially found it daunting to give and receive critique and to defend their work on their feet.

It's quite intimidating because she interrupts you a lot and she asks you a lot of questions, and she wants you to recall a lot of things. And so, from that experience alone ... I feel so much better about being on the spot and defending my work.

It was a strange feeling, receiving a paper with lots of red ink on it.... I think it's part of the learning process to recognize when there's a right style, and a right word.... It was very, very useful to me.

Communication skills were valued outside the research context, too, as students explained their work to colleagues in other fields and to people with a limited science background.

Learning to put your scientific research in terms of someone who doesn't have a scientific background so that they can understand, I think is just as important a skill as being able to explain it to other scientists.

Laboratory techniques and computer skills were thought to be particularly useful in future study and work, as were work organization and time management skills.

I think I've gained a lot of skills, practical skills that I could use career-wise.... I think the most valuable thing is just the raw skills, and I guess problem solving as well, that goes along with it.

Across their accounts, students emphasized how these skill gains also contributed to their feelings of confidence and identity as scientists.

Becoming a Scientist

This category (12%) includes gains in attitudes and behaviors necessary to become a researcher: taking ownership for a project, showing intellectual engagement and initiative, and becoming independent and creative in problem solving and decision making. Students saw up close how the profession operates, as their advisors managed papers, grants, peer review, conferences, and collaborations. Combined, these gains represent socialization into the set of skills, attitudes, and behaviors of a professional scientist. Faculty, with their deeper experience of the profession and longer view of students' research careers, could spot these gains more easily than did students.

To me, the mark of success in this kind of endeavor is ownership.... There's some transformation that occurs, where it suddenly becomes their project.

They approach me and say, "I know you always say I should at least run it by you before I use expensive reagents, but I did this on my own and look what I got!" ... That's a real transition point. That they want to surprise you by bringing something of themselves to it.

And I thought, just listening to [three students], "They're scientists!" They're sitting there having this conversation about the project. "Well, wouldn't you do this? What if you did that?" And that's just such a leap from when they started in the lab.

Faculty recognized such transformations as adoption of professional norms, while students simply expressed ownership and readiness to take on responsibility.

We felt like we actually had a responsibility for trying to, like, if we didn't figure it out, the problem wasn't going to get solved.

Just being able to sit down and concentrate on one thing and figure it out and ... really, really understand it, rather than just getting the big overview. And then, actually thinking about the problem critically and creatively and being, "OK. Now what can I change to have this effect and to have this outcome?" That's a whole new experience for me.

Students came to understand that research is messy, slow, and tedious; that many tries may be necessary before a procedure works; and that "failure" is often par for the course.

It's helped me to deal with failure in the laboratory. And it's not your fault. It's not anything you could have done. It's just the protocols that worked perfectly for so-and-so don't work for you because of reasons you didn't even think about and nobody thought about. It's helped me to be a better problem-solver, I think, to look at this and say, "Okay, we'll pinpoint what's going wrong. We'll see what other people have done. We'll see why ours is different and how we can change things so that it will work."

Lessons learned about the time, care, and persistence needed to succeed in research were viewed as especially transferable to later work and life in general.

Sometimes you just have to slog through things. That was kinda one of my biggest lessons. Sometimes there're no shortcuts. You just have to get in there and work at it. And it might take a while, but sometimes that's the only way to get it done.

I think the perseverance that it takes, the patience to be able to just keep working and not giving up on things, that is something that I think will be useful in other areas—learning to not expect things to happen right away, and suddenly, magically you have all your results.

Understanding the real nature of research also helped students begin to identify as scientists. They realized that it was necessary to acquire a tolerance for failure.

When I really realized some of the frustrations you can have with research, I think I learned that that's a part of being a scientist, is dealing with that.

Students' observations were largely framed in personal terms—connected to increased confidence and "feeling like a scientist." They did not yet recognize these gains as habits of the profession, as faculty do. Yet understanding how science works day to day and developing attributes of a practicing scientist are clearly transferable to future study and careers in science, while growth in patience and perseverance transfers to many professions.

Clarification, Confirmation, and Refinement of Career and Education Paths

UR is often presumed to lead students to pursue graduate school. However, it is important to distinguish claims that UR prompts students to *choose* a particular career path and more qualified claims that the experience can *clarify, confirm,* or *refine* their choice. To date, reliable evidence that UR programs can recruit students to graduate school comes only from studies of programs offering early research experiences to students *least* likely to have already developed aspirations to graduate education—women, students of color, and first-generation college students (Adhikari and Nolan 2002; Alexander, Foertsch, and Daffinrud 1998; Barlow and Villarejo 2004; Foertsch, Alexander, and Penberthy 1997; Hathaway, Nagda, and Gregerman 2002; Nagda et al. 1998; Russell et al. 2005b).

This category (11%) includes benefits of refinement of career interests. Students reported that UR increased interest and enthusiasm for their field, introduced them to a new field, and helped them select or confirm interest in a particular field.

I think it helped me decide what I like about chemistry…. When I'm in class, I'm not really thinking, "Do I like this or not?" It's more, "I have to turn in this homework assignment and study for this test." In research, it's more I really enjoy chemistry a lot more…. And being in lab is a lot different from studying textbooks.

I think the research I did last summer was helpful…. That, in combination with course work that I've taken, makes me think that I'd like to go into some facet of neurology … because I think the exposure to it has influenced me. I've always been interested in it, but it kind of reaffirmed that.

Doing research confirmed for many a desire to pursue research at the graduate level.

Graduate school has been an idea of mine since maybe my freshman year in college. But I didn't know for sure that that's what I wanted to do. I thought maybe I would take a year off … but I'm having such a great time—I just wanna go, go, go and continue on.

Again, discovering a temperamental fit to the demands of research was an important element of this clarification.

I think that's good if [people] do research when they're an undergraduate. Because if I would have [decided], … "Oh, man, I can't handle this. I don't want to do this," … then I could have switched my major or my focus…. Now I know.

Of 76 students, 7 found research *not* to be the career that they wanted.

I really do enjoy doing research, but I can't see myself doing it for my entire life. I can't see myself in a lab, day in and day out.

We counted these realizations as gains rather than as negative outcomes of UR because the students reported them as such, valuing the clarity reached in ruling out research as a career option.

In sum, we found no evidence that UR had prompted students to choose to pursue a research career or graduate education. Rather, it clarified, confirmed, and refined preexisting career ideas and reinforced students' interests and enthusiasm for their choices. For a few students, this clarity came from realizing that other interests drew them more than research.

Enhanced Preparation for Career and Graduate School

Some aspects of their UR experiences particularly prepared students for future work and education (10%). For students planning to pursue science, this stemmed from "real-world" science experience: carrying out a longer-term project, seeing theory and classroom knowledge applied to a research problem. Coauthoring articles or attending conferences connected them to professional networks and documented their achievements. Research experience left students feeling confident and prepared for new challenges.

Any time you work at something for a long time, you become more confident, you gain more confidence. And I'm confident at my ability to go to grad school and research in a lab there.

You're given a lot of freedom and responsibility to do things, so I'm really getting out of it how to go about a professional-type job or business, these kinds of things.

Gains from UR were seen to apply to many other professions that use science and the critical-thinking skills it fosters.

I have interests both in law and in psychology. It's part of the reason I am doing research, is to see if I like this more than the other area, and I might, I see myself even like trying to combine the two.... So if it doesn't have direct bearing on law, it still might have direct bearing on a career that I choose.

Just work habits that will benefit you in the future. Kind of like the independence and your study habits, as opposed to relying on faculty, ... to come up with your own problems, propose your own solutions to things, design your own experiment, set your own goals. And I think that's going to be really important for medical school and the future.

I decided I wanted to be a high school teacher.... Not only can I talk about biology, 'cause I love biology, I'm excited about it, but I also have the research foundation to how these things are built up. The field work, I think that's an asset to teaching that a lot of people wouldn't have, and I think that makes me more marketable.

The last quotation raises the question, Do students pursue UR simply to benefit their résumés? In a separate analysis, only 17% of 236 student statements about their motivations to undertake UR cited instrumental motives such as summer salary, résumé enhancement, and improved chances of admission to graduate or medical school, in contrast with 71% of statements citing intrinsic interest and a desire to try "real research." While students both anticipated and valued benefits to their future careers, they did not pursue UR solely to receive these benefits.

Conclusions

Our data show that UR is a powerful experience for students, developing skills, knowledge, attitudes, and behaviors that have a profound impact on their emergent adult identity. Students often cited the value of UR in shaping and strengthening their future directions. Students planning to continue in science internalized their "fit" to research and their field, advanced in their understanding of how science works and how to do it, and came to value collegial conversation, careful work, accurate communication, and determination. Future schoolteachers saw ways to incorporate authentic science experiences into their classrooms. Pre-med students gained insight into how new drugs might be developed and tested, and valued "thinking on their feet" as useful in a clinical setting.

While faculty tended to focus more on the benefits for science-bound students, they too saw benefits of UR for all students—in fostering science literacy and healthy skepticism and in developing resilience and persistence.

When they graduate, whether they are trying to function effectively in a graduate program or in some kind of a job, working on a project or as a community activist or as a parent, I think that whole process of understanding and experiencing is great liberal education.... Just to have the confidence that you can do it, and to know that things in life don't occur in nice, linear, stepwise pathways in the way that we envision them.

If I thought we had the resources, I would like to see every student have this experience. Because I think it teaches you a lot more about how science is done ... what goes on in a laboratory, how you arrive at answers to things. I think there is value in that for everyone.

While these quotations echo strongly national recommendations about "science for all Americans," the last speaker also raises an inherent dilemma in envisioning UR as part of general science education. Currently too few UR positions are available to place all students who seek them (Grabowski and Coon 2005). In our interviews, faculty spoke eloquently of the intensity of this specialized type of teaching, of the tensions in carrying out their own scholarship while supporting novice scientists through their learning curve, and of the personal and family costs of spending summers in the lab with students (Seymour, Hunter, and Laursen 2006).

Thus, if our work implies that UR should be offered to even more students, it also shows this to be a challenging goal. In determining whether we should as a society pursue this goal, both research and practice must contribute. Education researchers must fully document the value of UR as an educational, personal, and professional growth experience and track its long-term consequences. And UR practitioners must draw on this research base as they design and evaluate programs to provide a research opportunity for all who seek it.

References

Adhikari, N., and D. Nolan. 2002. "But what good came of it at last?": How to assess the value of undergraduate research. *Notices of the AMS* 49 (10): 1252–1257.

Alexander, B. B., J. A. Foertsch, and S. Daffinrud. July 1998. *The Spend a Summer With a Scientist program: An evaluation of program outcomes and the essential elements of success.* Madison: University of Wisconsin–Madison, LEAD Center.

Barlow, A., and M. Villarejo. 2004. Making a difference for minorities: Evaluation of an educational enrichment program. *Journal of Research in Science Teaching* 41 (9): 861–881.

Boyer Commission on Educating Undergraduates in the Research University. 2002. *Reinventing undergraduate education: Three years after the Boyer Report.* State University of New York-Stony Brook.

Bunnett, J. F. 1984. The education of butchers and bakers and public policy makers. *Journal of Chemical Education* 61 (6): 509–510.

Foertsch, J. A., B. B. Alexander, and D. L. Penberthy. June 1997. *Evaluation of the UW-Madison's summer undergraduate research programs: Final report.* Madison: University of Wisconsin—Madison, LEAD Center.

Grabowksi, J., and D. Coon. 2005. What is the market demand for NSF-sponsored summer REU positions in chemistry? Paper presented at the 229th American Chemical Society National Meeting, San Diego, CA.

Hathaway, R., B. Nagda, and S. Gregerman. 2002. The relationship of undergraduate research participation to graduate and professional educational pursuit: An empirical study. *Journal of College Student Development* 43 (5): 614–631.

Hunter, A-B., S. L. Laursen, and E. Seymour. 2006. Benefits of participating in undergraduate research in science: A comparative analysis of student and faculty perceptions. Paper presented at To Think and Act Like a Scientist: The Roles of Inquiry, Research, and Technology, Texas Tech University, Lubbock, TX, February 10–11.

Kardash, C. M. 2000. Evaluation of an undergraduate research experience: Perceptions of undergraduate interns and their faculty mentors. *Journal of Educational Psychology* 92 (1): 191–201.

Nagda, B. A., S. R. Gregerman, J. Jonides, W. von Hippel, and J. S. Lerner. 1998. Undergraduate student-faculty research partnerships affect student retention. *Review of Higher Education* 22 (1): 55–72.

Russell, S. H. 2005a. *Evaluation of NSF support for undergraduate research opportunities: 2003 NSF-program participant survey. Final report.* Menlo Park, CA: SRI International. *www.sri.com/policy/csted/reports*

Russell, S. H. 2005b. *Evaluation of NSF support for undergraduate research opportunities: Survey of STEM graduates. Draft Final Report.* Menlo Park, CA: SRI International. *www.sri.com/policy/csted/reports*

Seymour, E., A.-B. Hunter, and S. L. Laursen. 2006. The benefits and costs of faculty engagement in undergraduate research. Paper presented at To Think and Act Like a Scientist: The Roles of Inquiry, Research, and Technology, Texas Tech University, Lubbock, TX, February 10–11.

Seymour, E., A.-B. Hunter, S. L. Laursen, and T. DeAntoni. 2004. Establishing the benefits of research experiences for undergraduates in the sciences: First findings from a three-year study. *Science Education* 88 (4): 493–534.

CHAPTER 7

Concept Mapping in College Science

Joel J. Mintzes

Joel J. Mintzes is professor of biology at the University of North Carolina Wilmington. He earned a PhD in biological science education at Northwestern University and conducts research on environmental education and on conceptual development and cognitive processes in biology. He teaches courses in general and cell biology, zoology, and cognition, evolution, and behavior.

The results of hundreds of studies in science learning (Wandersee, Mintzes, and Novak 1994) combined with years of daily classroom experience suggest that many students have considerable difficulty assimilating and understanding fundamental concepts in the natural sciences. Sometimes problems associated with meaningful learning begin in the schools where memorization is rewarded at the expense of conceptual understanding (see Chapter 12 in this volume). While theoretical and empirical work concerning conceptual understanding is ongoing, applied research has focused largely on developing and evaluating practical tools to encourage and reward students who learn meaningfully. One such tool, the concept map, was developed in the early 1970s by Joseph D. Novak and his students at Cornell University, and it has been used widely at virtually every level and in all scientific disciplines.

Meaningful Learning

A concept map is a two-dimensional, hierarchical node-link diagram that depicts the most important concepts and propositions in a knowledge domain (Arnaudin et al. 1984; Wallace, Mintzes, and Markham 1992; Figure 7.1). Concepts are perceived regularities in objects or events that are designated by a sign or symbol (Novak 1998; Novak and Gowin 1984). For example, the three-letter English word *car* refers to a four-wheeled vehicle used for transporting passengers that is propelled by an internal combustion engine. As basic units of thought and language, concepts derive their meanings through connections with other concepts; the more connections a concept possesses, the more meaningful it is said to be. A proposition or principle is a statement of relationship between two or more concepts (All *cars* have *seats*), and a theory is a set of interrelated principles (*Cars, trucks, trains,* and *airplanes* are useful *vehicles* of *transportation*).

Figure 7.1

Example of Concept Map on Cells

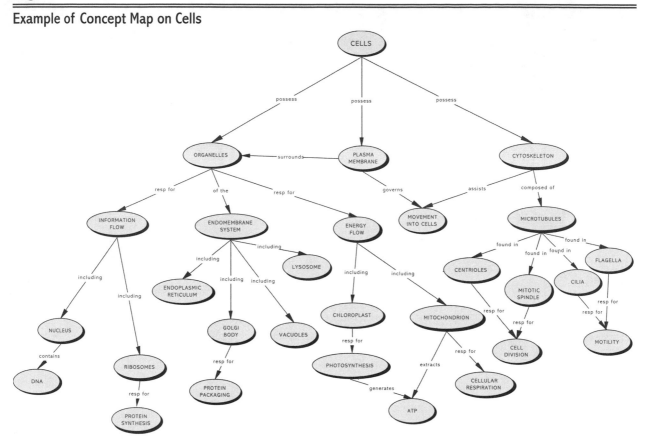

The concept mapping strategy was designed to accomplish several ends: (1) to help students (and faculty) recognize the difference between meaningful and rote learning, (2) to encourage and reward students who learn meaningfully, (3) to enable students to "externalize" and share their understandings and thereby to obtain feedback for their efforts, and (4) to help faculty assess and evaluate student success in meaningful learning.

Concept mapping grew out of a theory of meaningful verbal learning proposed originally by Ausubel (1963, 1968) and later elaborated (Ausubel, Novak, and Hanesian 1978) and expanded into a view of "personal meaning-making" and "knowledge-building" (Mintzes, Wandersee, and Novak 1998, 2000; Novak 1993) that has attracted many adherents in recent years. The fundamental principle of Ausubel's theory is the distinction between *meaningful* and *rote* learning.

When new concepts are learned meaningfully they are linked to concepts previously stored in long-term memory (LTM), resulting in strongly hierarchical, dendritic, and highly integrated frameworks of interrelated ideas. In the course of their careers, successful science students and scientists build complex frameworks of knowledge about objects and events in the natural world that enable them to solve novel problems and think critically within a scientific discipline. The building of such a framework depends on four cognitive processes: (1) *subsumption*, in which new, more specific concepts are linked to more general and inclusive concepts already possessed by the learner; (2) *differentiation*, in which the existing knowledge structure is progressively elaborated, refined, and clarified; (3) *integration*, in which the meaning of a new concept is modified and reconciled with existing concepts; and (4) *superordination*, in which new, more general, and more inclusive concepts are assimilated into and subsume existing concepts in the knowledge framework.

In contrast to meaningful learning, rote learning occurs when linkages to existing knowledge are minimal, and when new concepts are stored in an *arbitrary, verbatim,* and *nonsubstantive* fashion in LTM. The principal advantages of meaningful learning are that concepts are retained longer, subsequent learning becomes easier and more efficient, and the ultimate products of the learning experience (conceptual frameworks) become more useful to the individual.

Constructing Concept Maps

Fortunately, constructing a concept map seems to be a fairly "intuitive" exercise for most college students. Practical experience over the course of 30 years suggests that students can learn to construct a "good" map in a single laboratory period. It also seems that students benefit from a simple stepwise formula, which they can consult at a later time (Figure 7.2), and from an exemplary map (Figure 7.1), which depicts a significant number of concepts, relationships, levels of hierarchy, branching, and cross-links.

Figure 7.2

Six Steps to Concept Mapping

Step 1: Review a topic or conceptual domain: This may involve reading a section of a book or article, viewing a website or film, listening to a lecture and reading your notes, or simply reflecting on what you already know about a topical area. (Examples of conceptual domains are cells, chemical bonds, and laws of thermodynamics.)

Step 2: Identify the major concepts: Underline or list the 10 or 15 most important concepts on a sheet of paper. (Examples for cells include organelles, plasma membrane, cytoskeleton, endomembrane system, information flow, energy flow, microtubules, cellular respiration, photosynthesis, and protein packaging.)

Step 3: Arrange the concepts on paper: Where possible, organize them from most inclusive or most general (superordinate) to least inclusive or least general (subordinate).

Step 4: Link and label connections between concepts: Readers should be able to understand relationships between the concepts and to read the entire map from top to bottom.

Step 5: Branch out: Attempt to add as many additional subordinate concepts to your map as you can in order to display the depth and breadth of your knowledge about the topic.

Step 6: Make cross-links: Try to link and label connections between concepts that already appear on your map. Use arrowheads on the linking lines to indicate the intended reading direction.

Typically we begin our concept mapping sessions by engaging in a whole-class activity on the blackboard. Students are asked to think of a common concept (e.g., car, food, or sports) and then to generate a list of 10–12 additional concepts that they associate with the superordinate concept (e.g., for car, American, foreign, sedan, sports car, GM, Ford, Honda, Volkswagen, engine, transmission, and seats). Working in parallel in groups of three or four, students write the superordinate concept at the top of a large sheet of paper and enclose it in a box or oval. The students are then asked to organize their additional concepts "from most general or inclusive to least general or inclusive" and to arrange them beneath the superordinate concept on their paper.

Next, students are encouraged to link related concepts with connecting lines and to indicate the type of relationship between concepts by labeling the connections (e.g., the relational line between car and foreign is labeled "may be"). Sometimes it is necessary to punctuate the linking line with an arrowhead if the intended directional relationship is open to interpretation. When completed, a concept map should read from top to bottom. In the course of constructing their maps, students should be encouraged to "branch out," adding as many relevant subordinate concepts as they can, and to cross-link concepts in one part of the map with those in another.

We have found that the quality of students' concept maps improves with time and experience. We give students 30–40 minutes to complete their first maps. As students work, we circulate around the lab interjecting constructive suggestions when and where appropriate. General formatting problems often arise early in the exercise. For example, students often enclose whole sentences or propositions within a single box or oval; others fail to label a linking line or neglect cross-links. Throughout the period we remind students that concept maps are idiosyncratic representations of knowledge, and that there may be as many "correct" maps as there are students who draw them. We also point out that misconceptions are typically revealed as scientifically unacceptable connections between concepts. At the conclusion of this process, students are called on to share their maps with the class, and class members are encouraged to offer constructive feedback.

The last portion of the laboratory period is devoted to mapping a relevant section of the textbook. Students are asked to read a brief passage in their textbook and to underline or highlight the most important concepts. The new concept maps, which are begun in the laboratory and completed as a homework assignment, are treated as a "learning exercise" rather than a graded assignment. Subsequent concept maps are scored by the laboratory instructor and become a portion of the semester grade.

Scoring Concept Maps

Normally we ask students to construct 10–12 concept maps over the course of a semester. The first few maps are scored "holistically" or "qualitatively." Written comments are made directly on the maps indicating conceptual and formatting errors. For subsequent assignments, we make use of a scoring rubric (Figure 7.3), which assigns points based on the structural complexity and content validity of the map (Quinn, Mintzes, and Laws 2003).

For purposes of our assignments, structural complexity points (50%) are given for the total number of concepts, relationships, levels of hierarchy, branches, and cross-links. Content validity points (50%) are given for the total number of critical concepts and propositions depicted in a student's map based on comparison to the instructor's template map. Recognizing

Figure 7.3

Scoring Concept Maps (Using Example of Cells)

Structural Complexity (50%): One point is awarded for each of the following:
Concepts: Total number of nonredundant concepts
Relationships: Total number of scientifically acceptable and nonredundant propositions
Hierarchy: Maximum number of hierarchical levels possessing at least one branch
Branching: Total number of superordinate-to-subordinate branches
Cross-links: Total number of scientifically acceptable and nonredundant cross-links

Content Validity (50%): One point is awarded for each critical concept/proposition.
Critical Concepts:
    cells, plasma membrane, organelles, nucleus, mitochondrion, chloroplast, lysosome,
    endoplasmic reticulum, ribosome, golgi body, centriole, vacuole, cilium/flagellum
Critical Propositions:
    cells: structural/functional units
    plasma membrane: movement into/out of cell
    mitochondrion: cellular respiration
    chloroplast: photosynthesis
    lysosome: intracellular digestion
    endoplasmic reticulum: endomembrane system
    ribosome: protein synthesis
    golgi body: packaging
    centriole: cell division
    vacuole: storage
    cilium/flagellum: motility

that scoring can be a time-consuming and labor-intensive task, we encourage instructors to devise their own evaluative schemes that fit within the constraints of the local environment. Whatever scheme is devised, we suggest that students should be rewarded both for the complexity of their knowledge frameworks and for the completeness, inclusiveness, and accuracy of the knowledge they depict.

Variations in Concept Mapping

Concept mapping has proved to be a versatile strategy that can be implemented in many instructional settings and for a variety of purposes. In this chapter, emphasis has been placed on its use as a so-called metalearning device that encourages students who need help in "learning how to learn." In our own teaching we continue to rely on the concept map for this purpose but have also found it useful in many other ways.

As a tool for stimulating cooperative or collaborative learning in small discussion groups, the concept map has proved to be very helpful. Often we assign groups of three or four students to work together to construct a "consensus map," which stimulates discussion and enables students to externalize their understanding of a difficult concept and thereby to receive feedback and reinforcement for their efforts. Students who form study groups in preparation for examinations report that these cooperative activities are strongly motivational.

As an assessment tool the concept map has proved to be a valid and reliable measure of students' understanding. In our courses we frequently use a set of sequential or "successive maps" (Quinn, Mintzes, and Laws 2003) as an adjunct to traditional testing strategies (Mintzes, Wandersee, and Novak 2001). Students draw concept maps early in the semester and then, successively at intervals of four to five weeks, the maps are returned to them and they modify their depictions by adding or deleting new concepts and relationships. The effect of this strategy is to enable the students to visualize the way their knowledge frameworks are "restructured" during the course of the semester.

Apart from their use as learning tools, we have found concept maps quite helpful in instructional and curricular planning. We use concept maps to gain a "bird's-eye view" or global perspective on the instructional unit and to help us think through a sequence of new lectures ensuring that they fit together in an integrated and potentially meaningful way. They also help us to identify omissions or weaknesses in our courses. Finally, as faculty members within a large department, we have found that concept maps help us communicate the content of our courses and thereby make useful contributions to large-scale curricular revisions.

Research on Concept Maps

Research on the use of concept maps as learning and study tools is quite extensive, with individual reports numbering in the hundreds, and studies that explore the effects of concept mapping spanning a period of more than 30 years (Edmondson 2000; Fisher, Wandersee, and Moody 2000; Mintzes, Wandersee, and Novak 1998, 2000; Novak 1998). For college science instructors, two questions are of principal importance: (1) Is the concept map a valid measure of conceptual understanding? and (2) Do concept maps significantly enhance meaningful learning in scientific disciplines?

Validity

Research on the validity of concept maps has taken several directions. Among the most common and basic studies are those that correlate concept map scores with other measures of achievement. One of the earliest studies (Novak, Gowin, and Johansen 1983) revealed that mapping scores were substantially unrelated to scores on the verbal and mathematics portions of the SAT, the common entrance examination at selective colleges and universities in the United States. The findings were surprising inasmuch as the SAT is often touted as a strong predictor of college success. In contrast, a study by Schau and Mattern (1997) reported unusually high correlation coefficients of approximately 0.85 between concept map scores and final course grades in an introductory statistics course for graduate students. In the latter study, subjects completed a "select and fill-in" variation of the concept map. However, most reported correlational studies have found substantially lower coefficients, ranging from 0.2 to 0.5. The logical conclusion, that achievement tests and concept maps measure different but overlapping dimensions of learning, has been borne out by a host of subsequent studies (e.g., Shavelson and Ruiz-Primo 2000).

Experimental studies that vary treatments in well-controlled environments are uncommon. In one such study (Wallace and Mintzes 1990), college students were randomly assigned to a treatment group that received computer-assisted instruction in marine biology and a placebo group. Pre- and posttreatment concept maps on marine life zones revealed significant differences ($P < 0.05$) in the structural complexity of students' knowledge favoring those in the experimental group. In a follow-up study (Markham, Mintzes, and Jones 1994), juniors and seniors who enrolled in a college-level mammalogy course were compared with freshmen taking an introductory biology course for nonmajors. Findings suggested significant differences ($P < 0.05$) favoring the mammalogy students, and these results were supported by multidimensional scaling, which revealed substantially more complex knowledge among the juniors and seniors.

Another series of studies explored the validity of the successive concept mapping strategy (Martin, Mintzes, and Clavijo 2000; Pearsall, Skipper, and Mintzes 1994; Quinn, Mintzes, and Laws 2003). In these studies, it was shown that students' knowledge becomes sequentially more complex and "expert-like" over the course of a semester. Indeed, a stepwise pattern of significant differences ($P < 0.05$) was found in the number of concepts, relationships, levels of hierarchy, branching, and cross-links as students progressed through the courses. It has also been shown that the content of students' knowledge becomes more like that of professional biologists. Follow-up investigations (Barney, Mintzes, and Yen 2005; Thompson and Mintzes 2001) revealed that gains in students' concept map scores were significantly correlated ($P < 0.05$) with positive attitudes in the knowledge domain.

The general conclusion we draw from these and other studies of validity is that concept maps possess many of the characteristics that psychometric experts look for in the best measures of conceptual understanding. In fact, Shavelson and Ruiz-Primo (2000) of Stanford University report "generalizability coefficients" of approximately 0.90 (on a scale of 0.0 to 1.0), which suggests that concept maps do a better job of tapping into and representing scientific knowledge than almost any known alternative.

Meaningful Learning

The second issue that concerns college science teachers is evidence that concept mapping enhances meaningful learning when it is integrated into the regular classroom and laboratory routine. Evidence for this claim comes from a host of studies. One early study by Heinze-Fry and Novak (1990) investigated the effects of concept mapping on "long-term movement toward meaningful learning" in an auto-tutorial biology course at Cornell University. The results suggest that concept maps enhance learning, but the effects are gradual in nature. Subsequent studies on the effectiveness of concept mapping as a mediator of meaningful learning have generally produced positive findings (Chang, Chen, and Sung 2002; Daley 2002; Esiobu and Soyibo 1995; Jegede, Alaiyemola, and Okebukola 1990; Odom and Kelly 2001; Richie and Volkl 2000; Roth and Roychoudhury 1993; Santhanam, Leach, and Dawson 1998; Sungur, Tekkaya, and Gehan 2001; Tan 2000; Trowbridge and Wandersee 1994). A few studies have found "no significant effect" (Brandt et al. 2001; Markow and Lonning 1998; Nicoll, Francisco, and Nakleh 2001); all of these studies were conducted within high school and college chemistry courses.

In addition to the positive effects on cognitive processing and knowledge restructuring, studies also revealed that concept mapping reduces student anxiety (Jegede, Alaiyemola, and Okebukola 1990), encourages sustained verbal discourse (Roth and Roychoudhury 1993), enhances text comprehension (Chang, Chen, and Sung 2002), facilitates cooperative effort (Esiobu and Soyibo 1995), and develops higher-order thinking skills (Daley 2002).

In the only publication of its kind, Horton and colleagues (1993) reported a meta-analysis of 19 studies that investigated the effectiveness of concept mapping as an instructional strategy. The results indicate that concept mapping has a moderately positive effect on both achievement and attitudes in a wide variety of science courses. The effects varied somewhat depending on the knowledge domain; apparently biology achievement and attitudes were most positively affected by the intervention.

References

Arnaudin, M. W., J. J. Mintzes, C. S. Dunn, and T. H. Shafer. 1984. Concept mapping in college science teaching. *Journal of College Science Teaching* 14 (2): 117–121.

Ausubel, D. P. 1963. *The psychology of meaningful verbal learning.* New York: Grune & Stratton.

Ausubel, D. P. 1968. *Educational psychology: A cognitive view.* New York: Holt, Rinehart and Winston.

Ausubel, D. P., J. D. Novak, and H. Hanesian. 1978. *Educational psychology: A cognitive view.* 2nd ed. New York: Holt, Rinehart and Winston.

Barney, E., J. Mintzes, and C.-F. Yen. 2005. Assessing knowledge, attitudes and behavior toward charismatic megafauna: The case of dolphins. *Journal of Environmental Education* 36 (2): 41–55.

Brandt, L., J. Elen, J. Hellemans, L. Heerman, I. Couwenberg, L. Volckaert, and H. Morisse. 2001. The impact of concept mapping and visualization on the learning of secondary school chemistry students. *International Journal of Science Education* 23 (12): 1303–1313.

Chang, K-E., I. Chen, and Y. Sung. 2002. The effect of concept mapping to enhance text comprehension and summarization. *Journal of Experimental Education* 71 (1): 5–23.

Daley, B. J. 2002. Facilitating learning with adult students through concept mapping. *Journal of Continuing Higher Education* 50 (1): 21–31.

Edmondson, K. M. 2000. Assessing science understanding through concept maps. In *Assessing science understanding,* eds. J. J. Mintzes, J. H. Wandersee, and J. D. Novak, 15–40. San Diego, CA: Academic Press.

Esiobu, G.O., and K. Soyibo. 1995. Effects of concept and vee mappings under three learning modes on students' cognitive achievement in ecology and genetics. *Journal of Research in Science Teaching* 32 (9): 971–995.

Fisher, K. M., J. H. Wandersee, and D. E. Moody. 2000. *Mapping biology knowledge.* Dordrecht, The Netherlands: Kluwer Academic.

Heinze-Fry, J., and J. D. Novak. 1990. Concept mapping brings long-term movement toward meaningful learning. *Science Education* 74 (4): 461–472.

Horton, P. B., A. A. McConney, M. Gallo, A. L. Woods, G. J. Senn, and D. Hamelin. 1993. An investigation of the effectiveness of concept mapping as an instructional tool. *Science Education* 77 (1): 95–111.

Jegede, O. J., F. F. Alaiyemola, and P. A. O. Okebukola. 1990. The effect of concept mapping on students' anxiety and achievement in biology. *Journal of Research in Science Teaching* 27 (10): 951–960.

Markham, K. M., J. J. Mintzes, and M. G. Jones. 1994. The concept map as a research and evaluation tool: Further evidence of validity. *Journal of Research in Science Teaching* 31 (1): 1–11.

Markow, P. G., and R. A. Lonning. 1998. Usefulness of concept maps in college chemistry laboratories: Students' perceptions and effects on achievement. *Journal of Research in Science Teaching* 35 (9): 1015–1029.

Martin, B. L., J. J. Mintzes, and I. E. Clavijo. 2000. Restructuring knowledge in biology: Cognitive processes and metacognitive reflections. *International Journal of Science Education* 22: 303–323.

Mintzes, J. J., J. H. Wandersee, and J. D. Novak. 1998. *Teaching science for understanding.* San Diego, CA: Academic Press.

Mintzes, J. J., J. H. Wandersee, and J. D. Novak, eds. 2000. *Assessing science understanding.* San Diego, CA: Academic Press.

Mintzes, J. J., J. H. Wandersee, and J. D. Novak. 2001. Assessing understanding in biology. *Journal of Biological Education* 35 (3): 118–124.

Nicoll, G., J. Francisco, and M. Nakleh. 2001. An investigation of the value of concept maps in general chemistry. *Journal of Chemical Education* 78 (8): 1111–1117.

Novak, J. D. 1993. Human constructivism: A unification of psychological and epistemological phenomena in meaning making. *International Journal of Personal Construct Psychology* 6: 167–193.

Novak, J. D. 1998. *Learning, creating and using knowledge: Concept maps as facilitative tools in schools and corporations.* Mahwah, NJ: Erlbaum.

Novak, J. D., and D. B. Gowin. 1984. *Learning how to learn.* New York: Cambridge University Press.

Novak, J. D., D. B. Gowin, and G. T. Johansen. 1983. The use of concept mapping and knowledge vee mapping with junior high school science students. *Science Education* 67 (5): 625–645.

Odom, A. L., and P. V. Kelly. 2001. Integrating concept mapping and the learning cycle to teach diffusion and osmosis to high school biology students. *Science Education* 85 (6): 615–635.

Pearsall, N. R., J. J. Skipper, and J. J. Mintzes. 1994. Knowledge restructuring in the life sciences: A longitudinal study of conceptual change in biology. *Science Education* 81 (2): 193–215.

Quinn, H. J., J. J. Mintzes, and R. A. Laws. 2003. Successive concept mapping: Assessing understanding in college science classes. *Journal of College Science Teaching* 33 (3): 12–17.

Richie, D., and C. Volkl. 2000. Effectiveness of two generative learning strategies in the science classroom. *School Science and Mathematics* 100 (2): 83–89.

Roth, W-M., and A. Roychoudhury. 1993. The concept map as a tool for the collaborative construction of knowledge: A microanalysis of high school physics students. *Journal of Research in Science Teaching* 30 (5): 503–534.

Santhanam, E., C. Leach, and C. Dawson. 1998. Concept mapping: How should it be introduced, and is there evidence for long term benefit? *Higher Education* 35 (3): 317–328.

Schau, C., and N. Mattern. 1997. Use of map techniques in teaching statistics. *The American Statistician* 51 (2): 171–175.

Shavelson, R., and M. Ruiz-Primo. 2000. On the psychometrics of assessing science understanding. In *Assessing science understanding,* eds. J. J. Mintzes, J. H. Wandersee, and J. D. Novak, 303–341. San Diego, CA: Academic Press.

Sungur, S., C. Tekkaya, and O. Gehan. 2001. The contribution of conceptual change texts accompanied by concept mapping to students' understanding of the human circulatory system. *School Science and Mathematics* 101 (2): 91–101.

Tan, S. C. 2000. The effects of incorporating concept mapping into computer assisted instruction. *Journal of Educational Computing Research* 23 (2): 113–131.

Thompson, T. L., and J. J. Mintzes. 2001. Cognitive structure and the affective domain: On knowing and feeling in biology. *International Journal of Science Education* 24 (6): 645–660.

Trowbridge, J. E., and J. H. Wandersee. 1994. Identifying critical junctures in a college course on evolution. *Journal of Research in Science Teaching* 31 (5): 459–473.

Wallace, J. D., and J. J. Mintzes. 1990. The concept map as a research tool: Exploring conceptual change in biology. *Journal of Research in Science Teaching* 27 (10): 1033–1052.

Wallace, J. D., J. J. Mintzes, and K. M. Markham. 1992. Concept mapping in college science teaching: What the research says. *Journal of College Science Teaching* 22 (2): 84–86.

Wandersee, J. H., J. J. Mintzes, and J. D. Novak. 1994. Research on alternative conceptions in science. In *Handbook of research on science teaching and learning,* ed. D. Gabel, 177–210. New York: Macmillan.

CHAPTER 8

Peer Instruction:
Making Science Engaging

Jessica L. Rosenberg, Mercedes Lorenzo, and Eric Mazur

Jessica L. Rosenberg is a National Science Foundation (NSF) postdoctoral fellow at the Harvard-Smithsonian Center for Astrophysics. She earned a PhD in astronomy at the University of Massachusetts and conducts research on extra-galactic surveys of gas-rich and star-forming galaxies and on the use of active engagement techniques in science teaching. She teaches introductory and observational astronomy.

Mercedes Lorenzo is a visiting researcher in physics education at Harvard University and a high school teacher in physics and chemistry at IES Universidad Laboral in Spain. She earned a PhD in chemistry at the University of Murcia in Spain and conducts research on interactive teaching methods, students' alternative conceptions, and gender issues in science teaching.

Eric Mazur is Gordon McKay Professor of Applied Physics and professor of physics at Harvard University. He earned a PhD at Leiden University in physics and conducts research in nano- and bio-photonics and in gender issues in introductory physics. He teaches introductory physics, electromagnetism, fluid dynamics, and laser spectroscopy.

Science is a creative process where the synthesis of new ideas requires discussion and debate. However, the traditional model for teaching assumes that all information presented to students is automatically learned. As a result, most students leave their introductory science courses frustrated and without a solid conceptual understanding. At the same time, instructors feel that students have not lived up to their expectations, yet they cannot identify the problem. Peer Instruction (PI) is an interactive approach that was designed to improve the learning process. This approach provides students with greater opportunity for synthesizing the concepts while instructors get timely feedback that can help focus the instruction on the points that are the most difficult for the students. PI is flexible and easy to use on its own or in conjunction with other teaching methods. This chapter discusses the motivation for using PI and the mechanics of implementing it in the classroom.

Why Use PI?

Science instructors are often faced with the problem that students leave their courses without a good grasp of the concepts, in some cases even in spite of having obtained good grades in the course (Crouch and Mazur 2001). The primary goal of PI (Mazur 1997) is to improve students' conceptual understanding of the course material.

The basic premises of PI are that students need an opportunity to discuss the concepts with one another and that instructors need timely feedback on what the students do and do not understand. Students are given time in class to explore their understanding of the material by participating in a genuine scientific discussion. At the same time, instructors can gain valuable feedback by listening in on these conversations. Even more important for the instructor, feedback is received from all of the students in response to the administration of a conceptual test (see the section on ConcepTests later in this chapter). A full description of the PI method is presented in a later section.

New teaching methods can be daunting to implement, but the modular nature of PI allows for as much or as little implementation as an instructor is comfortable with. PI is not a rejection of the lecture format, but a supplement that can help engage students who have a range of learning styles. The research shows that PI is an effective method for improving student learning.

The Achievements of PI

Research has shown that students in courses using interactive engagement techniques, including PI, achieve a much greater gain in conceptual understanding than students in traditional lecture courses while also improving their ability to solve quantitative problems (Crouch and Mazur 2001; Hake 1998).

To assess students' conceptual understanding of Newtonian mechanics, Hestenes, Wells, and Swackhammer (1992) developed the Force Concept Inventory (FCI), which was revised by Halloun, Hake, Mosca, and Hestenes in 1995 (Mazur 1997). Many instructors use the FCI as a measure of the effectiveness of an instructional method by giving the test before and after their course. The gain in the students' scores then provides a measure of the gain in their conceptual understanding of Newtonian mechanics. Figure 8.1 shows the average gain on the FCI for tradi-

Figure 8.1

The Impact of Interactive Engagement on Force Concept Inventory (FCI) Score

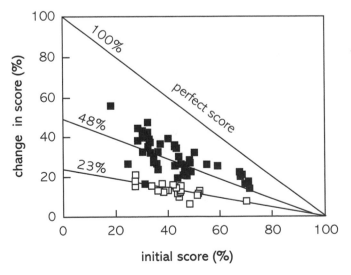

Each square represents the average gain in score vs. the average initial score for all of the students in a class. The open squares show the gain in FCI score in lecture-based courses (average gain out of maximum possible = 23%); the filled squares show the gain for active engagement courses (average gain out of maximum possible = 48%). The "perfect score" line shows the gain required to take students to a score of 100%.

tional lecture courses and interactive engagement courses as a function of the initial score. Each point represents the average for all of the students in a particular class. In traditional lectures, students, on average, only realize 23% of the maximum possible gain at the end of the course, whereas in interactive engagement courses they realize 48% of the possible gain (Hake 1998). For PI specifically, students realize 49–74% of the possible gain (Crouch and Mazur 2001).

Time spent on developing conceptual understanding does not jeopardize students' quantitative problem solving. The top panel in Figure 8.2 shows the relationship between student scores on a single conceptual and conventional (quantitative) problem on the same subject in a traditional lecture course. Note that the size of the points is proportional to the number of students who got that score. The bottom panel is the same plot for students in a PI course. The dashed lines show the average scores on the conceptual and conventional problems. Only a small fraction of students in the traditional lecture course got the conceptual question correct. In fact, there are many students who got perfect scores on the conventional problem but only got 0–2 on the conceptual problem; these students have learned how to "plug and chug" without understanding the meaning of what they are doing. The scores on the conceptual problem for students in the PI course were greatly improved, while the difference in the scores on the conventional problem was small.

The Mechanics Baseline Test (MBT; Hestenes and Wells 1992) provides a quantitative measure of students' problem-solving ability. Like the FCI, the MBT is a standardized test that is often given to measure the effectiveness of an instructional method in a mechanics course. Figure 8.3 shows the MBT results for a study of problem solving in a traditional lecture course (1990) and in PI courses (1991–1997) for the full test and for the quantitative questions (Crouch and Mazur 2001). Despite the conceptual nature of the PI courses, the average MBT scores on the full test and specifically on the quantitative questions are higher than for the traditional course.

Figure 8.2

The Relationship Between Student Answers to a Conceptual and Conventional Problem on the Same Topic

The top panel is for students in a traditional lecture course; the bottom panel is for students in a Peer Instruction (PI) course. The size of the dots is proportional to the number of students with a given score. The dashed lines show the average scores. The students in the PI course show a large increase in their scores on the conceptual problem and only a small change on the conventional problem.

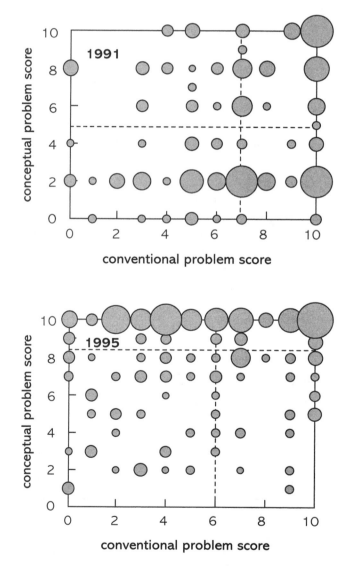

A gender gap exists in the FCI scores when students enter physics courses. In a study of Introductory Physics students at Harvard between 1990 and 1997, the average FCI pretest score was $72 \pm 1.7\%$ for men and $61 \pm 0.9\%$ for women (Lorenzo, Crouch, and Mazur 2006). Both male and female students gain a much better conceptual understanding in courses taught using PI; however, the gain for female students is much greater than for their male peers. The posttest gender gap (the difference between male and female scores) is reduced by only 9% in traditional lecture courses, but by 74% in courses using PI. Most notably, at the end of PI courses there is no statistically significant gender gap in the FCI scores.

The research shows that PI is an important technique for improving both conceptual and problem-solving skills in science courses. In addition, the method provides a way to close the achievement gap between male and female students while improving the achievement of all students.

The PI Method

The basic components of PI are (1) preclass reading assignments, (2) mini-lectures, (3) ConcepTests, and (4) discussion. When these components are added to a course, one must also consider how problem solving is to be incorporated and how exams are to be structured. Other elements can also be combined with PI, including traditional lecture and other interactive engagement techniques, but we do not discuss those here.

Preclass Reading Assignments

Preclass reading assignments are designed to motivate students and to engage them in the reading. The assignments consist of a text to be read along with several challenging conceptual questions, graded purely on effort. In addition, the students are always asked, "What did you find most confusing? If nothing, what did you find most interesting?" The students submit their answers to the reading questions electronically long enough before class that the instructor has time to review the answers (see the "Implementing PI" section later in this chapter for a discussion of adopting preclass reading with and without computer technology). The conceptual questions are designed to probe students' understanding of the material, not their ability to search for the appropriate answer in the text. Based on the knowledge gleaned from a review of their answers (not necessarily a thorough reading of all responses), the instructor can select the appropriate content to be discussed in detail in class.

Mini-Lectures

Each PI class consists of several mini-lectures that focus on key topics where students have difficulties

Figure 8.3

The Average Scores on the Mechanics Baseline Test (MBT) for an Introductory Physics Course Taught With Traditional Lecture (T; 1990) and With Peer Instruction (PI; 1991–1997)

The circles are for the full test, and the squares are for the quantitative questions. Reprinted with permission from C. H. Crouch and E. Mazur, "Peer Instruction: Ten Years of Experience and Results," *American Journal of Physics* 69: 970–977, 2001. Copyright 2001, American Association of Physics Teachers.

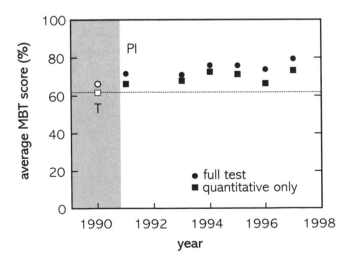

or misconceptions. These difficulties or misconceptions can be identified from previous teaching experience, student answers to the preclass reading, or the literature. Each mini-lecture is only about 10 minutes, so it must be concise and focused on a single subject. This is in contrast to standard lectures, which last for an entire class and tend to have the breadth and detail more comparable to the material covered in the textbook.

ConcepTests

The mini-lectures are interspersed with ConcepTests—short conceptual questions designed to probe student understanding of one of the concepts discussed. The ConcepTests, such as the sample shown in Figure 8.4, are based on misconceptions or student difficulties (see sidebar, "Writing and Vetting ConcepTests").

The ConcepTest is administered according to the following sequence:

1. Question posed (1 minute)
2. Students given time to think (1 minute)
3. Students record individual answers
4. Students convince their neighbors (optional, based on results of 3; 1–2 minutes)
5. Students record revised answers
6. Feedback to instructor: Tally of answers
7. Explanation of correct answer (2+ minutes)

As indicated in this sequence, the students are given time to formulate their answer (step 2) and then record it (step 3). Once they have committed to an answer, the students then discuss their answers with each other (step 4), as long as enough students have the correct answer (see "Discussion" section for details). After this discussion the students record their (possibly revised) answer again (step 5). This process forces students to think through and talk through the arguments being developed, providing them and the instructor with an assessment of their understanding of the concept.

Discussion

Whether to have students discuss their answers after a ConcepTest depends on what fraction of students get the correct answer. Figure 8.5 shows the percentage of correct ConcepTest answers after discussion as a function of the percentage of correct answers before discussion. Each data point corresponds to a single ConcepTest. The dashed line shows the trend

Figure 8.4

A Sample ConcepTest From a Newtonian Mechanics Course

A ball is thrown downward (not dropped) from the top of a tower. After being released, its downward acceleration is:

1. greater than g
2. exactly g
3. smaller than g
4. not covered in the reading assignment

Writing and Vetting ConcepTests

- Use questions based on student difficulties, mistakes, and misconceptions.
- Focus on a single concept.
- Ask questions that cannot be solved by relying on equations.
- Make sure questions and answers are clear and concise.
- Use only questions that are manageable in their level of difficulty.
- Keep track of questions that produce good discussion and improvement in understanding.
- Make use of existing question databases (e.g., *www.deas.harvard.edu/galileo* and *www.flaguide.org/tools/tools_technique.php*).

defined by these points. The aim of having students discuss their answers to a ConcepTest is to improve their understanding of the concept. The farther above the "no improvement" line the points are in Figure 8.5, the larger the fraction of students who moved from the incorrect answer before discussion to the correct answer after discussion. If the percentage of correct answers before discussion is too low (< 35%), then most of the students in the class have not understood the concept; in this case, slowing down, lecturing in more detail on the same subject, and then reassessing with another ConcepTest is more effective than a student discussion. If the percentage of correct answers before discussion is high (> 70%), then most students have understood the concept and one can proceed without discussion. The shaded region on Figure 8.5 highlights the prediscussion ConcepTest scores for which the largest fraction of students move to the correct answer after discussion. It is in this region that students derive the maximum benefit from discussing their answers with their peers.

Figure 8.6 shows the percentage of students who moved from the incorrect answer to the correct answer after discussion versus the percentage of students who got the correct answer both times. This figure shows that the fraction of students who are convinced to change their minds from the incorrect to the correct answer after discussion is larger when the initial percentage of students who understand the concept is larger.

Figure 8.5

Effect of Discussion on ConcepTest Scores

The plot shows ConcepTest score averages for the entire class before (*x*-axis) and after (*y*-axis) discussion. The solid line indicates where points would fall if discussion did not improve student scores. The shaded region shows where 35%–70% of students get the correct answer before discussion. This is the region in which discussion among the students produces the largest increase in correct answers.

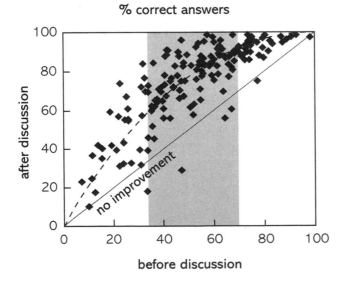

% correct answers

Problem Solving

Quantitative problem solving is an important aspect of many science courses and is entirely compatible with PI. As discussed in the earlier section on the achievements of PI, the improvement in conceptual understanding from PI does lead to better problem solving (Crouch and Mazur 2001).

Problem solving requires logical reasoning as well as mathematical skills. The problem with the way conventional problems are presented in a standard introductory textbook is that most textbooks test mathematical instead of analytical thinking skills. By adding conceptual questions to the curriculum, students are led to develop their logical reasoning skills as well as their mathematical skills, both of which help them become better problem solvers. The development of mathematical skills to complement the logical reasoning developed with PI requires time and practice. Time can be devoted during a mini-lecture or, more effectively, as part of small-group problem-solving sessions as discussed in the section on implementation of PI later in this chapter. Quantitative homework assignments also provide an opportunity for students to practice this skill.

Exams

One of the best ways to help students accept a new teaching method is to make the exams reflect the philosophy of the course. If only conceptual questions are addressed in class and in homework, then exams should contain only conceptual questions. Alternatively, if the students have been exposed to a mix of conceptual and mathematical questions, then the exams should reflect that balance. Students should not be faced with something completely new in a high-stakes, high-pressure situation. Adding conceptual questions on exams also reinforces that such questions are important and makes it more likely that the students will recognize the value of the ConcepTests.

Implementing PI

PI is designed to be flexible and easy to implement—one could ask a single ConcepTest, implement all of the components of PI, or do something in between. The modular nature of PI allows for experimentation with the method without total disruption of a previously established course design. In addition, PI can easily be combined with other classroom methods such as tutorials (e.g., Adams et al. 2003; McDermott, Schaffer, and the University of Washington Physics Education Group 2002), group work (see, e.g., *http://groups. physics.umn.edu/physed/Research/CGPS/GreenBook.html*), other active engagement techniques (see, e.g., *www.calstatela.edu/dept/chem/chem2/Active/index.htm*), or standard lecture.

Figure 8.6

Effect of the Percentage of Students Who Initially Get a ConcepTest Correct on the Postdiscussion Response of Students Who Initially Got It Incorrect

The plot shows the fraction of students who are convinced to change their minds from the incorrect to the correct answer after discussion vs. the percentage of students who got the correct answer both times.

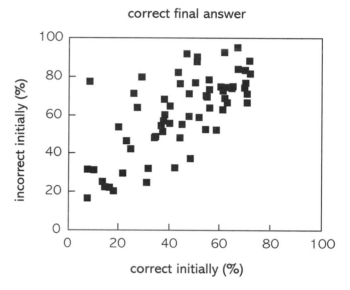

To convert a traditional lecture to a PI format, one must select the concepts in the lecture that are the most difficult for the students. The preclass reading assignments, prior knowledge of students' difficulties and misconceptions, and the literature can help guide this selection. The goal is to avoid spending significant amounts of class time on the material the students can obtain on their own. Mini-lectures (from one to six, depending on the overall class format and length) and the ConcepTests for each mini-lecture can then be based on the most difficult concepts of the material to be covered. Which and how many of the ConcepTests are administered can be based on the student scores on the ConcepTests and the misconceptions/difficulties that come to light in their discussions (see sidebar, p. 81).

In a PI course most of the quantitative problem solving is done outside class. Small-group sessions are an effective means of improving students' problem-solving skills. Quantitative problem solving can be incorporated as part of the homework and small-group sessions.

Technology is useful but not necessary for the implementation of PI. For the preclass reading assignments, technology is especially beneficial because it allows the instructor to view student answers to the reading questions before class (Novak et al. 1999). If computer access is limited, reading quizzes can be administered at the beginning of class to motivate students to do the reading ahead of time. The Interactive Learning Toolkit (for more information see *http://deas.harvard.edu/ilt*) can be used for the administration of preclass reading assignments and other pieces of a PI course (Blackboard [*www.blackboard.com*] and other online resources can also be used for this purpose). Unlike the preclass reading assignments, ConcepTests can easily be administered in multiple high- and low-tech ways. The most common examples are flashcards, personal response systems (PRS), and handheld computers.

- *Flashcards:* Each student is given a set of six or more cards labeled with letters or numbers (and sometimes color coded as well) to signal the answer to a question. Flashcards are an easy, low-tech way to gather student answers, but there is no permanent record of the answers provided by the students.
- *PRS:* Many institutions are now investing in radio or infrared devices that allow students to "click in" their answer, providing the instructor with an instantaneous histogram and a permanent record of the student responses. The disadvantage of this method is cost, but systems are getting cheaper and more commonly available. For more information on PRS, see *www.vanderbilt.edu/cft/resources/teaching_resources/technology/crs.htm*.
- *Handheld computers:* Many students come to class with a variety of communication or computing devices—cellular phones, palmtops, and laptops. Technology is now being developed so that these devices can all be used to provide responses to ConcepTests (for more information on this developing technology, see *http://mazur-www.deas.harvard.edu/lt3*).

While the improvisation required to use ConcepTests in the classroom may seem daunting at first, they often make teaching easier for the instructor and learning easier for the student. Students are given the opportunity to take a break from listening in order to think about and discuss the material being presented. The instructor is given a chance to listen to how students explain the material to one another. Students sometimes provide a completely different perspective on the material—one that is often more convincing to their peers because the students understand why the concepts are difficult. Putting ideas into words helps the students develop their understanding. At the same time, PI provides feedback to the instructor that is often lacking in the conventional classroom.

Summary

Research has shown that students often leave introductory science courses with little gain in understanding of the scientific concepts. Interactive engagement in the classroom using PI can increase students' understanding and can shrink the achievement gap between men and women. The method is easy to implement either within an existing course structure or as a redesign of a course. PI provides a dynamic environment in which instructors get feedback from students and students become active participants in the learning process. More information on PI, including an interactive DVD tutorial, is available at *www.teachingdvd.com*.

Recommendations

When deciding to implement a new teaching method in your course, there are issues to consider in terms of how you, your colleagues, and your students are going to respond to the changes. Here are a few suggestions to help make this change with PI:

1. *Convince yourself (and your colleagues) that changing the format of your course makes sense.* To this end, administering a benchmark test like the Force Concept Inventory (Hestenes, Wells, and Swackhammer 1992), the Mechanics Baseline Test (Hestenes and Wells 1992), the Astronomy Diagnostic Test (Zeilik et al. 1997), and the California Chemistry Diagnostic Test (Russell 1994) can provide useful data. Ideally you should administer the test both at the beginning and end of the semester—first during your conventional course and then when you are using PI. These data will provide a clear picture of what the changes to the course have accomplished.

2. *Motivate the students.* Students resist change, so explaining what you are doing, why you are making these changes, and how they will benefit is probably the most important thing you can do to make the change in your course succeed.

3. *Change the exams to reflect the change in the course format.* Students focus much, if not most, of their attention on exams, and their feelings about the course often reflect whether they felt that the exam adequately reflects the class activities. If most of the class time is spent on concepts, then giving exams that include conceptual questions is necessary for students to appreciate the time spent on conceptual material.

4. *Maintain adequate opportunities for problem solving.* For any course where problem solving is still an important part of the curriculum, there must be time devoted to developing this skill. Opportunities for students to sharpen their problem-solving skills include homework assignments and problem-solving sessions.

Acknowledgments

Mercedes Lorenzo thanks the Consejería de Educación de Castilla-La Mancha (Spain) for support during her leave of absence. Jessica L. Rosenberg thanks the NSF for support through grant AST-0302049.

References

Adams, J. P., E. E. Prather, T. F. Slater, and the CAPER Team. 2003. *Lecture tutorials for introductory astronomy.* Upper Saddle River, NJ: Prentice Hall.

Crouch, C. H., and E. Mazur. 2001. Peer Instruction: Ten years of experience and results. *American Journal of Physics* 69 (9): 970–977.

Hake, R. R. 1998. Interactive-engagement vs. traditional methods: A six-thousand-student survey of mechanics test data for introductory physics courses. *American Journal of Physics* 66 (1): 64–74.

Hestenes, D., and M. Wells. 1992. A mechanics baseline test. *The Physics Teacher* 30 (3): 159–166.

Hestenes, D., M. Wells, and G. Swackhammer. 1992. Force Concept Inventory. *The Physics Teacher* 30 (3): 141–151.

Lorenzo, M., C. H. Crouch, and E. Mazur. 2006. Reducing the gender gap in the physics classroom. *American Journal of Physics* 74: 118–122.

Mazur, E. 1997. *Peer Instruction: A user's manual.* Upper Saddle River, NJ: Prentice Hall.

McDermott, L. C., P. S. Schaffer, and the University of Washington Physics Education Group. 2002. *Tutorials in introductory physics.* Upper Saddle River, NJ: Prentice Hall.

Novak, G. M., E. T. Patterson, A. D. Gavrin, and W. Christian. 1999. *Just-in-Time Teaching: Blending active learning with web technology.* Upper Saddle River, NJ: Prentice Hall.

Russell, A. A. 1994. A rationally designed chemistry diagnostic test. *Journal of Chemical Education* 71 (4): 314–317.

Zeilik, M., C. Schau, N. Mattern, S. Hall, K. Teague, and W. Bisard. 1997. Conceptual astronomy: A novel model for teaching postsecondary science courses. *American Journal of Physics* 65 (10): 987–996.

CHAPTER 9

Open Laboratories in College Science

Susan Godbey, Tom Otieno, and Daniel Tofan

Susan Godbey is associate professor of chemistry at Eastern Kentucky University. She earned a PhD in analytical chemistry at the University of South Carolina and conducts research on environmental analysis and chemical education. She teaches introductory chemistry, chemistry for the health sciences, general chemistry, and analytical chemistry.

Tom Otieno is professor of chemistry at Eastern Kentucky University. He earned a PhD in inorganic chemistry at the University of British Columbia and conducts research on synthesis, structure, and properties of coordination compounds, and science education. He teaches chemistry for the health sciences, general chemistry, and inorganic chemistry.

Daniel Tofan is assistant professor of chemistry at Eastern Kentucky University. He earned a PhD in inorganic chemistry at Georgetown University and conducts research on chemical education, chemical information, and computers in chemical education. He teaches introductory and general chemistry.

The laboratory experience is an essential part of science learning. Traditionally, this experience has been provided to students in the form of regularly scheduled laboratory sessions. However, several factors, including scheduling flexibility to accommodate nontraditional students, space limitations, equipment costs, and staffing issues, have compelled some institutions to look for alternative models for laboratory teaching (Crane 1981; Davis et al. 2000; Hamilton and McMahon 1976; Hansen et al. 1996; Majerle, Utecht, and Guetzloff 1995).

One viable alternative to the conventional, regularly scheduled laboratory session is the open laboratory concept (see also Chapter 4 in this volume). In the present chapter, the authors use the open laboratory system developed at Eastern Kentucky University as a case study to provide insight into the system, including its benefits and challenges. The authors also report on plans to use current and emerging computer technologies to automate laboratory operations.

The "Open Lab" Concept

An *open lab* for science courses is broadly defined as any laboratory system in which students are required to complete the lab component of a course but are allowed to attend lab at any time it is open rather than being required to attend at a specific time. The open lab system is a versatile one, lending itself to implementation in different levels of institutions—including high schools, community colleges, and universities—and different scientific disciplines—including biology, chemistry, geology, and physics (Table 9.1). However, the use of the system is not well documented, with only a few relevant papers having been published (Crane 1981; Hamilton and McMahon 1976; Hansen et al. 1996). For this reason, many institutions may not be aware of the potential benefits of an open lab system. This chapter provides current and practical information to allow college science educators to critically evaluate the viability of adopting such a system at their institutions.

The general advantages and disadvantages of open lab systems are summarized in Figure 9.1. A major advantage of the open lab system over the conventional system is the scheduling flexibility it offers students. It has long been appreciated that this type of flexibility is important for students who have other demands on their time besides school (Hamilton and McMahon 1976). This issue has become increasingly important with the changing demographics of college students. Unlike the past when most students had education as their primary responsibility, an ever-increasing number of students now work full-time or part-time and have family obligations. Many students also commute rather than live on campus. The open lab system gives them more flexibility in scheduling for the laboratory experience and their other obligations. Because there are no specific lab sections in the open lab system, the system can also accommodate irregular blocks of time in instructor schedules.

The open lab allows much more efficient use of the laboratory space. A traditional lab is designed so that nearly all students can complete the lab in the allotted time, but many students complete experiments in less than the allotted time. In an open lab system, available space can be continuously used by other students. When significant constraints exist with regard to space and staffing, different courses can be taught in the same laboratory, and one instructor can over-

Table 9.1

Some Institutions Using Open Laboratory

Institution	Discipline[a]	Reference[b]
Calhoun Community College, Decatur, AL	Biology	*webnt.calhoun.edu/distance/Internet/Natural/Bio103/New/HTML/BIO103/help.html*
Capitol College, Laurel, MD	Physics	*www.capitol-college.edu/studentlife/facilities/chemlab.shtml*
Eastern Kentucky University, Richmond, KY	Chemistry	*http://people.eku.edu/Tofand/lab101-105/index.html*
Illinois Valley Community College, Oglesby, IL	Geology	*www.ivcc.edu/phillips/geology/geology.html*
Kennesaw State University, Kennesaw, GA	Biology	*http://science.kennesaw.edu/biophys/gened/1101labs/hrs-regs/index.htm*
Pacific Lutheran University, Tacoma, WA	Chemistry	*www.chem.plu.edu/openlab.html*
University of Arkansas at Little Rock, AR	Physics	*www.physics.ualr.edu/Open_Lab/instruct.html*

[a]The open lab systems at these institutions are used primarily at the freshman level.
[b]All websites were accessed on September 2, 2005.

Figure 9.1

Advantages and Disadvantages of Open Laboratory Systems

Advantages
- Allows students flexibility in scheduling lab attendance
- Permits students to spend more time if necessary to complete lab
- Encourages use of visual media such as videos, which provides a better format for presenting material to some students and can be viewed again if information is not understood
- Usually incorporates pretests to encourage lab preparation
- More consistent / less personnel-dependent instruction
- Allows more flexible scheduling of lab instructors
- Less instructor hours needed to staff lab because less wasted time in lab usage
- Grading inconsistencies minimized since grading duties shared by all instructors

Disadvantages
- Does not provide a single instructor to whom students may address their questions
- Requires significant administrative efforts, since modifications in labs require updating/remaking videos and adjusting pretest questions
- Allows procrastination, leading to crowded labs later in the week
- Some instructor time spent in check-in/check-out process
- Group work may require special accommodation
- Students may need to be more self-motivated than in the traditional lab format

see students involved in all courses and at all levels at the same time (Crane 1981; Hamilton and McMahon 1976), although combining different labs obviously complicates safety issues.

As a result of the efficient use of laboratory space, less equipment and fewer instructors are required, thereby saving on costs. The savings can be significant for laboratories serving large numbers of students. Finding qualified instructors to staff a large number of lab classes is often a challenge, so the savings in instructors may be particularly attractive.

The quality of the laboratory experience for students may be enhanced in a number of ways in an open lab. Unlike traditional labs, which assume that students have prepared by reading the laboratory procedure along with listening to short prelab talks by the instructor, in open lab systems alternative methods of preparation are prescribed. Students are generally required to conduct several prelab activities and demonstrate an understanding of the experiment before being allowed into the lab. These activities enhance student preparation and promote a successful laboratory experience that is less instructor dependent. As noted by other authors, consistency of instruction is a particular challenge in multisection laboratories staffed by diverse mixtures of full-time faculty members, graduate students, and part-time instructors (Majerle, Utecht, and Guetzloff 1995).

Open lab systems have many advantages, but there are also some challenges. Significant administrative effort is required to coordinate the various aspects of the typical system. Also, students may not feel they have a single person to whom they can address their questions, and group work may require special accommodation. Students may also need to be more self-motivated than in the traditional lab format.

The Original Open Lab System at Eastern Kentucky University

The open lab system at Eastern Kentucky University was developed in the mid-1970s to serve students in two courses: a traditional nonscience major / general education introductory chemistry course and a chemistry course for nursing majors. A preponderance of students enroll in the nursing course to fulfill a major requirement. A large proportion of students in the other course are also fulfilling major requirements, but a significant fraction choose the class to fulfill a general education science requirement.

Frequently, students in these two courses are required to take a second semester of chemistry to fulfill major requirements. The follow-up course for the nursing students introduced organic chemistry and biochemistry, while students in the other introductory course often advanced to a course that was primarily introductory organic chemistry. Although the courses served different types of students, there was a great deal of overlap in the lecture and laboratory content. It was expected that the same laboratory experiences could serve both groups of students, thus allowing the open lab system to be more efficient and cost-effective.

The initial open lab system had the following attributes:

1. Students were required to watch a video about each experiment, shown on campus television, as well as read the relevant material in the laboratory manual. The videos were produced by the university's Division of Media Resources in collaboration with the chemistry faculty and staff. Each week the appropriate video was shown at published intervals on campus cable. Students could view the videos more than once if they wished.

2. A laboratory pretest computer program was developed, and students were required to pass the pretest before attending the laboratory. The initial pretest program was written in the BASIC computer language and was accessible via networked campus computers or off-campus via modem. The pretest could be taken as many times as necessary, but there was a required waiting period of one hour after a failed attempt before another attempt could be made. An "admission ticket" for laboratory was printed after a successful attempt. The pretest consisted of random questions from a database developed for each experiment and covered safety, procedure, and concepts for the laboratory.

3. The laboratory was open and staffed during scheduled times each week. Students were allowed to attend lab once each week during any of the open hours, but only the lab scheduled for that week could be performed. The attending instructor checked the students in and out of lab and served as a resource to the students during lab (Figure 9.2).

The system substantially addressed the needs of students. It provided a great deal of flexibility for student schedules and allowed students to take as much time as needed to complete the laboratory experiment. The videos and pretest promoted student preparation and compensated for the lack of a "prelab lecture" by the lab instructor.

Recent Experiences at Eastern Kentucky University

This system operated for about 25 years; during this time, changes in staff and curriculum had an impact on the system. The chemistry faculty members involved in the creation of the system retired, the nursing program dropped the requirement for a follow-up chemistry course, the pretest program became outdated, and gradually changes were made in procedures without corresponding adjustments to the pretest databases and videos. Eventually, the direction

Figure 9.2

Checking Into the Lab

of the laboratory system needed to be reevaluated. In 1999 the chemistry department faculty assessed the advantages and disadvantages of investing the time and resources necessary to renew the system as opposed to converting back to traditional laboratory format for the two courses. Students in the courses were polled and found to favor the open lab system. Overall the practical advantages of the open lab system, particularly the savings in instructor hours in a time of critical instructor shortage, led to the retention of the open lab system.

Over the following couple of years, the open lab system was revamped in some ways, but the general principles of the system were retained. The pretest program was moved to the Blackboard system. All new videos were created, and the corresponding procedures and pretest databases were adjusted. The videos were made available via streaming video online as well as via a CD that was packaged with the laboratory manual. Eventually the laboratory manual was moved online and the CD that contained the videos was distributed to registered students in the laboratory, while the streaming video was retained as an optional way of accessing the videos.

The open lab system has been an overall success for Eastern Kentucky University. There has been a clear efficiency advantage in terms of staffing. During a typical semester it would have required about 20% more instructor hours to staff the lab in a standard non-open format. The open lab system also provides a sort of "entry-level" position for laboratory instructors. As is often the case in large freshman classes, the laboratories are staffed primarily by first-year graduate students.

More experienced instructors, including upper-level graduate students, are typically assigned to more advanced chemistry courses. The open lab system as operated at Eastern Kentucky University can be staffed with instructors possessing the requisite technical qualifications but who lack experience in teaching situations. After serving as instructors in the open lab system the instructors have usually developed the skills needed to supervise individual lab sections with confidence.

Eastern Kentucky University has experienced some administrative challenges with the open lab system. The pretest database, video, and written procedures need to be consistent for each experiment; therefore, changes in any of these components necessitate changes in the others. Changing the videos is especially problematic, requiring significant coordination and time in production as well as production costs. Thanks to the Division of Media Resources, most of the production costs of the videos have not been deducted from the chemistry department budget. Overall, the administration/maintenance of the system is a major undertaking and the person in charge of the lab needs to be supported appropriately by the university administration, especially in regard to reduction of duties in other areas.

Another interesting challenge of the open lab system involves student choices. When polled for preferences for lab days, students chose Tuesday and Wednesday, with only about 10% of students indicating a preference for attending lab on Thursday. However, with the open lab made available on Tuesday, Wednesday, and Thursday, over 50% of labs were actually completed on Thursday (Figure 9.3). Interestingly, statistical data collected over a number of semesters also reveal a small but consistent decline in lab scores as the week progresses (Table 9.2). Obviously, when students are afforded the freedom to choose which day to attend lab, many procrastinate and attend lab during the last available day of the week. Possibly, students procrastinate because they have not prepared for laboratory, accounting for the systematic decline in lab averages.

Future Directions for the Open Lab System at Eastern Kentucky University

Significant changes are planned for the open lab at Eastern Kentucky University to take advantage of existing and emerging computer technology. Three areas have been targeted for the introduction of new technologies or improvement of existing ones: pre- and postlab assignments, lab management, and grading of lab work.

Figure 9.3

Percent of Labs Completed During Each Open Lab Day

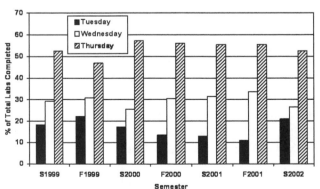

1. *Pre- and postlab assignments:* Custom software is being written to deliver prelab assignments. The software will allow numerical questions to be parameterized at will, creating a much more flexible question pool. Student responses, number of attempts, and other pertinent information will be saved in a local database, thus allowing collection of meaningful data for educational research. In a similar way, postlab assignments will be used to test what students have learned from performing an experiment and whether and how it helped them visualize the concepts learned in lecture. Use of these pre- and

Table 9.2

Differences in Average Scores for Eastern Kentucky University Chemistry Labs Completed on Specific Open Lab Days Compared With Overall Average

	Spring 1999	Fall 1999	Spring 2000	Fall 2000	Spring 2001	Fall 2001	Spring 2002	Average difference*
Tuesday	2.5	2.4	2.3	2.4	0.9	2.8	2.0	2.2(0.6)
Wednesday	0.6	0.9	0.0	0.4	0.3	0.6	1.0	0.5(0.3)
Thursday	-1.2	-1.7	-0.7	-0.8	-0.4	-0.9	-1.3	-1.0(0.4)

*Numbers in parentheses are standard deviations of the differences.

postlab quizzes will promote a more productive and safe laboratory experience.

2. *Lab management:* A computer-based system using custom software to check students in and out is being introduced. By communicating with the prelab assignment delivery software that will be implemented, the lab management program will be able to instantly check students' prelab scores and determine whether they did or did not pass the assignments. Data about check-in and check-out will be recorded automatically, with minimum assistance from the instructor. Thus, instructors will be able to focus more on supervising and helping the students than on collecting attendance information. Lab management will be further improved through the following methods:

a. The check-in process will become self-managed. Students will need to pass the prelab assignment, after which they will come to our check-in section, swipe their ID card, and be checked in automatically; the software will assign them a workstation number and any unknown samples needed for the experiment and will record the day and time of check-in without instructor assistance.

b. The system will be able to deny access into the lab to students who did not pass their prelabs or have defaulted in another prescribed task; it will also prevent a student from performing the same experiment twice (for whatever reason).

c. The instructor will carry a handheld computer (PDA) equipped with software that wirelessly communicates with the check-in station and updates the data about lab occupancy in real time; the instructor will instantly be able to see who is working in the lab at each station and will be able to obtain information about each student's prelab assignment, thus identifying areas of weakness and targeting help accordingly.

d. Upon completion, the instructor will verify that students have cleaned their workstation and will check the students out using the PDA, which will send to the mainframe data about the time of check-out and technique score.

e. The laboratory coordinator will be able to remotely connect to the management software and see a virtual picture of who's in the lab, since what time, what unknowns they are working on, and so on.

f. The instructors will be able to send messages to the coordinator from their PDAs in case assistance is needed.

One of the important uses of this system will be at the beginning of each semester, when signed safety agreements are collected from all students to allow them to go into the lab with a thorough knowledge of laboratory safety rules and guidelines. Signatures will be collected using an electronic pad connected to the computer, and the safety sheets will be stored in electronic format into the database, instead of keeping paper copies on file.

3. *Grading of lab work:* An automated grading system will be implemented. This will work well with experiments that require students to provide numerical results, while some of the qualitative questions may still be hand graded. It is anticipated that our laboratory will be equipped with computers at each workstation, which will also allow the use of interfaced probes for the collection of data. Using commercial and in-house software, data will be uploaded into the computer for each student, and the software will be able to grade the student's work. A lab report will be printed at the end of the experiment using a standard format filled with each student's data. The students will thus be able to leave the lab with a graded report in hand. At check-out, each student will be able to see a history of his or her lab performance.

These technological advances should be possible over the next few years, using technology now available. The Java programming language will be used to develop the essential parts of the future system: the assignment delivery component, the lab management component, the data interfacing and grading component, and the data storage mechanism.

In addition to enhancing student learning and improving the efficiency of the open laboratory, these advances will also allow the collection of a significant quantity of data to add to the educational research efforts in the area of the freshman chemistry laboratory. The system will provide an opportunity for novel applications of computer technology in science education as well. The improvements, although quite synergistic with open lab systems, can be applied in all sorts of laboratory environments. Other institutions may be encouraged to consider whether the use of the technology will improve laboratory experiences for their students.

Conclusions

Overall, the open lab system is an attractive alternative to traditionally scheduled laboratory experiences, especially when large numbers of students need to be served with limited laboratory space or when qualified instructors are in short supply. Students benefit by gaining the flexibility to attend lab at convenient times and the ability to spend more time completing a laboratory experience if necessary. The institution benefits by savings due to efficient use of space, equipment, and staff. The essential ingredient in the success of an open lab system is the reallocation of some of the savings due to the efficiency of the system into the administration, maintenance, and revision of the system. If an institution is willing to commit to this reallocation of resources, then the choice of an open lab system can work effectively and produce the expected efficiency.

References

Crane, D. W. 1981. The open laboratory—an alternative. *Journal of Chemical Education* 58 (10): 794–795.

Davis, D. D., B. R. Golden, P. Rhyne, and G. Schiffer. 2000. Unique laboratory experiences for the commuter university. *Reaching Through Teaching* 13 (2): 6.

Hamilton, H. H., and J. D. McMahon. 1976. An open laboratory approach for the community college. *Journal of Chemical Education* 53 (4): 246–247.

Hansen, L. D., J. L. Garner, B. J. Wilson, C. L. Cluff, and F. R. Nordmeyer. 1996. Teaching concepts in beginning chemistry with simple exploratory experiments. *Journal of Chemical Education* 73 (9): 840–842.

Majerle, R. S., R. E. Utecht, and C. J. Guetzloff. 1995. A different approach to the traditional chemistry lab experience. *Journal of Chemical Education* 72 (8): 718–719.

CHAPTER 10

New Physics Teaching and Assessment:
Laboratory- and Technology-Enhanced Active Learning

Robert J. Beichner, Yehudit Judy Dori, and John Belcher

Robert J. Beichner is Alumni Distinguished Professor of Physics at North Carolina State University. He earned a PhD in science education at the State University of New York / University at Buffalo and conducts research on active learning in large-enrollment classes. He teaches a physics education research seminar, introductory physics for scientists and engineers, and advanced physics laboratory techniques.

Yehudit Judy Dori is associate professor in the Department of Education in Technology and Science at the Technion-Israel Institute of Technology in Haifa, Israel, and a researcher in the Center for Educational Computing Initiatives at the Massachusetts Institute of Technology (MIT). She earned a PhD in science education at the Weizmann Institute of Science and conducts research on teaching, learning, and assessment of science curricula. She teaches courses on project assessment, science curriculum development, and research in science education.

John Belcher is Class of 1922 Professor of Physics at MIT and a researcher in the Center for Educational Computing Initiatives. He earned a PhD in physics at the California Institute of Technology and conducts research on space and astrophysical plasma physics and on large-enrollment introductory physics classes. He teaches introductory physics, electromagnetism, plasma physics, and astrophysics.

Active learning, which integrates experimental work, plays an important role in helping students create cognitive links between the world of mathematics and that of physics. We believe that teachers and students need to incorporate active learning, hands-on activities, and visualizations in the teaching and learning of scientific phenomena and processes, especially when dealing with abstract concepts such as electromagnetism.

For more than half a decade, two universities—North Carolina State University (NCSU) and Massachusetts Institute of Technology (MIT)—have been engaged in reforming their introductory physics courses. This chapter describes the instructional objectives that formed the basis of our reform efforts. After showing how revising the content led to a redesign of the classroom space, we set forth some of the new instructional activities that resulted from our efforts. Finally, we present and discuss the different types of assessments that were used to evaluate the efficacy of our changes.

Motivation

The underpinning of our efforts to reform the introductory calculus-based physics classes at our two institutions emanated from students' lack of interest in the subject matter and an accompanying high failure rate. Science and engineering education research indicates that students need to be engaged in the material they are studying. Hake (1998) illustrated clear differences in performance between traditional and interactive classes. Cummings and colleagues (1999) described and analyzed the first model of studio physics. Mazur (1997) presented his reasoning and method for increasing his students' engagement with his lectures (see also Chapter 8 in this volume). Of course, this idea is not confined to the teaching of physics. Engineering has probably made the most progress toward studying and implementing "engaging" instruction. Smith and colleagues (2005) outlined the history of implementing active engagement and described the research behind the pedagogy. In particular, they cited Astin (1993), who summarized data from more than 27,000 students enrolled at 309 different colleges. Astin found that interaction—among students and between students and faculty—had a much greater impact on college success, as measured on a variety of scales, than any other aspect of students' college experiences.

The book *How People Learn* (Bransford, Brown, and Cocking 1999) and its recent sequel, *How Students Learn* (Donovan and Bransford 2005), provide a useful framework for instruction in the classroom. Basically, they propose several interconnected perspectives on learning environments: learner centered, knowledge centered, and assessment centered, which are supported by the community. Effectively designed learning environments incorporate all these perspectives. While these approaches relate to learning in general, several methods have been developed that focus specifically on teaching physics in undergraduate courses (Laws 1997; McDermott and the Physics Education Group at the University of Washington 1996; McDermott, Shaffer, and the Physics Education Group at the University of Washington 2002; Sokoloff and Thornton 1997; Steinberg, Wittmann, and Redish 1997). The pedagogy we describe was developed with these ideas in mind.

Augmenting the altruistic "we want our students to learn more" motivation are external pressures. Administrators respond to student and faculty complaints when prerequisite classes are reported to be poor preparation for later work. There can be considerable persuasion applied by accrediting agencies. For us, the Accrediting Board for Engineering and Technology (ABET) had great import. Their newest criteria are quite different from those of the past. For example, there are no specific science course requirements. In fact, if it can be shown that engineering program graduates are able to "apply knowledge of science," whatever that might mean, it doesn't matter how they acquired that ability. Few engineering departments want the responsibility of teaching physics, but they could take it upon themselves if they decide that is the best plan of action. Thus it behooves physics departments to make a concerted effort to provide courses that are easily related to the ABET criteria (*www.abet.org/forms.shtml*). These criteria, besides their open-endedness, focus on "teamsmanship" (teamwork) and communication as well as experiment design and problem solving. Although these skills have supposedly always been important, engineering schools must now rigorously demonstrate that students indeed have these skills.

NCSU Mechanics and Electromagnetism Courses—
Objectives and Settings

The internal and external pressures may seem burdensome to physics instructors, but having these constraints actually makes course design easier because the "target" has been clearly specified. The NCSU effort is called SCALE-UP—Student-Centered Activities for Large Enrollment Undergraduate Programs. (For more information, visit the SCALE-UP website, *http://scaleup.ncsu.edu.*) The SCALE-UP guidelines at NCSU that were developed for the two-semester calculus-based introductory physics course are shown in the appendix at the end of this chapter. The first semester deals with mechanics and the second with electromagnetism.

The course objectives are behavior oriented—that is, they are written in terms of specific actions students should be able to complete after instruction of the entire two-course sequence. There are more detailed behaviors, primarily in the content areas that refer to each course and even down to the particular topical area. Creating objectives in this manner not only makes it easier for faculty and students to stay focused on the important parts of the course, but also makes assessment simpler.

Starting from a set of objectives that specified skills like communication and teamsmanship suggested that a complete redesign of the learning environment might be needed. After experimenting with different seating geometries, we discovered that round tables (6 or 7 ft. in diameter) were best at facilitating discussions between students and with instructors. We place three teams of three students at each table. The teams are structured to be heterogeneous within groups but homogeneous across groups. This ensures that students at all ability levels work together and learn from each other. We also structure the activities so that the stronger students want to help their teammates learn the material and weaker students feel a responsibility to do the best job they can.

A typical class will have students working on a series of activities. Brief periods of lecture, often less than 10 minutes, are interspersed with "tangibles" and "ponderables." The first type of activity involves hands-on observations or measurements (i.e., students work with something tangible). For example, early in the semester we ask students to find the thickness of a single page from their textbook. They then use the result to measure the diameter of a period at the end of a sentence in the book. Students invariably start by dividing the estimated or measured thickness of a large stack of the pages by the number of sheets of paper in the stack. Although they usually don't think of it in these terms until prompted, the reason for using many sheets at once is to increase the number of significant digits in the final answer. In a Socratic dialogue, students are asked questions about why they tackled the problem as they did. This is often done by having them consider what answers they would have gotten from a different approach. By recognizing for themselves how significant figures play a role in a measurement, they are much more likely to continue to consider the uncertainty in their measurements throughout the course.

Ponderables are problems and calculations for interesting, complex situations. For example, we ask them: "How far does a bowling ball travel down the lane before it stops skidding and is only rolling?" No other information is given, so students need to decide what parameters need to be estimated. The insight students gain into what happens to the frictional force when skidding stops and pure rolling begins makes it worth the effort. In some cases, ponderables involve programming in VPython. The computer activities are designed to promote a view of physics as a powerful way to understand situations using just a few fundamental principles. For example, early in the semester students write a simulation of an extra-solar planetary system. A few weeks later they make minor changes to their program and use it to simulate the Rutherford alpha particle experiment where atomic nuclei were discovered. The students note that a huge range of scale, from stellar to subatomic dimensions, can be accurately modeled with the same physical principles.

MIT Electromagnetism Course—Objectives and Settings

The TEAL (Technology Enabled Active Learning) Project at MIT is similar to the NCSU SCALE-UP effort, and the MIT effort was motivated by observing the NCSU effort in its early years. The two classrooms at MIT for teaching in this format have 12 tables, each 7 ft. in diameter, with each table accommodating three groups of three students, chosen heterogeneously within the group. In addition to the motivations discussed above, an additional factor in moving to an interactive engagement format at MIT was that the mainline introductory physics courses have not had a laboratory component for over 30 years, and we wanted to reintroduce a laboratory component into these courses (Dori and Belcher 2005a).

The TEAL Project began with two prototype courses (about 170 students each) in electromagnetism in fall 2001 and fall 2002, and moved to the large mainline course (550 students) in electromagnetism in spring 2003. A similar effort in mechanics was taught in prototype form in fall 2003 and fall 2004, and in the large mainline course in fall 2005. We discuss here the course in electromagnetism, since that is the more mature course with more extensive assessment. The majority of the students in the MIT introductory physics courses are engineering majors, and thus the objectives for the courses are broadly speaking the same as those listed in the appendix for NCSU.

Grades in the TEAL courses are not curved. Because collaboration is an element, it was important the class not be graded on a curve, either in fact or in appearance, to encourage students with stronger backgrounds to help students with weaker backgrounds. Also, the cutlines in the course were set in such a way that a student who consistently did not attend class could not get an A. This was a deliberate policy to encourage attendance, based on the belief that one of the reasons for the traditionally high failure rates was the lack of student engagement with the course, as reflected by the low attendance toward the end of the term in the lecture format (typically 40%).

Despite the fact that the spring 2003 learning gains were excellent compared with the standard lecture recitation format (see the assessment section later in this chapter), student acceptance of the new teaching format in spring 2003 was mixed. To improve this acceptance, in subsequent terms we have done more training of students in collaborative methods (e.g., group work) and more extensive training for course teaching staff in interactive engagement methods. We also increased the number of course teaching staff, and we perform fewer experiments (and the experiments are better integrated into the course material). We also rearranged individual classes to break our active-learning sessions into smaller units that can be more closely overseen by the teaching staff. Extensive course material for the spring 2005 version of the electromagnetism course can be found on the MIT OpenCourseWare site (*http://ocw.mit.edu*).

A unique feature of the TEAL learning environment is the large component centered on active and passive visualizations of electromagnetic phenomena (Dori and Belcher 2005b; see also Chapter 22 in this volume). This is especially important in electromagnetism because students have a hard time connecting the abstract mathematics of vector fields to their everyday experience. The TEAL visualization approach is designed to help students visualize, develop better intuition about, and build better conceptual models of electromagnetic phenomena. In the TEAL environment we incorporated advanced two-dimensional (2-D) and three-dimensional (3-D) visualizations to enable students to get a deeper view of the nature of various electromagnetism phenomena. Such visualizations allow students to gain insight into the way in which fields transmit forces by watching how the motions of objects evolve in time in response to those forces. They also allow students to intuitively relate the forces transmitted by electromagnetic fields to those transmitted by more familiar agents, for example, rubber bands and strings. This makes electromagnetic phenomena more concrete and more comprehensible, because it allows the students to apply electromagnetic stresses to other phenomena that they already understand. These visualizations are freely available for nonprofit educational use on the MIT OpenCourseWare site.

We exemplify the usefulness of the TEAL desktop experiments and Java 3-D visualizations through the Faraday's law desktop experiment done in class and its corresponding visualization. In the desktop experiment, the student moves a loop of wire along the axis of a strong rare earth magnet and measures the resultant eddy current in the loop using a computer interfaced to a current probe. In the associated Java applet (a virtual reconstruction of the real desktop experiment), the student can perform the same experiment and "see" both the eddy current in the ring and the effects of the additional magnetic field it produces on the total magnetic field. The field of the eddy current is generated in accord with Lenz's law—that is, the field is such as to try to keep the total magnetic flux through the wire loop from changing. In the virtual experiment (in contrast to the real experiment), the student can run the virtual resistance of the wire loop down to zero. He or she then can see that in this limit no magnetic field lines can cross the radius of the loop (e.g., the flux through the loop is constant), regardless of where the student moves the loop or how fast the student moves the loop. This simulation is a visceral (although virtual) example for the student of what Lenz's law means; it complements (but does not replace) the real experiment. Figure 10.1 shows the visualization of the magnetic field configuration around the ring as it moves past the magnet. The current in the ring is indicated by the small moving spheres. The motions of the field lines are in the direction of the local Poynting flux vector.

Assessing the Outcomes

Assessment of undergraduate students' achievements is changing, largely because today's students face a world that will demand new knowledge and abilities and that will require students to become lifelong learners. Current and future assessment should be based on the constructivist paradigm. In such an environment, the student becomes involved not just in the learning but in self-assessment while being responsible for the learning

Figure 10.1

The Falling Magnet With a Zero Resistance Ring

outcomes. Differences between "assessment of learning" and "assessment for learning" are described in the literature (Assessment Reform Group 1999; Dori 2003; Mitchell 1992). The former relates to assessment for grading and reporting, whereas the purpose of the latter is to enable students' meaningful learning through effective feedback.

Assessment of the NCSU Courses

The NCSU assessment plan was based on the objectives outlined in the appendix. We assessed conceptual understanding by taking advantage of some of the nationally standardized tests that have been developed for the topics of introductory physics courses. These tests were given over many semesters, in pre/posttest modes. Results were uniformly positive. We were especially encouraged by the fact that students in the top tier of the class showed the highest normalized gains, implying they benefited greatly by teaching their peers. We also randomly sampled problems from tests developed by teachers of traditional sections of the courses. In 7 out of 10 cases the experimental students significantly outperformed their cohorts. We also found that class attendance improved from roughly 70% to over 90% when the same teacher switched from traditional to interactive instruction, even though the attendance policy remained the same (attendance was voluntary and would not directly affect grades). By comparing the success rates of more than 16,000 students over a five-year time span, we found that students in the experimental sections failed less than half as often. For minorities and women the failure rates were one-fourth to one-fifth those seen in the traditional classes with similar students. We believe this is due to the social support network that is an outcome of the careful design of the learning environment and activities. Finally, we found that at-risk students from the experimental sections failed a later engineering statics course less than half as often as equivalent but traditionally taught students.

Assessment of the MIT Electromagnetism Course

To assess the effect of the visualizations and the pedagogical methods implemented in the TEAL Project, we examined the scores in conceptual pre- and posttests for the experimental (TEAL students) and the control (traditional lecture and recitation setting) groups. Both the pre- and posttests consisted of 20 multiple-choice conceptual questions from standardized tests (Maloney et al. 2001; Mazur 1997) augmented by questions that we devised (Dori and Belcher 2005a). Based on their pretest scores, students in both research groups were divided into three academic levels: high, intermediate, and low.

The difference in the net gain between the experimental and control groups was significant ($p < 0.0001$) for each academic level separately as well as for the entire population. These results suggest that the learning gains in TEAL are significantly greater than those obtained by the traditional lecture and recitation setting. The results are consistent with several studies of introductory physics education over the last two decades (Beichner et al., Forthcoming; Hake 2002). It is also in line with the much lower failure rates for the TEAL course of spring 2003 (a few percent) compared with traditional failure rates in recent years (from 7% to 13%).

To investigate the perceptions of spring 2003 students, we asked them to list the most important elements that contributed to their understanding of the subject matter taught in the TEAL Project and to explain their selection. We divided their responses into four categories: oral explanations in class, technology, written problems, and the textbook (Dori et al. 2003). The technology category included desktop experiments performed in groups, 2-D and 3-D visualizations, individual web-based home assignments turned in electronically, and individual real-time class responses to conceptual questions using a personal response system (PRS) accompanied by peer discussion. Written problems included both individual problem sets given as home assignments and analytic problems solved in class workshops.

The spring 2003 questionnaire was completed by 308 students. The results showed that about 40% favored the problem-solving method, about 22% selected the technology, 22% selected the textbook, and 16% favored the professor's oral explanations. Typical explanations students gave to their selection of technology-based teaching methods included elements of visualization, desktop experiments, PRS-based conceptual questions, and web-based assignments. Still, the teacher turned out to be indispensable for both the oral explanations and the problem-solving workshops.

Student surveys were also administered during spring 2004. The goal of this study was to locate patterns that may reveal how TEAL can be further improved from the student learning standpoint. Questionnaires were administered by the TEAL staff at the end of the term and completed by 74.4% of 508 students. After criteria for categorizing answers were developed based on the type of question asked and the responses generated, the survey answers were categorized and frequency percentages of answers were calculated. Figure 10.2 presents students' responses to the question "Would you recommend the TEAL Electromagnetism course to a fellow student?"

About half of the students responded that they would recommend TEAL to fellow students, while a quarter said they would not recommend TEAL. In response to the question "What are the pros and cons of working in groups in the classroom?" one student wrote,

The pros are that you get to learn from and teach your fellow classmates, which helps reinforce the information. If you are working with someone who is ahead of you, it's difficult to learn because you are trying to catch up but you are always pulling that person back. I found that it was a problem at the beginning of the semester when I was the one learning while the other people in my group were flying through all the questions. I felt like I was holding the group back. As the semester rolled on, I was able to catch up but it was difficult the first couple weeks.

Figure 10.2

Spring 2004 Survey Results: Students' Responses to the Question "Would you recommend the TEAL Electromagnetism course to a fellow student?"

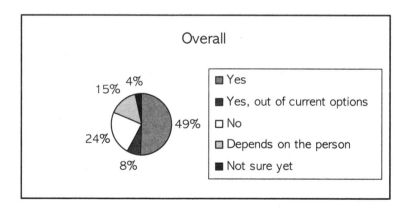

This response portrays the complexity of students' attitudes toward innovative elements in the TEAL environment (teamwork in this case).

Summarizing the results, we found that there is a large variation in the responses between the various classes. One cause that correlates well with the data is how responses varied with the professor teaching the class. Certain professors consistently had better results than others, especially over those who had never taught in the TEAL learning environments before. Another pattern that evolved was that students felt that TEAL might not be an effective environment for everyone because of differences in personal learning habits.

Conclusions

Science educators are facing increasing demands as they are asked to teach more content more effectively and to engage their students in scientific practices (Edelson 2001). The National Science Education Standards (National Research Council 1996) expressed strong disapproval of the traditional emphasis on memorization and recitation. They stressed the need to foster conceptual understanding and give students the firsthand experience of questioning, gathering evidence, and analyzing that resembles authentic scientific processes.

The methods by which science instructors were taught are often inconsistent with contemporary educational approaches. This state of affairs calls for a comprehensive conceptual change in the way science is taught in higher education. Such a change on the part of science faculty requires the development and implementation of new curricula and the adaptation of new teaching and assessment methods that foster conceptual understanding. The NCSU and MIT TEAL projects foster individual and group thinking, supported by hands-on activities, visualizations, and small- and large-group discussions for knowledge building. Aiming at enhancing conceptual understanding of mechanics and electromagnetism phenomena, these two projects are designed to actively engage students in the learning process, using technology-enabled methods as appropriate. One should bear in mind that in this type of basic physics course, students traditionally have been accustomed to classes that are made up of passive lectures that closely follow a particular textbook. Direct hands-on exposure to the phenomena under study, visualization of electromagnetic phenomena, and active learning in a collaborative setting were combined to achieve the desired effect on the students' learning outcomes.

Acknowledgments

We would like to thank the Fund for the Improvement of Postsecondary Education (FIPSE) program of the U.S. Department of Education (grants PB116B71905 and P116B000659), the National Science Foundation (grants DUE-9752313, DUE-0127050, and DUE-9981107), Hewlett-Packard, Apple Computer, and Pasco Scientific for their support. We especially appreciate the hard work of the many people who have played an important part in making the classroom work, including John Gastineau, Peg Gjertsen, Rich Felder, Joni Spurlin, Robert Egler, Chris Gould, and the teachers at the implementing sites.

The TEAL Project is supported by the d'Arbeloff Fund for Excellence in MIT Education, the Davis Educational Foundation, iCampus (the MIT/Microsoft Alliance), National Science Foundation grant 9950380, and the MIT School of Science and Department of Physics.

Judy Dori's work was funded in part by iCampus—the MIT/Microsoft Alliance for Educational Technology.

Appendix

North Carolina State University Objectives for the Two-Semester Introductory Physics Sequence

I. Students should develop a good functional understanding of physics. They should be able to:
- describe and explain physics concepts, including knowing where and when they apply
- apply physics concepts when solving problems and examining physical phenomena
- apply concepts in new contexts (transfer)

- translate between multiple representations of the same concept, for example: between words, equations, graphs, and diagrams
- combine concepts when analyzing a situation
- evaluate explanations of physical phenomena

II. Students should begin developing expert-like problem solving skills. They should be able to:
- satisfactorily solve standard textbook exercises
- apply all or part(s) of the GOAL expert problem-solving protocol in any context
- solve more challenging problems, including context-rich ("Real World") problems, estimation problems, multi-step problems, multi-concept problems, [and] problems requiring qualitative reasoning
- evaluate other people's written solutions and solution plans

III. Students should develop laboratory skills. They should be able to:
- interact with (set up, calibrate, set zero, determine uncertainty, etc.) apparatus and make measurements
- explain the underlying physical principles of the operation of the apparatus, measurements, physical situation being studied and analysis of data
- design, execute, analyze, and explain a scientific experiment to test a hypothesis
- evaluate someone else's experimental design

IV. Students should develop technology skills. They should be able to:
- use simulations to develop mathematical models of physical situations
- utilize a spreadsheet to graph and do curve fitting
- find information on the web
- use microcomputer, video, and web-based software and hardware for data collection and analysis

V. Students should improve their communication, interpersonal, and questioning skills. They should be able to:
- express understanding in written and oral forms by explaining their reasoning to peers
- demonstrate their knowledge and understanding of physics in written assignments
- discuss experimental observations and findings
- present a well-reasoned argument supported by observations and physical evidence
- evaluate oral arguments, both their own and those espoused by others
- function well in a group
- evaluate the functioning of their group

VI. Students should develop attitudes that are favorable for learning physics. They should:
- recognize that understanding physics means seeing the underlying concepts and principles instead of focusing on knowing and using equations
- see physics as a coherent framework of ideas that can be used to understand many different physical situations
- see what they are learning in the classroom as useful and strongly connected to the real world
- be cognizant of the scientific process/approach and how to apply it
- indicate a willingness to continue learning about physics and its applications
- see themselves as part of a classroom community of learners

References

Assessment Reform Group. 1999. *Assessment for learning: Beyond the black box.* Cambridge, England: Cambridge University, School of Education.

Astin, A. W. 1993. *What matters in college? Four critical years revisited.* San Francisco, CA: Jossey-Bass.

Beichner, R., J. Saul, D. Abbott, J. Morse, D. Deardorff, R. Allain, S. Bonham, M. Dancy, and J. Risley. Forthcoming. Student-centered activities for large enrollment undergraduate programs (SCALE-UP) project. In *PER* [Physics Education Research]-*based reform in university physics,* eds. E. F. Redish and P. J. Cooney. College Park, MD: American Association of Physics Teachers.

Bransford, J. D., A. L. Brown, and R. R. Cocking. 1999. *How people learn: Brain, mind, experience, and school.* Washington, DC: National Academy Press.

Cummings, K., J. Marx, R. Thornton, and D. Kuhl. 1999. Evaluating innovation in studio physics. *American Journal of Physics* 67 (S1): S38–S44.

Donovan, M. S., and J. D. Bransford. 2005. *How students learn: History, mathematics, and science in the classroom.* Washington, DC: National Academy Press.

Dori, Y. J. 2003. From nationwide standardized testing to school-based alternative embedded assessment in Israel: Students' performance in the "Matriculation 2000" project. *Journal of Research in Science Teaching* 40: 34–52.

Dori, Y. J., and J. W. Belcher. 2005a. How does technology-enabled active learning affect students' understanding of scientific concepts? *The Journal of the Learning Sciences* 14: 243–279.

Dori, Y. J., and J. W. Belcher. 2005b. Learning electromagnetism with visualizations and active learning. In *Visualization in science education*, ed. J. K. Gilbert, 187–216. Dordrecht, The Netherlands: Springer.

Dori, Y. J., J. W. Belcher, M. Bessette, M. Danziger, A. McKinney, and E. Hult. 2003. Technology for active learning. *Materials Today* 6: 44–49.

Edelson, D. C. 2001. Learning-for-use: A framework for the design of technology-supported inquiry activities. *Journal of Research in Science Teaching* 38: 355–385.

Hake, R. 1998. Interactive-engagement versus traditional methods: A six-thousand-student survey of mechanics test data for introductory physics courses. *American Journal of Physics* 66: 64–74.

Hake, R. 2002. Comment on "How do we know if we are doing a good job in physics teaching?" by Robert Ehrlich [American Journal of Physics 70 (1): 24–29 (2002)]. *American Journal of Physics* 70 (10): 1058–1059.

Laws, P. W. 1997. *The workshop physics activity guide: Modules 1–4.* New York: Wiley.

Maloney, D. P., T. L. O'Kuma, C. J. Hieggelke, and A. Van Heuvelen. 2001. Surveying students' conceptual knowledge of electricity and magnetism. *American Journal of Physics* 69 (S1): S12–S23.

Mazur, E. 1997. *Peer Instruction: A user's manual.* Upper Saddle River, NJ: Prentice Hall.

McDermott, L. C., and the University of Washington Physics Education Group. 1996. *Physics by inquiry.* New York: Wiley.

McDermott, L. C., P. S. Shaffer, and the University of Washington Physics Education Group. 2002. *Tutorials in introductory physics.* Upper Saddle River, NJ: Prentice Hall.

Mitchell, R. 1992. *Testing for learning: How new approaches to learning can improve American schools.* New York: Free Press.

National Research Council. 1996. *National science education standards.* Washington, DC: National Academy Press.

Smith, K. A., S. D. Sheppard, D. W. Johnson, and R. T. Johnson. 2005. Pedagogies of engagement: Classroom-based practices. *Journal of Engineering Education* 94: 87–101.

Sokoloff, D. R., and R. K. Thornton. 1997. Using interactive lecture demonstrations to create an active learning environment. *The Physics Teacher* 35: 340–347.

Steinberg, R. N., M. C. Wittmann, and E. F. Redish. 1997. Mathematical tutorials in introductory physics. In *The changing role of physics departments in modern universities: Proceedings of the International Conference on Undergraduate Physics Education*, eds. E. F. Redish and J. S. Rigden, 1075–1092. Woodbury, NY: American Institute of Physics.

Factors Affecting Learning

Given that many secondary school and college students have yet to develop formal and/or post-formal reasoning patterns, and that their reasoning deficiencies lead to difficulties in problem solving, understanding theoretical concepts, rejecting scientific misconceptions, and rejecting misconceptions about the nature of science and mathematics … more emphasis on teaching students how to reason scientifically is urged. —Anton E. Lawson

Perhaps of all the research that has been done in science education, the studies on misconceptions have been the most recognized by college teachers.... Unfortunately, too many college professors have not followed through by reorganizing course instruction and assessment in such a way as to encourage a greater chance for meaningful learning and more opportunities for students to recognize and seek to overcome their misconceptions. —Joseph D. Novak

Traditional biology instruction pays little attention to conceptual change, inquiry, how we know, or learning theory.... Conceptually sequenced topics would allow students to build conceptual schemes and modify their preconceptions. What would a section of an introductory biology course look like that reflected current knowledge of learning theory and conceptual change? —Linda W. Crow and Julie Harless

Students know which academic behaviors are important for success, and they are confident that they will earn high grades, attend lectures and help sessions, and take advantage of other opportunities to master the course material and raise their grade. Despite this optimism, many students do not follow through on their first-day-of-classes' expectations, and their grades suffer accordingly. —Randy Moore

A key instructional implication from the research on learning is that students need multiple opportunities to think deeply and purposefully about the content and to gain feedback on their learning.... Research has consistently

Unit III: Factors Affecting Learning

shown that all students, including college science students, learn more when actively engaged. Engagement can occur through increased interaction with the content itself, or it may be coupled with increased interaction with peers or the course instructor. —Catherine Ueckert and Julie Gess-Newsome

For many of us who have devoted our lives to teaching college students, our first goal is to encourage meaningful learning and conceptual understanding within our scientific discipline. As successful learners ourselves, we sometimes find it difficult to see why others have problems understanding what we so clearly grasp. Authors in this unit remind us of the many factors that affect successful learning in science and what we can do to facilitate it. Among the factors they discuss are the importance of formal reasoning ability, the structure of students' prior knowledge, the sequencing of instruction, the effort exerted by learners, and the opportunities to reflect deeply and to interact with others.

Well-known researcher Tony Lawson of Arizona State University summarizes his work on the importance of *formal and post-formal reasoning* in science learning. Although the ability to construct hypothetico-predictive arguments is central to the scientific enterprise, he suggests that most college students have yet to develop this higher level of reasoning. As a result, they are susceptible to a wide range of conceptual difficulties and errors in problem solving. To address these issues, Tony says that students must personally and repeatedly engage in the generation and testing of alternative hypotheses and theories in the form of laboratory and field exercises, readings, lectures, and discussions.

Joe Novak of Cornell University has spent nearly 50 years studying the importance of prior knowledge as "the single most important factor" affecting learning in science. In this chapter Joe reviews several important *principles derived from research on science learning.* He also discusses a new model for education based on the use of tools such as concept mapping that were designed by his research group to help students "learn how to learn."

Although most college science textbooks present a "logical," disciplinary perspective, they often fail to encourage conceptual change and deep learning. Linda Crow and Julie Harless of Montgomery College (Texas) suggest that the problem is due in part to the conventional way traditional textbooks *sequence the concepts,* ignoring what we know about human learning. In this chapter, Linda and Julie describe a revised, conceptually sequenced unit on genetics and compare its effectiveness with a conventionally sequenced unit on the same set of concepts.

Do introductory science courses reward *aptitude or effort*? Randy Moore of the University of Minnesota tells us that students believe their own effort to be the most important determinant of successful learning in their science courses, and, when given the opportunity, students even predict that they will exert the effort required to achieve their goals. In this chapter Randy describes a study that explores students' effort-related behaviors and whether those behaviors are consistent with their beliefs.

Catherine Ueckert and Julie Gess-Newsome of Northern Arizona University discuss the critical importance of *active engagement* and *interaction* in college science learning, suggesting that learners need to debate ideas, ask questions, compare answers, use evidence, consider alternatives, collect data, and apply knowledge. To encourage this kind of interaction and deep reflection, Catherine and Julie offer several strategies for the classroom teacher, including Just-in-Time Teaching, web-based modules, warm-up questions, classroom response systems, group concept maps, and minute papers.

CHAPTER 11

Developing Scientific Reasoning Patterns in College Biology

Anton E. Lawson

Anton E. Lawson is professor of organismal, integrative and systems biology at Arizona State University. He earned a PhD in biology education at the University of Oklahoma and conducts research on science teaching, cognition, cognitive development, nature of science, and epistemology. He teaches methods of teaching biology, the living world, teaching biology labs, and science education research.

In this chapter I describe the nature of scientific reasoning and argumentation and instructional strategies to help college students develop advanced scientific reasoning patterns and construct key biological concepts and theories. Biologists respond to causal questions with the generation and testing of alternative hypotheses through cycles of *hypothetico-predictive (H-P) argumentation*. Such arguments are employed to test causal claims that exist on at least two levels: a level at which the proposed causal entities are perceptible and a more advanced level at which they are imperceptible. The ability to construct H-P arguments at this higher level can be traced to preverbal reasoning of the child and the gradual internalization of verbally mediated arguments. Presumably the ability to construct and comprehend H-P arguments (an aspect of procedural knowledge) plays a role in the acquisition of conceptual knowledge (an aspect of declarative knowledge), because such arguments are used during alternative concept evaluation and conceptual change. Laboratory and field inquiries, discussions/lectures, and textbook readings that focus on the generation and debate of H-P arguments can improve students' conceptual understanding and general reasoning skills.

A long-held and central objective of science instruction is to help students develop scientific reasoning patterns. During the past few decades, considerable research has been undertaken to identify the nature of scientific reasoning patterns, their "natural" paths of development, and their role in concept acquisition, as well as how science instruction can help in their development. Currently, much is known about how to improve student reasoning skills, but few college instructors and curriculum developers are putting that knowledge to practical use. I hope this chapter will help more to do so.

Key Definitions and Clarifications

Scientific reasoning consists of an overall pattern of thought, which can be characterized as H-P, as well as several sub-patterns. Inhelder and Piaget (1958) referred to these sub-patterns as formal operational schemata (e.g., controlling variables, combinatorial reasoning, proportional reasoning, and correlational reasoning). Logicians often refer to them as "methods" or "forms" of argumentation such as argument by analogy, method of difference, method of agreement, and concomitant variation (e.g., Tidman and Kahane 2003; Warnick and Inch 1989).

Before discussing specific reasoning patterns and how students can gain skill in their use, a few definitions and clarifications are in order. A reasoning pattern is defined as a mental strategy, plan, or rule used to process information and derive conclusions that go beyond direct experience. As such, reasoning patterns are part of one's "how to" knowledge—one's procedural knowledge—as opposed to one's "that is" knowledge—one's declarative knowledge (e.g., Anderson 1980; Piaget 1970). Procedural knowledge, which is expressed through performance, is often implicit in the sense that we may not be conscious that we have it or know precisely when or how it was acquired. The word *development* is often used in conjunction with the acquisition of procedural knowledge. On the other hand, declarative knowledge is often explicit—that is, we often know that we have it and when and how it was acquired. The word *learning* is often used in conjunction with the acquisition of declarative knowledge.

Neurological research indicates that reasoning patterns, once acquired, reside in neural networks that are hierarchical in nature. The hierarchical networks culminate in single neurons located in the brain's prefrontal cortex (Wallis, Anderson, and Miller 2001). Interestingly, researchers have found that activity of the lateral prefrontal cortex in one or both brain hemispheres is associated with various psychological measures accessing differences in general intelligence (i.e., Spearman's g) (Duncan et al. 2000). Further, psychological measures of general intelligence have been found to be almost perfectly correlated with working memory capacity (Colom et al. 2001). Thus, we have the possibility that a primary value of reasoning patterns is to reduce the cognitive load on working memory, making reasoning more efficient and making reasoners appear more intelligent in a general sense.

What Is the Core Scientific Reasoning Pattern?

Science is largely about trying to explain puzzling observations of nature in terms of cause-and-effect relationships. Unfortunately, because many causes are not directly perceptible, explanation generation and testing is often an indirect process that employs a bit of a "trick." For example, with respect to the existence of atoms, Chown (2001) put it this way:

> There was no doubt atoms could explain some puzzling phenomena. But in truth they were merely one man's daydreams. Atoms, if they really existed, were far too small to be perceived directly by the senses. How then would it ever be possible to establish their reality? Fortunately, there was a way. The trick was to assume that atoms existed then deduce a logical consequence for the everyday world. If the consequence matched reality, then the idea of atoms was given a boost. If not, then it was time to look for a better idea. (p. 6)

The Greek Democritus (circa 460 BC to 370 BC) theorized that all matter is composed of tiny invisible and indivisible particles, which he named atoms. Although Democritus's idea seemed like a good one, it was not until the early 1800s and the work of John Dalton that atomic theory was tested by use of the following general reasoning pattern and evidence:

If ... matter consists of indivisible atoms that have specific weights and that combine in specific ways (atomic theory),
and ... combinations of atoms (molecules) are separated into their parts (imagined test),
then ... the weight ratios of those parts should be in simple whole-number ratios (expected result).
And ... when Dalton separated several gases (e.g., nitrous, nitrous oxide, nitrous acid) into their parts he found the weight ratios of those parts were in simple whole-number ratios (observed result).
Therefore ... atomic theory had been supported (conclusion).

This overall *If/then/Therefore* reasoning pattern has been characterized as hypothetico-predictive (or sometimes hypothetico-deductive) because it is initiated by the creative generation of a hypothesis/theory to possibly explain a puzzling observation, and is then followed by the generation of some sort of imagined test that yields one or more specific expected results (or predictions). Although the generation of expected results follows the linguistic *If/and/then* form known as deduction (e.g., *If* all crows are black *and* this bird is a crow *then* it deductively follows that this bird is black.), prediction generation is by no means automatic, because it rests on specific knowledge of the proposed explanation (or description) and its imagined test. To clarify this point, try to complete the following series of *If/and/then* deductive arguments:

1. *If* stick A is longer than stick B *and* stick B is longer than stick C *then* stick A is....
2. *If* all men are mortal *and* Socrates is a man *then* Socrates is....
3. *If* the three angles of a triangle sum to 180 degrees *and* one of the angles is 90 degrees *then* the other two angles sum to a total of....
4. *If* this hose-like object is the trunk of an elephant *and* a blind man feels his way to the other end *then* he should feel....
5. *If* this hose-like object is the nose of a Glomp *and* a blind man feels his way to the other end *then* he should feel....

Most people have little difficulty in deducing the correct "conclusion" (i.e., in generating the correct prediction) for statements 1 through 4, presumably because they have the requisite declarative knowledge of sticks, men, triangles, and elephants. But when they come to statement 5, they are unable to generate a prediction because they do not know about the nature of Glomps. The point is that prediction generation using the *If/and/then* linguistic form does not hinge on the use of a general all-purpose skill in deductive reasoning. Rather it depends on the presence or absence of specific declarative knowledge.

Prediction generation may also depend on a subconscious search through one's store of declarative knowledge until one "hits" on a relevant connection. To emphasize this "creative" aspect of prediction generation, and to provide a biological example of H-P reasoning, let's briefly consider the Nobel Prize–winning research of German physiologist Otto Loewi and his discovery of the chemical transmission of neural impulses.

As recounted by Koestler (1964), Loewi's story began in the early 1900s, when most biologists believed that all neural transmissions were electrical in nature. Nevertheless, it was puzzling at the time that the same type of electrical impulse traveling down a nerve excited some organs and inhibited others. Also puzzling was the observation that certain chemicals had precisely the same excitatory and inhibitory effect. But no one had yet linked this chemical effect with neural impulses. Thus, the question remained: How could the same type of electrical impulse make the activity of some organs speed up and others slow down?

No one had much of a clue until, during a discussion with a friend in 1903, it occurred to Loewi that one or more of these chemicals might be present at nerve endings and that an electrical impulse traveling down a nerve might initiate the release of one or another, which would then excite some organs and inhibit others. Unfortunately, not having a way to test this "chemical-transmission" hypothesis, Loewi forgot about it until 1920, when he literally dreamed up a way to test it. In Loewi's words (quoted in Koestler 1964):

The night before Easter Sunday of that year I awoke, turned on the light, and jotted down a few notes on a tiny slip of thin paper. Then I fell asleep again. It occurred to me at six o'clock in the morning that during the night I had written down something most important, but I was unable to decipher the scrawl. The next night, at three o'clock, the idea returned. It was the design of an experiment to determine whether or not the hypothesis of chemical transmission that I had uttered seventeen years ago was correct. I got up immediately, went to the laboratory, and performed a simple experiment on a frog heart according to the nocturnal design. (p. 205)

Loewi's nocturnal design involved dissecting out two frog hearts—the first with its nerves intact and the second with its nerves removed. He stimulated the first heart's vagus nerve several times to slow its heartbeat while the heart was bathed in a fluid. He then collected the fluid and applied it to the second heart. When he did, he found that its heartbeat also slowed. The fluid had the same effect on several other tissues as well. Therefore, Loewi had evidence that a chemical produced by the first heart had accumulated in the fluid and then when applied to the second heart, and to other tissues, caused their activity to also slow. He then repeated the experiment, this time stimulating the accelerator nerve of the first heart. And when the collected liquid was transferred to the second heart, its heartbeat speeded up. These results prompted Loewi to conclude "that the nerves do not influence the heart directly but liberate from their terminals specific chemical substances which, in their turn, cause the well-known modifications of the function of the heart characteristic of its nerves" (quoted in Koestler 1964, p. 205).

When Loewi's discovery is cast in terms of H-P reasoning, we get the following:

If ... diffusing chemicals transmit impulses (chemical-transmission hypothesis),
and ... a frog's vagus nerve is stimulated several times to slow its heartbeat while the heart is bathed in a fluid (imagined test),
then ... when that fluid is collected and applied to another frog's heart, its heartbeat should also slow (expected result). This result is expected because the imagined chemicals released by the stimulated nerve should collect in the fluid. So when the fluid is applied to the second heart, the chemicals in the fluid should produce the same effect. (This statement constitutes a *warrant,* i.e., a justification of why the prediction deductively follows).
And ... when Loewi applied the fluid to the second heart, he found that, as predicted, its heartbeat

slowed. The fluid had the same effect on several other tissues as well (observed result).
Therefore ... the chemical-transmission hypothesis was supported (conclusion).
    Further,
if ... diffusing chemicals transmit impulses (chemical-transmission hypothesis),
and ... a frog's accelerator nerve is stimulated several times to increase its heartbeat while the heart is bathed in a fluid (imagined test),
then ... when that fluid is collected and applied to another frog's heart, its heartbeat should also increase (expected result).
And ... when Loewi applied the fluid to the second heart, he found that, as predicted, its heartbeat increased (observed result).
Therefore ... the chemical-transmission hypothesis was again supported (conclusion).

How Does H-P Reasoning Develop?

Although most secondary school and college students have not developed skill in using H-P reasoning to test theoretical propositions such as those tested by Dalton and Loewi, children appear capable of a rudimentary form of H-P reasoning virtually at birth. We can be fairly certain of this because the pattern can be found in nonhumans. For example, Hauser (2000) conducted a revealing experiment with rhesus monkeys. First, a monkey was shown an eggplant—a favorite food item. In full view, the eggplant was then placed behind a screen. A second eggplant was then placed behind the screen. When the screen was lifted, the length of time the monkey looked at the two revealed eggplants was measured, which turned out to be about one second. Next, the conditions were changed. In the initial changed condition, one eggplant was placed behind the screen followed by a second eggplant. Then without the monkey knowing it, the second eggplant was removed. Now when the screen was lifted, the monkey looked at the unexpected single remaining eggplant for about three to four seconds. The same increase in looking time occurred when a third eggplant was secretly added and then revealed. Thus, the monkey had a clear expectation of seeing two eggplants and when either one or three eggplants unexpectedly showed up, the monkey was puzzled, as evidenced by the increase in looking time. In the first unexpected condition the monkey's "reasoning" can be summarized like this: *If* one eggplant is placed behind the screen, *and* another is added, *then* there should be two eggplants behind the screen. *But* there is only one eggplant. *Therefore I am puzzled and need to look at the puzzling situation longer.*

    If we assume that this pattern of H-P reasoning in humans is present at birth, then intellectual development involves a growing awareness (i.e., consciousness) of this reasoning pattern, increases in the contexts to which the pattern can be applied, and the development of associated reasoning sub-patterns. Let's see how this might work in terms of Piaget's formal operational stage of intellectual development (e.g., Inhelder and Piaget 1958; Piaget and Inhelder 1969) as well as a possible post-formal stage (Lawson et al. 2000a, 2000b). Note that use of the Piagetian stage labels does not imply acceptance of his theory concerning their underlying "logical" operations (e.g., Piaget's postulated combinatorial system and INRC [identity, negation, reciprocity, correlativity] group).

The Formal Operational Stage (Early to Late Adolescence)
Following a comprehensive literature review, Moshman (1998) came to the following conclusion: "In fact, there is surprisingly strong support for Piaget's 1924 proposal that formal or

hypothetico-deductive reasoning—deliberate deduction from propositions consciously recognized as hypothetical—plays an important role in the thinking of adolescents and adults but is rarely seen much before the age of 11 or 12" (p. 972). By "hypothetical" Moshman is referring to causal, as opposed to descriptive, hypotheses. For example, consider this question: What causes differences in the rates at which pendulums swing? To answer this causal question, one can use H-P reasoning (or "hypothetico-deductive" if you prefer) to generate and test alternative causal hypotheses (cf., Inhelder and Piaget 1958, Chapter 4). For example:

If changes in swing rates are caused by the amount of weight hanging on the end (causal weight hypothesis), *and* the weights are varied while holding other possible causes constant, *then* rate of pendulum swing should vary. *But* the rates do not vary. *Therefore* the weight hypothesis is not supported.

We should note that prior concrete reasoning (age 7 to about age 12) is about testing descriptive hypotheses, whereas formal reasoning is about testing causal hypotheses. The pendulum test involves an experiment in which the values of one possible cause are directly varied. The test also involves use of the very important control of variables reasoning sub-pattern.

The Post-Formal or "Theoretical" Stage (Late Adolescence and Early Adulthood)
Consider once again Loewi's test of his chemical-transmission hypothesis. The *If/and/then* argument summarizing his test went like this: *If* chemicals transmit impulses, *and* a frog's vagus nerve is stimulated to slow its heartbeat while the heart is bathed in a fluid, *then* when that fluid is applied to another frog's heart, its heartbeat should also slow. Although identical to prior reasoning in form, this argument differs from formal stage reasoning in at least two important ways. First, here the proposed cause is unseen (i.e., theoretical), whereas at the formal stage the proposed cause is observable. Second, in formal reasoning a proposed cause and the independent variable of an experiment designed to test it are one and the same, but this is not the case here. In Loewi's experiment, the independent variable was the presence or absence of an electrically stimulated heart, while the proposed cause was imaginary and unseen molecules. Also, because the proposed cause and the independent variable are not the same, a warrant, or theoretical rationale, is needed to link the two so that a reasonable test can be conducted. For these reasons, such reasoning is considered post-formal, or theoretical; it is more difficult than formal reasoning (e.g., Lawson et al. 2000a, 2000b) and is presumably not achieved until late adolescence after the final brain growth spurt at age 18 (Thatcher 1991; Thatcher, Walker, and Giudice 1987), if at all.

Why Is Intellectual Development Stage-Like?
Based on the previous arguments and evidence, we can understand why intellectual development is stage-like. In addition to probable maturational constraints, individuals construct something new during each stage that can be constructed only following the previous stage because the products of the previous stage are used in testing the possible constructions (i.e., the hypotheses) of the subsequent stage. For example, Dalton's testing of atomic theory required him to compare expected and observed weight ratios of separated gas molecules. Comparing ratios involves proportional reasoning, a formal stage construction. Thus, Dalton's reasoning and eventual support for atomic theory could not have occurred without his prior construction of a proportional reasoning pattern.

Similarly, testing formal stage hypotheses requires use of prior concrete stage constructions. Consider Inhelder and Piaget's bending rods task (Inhelder and Piaget 1958, Chapter 3). To test the causal hypothesis that variation in rod thickness causes variation in amount of rod bend (i.e., thinner rods bend more than thicker rods), one can reason like this:

If differences in rod bending are caused by rod thickness, *and* equal weights are hung on two rods that vary only in thickness, *then* the thinner rod should bend more. *And* the thinner rod does bend more. *Therefore* the thickness hypothesis is supported.

Thus, to test the causal thickness hypothesis (one can directly observe/sense thickness differences), we must determine which of the two rods bends more and which bends less. In other words, we need to have already constructed a concrete stage "distance" variable, which we can label as "distance of bending." So to test a formal stage causal hypothesis, we use a prior stage construction (i.e., conservation of distance/length).

Given that several studies have found that many secondary school and college students have yet to develop formal and/or post-formal reasoning patterns, and that their reasoning deficiencies lead to difficulties in problem solving, understanding theoretical concepts, rejecting scientific misconceptions, and rejecting misconceptions about the nature of science and mathematics (as reviewed in Lawson 2003), more emphasis on teaching students how to reason scientifically is urged. Thus, the key pedagogical question becomes, How can we help more students develop formal and then post-formal reasoning patterns?

How Can Instruction Help Students Develop Formal and Post-Formal Reasoning Patterns?

The key point in terms of the development of advanced reasoning patterns is that for progress to occur, students must personally and repeatedly engage in the generation and test of alternative hypotheses and theories. Progress is made when ideas are generated and tested, when mistakes are made, when ways of correcting those mistakes are suggested, and when students have an opportunity to reflect on their mistakes and the suggestions until they can disembed the successful reasoning patterns from the particulars of each test. This means that although lectures and textbook readings can and should discuss how biologists in the past have generated and tested alternative explanations (e.g., Lawson 2004), lab and field-based activities become the main vehicle for promoting intellectual development. But such activities cannot be "cookbook" in nature. Instead, they should allow students to explore nature and raise puzzling observations. The puzzling observations should then prompt students to generate and test alternative explanations with the following sorts of questions becoming the central focus of instruction:

- What did you observe?
- What is puzzling about what you observed?
- What questions are raised?
- What is the central causal question?
- What are some possible answers/explanations?
- How could these possibilities (alternative hypotheses) be tested?
- What does each hypothesis and imagined test lead you to expect to find (i.e., what are the predicted results of each hypothesis and imagined test)?

- What are your results?
- How do your results compare with your predictions?
- If the results do not match your predictions, is the mismatch due to a faulty hypothesis, to a faulty test, or both? Can you tell? Why or why not?
- If the results match your predictions, what conclusion should you draw? Have your results eliminated each of the identified alternatives? If not, what additional tests are needed?
- How can you be sure that the match or mismatch of results with predictions is not due to chance? If you cannot be sure, what can be done to at least reduce the likelihood of drawing an incorrect conclusion?

The appendix at the end of this chapter lists several example causal questions and *If/and/then* arguments embedded in 10 inquiry-based lab/field activities in a nonmajor biology course at Arizona State University. As has been mentioned, such arguments should be student generated. However, more instructor help is required at the outset than later in the course. The point is that these sorts of arguments are generated and used during inquiry, but typically remain on a subconscious plane. Consequently, when the arguments are generated in the course of answering these questions, students should write them on the board or in their notebooks, so they can be explicitly discussed, compared, and critiqued.

A significant problem in implementing an inquiry-based curriculum in which these sorts of arguments are repeatedly constructed and discussed is that instructors typically introduce so much declarative content that they leave too little time for students to explore nature, to question, to discuss, and to reflect on their hypotheses and their reasoning. Also, lab and field activities are often used to verify lecture content rather than to conduct "real" (real to the students, that is) inquiries. To help solve this problem you may decide to not closely articulate lectures with lab and field inquiries so that when students need to take several weeks to answer a particularly difficult question, they can do so. Another threat to success is the current rush to incorporate technology such as computers and videodisc players into instructional settings. These devices may be beneficial, but only as long as they do not replace actual hands-on, minds-on inquiries. Indeed, teachers would do well to keep firmly in mind that the primary purpose of American education is to help students become better thinkers (e.g., Educational Policies Commission 1961) and to remember the American Association for the Advancement of Science's central teaching principle: "Teaching should be consistent with the nature of scientific inquiry" (AAAS 1989, p. 147).

Many biology courses suffer from yet another problem. Having been designed largely by subject-matter experts, they are often structured to make sense from an already knowledgeable instructor's perspective, but not necessarily from the learner's perspective. Thus, courses often take a "micro-to-macro" approach, which begins at the highly abstract and theoretical atomic and molecular levels and only later addresses more familiar, less abstract topics at the organism, population, and community levels. Some recent textbooks have tried to remedy this problem by taking a "macro-to-micro" approach, starting big at the biome level and working their way down to ecosystems, communities, populations, organisms, and so on. But this approach also fails to recognize that inquiry, concept construction, and general intellectual development all progress from the familiar and perceptible to the unfamiliar and imperceptible. Students are organisms, not biomes, so student inquiries should start at the organism level and then move toward either progressively smaller or progressively larger levels of organization. The history of biology has much to offer in terms of helping us identify "natural" routes of inquiry, routes that past biologists have taken and routes that present students can also take—routes that should lead to students who know what science is and how to reason scientifically.

Appendix

Example Causal Questions and *If/and/then* Arguments Generated During 10 Lab/Field Inquiries in a Nonmajor Biology Course

Inquiry 1: Why does water rush up into a cylinder placed over a burning candle sitting in a pan of water when the candle burns out? *If* … the water rushes up because CO_2 produced by the burning candle escapes in the water, *and* … we invert a cylinder full of CO_2 in a pan of water, *then* … the CO_2 should dissolve in the water and the water should rise into the cylinder.

Inquiry 2: Why did the isopods move toward the right end of the tray? *If* … the isopods moved to the right end because that end was darker than the left end, *and* … we repeat the experiment making sure that the only difference between the two ends is the amount of light (e.g., same temperature and so on), *then* … the isopods should move toward the darker end of the tray.

Inquiry 3: What causes the differences in color of corn kernels on an ear of Indian corn? *If* … variation in the color of corn kernels on an ear of Indian corn is caused by genes, *and* … we count the numbers of different colors on an ear, *then* … color differences should occur in simple whole-number ratios (e.g., 1:1, 3:1, 1:2:1).

Inquiry 4: Why do some fruit flies have red eyes while others have brown eyes? *If* … the observed differences in fruit fly eye have an environmental basis, *and* … we mate red-eyed flies with brown-eyed flies and raise the offspring flies in identical environments, *then* … all the offspring flies should have similar eye color. Alternatively, *if* … the observed differences in fruit fly eye have a genetic basis, *then* … we might find that the color difference remains over several generations and may occur in some simple whole-number ratio (e.g., 3:1).

Inquiry 5: What caused present-day species diversity? *If* … organisms have evolved across time, *and* … we compare fossils from a series of sedimentary rock layers, *then* … fossils of intermediate species should be found in intermediate rock layers. Alternatively, *if* … organisms were created by a creator in their present-day forms, *then* … fossils of intermediate species should not be found in intermediate rock layers.

Inquiry 6: Why did the distribution of fur colors in a mouse population change following several generations of predation and reproduction? *If* … the observed pattern of fur colors in a mouse population following several generations of simulated predation is caused by directional selection, *and* … we repeat the selection process using two or more identical environments, *then* … the resulting pattern of fur colors should be similar in each environment. Alternatively, *if* … the observed pattern is caused by random selection, *then* … the resulting patterns should differ from one environment to the next.

Inquiry 7: Why do some women with breast implants develop connective tissue disease? *If* … breast implants cause connective tissue disease, *and* … a group of women with implants is compared to a similar group but without implants, *then* … disease incidence should be higher in the implant group than in the non-implant group.

Inquiry 8: Why is more grass growing on the north-facing slope of Tempe Butte than on the south-facing slope? *If* … lack of soil moisture on the south-facing slope keeps grass from growing there, *and* … a plot of ground on the south-facing slope is watered so that its moisture content is equal to that of the north-facing slope, *then* … more grass should grow on the plot—i.e., an amount equal to that on the north-facing slope. Alternatively, *if* … the sunlight itself is too intense for good grass growth on the south-facing slope (i.e., very intense rays disrupt the grasses' ability to conduct photosynthesis), *then* … the grass should not grow on the plot.

Inquiry 9: Why do red onion cell membranes appear to shrink when bathed in salt water? *If* … attractive forces of the salt ions (i.e., Na+ and Cl−) cause the polar water molecules to leave the cells, *and* … we weigh a dialysis bag filled with distilled water, place it in a salt solution for several minutes, and reweigh the bag, *then* … the bag should weigh less. Alternatively, *if* ... salt ions (i.e., Na+ and Cl−) push on the cell membranes and make then appear to shrink, *then* ... the bag should weigh the same. (Note that this test assumes that the dialysis bag has properties like the cell membranes.)

Inquiry 10: Why are most plants green? *If* ... plants are green because they reflect green light, *and* ... we shine green light on a growing water plant, *then* ... it should release very few, if any, oxygen bubbles. (Presumably photosynthesis requires light and takes place inside plant cells; thus if green light is reflected it does not get inside the cells and cannot drive photosynthesis). Alternatively, *if* ... plants are green because they absorb green light, *then* ... the plant should release a lot of oxygen bubbles.

References

American Association for the Advancement of Science (AAAS). 1989. *Science for all Americans.* Washington, DC: AAAS.

Anderson, J. R. 1980. *Cognitive psychology and its implications.* San Francisco: Freeman.

Chown, M. 2001. *The magic furnace: The search for the origin of atoms.* New York: Oxford University Press.

Colom, R., I. Rebollo, A. Palacios, M. Juan-Espinosa, and P. C. Kyllonen. 2001. Working memory is (almost) perfectly predicted by *g. Intelligence* 32: 277–296.

Duncan, J., R. J. Seitz, J. Kolodny, D. Bor, H. Herzog, A. Ahmed, F. N. Newell, and H. Emslie. 2000. A neural basis for general intelligence. *Science* 289: 457–460.

Educational Policies Commission. 1961. *The central purpose of American education.* Washington, DC: National Education Association.

Hauser, M. D. 2000. What do animals think about numbers? *American Scientist* 88: 144–151.

Inhelder, B., and J. Piaget. 1958. The growth of logical thinking from childhood to adolescence. New York: Basic Books.

Koestler, A. 1964. *The act of creation.* London: Hutchinson.

Lawson, A. E. 2003. *The neurological basis of learning, development and discovery: Implications for teaching science and mathematics.* Dordrecht, The Netherlands: Kluwer Academic Publishers.

Lawson, A. E. 2004. *Biology: An inquiry approach.* Dubuque, IA: Kendall/Hunt.

Lawson, A. E., B. Clark, E. Cramer-Meldrum, K. A. Falconer, Y. J. Kwon, and J. M. Sequist. 2000a. The development of reasoning skills in college biology: Do two levels of general hypothesis-testing skills exist? *Journal of Research in Science Teaching* 37: 81–101.

Lawson, A. E., N. Drake, J. Johnson, Y. J. Kwon, and C. Scarpone. 2000b. How good are students at testing alternative explanations of unseen entities? *American Biology Teacher* 62: 249–255.

Moshman, D. 1998. Cognitive development beyond childhood. In *Handbook of child psychology.* Vol. 2, *Cognition, perception, and language* (5th ed.), eds. D. Kuhn and R. S. Siegler. New York: Wiley.

Piaget, J. 1970. *Genetic epistemology.* New York: Norton.

Piaget, J., and B. Inhelder. 1969. *The psychology of the child.* New York: Basic Books.

Thatcher, R. W. 1991. Maturation of the human frontal lobes: Physiological basis of staging. *Developmental Neuropsychology* 7: 397–419.

Thatcher, R. W., R. A. Walker, and S. Giudice. 1987. Human cerebral hemispheres develop at different rates and ages. *Science* 236: 1110–1113.

Tidman, P., and H. Kahane. 2003. *Logic and philosophy.* 9th ed. Belmont, CA: Wadsworth/Thomson.

Wallis, J. D., K. C. Anderson, and E. K. Miller. 2001. Single neurons in prefrontal cortex encode abstract rules. *Nature* 411: 953–956.

Warnick, B., and E. S. Inch. 1989. *Critical thinking and communication: The use of reason in argument.* New York: Macmillan.

CHAPTER 12

Learning Science and the Science of Learning

Joseph D. Novak

Joseph D. Novak is professor emeritus of science education and biological sciences at Cornell University and senior research scientist at the Florida Institute for Human and Machine Cognition in Pensacola. He earned a PhD in science education and biology at the University of Minnesota and conducts research on learning theory, knowledge and knowledge creation, metacognition, and epistemology. He teaches courses in learning theory applied to science education and metacognitive processes.

In 1988, at the invitation of the journal editors, I published an article by the same title as this chapter in the journal *Studies in Science Education*. In this chapter I recap some of the key points made in that article, present some more recent work, and discuss what I believe have been important advances since 1988 and the implications of these advances for learning science, or learning any subject for that matter.

Principles Derived From Research on Science Learning

In the original article, I presented what I regarded as eight valid principles that derived from research on science learning. These remain the key valid principles today, so I shall review and update them briefly, add one more principle, and then move on to some related, newer ideas.

Principle 1. Concepts are acquired early in life.

This principle is now more clearly established than in 1988. Numerous studies have shown that even infants begin to acquire rudimentary concepts and that these are developed over time (Carey 1985; Gelman 2003). In a paper posted on the internet, Gelman (1999) observed that four key themes had emerged from recent research:

- *Theme 1. Concepts are tools and as such have powerful implications for children's reasoning—both positive and negative.*
- *Theme 2. Children's early concepts are not necessarily concrete or perceptually based. Even preschool children are capable of reasoning about non-obvious, subtle, and abstract concepts.*
- *Theme 3. Children's concepts are not uniform across content areas, across individuals, or across tasks.*
- *Theme 4. Children's concepts reflect their emerging "theories" about the world. To the extent that children's theories are inaccurate, their conceptions are also biased.*

Gelman goes on to identify four myths that have been shattered by recent research:

- *Myth 1. The sole function of concepts is to organize experience efficiently.*
- *Myth 2. There is qualitative change in children's concepts over time, with major shifts between four and seven years.*
- *Myth 3. Until about age 7, most children are unable to reason about abstract concepts or non-obvious features.*
- *Myth 4. Children's concepts start out perceptually-based, becoming conceptual with development.*

In our research program at Purdue University and Cornell University, which is sometimes referred to as the Meaningful Learning Research Group (see *www.mlrg.org*), we held to the kind of themes Gelman identifies, and we eschewed the above myths. Our early research with children showed that they are far more capable of acquiring abstract scientific concepts than was commonly believed by the vast majority of science educators, who generally subscribed to the above myths (Novak 1964, 1982). In 1965, we began the design of audio-tutorial lessons (Novak 1972) to teach basic science concepts to 6- to 7-year-old children, building on ideas from Ausubel's cognitive psychology (1963, 1968) and curriculum ideas that focused on a few fundamental science concepts (Novak 1964). We also drew on ideas in an elementary science textbook series that I coauthored (Novak, Meister, et al. 1966). By 1971, we had a sufficient pool of tested lessons to begin a 12-year longitudinal study with 197 first-grade children receiving these lessons in grades 1 and 2, and a comparable sample of 48 children not receiving these lessons. What the research clearly showed was that instruction in basic science concepts very significantly influenced later learning of science (Novak 2003; Novak and Musonda 1991). This contrasts with some of the recommendations in the *Benchmarks for Science Literacy* (American Association for the Advancement of Science 1993) and the *National Science Education Standards* (National Research Council 1996).

Another outcome of our 12-year study was the necessity to find a better way to record and follow specific changes in children's conceptual understanding. Working initially with transcripts from interviews, we found it difficult to observe specific improvements in the children's concept and propositional meanings. However, when we converted these transcripts into what we call concept maps, specific changes in conceptual understanding were easily observed. Thus out of research necessity, a new tool was created for studying changes in conceptual understanding and the structure of knowledge. Concept maps differ from other forms of knowledge representation in that they show single concepts in the nodes, nodes are connected with "linking words" to form meaningful propositions, and a hierarchy is created from the most general concept(s) at the top to the most specific and least inclusive concepts at the bottom (see Chapter 7 in this volume). Later we found that this new tool was also effective for designing instruction, helping students to learn, capturing and preserving expert knowledge, and many other applications (Novak 1998; Novak and Gowin 1984). Figure 12.1 shows an example of a concept map drawn from an interview with a second-grade child (named Paul), and Figure 12.2 shows a concept map drawn from an interview with the same child in grade 12. The figures clearly show the child's gains in concept understanding. Figure 12.1 shows that Paul has acquired some concepts pertinent to understanding the nature of matter and energy. Figure 12.2 shows that Paul has acquired and integrated the meanings of many new concepts dealing with the nature of matter and energy. He is characteristic of students who learn meaningfully.

Unfortunately, some leaders of national science education organizations continue to believe in the myths listed earlier in this chapter. Moreover, some of those leaders still do not acknowledge the power and value of using concept mapping as a metacognitive learning tool and a tool for the New Model for Education described later in this chapter. One of the reasons we see the persistence of science misconceptions, so dramatically illustrated in the videotaped interviews with Harvard graduates, alumni, and faculty in the Private Universe Project (Schneps 1989), derives from the failure of school and university instruction to move learners away from rote learning and toward high levels of meaningful learning (Novak 2002).

Figure 12.1

Concept Map From the End of Grade 2

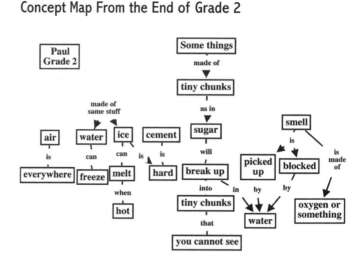

Figure 12.2

Concept Map From the End of Grade 12

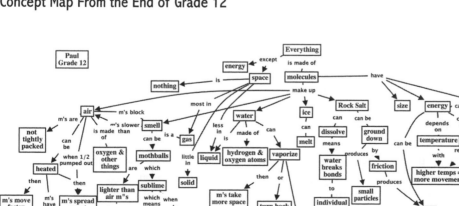

Principle 2. Misconceptions are acquired early and are resistant to modification.
For a variety of reasons, children and adults acquire faulty ideas about how the universe works, as well as faulty ideas in mathematics and other disciplines. These faulty ideas are sometimes called alternative conceptions or naive concepts but are most commonly called misconceptions. These misconceptions present problems to the learner and the teacher in that they derive from incorrect concept meanings and/or relationships between concept meanings (Novak 2002). Moreover, when new, related information is presented, the misconceptions function to "anchor" or subsume the new information incorrectly into cognitive structure, and the net effect is often that the misconception is strengthened rather than remediated. From 1983 to 1997 our research group held four international seminars on misconceptions in science and mathematics at Cornell University, and the papers in proceedings from these seminars abundantly illustrated these problems (see *www.mlrg.org/mlrgarticles.html*). Also illustrated in the papers of these proceedings are a variety of instructional efforts to overcome misconceptions, often with limited success.

Perhaps of all the research that has been done in science education, the studies on misconceptions have been the most recognized by college teachers. An earlier review of research on misconceptions has been widely cited in articles on college science teaching (Wandersee, Mintzes, and Novak 1994). Unfortunately, too many college professors have not followed through by reorganizing course instruction and assessment in such a way as to encourage a greater chance for meaningful learning and more opportunities for students to recognize and seek to overcome their misconceptions. It is hoped that this volume may help to resolve this difficulty.

Principle 3. Prior knowledge influences new learning.
While misconceptions impede learning of new related ideas, valid concepts and propositions held by students can substantially enhance meaningful learning of new materials. Fundamental to current *constructivist* views on science learning is that we must begin with consideration of what the student already knows and build on this understanding. Also, it is recognized that only the learner can choose to assimilate new knowledge into his or her current knowledge, and this learning must be an active process. The use of concept maps can serve a twofold purpose, first in identifying for learners and professors what learners know about a given topic prior to study of the topic, and subsequently to facilitate new meaningful learning. The primary change that has occurred since 1988 is the almost universal acceptance of the validity of this principle, and considerable research that adds support to it. Not only is it becoming generally accepted that learners must build on their prior knowledge, this constructivist view of learning also extends to the way humans create new knowledge (Novak 1993).

Principle 4. Information-processing capacity is limited.
In 1956, Miller proposed that the working memory of the human brain is limited in its ability to process information to about seven, plus or minus two, "chunks." There has been much research since 1988 that raises issues about the nature of working memory, but the idea that our minds are limited in processing information has been generally supported. This means that to develop complex bodies of information in our long-term memories, there must be iterative processing of the information, seven or less chunks at a time, and the gradual construction of the complex body of information. One of the reasons concept maps may facilitate such learning is that the concept maps can serve as a kind of scaffolding in the information-processing

sequence, helping to build complex knowledge structures. This idea will be explored further in the section on the New Model for Education.

Principle 5. Most knowledge is stored hierarchically.

Although this principle is still controversial, there is growing psychological and neurological evidence that storage of knowledge in long-term memory is hierarchical (Gazzaniga and Heatherton 2002). It would appear to follow that learning tools such as concept maps that encourage hierarchical organization of knowledge would enhance knowledge acquisition, storage, and retrieval.

Principle 6. Learners are seldom conscious of their cognitive processes.

Some of our more recent studies have shown that learners in general have a poor understanding of how they learn (Edmondson and Novak 1993; Novak 1998). Research by others on *metacognition*, or thinking about thinking, also shows that most teachers and students have little awareness of how our minds work and how to improve learning (Bransford, Brown, and Cocking 1999). This is currently an important area of research, and we can expect that there will be significant advances in the application of metacognitive strategies to help students understand their own learning and to improve meaningful learning. Once again, concept maps stand out as an important metacognitive tool, and we are seeing greater use of this tool at all educational levels (Novak 1985, 1998).

Principle 7. Epistemological commitments of learners influence learning.

Most of the research we were doing just before my retirement at Cornell University focused on epistemological problems manifested both by individual learners (Chang 1995; Edmondson and Novak 1993) and by research groups in their efforts to create new knowledge (Novak and Iuli 1995). While many teachers and learners are not aware of the value of metacognitive skills to facilitate learning, there is even less awareness of the importance of understanding and applying ideas from constructivist epistemology to enhance learning from preschool to the research teams in universities (see Chapter 20 in this volume).

Principle 8. Thinking, feeling, and acting are integrated.

In the sciences there has long been an awareness that learning science is more than just learning the facts. This is one of the reasons why laboratory and field work in science have long been regarded as essential to building an understanding of science concepts and methods of work (Novak 1976). Over the years, the research of the Meaningful Learning Research Group has shown explicitly in many cases the important interactions that take place between a learner's thinking, feeling, and acting in the process of achieving really high levels of meaningful learning. In fact, we see such an important interplay between the integration of thinking, feeling, and acting and meaningful learning that I have come to believe that this interplay is the necessary foundation for an individual's capability to achieve high levels of commitment and responsibility. This is the cornerstone of my theory of education (Novak 1977, 1998).

Principle 9. Learning takes place in a context.

The recognition that learning occurs in a context goes back at least to the work of Schwab (1973), but it has been reincarnated under the label *situated cognition* (Brown, Collins, and

Duguid 1989). Much of the literature on this subject fails to recognize the complex nature of meaningful learning and the fact that when learning is done largely by rote, this learning is highly situated; that is, it is not transferable to similar tasks or problem situations. I do not see *situativity* as a separate principle of learning, but rather as a component of the rote to meaningful learning continuum that can be explained more comprehensively by Ausubel's (1963, 1968) assimilation theory of learning.

Development of the Internet and CmapTools

Perhaps the most important advance that has occurred since 1988 is the explosive development of the internet. It is now possible to find information on virtually any subject in a matter of seconds, assuming one has a relatively new computer and high-speed internet access. With the prices of computers declining, and their computing and storage capacity increasing rapidly, good computers are becoming available to virtually every child, even in developing countries if there is a national commitment to leapfrogging education into the 21st century. Unfortunately, access to such technology is limited in U.S. schools by bureaucratic inertia and resistance to change, even when funds are available.

Although we have been using concept maps to aid learning since the early 1970s, the development of new software to facilitate the building and use of concept maps has added a very significant new dimension to this work. At the Florida Institute for Human and Machine Cognition (IHMC), a team has been working for some 10 years to develop a very robust and highly functional concept mapping tool called CmapTools. This software is available to nonprofit groups at no cost, and currently it is being used in some 150 countries around the world. The software and other resource materials can be downloaded at *http://cmap.ihmc.us*. Another website shows the locations where CmapTools has been actively connected to the IHMC server in the past 24 hours (*http://pictor.ihmc.us/gl*). Currently there are some 300 downloads of CmapTools per day. Although there are a number of software programs that can be used to make concept maps, CmapTools was designed specifically for this purpose and supports the making of concept maps that conform to the criteria we use to judge good concept maps. The concept maps shown in this chapter were made with CmapTools. A number of papers describing CmapTools and applications have been published (Cañas, Carff, et al. 2005; Cañas, Ford, and Coffey 1994; Cañas, Ford et al. 1995, 2001; Cañas, Hill, et al. 2004).

The Development and Implementation of a New Model for Education

As noted earlier, the explosive growth of the internet has created new opportunities for education. The problem is not to find information but how to organize and use this information. This is where CmapTools combined with "expert skeleton" concept maps presents a unique opportunity for facilitating meaningful learning. We call these small concept maps, perhaps containing only 6–10 concepts and propositional linkages, expert skeleton concept maps because they are prepared by an expert in the field and they serve as a starting point for learners, who then add concepts and propositions to put more "intellectual meat" on the skeleton map using the internet and other resources. Currently we are working with a group in Italy that is implementing the New Model for Education using expert skeleton concept maps based on an elementary science textbook series (Novak, Meister, et al. 1966). Scanned copies of the latter books have been made available on DVD, and these books are being translated into Italian. Figure 12.3 shows an example of one of these expert skeleton concept maps, drawn from ideas in pages 138–139 of the fourth-grade science book *The Expanding World of Science* (Novak, Meister, et al. 1966, Book 4).

Figure 12.3

Expert Skeleton Concept Map Drawn From Ideas on Pages 138–139 (Grade 4) of *The Expanding World of Science* (Novak, Meister, et al. 1966)

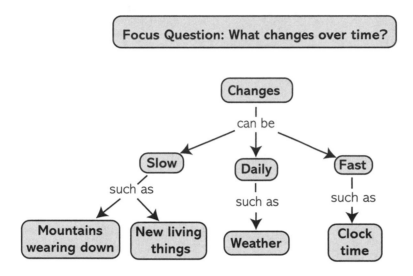

Expert skeleton concept maps can serve as a valid starting point for understanding changes over time. Of course, it would be very poor science teaching to have students memorize such concept maps and do nothing more. Instead, we ask the students to use text and internet resources to identify new, pertinent concepts and to incorporate these into their concept maps appropriately. This requires that they seek to screen the resources to find pertinent concepts and also to find meaningful ways to integrate new concepts into their growing concept map and their growing cognitive structure. Research suggests that it is better if students work in small groups to collaborate in their learning (Qin, Johnson, and Johnson 1995), and CmapTools provides for both synchronous and asynchronous collaboration in building concept maps. Any resource that can be digitized can be added to a concept map and accessed by simply clicking on the icon representing the resource and selecting the desired resource name. There can be several different types of resources attached to a concept, such as photos, graphs, tables, video clips, and URLs for websites. All that is required to attach a resource is to drag the symbol representing the resource and drop it onto the appropriate concept. Figure 12.4 shows the result of adding three concepts and several resources to Figure 12.3.

Current work under way with 150 teachers in grades 4–6 in Italy is not only showing the viability of the New Model for Education but also producing data that should document the high success of the program. A similar program is being initiated in a project with 150 schools in Panama, with the goal of reaching 1,000 schools. Both of these projects are funded by their respective ministries of education and have the potential for becoming nationwide, in all curriculum areas. It is expected that similar programs will develop at the university level.

Figure 12.4

Expansion of Figure 12.3 With Three Concepts (*Italic Type*) and Images of Three Resources Accessed by Clicking on the Icons Attached to the Concepts

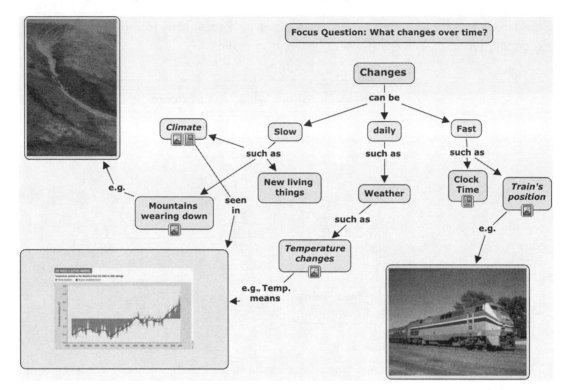

Although students or adults can work with expert skeleton concept maps at home or anywhere with an internet connection, the classroom setting with a good teacher can do much to enrich the experience. In addition to coaching and providing feedback to individual students and groups, the teacher might organize reporting sessions where work groups present the product of their work in show-and-tell sessions with comments and suggestions by other study groups. More importantly, the teacher can also arrange for "hands-on" laboratory and field studies, or even simple demonstrations, to add real-world experiences needed for building rich conceptual meanings for the concepts studied. Ideally, we would expect laboratory and field experiences to constitute the larger fraction of study time. An advantage over the usual lab and field study is that the student can enter into the work with at least rudimentary conceptual understanding of what they are researching, much more like the real-world case of scientists' work. Moreover, misconceptions are more likely to be uncovered and made conceptually explicit, thus facilitating remediation of the misconceptions (Novak 2002). Typically students progress through laboratory studies, including those designed to be "inquiry oriented," with little *conceptual* understanding of what they are doing, and little gain in their comprehension of the science involved (Heinze-Frey and Novak 1990; Taylor 1996).

The use of concept maps according to the New Model for Education is still in its infancy. David Macias Ferrer at the Instituto de Estudios Superiores de Tamaulipas in Mexico is doing work in college mathematics (*www.geocities.com/dmacias_iest/Conceptual.html*). In Florida, the Florida Institute for Education is sponsoring a number of efforts to introduce concept mapping and New Model for Education practices at the school and university levels. Some very nice "expert" concept maps have been prepared for algebra and can be viewed at *http://cmap.ihms.us;* download CmapTools and click on All Places, UNF (USA), Algebra 1.

Part of my motivation for writing this chapter is to encourage experimentation in college science classes with the hope that in a few years we can build a body of evidence to support the value of using this new model in college courses, especially in distance learning settings, and also to develop and refine the practices based on data. Currently the New Model for Education appears to be on sound theoretical footing, and what relevant empirical data exist are highly encouraging.

References

American Association for the Advancement of Science. 1993. *Benchmarks for science literacy.* New York: Oxford University Press.

Ausubel, D. P. 1963. *The psychology of meaningful verbal learning.* New York: Grune & Stratton.

Ausubel, D. P. 1968. *Educational psychology: A cognitive view.* New York: Holt, Rinehart and Winston.

Bransford, J. D., A. L. Brown, and R. R. Cocking. 1999. *How people learn: Brain, mind, experience, and school.* Washington, DC: National Academy Press.

Brown, A. S., A. Collins, and P. Duguid. 1989. Situated cognition and the culture of learning. *Educational Researcher* 18 (1): 32–41.

Cañas, A. J., R. Carff, G. Hill, M. Carvalho, M. Arguedas, T. Eskridge, J. Lott, and R. Carvajal. 2005. Concept maps: Integrating knowledge and information visualization. In *Knowledge and information visualization: Searching for synergies* (Lecture Notes in Computer Science), eds. S.-O. Tergan and T. Keller, 205–219. Heidelberg, Germany: Springer-Verlag.

Cañas, A. J., K. M. Ford, and J. W. Coffey. 1994. Concept maps as a hypermedia navigational tool. Paper presented at the Seventh Florida Artificial Intelligence Research Symposium (FLAIRS), Pensacola, FL.

Cañas, A. J., K. M. Ford, G. Hill, J. Brennan, R. Carff, N. Suri, and J. Coffey. 1995. Quorum: Children collaborating throughout Latin America. Paper presented at the Sixth IFIP World Conference on Computers in Education, Birmingham, England.

Cañas, A. J., K. M. Ford, J. D. Novak, P. Hayes, T. Reichherzer, and S. Niranjan. 2001. Online concept maps: Enhancing collaborative learning by using technology with concept maps. *The Science Teacher* 68 (4): 49–51.

Cañas, A. J., G. Hill, R. Carff, N. Suri, J. Lott, T. Eskridge, G. Gómez, M. Arroyo, and R. Carvajal. 2004. CmapTools: A knowledge modeling and sharing environment. In *Concept maps: Theory, methodology, technology. Proceedings of the First International Conference on Concept Mapping,* eds. A. J. Cañas, J. D. Novak, and F. M. González, 125–133. Pamplona, Spain: Universidad Pública de Navarra.

Carey, S. 1985. *Conceptual change in childhood.* Cambridge, MA: MIT Press.

Chang, T. 1995. Ph.D. students' epistemological commitments and their knowledge construction. *Proceedings of the National Science Council* 5: 103–121.

Edmondson, K. M., and J. D. Novak. 1993. The interplay of scientific epistemological views, learning strategies, and attitudes of college students. *Journal of Research in Science Teaching* 32: 547–559.

Gazzaniga, M. S., and T. Heatherton. 2002. *Psychological science: Mind, brain, and behavior.* New York: W. W. Norton.

Gelman, S. A. 1999. Dialogue on early childhood science, mathematics, and technology education: A context for learning. Concept development in preschool children. *www.project2061.org/publications/earlychild/online/context/gelman.htm*

Gelman S. A. 2003. *The essential child: Origins of essentialism in everyday thought.* Oxford, England: Oxford University Press.

Heinze-Fry, J. A., and J. D. Novak. 1990. Concept mapping brings long-term movement toward meaningful learning. *Science Education* 74 (4): 461–472.

Miller, G. A. 1956. The magical number seven, plus or minus two: Some limits on our capacity for processing information. *Psychological Review* 63: 81–92.

National Research Council. 1996. *National science education standards.* Washington, DC: National Academy Press.

Novak, J. D. 1964. Importance of conceptual schemes for science teaching. *The Science Teacher* 31: 10–14.

Novak, J. D. 1972. The use of audio-tutorial methods in elementary school instruction. In *The audio-tutorial approach to learning through independent study and integrated experiences* (2nd ed.), eds. S. N. Postlethwait, J. D. Novak, and H. T. Murray, Jr. Minneapolis, MN: Burgess.

Novak, J. D. 1976. Understanding the learning process and effectiveness of teaching methods in the classroom, laboratory, and field. *Science Education* 60 (4): 493–512. Reprinted in Spanish in *Perfiles Educativos,* Numero 1, Julio-Agosto-Septiembre, 1978.

Novak, J. D. 1977. *A theory of education.* Ithaca, NY: Cornell University Press.

Novak, J. D. 1982. Psychological and epistemological alternatives to Piagetian developmental psychology with support from empirical studies in science education. In *Jean Piaget—consensus and controversy,* eds. S. Modgil and C. Modgil, 331–349. New York: Praeger.

Novak. J. D. 1985. Metalearning and metaknowledge strategies to help students learn how to learn. In *Cognitive structure and conceptual change,* eds. L. H. T. West and A. L. Pines, 189–209. Orlando, FL: Academic Press.

Novak, J. D. 1988. Learning science and the science of learning. *Studies in Science Education* 15: 77–101.

Novak, J. D. 1993. Human constructivism: A unification of psychological and epistemological phenomena in meaning making. *International Journal of Personal Construct Psychology* 6: 167–193.

Novak, J. D. 1998. *Metacognitive strategies to help students learning how to learn.* Research Matters - to the Science Teacher, No. 9802. Nashville, TN: National Association for Research in Science Teaching.

Novak, J. D. 2002. Meaningful learning: The essential factor for conceptual change in limited or appropriate propositional hierarchies (LIPHs) leading to empowerment of learners. *Science Education* 86: 548–571.

Novak, J. D. 2003. The promise of new ideas and new technology for improving teaching and learning. *Cell Biology Education* 2: 122–132. Also available online at *www.cellbioed.org/article.cfm?ArticleID=59.*

Novak, J. D., and D. B. Gowin. 1984. *Learning how to learn.* New York: Cambridge University Press.

Novak, J. D., and R. I. Iuli. 1995. Meaningful learning as the foundation for constructivist epistemology. In *Proceedings of the Third International History, Philosophy and Science Teaching Conference,* Vol. 2, eds. F. Finley, D. Allchin, D. Rhees, and S. Fifield, 873–896. Minneapolis: University of Minnesota.

Novak, J. D., M. Meister, W. W. Knox, and D. W. Sullivan. 1966. *The world of science series.* Books 1–6. Indianapolis, IN: Bobbs-Merrill.

Novak, J. D., and D. Musonda. 1991. A twelve-year longitudinal study of science concept learning. *American Educational Research Journal* 28: 117–153.

Qin, Z., D. W. Johnson, and R. T. Johnson. 1995. Cooperative versus competitive efforts and problem solving. *Review of Educational Research* 65 (Summer): 129–143.

Schneps, M. 1989. *Private Universe Project.* Cambridge, MA: Smithsonian Center for Astrophysics.

Schwab, J. J. 1973. The Practical 3: Translation into curriculum. *School Review* 81 (4): 501–522.

Taylor, M. R. 1996. *Student study guide for Campbell's Biology.* New York: Benjamin Cummings.

Wandersee, J. H., J. J. Mintzes, and J. D. Novak. 1994. Research on alternative conceptions in science. In *Handbook of research on science teaching and learning,* ed. D. L. Gabel, 177–210. New York: Macmillan.

CHAPTER 13

The Impact of a Conceptually Sequenced Genetics Unit in an Introductory College Biology Course

Linda W. Crow and Julie Harless

Linda W. Crow is professor of biology at Montgomery College, Conroe, Texas. She earned an EdD in science education and biology at the University of Houston and conducts research on photosynthesis, evolution, conceptual development in the teaching of science, and the application of technology to science learning. A former president of the Society for College Science Teachers, she teaches introductory biology, biology for nonmajors, and environmental biology.

Julie Harless is professor of biology at Montgomery College. She earned a PhD in biomedical sciences at the University of Texas and conducts research on learning theory and DNA repair. She teaches introductory biology, biology for nonmajors, and microbiology.

When comparing introductory college biology textbooks, it is interesting to note how similar they are. Although the number of topics and depth of coverage can vary depending on whether a book is for majors or for mixed majors, the most striking similarity among all these textbooks is the sequence of topics and the lack of attention paid to the results of learning research. The sequence that most college textbooks follow merely reflects the logic of the discipline. They begin with atomic structure, a very abstract concept, then continue with chemistry and biochemistry (equally abstract ideas), and end finally with the microscopic cell structure. Even large ideas such as evolution and inheritance come later in most sequences. Macroscopic investigations usually appear in the second half of the book.

Texts are filled with a recitation of the end points of biology, mostly ignoring the real science of how we know these facts. These texts also use an enormous biological vocabulary that surpasses the number of new words learned in the first year of a foreign language (Yager 1983). Students are told what biologists discovered. But this is not enough to have an impact on conceptual change and to promote deep learning (Carey 2000). Traditional biology instruction pays little attention to conceptual change, inquiry, how we know, or learning theory (see Chapter 31 in this volume). Conceptually sequenced topics would allow students to build conceptual schemes and modify their preconceptions. What would a section of an introductory biology course look like that reflected current knowledge of learning theory and conceptual change? This was the challenge undertaken in our biology program.

The basis of this conceptual and sequenced approach can be traced as far back as the work of Jerome Bruner. He stated that merely teaching specific topics or skills without showing their placement in a broader context is useless (Bruner 1960). Without understanding that broader context, the student will not be able to connect these individual topics into a meaningful pattern (Donovan and Bransford 2005). This isolated knowledge is readily lost.

Concepts can be thought of as mental constructions that represent some object, quantity, or phenomena (Carey 2000). These concepts provide a framework for individuals to make sense of the world around them. When we are children, concepts form as a result of experiences and are used to construct explanations and theories of how things work. These concepts and their resulting theories may be totally incorrect, but they do explain what an individual has experienced or, at least, what an individual thinks he or she has experienced.

The goal of conceptual change is to substitute one conceptual scheme for another. This may not be easily accomplished because of most individuals' general reluctance to admit that their explanation is incorrect (Watson and Kopnicek 1990). To have conceptual change occur, you must first provide some experience that challenges their current conceptual system (Posner et al. 1982). This is often referred to as a *discrepant event*. Next, a new conceptual explanation must be developed that is understood by the student and is plausible. Finally the new conceptual framework must be tested to see if it can be used in different contexts. This change is not easily done, but all students have the capacity to make this change in their conceptual frameworks (Carey 2000).

Methods

As a first step toward implementing current research, the presentation of the genetics section was revised and this section was placed at the beginning of the introductory biology course. First, a set of central concepts was identified in the genetics sequence that would enhance the development of critical-thinking skills and allow for the knowledge to be linked together. The identification of this set of basic concepts was intended to provide the basis of what we wanted students to know. Terms associated with these concepts were also identified. Second, a set of experiences was identified that would represent what students should be able to do and that would provide them with experiences with these concepts. Again, just telling them about these concepts would not be enough (Clement 1993; Driver, Guesne, and Tiberghien 1985). Third, a sequence was developed that built on the ideas of novice versus expert problem solving, building from concrete to abstract, linking new knowledge to previous knowledge and addressing the preconceptions that students possess (Bransford, Brown, and Cocking 1999). Genetics was chosen as our initial test case. Concepts and terms were identified to attempt to describe what we wanted students to know about genetics in our introductory biology course (Figure 13.1). This initial identification of central concepts and related phenomena is supported by the literature (Lawson 1995).

Figure 13.1

Genetic Concepts and Terms

Genetic Concepts
- Variation can be explained in part by heredity.
- Genetic traits can be controlled by many different genetic patterns.
- Phenotype of an individual results from an interaction between genotype and environment.
- Phenotype does not always reveal the genotype.
- Inheritance patterns can be predicted and modeled.
- Phenotype as detected by genotype is related to protein production.
- The inheritance of genes parallels the inheritance of chromosomes.
- Organisms have pairs of homologous chromosomes, which meiosis distributes.
- Each gamete contributes one chromosome to each pair.

Genetic Terms
polygenic, dichotomous, genotype, phenotype, recessive, dominant, homozygous, heterozygous, allele, gene, homologous chromosomes, pedigree symbols, Punnett square, basics of mitosis and meiosis

A sequence and associated experiences were developed that would center on building from concrete to abstract, allowing time for expert problem-solving strategies to develop, promoting inquiry, linking new knowledge to previous knowledge, addressing preconceptions, and providing novel situations to which the knowledge could be applied.

The revised sequence of the genetics unit follows, with a description of the learning phenomena presented along with the concepts and terms being addressed. Most students have some basic understanding of heritability, and this provides a starting point.

Day 1

Using themselves, students measure certain traits—hairline shape, handedness, straightness of little finger, dominant eye (eyeness), PTC (phenylthiocarbamide) tasting, height (in centimeters), quickness (how quickly a person can catch a falling object), arm span (in centimeters), hitchhiker's thumb, earlobe attachment, interlocking thumbs, and grip strength. Class data are collected in a table (see Table 13.1 for a sample). Students are asked to examine these data and compare the types of results collected for each trait. For example, how do the data collected for PTC tasting compare with the data collected for height? The goal is to have students realize that some traits are dichotomous and others are more infinite. The terms *dichotomous* and *polygenic* are introduced. Most students have already heard the terms *dominant* and *recessive,* but they may have some preconceptions about them. Many students think that the recessive trait is the one that is the least prevalent. Using the data the students begin to recognize that dominance and recessiveness do not relate to the frequency of these characteristics in the population. This naturally leads into describing and using the terms *phenotype* and *genotype, homozygous* and *heterozygous,* and *gene* and *allele.*

Finally, students are asked to graph two characteristics such as height and arm span or height and gripping strength. The goal is to have them recognize that some traits are linked or at least have an impact on one another. This leads to a lively discussion of what genetic and environmental influences would impact height and strength. Outside of class students can use their textbooks to look up some standard definitions of these terms, but they leave this first day with operational definitions and examples of each of them. The entire day provides a very broad concrete experience that enables students to connect their previous knowledge about genetics to themselves (a concrete experience), start applying more abstract concepts to themselves (moving from concrete to abstract), confront some misconceptions, and have some practice with analyzing data about themselves (again concrete to abstract).

Day 2

A short series of questions is given to the students to allow them to practice using their terminology. This reinforces the work of Day 1. Pedigree symbols are introduced, and students are asked to represent their family using these symbols. This exercise takes previous knowledge of their family and has students make an abstract representation of this concrete idea. Short case studies are used to introduce conventional genetic nomenclature. In groups they analyze these case studies, draw pedigrees, add genotypes, and propose inheritance patterns. A demonstration of genotype symbolism is provided on the board. This allows the students to see some expert strategies after they have tried their own strategies and apply their knowledge to a new situation (the case study). By using two or three case studies, students practice the strategy and are provided with more application situations.

Day 3

Students are given some simple genetic problems to work in small groups. During discussions either with individual groups or in a whole-class discussion, Punnett squares are introduced as an expert strategy. The ideas of probability and ratios are introduced. Two labs are used—one with *Drosophila* and the other using albino corn plants as hands-on applications of monohybrid crosses.

Day 4

More difficult genetic problems are provided along with case studies that focus on the connection between genotype, phenotype, and protein production. Punnett squares are needed to solve these problems, providing more practice using the expert strategy for problem solving. Diseases such as Tay-Sachs and conditions such as phenylketonuria (PKU) and osteogenesis imperfecta are used as examples of the important link between genotype and protein production. The activities during this day allow students to see expert strategies and apply their knowledge to a new situation.

Day 5

Special inheritance patterns such as incomplete dominance, co-dominance, and sex-linked characteristics are introduced. Problems using these inheritance patterns are provided to the

Table 13.1

Sample of Student Genetics Data Used on Day 1

Student Initials	Gender M/F	Hand R/L	Eyed R/L	Quickness #R	Quickness #L	HT #	AS #	WP Yes/No	Ears attached Yes/No	Thumb HH/S	Little finger B/S	Interlock on top R/L	PTC taster Yes/No	Grip #
RH	M	R	R	19	18	181	183	No	Yes	HH	B	L	Yes	55
ZD	M	R	R	24	26	182	176	Yes	Yes	HH	S	L	No	56
SS	F	R	R	16	14	172	167	No	No	HH	S	L	Yes	11
NM	F	R	L	19	17	170	173	No	No	HH	S	L	No	17
BR	M	L	R	28	16	195	197	No	no	HH	S	L	No	37
JL	F	R	L	13	13	165	160	No	Yes	HH	S	L	Yes	39
ML	M	R	L	22	24	176	169	No	n	S	S	L	Yes	38
AB	F	R	R	15	17	172	166	No	No	S	B	R	No	14
CH	F	L	R	22	16	168	160	No	No	HH	S	L	Yes	24
NK	M	R	R	6	15	175	173	Yes	Yes	HH	S	R	Yes	51
JH	F	R	R	34	37	173	167	No	Yes	S	S	L	No	26
GS	F	R	R	38	32	163	152	Yes	No	HH	S	R	No	5
AR	F	R	R	40	36	160	157	No	No	S	S	L	Yes	6
CH	M	R	R	26	30	193	195	Yes	Yes	HH	B	L	No	59

Note: M/F = male or female; R/L = right or left; Quickness = quickness in centimeters; HT = height in centimeters; AS = arm span in centimeters; WP = widow's peak; HH/S = hitchhiker's thumb or straight; B/S = bent or straight; PTC = phenylthiocarbamide.

students. Chromosomes are introduced as structures that contain genes. An electronic karyotyping lab is done to further define chromosomes as autosomes and sex chromosomes. Again, a concrete experience is used along with continuous linking of concepts and terms.

Days 6 and 7

A study of cell reproduction is done with a particular focus on meiosis. Homologous chromosomes are highlighted to provide a basis for further study of inheritance patterns. Some time is spent working with students to understand the importance of meiosis in understanding genetic patterns.

Day 8

Dihybrid crosses are introduced, linking them closely to the behavior of chromosomes during meiosis. Students are divided into groups to analyze dihybrid crosses and predict outcomes. Again students are applying what they have learned to a new situation. Students are asked to describe how genes are sorted out during meiosis.

This approach is quite different from most approaches to genetics, which usually begin with the abstract. Beginning with Day 1 the emphasis has been on building from concrete to abstract, linking knowledge together, allowing some inquiry, and providing demonstrations of expert strategies.

Results

To assess the effectiveness of this resequencing approach, test scores from previous semesters were compared with test scores from the classes using this new sequence. The test (exam 1) used in both cases had both knowledge-level questions and questions that tested higher-order thinking. The question types and levels were consistent across the semesters. The activities used in the revision were also used in previous semesters, so any changes in scores can be attributed to the sequencing effects. Two professors were used in this study, and their data were pooled to achieve some randomness. In addition to this comparison, the scores on the second test (exam 2) covering material that had not been resequenced were compared to detect any unforeseen differences between the groups. Finally the distribution of scores on the exam was examined to see if there were different impacts depending on the achievement level.

Results of this restructuring were analyzed using an analysis of variance (ANOVA). The previous semesters were used as the control group. Results from nine previous semesters' exams (control) ($n = 180$) were compared with seven revised (experimental) classes ($n = 80$).

The average exam score using the traditional presentation is 66.6; with the revised sequence the average exam score is 72.4. ANOVA shows a significant difference ($P = 0.002$) between the two groups. This contrasts sharply with the results from the same students on exam 2, where there is less than a 1-point difference in exam 2 averages ($P = 0.73$).

As an internal control, individual student scores on exam 1 and exam 2 were compared. The difference between exam 1 and exam 2 scores controls for individual student achievement level and isolates the effect of revisions. Students in the control group averaged 1.3 points higher on the first exam than on the second. Students taught the new resequenced format averaged 6.6 points higher on the exam over revised material than on the exam over unchanged material. ANOVA indicates that this difference is significant ($P = 0.01$).

When examining grade distributions we found some striking changes. The most dramatic changes were in the "high F" and "D" categories (50–69). This group decreased and the "C" and "A" groups increased. In the control group, 66% of the students passed (42% C or better); in the revised group, 80% passed (60% C or better).

Conclusions

These results provide some hope that introductory biology courses can be modified to incorporate learning theory while still meeting the needs of the syllabus. Current textbooks continue to reflect the logic of discipline, and introductory biology courses suffer from an overemphasis on coverage. Perhaps by developing concepts from a macro perspective to a micro perspective, tying this knowledge to phenomena, providing opportunities to demonstrate expert approaches, and linking knowledge together in a meaningful fashion, introductory biology courses can be more effective, increase student achievement, and provide a more successful science experience for students who may be high achievers (see also Chapter 12 in this volume).

The next step is, of course, to attempt to resequence the entire course and still maintain the demands of the syllabus. There are some general rules to follow in expanding this approach to the rest of the course. To initiate this process, research concerning student misconceptions should be reviewed to reveal common mistakes in student thinking. Then, disregarding the usual order found in textbooks, a new sequence should be developed based on the following tenets:

- Attach new information to previous knowledge.
- Proceed from concrete to abstract representations.
- Begin with big ideas and lead to smaller ones.
- Focus on how we know, not just on the end points of science.
- Relate concepts to the underlying themes of biology such as evolution and structure function.
- Allow students to apply information and concepts in several contexts and revisit ideas in successive chapters.
- Provide experiences and information that challenge certain biological misconceptions and encourage conceptual changes.

If resequencing the genetics section has such positive results, then reorganizing the entire course could have larger effects and overall retention and learning could be improved.

References

Bransford, J. D., A. L. Brown, and R. Cocking. 1999. *How people learn: Brain, mind, experience, and school*. Washington, DC: National Academy Press.

Bruner, J. 1960. *The process of education*. Cambridge, MA: Harvard University Press.

Carey, S. 2000. Science education as conceptual change. *Journal of Applied Development Psychology* 21 (1): 13–19.

Clement, J. 1993. Using bridging analogies and anchoring institutions to deal with students' preconceptions in physics. *Journal of Research in Science Teaching* 30 (10): 1241–1257.

Donovan, M. S., and J. D. Bransford. 2005. *How students learn: History, mathematics, and science in the classroom*. Washington DC: National Academy Press.

Driver, R., E. Guesne, and A. Tiberghien. 1985. Some features of children's ideas and their implications for teaching. In *Children's ideas in science*, 193–201. Berkshire, England: Open University Press.

Lawson, A. E. 1995. *Science teaching and the development of thinking.* Belmont, CA: Wadsworth.

Posner, G. J., K. A. Strike, P. W. Hewson, and W. A. Gertzog. 1982. Accommodation of a scientific conception: Toward a theory of conceptual change. *Science Education* 66: 211–227.

Watson, B., and Kopnicek, R. 1990. Teaching for conceptual change: Confronting children's experience. *Phi Delta Kappan* (May): 680–684.

Yager, R. 1983. The importance of terminology in teaching K–12 science. *Journal of Research in Science Teaching* 20 (6): 577–588.

CHAPTER 14

Do Introductory Science Courses Select for Effort or Aptitude?

Randy Moore

Randy Moore is professor of biology at the University of Minnesota. He earned a PhD in biology at the University of California at Los Angeles (UCLA) and conducts research in evolution and science education. He teaches courses in introductory biology, evolution, and understanding the evolution-creationism controversy.

On the first day of classes, students in introductory biology courses believe that effort is the most accurate predictor of their academic success. Students know which academic behaviors are important for success, and they are confident that they will earn high grades, attend lectures and help sessions, and take advantage of other opportunities to master the course material and raise their grade. Despite this optimism, many students do not follow through on their first-day-of-classes' expectations, and their grades suffer accordingly. When asked about their academic behaviors, many students provide misleading answers. Academic success in introductory science courses is strongly associated with effort-based behaviors, but only weakly associated with aptitude. The relevant research findings are discussed in this chapter relative to how instructors can help students succeed in introductory science courses.

It Happens Every Semester

I've lost track of how many times I've had the following conversation with a student:

Student: I'm having trouble in your course. Can you tell me what I'm doing wrong? I did everything that you told us to do to get ready for the exam.

Randy: Thanks for coming to see me. How did you prepare for the exam?

Student: I studied the class notes, did the assignments, went to the help sessions, and read the corresponding chapters in the textbook.

Randy:	You did all of the assignments?
Student:	Yes.
Randy:	You read and studied all of the assigned chapters in the textbook before class?
Student:	Yes.
Randy:	You came to the help session?
Student:	Yes.
Randy:	You came to class every day and paid attention?
Student:	Yes; every day.
Randy:	You did all of those things? Really? What did you make on the exam?
Student:	I failed.
Randy:	(*long pause*) Hmmm….

Although we know that following our advice won't automatically produce As, we also know that students who follow our advice should not fail. So what could be the problem here? How could students be following our advice and still be failing our courses?

Our Students

Despite decades of science education reform, increasingly large numbers of underprepared students are entering college science courses. Although many colleges and universities have implemented programs to help these students, introductory science courses continue to have higher failure rates than other courses (Congos, Langsam, and Schoeps 1997). These higher failure rates are often attributed to students' poor preparation; for example, more than three-fourths of college freshmen who took the ACT in 2004 were not prepared for college-level biology (Cavanagh 2004; see also Chapter 33 in this volume). But is the explanation that simple? In some instances, it probably is; the academic outcomes of students at academic extremes are easy to predict—National Merit Scholars do well, and functionally illiterate students do not. However, the academic outcomes of "average" students are not as easy to predict—many privileged students who are seemingly well prepared for college often struggle, whereas others succeed despite having to overcome significant obstacles. What is the primary determinant of success for these students?

In this investigation I tried to determine the relative importance of effort and aptitude for the success of students in an introductory biology course. Given the unreliability of self-reported data about academic behaviors (Caron, Whitbourne, and Halgin 1992; Sappington, Kinsey, and Munsayac 2002), I restricted my study to measures of academic outcomes (e.g., grades) and behaviors (e.g., class attendance) that could be easily and objectively measured.

Methods

This study was conducted from 2002 to 2005 in several large sections of a traditional four-credit introductory "mixed-majors" biology course at the University of Minnesota. All sections of the course met near the same time of day and were taught by the same instructor in the same classroom in the same way (e.g., the same syllabus, textbook, sequence of topics, grading policy, exams, and pedagogical techniques). The course syllabus included the following statement about the importance of class attendance and academic engagement for academic success: "I expect you to prepare for and attend every class. This is important because class attendance is usually a strong indicator of course performance." I also discussed these statements and the importance of attendance and course engagement on the first day of class.

This study included a total of 1,588 students, and each subgroup included at least 328 students. The students in the total sample were ethnically diverse: 51% Anglo, 21% African American, 5% Chicano/Latino, 20% Asian American, and 3% other or missing information. Each subgroup of the study was similarly diverse. The students had an average high school graduation percentile ranking of 54 and an average composite ACT score of 20. Approximately half of the students were females, and virtually all of the students (98%) had taken a biology course in high school.

Measures of Academic Aptitude and Effort

I measured the following aspects of these students' academic aptitude and effort:

- *ACT scores and high school graduation percentiles:* I used institutional records to obtain students' Academic Aptitude Ratings (AAR); the AAR is calculated for each student as the high school graduation percentile plus two times the ACT composite score. This part of the study included 896 students.
- *Attendance at lectures:* I recorded attendance at every class for all 1,588 students.
- *Attendance at help sessions:* Help sessions were held before each exam and were conducted by teaching assistants who had no knowledge of, or input regarding, any of the exams. Attendance at the help sessions was optional, and students who attended help sessions received no points or "inside information" about upcoming exams. Attendance was recorded at each help session, and students were considered attendees if they attended at least one help session. This part of the study included 328 students.
- *Submission of extra-credit work:* Students could earn one-third of the points that they had missed on each lecture exam if they wrote a one-page essay about each of the questions that they missed on the exam. Students had up to six weeks to write and submit these essays, and the extra-credit points were guaranteed for any reasonable effort. Points earned by students who submitted extra-credit work were excluded from all calculations of grades in this study. Students who completed at least one extra-credit assignment were counted in this study. This part of the study included 328 students.
- *Compliance with reading assignments:* The course syllabus stated prominently that "Reading assignments are strict requirements for this course." I emphasized on the first day of classes that, as was noted in bold print in the syllabus, the first assignment was "to read the entire syllabus before the beginning of the next class." This part of the study included all 1,588 students.

The syllabus included a section entitled "Your First Assignment" that was printed in a bold font and stated, "Your final grade will be raised by 1% if you e-mail the word 'bonus' to [the instructor] before the start of the second class." All students had access to e-mail, but they could have also obtained the reward by calling me, coming to my office, seeing me outside of class, or leaving a message that indicated that they had read the entire syllabus before the second class. I did not distribute syllabi until the end of the first class to prevent variance among students reading them during class.

On the second day of classes, I administered a survey to 468 students that asked the following question: "Your first assignment was to read the entire syllabus. Did you read the entire syllabus?" All students who had read the entire syllabus would presumably have been eager to earn a bonus point for doing so. Students who missed the first class were not included in the survey.

Students' Expectations

On the first day of classes, I gave all 1,588 students a survey that asked the following questions:

- What grade do you expect to earn in this course?
- What percentage of classes will you attend?
- Will you do extra-credit work if given an opportunity to do so?
- Will you come to help sessions before exams?
- Do you believe that you will earn a higher grade in this course if you attend class regularly?
- Will you respond honestly to questions about class attendance and other academic behaviors?
- Which of the following is most responsible for your grades: your own ability, your own effort, the ease or difficulty of the course, or luck?

Students were told throughout the semester to keep a record of their class attendance, and on the last day of class they were told to know their rate of class attendance for the final exam. At the final exam, I asked all of the students (1,588) to list (a) the percentage of classes that they had attended and (b) whether they had attended a help session during the semester.

Results

On the first day of classes, students predicted that they would attend an average of 87% of classes. Approximately 55% of students predicted that they would earn an A, 41% predicted that they would earn a B, 4% predicted they would earn a C, and no students predicted that they would earn a D or F. Virtually all (i.e., 96%) of students believed that they would make a higher grade in the course if they attended class regularly. Approximately 93% of the students who predicted they would earn an A also predicted they would attend 81%–100% of classes, 81% of students who predicted they would earn a B claimed they would attend 81%–100% of classes, and 14% of students who predicted they would earn a C also predicted they would attend 81%–100% of classes.

Table 14.1 compares the claims made by students about their academic behaviors (i.e., attending class, doing extra-credit work, and attending help sessions) and grades on the first week and last week of classes with their actual behaviors and grades. Most students fell short of their predicted behaviors and grades.

Table 14.2 shows how students' final grades in the course were related to their average attendance rates and AAR scores. The correlation coefficient for class attendance and course grade was 0.74, and the coefficient of determination for these variables was 0.55 (i.e., variation in students' rates of class attendance accounted for 55% of the variation in students' grades). The correlation coefficient for AAR and course grade was 0.17, and the coefficient of determination for these variables was 0.03 (i.e., variation in students' AAR scores accounted for 3% of the variability in students' grades). Students' responses to the question "Which of the following is most responsible for your grades?" were as follows: my own ability, 12%; my own effort, 83%; the ease or difficulty of the course, 4%; good or bad luck, 1%.

Table 14.1

Comparison of Students' Predictions and Claims About Their Academic Behaviors and Grades During the First and Last Weeks of Class With Actual Behaviors and Outcomes

Prediction	Predicted during first week	Claimed during last week	Actual
I will attend/attended a help session.	84	41	28
I will attend/attended approximately ____% of classes.	89	85	69
I will do an extra-credit assignment if given an opportunity to do so.	85		24
My course grade will be ____%.	92		70

Note: Numbers in the table are means (*N* > 328).

Although 95% of students claimed on the first day of class that they would respond honestly to questions about their academic behaviors, many students lied about their academic behaviors. For example, 41% claimed that they had attended a help session, but only 28% had actually attended one (Table 14.1). Similarly, although 74% of students claimed that they had read the entire syllabus (as instructed), only 1% of the students had submitted the "bonus" e-mail or message. During subsequent years, the percentage of responses rose steadily to 32% as "word got out" about the assignment.

Table 14.2

Association of Students' Final Grades in an Introductory Biology Course With Average Academic Aptitude Ratings (AAR) Scores and Attendance Rates

Grade	% of students earning grade	Average attendance, %	Average AAR
A	9	92	97
B	26	79	96
C	30	70	92
D	16	61	92
F	19	34	91

Note: Numbers in the table are means.

Approximately 28% of students attended at least one help session. These students were three times more likely to earn an A and five times less likely to earn an F than were students who attended no help sessions. Approximately 24% of students submitted at least one extra-credit assignment; these students were three times more likely to earn an A and nine times less likely to earn an F than were students who did not submit an extra-credit assignment.

Discussion

Students know that their effort, and not their aptitude, will be the primary determinant of their success in introductory science courses.

On the first day of classes, more than 80% of 1,588 first-year biology students believed that their grade in introductory biology would be determined primarily by their effort, and not by their aptitude, luck, or the ease or difficulty of the course. Students know which effort-based behaviors are important for academic success; that is, they know that attending class, doing extra-credit work, and attending help sessions will help them earn higher grades (Moore 2003). This is consistent with the fact that students who predicted they would earn an A in the course linked their performance with an average attendance rate of 93%, whereas those who believed they would earn a C predicted that they would attend only 73% of classes. These results support earlier studies (Moore 2003) and indicate that most students in introductory science courses know which academic behaviors are important for success.

Students are highly confident that they will work hard enough and exhibit the behaviors necessary to earn high grades in introductory science courses.

On the first day of classes, students predict that they will attend an average of 89% of classes; large majorities also predict that they will attend help sessions and do extra-credit work if given an opportunity to do so (Table 14.1). In light of this confidence about their predicted level of effort, it is not surprising that more than 90% of students in introductory biology believe they will earn an A or B in the course (Moore 2003), despite the fact that many students have had negative experiences in earlier science courses (Congos, Langsam, and Schoeps 1997). These results indicate that most introductory biology students are optimistic on the first day of classes about their commitment toward, and the probable outcome of, their upcoming academic experience in introductory biology courses.

Students who do exhibit these behaviors usually do well in introductory science courses, regardless of their admission scores and academic histories.

Students with the highest rates of participation in extra-credit opportunities and highest rates of attendance in class and at help sessions earned higher grades than students who ignored extra-credit opportunities and did not regularly attend class or help sessions (Moore et al. 2003). That is, the impact of the motivation-related behaviors studied here far exceeded that of aptitude for students' success in introductory biology. These data are consistent with other studies (Launius 1997; Moore 2003, 2004; Thomas and Higbee 2000; Wiley 1992) and indicate that (a) academic motivation is the most important factor for success in introductory science courses, and (b) scores on standardized admissions tests (e.g., ACT) are not destiny. The importance of effort and motivation for academic success was summarized this way by Thompson (2002): "If a student ever complains about a grade or how tough the course is, one of the first things I look at is class attendance. That usually says it all" (p. B5). Thomas and Higbee (2000) were more succinct when they concluded that "nothing replaces being present in class" (p. 229).

Although students are confident they will work hard and succeed in introductory science courses, most students' confidence is unjustified; their efforts do not match their predictions.

Although virtually all first-year students are confident on the first day of classes that they will work hard and earn high grades, many students fall short of their predicted effort; they do not come to class as much, attend help sessions as much, or do extra-credit work as much as they predicted they would (Table 14.1). These discrepancies in their predicted effort and actual effort correlate positively with corresponding differences in their predicted and actual grades in the course: On average, students who earn the highest grades are also the students most likely to attend class, attend help sessions, and engage in course-related opportunities. These results are consistent with previous reports (Friedman, Rodriguez, and McComb 2001; Romer 1993) and indicate that many students (a) do not follow through on their academic intentions and (b) have behaviors that are inconsistent with academic success (Pintrich and Garcia 1994; Van-Zile-Tamsen, and Livingston 1999; Yaworski, Weber, and Ibrahim 2000). Virtually all students know that attending class, doing extra-credit work, and attending help sessions will probably improve their grade, yet many choose to ignore these opportunities.

Students often provide misleading information about their academic behaviors.

Although input from students can often be useful for improving academic programs and procedures, students' responses about their own academic performances are often unreliable (Table 14.1; Caron, Whitbourne, and Halgin 1992; Sappington, Kinsey, and Munsayac 2002). More than 90% of the students in this study indicated that they would respond honestly to questions about their academic behaviors, yet many more students claimed that they came to class, did assigned work, and attended help sessions than actually did these things. These misrepresentations have important consequences, for they complicate instructors' and advisors' efforts to help students succeed. When we try to identify and remedy behaviors that impede success, many students will mislead us with answers that are not true. Our responses to these misrepresentations (e.g., sending students for tests of reading comprehension, routing students to remedial courses) may unnecessarily divert resources and impede students' success when, in fact, the underlying problem may be that the students simply haven't tried very hard (e.g., they haven't come to class, haven't attended help sessions, and haven't participated in course-related opportunities). Because these misrepresentations can mislead instructors and academic advisors and thereby hinder our abilities to help students, instructors should not rely on these responses when designing strategies and interventions for improving students' academic performance.

Aptitude, Motivation, and Success in Introductory Science Courses

Data presented here and elsewhere (Yaworski, Weber, and Ibrahim 2000) indicate that many students have motivation-related behaviors that impede their success in introductory science courses. The apathy and detrimental academic behaviors that typify unsuccessful students often begin in high school (Gehring 2003; Peterson and Colangelo 1996). However, since these poor academic behaviors in high school have been rewarded with the highest grades on record (Young 2002), it's not surprising that many first-year students believe that they are prepared for college, that college is merely the 13th grade, and that the same amount of effort that produced their high grades in high school will produce the same grades in college (Toppo 2005; Young 2002). When it does not, many students do not change their academic behaviors; they continue to miss classes and ignore course-related opportunities and, as a result, often continue to fail. This is why most students who earn failing grades during their first semester continue the same behaviors and, not surprisingly, make similar grades during their second semester (Moore 2004). Instructors should use quantitative data such as those shown in Table 14.1 to convince students of the probable outcomes of their academic behaviors. Commitment is essential; without it, students' other traits (e.g., aptitude) don't matter.

Of course, the correlations noted here are not perfect, and what I report does not explain all academic behaviors and outcomes; after all, students' academic success is influenced by many factors (Higbee, Lundell, and Arendale 2005). However, the primary determinant of many students' academic success in introductory science courses is academic motivation, which is expressed in behaviors such as class attendance and course engagement. This is why many students who drop out of college list a lack of motivation as the top reason for their academic failures (Wambach et al. 2003). In introductory science courses such as the one studied here, it is usually a lack of academic motivation that uncouples many students' academic goals from their academic outcomes.

References

Caron, M. D., S. K. Whitbourne, and R. P. Halgin. 1992. Fraudulent excuse making among college students. *Teaching of Psychology* 19 (2): 90–93.

Cavanagh, S. 2004. Students ill-prepared for college, ACT warns. *Education Week* 24 (8): 5.

Congos, D. H., D. M. Langsam, and N. Schoeps. 1997. Supplemental instruction: A successful approach to learning how to learn college introductory biology. *Journal of Teaching and Learning* 2 (1): 2–17.

Friedman, P., F. Rodriguez, and J. McComb. 2001. Why students do and do not attend classes. *College Teaching* 49 (4): 124–133.

Gehring, J. 2003. Report examines motivation among students. *Education Week* 23 (15): 17.

Higbee, J. L., D. B. Lundell, and D. Arendale. 2005. *The general college vision: Integrating intellectual growth, multicultural perspectives, and student development.* Minneapolis: University of Minnesota, General College, Center for Research on Developmental Education and Urban Literacy.

Launius, M. H. 1997. College student attendance: Attitudes and academic performance. *College Student Journal* 31: 86–92.

Moore, R. 2003. Does improving developmental education students' understanding of the importance of class attendance improve students' class attendance and academic performance? *Research and Teaching in Developmental Education* 20 (2): 24–39.

Moore, R. 2004. The importance of a good start. In *Best practices for access and retention in higher education,* eds. I. M. Duranczyk, J. L. Higbee, and D. B. Lundell, 115–123. Minneapolis: University of Minnesota, General College, Center for Research on Developmental Education and Urban Literacy.

Moore, R., M. Jensen, J. Hatch, I. Duranczyk, and L. Koch. 2003. Showing up: The importance of class attendance for academic success in introductory science classes. *American Biology Teacher* 65 (5): 325–329.

Peterson, J. S., and N. Colangelo. 1996. Gifted achievers and underachievers: A comparison of patterns found in school files. *Journal of Counseling and Development* 74 (3): 399–407.

Pintrich, P. R., and T. Garcia. 1994. Self-regulated learning in college students: Knowledge, strategies and motivation. In *Student motivation, cognition and learning: Essays in honor of Wilbur J. McKeachie,* eds. P. R. Pintrich and D. R. Brown, 113–133. Hillsdale, NJ: Erlbaum.

Romer, R. 1993. Do students go to class? Should they? *Journal of Economic Perspectives* 7 (3): 167–174.

Sappington, J., K. Kinsey, and K. Munsayac. 2002. Two studies of reading compliance among college students. *Teaching of Psychology* 29: 272–274.

Thomas, P. V., and J. L. Higbee. 2000. The relationship between involvement and success in developmental algebra. *Journal of College Reading and Learning* 30 (2): 222–232.

Thompson, B. 2002. If I quiz them, they will come. *The Chronicle of Higher Education* 48 (41): B5.

Toppo, G. *USA Today*. 2005. Groups call for comprehensive reform for U.S. high schools. February 28, p. 6D.

VanZile-Tamsen, C., and J. A. Livingston. 1999. The differential impact of motivation on the self-regulated strategy use of high- and low-achieving college students. *Journal of College Student Development* 40 (1): 54–60.

Wambach, C., J. Hatfield, J. Franko, and A. Mayer. 2003. *General College persisters and leavers: A comparative study*. Minneapolis: University of Minnesota, General College, Office of Research and Evaluation.

Wiley, C. 1992. Predicting business course grades from class attendance and other objective student characteristics. *College Student Journal* 26: 497–501.

Yaworski, J., R. M. Weber, and N. Ibrahim. 2000. What makes students succeed or fail? The voices of developmental college students. *Journal of College Reading and Learning* 30 (2): 195–221.

Young, J. R. 2002. Homework? What homework? *The Chronicle of Higher Education* 49 (15): A35–A37.

CHAPTER 15

Active Learning in the College Science Classroom

Catherine Ueckert and Julie Gess-Newsome

Catherine Ueckert is associate professor at Northern Arizona University. She earned a PhD in science education at the University of Nebraska and conducts research on place-based learning and how students learn. She teaches courses on college science teaching, middle/secondary science teaching methods, supervision of secondary student teachers, and unity of life.

Julie Gess-Newsome is professor and Walkup Distinguished Professor of Science Education at Northern Arizona University. She earned a PhD in science education at Oregon State University and conducts research on teacher cognition, pedagogical content knowledge, and professional development. She teaches courses on college science teaching, elementary/middle/secondary science teaching methods, science curriculum and instruction, and assessment.

We've all heard the statement, "I've never learned this topic as well as I did when I prepared to teach it." As college instructors, we have probably all experienced this phenomenon. But why is this statement true? As we prepare to teach, we closely examine what we want students to know, organize our thinking about what topics and concepts are the most important, make connections across the ideas as well as to real-life applications, and craft an instructional strategy that we hope will powerfully engage our students in learning. This interaction with the course material results in a great deal of learning for the instructor, especially the first-year instructor. Unfortunately, the product of this experience is often passive reception of our knowledge by students. How can we reverse this scenario to make our students partners in the active-learning process?

Why the Emphasis on Active Learning?

Traditional forms of teaching involve the transmission of knowledge from an authority (the teacher or text) to the student. In such instances, learning from a student perspective means reciting knowledge as evidence of learning. Those students who know the most facts are the "winners" in the game of science, a practice that increases competition and reinforces working in isolation.

While such practices are certainly effective for a subset of the population, changes since the mid-1970s have caused us to rethink these early teaching traditions. First, *the world has changed*. In examining the needs of the future workforce, the Business-Higher Education Forum (2003) identified nine key attributes for today's workplace: leadership, teamwork, problem solving, time management, self-management, adaptability, analytical thinking, global consciousness, and strong communication skills (listening, speaking, reading, and writing). These skills clearly require different teaching practices than have been used in the past.

Second, *our goals for science learning have changed*. Factual knowledge in isolation is no longer sufficient. The understandings needed for scientific literacy are much more complex. Not only do people need to understand the content of science, they need to recognize the strengths and limitations of science as a way of making sense of the world around us. All individuals need to know how science is done, how knowledge is tested and advanced, what questions can and cannot be answered by science, and how scientific inquiry and knowledge can be applied to problem solving. These goals are reinforced in the National Science Education Standards (National Research Council [NRC] 1996), where understanding the unifying concepts and processes in science, science as inquiry, the history and nature of science, and science in social and personal perspectives are emphasized as equal in importance to the learning of key concepts in physical, life, Earth, and space sciences.

Third, *our understanding of how people learn has advanced*. We know that understanding involves more than just knowing facts and vocabulary. To build understanding, we must recognize the incoming conceptions that learners have and work to either add to or modify those understandings. This process of change is facilitated by active engagement with the content and is stimulated in social settings. Learning occurs best when the learner takes control of the learning process (metacognition) by recognizing when he or she does and does not understand. A sign of deep understanding is found in the ability to apply information to new contexts (transfer), though transfer can only occur when the learner is aware of the underlying principles and themes that ground their thinking (Bransford, Brown, and Cocking 1999; NRC 2000). A key instructional implication from the research on learning is that students need multiple opportunities to think deeply and purposefully about the content and to gain feedback on their learning.

What Does Active Learning Look Like?

Research has consistently shown that all students, including college science students, learn more when actively engaged. Engagement can occur through increased interaction with the content itself, or it may be coupled with increased interaction with peers or the course instructor (see Chapter 5 in this volume). In an active-learning environment, students debate ideas, ask questions and compare answers to what is known, use evidence to develop explanations, consider alternatives, and make ideas public while recognizing that explanations may change following discussion. In other cases, students may work in groups to collect data in real-life contexts or apply knowledge gained in the classroom to societal problems. The power of such increased interaction with content and peers is the opportunity to make thinking explicit and to gain feedback about the effectiveness of individual learning strategies. These strategies not only mirror many of the processes of scientific inquiry and accommodate different interests and learning preferences, but they are also helpful in attracting and retaining women and students of color in the sciences.

Active learning can take many forms. Laboratory experiences come readily to mind. But, while laboratories offer the powerful potential for learning, not all college science courses can afford such opportunities. Therefore, this chapter will focus on active-learning strategies that can be used in all classrooms. Although these strategies can be used at any time in a learning sequence, we have organized the strategies by their logical placement in instruction.

Engaging the Learner With the Content

One of the most important parts of the instructional sequence is the introduction. The strategies presented in this section act as tools to introduce a topic or focus student attention prior to or at the start of the sequence. These strategies alert students to the instructional objectives and provide feedback to the instructor about incoming students' conceptions.

Just-in-Time Teaching

Just-in-Time Teaching (JiTT) is a teaching and learning strategy that focuses on using knowledge about student learning, collected on the web, to adjust classroom practice. In the JiTT process developed by Novak and colleagues (1999), the instructor analyzes an upcoming instructional sequence and crafts two to four conceptually rich open-ended questions based on the content for the day and the reading assignments. These questions are placed on the web. The following are examples of the questions:

- *Using the ideas in section X, how do you interpret the following situation?*
- *In your own words, explain the meaning of "Y" as it is used in Chapter 3.*
- *Examine figure Z and explain what it means in nontechnical terms.*

At least two hours before class, the student attempts to answer the questions on the web. Students may earn credit for simply submitting their answers, or they may be graded on the correctness of the answers. Assigning some level of course credit will help motivate students to complete the questions. The instructor gathers the answers and analyzes them for the level of understanding and common errors. The upcoming instruction is then adjusted "just in time" by decreasing time spent on mastered concepts and increasing time spent on difficult concepts. The instructor may present sample student responses, including both strong and weak answers, as a pedagogical tool for fostering discussion in an interactive setting. The cycle is repeated several times each week, encouraging students to stay current with the content and structuring their learning time outside of the classroom.

JiTT techniques have been the focus of a number of grants. Additional examples of JiTT methods used in physics can be found at *http://webphysics.iupui.edu/jitt.html*, and examples used in the geosciences can be found at *http://serc.carleton.edu/introgeo/justintime.*

Web-Based Modules

Instructor-created web-based modules are short interactive extensions of classroom lectures that may include activities, short videos, simulations, links to pertinent websites, and quizzes.

For instance, a biology lecture on organic molecules may be followed by a module on functional groups. Students are able to click and drag various functional groups to a base molecule such as ethane. As the functional group changes, so do the properties of the molecule formed. Links to these newly formed molecules provide additional information.

The technology-enhanced learning environments (see Chapter 22 in this volume) help meet the learning needs of a diverse student population while providing activities that require students to think, reflect, connect, and apply information (McKeachie 2002). The activities and links allow students to access materials that are of personal interest and to check for conceptual understanding. Web-based modules may have a positive impact on student motivation due to a novel learning approach that encourages student curiosity and the personal control of the time and place of access.

Warm-Up Questions

The first few minutes of class are often busy ones for the instructor. To turn this transition time into learning time, consider posting a question or problem on the board or screen for students to answer as class begins. These questions, often called "bell work" because the work should commence with the signal for the start of class, allow students a few minutes to capture their own thoughts and focus on the content of the day. Questions may act as a form of review or application from prior work, be based on reading assignments, or elicit thinking about the topic of the day. The answers to these questions can be submitted for review or simply kept in a journal by students. To gain feedback for teaching, the instructor can collect a random set of journals each day or week to review. Maintaining the journal may constitute a portion of the course grade.

Interacting With Student Knowledge Construction

In contrast to the previous strategies, the strategies described in this section are designed to maintain student engagement with the content and each other during the body of the instructional sequence. These strategies increase interest and motivation and act as midpoint checks for student understanding and pacing guides for the instructor.

Questioning Techniques

The most obvious way to find out what students know is to ask them. But in large classes, this strategy can be intimidating! Questions can be used to elicit ideas, guide thought processes, probe for understanding, increase involvement, and facilitate analysis or synthesis of an idea. To ask effective questions, an instructor must use skill in asking the question, as well as recognize its purpose. In addition to stating the question verbally, the instructor should post the question on the board or screen so that students have time to carefully study the question. Give students time to think and process the question and their answer. This wait time, often suggested as three seconds after posing the question, has been shown to improve both the quality and the length of the answers. Ask several students to explain the thinking behind their answer. The explanation reveals both logic and potential misconceptions.

Closed questions have a single answer that may be simply stated in a choral response (2 + 2 is ?) or selected from a list, such as a multiple-choice question. Closed questions offer a quick way to assess factual learning and can be used throughout a lesson to increase motivation, change the pacing, and provide feedback to both the students and the instructor. Answers can be collected in a number of ways. Although choral responses are quick, they provide the instructor with limited information about student thinking or variations in their thinking. Choral responses also allow some students to opt out of participation. More effective techniques collect answers from all students quickly and in an active way. A show of hands can work well for agreement or disagreement with a statement, as can a signal of thumbs up, thumbs down, or neutral. Colored pieces of paper with the letters A, B, C, and D on them can be used to collect answers to multiple-choice questions, allowing the instructor to get a quick visual scan of the diversity of answers. Classroom response systems (see next section) are another way to collect such data. In other instances, white boards and markers can be used to collect graphical information, such as the rate of a reaction over time.

Open questions ask students to craft explanations, state relationships, evaluate an idea, or apply a concept to a new setting. Stems for open questions that encourage learning include

- What did you observe?
- What do you think happened?
- How do we know?
- How does this compare to…?
- What other factors might be involved?
- How could we find out?
- How could we test this idea?
- What evidence do we have for…?

Because the answers to open-ended questions are unlimited, they are not conducive to choral responses. Instead, consider having students record their answers in writing (see section on minute papers later in this chapter) or share their explanations with a partner (see section on think-pair-share later in this chapter). As an instructor, you will then need to determine how to collect or present representative answers so that students can gain feedback on their thinking. Calling on random groups to report out to the class is one strategy, as is reading selected answers and discussing them the next day. The important point is to engage students in thinking about the topic and to collect the feedback to adjust teaching and student learning.

Classroom Response Systems

Classroom response systems, or "clickers," allow an instructor to pose a question and collect student responses through the use of a remote control–like system. Each student has a battery-powered clicker with a number of labeled buttons (a, b, c, etc., or 1, 2, 3, etc.). Classroom receivers collect and tally the student signals electronically and post the information in graphic form. Since names are not attached, the instructor can assess student thinking without the risk of embarrassment. For more information on how to implement such a system, see Duncan (2005).

Clickers enhance interactive teaching by actively involving students in the learning process. Students interact with the lecture material at a personal level and with peer-to-peer interactions, resulting in increased learning and retention of concepts. Every student will be questioned and their answers recorded several times during the class. As a result class attendance tends to increase (Burnstein and Lederman 2001; Jackson, Trees, and Dickerson 2004).

Instructors like the energy that clickers bring to the classroom. Clickers enable instructors to frequently check for understanding and assess students' prior knowledge and misconceptions before beginning a new topic. Both simple recall and conceptual questions can be used. Recall questions can be used to determine if students have read the assignment but may reinforce memorization of facts as opposed to the development of conceptual understanding. Conceptual questions, while providing students with feedback, are most effective when coupled with peer discussions. Students can answer the concept-based question individually, see the correct answer, and then discuss with a peer or peers. Effective peer discussions require that about half of the students know the correct answer (Duncan 2005). Another strategy is for students to discuss the question, try to convince each other of the correct answer, and then answer the question. Working in small groups this way facilitates deeper thinking, clarifies conceptual understanding, and allows for the exploration of ideas, while diminishing student anxiety (Mazur 1997; see also Chapter 8 in this volume).

Think-Pair-Share Structures

Think-pair-share is a cooperative learning strategy that probes student thinking, challenges students' prior knowledge, and engages students in peer discussions. Students are asked to think about a question, issue, or problem for a minute, spend a minute recording their thoughts, and then share their thinking with a partner. The pair then continues the discussion to arrive at a consensus that is presented to the class. A safe learning environment in which all answers and opinions are valued is required for this strategy to be effective. Instructors need to visit student groups to listen to answers, ask probing questions, and reinforce productive discussion behaviors.

The think-pair-share strategy may be used for students to summarize an assigned reading or the main points of a lecture, react to an issue, determine the solution to a problem, check and clarify notes, or defend a reaction to a lecture point (Johnson, Johnson, and Smith 1998). This strategy leads to the expression of different viewpoints and synthesis of information, while lowering student anxiety because students are working with peers. Through discussion, students often find gaps in understanding, and listening to peers may lead to new insights.

Evaluating Learning

While closely aligned with engagement strategies, closure strategies help students extend, apply, or synthesize learning and provide feedback regarding the quality of the learning that has occurred.

Group Concept Maps

A concept map is a tool to help organize information and review ideas, synthesize disjointed facts and ideas, reinforce previously learned concepts, and show the relationship among ideas. Concept maps require students to use their current knowledge to develop hierarchies of ideas and their relationships. Instructors should model what is expected and provide students with steps to completing a concept map (Uno 2002; see also Chapter 7 in this volume).

Group concept maps are more complex than individual concept maps. Overarching ideas and interconnections are discovered through active student discussions of topics and how they relate and interrelate. Group concept maps can be open-ended, with the students selecting the words and linking them, or the words can be selected by the instructor while students create the map and show the linkages. For instance, students could be instructed to make a concept map using 25 provided words and two wild cards. The product is then presented and explained to the class, which allows the instructor to evaluate student understanding.

Minute Paper

The minute paper is a popular technique used to collect quick, formative feedback from a group of students (Angelo and Cross 1993). The process is quite simple. At the end of the class period, the instructor poses one or more open-ended questions about the day's content. The following are typical stems: "What are the two [three, four, five] most significant [central, useful, meaningful, surprising, disturbing, confusing] things you have learned during this session? "What questions do you still have?" The question can remain general or can be targeted to a particular concept.

The students answer the questions either on their own papers or on a 3×5 card and submit them before leaving class. The instructor tells the students to either sign the papers or cards or to submit them anonymously, depending on the purpose of the assignment. Anonymous responses may increase student comfort with providing feedback. Signed responses may also act as a tool to collect attendance and allow for personal responses to students. Once the responses are collected, the instructor reads them and groups them according to common answers. Most instructors find that they can read and group about four responses in a minute. If the responses are used for attendance purposes and if the instructor chooses to respond to the students, processing will take about one minute per paper. This information can be used to adjust the teaching for the following day, and answers should be discussed with the class.

Variations of this technique include collecting minute papers from only one recitation section rather than the whole class, having students e-mail their responses, or posting responses to a web site. In all cases, a minute paper allows students to review and synthesize the information presented and to restate it in their own terms, and it allows the instructor access to student learning. The process aids in concept retention and fosters higher-order thinking skills, particularly when the technique is used on a regular basis.

Bonus Point Questions

Many students comprehend and retain material better when tested frequently. In fact, short tests at the end of each day's lecture can double the retention of the lecture material on an exam (Uno 2002). Daily quizzes encourage students to review presented material and read the text on a regular basis instead of cramming the night before an exam and provide students with examples of the level of comprehension required to be successful in the course. Giving and grading daily quizzes, however, is time-consuming. One alternative is to have the students answer a single multiple-choice question on a 3×5 card. The answer would include the student's name, the letter of their selected answer, and an explanation of why they believe their answer to be correct. This last step stimulates students to reflect about concepts, helps uncover gaps in their understanding, fosters refinement and revision of knowledge, and alerts the instructor to potential misconceptions prior to the exam. The cards are quickly graded by scanning for the correct letter choice and only reading the explanations on those cards. Each correct answer is worth 1 point of extra credit. It is possible to have the correct letter answer but not receive a bonus point if an explanation is lacking or incorrect.

This is a low-risk strategy for assessing student knowledge because there is no penalty for not knowing the answer, and it provides a student incentive for learning through the extra credit point. Common errors and misconceptions can be discussed in class at the beginning of the following period. The cards can also used to monitor attendance, and cheating is kept in check by requiring students to explain their answers.

Summary

Active-learning strategies can be used throughout the course to involve students in the learning process. The opportunities for students to interact with lecture materials and to apply, integrate, and make sense of the course content leads to increased learning (Michael and Modell 2003). In addition, many of the strategies described here have been shown to increase attendance, improve student motivation, aid in the recruitment and retention of underrepresented populations in science, and ultimately improve student course success. In the process, learning becomes a personal and active process. Students are challenged to read, think, and interact with the lecture material by answering questions and engaging in peer-to-peer discussions, helping them gain a sense of accomplishment and satisfaction through learning. Perhaps as important, through the use of active-learning techniques, the instructor becomes a partner in student learning, which can renew enthusiasm for teaching while gaining continual feedback that can be used to adjust classroom practice. Through active-learning strategies, everyone can be a winner in the game of science!

References

Angelo, T., and P. Cross. 1993. *Classroom assessment techniques.* 2nd ed. San Francisco: Jossey-Bass.

Bransford, J.D., A. L. Brown, and R. R. Cocking. 1999. *How people learn: Brain, mind, experience, and school.* Washington, DC: National Academy Press.

Burnstein, R., and L. Lederman. 2001. Using wireless keypads in lecture classes. *The Physics Teacher* 39: 8–11.

Business-Higher Education Forum. 2003. *Building a nation of learners: The need for changes in teaching and learning to meet global challenges.* Washington, DC: Business-Higher Education Forum.

Duncan, D. 2005. *Clickers in the classroom: How to enhance science teaching using classroom response systems.* San Francisco: Pearson/Addison Wesley.

Jackson, M. H., A. R. Trees, and J. A. Dickerson. 2004. The learning environment in clicker classrooms: Student processes of learning and involvement in large courses using student response systems. Paper presented at the National Communication Association Conference, Chicago, IL.

Johnson, D., R. Johnson, and K. Smith. 1998. *Active learning: Cooperation in the college classroom.* Edina, MN: Interaction Book Company.

Mazur, E. 1997. *Peer Instruction: A user's manual.* Upper Saddle River, NJ: Prentice Hall.

McKeachie, W. J. 2002. *McKeachie's teaching tips: Strategies, research, and theory for college and university teachers.* 11th ed. Boston: Houghton Mifflin.

Michael, J. A., and H. I. Modell. 2003. *Active learning in secondary and college science classrooms.* Mahwah, NJ: Erlbaum.

National Research Council (NRC). 1996. *National science education standards.* Washington, DC: National Academy Press.

National Research Council (NRC). 2000. *Inquiry and the national science education standards: A guide for teaching and learning.* Washington, DC: National Academy Press.

Novak, G. M., E. T. Patterson, A. D. Gavrin, and W. Christian. 1999. *Just-in-Time Teaching: Blending active learning with web technology.* Upper Saddle River, NJ: Prentice Hall.

Uno, G. 2002. *Handbook on teaching undergraduate science courses: A survival training manual.* Pacific Grove, CA: Brooks/Cole.

Innovative Teaching Approaches

Learning how to tackle scientific literature is a daunting task. It is clear that learning how to read primary literature is a skill that is developed throughout one's scientific career. With guidance, practice, and consistent exposure, students can begin developing these skills in their undergraduate science courses. —Brian Rybarczyk

When designing college science courses, we sometimes forget that real science is done not only at the desk and the laboratory bench, but also in the field. Thus, authentic course work calls for a field component. [It is] often the most inspiring and memorable feature of a course. —James H. Wandersee and Renee M. Clary

Storytelling permeates the human experience. It is found on street corners, in bars, in living rooms, and playgrounds; it exists wherever people gather, be it around campfires or TV sets. Stories set cultural norms, provide us with heroes and demons, warn us of folly, and give us reason to hope for better days. They are with us from the day we are born until the moment when we shuffle off this mortal coil. They make us human. Not surprisingly, great teachers are often great storytellers. —Clyde Freeman Herreid

By mating ideas and methods from scientists like Charles Darwin with those of poets like Emily Dickinson, students discover new perspectives on scientific issues that are rich in both content and personal meaning because they arise from the student's own creativity. —Jerry A. Waldvogel

Focusing on a learning environment that emphasizes only content knowledge through problem-solving and critical-thinking skills, some science instructors could be shortchanging their students.... We need to expand our pedagogies and embrace learning strategies that integrate the development of effective citizenry, as well as respect for others' identities and cultures. —Maureen A. Scharberg

For decades, reports, presentations, and articles have recommended that rather than serve as a place to verify facts and concepts presented in lecture, laboratories should provide opportunities for students to engage in activities such as asking questions, formulating hypotheses, designing experiments, collecting and analyzing data, and interpreting and presenting results in a formal (oral or written) manner. In short, we should give students practice acting like scientists if we want them to become scientists or scientifically literate citizens. —Donald P. French and Connie P. Russell

Are students of the 21st century really that different from those of the 20th, and if so, what does that mean for college science teachers? For many of us, one of the attractions of our profession is the opportunity it affords to try new approaches and to tinker with and modify old ones. The challenge of a new generation of students requires us to reflect on our daily practices and to accommodate them to an entirely different set of demands and expectations. Meeting these new expectations with innovative solutions can be a stimulating and rejuvenating process. In this unit several authors describe some of the problems they've encountered in working with college science students and the solutions they have devised.

Brian Rybarczyk of the University of North Carolina at Chapel Hill describes the long-standing problem of introducing students to the *primary research literature* in science. Among the issues he addresses are the challenges of using peer-reviewed research articles in undergraduate science courses, where to find and how to select such articles, and ways of integrating current research articles into the undergraduate course.

Jim Wandersee of Louisiana State University and Renee Clary of Northwestern State University (Louisiana) discuss the unique value of *fieldwork* in college biology and geology courses. As a teaching tool, field experiences offer a matchless opportunity to motivate students, to encourage them to integrate and apply their knowledge in a natural environment, and to gain practical skills in observation, sampling, collection, and analysis of data. Jim and Renee describe several interesting field-based programs at universities in various regions of the United States.

Clyde "Kip" Herreid offers an overview of the well-known *case studies* approach he has pioneered in the biology department at the University at Buffalo. The website he and his colleagues maintain contains several hundred cases in virtually every science discipline, ranging from anatomy and physiology to physics and engineering. Each case presents an intriguing and sometimes controversial story that draws students into an active-learning context and poses questions for discussion and collaborative activity. Kip discusses several methods for integrating cases into undergraduate science courses and some of the strengths and weaknesses of these methods.

Jerry Waldvogel of Clemson University reminds us that undergraduate courses can serve as a unique vehicle for helping students integrate scientific and humanistic knowledge and values. He encourages us to think about the long-standing separation between the humanities and natural sciences and describes his efforts to use *poetry* as a way of stimulating creativity, connectivity, and critical thinking. Included in the chapter are three of his students' original poems.

In the chemistry department of San Jose State University, Maureen Scharberg encourages students to venture beyond the traditional goals of mastering content knowledge and analytical skills; she seeks to prepare them for the 21st century workforce. In addition to the conventional goals of science courses, Maureen focuses on leadership skills, teamwork, problem solving, time management, self-management, adaptability, global consciousness, and communication. In her chapter she describes her efforts to create *learning partnerships,* which encourage students to reflect on and explore their own values and to learn respect for others' identities and cultures.

At Oklahoma State University, Don French and Connie Russell converted their traditional, verification-style laboratory in biology into an opportunity for *investigation*. Inquiry laboratories enable students to experience the creative side of science, to learn about experimental design, to engage in scientific thinking, and to wrestle with rules of evidence as they make observations, pose questions, formulate and test hypotheses, draw conclusions, and communicate their results. In this chapter Don and Connie provide a research-based rationale for inquiry-style laboratories, a model based on their own experiences, and a set of recommendations for those who would follow their lead. An assessment of their revised course is included.

CHAPTER 16

Incorporating Primary Literature Into Science Learning

Brian Rybarczyk

Brian Rybarczyk is coordinator of undergraduate initiatives for the Partnership for Minority Advancement in the Biomolecular Sciences at the Institute for Science Learning, University of North Carolina at Chapel Hill. He earned a PhD in pathology at the University of Rochester and conducts research in the mechanisms of disease and molecular evolution. He teaches courses in the molecular basis of disease and general biology.

How do you eat an elephant? ... One bite at a time.

Why is it important for undergraduate students to learn how to read scientific literature in science courses? Educational initiatives such as Beyond Bio 101 (Howard Hughes Medical Institute, n.d.), BIO2010 (National Research Council, Board on Life Sciences 2003), and Project 2061 of the American Association for the Advancement of Science (*www.project2061.org*) call for changes in science education that promote the development of students' scientific skills, such as interpreting data, applying concepts, and synthesizing information. Although these initiatives do not explicitly recommend incorporating primary literature as a component of undergraduate science education, instruction with primary literature can promote these skills.

In this chapter *primary literature* refers to original, research-based articles found in peer-reviewed journals. The goals for learning how to read primary literature support the overarching goals of students' scientific skills development and specifically include (1) gaining important insights into the nature of science as a process (based on experiments) rather than as a collection of facts (as presented in traditional textbooks), (2) engaging with the primary form of scientific communication, (3) developing deeper learning associated with hands-on research projects, (4) building analytical skills, (5) synthesizing bodies of literature creating an interdisciplinary perspective on the nature of science, and (6) keeping abreast with current scientific knowledge.

Challenges Faced When Using Primary Literature as a Learning Tool

Instructors may not readily incorporate primary scientific literature into course work because (a) they may feel that they are not able to cover sufficient content if time is spent analyzing an article with students, (b) they don't want to take the time to teach students how to read primary literature, or (c) they may not see the value of incorporating primary literature in their courses. If instructors do assign primary literature, it is usually as a supplement to textbook reading and sufficient time is not always designated for teaching students how to read a primary journal article. From the student perspective, students may feel overwhelmed with unfamiliar terminology, may be confused about identifying what is important and what is not, may have to deal with gaps in knowledge, and may fear that they have to comprehend the entire article on first pass, determine how the article fits into a larger body of scientific inquiry, and articulate the implications of the research findings. Students are faced with learning the purpose of each section of an article, how to summarize results and analyze data, and how to propose future research directions.

Science education literature describes numerous methods that guide instructors in helping students develop skills while reading primary literature such as critical analysis, generating alternative explanations, designing experiments, seeing science as a process rather than a collection of facts, improving communication skills, and building confidence in discussing and interpreting science. Instructors should remember that students need time to develop these skills throughout their undergraduate years. With some creativity, instructors can integrate primary literature into their courses without compromising time and content coverage. This chapter is designed to assist undergraduate science faculty in guiding students' scientific literacy using primary literature. Sections of the chapter cover where to find applicable scientific literature suited for courses, how to select appropriate journal articles, and strategies and additional pedagogical ideas for incorporating primary literature into courses.

Where to Find Journal Articles for a Course

You have decided that incorporating primary literature will be a valuable component of your course. Now, where do you find the articles most appropriate for student learning? Sources of scientific literature include general, peer-reviewed research journals (e.g., *Science* and *Nature*), discipline-specific peer-reviewed research journals, and open-source journals. Table 16.1 lists resources, searchable databases, and open-access publishers. Check with your campus library for a complete list of subscriptions (both electronic and paper) for journals of interest. It is also helpful to consult science news journals such as *The Scientist* and *New Scientist* for reviews on the latest research findings. The articles in these journals contain references to primary literature cited. These articles might also serve as a springboard into primary literature for students since they give both a general overview and multiple perspectives and describe conflicting data.

Selecting Articles for a Course

Once you have narrowed down the most important research articles that will enhance the students' learning experiences in your course, how do you select the most appropriate articles that support the content, keeping in mind the students' limited outside class time and realistic expectations? Some general questions to ask are the following: Should students develop an understanding of the material or develop critical analysis skills? Should students gain knowledge

Table 16.1

Sources of Scientific Literature

Source	Description	Website
Science	Original research	*http://intl.sciencemag.org*
Nature	Original research	*www.nature.com*
BioMed Central	Open access publisher	*www.biomedcentral.com*
PubMed Central	Access to life science journals	*www.pubmedcentral.nih.gov*
Directory of Open Access Journals	Comprehensive list of open access journals in multiple disciplines	*www.doaj.org*
Public Library of Science (PLoS)	Open-source publications of research articles covering biology, genetics, medicine, pathogens, and so forth	*www.plos.org*
The Scientist	Science news journal	*www.the-scientist.com*
New Scientist	Science news journal	*www.newscientist.com*

of a specific concept, learn how a technique is performed, or compare different experimental approaches to similar research questions? Additional questions (from Muench 2000, pp. 256, 257, and 259) include

- What are the educational goals of the course?
- What are the goals of the assignments?
- What concepts must the reader understand?
- Is the relationship between the data and the conclusions simple and direct or complex and abstract?
- What else can the student learn from the paper?

Generally, it is best to choose papers that fit well with course concepts without extraneous background or additional knowledge beyond students' knowledge. Select articles with "hooks," such as papers with obvious practical or social significance or that deal with current controversies in the news. Initially, use articles that incorporate a limited number of experimental steps. This will decrease students' frustrations with conceptual comprehension. Another strategy is to select multiple articles from the same investigator or the same line of inquiry to demonstrate the iterative process of science. Students can then see how a particular line of evidence is developed and how a research question is investigated over time as new findings are discovered. Chosen articles should illustrate concepts as well as engage in the process of science. As a general rule of thumb, keep in mind your audience: for nonmajors, use articles written for a general scientific audience; for majors, choose discipline-specific literature.

Techniques to Incorporate Literature as Learning Experiences

You have decided that incorporating scientific literature into your course will greatly benefit your students and you have selected key articles that will augment the course content. Now, how do you effectively incorporate the literature into the learning environment? The following subsections provide an overview of published articles describing how other instructors have successfully incorporated primary literature into their science courses and curriculum.

Process-Based Approach

A process-based approach is a formulation of stages or steps that guide students through reading primary literature. The main goals of the approach are to expose students to research methods, research questions, critical analysis of conclusions, the ways scientists solve questions, and an emphasis on research as a process. One version of this approach integrated four research studies highlighting concepts in a biology curriculum (Yarden, Brill, and Falk 2001). The strategies for implementation include modifying sections of an article with explanatory information, deleting extraneous details, focusing on the main figures of an article, and expanding the discussion section with explanations of implicit assumptions. Questions to think about are added for students as they read the article, guiding the entire process.

A second process-based approach sets goals of sophisticated subject-matter mastery and the development of process skills (DebBurman 2002). The approach involves a series of five steps, the first of which is multiple readings of one article. The students read the article with the instructor and other students, then the students present a summarized version of the paper to their peers. The second step involves students summarizing other articles and writing a review report as if it were going to be published in a newspaper. Third, students write a review about a disease of their choice, using primary literature sources, and, fourth, they present the disease in a symposium forum. Finally, the students write a lab report in the format of a primary journal article focused on a lab experiment they are performing in the course. Two keys to the success of this approach are incorporating guided discussions and consistent contacts with the instructor throughout the five-step process.

Progressive Approach

Other instructors introduce scientific literature to students using a progressive approach. This approach distills down individual parts of a primary journal article, allowing students to focus on specific parts of the article instead of the entire article all at once. Guided literature explorations are used in which students are exposed to primary literature in an introductory biology course by initially exploring basic statistics, graph interpretations, and how to perform a library search (Smith 2001). Students then work with individual parts of a paper, with the instructor providing a summary of the introduction and methods section. Students are then given tables and figures and asked to draw conclusions. Next, students are provided the authors' actual wording (still abbreviated) with the figures and tables and asked to interpret and draw conclusions from results. Finally, students are given an entire paper along with a set of guiding questions. Building students' confidence first will allow for decreased apprehension and increased comprehension.

A similar progressive approach was proposed by choosing articles from sources written for general scientists to introduce students to primary literature (Herman 1999). The instructor provides the students with just the introduction section, and the students have to define unfamiliar terms and phrases. The students then answer questions about the content within the introduction section and discuss the answers in small groups. The same strategy is used for subsequent sections of the paper. The results of such an approach indicated that students developed more technically sophisticated research projects, increased retention of content, and learned how to apply knowledge to new articles.

Student Presentation Approach

At scientific conferences, scientists communicate results from research studies through oral and poster presentations. Simulating scientific symposia is another effective method for students to interact with primary literature. Students read and prepare a class presentation that explains the research from an article to other students (Houde 2000). Explaining a topic to others is an effective way to ensure that students comprehend what they are reading, analyze the experimental methods, and evaluate results. This approach also develops students' oral communication skills and confidence in translating science to others. It is essential that instructors create a grading rubric for these activities so students know what is expected during the presentation. Students reported increased confidence in presenting information found in research articles, interpreting graphs, and working with statistical analyses.

Another example describes using poster presentations to build students' skills in reading scientific literature, communication, and collaboration with peers in a cell physiology course (Mulnix 2003). Small groups of students read and present the results of an article to their peers in a visual format (scientific poster). They develop skills in communication and group work and build their confidence as a result of this exercise. This approach can be modified and used in other science courses.

Analytical Approach

For students in the sciences, it is as important to develop and master analytic skills as it is to comprehend the content of a scientific article. An analytical approach for incorporating primary literature into courses focuses on developing students' critical analysis skills. Instructors provide students with guidelines for reading a paper and ask the students to highlight important points in the article. Then, students write a critique of the article before the class discussion, including an evaluation of the strength of the data presented and the authors' interpretations (Janick-Buckner 1997). During class, students proceed through the paper, analyzing each figure for experimental design and interpretations of the results. During this student-centered discussion, the instructor becomes a facilitator/moderator, ensuring that students are on task and addressing other issues raised by the students. Student feedback indicated perceived improved skills in reading primary literature, designing experiments, and interpreting data using this approach.

An alternative method is a four-tier approach in a computer-conferencing environment to develop students' analytical skills (Klemm 2002). The four tiers of this inquiry model include understanding the content of the article, assessing the experimental strategies and methods, integrating the paper into a broader context of knowledge, and creating new insights. Students are grouped into small teams and asked to identify parts of the paper that they do not understand and parts for which they need additional information. Each group comments on other students' annotations and provides answers to other students' questions. Next, students critique the methods, results, and conclusions presented in the paper. These comments are focused on addressing the experimental biases, alternative explanations of results, adequacy of statistical methods, and quality of supportive evidence. Students then integrate the article into a context of what is already known about the topic, analyze the paper from interdisciplinary perspectives, and appraise the article's significance. Students propose questions, new hypotheses, and experimental designs as next steps in the research process. Results of this approach have shown increased individual student accountability for work contributed, increased ownership in the learning process, and improved analytical skills.

Case Study Approach

Case studies are pedagogical tools that incorporate an engaging and/or controversial story, usually a dilemma, focused on contemporary issues in science and supported with thought-provoking questions (see Chapter 18 in this volume). Case studies provide a context in which students develop collaboration skills, analysis and critical-thinking skills, and communication skills. Primary literature can be transformed into case studies (Camill 2000; Herreid 1994). One example describes how data collected by environmental biologists are compiled into an interrupted case study format (Camill 2000). The case study engages students in the process of science through selected data and information about wetland ecology. Students interpret the data in response to real-world ecological issues and dilemmas such as wetland function, wetland protection, government regulations, and long-term impacts of ecological change. Tips for using cases based on primary literature include identification of articles that best represent the concepts students should grasp, exposure of students to laboratory techniques and field-work protocols, and working through the scientific process with actual data.

In a slightly different use of case studies, an instructor provides students with cases focused on a wide range of topics, including HIV/AIDS, biodiversity, and drug abuse, and asks them to research possible solutions to questions presented in the case based on primary research articles (Mangurian et al. 2001). Students select a case of interest, collect references, and analyze the references to answer the questions posed. Again, the case provides a context for the activity and a rationale for using primary literature. Students also learn how to distinguish between scientifically valid and nonreliable sources of scientific information.

Concept Map Approach

A concept map is a graphical representation that illustrates connections between concepts, ideas, topics, and facts (Novak, Gowin, and Johansen 1983; see also Chapter 7 in this volume). Students can use concept mapping techniques while reading primary literature to compare and contrast scientific theories and to elucidate experimental approaches. One example of this approach used the classic 1953 Watson and Crick paper describing the structure of DNA; students illustrated differences between hypothesized DNA structures (Kinchin 2005). This approach to reading primary literature can be applied to other articles that describe conflicting data from multiple research laboratories, alternative explanations for experimental data, and complex experimental designs or intricate results. For visuospatial learners who rely more heavily on graphics rather than text as a main learning input, this approach may augment their level of comprehension and subject mastery and allow them to demonstrate comprehension more effectively.

Additional Ways to Use Primary Literature

Additional pedagogical techniques that actively engage students with research-based scientific literature leading to increased scientific literacy are listed on page 165.

- *Ask students to perform data analysis in small groups:* Each group analyzes one figure, graph, or table from a journal article and discusses the content with their peers. The students communicate their observations and generate conclusions from the data. The instructor can omit the accompanying figure legends so that the students practice describing the data. Once all groups analyze the assigned figures, each group presents the data, the class discusses the observations together, and students create overall conclusions from the complete data set.

- *Omit the title of the journal article:* After a complete analysis of the article, students create a title that appropriately describes the main point(s) of the article. Instructors can provide titles from other articles as examples.

- *Omit the abstract of the article:* Instructors provide the students with only the figures and tables. After data analysis, students write an abstract that summarizes the paper based on the figures alone.

- *Provide conflicting data sets from different research studies that address the same research question:* Students hypothesize reasons for the conflicting results, generate explanations to rectify the differences, and discuss the implications of conflicting data in the scientific community.

- *Ask students to investigate experimental methods:* From a written description of experimental methods, students diagram the procedures in a flowchart and indicate expected results at each step in the procedure. This approach is ideally suited for laboratory-based courses.

- *Ask students to interpret text explanations of results:* From a written description of experimental results, students draw graphs and charts of the experimental results in visual form.

- *Incorporate articles found in science news journals such as* The Scientist *and* New Scientist: The types of articles found in these journals typically integrate bodies of research based on multiple primary literature articles and could serve as an introduction to a body of research.

- *Ask students to perform data manipulation:* With the call for data sharing in the scientific community, journals now encourage or require authors to make their data freely accessible via web pages or deposit them in locally managed or national databases (e.g., the National Center for Biotechnology Information, *www.ncbi.nih.gov*). Examples of available biological data include gene expression quantification from microarray analyses, DNA and protein sequences generated from experiments, and protein structure information. Some learning modules have already been created based on original data from primary literature, allowing students to manipulate real experimental data (see *http://bioquest. org/bedrock*). Using the internet, students can access the data and recreate the experiments, formulate new hypotheses and research questions, test alternative hypotheses, and draw novel conclusions.

Summary

Learning how to tackle scientific literature is a daunting task. It is clear that learning how to read primary literature is a skill that is developed throughout one's scientific career. With guidance, practice, and consistent exposure, students can begin developing these skills in their undergraduate science courses. Many approaches have been shown to be effective. This chapter has reviewed the importance of students interacting with primary literature, where to locate primary literature that supports course content, how to determine which articles to include, and multiple approaches for integrating scientific literature into courses. Collectively, the following general themes can be gleaned from the pedagogical approaches: gradually incorporate aspects of scientific literature into a course or curriculum rather than forcing students to read an entire article all at once; ensure students don't get frustrated with unfamiliar terminology; develop analytical skills, draw connections, and reinforce the relevance between articles chosen and course content. As a result, students will approach subsequent research articles with less apprehension and will be able to effectively communicate research discoveries to others and to critically analyze bodies of experimental research—skills that are essential for their advancement in science.

References

Camill, P. 2000. Using journal articles in an environmental biology course. *Journal of College Science Teaching* 30 (1): 38–43.

Committee on Undergraduate Biology Education to Prepare Research Scientists for the 21st Century. 2003. *BIO2010: Transforming undergraduate education for future research biologists.* Washington, DC: National Academies Press.

DebBurman, S. K. 2002. Learning how scientists work: Experiential research projects to promote cell biology learning and scientific process skills. *Cell Biology Education* 1: 154–172.

Herman, C. 1999. Reading the literature in the jargon-intensive field of molecular genetics. *Journal of College Science Teaching* 28 (4): 252–253.

Herreid, C. F. 1994. Journal articles as case studies—*The New England Journal of Medicine* on breast cancer. *Journal of College Science Teaching* 23 (6): 349–355.

Houde, A. 2000. Student symposia on primary research articles. *Journal of College Science Teaching* 30 (3): 184–187.

Howard Hughes Medical Institute. n.d. *Beyond Bio 101: The transformation of undergraduate biology education. www. hhmi.org/BeyondBio101*

Janick-Buckner, D. 1997. Getting undergraduates to critically read and discuss primary literature. *Journal of College Science Teaching* 27 (1): 29–32.

Kinchin, I. M. 2005. Reading scientific papers for understanding: Revisiting Watson and Crick (1953). *Journal of Biological Education* 39 (2): 73–75.

Klemm, W. R. 2002. FORUM for case study learning. *Journal of College Science Teaching* 31 (5): 298–302.

Mangurian, L., S. Feldman, J. Clements, and L. Boucher. 2001. Analyzing and communicating scientific information: A Towson Transition Course to hone students' scientific skills. *Journal of College Science Teaching* 30 (7): 440–445.

Muench, S. B. 2000. Choosing primary literature in biology to achieve specific educational goals. *Journal of College Science Teaching* 29 (4): 255–260.

Mulnix, A. B. 2003. Investigations of protein structure and function using the scientific literature: An assignment for an undergraduate cell physiology course. *Cell Biology Education* 2: 248–255.

Novak, J. D., D. B. Gowin, and G. T. Johansen. 1983. The use of concept mapping and knowledge vee mapping with junior high school science students. *Science Education* 67 (5): 625–645.

Smith, G. R. 2001. Guided literature explorations. *Journal of College Science Teaching* 30 (7): 465–469.

Yarden, A., G. Brill, and H. Falk. 2001. Primary literature as a basis for a high-school biology curriculum. *Journal of Biological Education* 35 (4): 190–195.

CHAPTER 17

Fieldwork:
New Directions and Exemplars in Informal Science Education Research

James H. Wandersee and Renee M. Clary

James H. Wandersee is William LeBlanc Alumni Association Professor of Biology Education at Louisiana State University. He earned a PhD in curriculum and instruction (science) at Marquette University and completed postdoctoral work in biology education at Cornell University. He conducts research in biology and geobiology instruction, scientific visualization, and the history of science. He also teaches numerous courses in science education.

Renee M. Clary teaches courses in geology and geology education in the Geosciences Department at Mississippi State University. She earned a PhD in curriculum and instruction (geoscience) at Louisiana State University and conducts research in geology and geobiology instruction, scientific visualization, the history of science, and the incorporation of technology in online and traditional classrooms. A fellow of the Geological Society of London, she cofounded EarthScholars research group in 2002 with James H. Wandersee.

M ost scientists would agree that some combination of content, process, and application drives them professionally and attracts many students to scientific pursuits (Camill 2000; Felder 1993). To deliver this constructive mixture within a college science course requires something other than a plethora of PowerPoint slides, heavy reading assignments, and the threat of regular pencil-and-paper tests.

So why doesn't all college science instruction provide this desired richness of process, content, and application? In courses that lack active-learning strategies (Michael and Modell 2003), the majority of class time is spent in formal lectures, occasional demonstrations, and the teaching laboratory's tranquilizing analogue of lecture—replicating cookbook laboratory exercises and performing verification activities (Camill 2000; McComas 1996).

The Importance of Fieldwork in Informal Science Education Settings

While such approaches may sometimes do a passable job of teaching content and process, we think that field experiences within informal science education settings are essential for motivating learning and for driving knowledge application and knowledge integration. Without those three field-based course components, the probability of student meaning-making is diminished.

King (1998) observed that "particularly in the case of modular degree courses, fieldwork can address and resolve the problem of compartmentalization of knowledge" (p. 1). We consider compartmentalization to be a major impediment to meaningful and mindful learning. We think students' disinterest in particular science topics and their failure to transfer what they have learned in the classroom to novel situations often stem from their lack of applicable and integrative experiences in real-world settings. College science teachers often emphasize *final form science* (Duschl 1990) and teach a *rhetoric of conclusions* (Schwab 1962) in an attempt to accelerate instruction and satisfy their department's expectations for substantial content coverage. In contrast, fieldwork helps students notice and identify relevant objects and phenomena of scientific interest within their natural settings (Wandersee and Schussler 2001) and, more importantly, begin to understand *how we know what we know* in science.

Fieldwork-Based Scientific Discoveries

Fieldwork can teach our students that although controlled experiments are one route to scientific knowledge, they are by no means the only route (McComas 1996). Sometimes nature conducts the experiment for us, and, from astronomy to zoology, many important discoveries have been and continue to be based on field observations.

An article published in the journal *Science* reported that, after more than 7,000 hours of field observation by a team of Cornell University researchers within 550,000 acres of swamps in Arkansas, at least one ivory-billed woodpecker—previously thought by many ornithological experts to have gone extinct—had been sighted (Milius 2005). Most conservationists and birders were ecstatic (Gorman and Revkin 2005). However, another team of bird authorities questioned the limited quantity and the resolution quality of the recorded data that were used to make the initial claim of species rediscovery. The dispute was resolved when subsequent analysis of 17,000 hours of audio recordings made that winter were compared with 1930s archived recordings made in Louisiana of the bird's vocalizations and drumming. In fact, this new and more robust audio data, along with the benchmark data, convinced the skeptics that at least two members of the species are present in Arkansas.

Observing is not just perceiving, it is also the processing of information from sensory experience into forms that make thinking about it and making sense of it possible. To remove as many confounds as possible, observation and instrumental sampling should be conducted in places where the objects or events actually occur in nature. For example, most astronomers agree that Mauna Kea on the big island of Hawaii is the best astronomical observation site in the world because of optimal viewing conditions and instrumentation advantages (Dayton 2005). In addition, many scientific questions, such as the one about extinction, can only be answered in the field. Making careful field observations in carefully chosen locations, whether via human senses or by instrumentation, is often the keystone of scientific research programs.

Many scientific hypotheses originate in fieldwork. If we want students to think like scientists, for many disciplines fieldwork is essential. Paleobotanist Jennifer McElwain (Mullen

2004) asked her graduate students to collect leaf samples of living black oak trees at various altitudes in California. Using their own field-collected specimens, she taught them how to measure the density of leaf stomata in the laboratory. This work ultimately led to a mathematical relationship between stomatal density and altitude. She then applied this knowledge to fossilized black oak leaves to make paleoelevation estimates. The students learned that fieldwork can fuel laboratory work, and, in this case, the research findings led to methodological advances and improved theorizing in paleobotany.

Taking Students Into the Field

When designing college science courses, we sometimes forget that real science is done not only at the desk and the laboratory bench but also in the field. Thus, authentic course work calls for a field component. Often the most inspiring and memorable feature of a course, fieldwork may also require the most planning and effort. Inclement weather can sometimes make learning opportunities a bit less structured and predictable. Land access and safety practices are other key considerations. Fortunately, nature preserves, state and national forests, national parks, nature centers, arboretums, botanical gardens, fossil parks, zoos, and the like often have science education specialists available to help instructors in planning for teaching, choosing optimal locations for particular kinds of fieldwork, and tending to basic group needs—from parking places to picnic areas and restrooms. We recommend these sites especially to college science teachers who have never incorporated fieldwork into their courses. In weighing options, also consider the range of on-campus and field sites associated with your own college or university.

It is good to keep in mind that informal science education is learning that occurs outside of school. Whether it is open-ended or semistructured, it always involves more student choices and self-direction. It is less sequential but more experiential and exploratory than classroom science. It is a fine way to learn about scientific processes and to see applications, as well as to recognize the need to learn more science content.

Butler, Hall-Wallace, and Burgess (2000), a biology-geology teaching team that taught a freshman science seminar at the University of Arizona entitled "A Sense of Place," wrote, "Designed for students with little or no background in geology or biology, we emphasize teaching students to make careful and objective observations of their surroundings and to interpret the observations in the context of geologic and ecological systems" (p. 253). They said that teaching this seminar "reinforced for us the effectiveness of field experiences for integrating scientific concepts and teaching the scientific skill of observation" (p. 255). They also found that college students' attitudes toward science improved when they did fieldwork. This finding is supported by many other research studies, which they cited. Some students who completed this course commented on how relevant it was because it offered them "powerful local examples of many geological and ecological principles" (p. 254). Similarly, Abrams (1995) found that teaching biology with local examples rather than exotic ones improved student learning.

Our Stance on Integrative and Fieldwork-Driven Teaching

We ourselves are strong advocates of fieldwork-driven teaching and learning and of teaching for science knowledge integration. We like our students to raise initial questions and record personal "wonderings" in the field, often leading to the collection of specimens or samples that they can analyze in the laboratory and relate to the lectures. Similar to the aforementioned

University of Arizona team, our own EarthScholars research group (*www.EarthScholars.com*) comprises a botanist/biology educator and a geologist/geology educator. By working within and across scientific fields together, we are continually amazed at the insights, connections, and benefits we gain. All of our research studies focus on integrating biological and geological knowledge—both past and present, both graphic and textual—and its effects on student and public understanding of science in both formal and informal learning environments.

In this chapter we have selected a small set of field-based geology education and biology education research studies to demonstrate that the college science education research literature can help you teach your students more effectively in informal science education settings, while making your job and life more interesting. We begin with a field site study conducted by our research group, and we then summarize and discuss several studies that may apply to college geology and college biology teachers.

An Informal Geoscience Education Success Story: The Texas Geology Trail, University of North Texas

Some university campuses have developed trails to showcase local geology and geology-related building materials. Many of these trails use large areas with pathways that meander through sprawling university campuses and waypoints separated by vast distances. In contrast, at the University of North Texas (UNT), Professor Reid Ferring designed the Preston, Grant and Savannah Troutt Texas Geology Trail with $35,000 and leftover space adjacent to the Environmental Education, Science and Technology Building (see Figure 17.1).

Figure 17.1

An overhead view of the outdoor education area at Elm Fork Education Center, Denton, Texas. Note that the Texas Geology Trail runs along the area's left perimeter. (Photograph courtesy of Elm Fork Education Center.)

Trail Description

The trail features Texas rocks placed along a geological time sidewalk, labeled from the Achaean eon to the Quaternary period (see Figure 17.2). The trail begins in a mini-amphitheater with a wall-mounted, generalized geological map of Texas. Large rocks along the trail illustrate more than two billion years of Texas geological history, beginning with Proterozoic rocks and culminating with Cretaceous period specimens. The project is not yet finished—even more rocks will arrive, and the hinged propane tanks interspersed alongside the trail will open to reveal dioramas (see Figure 17.3).

History of Trail and Current Usage

We visited the Texas Geology Trail in April 2005 and spoke with Professor Ferring, Brian Wheeler (Elm Fork Education Center Exhibit Coordinator), and center docents about the trail's usage and plans for further development. We also observed local students and teachers who were visiting the center, and we gathered local documents about the site.

Dr. Ferring's idea for a geology trail was made possible through an alumna's monetary gift, coupled with material and labor donations from the Texas Aggregates and Concrete Association.

Figure 17.2

View from the beginning of the trail, heading up through geological time. Note the inset granite markers denoting geological time units within the walkway. (Photograph by R. Clary.)

Figure 17.3

View from midtrail, looking back toward the amphitheater. Hinged propane tanks will eventually open to reveal dioramas. (Photograph by R. Clary.)

Although the trail officially opened in June 2001, funding was consumed when the project was 66% complete. Currently, visitors to UNT can view the trail during Elm Fork Education Center's operating hours. The trail is used for university physical geology laboratory exercises, as well as for a one-week summer geology program for older elementary students. Although the Elm Fork Education Center serves 15,000 elementary students a year, the geology trail's role is currently rather peripheral to its programs.

Analysis of UNT Texas Geology Trail

The trail functions as a secure outdoor learning laboratory, providing a visual and tactile representation of the geological history of the state. Fortunately, Texas has great diversity in its rock types and ages. Rock placement moves beyond simple rock garden display to angled compilations that resemble naturally occurring outcrops. Many of the rocks are large and impressive. We think the trail is adaptable to curriculum goals in elementary through college educational settings.

There are some limitations. The security of the site, behind a tall fence, is not only a strength but also a liability: the site is not accessible to the public beyond UNT business hours. Unfortunately, time constraints dictated sidewalk development before the huge rocks arrived; thus the path's geological timeline is not to scale, nor is it explained. Rocks are not well aligned with their sidewalk period labels because of lack of space, rock size, and trail layout. In addition, not all rocks are labeled, and there is currently no trail guide or trail signage system for self-interpretation.

We do think that this unique and innovative informal geology trail could become a fine geobiology trail as well. At the present, even the period-linked living plants the designer intended are missing. The trail could be improved through rock correlation with the Texas geological map and correct positioning within an identified timeline. We suggest that an *evolutionary history of the Earth* theme be implemented, including period-linked animal representations and some fossil replicas, as well as the trailside plant inclusion. This will successfully integrate biological information within the trail for an effective geobiological experience. The trail also presents opportunities for rock types to be developed and linked to the rock cycle, as well as for their integration within the theory of plate tectonics. We suggest that thin sections of rocks, quarry photographs, and economic geology examples be added; these offer potential for further interpretive development within the trail. Our own research on writing high-quality interpretive science trail signs may also be useful (Wandersee and Clary, Forthcoming).

Summary

The UNT Texas Geology Trail demonstrates that a workable, multileveled outdoor learning laboratory based on geological time can be developed with limited capital and space. The trail is tied to local geology, geography, and the economy of the state and has the potential to incorporate the biology and evolutionary life history of Texas. This compact, building-side trail provides a model for other institutions to emulate, customize, and improve. The trail is also an excellent example of a partnership among an institution, its alumni, and industry within the state. We think it could serve as a sound prototype for researchers and institutions seeking outside funding for similar projects.

Informal Geology and Biology Education: Research and New Directions

Field excursions have always been popular in the geosciences. However, informal geoscience education has evolved far beyond the instructor-centered geology field trip of the past. As in geology, biology field trips and fieldwork have been standard in various specialized courses but less common in introductory courses or courses for nonmajors. Ironically, it is often fieldwork that motivates and convinces someone to major in geology or biology—thus we think fieldwork and informal science education experiences should be "front-loaded" in today's college science curricula. Our survey of recent science education research studies revealed that modern informal education in geology and biology tends to be increasingly multidisciplinary, innovative in its implementation of technology, and practically and locally adapted.

Integrated, Multidisciplinary Field Approaches

Although the previously mentioned University of Arizona teacher-researchers also designed a freshman course with a geology-biology focus, a University of Vermont course has several additional teaching dimensions. Drake and associates (1997) developed their introductory, multidisciplinary science course as a year-long, residentially based course for new students interested in science. Using local geology and biology as context, a small group of students was involved in a series of five experiential research projects around Lake Champlain and the Green Mountains during the fall semester. Each field experience was scaffolded by supplemental exercises, data analysis, and scientific communication. The spring semester shifted to students' independent study projects and was supplemented with weekly guest lectures.

High course satisfaction levels were reported by both students and instructors. Those students whose science interest was piqued in this course could continue in the geology program, substituting this field-based course for an introductory geology course. Drake and associates (1997) reported that students' "lack of exposure to subject matter is made up for by the enthusiasm and field experience" (p. 235). Improved student-faculty interactions early in a student's undergraduate program led to recruitment of more geology majors from this program than the traditional introductory course.

Innovative Technology Use in Informal Geology and Biology Field Education

Since technological advances are rapid and new research tools are continually being introduced and implemented within geology and biology, many educators acknowledge the need for students to experience technology integration in multidisciplinary informal educational settings. Authentic research experiences should involve authentic research tools. Woltemade and Stanitski-Martin (2002) studied their students' research experiences, based on comparisons of Next Generation Weather Radar (NEXRAD) estimates with field rain gauge measurements. Students used global positioning systems (GPS), geographic information systems (GIS), and an assortment of internet and computer graphic analysis tools. Woltemade and Stanitski-Martin based their study on research supporting effectiveness of small research groups, authentic research experience, problem-solving procedures, and the integration of field research and classroom instruction.

The investigation, based within a Pennsylvania watershed, involved four undergraduate students, three graduate students, and two faculty members. Across six months, the team monitored 63 rainfall events and analyzed discrepancies between field data and NEXRAD estimates. Students subsequently presented their research at a professional meeting. Postproject surveys revealed success on the four identified premises of quality teaching. The researchers estimated that the course could be scaled up to serve 20 students. We can also personally attest that informal field experiences, integrated with advanced analytical geochemistry instrumentation, can enhance students' authentic experiences (Clary et al., Forthcoming).

In biology education, using their own field-collected and greenhouse-cultivated medicinal plants, Hispanic and Native American students enrolled in the Medicinal Plants of the Southwest summer workshop at the University of New Mexico discovered the chemical and biological basis of their chosen plant's antimicrobial activity. This 2005 study, conducted by O'Connell and Lara, showed that the course attracted two kinds of students: students already interested in biomedical careers and those with an interest and some family knowledge of medicinal plants who had never considered biomedical careers. The students learned to use gas chromatograph / mass spectrometer chromatograms to analyze their field-collected target plants' extract profile. Following the first three seven-week summer workshops conducted by these teacher-researchers, 59% of the participants pursued a biomedical career and 85% agreed that the workshop sparked an interest in graduate school, while 80% said it helped them do college science course work.

Practical, Locally Adapted Informal Education Experiences

Weiss and Walters (2004) incorporated space technology tools in their informal geoscience experience but saw benefits in keeping the informal education site within the university campus. Their campus tour, developed for introductory geology students, incorporated GPS receivers. The researchers' goals were to provide self-paced opportunities for students to explore geological concepts in their everyday surroundings and to introduce them to GPS technology, a research tool with multidisciplinary applications.

For the actual walking tour, students worked in small groups, answered questions concerning a variety of geological materials and processes, and used GPS receivers to label campus map points and track GPS-stored waypoints. The researchers evaluated students' answers to map questions on the final laboratory test and reported that students who participated in the geology walking tour scored an average of 13% higher.

This type of informal education experience does not have to be on-campus. Wetzel (2002) incorporated geological building materials accessible within walking distance off-campus as resources for student research.

Haines and Blake (2005) of Towson University studied a senior-level field biology course for preservice elementary and middle school teachers who have already earned 14 science credits. It was devoted to ecology, human impacts on the local environment, and teaching. There were (a) three freshwater field trips (stream water quality testing, seining wetland organisms for habitat quality assessment, and touring a wastewater treatment plant), (b) one saltwater field trip (onboard an oyster rig in Chesapeake Bay to sample biodiversity), and (c) a student-planned environmental action project (creating a school-based outdoor native plant garden that maximizes runoff use and prevents it from entering Chesapeake Bay). When asked to compare the value of course components, students consistently ranked the five field experiences of highest value to them as future teachers—boosting their science content, process, and application knowledge. Many comments indicated surprise at how fragile the nearby Chesapeake Bay ecosystem is.

Conclusions

We have included only a small, selected sample of all the geology and biology education field-based research studies available to inform the college science teacher. Whatever your field of interest, you will find studies published in science education research books and journals that can improve your own teaching. The 1999 National Science Teacher Association's position statement on informal science education noted that informal science learning experiences and institutions offer powerful means to give students "direct access to scientists and other career role models in the sciences, as well as to opportunities for authentic science study." Such direct access is considered a valuable privilege by most college students. Instructors working with their students at a field site are much more accessible to students on a conversational basis and can show students that they actually *do* science as well as *teach* it. Often, a student's science major choice is based on getting to know a scientist. Some college courses may not be adaptable to fieldwork—so if yours *is*, consider it to be another powerful teaching option.

If you still do not think fieldwork in college science courses matters, consider English professor Susan Naomi Bernstein's inspirational 2003 essay. In "A Limestone Way of Learning," Bernstein praised the value of science fieldwork:

> *Now, more than two decades later, I still remember the feel of the limestone underneath my fingers and the look of the delicate water droplets on the spider webs. I also remember the wisdom of my elderly professor, who understood what I had learned from the course even if I could not replicate the terms on a diagram. Clearly, I did not choose to major in geology, but I left the course with a layperson's strong (indeed, lifelong) appreciation for the subject. (p. B5)*

References

Abrams, E. 1995. A comparison of the effects of multiple visual examples and nonexamples versus prototypical examples on science concept learning: An exploratory study based upon the concept of photosynthesis. PhD diss., Louisiana State University. [UMI order no. 9425216]

Bernstein, S. 2003. A limestone way of learning. *The Chronicle of Higher Education* 50 (7): B5.

Butler, R., M. Hall-Wallace, and T. Burgess. 2000. A sense of place: At home with local natural history. *Journal of College Science Teaching* 30 (4): 252–255.

Camill, P. 2000. Using journal articles in an environmental biology course. *Journal of College Science Teaching* 30: 38–43.

Clary, R., D. Gresham, F. Bases, E. Hamlin, N. Bergeron, C. Petry, M. LaGrange, and E. Fischer. Forthcoming. Sediment and water analysis adjacent to an active scrap yard and archived Superfund site, Lafayette Parish, Louisiana. In *Gulf Coast Association of Geological Societies Transactions* Vol. 55.

Dayton, K. *Honolulu Advertiser.* 2005. NASA still wants more scopes on Mauna Kea. August 6. Also available online at *www.honoluluadvertiser.com/apps/pbcs.dll/article?AID=/20050806/NEWS0101/508060335/1003/NEWS.*

Drake, J., I. Worley, and C. Mehrtens. 1997. An introductory-level field-based course in geology and biology. *Journal of Geoscience Education* 45: 234–237.

Duschl, R. 1990. *Restructuring science education: The importance of theories and their development.* New York: Teachers College Press.

Felder, R. 1993. Reaching the second tier: Learning and teaching styles in college science education. *Journal of College Science Teaching* 23: 286–290.

Gorman, J., and A. Revkin. *New York Times.* 2005. Vindication for a bird and its fans. August 2. Also available online at *www.nytimes.com/2005/08/02/science/02bird.html?pagewanted=print.*

Haines, S., and R. Blake, Jr. 2005. Field and natural science. *Journal of College Science Teaching* 34 (7): 28–31.

King, H. 1998. The UK geoscience fieldwork symposium. In *Proceedings of the UK Geosciences Fieldwork Symposium,* eds. H. King, D. Hawley, and N. Thomas, 1–6. [Plymouth, England]: UK Geosciences Education Consortium and the Earth Science Teachers Association. Also available online at *www.gees.ac.uk/essd/field.htm#KingH.*

McComas, W. 1996. Ten myths of science: Reexamining what we think we know about the nature of science. *School Science and Mathematics* 96: 10–16.

Michael, J., and H. Modell. 2003. *Active learning in secondary and college science classrooms: A working model for helping the learner to learn.* Mahwah, NJ: Erlbaum.

Milius, S. 2005. Comeback bird: Tales from the search for the ivory-billed woodpecker. *Science News* 167: 376–378.

Mullen, W. *Daily Item.* 2004. Paleobotanist reads fossil leaves to determine ancient geology. December 5. Also available online at *www.dailyitem.com/archive/2004/1205/fea/stories/04fea.htm.*

National Science Teachers Association. 1999. NSTA position statement: Informal science education. *www.nsta.org/positionstatement&psid=13*

O'Connell, M., and A. Lara. 2005. From Curanderas to gas chromatography. *Journal of College Science Teaching* 34 (4): 26–30.

Schwab, J. 1962. The teaching of science as inquiry. In *The teaching of science*, eds. J. Schwab and P. Brandwein, 1–104. Cambridge, MA: Harvard University Press.

Wandersee, J., and R. Clary. Forthcoming. Learning on the trail: A content analysis of a university arboretum's exemplary interpretive science signage system. *American Biology Teacher.*

Wandersee, J., and E. Schussler. 2001. Toward a theory of plant blindness. *Plant Science Bulletin* 47 (1): 2–9.

Weiss, D., and J. Walters. 2004. Incorporating GPS technology with a campus geology walking tour. *Journal of Geoscience Education* 52: 186–190.

Wetzel, L. 2002. Building stones as resources for student research. *Journal of Geoscience Education* 50: 404–409.

Woltemade, C., and D. Stanitski-Martin. 2002. A student-centered field project comparing NEXRAD and rain gauge precipitation values in mountainous terrain. *Journal of Geoscience Education* 50: 296–302.

CHAPTER 18

Using Case Studies to Teach Science

Clyde Freeman Herreid

Clyde Freeman Herreid is Distinguished Teaching Professor at the State University of New York / University at Buffalo. He earned a PhD in zoology and entomology at Pennsylvania State University and conducts research on the use of innovative teaching methods in science. He teaches courses in evolutionary biology, comparative physiology and ecology, comparative behavior, and general biology.

I will tell you something about stories; they aren't just entertainment. Don't be fooled. They are all we have, you see, all we have to fight off illness and death. You don't have anything if you don't have the stories.

—Leslie Marmon Silko, Laguna Tribe
(Silko 1977, p. 2)

Storytelling permeates the human experience. It is found on street corners, in bars, in living rooms, and playgrounds; it exists wherever people gather, be it around campfires or TV sets. Stories set cultural norms, provide us with heroes and demons, warn us of folly, and give us reason to hope for better days. They are with us from the day we are born until the moment when we shuffle off this mortal coil. They make us human. Not surprisingly, great teachers are often great storytellers.

A Brief History of Case Study Teaching

Storytelling as a formal educational device arguably entered the didactic scene about 100 years ago with case study teaching at Harvard (Herreid 1994). There in the law and business schools instructors and students analyzed realistic stories as exemplars of good and bad practice. They were stories with an educational message, perhaps the best definition of case studies. It shouldn't come as a surprise to learn that students learn better if they have a "context." This case study approach has also been long used in medical school in the "grand rounds" but most notably was instituted as problem-based learning (PBL) at McMaster University in Canada,

---

The chapter is adapted from an essay on the American Institute of Biological Sciences website *ActionBioscience.org* and is used with permission.

spreading from there to throughout the world. The entry of the case study approach and PBL into the undergraduate classroom can be primarily traced to two institutions. A dozen years ago, the University of Delaware began to introduce PBL across the curriculum, and the University at Buffalo pioneered the use of cases on a large scale in science, mathematics, and engineering.

Case-Based Teaching Today

In its original form, cases were largely self-contained stories that were written and analyzed via the discussion method in the classroom—exemplified by Professor Kingsfield in the movie and TV series *The Paper Chase*. With an intensive cross-examination style, the professor badgered the poor students with persistent questions. Although there are more benign versions of this discussion method, it is still the method of choice for many law and business schools.

Nonetheless, storytelling does not have to be limited to either the traditional discussion formula advocated in law and business schools or to using student groups as in PBL. Rather, there are many other ways to tell the "story with an educational message" (Herreid 1994, 1998a).

Lecture Method

In the 1970s, Richard Eakin at the University of California at Berkeley was famous for dressing as well-known scientists (e.g., Darwin, Mendel, and Pasteur) and lecturing to wide-eyed students in the first person. It was as if these famous personages actually visited their classroom. Chemist James Connant championed the use of lecture cases in the 1940s at Harvard, giving an entire course in science centered on great discoveries. Both of these approaches are surely compelling alternatives to the straightforward preachy lecture.

Whole-Class Discussion Method

The original case study teaching was some variant of the Socratic method. It was largely an interaction between a student and the professor, with other students listening and occasional student-student involvement. But there are many more variations on the discussion method than that, cases that unfold in the form of role-playing, debates, trials, and public hearings, all within the framework of the whole class participating (Herreid 1998a).

Characteristics of a Good Discussion Case

There are several key characteristics found in the best business case studies. They seem to hold true in the sciences as well (Herreid 1997). The cases tend to share the following characteristics:

- They are short. One to three pages works well for most faculty, something that can be covered in a single class period. Yet some excellent cases can extend for several weeks or even over an entire semester.
- They are controversial. However, care must be taken because students can be swept up with the controversy and competitive nature of the discussion rather then giving the topic careful analysis.
- They have dialogue. Although difficult to write well, dialogue makes the cases appear more real to the reader.
- They have interesting characters.

- They are relevant to students.
- They have a dilemma to be solved. Such decision cases force the reader to be involved in the outcome of the discussion because they cannot sit on the sidelines—they must take a position.
- They are contemporary. Although historical cases are interesting to experts, students greatly prefer topics in the news.
- They are real rather than fabricated. It is hard to get involved in a generic case, although a fantasy case—say, involving Spiderman—does capture interest.
- They have learning objectives (why else use them?) and have lessons that can be generalized to other situations.

With that said, let me hurriedly say that many fine cases don't have these characteristics at all—and I have written some myself.

Open Versus Closed Cases

There are other considerations to think about in selecting case studies, and one is the open or closed nature of the case (Cliff and Nesbitt 2005). Most cases used by business schools are open, meaning there are several plausible solutions—reasonable people can differ. The student must sift through the facts, evaluate them, and weigh the possible options and consequences of the decision he must suggest. For instance, the question "Should the United States sign the Kyoto Treaty?" clearly has people on different sides. This type of case is set at the high end of Bloom's taxonomy of knowledge, where synthesis, analysis, and evaluation have a high priority (Bloom et al. 1956).

At the other end of the scale are cases that may be considered closed. These cases do have right and wrong answers. Cases of this type put a premium on facts, principles, and definitions. They focus on the lower end of Bloom's taxonomy of knowledge. Many medical school cases are like this, where the patient has a particular complaint and the correct diagnosis is essential, and woe (not to mention malpractice suits) be to the student or physician who gets it wrong.

Small Groups

PBL is only one form of case instruction, albeit one of the very best. In its original incarnation used at McMaster University Medical School, about a dozen students along with a faculty facilitator puzzled out patient problems. For each case they would follow the same sequence: The first day, they would be given some details about a patient's symptoms. They would separate out the things they knew and those they didn't. The students would then seek information from texts or the internet to assist in their deliberations. When they gathered together for the next class, they would pool their information and again determine what was or was not known. At this time they might receive additional information, perhaps some clinical test results or a new complication. Once again they would reanalyze the situation and seek more information. As a rule, after a couple of cycles of this, they would finalize their diagnosis and receive their next case. The PBL approach has been praised as producing students with increased analytical skills and talents for teamwork and independent learning.

The use of the original PBL has come under criticism because of the heavy investment of faculty time (Glew 2003). As a result PBL has been so much modified that it can hardly be recognized. One sees the phrase used for large classes and small, with facilitators and without

(Herreid 2003). The only unifying feature might be that these cases begin with problems to be solved and not all of the information is given at once.

A favorite method of many science faculty is a variation of PBL called the *interrupted case* (Herreid 2005). Like PBL it uses progressive disclosure of information rather than giving away the entire story line at the outset. The approach differs from PBL only in the fact that in the interrupted method the case is accomplished in a single class period. The power of both approaches is that receiving information piecemeal mimics the way that scientists actually have to analyze problems. And the method provides obvious structure to the discussion, an important point for those students who do not appreciate a freewheeling conversation.

The *jigsaw* approach is a robust way to use cases and small groups (Herreid 2000). First, student groups are given different pieces of information and asked to come to a consensus about a problem. Each group may represent a different stakeholder. Take a case of overfishing near the Galapagos Islands. When the government of Ecuador clamped down on this illegal activity, bands of fishermen took over the Charles Darwin Research Station and held the scientists hostage. An instructor running this case might set up different groups to represent the scientists, the fishermen, the tourists, the shop owners, and the politicians. After the groups establish their initial positions, the teacher sets up new groups, each with one representative from the former groups, and they are responsible for hammering out a compromise policy.

Individual Case Instruction

Cases can be done in a tutorial setting or by individual assignment. One of the most interesting approaches is to use a *dialogue case* (Herreid 1999). Here the instructor gives a student the task of writing a short play about a controversial subject, such as the use of stem cells for research. The student is asked to write a verbal exchange that might take place on this topic between intelligent, informed people on opposite sides of the question. He or she must write at least 20 comments and responses for each protagonist. The comments must be substantial rather than frivolous or superficial (such as "Sally, you're a jerk!"). At the end of the paper the student must write his or her own opinion along with a reference section. Not surprisingly, students often change sides after completing such an assignment—not a bad result.

Mixed Methods

There are many hybrid approaches. Commonly instructors start cases working with small groups and finish by running general discussions with the whole class.

One of the most frequently used methods, the *direct case method,* does not fit neatly into any one category. This technique is a favorite of teachers of anatomy and physiology courses, where the coverage of material is of paramount concern (Cliff and Nesbitt Curtin 2000; Cliff and Wright 1996). In this approach the case is often one or two paragraphs that outline a patient's symptoms, say high blood pressure. This is followed by a series of questions. The students receive the case and questions at the beginning of the unit dealing with the cardiovascular system. They work individually over the next several days to find the answers to the questions, consulting any authority. Meanwhile, the instructor gives a series of traditional lectures on the subject. At the end of the unit, one class period is set aside to deal with the questions; the instructor collects the student papers and then runs a discussion over the topic, keeping track of the students and their responses. The cycle is repeated with each unit: beginning with presentation of a case and questions, followed by lectures, and ending with papers turned in and a discussion.

Another favorite method is *constructive controversy,* which I prefer to call *intimate debate.* Traditionally, debates involve two teams arguing opposite sides of a proposition. The purpose of the debate in a school situation is primarily to hone the argumentative skills of the participants, historically in preparation for a lawyer's career. To win is the primary goal; compromise is not an option.

The approach is different in intimate debate. Say there are 24 students in a class. They are divided into six teams of four students. Three of the teams receive a written fact sheet favoring the "pro" side of the proposition, while three teams receive information supporting the "con" side. In their teams they discuss the best possible points they can use to advance their position. After 15 minutes the instructor takes two people from the pro group and two from the con group and switches them. So the new arrangement has two pros facing two cons across a table. At a signal from the teacher, the pro students have four minutes to make their best case to the con students, who have to listen without comment. (The cons must take careful notes because they will shortly have to reverse roles and take the pro position but will not have the fact sheet of the pros to use—only the notes they have taken.) The cons then have four minutes to respond with their side of the argument, again without comment from the other side.

At this point the instructor tells the two groups to switch sides—i.e., the pro group must take the con position and vice versa using only their notes. It is useful to give the students three minutes to gather their thoughts and have a quick caucus, each pair conferring briefly. Then the new pro group has two minutes to make their points followed by two minutes of response by the new con group. The students then abandon their roles and see if they can come up with a solution to the problem; they are not limited to the arguments they have made but can choose a compromise position. This typically takes only a few minutes. Finally the instructor runs a full-scale class discussion while polling the groups on their thoughts. The virtue of the method is that the strengths and weaknesses of the positions are exposed and alternative solutions are explored. Winning isn't the goal, understanding the issues and problem solving are.

Virtues and Weaknesses of the Different Methods

Some teachers see "cases" as different from "problems." As stated by a reviewer of this chapter, "One engages the student in a human context and a narrative learning style; the other is oriented towards skill-development (in problem analysis, problem solving, perhaps persuasion)." I don't think the distinction is this clear. Many narrative cases have a strong component of skill development, as in medical cases (Herreid 2000) or lab-based cases or, indeed, many business cases where accounts need to be analyzed.

The instructor should have a clear view of what he or she wishes to accomplish with the case, and then design it to do the job. Lecture cases are still lectures and have the same limitations as any other lecture; they may be more fascinating as stories but the listener is passive. There is evidence that regardless of the expertise of the lecturer student performance does not differ on exams (Birx and Foster 1993).

Discussion cases with the whole class have limitations as well: Students are often reluctant to speak out, and a few individuals may dominate the discussion. Also, in large classes only a few individuals can contribute. And few science faculty have had experience leading good discussions.

Small-group cases appear to be the easiest cases to teach for faculty; they do not demand the questioning and listening skills that many of us have not acquired. Instead, a case may be given to small groups to analyze, and a team representative can report on the groups' deliberations. Faculty are then in an ideal position to comment. Students are more apt to participate in small groups of, say, five people, and if they don't prepare it is immediately evident.

A meta-analysis of over 1,200 studies in which researchers compared the performance of students educated using cooperative learning strategies (including case studies) with those taught by the lecture method showed that cooperative learning promoted greater learning and greater retention in verbal, mathematical, and physical skills. Students enjoyed the experience more, had better attitudes toward the subject, developed better social skills, became more articulate, and became more tolerant of differing viewpoints than with the lecture style (Johnson and Johnson 1989, 1993).

Barriers to the Case Method

College faculty face three major barriers when they shift to a new method of teaching: themselves, the students, and other faculty and administrators (Herreid 1998b). And if we consider the K–12 classroom, we should add the parents as a potential barrier. Novelty is worrisome and risky.

The faculty barriers are fairly obvious. It takes time to convert your course, and there are always a thousand other things to do—like research. (Not surprisingly, most faculty that attend teaching workshops come from teaching institutions). Then there is the question of content coverage; the case approach often does not permit instructors to cover as much material as with lectures—never mind that most students forget the information the moment the final is over. Control is an issue with some instructors; they are worried about relinquishing the floor to students—who knows what they will say? And they don't know how to run a discussion; indeed, they may never have seen a discussion in a science classroom. (What happens when no one talks?) Finally, some of us just don't want to give up center stage. "What will happen to my teaching evaluations and how will I get the praise and recognition that I so love?"

The students have their issues too. They like the familiar. They have grown up with the lecture method and know how to cope with it, even if they aren't doing sterling work. If you suddenly throw them into uncharted waters, they don't know what will happen even if you tell them that the results will be better. This can be especially threatening to the preprofessional health students and honors students, who do rather well with the lecture method. (Most faculty have clearly survived quite well, too, and have their own experiences to fall back on when trying to justify not changing.)

Our colleagues and administrators may stand in the way. They may not give a fig about what you do in the classroom, but if trouble starts brewing they are sure to have an opinion and get into the act. Consider the cautionary tale of the chaotic events at Duke University a couple of years ago when the chemistry department tried to introduce cases into its introductory chemistry class (Herreid 2004).

Finally, parents can act as a barrier if they believe that a new method of instruction puts their child at a disadvantage, especially if it involves a controversial topic such as evolution or sex education.

Impact of the Case Teaching Method

In spite of the long history of case-based instruction in business and law, there has been little effort to evaluate the method. However, PBL has been intensively studied, and the results of 43 carefully conducted studies have been summarized in a meta-analysis (Dochy et al. 2003). The results clearly indicate that PBL has a major positive impact on the development of skills of students and that the retention of knowledge is improved compared with standard lectures.

Through workshops and conferences, thousands of faculty have now been trained in using cases, and many have transformed their classrooms. In a recent unpublished review commissioned by the National Center for Case Teaching in Science, 152 faculty were surveyed after they had attended a five-day summer workshop or a two-day conference. Even though these faculty were predisposed toward the method, the results are of interest: 97% reported that students taught with cases learned new ways to think about an issue; 95% reported that students took a more active part in the learning process; 92% reported that students were more engaged in classes; 84% reported that students in classes using case studies were glad case studies were being used; 59% said that students were more likely to do independent research outside the classroom to improve their understanding of the material (only 5% said that they were less likely to do independent research); and 68% said that students demonstrated, in some way, that they learned more in classes using case studies (only 2% said that they learned less).

Evaluation of the strengths of the different case methods is in its infancy, and we must wait for data to accumulate. But it appears that the case method has developed an important following. Several journals routinely publish articles with cases or assessing the method. The *Journal of College Science Teaching* has a regular column dealing with the case teaching method, and it publishes an annual issue devoted solely to case studies. The websites of the University of Delaware (Problem-Based Learning Clearinghouse at *https://chico.nss.udel.edu/Pbl*) and the University at Buffalo (National Center for Case Study Teaching in Science at *http://ublib.buffalo.edu/libraries/projects/cases/case.html*) have several hundred cases with teaching notes available for teachers. They are regularly downloaded by university and college faculty and by K–12 teachers who are cutting and pasting these cases for their students. The traffic on the website of the National Center for Case Study Teaching in Science is impressive; there are several million hits in the course of a year and over a thousand visitors a day.

Case study teaching has gained a strong foothold in science education. Perhaps it is not for everybody, but it is here to stay. It is the stories that hook us. A well-told story will be remembered, and with it the educational message: *You don't have anything if you don't have the stories.*

Acknowledgment

This material is based on work supported by the National Science Foundation under Grant 0341279. Any opinions, findings, conclusions, or recommendations expressed in this material are those of the author and do not necessarily reflect the views of the National Science Foundation.

References

Birx, J., and J. Foster. 1993. The importance of lecture in general chemistry course performance. *Journal of Chemical Education* 70: 180–182.

Bloom, B. S., M. B. Englehart, E. J. Furst, W. H. Hill, and D. R. Krathwohl. 1956. *Taxonomy of educational objectives: The classification of educational goals. Handbook I: Cognitive domain.* New York: Longmans, Green.

Cliff, W. H., and L. M. Nesbitt. 2005. An open or shut case? *Journal of College Science Teaching* 34 (4): 14–17.

Cliff, W. H., and L. Nesbitt Curtin. 2000. The directed case method. *Journal of College Science Teaching* 30 (1): 64–66.

Cliff, W. H., and A. W. Wright. 1996. Directed case study method for teaching human anatomy and physiology. *Advances in Physiology Education* 15: S19–S28.

Dochy, F., M. Segers, P. Van den Bossche, and D. Gijbels. 2003. Effects of problem-based learning: A meta-analysis.

Learning and Instruction 13: 533–568.

Glew, R. H. 2003. The problem with problem-based medical school education: Promises not kept. *Biochemistry and Molecular Biology Education* 31: 52–56.

Herreid, C. F. 1994. Case studies in science—a novel method for science education. *Journal of College Science Teaching* 23 (4): 221–229.

Herreid, C. F. 1997. What makes a good case? *Journal of College Science Teaching* 27 (3): 163–165.

Herreid, C. F. 1998a. Sorting potatoes for Miss Bonner. *Journal of College Science Teaching* 27 (4): 236–239.

Herreid, C. F. 1998b. Why isn't cooperative learning used to teach science? *BioScience* 48: 553–559.

Herreid, C. F. 1999. Dialogues as case studies—a discussion on human cloning. *Journal of College Science Teaching* 29: 245–249.

Herreid, C. F. 2000. Jigsaw: A case study method where students become experts. *http://ublib.buffalo.edu/libraries/projects/cases/teaching/jigsaw.html*

Herreid, C. F. 2003. The death of problem-based learning? *Journal of College Science Teaching* 32 (6): 364–366.

Herreid, C. F. 2004. Why a case-based course failed: An analysis of an ill-fated experiment. *Journal of College Science Teaching* 33 (3): 8–11.

Herreid, C. F. 2005. The interrupted case method. *Journal of College Science Teaching* 35 (2): 4–5.

Johnson, D. W., and R. T. Johnson. 1989. *Cooperation and competition: Theory and research.* Edina, MN: Interaction Book Company.

Johnson, D. W., and R. T. Johnson. 1993. Cooperative learning: Where we have been, where we are going. *Cooperative Learning and Teaching Newsletter* 3(2): 6–9.

Silko, L. M. 1977. *Ceremony.* New York: Viking.

CHAPTER 19

Mating Darwin With Dickinson:

How Writing Creative Poetry in Biology Helps Students Think Critically and Build Personal Connections to Course Content

Jerry A. Waldvogel

Jerry A. Waldvogel is associate professor of biological sciences at Clemson University. He earned a PhD in behavioral biology at Cornell University and conducts research on innovative teaching practices that promote creative and critical thinking, and on the behavioral ecology and sensory physiology of animal orientation systems. He teaches general biology for majors and nonmajors, evolution and creationism, and field methods in ecology and animal behavior.

We are all familiar with the many national efforts to reform K–16 science teaching into a more meaningful educational experience for our students. Beginning with the publication of *Science for All Americans* (Rutherford and Ahlgren 1990) and continuing through *Benchmarks for Science Literacy* (American Association for the Advancement of Science 1993), the *National Science Education Standards* (National Research Council 1996), *Reinventing Undergraduate Education* (Boyer Higher Education Commission 1998), and most recently *BIO2010* (Committee on Undergraduate Biology Education to Prepare Research Scientists for the 21st Century 2003), the recommendation has been to create an educational environment that not only helps students master necessary content material but also encourages them to build personally meaningful connections between science and important social issues that require the application of scientific reasoning skills.

These reform efforts appear to be having some positive effects on K–12 science literacy as measured by the 2003 Trends in International Mathematics and Science Study (TIMSS) (Gonzalez et al. 2004). Nevertheless, the improvements are being met with only cautious optimism; important questions remain regarding the extent to which the changes are truly indicative of permanent and systemic educational reform (Bybee and Kennedy 2005). Indeed, recent public surveys indicate that the American population at large remains woefully ignorant of science, with only 20%–25% of those surveyed being "scientifically savvy and alert" (Dean 2005). In a world where acid rain, infectious diseases, and cloning are all daily topics in newspapers and TV talk shows, the vast majority of the American public is not sufficiently knowledgeable about science to competently discuss these topics. Although a much-needed change in the winds of science literacy may be starting to blow in the lower grade levels, so far that wind appears to be but a gentle breeze for the population as a whole.

College education is not immune from the problem of inadequate science literacy. Although research shows that more-educated people tend to have a better knowledge of science (Miller 1995), it nevertheless remains true that most of today's college students still labor under the misconception that there is little, if any, connection between science and their other courses of study (Waldvogel 2004a). This disconnect is due partly to our own failure as academicians to communicate effectively with each other, or with the general public, about the important relationships between our disciplines (the so-called ivory tower or vertical silo mentalities). But an equally important part of the problem lies in our failure to *require* students to make such connections by providing learning opportunities specifically designed to engage them in the process of forming conceptual links among diverse ideas (Waldvogel 2004b; Young et al. 2003). While calls are currently being made to mandate these kinds of curriculum standards at the college level (National Center for Public Policy and Higher Education 2004), such ideas are only in the discussion stage and face considerable institutional and political obstacles to their implementation. It thus appears that, at least in the short term, any meaningful change in science literacy at the college level will have to depend on the actions of classroom instructors and those charged with developing science curricula on individual college campuses.

The problem is perhaps best illustrated with an example. Young (2006) relates the story of one biology student who, in her senior year, wrote a report for a biology class that the professor labeled as "semi-literate," even though the girl had received a strong B in her first-year composition course. After talking with this student, Young discovered she had assumed that because this paper was for a biology course she did not need to be concerned with issues such as having a focused introduction, purposeful organization, thoughtful analysis, or attention to spelling and grammar. Such issues, the student reasoned, were only relevant in English classes. It also turned out that this assignment was the very first time in her major curriculum where she had been asked to do any serious discipline-specific writing requiring her to link the ideas of her freshmen composition course with the content of her science major. An important take-home lesson from this example is for us to recognize the deeply rooted, indeed institutionalized, failure of collegiate instruction to connect ideas across disciplines in a meaningful manner.

The regular occurrence of such scenarios is what motivated Young and others to develop the Writing Across the Curriculum (WAC) concept. During the past decade, WAC programs have become increasingly commonplace on college campuses, and they are today showing signs of redefining our students' relationship to their work (Young 2006). Several years ago at Clemson University we modified the WAC concept and created a Poetry Across the Curriculum (PAC) program in which students were asked to creatively approach the study of their course content from a more nontraditional form of written communication, the poem (Connor-Greene et al. 2005). It is this genre of creative expression that I have successfully used in my introductory biology courses as a means of helping students forge more meaningful connections between science and other disciplines.

Methods for Encouraging Connectivity, Creativity, and Critical Thought

Poetry is by no means the only way to encourage the development of cross-disciplinary connectivity, creativity, and critical thinking in students. A number of other innovative teaching methods, including various forms of visual art, problem-based learning, and service learning have been used to help students make connections and seek alternative perspectives.

At the high school level, Dambekalns (2005) has combined the visual arts with geography and earth science. Her students use geospatial technology such as global information systems to create silk batiks of the areas they are studying, thus providing a scientific foundation for creative expression. Likewise, Stokes (2001) has used the ancient art of Japanese fish printing to link vertebrate anatomy and taxonomic classification with studies of cultural history.

Applying course content to real-world problems, typically known as problem-based learning or case studies (Herreid 2004; Hmelo and Evensen 2000) is yet another way to help students forge interdisciplinary connections and enhance critical thinking. A growing body of evidence now indicates that the process of identifying and defining problems, determining which content to apply to the solution of those problems, and understanding the variety of perspectives involved in any real-world problem are all important aspects of building interdisciplinary connections. Similarly, the use of service learning, in which course content is applied to specific community service projects, puts students in situations where they must assess, plan, execute, and then reflect on the success of their projects in the context of the complexity of solving real-world problems (Waldvogel 2005).

Although the evidence shows that these methods are all effective instructional tools, a drawback with each of them is that they require a significant degree of instructor design and classroom management for effective implementation. Having students write creative poetry, on the other hand, is a much less labor-intensive way to promote critical thinking and to foster the building of cross-disciplinary connections. In other words, by mating ideas and methods from scientists like Charles Darwin with those of poets like Emily Dickinson, students discover new perspectives on scientific issues that are rich in both content and personal meaning because they arise from the student's own creativity.

Making Poetry Work in the Science Classroom

Exactly how an instructor decides to use creative poetry writing in the classroom is as varied as the disciplines in which it has been used (see Young et al. 2003 for examples). Some instructors grade assignments based on student creativity, others on the accuracy of the content being discussed, and others on simply doing the assignment sincerely. Some instructors do not give formal grades at all. In my introductory biology classes, poetry assignments account for 5%–10% of the course grade, and the evaluation of student work is based on three primary criteria. The first is the *accuracy* of the science being described. Students must demonstrate that they correctly understand the foundational biology content around which their poems revolve. The second criterion is *effort*. Students must show work that is indicative of thoughtful consideration about the topic being discussed. Poems that look as though they were dashed off shortly before class do not receive full credit. The third criterion is *basic grammar and spelling*. Unless incorrect grammar or spelling is an intentional part of the poem, students must use proper grammar and spell correctly.

What I do not use as a grading criterion is the *quality of the poetry* itself. My students are allowed to use whatever style of poetry they wish, and since I am not a trained poet myself, I do not feel qualified to formally assess them on this aspect of their work. I typically receive rhymed verses, but students will also use nonrhyming forms, visual poetry, haiku, and other styles. My only requirement is that their poems be at least 10 lines long. If haiku is submitted (which has a strict syllabic pattern and line format), then the student must create at least three separate haiku poems to meet the 10-line minimum. My poetry assignments are typically given at the end of a class lecture or discussion and are based loosely on the topic of that class period. Completed poems are usually due at the beginning of the next class meeting.

After I have read and graded the students' poetry, I return the poems and encourage volunteers to read their work out loud to the entire class. This serves two purposes. The first is to give the students a range of examples regarding the style, form, and emphasis that can be placed on a given topic. The second is for the class to appreciate the rather high quality of thinking and originality that is apparent in many of the poems. If students are uneasy about reading their work in public, I will often ask permission to read it aloud for them. But if they really do not want to share their work, perhaps because it is too private, I never force them to do so.

The initial student reaction to these assignments is a mixture of trepidation and excitement. Since my classes tend to be a blend of both science majors and nonscience majors, the previous knowledge of biology varies widely within the class. For those with little or no biology background, the task of understanding a topic well enough to be genuinely creative about it can be somewhat daunting. Moreover, the range of personal comfort with writing creative poetry also varies with a student's previous experience. Some students often write personal poetry, others do so only when required by course work. What is virtually universal, however, is the rapid increase in the students' interest for these assignments as they gain confidence expressing themselves in novel ways. I believe that my de-emphasis of the structural details of writing poetry has facilitated this process. Over time the students become increasingly comfortable with the new biology content they encounter as poetry allows them to find more interesting and relevant ways to relate that content to their personal lives.

Example Poems and Student Reflections

Three poems, all written by first-year students from my introductory biology classes, illustrate the creativity and personal connectivity that emerge through these assignments. One student was a mathematics major, one an animal science major, and the other a graphic communications major.

Maureen McHugh's "Fertilization Poem" (Figure 19.1) was one of the first biology poems that I ever received, and to this day it remains one of the most creative. After a series of lectures on the basics of reproduction and the scope of reproductive strategies used by animals, Maureen chose "poetic art" to contrast the reproductive investments of males and females.

Evolutionary theory argues that, because of their abundant and easily manufactured sperm, males should be rather cavalier about (and eager for) mating opportunities. Females, on the other

Figure 19.1

"Fertilization Poem"

"Fertilization Poem," by Maureen McHugh, is an example of how poetry can be combined with visual art to striking effect in a biology course. This poem is reprinted with permission from *Across the Disciplines*.

Figure 19.2

"Wacko-Tobacco"

"Wacko-Tobacco," a poem by Kara Davis, takes both a light-hearted and serious view of the health risks associated with tobacco use as seen through the eyes of college roommates.

Dear Stevie:

Roomie, I do love you so,
But this chewing snuff has got to go!
Our room is laced in bottles and cans,
And a smell that lingers with your hair and hands.
Your constant spitting while I'm trying to work
Has led me to act a bit like a jerk.
I'm sorry, really, but think how I feel,
When you're sucking your teeth and tapping your wheel.
And what about Josie when he kisses you sweet?
A surprise sure awaits that tastes of rank feet!
If not for us, then quit for just you,
The scary stats prove all too true.
Ulcers, cancer, heart disease, even death,
A hell of a case of God-awful bad breath!
Besides that, darling, you are a girl!
Think of social stigmas, your place in the world.
If you're stressed take runs, naps, showers.
Set small goals; a few days, several hours.
Baby steps, baby steps, you'll pull right through,
And there'll be a much happier, healthier you!

hand, need to protect their valuable eggs and thus should be choosy when selecting mates. Maureen takes this evolutionary battle of the sexes and translates it into a witty exchange between the stereotyped pickup lines of men and the more discerning response of a woman. She humorously but accurately depicts the fundamental biology by casting the men's abrupt lines as competitive sperm swimming about the egg, comparing these with the lengthy and thoughtful response of the woman shown in the coiled text of her egg. Not only is the visual layout accurate in its anatomical depiction, it also forces the reader to physically engage in the poem by rotating the page in order to read what is being said. I find Maureen's design as absorbing and fundamentally important to the learning being demonstrated as is the process of fertilization to life itself.

Kara Davis is the author of "Wacko-Tobacco" (Figure 19. 2), a poem written in response to my challenge to produce a persuasive argument for quitting tobacco aimed at a friend or relative. As we begin reading her poem, we logically assume that "Dear Stevie" refers to a male friend, mainly because of the common stereotype that men are the ones who use chewing tobacco. Quickly, however, clues are given that Stevie is actually Kara's *female* roommate. This plot twist adds to the impact of the poem and makes us want to read further. In addition, Kara's amusing description of the practical side effects of chewing tobacco (empty cans left around the room, annoying tapping sounds, and bad breath) stands in stark contrast to the typical warnings of the serious health risks of cancer and gum disease that result from this unnecessary habit. The unusual mixture of hard scientific facts coupled with the familiar banter of college roommates stands out clearly in the poem, making the connections between biology, health, and personal relationships more realistic than they otherwise would be if the poem had taken a more unemotional or clinical view of tobacco use by young people.

Tiffany Voss wrote "Evolution in School" (Figure 19.3). Her poem was written in response to my request for student opinions on how they personally reconcile the scientific description of human origins with their own socio-religious perspectives on the topic. In particular, I asked them to include comments on whether the evolutionary origins of humans should be taught in public school science classes. Tiffany's poem is an example of the "middle ground" that many students take when asked about this issue. She acknowledges the scientific power of Darwin's explanation for human origins but also stands firmly by her Christian viewpoint. Instead of forcing herself into the predicament of having to choose one view over the other,

Figure 19.3

"Evolution in School"

"Evolution in School," a poem by Tiffany Voss, strikes a thoughtful middle ground in the ongoing battle between scientific and religious viewpoints regarding the teaching of human evolution in public schools.

Evolution in School

Many scientists try to prove,
Facts and theories of all sorts
They want fame and cash,
But did not make it playing sports.

This is fine and dandy,
With their work I have no qualms
Some people on the other hand,
Think some scientists are wrong.

Darwin was a scientist,
Who has angered many nations.
He believes that evolution,
Was more likely than creation.

Due to natural selection,
Darwin hypothesized
That animals were simpler,
Before humans were on the rise.

He believes that simple cells,
To evolution, were the key.
He also thinks that humans,
Are related to monkeys.

Fossil evidence suggests,
That Darwin's right on track.
However, many people,
Wish he'd take his theories back.

They believe that God created,
Adam and Eve and you,
To this I will not argue,
For I am a Christian too.

These spiritual beliefs,
In my most excellent conclusion,
Cannot belong in schools,
They'd lead to other religions' exclusion.

In school there should be teachings,
Of the evolutionary view.
These teachings don't need belief,
Just understanding them will do.

The ideas of creation,
Also need their space.
In churches, temples, Bibles,
And homes is their place.

Adam and Eve were created,
There is no doubt from me.
However, God could have set it up,
So they evolved from chimpanzees.

she demonstrates her knowledge of the separate intellectual roles that science and religion play in helping humans to understand the world and their role in it. By making comparisons and connections between science and religion as philosophical enterprises, Tiffany leads us to the conclusion that each has its proper place in society, but that we err in thinking either is capable of explaining away the other. She ends by suggesting that science and theology could be intertwined if indeed God is responsible for the evolution of Adam and Eve from a chimpanzee-like ancestor, a point underscored by her including some original artwork alongside the verse (not shown here). Clearly, whether you agree with Tiffany's interpretation or not, it is obvious that she has wrestled with one of the most contentious interfaces between modern science and religion in an intellectually meaningful fashion.

It is important to note that none of these three poems is necessarily a fine example of poetry per se. Serious critics of poetic style and meaning might find much fault with each of the poems, but recall that my assignments de-emphasize the mechanics of poetic style (e.g., cadence, verse structure, and rhyme scheme) in favor of science content, creativity, and connection to nonscientific perspectives. With this focus, I believe students feel more secure and confident in developing personal meaning from science through the use of creative poetry writing.

In an attempt to quantify student reactions to the use of poetry in my classes, as part of the end-of-year course evaluation process I administered a short opinion survey to a subset of students who were chosen at random from the entire class. Students were asked to answer nine questions using a modified Likert scale, where a response of 1 indicates strong disagreement with the statement and a response of 4 indicates strong agreement. The mean responses ($N = 43$ students) are shown in Table 19.1.

Table 19.1

Survey Data From 43 Introductory Biology Students at Clemson University Who Wrote Poems About Some Aspect of Biology and Society in 2002–2004

Reflection Question	Mean Score
1. Writing creative poetry is a valuable learning experience in an introductory biology class.	3.6
2. The material that I learned while writing poetry enhanced my overall understanding of biology as a subject.	3.1
3. The material that I learned while writing poetry enhanced my understanding of the connection between biology and other disciplines.	3.7
4. Writing poetry improved my ability to think *critically* about science.	3.2
5. Writing poetry improved my ability to think *creatively* about science.	3.5
6. My written communication skills improved because of writing poetry.	3.2
7. I will remember the topics about which I wrote poems better than if I had not written those poems.	2.9
8. Writing poetry for a biology class is a reasonable kind of assignment.	3.1
9. I recommend keeping poetry assignments in future biology classes.	3.0

Note: Mean response scores are based on a modified Likert scale ranging from 1 (strongly disagree) to 4 (strongly agree).

Overall, my students were favorably inclined toward the use of creative poetry writing in their introductory biology course. Mean responses were all on the "agree" side of the response scale, ranging from 2.9 to 3.7 (73%–93%). Of particular note are the high levels of agreement with statements that writing creative poetry is a valuable exercise, that students make better connections between science and society as a result of writing poetry, and that writing poetry encourages them to think more creatively about science.

I also asked my students to provide anonymous written reflections on the use of creative poetry writing in biology. Again, the responses were largely favorable, with the following four examples being typical:

The poetry assignments, while very challenging at first, were one of the best things about his course. They really got me thinking about a topic and trying to find some new way of looking at it from a different perspective.

Until this course, I thought poetry was pretty much junk! I have never been good at writing or interpreting it. But once I got to use it to talk about things that really mattered to me as a science major, I found a whole new "voice" for expressing my ideas. I hope I get to do more of this in future biology classes.

My own poetry wasn't so great, but I was amazed at how well the rest of the class did on their poems. Some of the people in this class are really talented at expressing their ideas in poems, and their work made me think differently about the topics we wrote on. I will certainly remember those discussions and topics better than I would probably have done were it not for the poetry assignments.

I liked the poetry assignments in biology—so much so that I've asked my economics professor if it's okay to write poems for that class too!

Conclusions

Poetry writing is a simple yet effective way to stimulate creative and critical thought in science students. Course management and grading issues are minimal compared with other kinds of nontraditional teaching such as case studies or service learning. Most students like writing poetry, and by their own accounts they learn new and different ways of viewing the world that lead them to a richer understanding of science that includes a more personal connection to course content. Creative poetry writing is thus one tool that can help achieve the goal of enhancing science literacy and creating more effective classroom learning environments.

Acknowledgments

I thank my biology students at Clemson University for taking part in the poetry assignments described in this paper, especially Maureen McHugh, Kara Davis, and Tiffany Voss, who granted me permission to use their work as examples. The editors of *Across the Disciplines* graciously granted permission to reprint the McHugh poem here. I also thank my Clemson faculty colleagues in the Poetry Across the Curriculum project for their insight regarding novel ways of teaching. In particular, Art Young, Patricia Connor-Greene, and Catherine Paul have given especially cogent advice on how I might use poetry in the biology classroom. Elizabeth Wright generated electronic versions of some of the poems used in this paper. This work was supported in part by funds from the Roy and Marnie Pearce Center for Communications at Clemson University.

References

American Association for the Advancement of Science. 1993. *Benchmarks for science literacy*. New York: Oxford University Press.

Boyer Higher Education Commission. 1998. *Reinventing undergraduate education: A blueprint for America's research universities*. New York: Carnegie Foundation.

Bybee, R. W., and D. Kennedy. 2005. Editorial: Math and science achievement. *Science* 307: 481.

Committee on Undergraduate Biology Education to Prepare Research Scientists for the 21st Century. 2003. *BIO2010: Transforming undergraduate education for future research biologists*. Washington, DC: National Academies Press.

Connor-Greene, P. A., A. Young, C. Paul, and J. W. Murdoch. 2005. Poetry: It's not just for English class anymore. *Teaching of Psychology* 32 (2): 215–221.

Dambekalns, L. 2005. Earth view, art view. *The Science Teacher* 72 (1): 43–47.

Dean, C. *New York Times*. 2005. Scientist at work—Jon Miller; Scientific savvy? In U.S., not much. August 30.

Gonzales, P., J. C. Guzman, L. Partelow, E. Pahlke, L. Jocelyn, D. Kastberg, and T. Williams. 2004. *Highlights From the Trends in International Mathematics and Science Study (TIMSS) 2003*. NCES 2005-005. Washington, DC: National Center for Education Statistics.

Herreid, C. F. 2004. Can case studies be used to teach critical thinking? *Journal of College Science Teaching* 33 (6): 12–14.

Hmelo, C. E., and D. H. Evensen. 2000. Introduction to problem-based learning: Gaining insights on learning interactions through multiple methods of inquiry. In *Problem-based learning: A research perspective on learning interactions,* eds. D. H. Evensen and C. E. Hmelo, 1–16. Mahwah, NJ: Erlbaum.

Miller, J. D. 1995. *The public understanding of science and technology in the United States, 1995: A report to the National Science Foundation, Washington, DC*. Chicago: Chicago Academy of Sciences.

National Center for Public Policy and Higher Education (NCPPHE). 2004. *Measuring up 2004: The national report card on higher education*. San Jose, CA: NCPPHE.

National Research Council. 1996. *National science education standards*. Washington, DC: National Academy Press.

Rutherford, F. J., and A. Ahlgren. 1990. *Science for all Americans*. New York: Oxford University Press.

Stokes, N. C. 2001. The fine art of science. *The Science Teacher* 68 (3): 22–24.

Waldvogel, J. A. 2004a. Implications of future biological research for the biology curriculum. In *Biology and the physics-first curriculum: A symposium celebrating BSCS's 45th Anniversary,* eds. R. Bybee and A. Gardner, 15–19. Colorado Springs, CO: Biological Sciences Curriculum Study.

Waldvogel, J. A. 2004b. Writing poetry to assess creative and critical thinking in the sciences. In *Teaching tips: Innovations in undergraduate science instruction,* eds. M. Druger, E. D. Siebert, and L. M. Crow, 58–59. Arlington, VA: NSTA Press.

Waldvogel, J. A. 2005. Assessing effectiveness and student satisfaction for two service learning projects in a college introductory biology course. *Creative College Teaching Journal* 2 (1): 78–89.

Young, A. 2006. *Teaching writing across the curriculum*. 4th ed. Upper Saddle River, NJ: Pearson Education.

Young, A., P. Connor-Greene, C. Paul, and J. Waldvogel. 2003. Poetry across the curriculum: Four disciplinary perspectives. *Language and Learning Across the Disciplines* 6 (2): 14–44.

CHAPTER 20

Constructive-Developmental Pedagogy in Chemistry

Maureen A. Scharberg

Maureen A. Scharberg is director of the Science Education Program and professor of chemistry at San Jose State University. She earned a PhD in chemistry at the University of California at Davis and conducts research on curriculum development in undergraduate chemistry and professional development in chemistry for K–12 teachers. She teaches courses in introductory and general chemistry.

In today's undergraduate chemistry classroom, instructors are adopting learning strategies based on research outcomes of how students learn science and chemistry (National Research Council 2003; Pienta, Cooper, and Greenbowe 2005). Specifically, they are developing and implementing active learning environments that build on chemical principles and students' previous learning experiences involving peer learning and problem-based, collaborative laboratories. The ultimate goal of these efforts is to prepare undergraduates for the 21st century workforce.

This chapter reflects on research in constructive-developmental (CD) pedagogy having application to today's undergraduate science classroom. The focus will be on the undergraduate chemistry curriculum and pedagogy. I will explore the extent to which teaching strategies in undergraduate chemical education meet the criteria for preparing today's students for the 21st century workforce.

Elements of a 21st Century Education

It matters not only what we know but also how we know it, how we use what we know, how we work with others who have different expertise than our own, and how well we respond to unexpected challenges that we encounter. (Ramaley and Haggett 2005)

This statement of Dr. Ramaley and Dr. Haggett is in response to the Business-Higher Education Forum's report, *Building a Nation of Learners* (2003). This report described nine elements that are critical for success in today's workplace: leadership, teamwork, problem solving, time management, self-management, adaptability, analytical thinking, global consciousness, and strong communication skills.

The Business-Higher Education Forum was not alone in its position. Similar viewpoints were noted from other publications of professional organizations. These publications include *Powerful Partnerships,* which is a joint report from the American Association of Higher Education, the American College Personnel Association, and the National Association of Student Personnel Administrators (1998), and *Greater Expectations: A New Vision for Learning as a Nation Goes to College,* from the Association of American Colleges and Universities (2002). In the latter report, the authors defined the intentional learner:

> *Becoming … an intentional learner means developing self-awareness about the reason for study, the learning process itself, and how education is used. Intentional learners are integrative thinkers who can see connections in seemingly disparate information and draw on a wide range of knowledge to make decisions. They adapt skills learned in one situation to problems encountered in another: in the classroom, the workplace, their communities, or their personal lives.*
>
> *For intentional learners, intellectual study connects to personal life, formal education to work, and knowledge to social responsibility. Through understanding the power and implications of education, learners who are intentional consciously choose to act in ethical and responsible ways.* (pp. 21–22)

The Constructive-Developmental Framework

Focusing on a learning environment that emphasizes only content knowledge through problem-solving and critical-thinking skills, some science instructors could be shortchanging their students and thus not meeting the elements required of the 21st century workforce. We need to expand our pedagogies and embrace learning strategies that integrate the development of effective citizenry, as well as respect for others' identities and cultures (see Chapter 37 in this volume). CD pedagogy (Belenky et al. 1986; Daloz 1986; Ignelzi 2000; Kegan 1994; King and Kitchener 2002; Ladson-Billings 1994; Perry 1970) provides a framework for designing an undergraduate science curriculum to meet the requirements of the 21st century workforce. The CD framework suggests three objectives that must be integrated into our undergraduate science classrooms:

- *Cognitive development and maturity:* Students should construct knowledge through application of critical-thinking skills and problem-solving techniques. Students transition from accepting knowledge to constructing knowledge. The final outcome will be adult learners with strong skills in problem solving, analytical thinking, and communication skills.
- *Integrated identity:* Students should be confident about who they are as individuals. They should reflect, explore, and choose their own values. Essentially, they are responsible for their own learning. To achieve integrated identity, students transition from adopting values for external approval to exploring and choosing their own values. The final outcome will be adult learners with skills in leadership, time management, and self-management.
- *Working with and respecting others:* Students should be respectful of others' particular identities and cultures and should be open to other perspectives. Students transition

from depending on relationships to gaining the approval of others. The final outcome will be adult learners with skills in teamwork, global consciousness, and adaptability to a variety of situations.

Learning Partnerships

Though teaching and learning strategies that are consistent with the CD framework are adaptable to any area of science, I have chosen chemistry as the illustrative example. One strategy that fosters CD objectives is the learning partnership.

Baxter Magolda's longitudinal (1986–2003) research study (Baxter Magolda 1992, 2001, 2004) tracked college students through various stages and aspects of their lives. The initial interviews covered students' undergraduate curricular and co-curricular activities and experiences. Their undergraduate instructors were also interviewed. In the postcollege years, the students were interviewed about their graduate or professional education, their employment opportunities and careers, and their personal and community lives. The results of Baxter Magolda's qualitative research based on over 900 interviews strongly support CD pedagogy (Belenky et al. 1986; Daloz 1986; Ignelzi 2000; Kegan 1994; King and Kitchener 2002; Ladson-Billings 1994; Perry 1970). Further, it led her to describe a learning partnership between faculty and students that fosters students' self-authorships in defining what their roles in society are, what they believe and value, and what they seek in their adult working relationships.

Three assumptions underlie the learning partnership (Baxter Magolda 2004):

1. Knowledge is complex and socially constructed. This assumption focuses on students' capabilities to choose wisely from many sources.
2. Knowing oneself is key for constructing one's knowledge. This assumption provides mechanisms for students to define how they learn, how they achieve their goals, and how they work with others.
3. Knowledge is mutually constructed among peers through shared authority and expertise.

Baxter Magolda found that instructors in her study did not directly state these assumptions overtly, but they were key components of their enacted curriculum. These assumptions were noted in supporting the following *three principles of self-authorship* that were observed in her participants' undergraduate experiences and beyond:

1. Validate students as learners and value their experiences. The curriculum should be meaningful, engaging, and connecting to students.
2. Use active-learning strategies where students and educators construct knowledge together that takes students' previous experience and evidence into account.
3. Develop a combined perspective on students' learning and their development as a contributing member of society.

Promoting Self-Authorship in the Undergraduate Chemistry Curriculum

Validate Students as Learners by Creating Meaningful Experiences
Baxter Magolda points out that instructors must validate their students as learners and engage

students in challenging yet meaningful ways. The ultimate goal is to help students develop their minds and to help them transition to becoming self-authors. In Wink's (2005) chapter entitled "Relevance and Learning Theories" in *Chemists' Guide to Effective Teaching,* he presents an excellent review on how relevance is addressed in chemistry. Science educators need to constantly answer two questions: "Why do our students need to learn this particular concept?" and "How can I create relevant and meaningful learning experiences in chemistry?" If we cannot justify our responses to these questions, then we need to revise the curriculum.

However, providing students with "real-world" experiences may not be enough; students must be open to learning and find value in the experience. Wink discussed four essentials to a meaningful and relevant curriculum. Typically, when one or more of these components is missing, learning problems arise. The four components of a meaningful and relevant curriculum are the particular student, the mediator, the course materials, and the assessment strategy.

Engaging particular students can be especially challenging in today's diverse classroom. In my nonmajors introductory chemistry course, there are students from almost every disciplinary major as well as those who plan to become science and engineering majors. The most rapidly growing minority group (with respect to major field) at San Jose State University is "none of the above" (mixed-race students who do not fit into any ethnic category). Some of them are concurrently enrolled in remedial math or English courses. My students are multidimensional with respect to their career goals, academic programs, cultural attributes, and learning styles. Yet I validate all of them as being able to learn chemistry because, regardless of their previous experiences in chemistry, I respect them as having the potential to learn fundamental chemical principles.

In accepting them as having the capabilities to learn chemistry, I assume that all students in this nonmajors learning environment can relate to consumer chemistry. In fact, many of them are unaware of the importance that chemistry plays in their everyday lives and are amazed to discover that all of them are chemists, in one way or another. As the mediator of this course, I choose the course materials very carefully and purposefully to emphasize the role chemistry plays in their everyday lives. Demonstrations or other student-centered activities are conducted in lecture, structured according to the framework presented in the American Chemical Society's Chemistry project (Bell 2005).

The curriculum in Bell's textbook is presented as carefully chosen and relevant student-led or demonstration activities. The activities introduce and build students' understanding of particular and relevant phenomena in chemistry. Then, a series of questions asks students to discuss and develop a hypothesis or explanation. All activities are presented as questions. By posing a question, the instructor can ascertain students' understanding and begin to address any misconceptions. The ensuing dialogue between students and instructor, with the instructor as a mediator, allows a relationship of fostering and promoting acceptance of students as developing learners of chemistry.

Many of the laboratories in this nonmajors chemistry course require students to design their own experiments or to bring in household products for determining their densities, conductive properties, or pH. Thus, students have some ownership of the materials and are engaged in the explorations.

A wide variety of out-of-class activities are provided for students to master each week. The weekly assessments (i.e., quizzes), given during the first 30 minutes of laboratory, also allow students to demonstrate what they know and how they know it. These quizzes are graded during the laboratory, and feedback is given to students before they leave the laboratory that day. This mechanism allows students to assess their individual understanding of a particular concept as well as to address any misunderstandings.

Use Active Learning Where Students and Educators Construct Knowledge Together
Constructing knowledge in chemistry is heavily rooted in Piaget's theory of intelligence (Piaget 1964, 1972). Piaget distinguished between two types of knowledge: knowledge gained through the sensory experiences and knowledge that builds intelligence. Abraham (2005) presents an excellent review that addresses constructing knowledge in chemistry using Piaget's theory as well as other learning theories, in *Chemists' Guide to Effective Teaching*. Also, Dudley Herron's book provides a thorough description on how Piagetian theory applies to the chemistry classroom (Herron 1996).

Chemical educators are becoming increasingly aware of how students construct knowledge through creating an active-learning environment where students are actively engaged in learning. In fact, there are many different and effective methods of creating an active-learning environment in today's chemistry classroom, as described in *Chemists' Guide to Effective Teaching* (Pienta, Cooper, and Greenbowe 2005).

One active-learning strategy that I have incorporated into both the lectures and laboratories is the *guided inquiry approach*, based on Farrell, Moog, and Spencer (1999). This approach creates a learning environment that models the scientific method through the use of the learning cycle (Abraham and Renner 1986; Spencer 1999). The learning cycle is said to provide a deeper learning experience that enhances students' critical-thinking and problem-solving skills and improves students' ability to apply their knowledge to new situations.

Farrell, Moog, and Spencer's learning cycle worksheets involve three main components: Model and Information Sections, Critical Thinking Questions, and Exercises and Problems. In my nonmajors chemistry class, I have used these types of worksheets to help students learn to classify matter, and to understand atomic theory, stoichiometry and moles, and nuclear chemistry. In laboratories, many of the experiments allow students to explore, gather data, and then discuss their outcomes and ideas with the laboratory instructor, who guides them through relevant questions after the experiment. Tied together as a weekly unit, homework exercises and problems allow extra practice in their skills and problem-solving capabilities.

Using a constructivist approach to learning may have some negative consequences. Since students bring their previous experiences in chemistry to our classrooms, they often bring their misconceptions as well. Nonmajors also bring their fears, anxieties, and lack of confidence in chemistry to the classroom. In dealing with anxieties and lack of confidence, creating a learning partnership reassures students and sets their minds at ease as long as they have access to a variety of learning tools.

An excellent resource for diagnosing misconceptions in chemistry is the Chemical Concepts Inventory (American Chemical Society, Division of Chemical Education 2005). By becoming involved in constructing students' knowledge in chemistry, we can then identify and correct these misconceptions. As Bodner (1986) states in his well-known paper,

The only way to get rid of an old theory is by constructing a new theory that does a better job at explaining the experimental evidence or finds a more appropriate set of experimental facts to explain. The only way to replace a misconcept is by constructing a new concept that more

appropriately explains our experiences. (p. 876)

Develop a Combined Perspective on Students' Learning and Their Development as Contributing Members of Society

In addition to constructing knowledge and providing relevant learning experiences in chemistry, the chemistry classroom should enable students to become contributing members of society. Small-group learning experiences for both lecture and laboratory, such as those described by Cooper (2005) in her chapter "An Introduction to Small-Group Learning" in *Chemists' Guide to Effective Teaching,* can be very valuable. The versatility of small-group learning experiences cannot be overestimated. Whether one chooses collaborative learning, cooperative learning, or peer-led learning groups, the research (Johnson, Johnson, and Smith 1998) suggests that small groups facilitate knowledge-based outcomes and greater acceptance of diversity, greater social support, and greater social competencies.

Many of my nonmajors laboratories require students to work together in collecting and analyzing data from their experiments. In end-of-semester reflective papers, students often comment that working in group environments gave them experience in working with a diverse group of students. They also state that these experiences helped them develop the communication skills that will be required for their future careers.

Undergraduate research experiences in both academic and industrial settings provide students with opportunities to work in teams with other scientists. If students are allowed to present their results at a scientific meeting or forum, they learn how to effectively present and communicate their research findings. They also gain the satisfaction of contributing to the ever-growing body of scientific knowledge.

Service learning experiences, such as those implemented in elementary schools by Kalamazoo College students, are gaining recognition by chemistry educators (Esson, Stevens-Truss, and Thomas 2005). The evidence suggests that these courses enhance interpersonal and leadership skills, increase community engagement, and improve self-esteem and self-confidence. Whether such experiences actually help college students learn chemistry has been questioned. But there is some evidence that they may encourage some students to select chemistry as their college major.

Conclusion

Promoting self-authorship through a constructive-developmental pedagogy provides undergraduate science students with a wide variety of learning opportunities that prepares them for the 21st century workforce. Such a framework encourages a deep understanding of one's own area of science and develops skills in working with a diverse group of people and exploring and defining one's roles in society.

Although an individual course may possess the characteristics required for self-authorship, the students' programs of study as well as the undergraduate institution must also value, support, and promote students' transitions to becoming self-authors. As science educators, we must begin to look beyond our own course and to entire undergraduate programs of study in the sciences to ensure that these programs collectively are preparing students for the 21st century workforce. We need to urge our campus leaders, as a whole, to also support, value, and sustain these learning partnerships as an integral part of our university missions.

References

Abraham, M. R. 2005. Relevance and learning theories. In *Chemists' guide to effective teaching,* eds. N. J. Pienta, M. M. Cooper, and T. J. Greenbowe, 41–52. Upper Saddle River, NJ: Pearson Prentice Hall.

Abraham, M. R., and J. W. Renner. 1986. The sequence of learning cycle activities in high school chemistry. *Journal of Research in Science Teaching* 23 (2): 121–143.

American Association of Higher Education (AAHE) / American College Personnel Association (ACPA) / National Association of Student Personnel Administrators (NASPA). 1998. *Powerful partnerships: A shared responsibility for learning.* Washington, DC: AAHE / ACPA / NASPA.

American Chemical Society, Division of Chemical Education. Conceptual Questions (CQs): The Chemical Concepts Inventory. *http://jchemed.chem.wisc.edu/JCEWWW/Features/CqandChP/CQs/ConceptsInventory/CCIIntro.html*

Association of American Colleges and Universities (AACU). 2002. *Greater expectations: A new vision of learning as a nation goes to college.* Washington, DC: AACU.

Baxter Magolda, M. B. 1992. *Knowing and reasoning in college: Gender-related patterns in students' intellectual development.* San Francisco: Jossey-Bass.

Baxter Magolda, M. B. 2001. *Making their own way: Narratives for transforming higher education to promote self-development.* Sterling, VA: Stylus.

Baxter Magolda, M. B. 2004. *Learning partnerships: Theory and models of practice to educate for self-authorship.* Sterling, VA: Stylus.

Belenky, M., B. M. Clinchy, N. Goldberger, and J. Tarule. 1986. *Women's ways of knowing: The development of self, voice, and mind.* New York: Basic Books.

Bell, J. A. 2005. *Chemistry: A project of the American Chemical Society.* New York: W. H. Freeman.

Bodner, G. M. 1986. Constructivism. A theory of knowledge. *Journal of Chemical Education* 63 (10): 873–878.

Business-Higher Education Forum. 2003. *Building a nation of learners: The need for changes in teaching and learning to meet global challenges.* Washington, DC: Business-Higher Education Forum.

Cooper, M. M. 2005. An introduction to small-group learning. In *Chemists' guide to effective teaching,* eds. N. J. Pienta, M. M. Cooper, and T. J. Greenbowe, 117–128. Upper Saddle River, NJ: Pearson Prentice Hall.

Daloz, L. A. 1986. *Effective teaching and mentoring: Realizing the transformational power of adult learning experiences.* San Francisco: Jossey-Bass.

Esson, J. M., R. Stevens-Truss, and A. Thomas. 2005. Service-learning in introductory chemistry: Supplementing chemistry curriculum in elementary schools. *Journal of Chemical Education* 82 (8): 1168–1173.

Farrell, J. J., R. S. Moog, and J. N. Spencer. 1999. A guided inquiry general chemistry course. *Journal of Chemical Education* 76 (4): 570–574.

Herron, J. D. 1996. *The chemistry classroom: Formulas for successful teaching.* Washington, DC: American Chemical Society.

Ignelzi, M. 2000. Meaning-making in the learning and teaching process. In *Teaching to promote intellectual and personal maturity incorporating students' worldviews and identities into the learning process* (New Directions for Teaching and Learning, No. 82), ed. M. B. Baxter Magolda, 5–14. San Francisco: Jossey-Bass.

Johnson, D., R. Johnson, and K. Smith. 1998. *Active learning: Cooperation in the college classroom.* Edina, MN: Interaction Book Company.

Kegan, R. 1994. *In over our heads: The mental demands of modern life.* Cambridge, MA: Harvard University Press.

King, P. M., and K. S. Kitchener. 2002. The reflective judgment model: Twenty years of research on epistemic cognition. In *Personal epistemology: The psychology of beliefs about knowledge and knowing,* eds. B. K. Hofer and P. R. Pintrich, 37–61. Mahwah, NJ: Erlbaum.

Ladson-Billings, G. 1994. *The dreamkeepers: Successful teachers of African American children.* San Francisco: Jossey-Bass.

National Research Council. 2003. *How people learn.* Washington, DC: National Academy Press.

Perry, W. J. 1970. *Forms of intellectual and ethical development in the college years: A scheme.* Troy, MO: Holt, Rinehart and Winston.

Piaget, J. 1964. Development and learning. *Journal of Research in Science Teaching* 2: 176–186.

Piaget, J. 1972. Intellectual evolution from adolescence to adulthood. *Human Development* 15: 1–12.

Pienta, N. J., M. M. Cooper, and T. J. Greenbowe. 2005. *Chemists' guide to effective teaching.* Upper Saddle River, NJ: Pearson Prentice Hall.

Ramaley, J. A., and R. R. Haggett. 2005. Engaged and engaging science: A component of a good liberal education. *Peer Review* 7 (2): 8–12. Also available online at *www.aacu.org/peerreview/pr-wi05/pr-wi05contents.cfm.*

Spencer, J. N. 1999. New directions in teaching chemistry: A philosophical and pedagogical basis. *Journal of Chemical Education* 76 (4): 566–569.

Wink, D. J. 2005. Relevance and learning theories. In *Chemists' guide to effective teaching,* eds. N. J. Pienta, M. M. Cooper, and T. J. Greenbowe, 53–66. Upper Saddle River, NJ: Pearson Prentice Hall.

CHAPTER 21

Converting Your Lab From Verification to Inquiry

Donald P. French and Connie P. Russell

Donald P. French is professor of zoology at Oklahoma State University and president of the Society for College Science Teachers. He earned a PhD in zoology at Indiana University and conducts research in animal behavior and science education. He teaches courses in introductory biology and the teaching of zoology.

Connie P. Russell is associate professor of biology at Angelo State University in Texas. She earned a PhD in zoology at Oklahoma State University and conducts research in science education. She teaches principles of biology, general zoology, human anatomy, and advanced instructional methods in science education.

For decades, reports, presentations, and articles have recommended that rather than serve as a place to verify facts and concepts presented in lecture, laboratories should provide opportunities for students to engage in activities such as asking questions, formulating hypotheses, designing experiments, collecting and analyzing data, and interpreting and presenting results in a formal (oral or written) manner. In short, we should give students practice acting like scientists if we want them to become scientists or scientifically literate citizens. This chapter offers insight into how to create laboratories that provide students with research experiences within the constraints of time, resources, and course formats that most faculty face. It provides a research-based rationale for investigative or inquiry-based labs; an example of their implementation in a large-enrollment, introductory course for mixed majors; and recommendations for converting labs.

Rationale for Inquiry-Based Labs

The call for labs in which college students make decisions about experiments they do is not new. In 1969, Holt and colleagues argued that traditional labs do not accomplish the goal of training the next generation of scientists and even questioned whether they met their traditional goals of illustrating concepts, teaching techniques, engendering a positive attitude, and encouraging discussion. Thornton (1972) provided a rationale for and examples of laboratories in which students designed and conducted experiments. Subsequently, there have been many articles discussing various laboratories in which students design at least one experimental component. For example, there are courses in which the students conduct an open inquiry (i.e., students decide their own question and formulate the hypothesis and experiment) for the entire semester (Heady 1993). In other courses, an open-ended experiment is conducted for several weeks near the end of the course, after students have done a series of traditional or somewhat inquiry-based labs (Luckie et al. 2004).

Just as the percentage of the course devoted to inquiry-based labs varies, so does the degree or type of inquiry used. Sundberg and Moncada (1994), Grant and Vatnick (1998), Basey and colleagues (2000), and others characterized labs with respect to the level of inquiry. On one end of the spectrum is the "cookbook" or traditional experimental laboratory. Here the instructor determines the question asked and hypothesis tested, makes predictions, chooses the specific steps of the method used, and decides what data should be collected, the analysis that should be used, and the one answer/conclusion that should be reached. Such a lab may be useful for teaching techniques (Ault 2002) and for ensuring a breadth of topic coverage, but it will not help develop scientific thinking and process skills.

On the other end of the spectrum are labs labeled "free inquiry," "discovery," "open-induction," or something similar, where students determine all experimental components. Between these two are many variations, in which students determine more (inquiry) or fewer (traditional) of the individual components, resulting in more or fewer possible "correct" outcomes.

Faculty considering inquiry labs typically worry about loss of content, students missing techniques or concepts or developing more misconceptions, the time required for developing or teaching such labs, and whether labs will integrate with lecture. The validity of these concerns depends on the nature and degree of inquiry. The concerns are offset by what is not being taught in more traditional labs—creativity, experimental design, scientific thinking, and the rules of evidence used by scientists in developing arguments. Faculty concerned about content loss also ignore the difference between exposing students to techniques or concepts, as happens in traditional labs where little time is devoted to mastering skills or concepts, and having students develop a deep understanding of concepts and true competency skills, which results when more time and thought are devoted to using skills and concepts to solve meaningful problems.

Evidence that inquiry-based labs are effective is extensive. Luckie and colleagues (2004) reported that students' scores on an exam created from practice questions from the Medical College Admissions Test increased significantly after converting to inquiry-based labs. They also found that 78% of the comments from students in inquiry-based labs were positive, while only 20% of those from traditional labs were. Myers and Burgess (2003) found that students completing inquiry-based labs critiqued and designed experiments better than those who did not. Keefer (1998) found immediate and long-term (several semesters) gains in student understanding of projectile motion when students participated in a structured inquiry-based lab (i.e., students were given the problem). Suits (2004) found that science and engineering majors (SEM) taught chemistry via inquiry scored better on tests of investigative skills (designing, conducting, and interpreting and reporting results for experiments) than those not taught by inquiry. Non-SEM students in the inquiry-based group also did better than majors in the traditional group in writing discussions.

Modification of Existing Laboratories

In 1997, we elected to create new laboratories at Oklahoma State University to provide many students (up to 1,100 each semester) with highly diverse backgrounds (i.e., all majors) with meaningful experiences designing and conducting experiments to test hypotheses that they developed. In designing the labs, we followed a framework based on several guidelines and constraints. Because multiple instructors taught many laboratory sections, we had to consider cost, logistics, and variations in teaching experience and content background. We were interested in modifying existing laboratories to take advantage of existing equipment, tested procedures, and concepts taught in lecture. We wanted to cover a breadth of topics similar to the lecture course so we could integrate the students' lecture and lab experiences and use opportunities during our scenario-based (case-based/problem-based) lectures (see Chapter 18 in this volume) to introduce labs and discuss results. This meant that students would have to complete labs in one lab period, which would also prevent students from losing focus or forgetting the point of the lab (Sundberg, Armstrong, et al. 2000; Sundberg and Moncada 1994).

By modifying existing labs, a strategy others have suggested (DeGolier 2002; Deters 2004; Glasson and McKenzie 1997; Shiland 1999), we were more confident that the outcomes of experiments would depend on students' designs and hypotheses and not technical or instructor issues. Modifying existing labs also let us convert to inquiry labs far faster than the one- to two-year time scale that Sundberg and colleagues (2000) estimated for creating a whole semester's worth of inquiry-based labs.

Because our first-year students' backgrounds are highly diverse, we expected that they would not all be prepared to ask meaningful questions and deal with the organizational and time requirements needed for meaningful open inquiry. Therefore, we chose to structure the laboratory by presenting students with open-ended questions (Leonard 1991) and not to use a free-inquiry format. This choice has been supported by several subsequent studies. Mayer (2004) reviewed the literature on guided and open-ended inquiry since the 1960s and concluded that students learning through guided inquiry developed more meaningful understanding of scientific concepts as indicated by their ability to transfer their understanding to new situations. This review was not of college-level students and so may not fully describe the learning process at the postsecondary level. However, many acknowledge the need for some type of instruction or experience to precede open inquiry (Colburn 2004; Darling 2001; Glasson and McKenzie 1997). Wallace and colleagues (2003) found that college students differed in their thinking strategies, so many need explicit instructions in developing strategies suited to science as a creative and changing endeavor. Marbach-Ad and Classen (2001) concluded that students cannot conduct good open-ended investigations without sufficient background knowledge and direct instruction on developing questions. Our format was designed to provide needed guidance and structure to inexperienced students, while permitting as much practice with experimental design and using critical-thinking skills as possible.

Our Design

To start each investigation, we pose a general *question,* such as "Why do metabolic rates of different animals change differently as temperatures vary?" or "Why is diffusion through a membrane faster sometimes?" This is followed by a *scenario* (short story) that provides a context and observations students can use to develop and justify their *hypotheses.* We require that students submit their hypotheses and short plans for their experiments individually using the one-page *planning form* described later in this section. Students receive constructive feedback on these forms at the beginning of the laboratory period; then, working in groups of three to four, they choose which hypothesis to test and how to test it. They then submit a brief *research proposal* to inform the lab instructor of their final plan. Students have three hours to conduct their experiment, analyze their data, and collaboratively write a short *lab report* (typically two to three pages) following a standard format (Title, Introduction, Methods, Results, Discussion).

When designing experiments, students search the reference sections of their lab manuals (French 2005a; Russell and French 2005) for possible techniques and the operating instructions for the available equipment they select. The manuals also include guides on how to conduct a laboratory successfully and how to write a lab report, divided into sections that correspond to each item of the *grading scheme* (rubric). We also developed a series of *prelab exercises* (online and hands-on activities) and *laboratory study guide web pages* to provide hints, skills development, further background material, and guidance. The laboratory study guides can be viewed at *http://zoology.okstate.edu/zoo_lrc/biol1114/study_guides/labs*.

To develop investigations, we followed a general protocol. First we made up a list of target concepts, laboratory skills, and analytical skills that we thought students might learn during the course of a lab. Some were very broad and traditional (e.g., osmosis; graphing; use of a spectrophotometer) and others were narrower and unusual (surface-area-to-volume ratios; use of a dissolved oxygen probe). The concepts were those that the course developers thought important and were discussed in lecture at least once. Many concepts were covered in traditional labs we had done previously or found in traditional lab manuals. By starting with such labs, we were able to use equipment we had or could obtain easily. We were also able to start with protocols that consistently led to reliable and meaningful results. We chose experiments that would allow students flexibility in choosing independent variables; for example, in investigating transpiration rate, students could choose temperature, humidity, light intensity, wavelength of light, wind speed, CO_2 concentration, or pH of water.

We were not especially concerned with mastery of any particular piece of laboratory equipment by every student. Equipment that scientists use changes, varies from discipline to discipline, and typically requires extensive use before it is mastered (Holt et al. 1969). Sundberg and Moncada (1994) found that complex equipment may interfere with students' understanding of the phenomena they are trying to measure. On the other hand, computer systems and software that we use repeatedly (and are increasingly used in our upper-division courses) permit rapid data collection and analysis, allowing students to spend more time interpreting and performing additional experiments. We expected students would be more likely to master equipment that they select. By using instruments and computers repeatedly to generate reliable data quickly, students can spend more time thinking critically rather than spending substantial lab time setting up and mastering equipment most will never use again.

Once we had identified concept areas that would serve as domains for investigations, we created questions that could be answered by testable hypotheses. Given the constraints of class size and student and instructor experience and time, we chose to limit the scope of the investigations by posing questions as a means of stimulating scientific thinking. All our questions began with "Why," to reinforce the nature of hypotheses as being causal (McPherson 2001). For example, we used the question "Why do plants transpire water faster under certain environmental conditions?" rather than "What factors affect transpiration?"

We then wrote a story for each investigation to provide a real-world context and observations that would lead students to the question and to possible hypotheses. For example, when students investigate diffusion, they read that they work for a manufacturer of dialysis machines, and they read about how those machines work and some issues and observations made by those who work there. This alternative to requiring students to do literature searches reduces the time and training needed to prepare for each lab and therefore increases the number of investigative labs and opportunities to develop skills in formulating and testing hypotheses, experimental design, and data analysis that we can offer students. We do encourage students to review the literature, provide them with guides that explain how to do so, and reward those who cite and discuss articles in their reports.

Planning Form

One problem instructors face is getting the students to prepare for lab (Henderson and Buising 2001; Trautwein, Racke, and Hillman 1996), and prelab lectures and quizzes are typical solutions. Students must prepare more for inquiry-based labs (Sundberg and Moncada 1994; Tsaparlis and Gorezi 2005) because they do not follow specific directions or answer simple questions, but Stewart (1988) found that students came better prepared for inquiry labs than for traditional labs. To help students prepare for lab, to assess whether they need additional assistance, and to plan for unusual supplies, we developed a short planning form for students to complete before lab. The planning form consists of two basic sections.

In the first section, the students describe observations that led to the questions under investigation; propose a hypothesis that is relevant and testable within the context of the lab; briefly outline their experiment, including identifying experimental and control groups, method, and independent and dependent variables (by simple graph); predict results that would indicate whether their hypothesis was supported or not; list references for use in their report; and answer questions concerning relevant scientific concepts or techniques.

In the second section, students answer questions to indicate whether they completed their prelab exercises. We developed prelab exercises to familiarize students with concepts or techniques that could be useful. Some examples include learning to use Microsoft Excel to graph the mass, surface area, and volume of objects and predict one from the other; measuring temperatures using computer-based temperature probes; describing the mode of action of specific antibiotics; and identifying organisms that are good indicators of water quality. Students must complete some exercises (e.g., learning to load a gel) outside lab time at stations set up for that purpose; they can complete others online. To satisfy students' requests, we created online versions of many exercises that students originally performed on-campus. This allows flexibility and suits students' preferences for online or hands-on. Interestingly, many students complete both.

Lab Manuals

To provide the students with the information they need while encouraging them to take responsibility for planning and preparation, we authored lab manuals with an unusual format (French 2005a; Russell and French 2005). We wanted the manuals to serve as resource guides that described procedures and techniques clearly, without providing step-by-step solutions to problems or details of specific experiments. Therefore the lab manuals were divided into three sections. The first section provides course information (expectations, philosophy of inquiry labs, directions for using the manual, discussion of plagiarism, discussion of peer review) and guidelines and recommendations for how to design and complete experiments and write lab reports successfully. The second section provides information on what equipment and supplies are available; how to operate the computer; how to use word-processing and spreadsheet software; how to use lab equipment, including microscopes, video cameras, and computer-based sensors; how to measure volumes, mass, and surfaces; how to perform statistical analyses; and how to search for articles in our library. The third section includes the investigations, planning forms, and grading rubrics. Besides the questions and scenarios described above, the investigation chapters include lists of potentially useful concepts, directions for using investigation-specific techniques or equipment, special instructions, and safety hints. We opted to include techniques specific to one investigation with that investigation so as to reduce unnecessary searching and frustration. For example, a temperature probe is useful in many different situations, so directions for its use are found in the reference section, but calculating a Palmer Index is only useful in our water quality investigation and is found there. Including safety hints in the manual and the lab instructors' remarks is very important in an inquiry lab, where students are not following set procedures (Deters 2004; Sundberg, Armstrong, et al. 2000).

Equipment

Equipment is distributed depending on how often it will be used. Like Luckie and colleagues (2004), we provide each group a set of frequently used equipment in the lab bench drawers. Each group can choose to use any of those items as they wish and without having to share. Students sitting at that lab bench in other lab sections use the same equipment. More fragile or specialized equipment resides in a separate room and can be requested as needed. Equipment that will only be used during one lab (e.g., gel electrophoresis chambers) is put out only for that lab.

Assessment of Our Method

How well does our method work? During extensive observations of students, we found a positive correlation between time spent on task (i.e., setting up, conducting experiments, analyzing data) and achievement in inquiry-based laboratories (Russell and French 2001). We did not find this same correlation in traditional labs. Additionally, although males and females participated differently in traditional labs, no such gender differences were found in inquiry-based labs. This is consistent with Shepardson (1997), who found that in traditional labs, students spent more time interpreting directions, but in inquiry labs, they spent more time analyzing and interpreting results. Students interacted more with their teachers in traditional labs but interacted more with other students in inquiry labs.

In a recent end-of-semester survey, we found that 81% of students ($N = 683$) either agreed or strongly agreed (based on a 5-point Likert-type scale) with the statement "I think the lab helped me better understand how scientists discover how things work"; only 7% disagreed. We also found that 78% strongly agreed or agreed and 7% disagreed with the statement "I liked working in labs where I could control the outcome by designing my own experiments." (The remaining students were neutral in their opinions.) However, in discussions with students and in open-ended comments on surveys, we find that many students are still ambivalent about inquiry labs. This observation has been made by others (Henderson and Buising 2001; Stukus and Lennox 1995; Sundberg and Moncada 1994) and has been attributed to students' feelings of uncertainty, reaction to the rigor of the work required, and lack of organizational skills.

We also investigated whether our prelab exercises helped students prepare for lab and found that students who did prelab exercises scored higher on their planning forms and groups that scored higher on planning forms scored higher on lab reports, but these relationships appear to be affected by the instructor, many of whom are teaching inquiry-based labs for the first time (Gentry and French, manuscript in preparation). This is consistent with studies that have discussed the importance of having experienced instructors in inquiry labs (French and Russell 2002; Glasson and McKenzie 1997; Sundberg, Armstrong, et al. 2000).

Recommendations

Converting to inquiry-based labs can appear daunting, especially for large-enrollment courses. It is easier if one modifies existing labs with the goal of creating a research experience for students (French 2005b). To do this, one should

- select labs that can be completed in one period,
- allow students to select variables and methods that can result in multiple successful outcomes,
- provide a short scenario for each lab to introduce a question in a real-world context,
- ask an open-ended question in each lab that leads to multiple testable hypotheses,
- provide a general set of equipment and techniques from which students can choose,
- provide support (prelab exercises, lab manual of resources, online guides) to help students prepare for lab,
- require short written proposals from individuals to encourage and assess preparedness and provide feedback on these before lab starts, and
- allow students to work in groups to design, conduct, and report on experiments.

Although making the transition from traditional laboratory exercises to inquiry-based investigations can be challenging, the return in improved critical-thinking skills, student attitude toward science, and achievement in courses using the strategy makes it worth the effort.

Acknowledgment

This material is based on research partially supported by the National Science Foundation under awards DUE 9752402 and DUE 9851458. Any opinions, findings, and conclusions or recommendations expressed in the chapter are those of the authors and do not necessarily reflect the views of the National Science Foundation.

References

Ault, A. 2002. What's wrong with cookbooks? *Journal of Chemical Education* 79: 1177.

Basey, J. M., T. N. Mendelow, and C. N. Ramos. 2000. Current trends of community college lab curricula in biology: An analysis of inquiry, technology. *Journal of Biological Education* 34: 80–86.

Colburn, A. 2004. Focusing labs on the nature of science. *The Science Teacher* 71 (9): 32–35.

Darling, R. 2001. Don't settle for imitation laboratory assignments: Introducing students to semester-long independent study projects. *Journal of College Science Teaching* 31: 102–105.

DeGolier, T. 2002. Using a guided-inquiry approach for investigating metabolic rate in mice. *American Biology Teacher* 64: 449–454.

Deters, K. 2004. Inquiry in the chemistry classroom. *The Science Teacher* 71 (10): 42–45.

French, D. P. 2005a. *Investigating biology: A laboratory resource manual.* 2005 ed. Fort Worth, TX: Fountainhead Press.

French, D. P. 2005b. Was inquiry a mistake? It's all in the name. *Journal of College Science Teaching* 35: 60–62.

French, D. P., and C. P. Russell. 2002. Do graduate teaching assistants benefit from teaching inquiry-based laboratories? *Bioscience* 52: 1036–1041.

Gentry, M. R., and D. P. French. Manuscript in preparation. The effect of pre-class activities on student performance in inquiry-based labs.

Glasson, G. E., and W. L. McKenzie. 1997. Investigative learning in undergraduate freshman biology laboratories. *Journal of College Science Teaching* 27: 189–193.

Grant, B., and W. Vatnick. 1998. A multi-week inquiry for an undergraduate introductory biology laboratory. *Journal of College Science Teaching* 28: 109–112.

Heady, J. E. 1993. Teaching embryology without lectures and without traditional laboratories—an adventure in innovation. *Journal of College Science Teaching* 23: 87–91.

Henderson, L., and C. Buising. 2001. A research-based molecular biology laboratory. *Journal of College Science Teaching* 30: 322–327.

Holt, C. E., P. Abramoff, L. V. Wilcox, and D. L. Abell. 1969. Investigative laboratory programs in biology: A position paper of the commission on undergraduate education in the biological sciences. *Bioscience* 19: 1104–1107.

Keefer, R. 1998. Criteria for designing inquiry activities that are effective for teaching and learning science concepts. *Journal of College Science Teaching* 28: 159–165.

Leonard, W. H. 1991. A recipe for uncookbooking laboratory investigations. *Journal of College Science Teaching* 21: 84–87.

Luckie, D. B., J. J. Maleszewski, S. D. Loznak, and M. Krha. 2004. Infusion of collaborative inquiry throughout a biology curriculum increases student learning: A four-year study of "Teams and Streams." *Advances in Physiological Education* 287: 199–209.

Marbach-Ad, G., and L. A. Classen. 2001. Improving students' questions in inquiry labs. *American Biology Teacher* 63: 410–419.

Mayer, R. E. 2004. Should there be a three-strikes rule against pure discovery learning?: The case for guided methods of instruction. *American Psychologist* 59: 14–19.

McPherson G. R. 2001. Teaching and learning the scientific method. *American Biology Teacher* 63: 242–245.

Myers, M. J., and A.B. Burgess. 2003. Inquiry-based laboratory course improves students' ability to design experiments and interpret data. *Advances in Physiological Education* 27 (1): 26–33.

Russell, C. P., and D. P. French. 2001. Factors affecting participation in traditional and inquiry-based laboratories. *Journal of College Science Teaching* 31: 225–229.

Russell, C. P., and D. P. French. 2005. *Biological investigations: A laboratory resource guide.* Fort Worth, TX: Fountainhead Press.

Shepardson, D. P. 1997. The nature of student thinking in life science laboratories. *School Science and Mathematics* 97: 37–44.

Shiland, T. W. 1999. Constructivism: the implications for laboratory work. *Journal of Chemical Education* 76 (1): 107–109

Stewart, B. Y. 1988. The surprise element of a student-designed laboratory experiment. *Journal of College Science Teaching* 17: 269–270.

Stukus, P., and J. E. Lennox. 1995. Use of an investigative semester-length laboratory project in an introductory microbiology course. *Journal of College Science Teaching* 25: 135–139.

Suits, J. P. 2004. Assessing investigative skill development in inquiry-based and traditional college science laboratory courses. *School Science and Mathematics* 104: 248–257.

Sundberg, M. D., J. E. Armstrong, M. Dini, and W. Wischusen. 2000. Some practical tips for instituting investigative biology laboratories. *Journal of College Science Teaching* 29 (5): 353–359.

Sundberg, M. D., and G. J. Moncada. 1994. Creating effective investigative laboratories for undergraduates. *BioScience* 44: 698–704.

Thornton, J. W., ed. 1972. *The laboratory: A place to investigate.* Commission on Undergraduate Education in the Biological Sciences, Pub. No. 33. Washington, DC: AIBS Education Division.

Trautwein, S. N., A. Racke, and B. Hillman. 1996. Cooperative learning in the anatomy laboratory. *Journal of College Science Teaching* 26: 183–188.

Tsaparlis, G., and M. Gorezi. 2005. A modification of a conventional expository physical chemistry laboratory to accommodate an inquiry/project-based component: Method and students' evaluation. *Canadian Journal of Science, Mathematics, and Technology Education* 5: 111–131.

Wallace, C. S., M. Y. Tsoi, J. Calkin, and M. Darley. 2003. Learning from inquiry-based laboratories in non-major biology: An interpretive study of the relationships among inquiry experience, epistemologies, and conceptual growth. *Journal of Research in Science Teaching* 40: 986–1024.

UNIT V
Use of Technology

While the use of technology-enriched environments ... is becoming increasingly common, this by no means implies that technology is either well used or well understood. Educational technologies can boost learning and better chemistry understanding only if they are wisely used and judiciously coordinated with course goals.... The integration of technology-enriched environments can achieve many positive outcomes [that] .... inculcate in students intrinsic motivation to learn in addition to a deep understanding of class content compared with traditional lectures. —Miri Barak

Since 1998, ... [we] have been using animations to help students construct an understanding of processes such as cellular respiration, photosynthesis, action potentials, and synaptic transmission in a large-enrollment ..., multi-section ..., mixed-majors, general education, introductory biology course. We present the animations as part of larger scenarios in which we have introduced a real-life context, posed a general question, or set up a problem to be solved. —Donald P. French

Carefully chosen and properly used instructional technology can increase student learning and student interest. Poorly used instructional technology can do the opposite.... The decision to use instructional technology, or any educational tool, should be centered on student learning. —Timothy Champion and Andrea Novicki

The chemistry pedagogy courses were developed within a mastery framework. They focus on repeatable testing with feedback and use links to existing web-based curriculum resources. Teachers enroll and work asynchronously and receive credit once they demonstrate success with 93% of the items. —David W. Brooks and Kent J. Crippen

Recent studies confirm what undergraduate science instructors already know: Students are increasingly using the internet as the primary source of science information for reports, projects, presentations, and other class assignments. While the internet has unquestionably revolutionized information dissemination and access, it is also clear that the quality, validity, and accuracy of science information on the internet are extremely variable. —Jory P. Weintraub

213

Perhaps the most far-reaching event to impact college science teaching in recent years is the revolution in information technology. In the "flattened world" (Friedman 2005) of the 21st century, knowledge is freely available to those with access, and the privileged position of knowledge producers and disseminators has been forever altered. What does this mean for college science teachers? In this unit several authors present their views on how best to accommodate our teaching to the technological changes we have experienced. Topics include the use of technology-enhanced learning environments; the use of animations to enhance lectures; the value of interactive, web-based instruction; and the use of the internet as a primary source of science information.

Miri Barak of the Technion-Israel Institute of Technology reviews the research on *technology-enriched learning environments* in college chemistry. Summarizing current research and practice, she provides an overview of the use of technology in the areas of information seeking and problem solving, computer-based modeling and simulations, computers in laboratory work and simulations, and the computer in collaborative learning and knowledge sharing. The chapter offers a number of useful sources of additional information and valuable websites.

Donald French has revamped his introductory biology course at Oklahoma State University, incorporating *animated presentations* as one component of an inquiry-oriented effort to encourage students to ask questions, make observations, formulate and test hypotheses, and draw conclusion from data. In this chapter, Don discusses what cognitive theory has to say about animations, how to use animations to encourage active engagement in large lectures, and where to acquire animated materials. He concludes with some recommendations on the use of animations in college science teaching.

In their wide-ranging *review of technology* in college science teaching, Timothy Champion and Andrea Novicki of Johnson C. Smith University describe and provide empirical support for three broad areas of application: face-to-face teaching, communication outside the classroom, and learning assignments. In the area of teaching they discuss presentation software (i.e., PowerPoint), animations, classroom response systems (i.e., "clickers"), interactive whiteboards and tablet PCs, simulations, and probeware. In communication, they touch on course management systems, e-mail, and distance learning. And in learning assignments they discuss wikis, blogs, discussion boards, online assignments, concept mapping, and Calibrated Peer Review software.

David Brooks of the University of Nebraska and Kent Crippen of the University of Nevada describe their work on *web-based practice and assessment* using a mastery learning model in chemistry. Their learning systems aim to develop both conceptual and procedural knowledge with special attention to problem-solving ability, and they have been used to teach pedagogy to high school science teachers and undergraduate general chemistry students. The system makes use of a wide variety of response items, including essay, short answer, fill-in-the-blank, ranking, matching, categorization, multiple choice, true/false, image, and more complex formats.

Jory Weintraub of the National Evolutionary Synthesis Center (a collaborative effort of Duke University, University of North Carolina at Chapel Hill, and North Carolina State University) tells us how undergraduate students *use the internet* as a primary source in their search for high-quality, useful, and scientifically valid information. His primary focus is on teaching students to read sources skeptically and to analyze information critically. Among the sources he recommends is his own website, "Evaluating the Accuracy of Science Information on the Internet."

Reference

Friedman, T. L. 2005. *The world is flat: A brief history of the twenty-first century.* New York: Farrar, Straus and Giroux.

CHAPTER 22

Technology-Enriched Learning Environments in University Chemistry

Miri Barak

Miri Barak is senior researcher in the Department of Education in Technology and Science at Technion-Israel Institute of Technology, Haifa. She earned a PhD in chemistry and biochemistry education at the Technion and conducts research in chemical education, educational technologies, and computerized molecular modeling. She teaches science and technology courses.

Science and technology courses in higher education have traditionally been composed of three elements—lecture, recitation, and evaluation—and have been conducted in lecture-based, teacher-centered settings. In recent years, a growing number of university-level courses are exploring the possibilities of integrating technology-enriched environments (see Chapter 10 in this volume). This chapter presents an overview of recent studies on the integration of technology-enriched environments into college-level chemistry courses and the effect of these environments on students' learning.

Chemistry Education and Technology-Enriched Learning Environments

Technology-enriched environments, also referred to as web-based environments or ICT (information and communication technologies), are rapidly emerging as an important tool for teaching chemistry in higher education (Donovan and Nakhleh 2001; Dori, Barak, and Adir 2003). Indeed, discovering the scope of information available over the web and how to use it is an important part of the undergraduate education of every chemistry student (Murov 2001). Along this line, a large number of websites that focus on chemistry topics have been developed for academic purposes. Lecture notes, homework projects, online books, and complete courses in chemistry are now available on the web.

Exemplary online chemistry courses can be found at the Open CourseWare website of the Massachusetts Institute of Technology (MIT; *http://ocw.mit.edu/OcwWeb/Chemistry/index.htm*),

which includes problem sets and lecture handouts of organic, physical, and biological chemistry, as well as laboratory assignments, readings, and recitations. The National Institute of Standards and Technology Chemistry WebBook (*http://webbook.nist.gov/chemistry*) is another web-based resource that provides access to chemical and physical properties, data, search options, models, and tools. Another online resource is the Computational Chemistry Comparison and Benchmark DataBase (*http://srdata.nist.gov/cccbdb*), which provides experimental and computational thermochemical data for gas-phase atoms and molecules. These are only a few examples of the vast chemical information, data, and resources that can be found on the web.

Integrating technology in a coherent and authentic way into curricula is a significant and imperative challenge, especially in higher-education institutions (Barak, Forthcoming; Barak and Dori 2005). Such integration can be classified into four educational applications: (a) information seeking and problem solving, (b) computerized modeling and simulations, (c) computer-based laboratories and real-time graphing, and (d) collaborative learning and knowledge sharing.

Information Seeking and Problem Solving

The web is a valuable resource for chemistry information. Use of the web can save considerable library research time as it provides users with rapidly growing chemistry references. The information that can be found on the web ranges from chemical and physical properties of elements, isotopes, and compounds to significant figures and unit conversions.

The web's capability of being a constant resource for new information, as well as its availability and accessibility, gives rise to educational assignments that focus on information seeking and problem solving in a real-world context and inquiry-based setting. A well thought-out use of the web might promote students' ability to develop a logical sequence of steps toward solving chemical problems or investigating molecular systems. Indeed, information seeking, inquiry-based learning, and exploring resources via networks were found to be beneficial for higher-education chemistry learning and teaching (Dori, Barak, and Adir 2003; Glaser and Poole 1999).

Barak and Dori (2005) investigated the integration of web-based tools for enhancing project-based learning among general chemistry students. The project included topics such as molecules in daily life, elements in the periodic table, and scientific theories. Each assignment required an authentic investigation of concepts and theories, solutions to real-world problems, and use of the web for supporting this process of inquiry. The study indicated that incorporating ICT-rich learning environments into freshman chemistry courses enhanced students' understanding of chemical concepts, scientific theories, and molecular structures.

Wamser (2003) reported on a chemistry course website that holds a list containing over 200 molecules. Students in organic chemistry classes were assigned a unique set of biologically relevant molecules to report on as optional extra-credit assignments. Their report had to include the assigned molecule's molecular formula, hybridization, functional groups, number of stereocenters, and biological relevance. Students could use a book for their answer, but they were encouraged to use the web as their source of information (e.g., the ChemFinder website, *http://chemfinder.cambridgesoft.com*). Investigating the affective domain, the researcher found students' responses to the online exercise to be highly positive. Positive results of the use of web capabilities were also presented by Donovan and Nakhleh (2001), who found that students who use the course website value this resource of information and the visualization that it offers.

Having access to a vast library of information sources, statistics, quotations, graphic images, sound files, and free download programs is a tremendous benefit for students. However, the spectrum of material on the web runs from the useful and important to the pointless, biased, and misleading (Barak, Forthcoming; Burbules and Callister 2000; see also Chapter 26 in this volume). In their search for a certain concept, topic, or data, students might be exposed to misinformation, disinformation, or useless information that might result in misunderstanding and misconceptions. It is therefore recommended not to send students on a random quest, but rather to direct them to approved educational websites such as an online encyclopedia and websites of known universities and authorized institutions.

Computerized Modeling and Simulations

Modeling and simulations are used in chemistry research for describing, explaining, and exploring phenomena, processes, and abstract ideas (Dori and Barak 2001). Models stimulate their creators and viewers to pose questions that take them beyond the original phenomenon and, therefore, might assist them in formulating new hypotheses. These capabilities have opened the way for advanced research in chemistry, resulting in, among other things, a Nobel Prize in chemistry awarded to John Pople in 1998 (see *http://nobelprize.org/chemistry/laureates/1998*). Computational chemistry, modeling, and simulations, which are well integrated into chemistry research, are slowly finding their way into chemistry teaching.

Static graphics of chemical structures found in textbooks may help learners to form two-dimensional (2-D) mental images, but computers can provide three-dimensional (3-D) visualizations. Computerized molecular modeling tools such as MDL ISIS/Draw and Chime (*www.mdli.com*) and Viewer-Pro (*www.accelrys.com*) enable dynamic, interactive, 3-D simulations of molecular formulas and their spatial structure (Figure 22.1). These web-based tools facilitate the drawing and manipulating of virtual molecules and the prediction of molecular spatial structure through energy minimization calculations based on quantum mechanics.

Computerized molecular modeling allows students to view, rotate, and measure virtual molecules, as well as modify or construct new ones. These visualization tools make the abstract real and thus help students understand chemical concepts (Barak and Dori 2005; Barnea and Dori 1999; Dori and Barak 2001). Williamson and Abraham (1995) studied the effect of computer animations on college student mental models of chemical

Figure 22.1

A Computerized Molecular Model of Caffeine

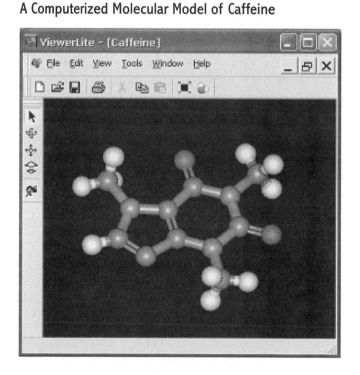

phenomena. The researchers indicated that the animations helped students understand the subject matter better while improving their ability to construct dynamic mental models of chemical processes.

Majors in the Department of Chemistry and Biochemistry at California State University, Fullerton, were introduced to chemical computation early in the undergraduate curriculum in an electronic classroom equipped with networked Silicon Graphics workstations (Kantard-jieff, Hardinger, and Van Willis 1999). Lipkowitz and colleagues (1999) used computational chemistry as a bridge between the disciplines of geology and chemistry. They presented four assignments in which computational chemistry was integrated into an undergraduate geology course on the topic of mineralogy. In both studies students were engaged in exploration activities whereby they learned how to use modern software packages as tools to understand chemistry and nature.

Dori, Barak, and Adir (2003) described a web-based general chemistry course that encouraged its students to participate in a computerized molecular modeling project. Their findings indicated that ICT-enhanced teaching positively affects students' achievement, provided the students are actively engaged in constructing the computerized models. These results are in line with the findings of Donovan and Nakhleh (2001), who concluded that the website used in their general chemistry course was instrumental in visualizing and understanding chemistry.

Cox and colleagues (2003) developed interactive physics-based curricular materials that helped their students learn concepts of thermodynamics, with a particular focus on kinetic theory models. The simulations helped students visualize ideal gas particle dynamics and develop a conceptual framework for problem solving.

Indeed, among the many advantages of using innovative technologies in chemical education, computerized molecular modeling and simulations are significantly important for students' chemical understanding and spatial ability (Barak and Dori 2005; Barnea and Dori 1999; Dori and Barak 2001).

Computer-Based Laboratories and Real-Time Graphing

Computers used as laboratory tools may offer a fundamentally new way for aiding students' construction of science concepts. Designated software and probes can help students collect, record, and graph data. They can provide opportunities for asking and refining questions, making predictions, designing plans or experiments, collecting and analyzing data, debating ideas, communicating ideas, drawing conclusions, and asking new questions (Linn, Layman, and Nachmias 1987). Probes can be used to collect laboratory data such as temperature, motion, force, pH, sound, light, and pressure. Since most of the technical work in technology environments is done in real time by the computer, students can spend more time solving problems, generating their own knowledge, and using higher-order thinking skills.

Real-time graphing, formerly known as microcomputer-based laboratories (MBL), offers a dynamic representation of the relationships between at least two variables such as time, pH, and/or temperature. Its value lies in the ease with which data can be collected by various probes and then stored in a computer or a calculator. It allows for frequent repetition and provides opportunities to experience graphical chemical and physical phenomena. The ability to access data over time intervals of varying durations and the power to rapidly process and display the collected data leave more time for students to test hypotheses, manipulate variables, and explore relationships (Russell, Lucas, and McRobbie 2004).

Papadopoulos and Limniou (2003) describe a pH titration simulator that allows students to run realistic experiments and receive sample data as part of the process of learning how to carry out a titration. They found that computer laboratories provide an extremely versatile way to ensure that students can gain experience with a wider variety of indicators and titrations than would be possible in the physical laboratory.

Using an interactive software program, Virtual Chemistry Laboratory (VCL), Martínez-Jiménez and colleagues (2003) conducted an experiment to assess the software's influence on student understanding of some basic organic chemistry laboratory techniques. They concluded that the use of VCL helped students gain a better understanding of the techniques and basic concepts used in the laboratory work. VCL particularly contributed to the progress of students with the greatest learning difficulties. Along this line, Stratford, Krajcik, and Soloway (1998) found that the use of computer-based laboratories enables students to connect between multiple representations of scientific phenomena and processes.

Dori and colleagues (2004) reported on a project that aimed at integrating computerized experiments into chemistry teaching in order to foster students' higher-order thinking skills, to teach in an up-to-date environment, and to motivate and stimulate the students. They found a significant improvement in students' question posing, scientific inquiry, and graphing skills, as well as in students' satisfaction with the computerized learning environment and the case-based inquiry approach.

Overall, studies have indicated that computer-based laboratories and real-time graphing can serve as a platform for incorporating inquiry strategies, which can help students collect and interpret online data. Technology-enhanced laboratories were found to foster conceptual understanding and transfer between chemical representations (Dori et al. 2004; H. Wu, Krajcik, and Soloway 2001).

Collaborative Learning and Knowledge Sharing

It is well established that learning is influenced by participation in a community and that learners construct their knowledge through social interaction with peers (Bruner 1990; Vygotsky 1978). The notion of small learning communities and online teamwork is gaining much traction in contemporary research on technology-enriched environments. There are only a few examples of such efforts in undergraduate courses, and this is an important field that is yet to be studied.

QSIA (*http://qsia.haifa.ac.il*)—an acronym for Questions Sharing, Information and Assessment—is one example of an online system that was specially developed for knowledge management and sharing (Barak and Rafaeli 2004; Rafaeli et al. 2004). The QSIA system facilitates the generation of learning

Figure 22.2

Sharing Knowledge Items via the QSIA System

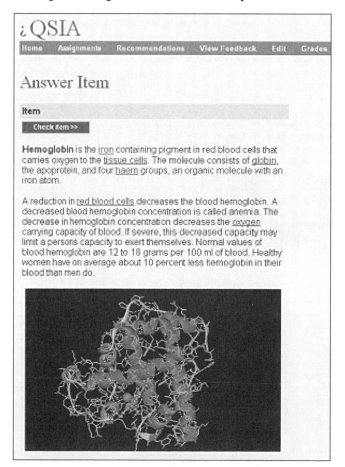

objects and assignments and their distribution among peer teachers and students (Figure 22.2). A study conducted to investigate students' use of QSIA provided evidence that web-based activities can serve as both learning and assessment enhancers in higher education by promoting active learning, constructive feedback, and knowledge sharing (Barak and Rafaeli 2004).

Glaser and Poole (1999) reported on the use of group research projects in an undergraduate course in organic chemistry to build small learning communities. Students were engaged in group research projects via online resources and developed reports that were published online. They also worked together in groups to review the online reports of their peers. This work was facilitated by the use of electronic media, including the course website, e-mail, and an electronic discussion list.

The Physical Chemistry Online (PCOL) consortium is a collaborative initiative engaging faculty and students from geographically dispersed institutions in short-duration activities. PCOL focuses on context-rich scenarios and uses e-mail, discussion boards, and the web for communication and information distribution (Towns et al. 2001). Chemistry Is in the News (CIITN) is a similar project that enhances chemistry learning experiences through collaboration among students and faculty from different academic institutions. It aims at developing scientific and media literacy by engaging students in learning activities that are based on authentic news. The CIITN web tool was developed to support online creation and peer review of team projects conducted as part of an organic chemistry course. Students who participated in this project demonstrated positive attitudes toward the use of the CIITN web tool, though efforts to improve its interface and attractiveness are still required (Z. Wu and Glaser 2004).

In another study, White and his colleagues (2000) reported on a seminar course for chemistry and biochemistry majors. Small groups of students worked together to create informative websites that took positions on important societal issues related to chemistry. Throughout the course, the instructors placed particular emphasis on developing students' ability to work cooperatively, locate and evaluate information, make informed judgments based on available information, and logically develop and defend their positions. This exemplary course and the studies reported above indicate the significance of fostering collaborative learning and knowledge sharing among students and lecturers (within the university and across universities) via communication technologies.

Conclusion

While the use of technology-enriched environments in chemistry higher education is becoming increasingly common, this by no means implies that technology is either well used or well understood. Educational technologies can boost learning and better chemistry understanding only if they are wisely used and judiciously coordinated with course goals. When properly done, the integration of technology-enriched environments can achieve many positive outcomes in student learning and faculty teaching. Such positive outcomes inculcate in students intrinsic motivation to learn in addition to a deep understanding of class content compared with traditional lectures. It can also be professionally rewarding for the faculty who provide it. The instructor's sustained commitment and the instructional setting play a critical role in shaping an environment that will allow for an active, constructivist, and meaningful learning setting.

References

Barak, M. Forthcoming. Transitions from traditional to ICT-enhanced learning environments in undergraduate chemistry courses. *Computers & Education*. Also available online at *www.sciencedirect.com*.

Barak, M., and Y. J. Dori. 2005. Enhancing undergraduate students' chemistry understanding through project-based learning in an IT environment. *Science Education* 89 (1): 117–139.

Barak, M., and S. Rafaeli. 2004. Online question-posing and peer-assessment as means for web-based knowledge sharing. *International Journal of Human-Computer Studies* 61 (1): 84–103.

Barnea, N., and Y. J. Dori. 1999. High-school chemistry students' performance and gender differences in a computerized molecular modeling learning environment. *Journal of Science Education and Technology* 8 (4): 257–271.

Bruner, J. S. 1990. *Acts of meaning.* Cambridge, MA: Harvard University Press.

Burbules, N. C., and T. A. Callister. 2000. *Watch IT: The risks and promises of information technologies for education.* Oxford, England: Westview Press.

Cox, A. J., M. Belloni, M. Dancy, and W. Christian. 2003. Physlets in introductory physics. *Physics Education* 38 (5): 433–440.

Donovan, W. J., and M. B. Nakhleh. 2001. Students' use of web-based tutorial materials and their understanding of chemistry concepts. *Journal of Chemical Education* 78: 975–980.

Dori, Y. J., and M. Barak. 2001. Virtual and physical molecular modeling: Fostering model perception and spatial understanding. *Educational Technology and Society* 4 (1): 61–74.

Dori, Y. J., M. Barak, and N. Adir. 2003. A web-based chemistry course as a means to foster freshmen learning. *Journal of Chemical Education* 80 (9): 1084–1092.

Dori, Y. J., I. Sasson, Z. Kaberman, and O. Herscovitz. 2004. Integrating case-based computerized laboratories into high school chemistry. *The Chemical Educator* 9: 1–5.

Glaser, R. E., and M. L. Poole. 1999. Organic chemistry online: Building collaborative learning communities through electronic communication tools. *Journal of Chemical Education* 76: 699–703.

Kantardjieff, K. A., S. A. Hardinger, and W. J. Van Willis. 1999. Introducing computers early in the undergraduate chemistry curriculum. *Journal of Chemical Education* 76: 694–697.

Linn, M. C., J. W. Layman, and R. Nachmias. 1987. Cognitive consequences of microcomputer-based laboratories: Graphing skills development. *Contemporary Education Psychology* 12 (3): 244–253.

Lipkowitz, K. B., M. Jalaie, D. Robertson, and A. Barth. 1999. Interdisciplinary learning with computational chemistry: A collaboration between chemistry and geology. *Journal of Chemical Education* 76: 684–687.

Martínez-Jiménez, P., A. Pontes-Pedrajas, M. S. Climent-Bellido, and J. Polo. 2003. Learning in chemistry with virtual laboratories. *Journal of Chemical Education* 80 (3): 346–347.

Murov, S. 2001. Exploring chemistry resources on the internet. *Journal of Chemical Education* 78 (10): 1429–1431.

Papadopoulos, N., and M. Limniou. 2003. pH titration simulator. *Journal of Chemical Education* 80 (6): 709.

Rafaeli, S., M. Barak, Y. Dan-Gur, and E. Toch. 2004. QSIA—a web-based environment for learning, assessing and knowledge sharing in communities. *Computers & Education* 43 (3): 273–289.

Russell, D. W., K. B. Lucas, and C. J. McRobbie. 2004. Role of the microcomputer-based laboratory display in supporting the construction of new understanding in thermal physics. *Journal of Research in Science Education* 41: 165–185.

Stratford, S. J., J. Krajcik, and E. Soloway. 1998. Secondary students' dynamic modeling processes: Analyzing, reasoning about, synthesizing, and testing models of stream ecosystems. *Journal of Science Education and Technology* 7 (3): 215–234.

Towns, M., D. Sauder, D. Whisnant, and T. J. Zielinski. 2001. Physical Chemistry On Line: Interinstitutional collaboration at a distance. *Journal of Chemical Education* 78 (3): 414–415.

Vygotsky, L. 1978. Interaction between learning and development. In *Mind in society: The development of higher psychological functions,* eds. M. Cole, V. John-Steiner, S. Scribner, and E. Souberman, 79–91. Cambridge, MA: Harvard University Press.

Wamser, C. C. 2003. E-mail molecules—individualizing the large lecture class. *Journal of Chemical Education* 80 (11): 1267–1270.

White, H. B., M. V. Johnston, and M. Panar. 2000. Senior seminar focusing on societal issues related to chemistry and biochemistry. *Journal of Chemical Education* 77 (12): 1590–1593.

Williamson, V. M., and M. R. Abraham. 1995. The effects of computer animation on the particulate mental models of college chemistry students. *Journal of Research in Science Teaching* 32: 521–534.

Wu, H., J. S. Krajcik, and E. Soloway. 2001. Promoting understanding of chemical representations: Students' use of visualization tools in the classroom. *Journal of Research in Science Teaching* 38 (7): 821–842.

Wu, Z., and R. E. Glaser. 2004. Software for the synergistic integration of science with ICT education. *Journal of Information Technology Education* 3: 325–339.

CHAPTER 23

Animating Your Lecture

Donald P. French

Donald P. French is professor of zoology at Oklahoma State University and president of the Society for College Science Teachers. He earned a PhD in zoology at Indiana University and conducts research in animal behavior and science education. He teaches courses in introductory biology and the teaching of zoology.

Advances in technology and cost reductions have made computers available for classroom use on most, if not all, college campuses. Consequently, faculty are encouraged to use presentation software in their classrooms. Faculty are also encouraged to follow the lead of many educators in changing the way they teach to better reflect how students learn (Donovan and Bransford 2005). Unfortunately, these two reform efforts (teaching with technology and inquiry-based teaching) can conflict.

Instructors commonly use presentation software (e.g., PowerPoint) the same way they use overheads and 35 mm slides (Crow 2005). Although presentation software technology allows faculty to create more legible and attractive visuals, it can promote teaching practices that have negative effects. This is especially true when instructors present a lot of text faster than they (or their students) might write.

As it is commonly used, presentation software can present a deceptively attractive barrier to active learning. Classrooms remain teacher centered, with didactic lectures and student engagement limited to note taking. This differs from a student-centered classroom, in which students engage in active learning by making observations, cooperative problem solving, and other activities that place a greater responsibility on students for reflecting on and formulating questions about the material that is the focus of discussion.

There is evidence that the use of presentation software can increase student learning (e.g., Mantei 2000) or retention (Moore and Miller 1996; Powers 1998), typically in the form of data from surveys. For example, Griffin (2003) reported that students thought his use of Power-Point resulted in more organized lectures and encouraged class participation. However, Szabo and Hastings (2000) found that when they controlled for the level of subject difficulty, Pow-erPoint presentations were no more effective than overheads. Norvig (2003) explains this as resulting from the design of PowerPoint presentations, in which the speaker reduces information to short phrases without complex graphs or charts and conveys the idea that the answers found in the bulleted points are simple and definitive.

Animations (rapidly changing sequences of drawn objects that simulate motion as in a movie) have also been advocated for classroom use for years (Hall 1996), and there is good evidence to support the value of this practice. Williamson and Abraham (1995) found that students taught using animations scored higher on tests of conceptual understanding of chemical phenomena than those taught without animations. They proposed that animations may help students form dynamic mental models that are longer lasting and more like those of experts. Sanger and Greenbowe (1997) found that, compared with those taught without animations, fewer students taught using animations in lecture developed misconceptions about molecular-level chemical processes. Sanger, Brecheisen, and Hynek (2001) also found animations effective in reducing students' misconceptions in biology, and Lowe (2003) found them effective in assisting students studying meteorology. Guided explorations using visualizations helped college students engage in active learning and construct knowledge (Khoo and Koh 1998).

There is general agreement that it is not the use of multimedia and animations but how they are used that is important (Mayer and Moreno 2002). Therefore, this chapter focuses on how to use animations in a classroom. Following a discussion of what cognitive theory tells us about designing and using multimedia, I explain how animations can be used in a classroom to encourage active learning and how to create and acquire animations to use in your classroom. The chapter concludes with guidelines for using animations in lecture.

Application of Cognitive Theory to the Design and Use of Multimedia

Application of cognitive psychology to the design and use of multimedia (i.e., information presented using a combination of at least two sensory stimuli, typically visual and auditory) has led to valuable findings and models. Although much of the research has focused on individual student use of computer-assisted instruction, it also applies to more general classroom use. Dual-coding theory (Paivio 1986) has been combined with other learning theories (Mayer 1997) to explain that people receive, separate, identify, and integrate information from visual and auditory channels and use separate systems dedicated to processing information from each of these channels. Each of the systems has a maximum capacity. Providing information in two modalities facilitates learning if the students can hold the two representations (visual and auditory) in short-term memory and integrate them. Once information is acquired and processed, cues from only one modality allow retrieval.

Unfortunately, instructors can present information in ways that make it difficult for students to acquire and process it. This occurs when students must concentrate on finding pertinent information amid all the stimuli presented, receive excess information on one or both channels, or cannot hold the representations of the information in memory long enough to integrate and process them (Mayer and Moreno 2003).

For example, animations are more effective if accompanied by narration alone than if accompanied by text (Moreno and Mayer 1999) or narration and text (Mayer and Moreno 2003). This may be because the text provides more visual information that must be processed by the same system that is processing the information from the animation. Alternatively, this may result from the observer having to split attention between the text and the animation and therefore missing part of the animation. The latter explanation is consistent with experiments showing that text placed close to the animation is more effective than text farther away (Moreno and Mayer 1999). Narration and animations are more effective if presented concurrently rather than sequentially (Mayer, Moreno, et al. 1999; Mayer and Sims 1994). This supports the assertion that for people to develop a representation of a concept from audiovisual information they must hold both representations in working memory simultaneously. This demands less effort if the learner does not have to hold one data set while waiting to accumulate the other. It also appears that live narration is more effective than recorded (Burke, Greenbowe, and Windschitl 1998).

An animation that presents irrelevant information or excess information can also impede learning. Animations without narration are ineffective if students cannot determine to what the elements and actions within the animation refer (Mayer and Anderson 1991). Mayer, Heiser, and Lonn (2001) found that music that accompanied a narration reduced the effectiveness of the narrated animation and suggested that narrations should be short and simple. They also suggested omitting interesting video clips or stories if they are not directly pertinent to the current concept. To reduce the problem of too much relevant information at once, Mayer and Moreno (2003) recommend using cues (e.g., arrows) to highlight the portion of an animation under discussion, breaking the animation into segments and allowing time for processing between segments, or allowing students to control the pace of the animation. Failure to give students control may have substantial effects on student learning. Tabbers and Martens (2004) found that when students controlled the pace of the animation, concurrent text displays rather than narrations led to higher posttest scores. This suggests that the technique that is best may be situation dependent.

Lowe (1999, 2003) found that students focused on components of animations that remained longer on the screen and were more readily distinguished from the other components of animation or background. Thus, animations may only help students construct knowledge about these components. Lowe also found that complex animations may exacerbate split-attention effects—too much visual information prevents students from following and understanding individual elements.

Yang, Andre, and Greenbowe (2003) found that animations were more effective than static illustrations as aids to student learning about electrochemical processes. They verbally described the processes while presenting images or 8- to 10-second animations to students in large-enrollment introductory chemistry lectures. Students could, and did, ask to have the animations repeated. They concluded that the animations were effective because they provided information not present in static illustrations, increased students' interest, encouraged students to spend more time studying them, or some combination of these effects. They also found, as did Mayer and Sims (1994), that students with higher spatial ability (the ability to imagine objects rotating in two or three dimensions and the effect of the rotations on their appearance) benefited more from animations than those with lower spatial ability. Carter, Larussa, and Bodner (1987) found a positive relationship between spatial ability and test scores in general chemistry.

Can animations help us engage students in activities that promote their construction of concepts through interactions with other students? Perhaps the key is using animations to provide information about the duration, rate, or sequence of steps within processes and guiding students through the process of making observations and asking questions.

An Example of the Use of Animation in a Large Lecture Classroom

Since 1998, the faculty teaching introductory biology at Oklahoma State University have been using animations to help students construct an understanding of processes such as cellular respiration, photosynthesis, action potentials, and synaptic transmission in a large-enrollment (125–215 students per section), multisection (4–6 sections per semester), mixed-majors, general education, introductory biology course. We present the animations as part of larger scenarios in which we have introduced a real-life context, posed a general question, or set up a problem to be solved. Some example contexts are

- trying to determine what compound might serve as an antidote for a child poisoned by consuming a plant that produces an acetylcholinesterase inhibitor,
- determining why a botanical preparation used by native peoples of the Amazon causes fish to become lethargic and "gasp" at the surface of a stream, and
- explaining the effects uncouplers have on adenosine triphosphate (ATP) formation in cellular respiration or photosynthesis.

We lead our students from the real-world applications to the underlying processes through a series of multimedia presentations, questions, discussions, and mini-lectures. Once we have agreed that the answer is within the process, it becomes time for the students to understand the process.

We do not build up to the process by presenting detailed information about each of the components or participants in the process. Instead, we rely on the animation to cue students in to particular components, then address the necessary topics or concepts on a need-to-know basis—that is, when the students' questions indicate that they are ready to discuss that component. To facilitate student note taking while they are observing and discussing the animation, we provide a diagram of the static, background portion of the animation. We tell the students, who work in semester-long groups of three or four, that they are free to ask any questions they want and that they should record what they observe by both drawing and describing the steps in a narrative. When we start the activity, we ask the students to record what they observe in the animation for a few minutes while the animation runs repeatedly. During this time, the instructor and graduate facilitators interact with the groups, assisting them by clarifying expectations and prompting them with questions (French and Russell 2001). We explain that we do not expect them to know what everything they are observing is (yet) and that simple descriptors (H^+, blue dot, brown circle) are acceptable.

After a few minutes, we ask the students to describe and explain what they have seen and ask whatever questions they wish. The types of questions students ask depend on their prior knowledge and experience. It is common for students to ask initially a question such as "What are those pink things?" Whenever possible, our responses are questions that can elicit the answer from students by leading them through what they have observed: What do you see it doing? What do you think the change signifies? What have you observed that makes you suggest that? How would you explain what you see happening? At this point, students are able to identify and name items like electron acceptors or to explain the role of neurotransmitters among themselves. Students' questions and answers help us uncover misconceptions or insufficient knowledge. We designed the software so that we can easily access animations that can help the students answer their own questions. For example, for a student who does not understand why we might call a hydrogen ion a proton, the instructor can access an interactive figure of water to illustrate dissociation and the parts of the atom.

With time, students begin asking questions leading to other relevant processes. For example, when observing the electron transport system in cellular respiration they ask, "Where do the NADH come from?" and during the light reactions of photosynthesis they ask, "Where are the NADPH going?" This allows the instructor to follow the students' lead into the Krebs cycle or the Calvin cycle. Eventually we reach discussions of the effect of interventions on the system at the microscopic and macroscopic level, which we can illustrate using animations after soliciting student hypotheses and predictions. To facilitate information transfer, we created similar animations to represent similar processes so students can apply their previous knowledge to explaining subsequent processes. For example, students require little time before they start identifying ATP synthase and explaining its action in the light reactions of photosynthesis after seeing it weeks earlier during cellular respiration. To monitor student understanding we use formative assessments, including diagrams and explanations that students produce in class and note cards on which students make hypotheses and predictions. Students also use personal response systems to answer multiple-choice questions that test their ability to apply their knowledge.

Creating and Acquiring Animations

We create our own animations and use those of others. To contain and control all of our images, video, audio, animations, and text, my students and I used Macromedia Authorware (*www.macromedia. com/software/authorware*) to create presentations. This software is designed for authoring computer-based instruction lessons and allows fine control and a high degree of interactivity. This allows us to manage the flow of our lessons and the cognitive load to fit student needs.

Figure 23.1

An Example of the Software Developed and Used by the Author

The main screen has clickable elements that animate when triggered. The buttons at the bottom allow rapid navigation to other animations or lesson components. The drop-down menus at the top of the screen allow access to elements on the web, videos, and other lesson chapters.

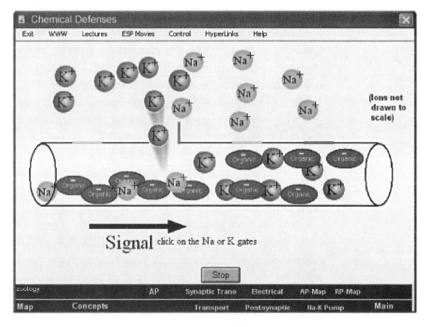

Navigation bars and drop-down menus allow us to quickly jump to the animations or other items as needed (see Figure 23.1). To show a minimum amount of text on the screen, except for predetermined questions, we use roll-over areas and clickable objects that trigger labels or other text to appear. The story portions of our presentations are accompanied by recorded audio, but the instructors describe all animations or interactive figures as needed, using controls to start, stop, pause, and select which components can be seen. While Authorware has moderate capabilities for animation, it also can import and control far more elaborate animations created with Macromedia Flash or Director (*www.macromedia.com*) or those in GIF or digital movie formats.

Creating your own animations has great benefits and some drawbacks. Creating animations makes you think carefully about your own mental representation of the process. Deciding how to represent each of the components, how fast they should move relative to one another, and why, when, and how components appear forces you to rethink and research introductory topics that are outside your area of expertise. By creating your own animations, you can control the appearance and navigation. Because many commercially produced animations are designed for computer-based tutorials, they include text and audio that are not suited for lecture use, based on what is known about cognitive load. Although a pointer will work for cuing (my students enjoy it when I stand precariously on a chair), interactively highlighting components may make it easier for students to focus on the component you are discussing and reduce the searching that contributes to cognitive load. When possible, we created animations using the images from the textbook. This lets the students find equivalent illustrations in the textbook and reduces problems with transfer as students try to match the animation components with the corresponding textbook elements. We have learned that students cue on color; similar components in animations appear to be recognized more quickly when they are colored similarly, and confusion arises when they are colored differently or when dissimilar components are similar colors. Unfortunately, textbooks and commercial software also suffer from this flaw.

The drawbacks to creating your own animations are primarily related to time and money. Creating animations is time-consuming and the learning curves for products capable of more attractive and elaborate animations (e.g., Flash or Director) are considerable. You also run the risk of introducing your own misconceptions or inducing them in your students' minds as a result of your work. For example, many students developed the misconception that hydrogen ions become part of ATP during chemiosmosis because we did not separate the two far enough at the end of the animation. There are also issues of instructional design that stem from an understanding of cognitive learning that we as scientists (not designers) may not resolve well. For example, we had sound effects associated with an animation that confused the students into thinking that acetylcholinesterase sucked up the neurotransmitter rather than catalyzing its breakdown.

If you don't choose to create your own animations, where can you get them? Many textbook publishers now distribute animations. When choosing your textbook, consider the animations that accompany it. We use a set created to accompany *Life* (Lewis et al. 2004). The publisher was also happy to grant us permission to use animations and artwork from their other textbooks. Other publishers are most likely to act similarly.

Another source for animations is the web. Search engines will find many sources for many topics. However, browsing through the results can be time-consuming and leave you wondering whether what you found is really a good choice. Collections of useful materials are maintained by some scientific societies, including the American Society for Microbiology (*www.asm.org*) and the American Society for Cell Biology (*www.cellbioed.org/resources.cfm*), and by educational societies such as the National Science Teachers Association (*www.scilinks.org*) and the American

Association of Physics Teachers (*http://psrc.aapt.org*). Another excellent source is MERLOT (Multimedia Educational Resource for Learning and Online Teaching; *www.merlot.org*). MER-LOT is a community of college educators from a variety of fields who identify and catalog web-based learning objects and associated lessons and provide peer reviews. Started by a consortium of universities and systems of higher education, MERLOT provides free membership to individuals, a variety of tools for forming personal collections of resources, and mechanisms to support exchange of ideas among members. Nonmembers can avail themselves of the catalog and search engine, but they cannot contribute or personalize a collection.

If you do use animations produced by others, be aware of copyright restrictions that the authors have invoked. Properly cite the work, as requested by the author. Seek permission whenever possible.

Guidelines for Using Animations in Lecture

Research supports the goal of creating an active-learning classroom; animations can help you focus the students on a common task and help them form mental models of abstract concepts. Research has shown that animations accompanied by narration are effective at improving learning and are more so when instructors provide cues to help students focus their attention, avoid items that increase cognitive load (like redundant text and extraneous sounds or video), and reduce the pace of information flow (by breaking animations into components and providing time for processing between segments). Collaborative learning has also had positive effects in a variety of settings and is likely to lead to benefits when combined with the use of animations, although this has not been tested formally in a lecture setting. In a recent end-of-semester survey, 82% of our students ($N = 681$) agreed with the statement "Animations helped me understand processes like cellular respiration and photosynthesis better than the plain image"; only 8% disagreed.

Here are some suggestions for incorporating animations in the lecture classroom:

- Set up a context or question that leads to the process that is illustrated in the animation.
- Present the animation and give students some uninterrupted time to observe it and record their observations and questions.
- Provide printed images of the animation's static components for students to use for drawings and notes.
- Let the students work in groups to discuss and integrate their individual observations and questions.
- Allow students to ask questions, however simple.
- When answering a question, first encourage other students to answer the question; then, if needed, guide the students toward an answer using questions and the animation. Provide other animations or visuals that can help students derive or explain the answer themselves.
- If animations are complex, break them into components or cue students into components. Control the pace of the steps so that students have time to process information.
- Select or design animations using what is known about cognitive load and dual-coding theory to help students process information effectively.
- Remember that as complexity increases processing time increases. This can be reduced by timing, cuing, reducing irrelevant stimuli, and breaking animations into segments (but students need to know how components fit together from the start).

Acknowledgment

This material is based on research partially supported by the National Science Foundation under award DUE 9752402. Any opinions, findings, and conclusions or recommendations expressed in the chapter are those of the authors and do not necessarily reflect the views of the National Science Foundation.

References

Burke, K. A., T. J. Greenbowe, and M.A. Windschitl. 1998. Developing and using conceptual computer animations for chemistry instruction. *Journal of Chemical Education* 75 (12): 1658–1661.

Carter, C. S., M. A. Larussa, and G. M. Bodner. 1987. A study of two measures of spatial ability as predictors of success in different levels of general chemistry. *Journal of College Science Teaching* 19: 697–710.

Crow, L. 2005. PowerPoint queens and online kings. *Journal of College Science Teaching* 34 (4): 72–73.

Donovan, M. S., and J. D. Bransford, eds. 2005. *How students learn: Science in the classroom.* Washington, DC: National Academies Press.

French, D. P., and C. P. Russell. 2001. The lecture facilitator: Sorcerer's apprentice. *Journal of College Science Teaching* 31 (2): 116–121.

Griffin, J. D. 2003. Technology in the teaching of neuroscience: Enhanced student learning. *Advances in Physiology Education* 27 (3): 146–155.

Hall, D. 1996. Computer-based animations in large enrollment lectures: Visual reinforcement of biological concepts. *Journal of College Science Teaching* 25 (6): 421–425.

Khoo, G., and T. Koh. 1998. Using visualization and simulation tools in tertiary science education. *Journal of Computers in Mathematics and Science Teaching* 17: 5–20.

Lewis, R., D. Gaffin, M. Hoefnagels, and B. Parker. 2004. *Life.* 5th ed. New York: McGraw-Hill.

Lowe, R. K. 1999. Extracting information from an animation during complex visual processing. *European Journal of the Psychology of Education* 14: 225–244.

Lowe, R. K. 2003. Animation and learning: Selective processing of information in dynamic graphics. *Learning and Instruction* 13: 157–176.

Mantei, E. J. 2000. Using internet class notes and PowerPoint in the physical geology lecture. *Journal of College Science Teaching* 29 (5): 301–305.

Mayer, R. E. 1997. Multimedia learning: Are we asking the right questions? *Educational Psychologist* 32 (1): 1–19.

Mayer, R. E., and R. B. Anderson. 1991. Animations need narrations: An experimental test of a dual-coding hypothesis. *Journal of Educational Psychology* 83: 484–490.

Mayer, R. E., J. Heiser, and S. Lonn. 2001. Cognitive constraints on multimedia learning: When presenting more material results in less understanding. *Journal of Educational Psychology* 93: 187–198.

Mayer, R. E., and R. Moreno. 2002. Animations as an aid to multimedia learning. *Educational Psychology Review* 14 (1): 87–99.

Mayer, R. E., and R. Moreno. 2003. Nine ways to reduce cognitive load in multimedia learning. *Educational Psychologist* 38 (1):43–52.

Mayer, R. E., R. Moreno, M. Boire, and S. Vagge. 1999. Maximizing constructivist learning from multimedia communications by minimizing cognitive load. *Journal of Educational Psychology* 91: 638–643.

Mayer, R. E., and V. K. Sims. 1994. For whom is a picture worth a thousand words? Extensions of a dual-coding theory of multimedia learning. *Journal of Educational Psychology* 84: 389–460.

Moore, R., and I. Miller. 1996. How the use of multimedia affects student retention and learning. *Journal of College Science Teaching* 25 (4): 289–293.

Moreno, R., and R. E. Mayer. 1999. Cognitive principles of multimedia learning: The role of modality and contiguity. *Journal of Educational Psychology* 91: 358–368.

Norvig, P. 2003. PowerPoint: Shot with its own bullets. *The Lancet* 362: 343–344.

Paivio, A. 1986. *Mental representations: A dual coding approach.* Oxford, England: Oxford University Press.

Powers, P. 1998. One path to using multimedia in chemistry courses. *Journal of College Science Teaching* 27: 317–318.

Sanger, M. J., and T. J. Greenbowe. 1997. Students misconceptions in electrochemistry regarding current flow in electrolyte solutions and salt bridge. *Journal of Chemical Education* 74 (7): 819–823.

Sanger, M. J., D. M. Brecheisen, and B. M. Hynek. 2001. Can computer animations affect college biology students conceptions about diffusion and osmosis? *American Biology Teacher* 63 (2): 104–109.

Szabo, A., and N. Hastings. 2000. Using IT in the undergraduate classroom: Should we replace the blackboard with PowerPoint? *Computers & Education* 35: 175–187.

Tabbers, H. K., and R. L. Martens. 2004. Multimedia instructions and cognitive load theory: Effects of modality and cueing. *British Journal of Educational Psychology* 74: 71–81.

Williamson, V. M., and M. R. Abraham. 1995. The effect of computer animation on the particulate mental models of college chemistry students. *Journal of Research in Science Teaching* 32: 521–534.

Yang, E., T. Andre, and T. J. Greenbowe. 2003 Spatial ability and the impact of visualization/animation on learning electrochemistry. *International Journal of Science Education* 25 (3): 329–349.

CHAPTER 24

Instructional Technology:
A Review of Research and Recommendations for Use

Timothy Champion and Andrea Novicki

Timothy Champion is chair of natural sciences and mathematics and associate professor of chemistry at Johnson C. Smith University. He earned a doctorate of arts in chemistry at the University of Northern Colorado and conducts research on teaching and learning, assessment, curriculum development, and use of technology. He teaches general chemistry and is a feature editor of the *Journal of Chemical Education*.

Andrea Novicki is assistant professor of biology at Johnson C. Smith University. She earned a PhD in biological sciences at the University of California at Irvine and conducts research in education, neurobiology, endocrinology, and behavior. She teaches general biology, zoology, neurobiology, and physiology.

Students, administrators, and colleagues now routinely expect faculty to use instructional technology. What should we use and how should we use it to most effectively promote meaningful learning? No absolute answers to these questions exist, but we provide considerations from published reports and our own experience.

Carefully chosen and properly used instructional technology can increase student learning and student interest. Poorly used instructional technology can do the opposite; we have all experienced this phenomenon when victimized by an enthusiastic new PowerPoint user. The decision to use instructional technology, or any educational tool, should be centered on student learning. To evaluate any teaching innovation, consider the seven principles for effective undergraduate education (Chickering and Gamson 1987). They state that good practice in undergraduate education

1. encourages **contacts** between students and faculty
2. develops **reciprocity and cooperation** among students

3. *uses* **active** *learning techniques*
4. *gives prompt* **feedback**
5. *emphasizes* **time** *on task*
6. *communicates high* **expectations**
7. **respects** *diverse talents and ways of learning*

Appropriately selected, properly used instructional technology can be used to facilitate student learning using these principles (Chickering and Ehrmann 1996). The TLT Group (TLT stands for "teaching, learning, and technology") maintains a library of ideas for using technology to advance the seven principles at *www.tltgroup.org/Seven/Library_TOC.htm*. The ever-useful *McKeachie's Teaching Tips* contains a chapter on technology and teaching, with sound advice on selecting and using technology effectively (Zhu and Kaplan 2002). Teaching without technology may even be unethical if we are to prepare students for the challenges they will face in the future.

Does technology improve learning? Frustratingly, despite a review of many studies, there are still no clear answers. We have not moved beyond the "no significant difference" phenomenon documented by Thomas Russell (Western Cooperative for Educational Telecommunications [WCET] 2006) when he compiled the results of more than 355 comparative research studies and concluded that students in technology-based (typically, distance learning) courses learn as well as their on-campus, face-to-face counterparts (see *www.nosignificantdifference.org*). We could conclude that technology does not harm student learning, and in some cases, can facilitate learning.

Assessment of student learning is problematic, as exemplified by a comparison of a computer-based laboratory with a human-instructed laboratory at the University of California at Los Angeles (UCLA). The students taught using computers were much more enthusiastic about the course and about studying science and thought they learned more. However, comparison of test results showed no difference in learning, which supports the idea that we have not yet learned to measure important learning outcomes (Howard Hughes Medical Institute, n.d.). The difficulty in revealing positive learning outcomes plagues research in education. It does not necessarily mean that instructional technology does not facilitate learning, but that we may not be measuring learning appropriately. In general, students respond positively to the use of technology and report that the technology helped them learn, even in studies that do not find a detectable increase in student learning with technology. In many cases, the benefits to learning depend on how the technology is used, which brings us back to the principles of good practice described above.

Additional insights come from a National Research Council synthesis of how people learn (Commission on Behavioral and Social Sciences and Education [CBASSE] 2000). To facilitate learning, (1) student's prior understandings should be engaged, (2) students should have both factual knowledge in a conceptual framework and concepts made meaningful by factual contexts, and (3) students should use self-monitoring, or metacognitive, strategies. Appropriately designed technology can facilitate each of these processes.

We will discuss three overlapping uses for instructional technology in face-to-face teaching, communication outside the classroom, and learning assignments. We are uncomfortably aware that some of the technology described in this chapter will be outmoded soon. A review of research on the use of technology in science education published about 10 years ago discussed technologies that are no longer in use, although they were forerunners of current technology (e.g., hypercards and videodiscs) (Berger et al. 1994). Compared with that early technology, the technology available today provides more opportunity for contacts between students and faculty and encourages student cooperation.

Face-to-Face Teaching

Presentation Software

Presentation software and digital projectors are taking over from overhead projectors and blackboards as teaching tools. Victimized by poor presentations, some of our colleagues reject the use of presentation software in teaching (McDonald 2004; Tufte 2003). However, presentation software facilitates content organization and presentation for both distance learning and face-to-face classes (Keefe and Willett 2004). The use of presentation software is still contentious, but clear guidelines for best practices are emerging. Material is available to help presenters; an example is the web page "Getting the Most Out of PowerPoint" (Telg and Irani 2001; *http://training.ifas.ufl.edu/deft/produce/pptart.htm*), which has good design advice. However, even well-designed presentations may not be effective teaching tools. To increase meaningful student learning from multimedia presentations, consider these research-based principles (based on Mayer 2001):

- Words and pictures should be presented simultaneously rather than successively.
- Extraneous words, pictures, sounds, and transitions should be excluded, no matter how attractive or interesting.
- Presentations with graphics plus narration are more effective than graphics plus printed text. Least effective are presentations that include narration and printed text. In other words, reading the text from the screen actually inhibits learning.
- Too much information presented at once inhibits learning. Present information in bite-sized chunks.
- Presentations should help learners to select, organize, and integrate information. Use clear headings, arrows, outlines, and concrete examples. Incorporate active learning to facilitate integration.
- Well-designed presentations increase learning more for introductory courses than for experienced learners, so if you must choose, focus your efforts on your novice learners.

Many textbooks come with packaged PowerPoint presentations. Often, these presentations are text-heavy chapter outlines, but they can be a time-saving starting place for creating effective presentations.

Animations

Since the early days of technology, instructors have been enchanted by the power of technology to deliver audiovisual learning materials (Dale 1946). We are still working out the best way to do this. Animations hold great potential for teaching science because they facilitate student understanding of processes and help students visualize abstract concepts.

A review of research comparing learning with animations versus learning with static pictures does not support this potential (Tversky, Morrison, and Betrancourt 2002). This metastudy rigorously excluded studies that did not compare noninteractive animations with still figures containing exactly the same information. However, most animations available to college science instructors contain more information than is available in still figures. Some are interactive and can be implemented using the principles for effective education in ways that simple narration cannot.

Research has yielded some guidelines for effective use of animations, which are similar to the guidelines for using presentation software:

- Animation plus narration results in deeper learning compared with narration alone.
- Animation and corresponding text should be near each other on the screen.
- Narration and animation should be presented simultaneously rather than successively.
- All extraneous narration, sounds, and video should be excluded.
- The use of animation and narration is preferable to the use of animation and on-screen text.
- The use of animation and narration is preferable to the use of animation, narration, and on-screen text.
- Narration or on-screen text should be conversational rather than formal (Mayer and Moreno 2002).
- Structure and content of the animation should correspond to the desired internal representation of the learner.
- Structure and content should be readily and accurately perceived and comprehended (i.e., animations should be schematic and simple) (Tversky, Morrison, and Betrancourt 2002).
- Student retention is significantly increased when students are presented with an animation and then allowed to study it (McClean et al. 2005).

There are many excellent animations available to science instructors; textbooks usually come with animations online or on a CD, and there are many excellent sources for finding animations online. One such repository is MERLOT (Multimedia Educational Resource for Learning and Online Teaching) at *www.merlot.org* (Figure 24.1).

Classroom Response Systems

Classroom response systems (aka "clickers") allow students to immediately respond to questions through an electronic unit. The students' aggregate responses can be presented graphically to the class (Figure 24.2). These systems are generally used in large lecture halls and are thought to increase communication between the students and the instructor, allow for immediate feedback for both students and instructors, and increase student participation. Electronic response systems have been used since the 1960s, but studies have not yet documented an increase in student academic achievement (reviewed in Judson and Sawada 2002). However, both students and faculty generally enjoy using these systems ("No Wrong Answer" 2005), although technical problems still arise (Hatch, Jensen, and Moore 2005). Classroom response systems do result in increased learning when used with social constructivist pedagogy (CBASSE 2000; Judson and Sawada 2002). In other words, using classroom response systems is fun for the instructor; the students believe that it aids their learning; and if the system is used as a springboard for student discussions, it may result in meaningful learning.

Figure 24.1

Screenshot of MERLOT Showing the Numbers of Science Learning Objects Arranged by Subject, and an Example of an Item (Physlets)

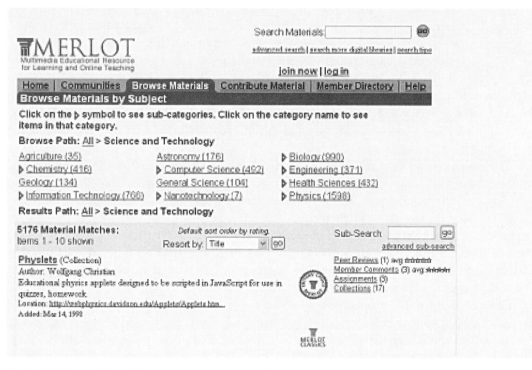

Reprinted with permission from *www.merlot.org/artifact/BrowseArtifacts.po?catcode=100&browsecat=100* (accessed December 2, 2005).

Figure 24.2

A Classroom Response System in Use

Students respond to a question on the screen behind the instructor by pressing the appropriate buttons on their response units. The aggregate responses are shown on the screen (21 students selected item A, 2 students selected item B).

Reprinted with permission from "eInstruction—The Global Leader in Interactive Response Systems" at *www.einstruction.com*.

Interactive Whiteboards and Tablet PCs

An interactive whiteboard is a touch-sensitive projection screen that allows the user to both annotate and navigate using the screen. Users can display, write on, and interact with computer-based resources (like PowerPoint, digital animations, and web pages) and save notes written on the board. Most of the published research on interactive whiteboards in education focuses on their use in primary and secondary schools (British Educational Communications and Technology Agency 2003; Smith et al. 2005). In general, students and teachers find the boards easy to use and helpful in promoting interactivity and increased student engagement. However, there is insufficient evidence for an impact on student learning. Because interactive whiteboards are relatively new, all of the results may reflect novelty. After instructors have had time to work out the best ways to use this technology, studies may document an increase in student learning; conversely, after users become accustomed to the interactive whiteboards, studies may find that they do not increase engagement.

The combination of a tablet PC and digital projector can function like an interactive whiteboard in any classroom with a digital projector. Both interactive whiteboards and tablet PCs display a computer screen, but with the tablet PC the presenter navigates and writes on the PC rather than the projected image. One advantage of the tablet PC is that the instructor can face the classroom instead of turning around to write on the board. The individual writing on the board does not block the projector. If the tablet PC is used with a wireless projector, the instructor can roam the classroom. For instructors with limited mobility, a tablet PC may be an ideal presentation tool.

Cox and Rogers (2005) reported that tablet PCs provide the ability to write and highlight formulas easily and to archive the notes, which improves teaching effectiveness. Mock (2004) uses a tablet PC to teach computer science; he records audio simultaneously with his notes to make his classroom presentation available to the students. This approach could facilitate online and distance learning.

The use of either interactive whiteboards or tablet PCs can address some of the criticisms of PowerPoint presentations, by allowing users to annotate during the presentation, increasing the spontaneity of instruction, and promoting interactions between faculty and students.

Interactive Animations, Simulations, and Virtual Laboratories

Interactive animations range in time from only a minute or two to virtual laboratories that span several classes. The interactive nature of these tools allows them to be used for presentations, for assignments, and as virtual laboratories. Interactive Java applets can be used in both lecture situations and as homework assignments when class size and costs make demonstrations or laboratories difficult (Corder 2005). Some studies in which web modules have been assigned to complement a course have shown no effect on student learning (Kesner and Linzey 2005); other studies have shown that use of these modules improves student learning (Loegering and Edge 2001). Overall, student response to these modules is positive. Simulations with interactivity that connect students in a community have been very successful in precollege classes (CBASSE 2000).

In some cases, computer-based simulations are more efficient in terms of time without decreasing student learning, and they can actually increase student learning compared with traditional laboratories (Gibbons et al. 2004). One study compared attitudes and student achievement after a virtual field trip and an actual field trip and found that there was little

difference (Garner and Gallo 2005)! Virtual labs can facilitate student learning by removing the distractions and tediousness of some laboratories, but they cannot substitute for hands-on laboratories when the goal is to teach techniques.

There are commercial as well as online sources for interactive animations and simulations (Figure 24.3 shows an example of an online laboratory exercise). These resources may be part of collections called learning object repositories, which are websites that allow access to a wide variety of resources called learning objects. A learning object is a resource or set of resources designed to be instructional that can be reused in other learning environments. These resources are freely available for use in your class. MERLOT, mentioned earlier in the chapter, is a learning object repository.

Figure 24.3

Online Laboratory Exercise Produced by Howard Hughes Medical Institute to Lead Users Through the Process of Making Transgenic Flies

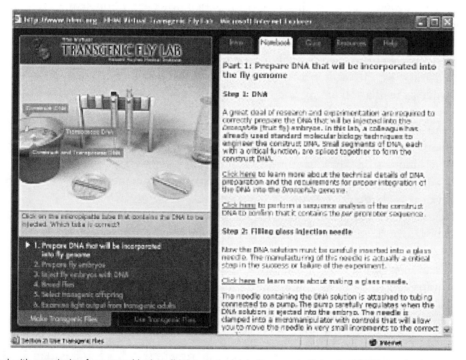

Reprinted with permission from *www.hhmi.org/biointeractive/vlabs/transgenic_fly/content/2000start.html* (accessed December 2, 2005).

Probeware / Data Acquisition Systems

Probeware consists of equipment and software used to gather and analyze data (such as pH, temperature, dissolved oxygen, and pressure) and is connected to a calculator, a computer, or a handheld device. These systems allow students to perform experiments and collect data for analysis (Figure 24.4). Probeware is used in chemistry, environmental science, physics, and life

Figure 24.4

Students Using Probeware to Produce Real-Time Graphs

Reprinted with permission from Vernier Software & Technology; *www.vernier.com/physiology/index.html*.

sciences. The use of probeware and its attendant calculators or computers may be the least controversial use of technology in science teaching. The advantages are numerous:

- They are quick and easy to use.
- Data replace qualitative observations.
- Data are collected in real time.
- Data are graphed instantaneously.
- The equipment is similar or identical to equipment used in "real" scientific research.

One of the documented strengths of using probeware is that a graph is produced in real time, promoting student connections between the laboratory process and the data collected and facilitating data interpretation and conclusions (Krajcik and Layman 1992; Lapp 2001; Marcum-Dietrich and Ford 2002). Probeware has also been used to facilitate undergraduate research (Sales, Ragan, and Murphy 2001), allowing the faculty mentor to teach experimental design, sampling rates, and ethical issues as well as obtaining and analyzing data. However, using probeware in even a 15- to 25-student setting can pose some logistical challenges. Issuing and recovering components, ensuring that software is installed and functioning, and dealing with student mistakes in setting up systems can be difficult challenges. As probeware progresses to USB interfaces and students increasingly have laptops, this gets easier. Brown (2005) reviewed five probeware packages; we provide a list of manufacturers with contact information in the appendix at the end of this chapter.

Computer-based data acquisition systems hold a special place in the physiology/neuroscience laboratory. Traditional laboratories have been taught using oscilloscopes, amplifiers, and balky chart recorders. Students are quickly overwhelmed by all of the buttons, knobs, and switches, and instructors must spend at least one laboratory session training the students to use the equipment. When this equipment is replaced by a computer, students easily learn the software and focus on the results rather than the equipment.

Good practices using probeware and data acquisition systems engage the students in

- making predictions before performing an experiment (Krajcik and Layman 1992; Lapp 2001) and
- deciding what to measure and how to interpret the results (The Probeware Group 2003).

Data Analysis and Reporting
Technology provides many tools for analyzing and reporting data. In our view, teaching a science class without using this technology is not preparing students for the future. Digital cameras, spreadsheet and graphing programs, and statistical packages should be used in teaching laboratories just as they are in research laboratories.

Communication Outside the Classroom

Course Management Systems

Course management systems have many names: virtual learning environments (VLEs), course-management software packages (CMSPs), learning management systems (LMSs), e-course-ware, e-learning courseware, and managed learning environments (MLEs). There are more than 40 different packages currently available. Generally, one course management system is adopted and supported throughout a university. These systems provide discussion boards; online chat; e-mail; online calendars; access to syllabi, handouts, and websites; announcement boards; online assignments; quizzes and exams; grading tools; and the ability to track student use. Course management systems are useful for face-to-face, online, and blended courses. Blackboard, Moodle, Sakai, and WebCT are commonly used systems (see the appendix for URLs; see also Figure 24.5). Currently, course management systems are used to improve access to course materials, and they may be used to improve instructor-student and student-student communication. Course management systems can also be used as a communication tool for departments, programs, and student organizations.

There are several alternatives to using course management systems while allowing for similar functionality. Some textbooks allow you to set up a course web page on their sites, which provide access to materials that complement the text and may provide access to online quizzes and allow students to track their grades. WebAssign is a website specifically designed for assigning and grading online homework for large college science classes, discussed in the "Learning Assignments" section later in this chapter. Alternatively, instructors can provide web pages or blogs (see "Learning Assignments" section) to allow student access to resources instead of using a course management system.

Although course management systems have tools to promote all seven of the principles for effective undergraduate education (Chickering and Gamson 1987), the best practices for student learning have not yet been elucidated, perhaps because faculty are just beginning to use these systems.

E-Mail

E-mail and other communication methods (Listservs, newsgroups, class discussion boards, electronic bulletin boards) can be used to promote interactions among students and between the students and instructor. Most course management systems allow the instructor to e-mail all students or just one, facilitating communication. E-mail has the advantage of being private, thereby allowing shy students an opportunity to interact with the instructor in a nonthreatening way. E-mail increases communication with the instructor (Brown 2001; Marbach-Ad and Sokolove 2001). Like all techniques, this requires some student training. Students should be reminded to check their e-mail, instructed on creating short and specific subject lines, and notified about when they can expect a response from the instructor.

Distance Learning

All of the technology discussed in this chapter can be used in distance learning courses, which is beyond the scope of this review. Distance learning can be synchronous (the instructor and students are present electronically at the same time for presentations and discussions), asynchronous (participants learn at their own pace, on their own schedule), or a blend of the

Figure 24.5

Course Management Systems: Blackboard (top), WebCT (middle), Moodle (bottom)

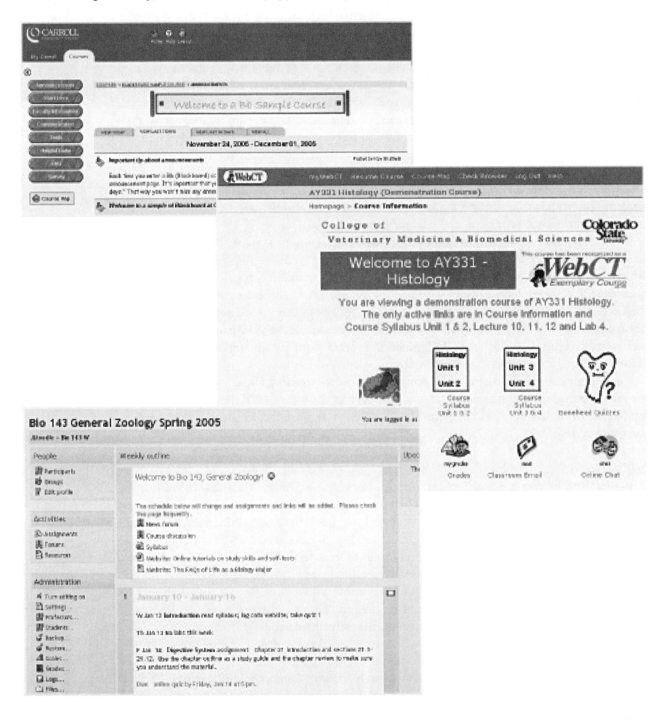

Sources: Blackboard sample course at Carroll Community College, *http://carrollcc.blackboard.com*; WebCT sample course at Colorado State University can be accessed via *www.ois.colostate.edu/SampleWebCTCourses/index.html*; and Moodle at Johnson C. Smith University, *http://hermes.jcsu.edu*.

two. Asynchronous distance learning is an updated version of the correspondence course, but current distance learning courses have technology components, which may include video teleconferencing, television, videos, and discussions.

Learning Assignments

Blogs, Wikis, and Discussion Boards

Blogs, wikis, and discussion boards are all ways of increasing communication among students and between students and instructors. Each of these techniques can be used to apply several of the good practices in undergraduate education; they can be used to foster communication and cooperation, promote discussion, address class concerns, extend learning beyond the classroom, and develop writing skills. The best practices for their use in science education are not yet available.

Blog is short for weblog, which is a running online journal that contains text, links, and comments. New entries are placed at the top of the page, moving older entries toward the bottom. Blogs are easy to use, because they do not require special web-authoring software or specialized knowledge. Blogs allow others to comment on the writer's ideas, which can be a powerful teaching tool. Blogs can be similar to journals or can be much more, including an exchange of ideas, reflection, synthesis, and communication. See *www.weblogg-ed.com* for an example of a blog, this one containing discussions about using blogs in education. Blogs can be used for Just-in-Time Teaching (discussed below in the "Online Assignment Submission" section) and to share student experiences, engage students in reflection, promote peer review, and develop writing skills (Glogoff 2005). Blogs can replace class web pages by providing internet links to course content, organizing classroom discussions, and providing summaries of readings. Student posts can be used as part of a class grade (Downes 2004). In the best case, blogging encourages reading, engaging in a community, and reflection (Downes 2004). A description of using blogs in a chemistry course to facilitate group projects, as well as a table comparing wikis, blogs, and threaded discussions, is located at *www.earlham.edu/~markp/sls/techie_blog.htm*.

A wiki is an interactive web page that can be modified by anyone who visits the site. Wikipedia (*http://en.wikipedia.org/wiki/Main_Page*), a free online encyclopedia, is an example. Any visitor can modify, add to, or create an entry. Users can add text, pictures, videos, and links. Wikis can be more collaborative than blogs but may take more knowledge on the part of the contributor, with a steeper learning curve than blogs.

Discussion boards or forums are online places where students and faculty can post questions or comments as part of the course web page, and they can be accessed by all. Some course management systems e-mail all new posts to all students in the class. One of the authors of this chapter (Novicki) has used discussion boards to address exam fairness, to answer questions about what is covered on the exam, and to resolve class management issues. However, if students are not required to read postings, they often do not, and even those who read them may not contribute constructively.

Challenges to using blogs, wikis, and discussion boards in learning are encountered in trying to encourage and reward student writing, obtain quality interactions, and assess student work. Instructors who use wikis and blogs must set up ground rules early (about how much and how frequently students must contribute, topics and language that are not acceptable, and how frequently students must consult the page). These technologies have the potential to be powerful learning tools because they can promote a combination of reflective writing and active, collaborative learning, both of which are proven techniques for effective learning.

Online Assignment Submission

Course management systems facilitate online assignment submission, in which the instructor can set up questions to be answered and graded online, promoting prompt feedback, communicating expectations, and providing more time to practice. WebAssign (*www.webassign.net*) is an online system specifically designed for collecting and grading homework in college science and mathematics.

Are online assignments good instructional tools? There are pros and cons (Bonham, Beichner, and Deardorff 2001). Automated homework permits practice, students get immediate feedback, and questions can be randomized for each student to prevent cheating. However, unless the assignment is constructed carefully, a computer cannot explain why a problem is wrong; grading by computer emphasizes getting the "right" answer instead of problem-solving skills; and, if multiple submissions are allowed, students may randomly guess instead of working on the problems.

Do online assignments increase learning? In an introductory physics class, there was no difference in exam grades between classes in which students submitted their homework online and classes in which students had homework graded by a hard-working teaching assistant. However, students reported that they liked the online system, even though there were initial technical difficulties (Bonham, Beichner, and Deardorff 2001). At many universities, the introductory science courses are large, and resources to grade student homework are not available. A comparison of student understanding of physics in courses with online, graded homework versus courses with nongraded homework showed a significant increase in student grades on a standardized exam for those students who submitted online homework (Cheng et al. 2004), but a similar study comparing multimedia online homework with rich feedback in chemistry versus homework that was graded based on completion (rather than correctness) did not detect a significant difference (Cole and Todd 2003).

A special use of online assignment submission is Just-in-Time Teaching, in which students complete web-based preparatory assignments (WarmUps) that are due online a few hours before class (Novak et al. 1999; see also Chapter 15 in this volume and *http://webphysics.iupui.edu/jitt/jitt.html*). The interactive classroom session focuses on both the content of the exercises and the student's prior knowledge and misconceptions. This technique has been shown to be effective in biology, chemistry, physics, and mathematics college teaching.

In summary, online homework is not about the technology; rather, it facilitates learning when it permits instructors to provide more feedback and time to practice. And, like other uses of technology in teaching, students like it.

Concept Mapping Software

Concept maps are graphic ways of organizing knowledge and have been demonstrated to increase meaningful learning (see Chapter 7 in this volume). Concept maps can be created in a classroom or as an assignment with paper and pencil. Paper-based maps are difficult or messy to modify, to build on, and to share between students at different locations. Software to make concept maps is available (see appendix), is easy to use, and allows students to work collaboratively, to refine concept maps over time, and to distribute their concept maps online to other students or to the instructor.

Calibrated Peer Review

Calibrated Peer Review (CPR) is a web-based tool that leads students through a writing assignment and peer review (see *http://cpr.molsci.ucla.edu*). It enables frequent writing assignments even in large classes. Student activities using CPR are listed in Table 24.1.

Table 24.1

Calibrated Peer Review Assignment Stages

Stage	Student Tasks
1: Text entry	1. Explore source material about the assigned topic. 2. Read the instructions for your assignment. 3. Write and submit text based on the source material.
2: Calibration and review	1. Evaluate several example texts, called calibration essays. 2. Receive feedback on your evaluations. 3. Evaluate your peers' text. 4. Evaluate your own submitted text.
3: Results	1. Receive results from your evaluation of your peers' text. 2. Receive results from your peers' evaluation of your text. 3. Receive an overall score for your assignment.

CPR has been successfully used in teaching chemistry (Russell and Pearson 2004) and biology (Robinson 2001), especially in combination with problem-based learning (Peleaz 2002). The following recommendations are made for the use of CPR:

- Introduce the tool to the students to prevent confusion (Russell and Pearson 2004).
- Prepare students for writing in a science class by discussing how much scientists write, including the practice of peer review, which the students will be practicing (Russell and Pearson 2004).
- Use the tool more than once in a class to overcome student unfamiliarity (Robinson 2001).
- Use a CPR assignment for first drafts of a final assignment that will be graded by the instructor (Champion, personal experience).

Conclusion

Does technology increase learning? One clear answer emerges from our review: It depends on how it is used. It is important that faculty practice the scholarship of teaching as they explore the use of technology in science education. Devising careful technology implementation plans with assessments and clearly communicating the conditions of the implementation and its results will help identify better practices.

In general, students enjoy and expect to use technology in learning, and they will be using technology in their careers. We believe that instructors should use technology appropriately.

In this chapter we have summarized the current uses of technology and listed the best practices as they are currently understood. We look forward to further experimentation to find the best way to use technology to facilitate meaningful learning.

Appendix
Electronic Resources

General Resources
Ideas for using technology to advance the "seven principles": *www.tltgroup.org/Seven/Library_TOC.htm*
Low Threshold Applications (LTAs; reliable, accessible, easy to learn, non-intimidating, and inexpensive applications of technology): *http://jade.mcli.dist.maricopa.edu/lta*
Summary of research on the use and design of animation as instructional tools: *www.cmu.edu/teaching/technology/animationresearch.html*

PowerPoint
PowerPoint tutorial: *www.actden.com/pp*
"Getting the Most Out of PowerPoint": *http://training.ifas.ufl.edu/deft/produce/pptart.htm*

Classroom Response Systems
Sample uses and a list of vendors: *www.foundationcoalition.org/publications/brochures/ers.doc*

Tablet PCs
Teaching chemistry with a tablet PC: *http://campus.murraystate.edu/academic/faculty/ricky.cox/tablet/rc_tablet.html*
Resources for using tablet PCs in the classroom: *www.math.uaa.alaska.edu/~afkjm/tablet*
The Tablet PC Education Blog: *http://tabletpceducation.blogspot.com*

Learning Object Repositories
MERLOT (Multimedia Educational Resource for Learning and Online Teaching): *www.merlot.org*
Lists of educational simulations primarily for younger students: *www.techtrekers.com/sim.htm*
Science resources for K–12 educators: *www.sciencenetlinks.com*
Games and demonstrations based on Nobel prizes: *http://nobelprize.org/search/games-simulations.html*
A peer-reviewed collection of web resources, available to *Journal of Chemical Education* subscribers: *www.jce.divched.org/JCEDLib/WebWare/collection/reviewed*
Biology articles on hot topics: *www.actionbioscience.org*
Lessons, problem-based learning resources, and help for teaching/learning on the web: *www.mcli.dist.maricopa.edu*

Probeware / Data Acquisition Systems
ADInstruments (specifically for the life sciences): *www.adinstruments.com*
BIOPAC Systems: *www.biopac.com*
Fourier Systems: *www.fouriersystems.com*
Imagiworks: *www.imagiworks.com*
National Instruments LabVIEW: *www.ni.com/labview*
Onset: *www.onsetcomp.com*
PASCO: *www.pasco.com*
Vernier Software & Technology: *www.vernier.com*

Course Management Systems
Blackboard (sample course): *http://carrollcc.blackboard.com* (log in with username sampleblackboard and password bb)
Moodle (sample course): *http://moodle.org/course/category.php?id=5*
Sakai: *www.sakaiproject.org*

WebCT (sample course): *www.ois.colostate.edu/SampleWebCTCourses/index.html*
WebAssign (not a course management system, but it facilitates online assignments): *www.webassign.net/index. html*
Comparison of course management systems: *www.edutools.info/course*

Blogs
   "Tools for the TEKS: Integrating Technology in the Classroom; Successful and Safe Educational Blogging" (a resource for all teachers at all levels): *www.wtvi.com/teks/04_05_articles/educational_blogging.html*
   To get started on blogs: *www.blogger.com*; *www.livejournal.com*; *www.sixapart.com/typepad*
   Comparison of blogs, wikis, and discussion boards: *www.earlham.edu/~markp/sls/techie_blog.htm*

Just-in-Time Teaching
   http://webphysics.iupui.edu/jitt/jitt.html

Concept Maps
   Inspiration Software: *www.inspiration.com*
   CmapTools (free, downloadable software for making concept maps): *http://cmap.ihmc.us*

Calibrated Peer Review
   http://cpr.molsci.ucla.edu

References

Berger, C. F., C. R. Lu, S. J. Belzer, and B. E. Voss. 1994. Research on the uses of technology in science education. In *Handbook of research on science teaching and learning,* ed. D. L. Gabel, 466–490. New York: Macmillan.

Bonham, S., R. Beichner, and D. Deardorff. 2001. Online homework: Does it make a difference? *The Physics Teacher* 39 (5): 293–296.

British Educational Communications and Technology Agency (Becta) ICT Research. 2003. *What the research says about interactive whiteboards. www.becta.org.uk/page_documents/research/wtrs_whiteboards.pdf*

Brown, D. G. 2001. The power of e-mail. *Syllabus.* July 1. *www.campus-technology.com/news_article.asp?ID=4160*

Brown, M. 2005. Real-time science. *Technology & Learning* 25 (9). *www.techlearning.com/showArticle.jhtml?articleID =160400808*

Cheng, K. K., B. A. Thacker, R. L. Cardenas, and C. Crouch. 2004. Using an online homework system enhances students' learning of physics concepts in an introductory physics course. *American Journal of Physics* 72 (1): 1447–1453.

Chickering, A. W., and. S. C. Ehrmann. 1996. Implementing the seven principles: Technology as lever. *AAHE Bulletin* 49 (2): 3–6. Also available online at *www.tltgroup.org/programs/seven.html.*

Chickering, A. W., and Z. F. Gamson. 1987. Seven principles for good practice in undergraduate education. *AAHE Bulletin* 39 (7): 3–7.

Cole, R. S., and J. B. Todd. 2003. Effects of web-based multimedia homework with immediate rich feedback on student learning in general chemistry. *Journal of Chemical Education* 80 (11): 1338–1343.

Commission on Behavioral and Social Sciences and Education (CBASSE). 2000. *How people learn: Brain, mind, experience, and school; expanded edition.* Washington, DC: National Academy Press. Also available online at *www.nap.edu.*

Corder, G. 2005. Teaching with Java applets. *Journal of College Science Teaching* 34 (6): 47–49.

Cox, J. R., and J. W. Rogers. 2005. Tablet PCs: Are they the next technopedagogical fad? *Journal of College Science Teaching* 34 (6): 7.

Dale, E. 1946. *Audio-visual methods in teaching.* New York: Dryden Press.

Downes, S. 2004. Educational blogging. *EDUCAUSE Review* 39 (5): 14–26. Also available online at *www.educause. edu/pub/er/erm04/erm0450.asp*.

Garner, L. C., and M. A. Gallo. 2005. Field trips and their effect on student achievement and attitudes. *Journal of College Science Teaching* 34 (5): 14–17.

Gibbons, N. J., C. Evans, A. Payne, K. Shah, and D. K. Griffin. 2004. Computer simulations improve university instructional laboratories. *Cell Biology Education* 3: 263–269.

Glogoff, S. 2005. Instructional blogging on campus: Identifying best practices. *Campus Technology. www.campus-technology.com/news_article.asp?ID=11311*

Hatch, J., M. Jensen, and R. Moore. 2005. Manna from heaven or "clickers" from hell. *Journal of College Science Teaching* 34 (7): 36–39.

Howard Hughes Medical Institute. n.d. *Beyond Bio 101: The transformation of undergraduate biology education. www. hhmi.org/BeyondBio101*

Judson, E., and D. Sawada. 2002. Learning from past and present: Electronic response systems in college lecture halls. *Journal of Computers in Mathematics and Science Teaching* 21 (2): 167–181.

Keefe, D. D., and J. D. Willett. 2004. A case for PowerPoint as a faculty authoring system. *Cell Biology Education* 3: 156–158.

Kesner, M. H., and A. V. Linzey. 2005. Can computer-based visual-spatial aids lead to increased student performance in anatomy and physiology? *American Biology Teacher* 67 (4): 206–212.

Krajcik, J. S., and J. W. Layman. 1992. Microcomputer-based laboratories in the science classroom. In *Research Matters – to the Science Teacher* (NARST Monograph No. 5), 101–108. National Association for Research in Science Teaching. *www.educ.sfu.ca/narstsite/publications/research/microcomputer.htm*

Lapp, D. A. 2001. How do students learn with data collection devices? Paper presented at the 13th Annual International Teachers Teaching With Technology (T^3) Conference, Columbus, OH. (ERIC Document Reproduction no. ED 465510)

Loegering, J. P., and D. W. Edge. 2001. An interactive website increases student participation and learning. *Journal of College Science Teaching* 31 (4): 252–257.

Marbach-Ad, G., and P. Sokolove. 2001. Creating direct channels of communication. *Journal of College Science Teaching* 31 (3): 178–182.

Marcum-Dietrich, N. I., and D. J. Ford. 2002. The place for the computer is in the laboratory: An investigation of the effect of computer probeware on student learning. *Journal of Computers in Mathematics and Science Teaching* 21 (4): 361–379.

Mayer, R. E. 2001. *Multimedia learning.* New York: Cambridge University Press.

Mayer, R. E., and R. Moreno. 2002. Animation as an aid to multimedia learning. *Educational Psychology Review* 14 (1): 87–99.

McClean, P., C. Johnson, R. Rogers, L. Daniels, J. Reber, B. M. Slator, J. Terpstra, and A. White. 2005. Molecular and cellular biology animations: Development and impact on student learning. *Cell Biology Education* 4: 169–179.

McDonald, K. 2004. Examining PowerPointlessness. *Cell Biology Education* 3: 160–161.

Mock, K. 2004. Teaching with tablet PC's. Paper presented at the Sixth Annual Northwestern Regional Conference of the Consortium for Computing Sciences in Colleges, Salem, OR. *www.math.uaa.alaska.edu/~afkjm/papers/mock-ccsc2004.pdf*

Novak, G. M., E. T. Patterson, A. D. Gavrin, and W. Christian. 1999. *Just-in-Time Teaching: Blending active learning with web technology.* Upper Saddle River, NJ: Prentice Hall.

No Wrong Answer: Click It. *Wired News.* 2005. May 15. *www.wired.com/news/culture/0,1284,67530,00.html*

Pelaez, N. J. 2002. Problem-based writing with peer review improves academic performance in physiology.

Advances in Physiology Education 26: 174–184. Also available online at *http://advan.physiology.org/cgi/content/full/26/3/174.*

The Probeware Group. 2003. *Probeware: A definition.* The Concord Consortium. *www.concord.org/work/software/ccprobeware/probeware_overview.pdf*

Robinson, R. 2001. An application to increase student reading and writing skills. *American Biology Teacher* 63 (7): 474–479.

Russell, J., and M. Pearson. 2004. Instructional technology jewels. *Journal of College Science Teaching* 33 (7): 24–28.

Sales, C. L., N. M. Ragan, and M. K. Murphy. 2001. Using calculator-based laboratory technology to conduct undergraduate chemical research. *Journal of Chemical Education* 78 (5): 694–696.

Smith, H. J., S. Higgins, K. Wall, and J. Miller. 2005. Interactive whiteboards: Boon or bandwagon? A critical review of the literature. *Journal of Computer Assisted Learning* 21 (2): 91–101.

Telg, R., and T. Irani. 2001. Getting the most out of PowerPoint. *http://training.ifas.ufl.edu/deft/produce/pptart.htm*

Tufte, E. 2003. The cognitive style of PowerPoint. Cheshire, CT: Graphics Press. Available from *www.edwardtufte.com.*

Tversky, B., J. B. Morrison, and M. Betrancourt. 2002. Animation: Can it facilitate? *International Journal of Human-Computer Studies* 57: 247–262.

Western Cooperative for Educational Telecommunications (WCET). 2006. *No significant difference phenomenon.* *www.nosignificantdifference.org*

Zhu, E., and M. Kaplan. 2002. Technology and teaching. In *McKeachie's teaching tips: Strategies, research, and theory for college and university teachers* (11th ed.), ed. W. J. McKeachie, 204–223. Boston: Houghton Mifflin.

CHAPTER 25

Web-Based Practice and Assessment Systems in Science

David W. Brooks and Kent J. Crippen

David W. Brooks is professor of chemistry education at the University of Nebraska-Lincoln. He earned a PhD in chemistry at Columbia University and conducts research on web-based learning systems. He teaches courses in instructional message design and technology.

Kent J. Crippen is assistant professor of science education and technology at the University of Nevada, Las Vegas. He earned a PhD in instructional technology at the University of Nebraska-Lincoln and conducts research on web-based learning systems. He teaches courses on applications of technology for secondary mathematics and science, use of the internet, and science content for teachers.

The Interactive Compensatory Model of Learning (ICML), developed by Schraw (Schraw, Brooks, and Crippen 2005), brings together three principal factors in successful learning: prior knowledge, ability, and motivation. Of these, prior knowledge provides the greatest influence on learning (Shapiro 2004). A recent modification of this model by Brooks interprets ability in terms of working memory capacity and motivation through a process of working memory utilization (Brooks and Shell, Forthcoming). As such, the ICML indicates that genetic, static intelligence has a much smaller influence than is often described and suggests instructors have many avenues for influencing learning. When viewed in the context of Schraw's model, learning environments that support practice with feedback target prior knowledge directly and should lead to substantial learning success.

Mastery learning provides a framework for setting a standard, high level of student performance and implies that an individual has acquired sufficiently all of the requisite knowledge and skills put forth in advance by an instructor. Corporate America has come to know mastery learning in the form of competency-based training (CBT). Student learning in a mastery model may be supported using repeatable testing with high-quality, individualized feedback. Mastery systems developed in the 1960s and 1970s were highly successful (Bloom 1984, 1976;

Keller and Sherman 1974; C. C. Kulik and Kulik 1987; J. A. Kulik, Kulik, and Bangert-Drowns 1990; J. A. Kulik, Kulik, and Carmichael 1974; J. A. Kulik, Kulik, and Cohen 1979). In spite of the generally demonstrable learning gains, the factors leading to the large-scale abandonment of such systems included management complexity, poor supporting infrastructure, and the requirement that teachers serve as managers (Silberman 1978).

We originally came at mastery learning through desktop computer-assisted instruction with videodisc technology. In 1987, Apple Computer created HyperCard, a software product that provided a means for managing visually rich, interactive learning systems based on videodiscs. The required supporting infrastructure was very expensive and limited the dissemination of such materials.

In the late 1990s it became clear that the internet in general and the World Wide Web in particular afforded an alternative infrastructure through which mastery learning systems could be implemented (Brooks 1997). Initial easy access to the web, first achieved with Mosaic but unleashed with Netscape Navigator, made widespread delivery of visually rich learning systems viable. Since that time, "browser" software and bandwidth have improved dramatically. Where once colleges had to provide much of the hardware for end users, today learners purchase their own hardware. The institution needs only to provide network access. Costly wired systems are giving way to lower-cost wireless systems. It is not surprising, therefore, that there have been numerous attempts to create web-based mastery learning practice systems (Brooks, Nolan, and Gallagher 2003; Penn, Nedeff, and Gozdzik 2000; see also *http://he-cda.wiley.com/WileyCDA/Section/id-107234.html*).

The client-server relationship offered by the web is advantageous for research and development of interactive learning materials. In a web-based system, although the learners can be nearly anywhere in the world, the server receiving and processing the information is in one place—and a change there affects the subsequent interactions of all learners with the system. It is as if a teacher could simply replace one chapter with another in a course textbook with little effort and cost and be assured that all students had access to the change. In addition to the ease of whole-scale modifications for users, the client-server model allows us to conduct nearly continuous learning research and to quickly implement systemic changes based on research findings. What has emerged is a model involving a continuous cycle of development, deployment within instruction, research, and then redevelopment.

In this chapter we describe the specific kinds of items that we have developed for use in automated practice systems and discuss some issues related to web-based learning. Next, we describe in broad terms other web implementations. We then describe the use of such systems in undergraduate and graduate chemistry courses. Finally, we speculate on the evolutionary paths these systems are likely to take in the near future.

Feedback Items

This section describes the kinds of items used to elicit responses from learners as we provide them with practice. In our opinion, one must interact with a web-based practice and feedback system to truly appreciate the power of the experience. Therefore, we recommend that readers contact one of the authors or visit a sample website (*http://dwbrr.unl.edu/Demo/CourseDemo/startdemo.html*) to enhance the reading experience. This website is the best way to appreciate the functioning of the tools described in this chapter. If this URL is unavailable, visit *http://dwb.unl.edu* and follow the "resource" links to find the current version and location of the paper.

Our learning systems aim to develop both conceptual and procedural knowledge, with special attention given to the notion of well-structured problem solving. A number of strategies are used in our practice systems to enable learners to demonstrate knowledge and understanding. These strategies manifest as a range of student response items developed specifically to demonstrate comprehension, reasoning, disposition, and problem-solving skill.

Essay

Demonstrating comprehension, reasoning, and articulating a position are all themes developed with the use of essay response items. Students complete extended responses to essay items that may involve writing sentences, paragraphs, or several paragraphs. Once an essay response is submitted, the learner is presented with a "model" response.

Due to the complexity of the response, essay items require evaluation by human experts. In our systems, once a student submits an essay response, an electronic message is dispatched to the instructor alerting him or her to log on, evaluate the response, and provide feedback. The learning system automatically converts URL references submitted by the learner into active hyperlinks. When responses are on focused topics, automated assessment is possible (Lemaire and Dessus 2001). In the future, automated evaluation and response to essay items is likely to become widespread. Another alternative to expert grading for essay responses is Calibrated Peer Review (CPR), an online approach developed by Chapman and Russell (Forthcoming) that involves training students to review the writing of other students (their peers).

The remaining item formats are used to develop knowledge, comprehension, and reasoning and involve automatic computer assessment with immediate feedback. To experience the way these practice (assessment) items function, visit the sample website (*http://dwbrr.unl.edu/Demo/ CourseDemo/startdemo.html*).

Short Answer

The powerful short-answer format facilitates practice on complex problems with numerical answers. Each short-answer problem is programmed separately so that random selections of problem components lead to the availability of scores to millions of problem variants. Perhaps the most important aspect of the short-answer format is that, after providing a response for evaluation, each learner receives a detailed, worked example of the problem using exactly the same given problem variants. This means that the problem might involve selections from as many as 50 chemical reactions with a very large (virtually infinite) range of amounts of substance.

One can think of short-answer items not just as practice tools but also as generators of worked examples. Worked examples have an extremely rich history of enhancing learning, especially when used to teach complex problem solving (Sweller and Cooper 1985; Sweller, van Merrienboer, and Paas 1998). A variety of scaffolding strategies can be used, allowing a learner to work up to complex problems through the presentation of simpler problem components. Substantial programming effort often is involved when developing these questions so that appropriate richness is available in the feedback to make that feedback meaningful. Short-answer items demand programming time and, therefore, are the most difficult to develop.

Some developers have chosen to produce shells or templates for short-answer problems such that 10 or 20 "patterns" of items may be used. We have eschewed this approach, but we often begin programming one question by copying a related or similar question and starting

from that point. Some operations, such as determining significant figures or setting bounds on the acceptable range of a numerical answer, are handled by generic functions.

Fill-in-the-Blank

Fill-in-the-blank items require recall rather than recognition. The answer-judging routines involve matching, and a list of acceptable responses is provided as basic feedback. Regular expressions can be used to strengthen the automatic grading of these items, eliminating the need for parsing of terms for precise matching of the learner's entry with an expected answer. Instead, all nonmatching responses are captured and examined periodically. This may lead to increasing the number of acceptable matches but more often leads to improving the feedback.

In addition to the list of accepted terms, the feedback for fill-in-the-blank items, when appropriate, focuses learners on those terms most often confused with one another. For example, chemical terms such as electronegativity and electron affinity are differentiated with item-specific feedback.

Ranking

The ranking item asks the learner to order a series of responses—for example, "Rank the following species according to size from smallest to largest radius: Na^+, K^+, Ar, and Cl^-." In this example, two rules allow the learner to choose a unique ranking. Such items have a very large number of options. The order in which the choices are presented is varied randomly. Sometimes five or six species may be pooled, from which only three or four are chosen, resulting in a large number of possible items. Each item is presented as a tabular array with radio buttons, and the learner is expected to "click" choices to make a response.

Matching

We use two matching or categorization formats. One displays radio buttons in a table and is used when the number of possibilities is constrained by a small range of choices. For example, a list of salts might be characterized as having acidic, neutral, or basic aqueous solutions. Another type of matching item provides options as pull-down menus. In this format, unrelated distractors often are provided. For example, one might have a series of equations related to gas laws and, from a pull-down menu, a list of names of persons generally associated with the discovery of those laws. So, one of the equations might be $PV = k$ and the pull-down list would include Boyle, Charles, Avogadro, and Einstein.

Categorization

Demonstrating knowledge of group characteristics can be done with a categorization question, where learners are asked to sort items into one of two categories. A list of items is presented in a checkbox format. For example, the question might be "Check those solutes whose 0.1 M aqueous solutions are expected to be good electrical conductors," and the accompanying list might include "HCl," "HF," "NaCl," "ethanol," and "NaF."

Multiple Choice and True/False

Multiple-choice items are built automatically from a collection of question stems with random assignment of the distractors and random ordering of the foils. Tailored feedback for known errors and misconceptions can be tied to both foils and distractors.

We also include a modified true/false item format in which several paired statements are used and the learner must identify each as true or false. Each statement has a true and a false version; perhaps two or three statements might be selected. One statement pair might be "In the van der Waals equation for an ideal gas, $a = b = 0$" and "In the van der Waals equation for an ideal gas, $a = b = 1$." The first statement is true; the second one is false. An item is developed by randomly selecting pairs of statements from among all of the available pairs and then randomly selecting the true or the false version of that statement.

Image
An image format requires the learners to interact with a picture or graph presented on their screen. For example, learners are asked to click the point on a schematic phase diagram where solid and vapor but no liquid are expected. This process requires them to click somewhere on a line in that graphical representation. Image-based formats also are useful for identifying components in laboratory activities (e.g., click on the beaker) or selecting functional groups or active sites in molecules (e.g., click on the peptide bond).

More Complex Formats
Complex item formats are continually under development. For example, a recent modification to the multiple-choice format includes an additional response where the learner chooses a statement from among several to justify her or his first choice. Java applets or Flash objects embedded within web pages offer opportunities for assessments of other kinds of learning. Issues remain for the development of web-based delivery of these types of formats, and the development time for the creation of such items is very long.

Summary
The range of intellectual skills for which one might want to provide automated practice still exceeds web-based capability. Nevertheless, the range of practice items is large and growing. The web-based delivery of writing instruction for elementary grades is under development. Systems in which learners practice speaking foreign languages also are envisioned. In spite of a few limitations, web-based practice today is better described in terms of what one *can* do than in terms of what one can't (yet) do.

Web-Based Learning
Though often very useful, sometimes even watching a learner work does not reveal to the observer the processes used by that learner to create a response. Web-based practice provides inherently less information for the teacher. However, much information still can be made available. The time elapsed between sending an item and receiving a response, as well as everything submitted with that response, is recorded in a log for each learner. An examination of each learner's log may provide an indication of the nature and extent of learning difficulty. Although not yet included in our chemistry software, it has proved possible to track all cursor movements and keystrokes and include them as part of the learner's record in software intended to teach writing in the early elementary grades.

Many users of web-based systems similar to those described previously focus on the assessment aspect of the tools. Our focus is on a standard but high level of student performance where the student acquires all of the requisite knowledge and skills put forth in advance by

the instructor. From the server side of the relationship, the nature of the feedback provided is critical. Learner effort is the critical variable on the client side. Experience suggests that many learners simply give up and stop using any form of web-based instruction.

Our systems differ philosophically and mechanically from those intended exclusively either to automate assessment or to track homework. Systems such as WebAssign (*www.webassign.net*) and OWL (*http://ccbit.cs.umass.edu/owl*) are used to manage homework assignments and homework-like practice. These systems are well received and widely used by teachers. Our systems are intended to support practice until mastery is achieved, a quite different notion from the limited, structured practice most often associated with homework.

We are aware of some teachers using systems like ours who encourage unlimited, web-based practice through a variety of strategies but maintain entirely conventional assessment with scheduled, in-classroom, proctored, pencil-and-paper testing (Garbin 2002). They report substantially improved learning in the context of using the practice systems.

Delivery Systems

Our delivery systems evolve continuously. Our choice of development software is guided by these basic principles: cost, flexibility, vendor/community support, features and stability, and potential use as a rapid application development environment. Our development software must be powerful in its function and feature set, yet accessible and affordable for teaching to our graduate students. In an older system, author Brooks used HyperCard, a Macintosh-specific application, as a back-end. This system was migrated successfully to Runtime Revolution using the Hyper-Card-like formats and strategies in 2004. In 2005, the system was migrated to one in which Transcript, the programming language of Runtime Revolution, was used to write scripts that directly manage server-side responses from web inputs. Web-based descriptions of the development of this system are available at *http://dwbrr.unl.edu/Demo/CourseDemo/startdemo.html*. Recognizing both that HyperCard is a database program of sorts and that its commercial future was bleak, author Crippen developed a system based on the FileMaker database application. This system involves smooth integration of student records. Features such as including tracking histories of learners from one course to the next were added. We use our systems as much for research as for teaching and have little interest in their commercial development.

There are excellent systems one can obtain commercially, however. The eGrade system developed by John Orr of the University of Nebraska is extremely powerful; see *http://he-cda.wiley.com/WileyCDA/Section/id-107234.html* for more information. This system has been used in over 100 courses by hundreds of Nebraska instructors in a wide range of disciplines. Although eGrade started in the mathematics and physics areas, it has now reached as far as the classics. Web-based practice is available on a 24/7 basis. Several rooms on campus provide proctored testing. Most instructors permit some form of practice, usually unlimited web-based practice, followed by on-campus testing in a controlled environment.

High schools are beginning to use systems like eGrade, and both science and mathematics teachers are beginning to share item pools. Though not labeled as such, mastery learning seems alive and well through the support of web-based practice systems.

John H. Penn, a chemist at West Virginia University, developed the WE-LEARN system. This system is commercially available and includes some useful chemistry item banks. A demonstration of learning improvements though the use of this system has been reported (Penn, Nedeff, and Gozdzik 2000).

A program called TestPilot developed at Purdue University also affords online practice support. TestPilot is most like eGrade; users of each system gravitate toward implementation of specific features that they find fit their practice styles. As time goes on, the features of these systems become more powerful and their ease of use increases.

Modern course management programs (Blackboard, WebCT) include some testing features. Although continuing to develop, these built-in assessment tools pale in comparison to those developed specifically for feedback and practice. Indeed, assessment rather than practice is usually the goal of management programs; they are not well designed in terms of supporting mastery. One virtue of these built-in approaches is that they are fully integrated with other aspects of course management. So, when a registrar adds a student to a course, the testing and record keeping for that student are set up automatically.

Example Applications

We have considerable experience with three different applications of practice systems. Using support from the National Science Foundation (ESI-9819377), we developed a series of 16 graduate courses in chemistry pedagogy aimed at high school chemistry teachers. These courses continue to be offered on a for-tuition basis through the University of Nebraska-Lincoln. Teachers may take them for graduate credit in either chemistry or teaching, learning, and teacher education. Of the 16, 3 are biochemistry courses available for credit in biochemistry or biological sciences. Historically, most teachers (7:1) choose to earn chemistry credit. Hundreds of teachers have received credit through these courses.

The chemistry pedagogy courses were developed within a mastery framework. They focus on repeatable testing with feedback and use links to existing web-based curriculum resources. Teachers enroll and work asynchronously and receive credit once they demonstrate success with 93% of the items. Content resources quickly became the biggest issue in delivery; the loss of access to those materials, dubbed "link rot," was the most serious problem encountered when offering the courses (Markwell and Brooks 2002, 2003).

The second general area of implementation has been in undergraduate general chemistry at the University of Nevada, Las Vegas. The web-based learning system used there targets the development of fundamental strategies for self-regulated learning. Results suggest that students use worked examples and self-explanation prompts extensively and perceive this intervention to be effective (Crippen and Earl 2004). Further, the combination of a worked example with a self-explanation prompt produces improvement in performance, problem-solving skill, and self-efficacy (Crippen and Earl, Forthcoming).

Finally, both authors have had extensive experience with a system used to support the descriptive chemistry question of the Advanced Placement (AP) chemistry test. Nearly every year since the inception of the program, the test has included an essay question in which students are given a group of eight statements like "a small piece of metallic sodium is added to a large beaker filled with cool distilled water." The student is expected to write formulas for reactants and products to describe any ensuing reaction (e.g., $Na + H_2O \rightarrow Na^+ + OH^- + H_2$). A "balanced" chemical equation is not required. Students have performed poorly on the items of this question. A desktop application was developed in 1988 to help teachers prepare students for this question. That application (a HyperCard "stack") used a large pool of items (from prior exams) to print a series of eight items selected to have a distribution similar to that of an AP question. Also, the application printed a key for the teacher. That software evolved into a

web-based system with tutoring and practice that is used annually by over 2,000 students. The research and development of this system has been foundational to our design principles (Crippen 2000; Crippen and Brooks 2001a, 2001b, 2002; Crippen, Brooks, and Abuloum 2000).

Perhaps one reason for the historically poor performance on this AP question is that over half of the students log on for the first time within two weeks of the AP test date. Usage peaks on the day before the AP test but falls essentially to 0 within 48 hours of giving the test. The same issue applies to all of the materials developed for web dissemination; they must be used and used properly for learning to be facilitated. We are driven by the notion that we can do better at supporting learning. Clearly, there are instances where the students can do better, too.

Future Effort

Motivation is a measure of how much working memory a learner consciously or subconsciously allocates to a learning task. One of the best ways to engage students in learning (i.e., to motivate) is through successful learning experiences. One reason for the success of mastery learning is that learners know that they are learning and derive satisfaction from newly acquired skills. Mastery learning can be problematic when the learning rate is low because the material is either too easy or too difficult for a learner. A much more subtle point is that, when a learning difficulty is encountered, the learner needs to have some working memory to allocate to the teaching. Therefore, we are focusing much effort on the types of scaffolding we provide learners based on their performance and in making practice systems highly adaptive. That is, we are attempting to design systems that adapt such that, when working on problems, the learner's cognitive load capacity is nearly fully used. When learning new material, the load will be lower, with capacity reserved for the deliberate integration or embedding of the new material within the learner's existing knowledge structures. With time, our software becomes faster and better able to tailor feedback to the individual needs of all learners.

If one accepts the notions of lifelong learning and change as they seem to be emerging at the outset of the 21st century, many standards and approaches of the past are likely to be revised. Perhaps the greatest challenge will be in determining which long-term intellectual skills must be in place for a person to successfully make use of just-in-time teaching materials, ones very likely to be delivered on the web. While this may seem both self-serving and counterintuitive, we speculate that more rather than fewer persons will be identified as teachers in that fast-moving world. Much of what those teachers will do is to create the just-in-time learning materials and help decide when the use of those materials will be enough to support the completion of complex tasks.

References

Bloom, B. S. 1976. *Human characteristics and school learning.* New York: McGraw-Hill.

Bloom, B. S. 1984. The 2 sigma problem: The search for methods of group instruction as effective as one-to-one tutoring. *Educational Researcher* 13: 4–16.

Brooks, D. W. 1997. *Web-teaching.* New York: Plenum Press.

Brooks, D. W., D. E. Nolan, and S. J. Gallagher. 2003. Automated testing. *Journal of Science Education and Technology* 12 (2): 183–185.

Brooks, D. W., and D. F. Shell. Forthcoming. Working memory, motivation, and teacher-initiated learning. *Journal of Science Education and Technology* 15 (1).

Chapman, O., and A. Russell. Forthcoming. Calibrated peer review. *Journal of Science Education and Technology* 15 (1).

Crippen, K. J. 2000. Analysis of learning at an advanced placement descriptive chemistry web site. PhD diss., University of Nebraska-Lincoln.

Crippen, K. J., and D. W. Brooks. 2001a. Learning difficult content using the web: Strategies make a difference. *Journal of Science Education and Technology* 10: 283–285.

Crippen, K. J., and D. W. Brooks. 2001b. Teaching advanced placement descriptive chemistry: Suggestions from a testing web site. *The Chemical Educator* 6 (5): 266–271.

Crippen, K. J., and D. W. Brooks. 2002. An analysis of student learning at a testing web site emphasizing descriptive chemistry. *Journal of Computers in Mathematics and Science Teaching* 21 (2): 183–201.

Crippen, K. J., D. W. Brooks, and A. Abuloum. 2000. A web-site supporting the AP descriptive chemistry question. *Journal of Chemical Education* 77: 1087–1088.

Crippen, K. J., and B. L. Earl. 2004. Considering the efficacy of web-based worked examples in introductory chemistry. *Journal of Computers in Mathematics and Science Teaching* 23 (2): 175–191.

Crippen, K. J., and B. L. Earl. Forthcoming. The impact of web-based worked examples and self-explanation on performance, problem solving, and self-efficacy. *Computers & Education.*

Garbin, C. P. 2002. A "technological make-over" for the psychological research methods & data analysis laboratory. *www-class.unl.edu/psycrs/peerev*

Keller, F. S., and J. G. Sherman. 1974. *Psi, the Keller Plan handbook: Essays on a personalized system of instruction.* Menlo Park, CA: W. A. Benjamin.

Kulik, C. C., and J. A. Kulik. 1987. Mastery testing and student learning: A meta-analysis. *Journal of Educational Technology Systems* 15: 325–345.

Kulik, J. A., C. C. Kulik, and R. L. Bangert-Drowns. 1990. Effectiveness of mastery learning programs: A meta-analysis. *Review of Educational Research* 60: 265–299.

Kulik, J. A., C. Kulik, and K. Carmichael. 1974. The Keller Plan in science teaching. *Science* 183: 379–383.

Kulik, J. A., C. C. Kulik, and P. A. Cohen. 1979. A meta-analysis of outcome studies of Keller's personalized system of instruction. *American Psychologist* 34: 307–318.

Lemaire, B., and P. Dessus. 2001. A system to assess the semantic content of student essays. *Journal of Educational Computing Research* 24 (3): 305–320.

Markwell, J., and D. W. Brooks. 2002. Broken links: Just how rapidly do science education hyperlinks go extinct? *Journal of Science Education and Technology* 11: 105–108.

Markwell, J., and D. W. Brooks. 2003. "Link rot" limits the usefulness of web-based educational materials in biochemistry and molecular biology. *Biochemistry and Molecular Biology Education* 31: 69–72.

Penn, J., V. M. Nedeff, and G. Gozdzik. 2000. Organic chemistry and the internet: A web-based approach to homework and testing using the WE-LEARN system. *Journal of Chemical Education* 77: 227–231.

Schraw, G., D. W. Brooks, and K. J. Crippen. 2005. Improving chemistry instruction using an interactive, compensatory model of learning. *Journal of Chemical Education* 82 (4): 637–640.

Shapiro, A. 2004. How including prior knowledge as a subject variable may change outcomes of learning research. *American Educational Research Journal* 41 (1): 159–189.

Silberman, R. 1978. The Keller Plan: A personal view. *Journal of Chemical Education* 55: 97–98.

Sweller, J., and G. Cooper. 1985. The use of worked examples as a substitute for problem solving in learning algebra. *Cognition and Instruction* 2: 59–89.

Sweller, J., J. van Merrienboer, and F. Paas. 1998. Cognitive architecture and instructional design. *Educational Psychology Review* 10 (3): 251–296.

CHAPTER 26

Teaching Students to Evaluate the Accuracy of Science Information on the Internet

Jory P. Weintraub

Jory P. Weintraub is science education and outreach manager at the National Evolutionary Synthesis Center (NESCent) in Durham, North Carolina. He earned a PhD in immunology at the University of North Carolina at Chapel Hill and conducts research in science education, instructional technology, and minority advancement in science. He teaches courses in immunology and the molecular basis of disease.

Recent studies confirm what undergraduate science instructors already know: Students are increasingly using the internet as the primary source of science information for reports, projects, presentations, and other class assignments. While the internet has unquestionably revolutionized information dissemination and access, it is also clear that the quality, validity, and accuracy of science information on the internet are extremely variable. This chapter addresses the issue of variable accuracy of science information on the internet, how to address this topic in undergraduate science courses, how to make students aware of this situation (if they are not already), and how to begin to train students to read and think critically about the information they obtain from the internet. Background will be provided on the extent to which students have adopted the internet as a primary source of information. This will be followed by an overview of a multidisciplinary, technology-enhanced, student-active module I have developed and used in undergraduate science instruction to build and refine students' critical thinking and analytical skills with respect to this timely and extremely important issue.

The Internet as a Primary Source of Science Information: Some Numbers

Pop quiz: Do you remember when television shows boasted that they were being broadcast "in living color" as opposed to high definition? Did listening to new music involve Peter Frampton and an 8-track tape player instead of Weezer and an iPod? Did you ever use a floppy disc that was actually floppy? If you answered "yes" to any of these questions, then you likely spent a great deal of your time as an undergraduate in a campus library (assuming you actually did research when it was assigned).

But, if you are in any way involved in undergraduate instruction today, you know that a current undergraduate student's typical default source for any information, including scientific information, is the internet, as opposed to books and journals accessed in a campus library. With the proliferation of computer laboratories on college campuses, increasing affordability of (and, often, university-mandated requirements for) student-owned personal computers, and an ever-expanding number of dormitory rooms being equipped with high-speed internet access, we have reached a point where a student can conceivably spend four (or more) years on a college campus without ever actually setting foot in a library.

Davis and Cohen (2001) found that during a period from 1996 through 1999 book citations decreased to 19%, while internet citations increased from 9% to 21% in undergraduate research papers. As expected, those patterns have shifted further in recent years, with a 2004 study revealing that 69% of surveyed students began their search for information on the internet, while a mere 17% accessed campus library resources for the same purpose (Abels, Griner, and Turqman 2004). In my own experience as an undergraduate instructor it is not uncommon to observe 100% of my students using the internet to obtain information for certain assignments.

There are many reasons for this—some valid (internet-based information is more up-to-date, multimedia resources can enhance student comprehension, physically disabled or off-campus students may have difficulty accessing library resources), and some questionable (it is "less work" than walking to the library, the library is filled with "old" books and information). Whatever the reasons, it is clear that today's point-and-click generation, which has come of age in the presence of the internet, sophisticated video-gaming technology, instant messaging, and cell phones, has a strong preference for the immediate gratification of technology-based information obtained easily and rapidly via the internet.

Why Is This a Problem? Accuracy and Permanence of Science Information on the Internet

Although there are many valid and compelling reasons to use the internet as a primary source of information for student research projects, the obvious risk is that the bulk of information (including scientific information) available online does not undergo any sort of peer-review process before being posted. This lack of quality control leads to a proliferation of "bad" science on the internet. As described in the journal *Nature*, Allen and colleagues (1999) found that the vast majority of websites on subjects such as evolution (87.8%), genetically modified organisms (82.8%), and endangered species (73.6%) were inaccurate or misleading. On average greater than 70% of the websites found via a search on these topics were not peer reviewed.

An additional concern is the permanence (or lack thereof) of websites on various scientific topics. Dellavalle and colleagues (2003) examined internet references in articles 27 months old or older in three prominent scientific journals (*Science, The New England Journal of Medicine,* and *JAMA* [the journal of the American Medical Association]) and found that 13% of these references were from sites that were inactive or no longer existed. Davis and Cohen (2001) reported that only 55% of URLs in 1999 bibliographies led to the correct website.

Clearly, if students are routinely citing references that are scientifically inaccurate or no longer accessible, this is an issue of major concern. But does this mean that the internet should not be used as a source of information for undergraduate science students?

The Real Issue: Critical Thinking and Reading

The question we need to ask is not whether students should use the internet as a source of scientific information. We know that they do and that they will continue to do so. Even if its use as an information source is restricted or prohibited in an undergraduate course, our students will continue to use the internet in nonacademic searches for information, including personal health information (Hansen et al. 2003).

Students are at risk of misinterpreting information or failing to identify inaccuracies in web-based science content because they are constantly being challenged to explore topics that are new and unfamiliar to them. Although this risk can't be eliminated, it can be greatly reduced by encouraging the development of students' critical thinking and reading skills. Indeed, doing so reinforces the very nature of science, which is to question, critique, and analyze rather than accept blindly.

The question, then, is what can we do as instructors to ensure that our students possess the critical thinking and reading skills necessary to assess accurately the validity of the information (scientific and otherwise) they find on the internet? It is clear from analyses such as that of Thompson (2003) that there is much room for improvement with respect to how students use the internet as a research tool.

How to Address This Challenge With Undergraduate Science Students: One Instructor's Approach

This challenge led to the development of a module entitled "Evaluating the Accuracy of Science Information on the Internet" (Weintraub 2000). This is a multiday, interdisciplinary module that involves both in-class activities and asynchronous, web-based exercises. A schematic overview of the module can be seen in Figure 26.1. It has been used over multiple semesters in upper-division undergraduate biology courses at several universities, with the following goals:

- to reinforce (or introduce) the concepts of *critical thinking* and *critical reading* to undergraduate science students,
- to challenge students with the notion that critical thinking and reading are two of the cornerstones of the scientific method, and
- to reiterate (or introduce) the idea that all scientific information—and particularly that found on the internet—should be questioned and assessed based on existing knowledge, the reputability of the source, and the author's expertise in the subject.

Figure 26.1

Evaluating the Accuracy of Science Information on the Internet: Module Overview

1. Short passages are assigned as prereading

2. In-class discussion of critical thinking

3. Follow-up assignment (asynchronous, online activities)

4. In-class follow-up discussion

Although these goals may seem fairly basic and obvious, informal in-class polling of students (junior and senior undergraduates) regularly reveals that a surprising number of them have never received a formal introduction to the concepts of critical thinking or critical reading and that they struggle to come up with even a basic definition of these concepts. Further, I have observed that although many students intuitively understand the process of critical thinking, a smaller number can effectively characterize the relationship between this process and scientific research or inquiry.

The module begins with a pre-reading assignment of several short passages, followed by a basic, in-class discussion of critical thinking and reading. The discussion, which is conducted in a highly interactive manner to increase student engagement, proceeds as follows:

1. Student volunteers are asked to define the term *critical thinking* aloud.
2. Several different definitions from various sources are presented and discussed.
3. The short passages that had been assigned as pre-reading are read aloud by student volunteers. The passages are analyzed and debated in small "breakout" groups, and then each group reports to the class, leading to further discussion.
4. Gradually, the focus of the discussion narrows to examine how critical thinking serves as a key element of the scientific method, which is briefly reviewed.
5. The discussion concludes with an emphasis on the need to use critical-thinking skills in assessing web-based science content.

This discussion is always spirited and lively, with most, if not all, students actively participating. A highlight of this discussion is an introduction to the tongue-in-cheek website "Dihydrogen Monoxide – DHMO Homepage" (*www.dhmo.org*). This site features graphic descriptions of the very real risks and hazards associated with the chemical compound DHMO. Some attentive students anticipate the punch line, but the majority typically develop a healthy concern for the threat until the instructor points out that DHMO is simply an alternate name for a compound known as H_2O. Of course, by then the point has been made and students are reminded of how easily individuals with basic web-authoring skills and an agenda can disseminate false or misleading information to an unsuspecting public.

Finally, several thought-provoking questions related to these topics are posed, and students are instructed to select one of these questions for the "discussion" portion of the assignment. Using a threaded discussion forum within the password-protected course website, students are required to (1) post a thoughtful and well-reasoned response to the question they have chosen and (2) post replies to the initial posts of at least two of their classmates. Typically, students demonstrate a great deal of enthusiasm for this portion of the activity, posting many more than the required two responses. Often, the online discussion and debate continue well beyond the completion of the assignment, as students develop a sense of pride and ownership of their personal opinions and responses.

The last segment of this assignment (Figure 26.1, step 4) is a second in-class discussion, this one focusing on the posts and replies from the discussion board. During this second in-class discussion, it is not uncommon to see participation by the entire class, including those who were hesitant to be actively involved in the previous discussion. This increase in participation can likely be attributed to a number of factors, including increased self-confidence based on the practice students have received in exercising their critical-thinking skills and an increased comfort level from having interacted online with their classmates over the preceding days.

By the conclusion of this assignment, students have spent several days discussing and actively debating issues associated with critical thinking and its utility in assessing the accuracy of science information on the internet. They have typically exercised their own critical thinking and reading skills in the process and have developed a new awareness of the potential pitfalls associated with using the internet as a primary source of science information. Additional benefits might include an increased comfort level with course technology usage (via the discussion board activity) and a new familiarity with their classmates.

Several "housekeeping" issues are worth mentioning:

- Students are clearly instructed not to "flame" or attack their classmates based on their opinions and are informed that doing so will result in deduction of points.
- Students are clearly informed that points for this assignment will be distributed solely on participation and completion of the assigned tasks (posting a response to a question of their choice and replying to at least two of their classmates' posts) and that they will not be evaluated or graded on their opinions or viewpoints.
- The instructor does not contribute to, or comment on, the discussion board posts. The instructor may, however, contribute to in-class discussions.
- This module is typically implemented at the outset of a course and is therefore not dependent on any specific knowledge of course content. As such, it can be implemented in any science course or, for that matter, any course in which critical thinking might be appropriately addressed.

Does It Work? Students Respond....

Since this is a nontraditional activity, especially for an upper-level science course, initial student reactions to this module typically range from enthusiasm to bemusement to open questioning of whether or not it is useful or appropriate for such a course. However, upon completion of the module, the general consensus is that the activity has been valuable and enjoyable. Several comments taken from course evaluations support this view:

The activity really made me think about questioning the websites I find—a thought which had never occurred to me before.

I enjoyed the in-class discussions and got a better sense for how important critical thinking is in doing science (or even reading about it).

I will definitely be more careful in the future when searching for science information online. I may even go to the library!

I wish we had done this during the first week of my freshman year instead of during my last semester of college. I might have done better (or at least learned more).

While the ultimate value of this module has yet to be formally and scientifically assessed, anecdotal data and observations clearly indicate that the activities are of benefit to students.

Final Thoughts

With the explosion of the internet it is easier than at any point in history to access information quickly and conveniently. However, it is also easier than ever to disseminate information, and to do so on a global scale. As with most phenomena, this has both advantages and liabilities, and everyone including students should be aware of both.

Critical-thinking skills have always been essential for one to function effectively and successfully in a complex world. As technologies such as the internet increase the complexity of our world at an unprecedented rate, critical thinking is more important than ever before. And, while it has always been essential for teachers to nurture and develop those skills, we are at a point in time where this may be the single most important job of educators, regardless of discipline.

William Butler Yeats said that "education is not the filling of a pail, but the lighting of a fire." Critical thinking is the spark that ignites that fire and the fuel that sustains it. This is truer in the age of the internet than ever before.

References

Abels, E., L. Griner, and M. Turqman. 2004. If you build it will they come? *Information Outlook* 8 (10): 13–17.

Allen, E. S., J. M. Burke, M. E. Welch, and L. H. Rieseberg. 1999. How reliable is science information on the web? *Nature* 402 (6763): 722.

Davis, P. M., and S. A. Cohen. 2001. The effect of the web on undergraduate citation behavior 1996-1999. *Journal of the American Society for Information Science and Technology* 52 (4): 309–314.

Dellavalle, R. P., E. J. Hester, L. F. Heilig, A. L. Drake, J. W. Kuntzman, M. Graber, and L. M. Schilling. 2003. Information science. Going, going, gone: Lost internet references. *Science* 302 (5646): 787–788.

Hansen, D. L., H. A. Derry, P. J. Resnick, and C. R. Richardson. 2003. Adolescents searching for health information on the internet: An observational study. *Journal of Medical Internet Research* 5 (4): e25.

Thompson, C. 2003. Information illiterate or lazy: How college students use the web for research. *Libraries and the Academy* 3 (2): 259–268.

Weintraub, J. P. 2000. Evaluating the accuracy of science information on the internet: Introduction to immunology. *www.unc.edu/cell/files/immunology/evaluating.html*

Meeting Special Challenges

Unfortunately, for the learning-disabled student, a "can't do science" attitude persists among K–12 teachers and administrators. Consequently, the learning-disabled student often is not required to engage in science-related course work and does not develop the necessary foundational skills that meet national science standards.... Negative attitudes faced by adult disabled individuals are similar to those faced by K–12 students. —Karen Benn Marshall

What do race, ethnicity, and gender have to do with the teaching of chemistry? In one sense, a great deal. By including a wider variety of examples and by removing those that implicitly exclude certain groups, an instructor can help students better connect what they are learning to the communities in which they live. Furthermore, inclusive instructional materials better represent the world in which students one day will work. —Catherine H. Middlecamp

Many colleges and universities offer undergraduate courses designed to promote an appreciation and understanding of cultural diversity, and to develop and foster international and intercultural competency.... The globalization of world economies, advances in information technologies, and the complex interconnections of global environmental issues are driving the initiative of providing students with a background and understanding of other cultures and nations. —Michael A. Fidanza

This study is exemplary because it examined the effectiveness of a specific, promising research tool for identifying alternative conceptions .... [and it revealed] the benefits of identifying gaps in student learning as a way to prevent or remediate alternative conceptions.... If researchers identify them, and college science teachers are made aware of these gaps, careful teaching may prevent alternative conceptions from forming. We think more knowledge-gap research findings would be valuable to college science instructors. —James H. Wandersee and Jewel J. Reuter

Calling attention to misconceptions and suggesting to students that they should be avoided is usually inadequate. Serious difficulties are not successfully addressed by telling students they are wrong and providing them with the "right answer." If students are expected to understand the scientifically accepted concepts, they need to go through a process termed conceptual change. —Luli Stern, Tamar Yechieli, and Joseph Nussbaum

In a perfect world, access to higher education and unqualified support for students, regardless of race, ethnicity, gender, culture, or disability, would be a fundamental premise on which all colleges and universities operate. Learning to appreciate human diversity would be central to our mission, and all faculty would be able and willing to help students with conceptual or learning problems. To what extent are we reaching these lofty goals? In this unit several authors discuss human diversity and its impact on college science learning. Included are chapters on identifying and helping learning-disabled students, including people of divergent ethnic and cultural backgrounds as well as women, introducing students to cultural diversity on a global scale, and working with students to overcome conceptual difficulties in science.

The world of *learning disabilities* is one with which most college science teachers are relatively unfamiliar, and yet a growing number of learning-disabled students are enrolling in colleges and universities and taking courses in the natural sciences. Karen Benn Marshall of Montgomery College (Maryland) discusses the nature of learning disabilities, attempts at "mainstreaming" learning-disabled students in pre-college science, how technology can be used to enhance their learning, and what college faculty can do to ensure their inclusion in college and university courses.

Cathy Middlecamp describes her efforts to achieve *ethnic, cultural, class, and gender inclusiveness* in her nonmajors chemistry courses at the University of Wisconsin–Madison. She suggests teaching science through a consideration of complex societal issues, embedding "core" disciplinary concepts within concentric sets of socially important human problems, such as air quality and nuclear energy. "Issues involving people (and the problems they face) have a rightful place in the science curriculum," says Cathy, and students who experience this kind of human-centered curriculum are better prepared to face the real world of culturally embedded problems.

Michael Fidanza of the Penn State University has developed Plants, Places, and People, a lecture course designed to encourage an understanding of *cultural diversity* and to develop international and intercultural competency through a study of agronomy, botany, and horticulture. He describes his use of collaborative group projects that focus on a culture and its economically important plants. An assessment of the course is included.

One special challenge that all faculty face is helping students overcome *conceptual difficulties* in science learning. Jim Wandersee and Jewel Reuter of Louisiana State University review recent research on conceptual problems encountered by college students in biology, chemistry, and physics, and they look at research on attempts to address common gaps in scientific knowledge. They describe some of the work they have done with visually scaffolded learning materials that are designed to encourage meaningful learning and conceptual understanding.

Israeli researchers Luli Stern, Tamar Yechieli, and Joseph Nussbaum describe the basic problem of *conceptual change* and what college teachers can do to encourage it, even among the "best and brightest." They remind us that learning science is an intellectually challenging task that is fraught with pitfalls, and misconceptions are a normal part of the learning process. Focusing on two knowledge areas, the particulate nature of matter and natural selection, they discuss ways of encouraging conceptual understanding in the most fundamental areas of natural science.

CHAPTER 27

Science, Technology, and the Learning Disabled:

A Review of the Literature

Karen Benn Marshall

Karen Benn Marshall is professor and chair of the Department of Biology at Montgomery College (Takoma Park/Silver Spring Campus), Maryland. She earned an MS degree in biology with a concentration in physiology at Alabama A&M University and is a third-year doctoral student in science education at Morgan State University. Her research interests are science and technology and the learning disabled, the disproportionate representation of African Americans in special education, and attitudes toward science and achievement in science. She teaches courses in anatomy and physiology, pathophysiology, and reproductive biology.

The lack of research studies that examine the use of technology as a tool to support the learning of science among the learning disabled is an important limitation of research in science teaching. For purposes of this chapter, technology is defined as a "wide range of electronic materials and methods for learning" (North Central Regional Educational Laboratory 2005). This chapter focuses specifically on the use of computer technology and has three objectives: (1) to summarize technology and science education research of the last decade as it relates to the learning disabled, (2) to identify potential computer technology tools that can be best used to support the learning of science by the learning disabled, and (3) to provide some recommendations for postsecondary science educators.

At the time this chapter was written in 2006, few researchers had conducted studies on the use of computer technology by the learning disabled to learn science. The research works reviewed for this chapter came primarily from three bodies of literature: technology, science education, and learning disabilities.

The Need for Scientific Literacy

Jarvis and Pell (2002) say that "scientifically literate people are better able to understand and participate in discussions about issues of our rapidly changing technological world, such as how drugs are tested, where waste is disposed, genetic engineering of food, value of space exploration, and fishing quotas" (p. 980). Furthermore, an understanding of scientific concepts helps students evaluate future scientific issues. According to Jarvis and Pell (2002), *scientific literacy* can be defined as a basic understanding of scientific concepts and the skills needed to engage in scientific experiences while retaining positive attitudes toward science. They suggest that the scientific education of young children should begin at the elementary school level, so that young children can develop a foundational understanding of science concepts and the ability to think critically and apply science ideas to their everyday lives.

A better understanding of how learning-disabled students learn science will help instructors identify which factors and types of science experiences are most effective in developing a scientific self-concept and influencing a lifelong interest in science. Unfortunately for the learning-disabled student, a "can't do science" attitude persists among K–12 teachers and administrators. Consequently, the learning-disabled student often is not required to engage in science-related course work and does not develop the necessary foundational skills that meet national science standards (Cunningham 1997). Cunningham reported that the negative attitudes faced by adult disabled individuals are similar to those faced by K–12 students. According to a National Science Foundation study (Task Force on Women, Minorities, and the Handicapped in Science and Technology 1989), a major obstacle that disabled individuals face is negative attitudes on the part of employers and teachers. Cunningham suggested that "this is particularly harmful, because not only does it deny or limit some students' entrance into the fields of science, engineering and math, but it almost ensures that those individuals will never be able to enter science, engineering or mathematics careers when they enter the work force" (p. 1).

Landrum and Tankersley (2004) referred to science "as something of an uninvited guest" in the schools (p. 207). Although educators and administrators do not invite science into their schools, science is not rejected by all educational professionals. Landrum and Tankersley believe that teachers have not yet developed a relationship with science and as a result they unconsciously avoid science. Accordingly, there "is more an indifference to science, or lack of awareness about the existing body of scientific evidence that might guide practice" (p. 207). As a result, "science drops by unannounced ... and [teachers and administrators] respond to this guest in different ways" (p. 207). The authors believe that "science does make it into schools on occasion, but its visits are random and unpredictable" (p. 211). This poses more of a problem for the learning-disabled student. A teacher's indifference to science or undeveloped relationship with science, coupled with a negative attitude that the learning-disabled student "can't do science," creates even more of a disparity and ultimately results in learning-disabled students who lack the necessary foundational skills in the sciences.

The Learning Disabled

According to federal guidelines, a learning disability is defined as "a disorder in one of more of the basic psychological processes involved in understanding or in using language, spoken or written, that may manifest itself in an imperfect ability to listen, think, speak, read, write, spell, or do mathematical calculations, including conditions such as perceptual disabilities, brain injury, minimal brain dysfunction, dyslexia, and developmental aphasia" (34 *Code of*

Federal Regulations §300.7(c)(10), quoted in National Dissemination Center for Children With Disabilities [NICHCY] 2004). This definition does not include "learning problems that are primarily the result of visual, hearing, or motor disabilities, of mental retardation, of emotional disturbance, or of environmental, cultural, or economic disadvantage" (NICHCY 2004).

The Individuals with Disabilities Education Act (IDEA), formerly the Education for All Handicapped Children Act (Public Law 94-142), guarantees that all students with disabilities will have the necessary accommodations to receive a public education. According to the No Child Left Behind Act of 2001 (NCLB; Public Law 107-110), all students should be provided access to the general education curriculum, scientifically based instruction, and assessments of performance. Because of these federal mandates, the focus has been to teach students with and without disabilities in the same general education classrooms. Terms such as *mainstreaming, inclusive classrooms,* and *least restrictive environment* have been used to either denote the practice or describe the teaching/learning environment. Data from the U.S. Department of Education (1999) indicate that students with disabilities receive 80% of their education in general education classrooms. According to Steele (2004), this trend is challenging to the teacher who is now responsible for providing instruction to students with even greater varying levels of ability.

Atwood and Oldham (1985) surveyed elementary school teachers and found that teachers viewed science as the easiest subject in which to include disabled students. The reasons cited by the teachers included that science is hands-on and that science requires a lot of group interaction. These characteristics appear to be advantageous for general education as well as learning-disabled students. Richardson (1994) found that when general education students are taught in the same classroom as disabled students, they appear to learn more of the content. Palincsar and colleagues (2001) reported that the inquiry approach to learning science and its focus on higher-order thinking and problem-solving skills could be problematic for the learning-disabled student. In some cases, specially designed activities need to be implemented to meet the needs of the learning-disabled student. Ormsbee and Finson (2000) believed that standard science activities are not designed appropriately for students with disabilities. Mastropieri and Scruggs (1994) suggested that students are more likely to perform poorly in science if they are not appropriately and actively engaged in learning. Even students who suffer from mild disabilities will have difficulty if the activities are visually unclear, difficult to follow, and contain difficult terms (Finson et al. 1997).

Academic Performance of Students With Learning Disabilities

In a study conducted by Donohoe and Zigmond (1990), almost 70% of learning-disabled ninth-grade students who enrolled in a science class received grades of D or below. Furthermore, learning-disabled ninth-grade students had lower grades than their non-learning-disabled peers who were also defined as low achievers. Harnisch and Wilkinson (1989) found that secondary school students with disabilities had lower performance levels in science and mathematics than in reading, vocabulary, and writing. Cawley, Kahn, and Tedesco (1989) reported that approximately 60% of learning-disabled students in grades 9–12 had grades of D or lower.

Opportunity to Learn

As cited by Cawley and Parmar (2001), the National Research Council suggests that "equal attention must be given to the assessment of opportunity to learn and to the assessment of student achievement. Students cannot be held accountable for achievement unless they are given adequate opportunity to learn science" (p. 106). The opportunity to learn includes but is not limited to experiences that introduce science concepts, processes, and skills (Cawley and Parmar 2001). For learning-disabled students, who have unique needs, it is necessary to modify the way science is taught, and computer technology is one possible tool for making science accessible to these students.

Why Computer Technology?

Kumar and Wilson (2000) reported that "computer technology could provide cognitively challenging environments for the development of analytical, critical thinking, reasoning and problem solving skills in students" (p. 200). In Carnine's view (1989), differences in performance between the learning disabled and their peers is a major challenge when attempting to mainstream students. Computer technology can be used to minimize these differences in performance. The additional demands placed on teachers who teach inclusion classes may be reduced as well. Accordingly, more time could be spent on instructional interactions than on implementing interventions (Carnine 1989).

This section describes the uses of anchor-based instruction, intelligent tutoring systems, collaborative learning systems, telecommunications networks, information organizers, and computer-based concept mapping as potential computer technology tools for the learning disabled.

Anchor-Based Instruction

Anchor-based instruction originated at the Cognition and Learning Technology Center of Vanderbilt University (Kumar and Wilson 2000). In anchored instruction, videodiscs are used to engage students in problem solving of real-world scenarios. In this instructional mode, students become absorbed in a variety of tasks and seek to find the most appropriate solutions for those tasks. By using videodiscs, students place themselves within the scenarios repeatedly and watch the images presented at their own pace. Anchored instruction may be a powerful tool for disabled students because it provides a variety of visual displays of concepts and of how these concepts are related to each other (Hofmeister, Engelmann, and Carnine 1989). Bransford and colleagues (1990) said that "the major goal of anchored instruction is to enable students to notice critical features of problem situations and to experience the changes in their perception and understanding of the anchor as they view the situation from new points of view" (p. 135).

Through the use of computer technology, instruction can be individualized to meet the needs of students. Science lessons can then be presented in the form of pictures, videos, or text, and hypermedia software tools can be used to enhance the presentations so that the needs of learning-disabled students are met. Each student can work at his or her own pace, and the learning-disabled student can do so without the stress of having to keep up. The student is able to follow the flexible instructions that are afforded through the use of software such as HyperCard.

Higgins and Boone (1990) found that learning-disabled students who received hypertext instruction received the highest scores on quizzes when compared with those who received lecture and lecture plus instruction that was hypertext based. Hypertext instructional tools allow teachers of learning-disabled students to provide simple, sequential, and pictorial instructions that have a greater chance of being understood (Kumar and Wilson 2000).

Intelligent Tutoring Systems

Intelligent tutoring systems are designed to provide one-on-one instruction. These software systems are encoded so that the necessary skills are taught while giving hints and coaching. Some of these systems are used quite frequently by military personnel in a variety of training applications, including the assessment and diagnosis of reading skill deficiencies. When the deficiencies have been determined, the tutoring system tailors instruction to meet the needs of the student. Built-in scaffolding builds on already mastered skills so that students can learn more difficult concepts.

Collaborative Learning Systems

Another type of computer-based instruction is the collaborative learning system, which offers an affordance called a learning companion. (An *affordance* is a visual clue that helps the user interface with the system.) The companion may be built into the system so that the computer is the companion and thus acts as a collaborator of the student. Examples of these types of systems include Alien Rescue (University of Texas at Austin), a role-playing game where the student assumes an assigned role and interacts with others (*http://jabba.edb.utexas.edu/liu/aliendb/home.htm*). Both intelligent tutoring systems and collaborative learning systems can be used to help learning-disabled students as they develop their higher-order thinking skills at their own pace (LaJoie and Lesgold 1989).

Telecommunications Networks

Science telecommunication networks are another tool that can be used to teach the learning disabled. The National Geographic Kids Network is one such network, in which elementary children in classrooms worldwide collaborate in a variety of projects through the use of computer technology and telecommunications activities. Students participating in this network spend time on "inquiry-oriented, hands-on instruction, strengthening science process and data analysis skills" (TERC 1990, p. 1). Cuffaro (1984) endorsed such activities, which provide "expanded access to the physical and social world, bringing it closer to [students]—even if indirectly—to be examined as it has not been before" (p. 565).

Information Organizers

Anderson-Inman and Tenny (1989) examined the usefulness of information organizers, such as word processors, databases, outliners, and hypertext systems, to promote effective studying and to help students comprehend and retain information. Using a computer-based outlining program, students studying perceptions and habits changed. Outlining programs such as MORE (Symantec) and The Learning Tool (Arborworks) are examples of programs that can be used "to help [learning-disabled] students study 'better' not harder" (Anderson-Inman and Tenny, p. 33).

Concept Mapping

Computer-based *concept mapping* (see Chapters 7 and 12 in this volume) is a technology tool that can be used to create and revise concept maps electronically. Software organizing tools can help learning-disabled students "facilitate information acquisition and syntheses on one topic through a variety of inter-related tasks over time" (Anderson-Inman and Zeitz 1993, p. 10). Computer-based concept mapping allows the student to actively participate in the process while making the necessary connections between concepts.

Recommendations for Postsecondary Educators

Bisagno and Haven (2002) noted that educators must customize computer technology to meet the individual needs of the college student, whereas at the elementary and secondary levels educators tend to design instruction to meet the needs of a group or groups of disabled learners, even when teaching inclusion classes. Sandock (n.d.) referred to learning disabilities as "hidden disabilities" because, unless students self-disclose their disabilities, instructors may not recognize that learning-disabled students are actually enrolled in their classes. Furthermore, at times the necessary accommodations cannot be made for the student unless he or she does self-disclose the disability, and many students are unwilling to disclose. Because it may be difficult to ascertain the needs of the learning-disabled student in the college classroom, the college instructor will need to use a variety of techniques that oftentimes are not needed in the K–12 science classroom.

Sandock (n.d.) recommended that faculty begin with a positive attitude—an attitude that helps all learners get past barriers to learning and the demonstration of knowledge. Her recommendation is that educators recognize that learning-disabled college students are capable of learning but that teaching style, delivery of content, patterns of organization, sequence of assignments, and assessment of content knowledge may have to be modified in an iterative process. A syllabus prepared before the beginning of a semester, lectures that are well organized and planned out, assignments that are detailed and specified with due dates, and assessments that are explained in detail are simple techniques that can be used to assist the learning-disabled college student.

Some of the items that can be included in the syllabus are a complete book list, a list of additional readings and where they can be found, specific course goals and objectives, specific exam and assignment due dates, detailed assignments and suggested reference sources, detailed grading and assessment methods, specific course policies, and lecture topics. The lectures given in class should be able to link to what was learned previously. The main lecture points should be available in written form along with the stated lecture objectives. A variety of teaching styles should be used to facilitate the various learning styles that students possess. Specific patterns of organization, such as cause-and-effect relationships, should also be identified. If possible, instructor notes should be given as a handout or made available on the internet. At the end of the lecture discussion, the instructor should clearly summarize and help all students draw the necessary conclusions. To adequately assess all students, particularly learning-disabled college students, instructors should create assessments that clearly allow students to show their mastery of course goals and objectives and subject content.

A very useful website for the college educator is *http://cte.udel.edu/disabilities.htm,* which contains an extensive collection of online resources for faculty and staff who teach college students with disabilities. The website was developed by Al Cavalier at the University of Delaware, School of Education, Center for Teaching Effectiveness. It covers relevant legislation, resource agencies, faculty and student guidebooks, online articles on college students and disabilities, and technology.

Any of the computer technology tools described earlier in this chapter, including anchor-based instruction, intelligent tutoring systems, collaborative learning systems, and telecommunications networks, can also be used to enhance the learning of college students with learning disabilities. However, it should not be assumed that one size fits all. As Bisagno and Haven (2002) noted, "the key to strategically matching the appropriate technology to an individual student resides in considering a number of things: 1) the learner's type and severity of [learning disability]; 2) his or her strengths and weaknesses, and preferred learning style; 3) the academic area(s) impacted by the [learning disability]; 4) the student's academic major; 5) the educational context or learning environment; and 6) the student's 'technology quotient,' or ease and comfort with using technology" (p. 26). These authors noted that if learning-disabled students, even those with severe disabilities, are provided with the appropriate technology tools, they can achieve success at the postsecondary level.

Conclusion

Although many new technologies have emerged, this review has revealed that little has changed since the 1980s with regard to the actual use of computer technology to teach science to the learning disabled. As always, more research is needed to find ways that computer technology can enhance science teaching among the learning disabled. Until more studies have been done in this area, the learning disabled will continue to be underrepresented in the sciences. Furthermore, the learning-disabled student will continue to be labeled as unable to "do science."

References

Anderson-Inman, L., and J. Tenny. 1989. Electronic studying: Information organizers to help students study "better" not "harder." *The Computing Teacher* 16 (8): 33–36.

Anderson-Inman, L., and L. Zeitz. 1993. Computer-based concept mapping: Active studying for active learners. *The Computing Teacher* 20 (1): 6–11.

Atwood, R. K., and B. R. Oldham. 1985. Teachers' perceptions of mainstreaming in an inquiry oriented elementary science program. *Science Education* 69: 619–624.

Bisagno, J. M., and R. M. Haven. 2002. Customizing technology solutions for college students with learning disabilities. *Perspectives* 28 (2): 21–26. Also available online at *www.ldonline.org/ld_indepth/technology/customizing_technology.html*.

Bransford, J. D., R. D. Sherwood, T. S. Hasselbring, C. K. Kinzer, and S. M. Williams. 1990. Anchored instruction: Why we need it and how technology can help. In *Cognition, education, and multimedia,* eds. D. Nix and R. Spiro, 115–141. Hillsdale, NJ: Erlbaum.

Carnine, D. 1989. Teaching complex content to learning disabled students: The role of technology. *Exceptional Children* 55 (6): 524.

Cawley, J., H. Kahn, and A. Tedesco. 1989. Vocational education and students with learning disabilities. *Journal of Learning Disabilities* 2: 630–634.

Cawley, J. F., and R. S. Parmar. 2001. Literacy proficiency and science for students with learning disabilities. *Reading & Writing Quarterly* 17: 105–125.

Cuffaro, H. K. 1984. Microcomputers in education: Why is earlier better? *Teachers College Record* 85 (65): 559–568.

Cunningham, C. 1997. Science, technology and math issues for K-12 students with disabilities. *Information Technology and Disabilities E-Journal,* Vol. IV. *www.rit.edu/~easi/itd/itdv04n4/article1.htm*

Donohoe, K., and N. Zigmond. 1990. Academic grades of ninth-grade urban learning disabled students and low achieving peers. *Exceptionality* I: 17–27.

Finson, K. D., C. K. Ormsbee, M. Jensen, and D. T. Powers. 1997. Science in the mainstream: Retooling science activities. *Journal of Science Teacher Education* 8 (3): 219–232.

Harnisch, D., and I. Wilkinson. 1989. Cognitive return of schooling for the handicapped: Preliminary findings from high school and beyond. Paper presented at the annual meeting of the American Educational Research Association, San Francisco, CA.

Higgins, K., and R. Boone. 1990. Hypertext computer study guides and the social studies achievement of students with learning disabilities, remedial students, and general education students. *Journal of Learning Disabilities* 23: 529–540.

Hofmeister, A.M., S. Engelmann, and D. Carnine. 1989. Developing and validating science education videodiscs. *Journal of Research in Science Teaching* 26: 665–677.

Jarvis, T., and A. Pell. 2002. Effect of the Challenger experience on elementary children's attitudes to science. *Journal of Research in Science Teaching* 39: 979–100.

Kumar, D., and C. L. Wilson. 2000. Computer technology, science education, and students with learning disabilities. In *The Jossey-Bass Reader on Technology and Learning*. San Francisco: Jossey-Bass.

LaJoie, S. P., and A. Lesgold. 1989. Apprenticeship training in the workplace: Computer-coached practice environment as new form of apprenticeship. *Machine-Mediated Learning* 3: 7–28.

Landrum, T. J., and M. Tankersley. 2004. Science in the schoolhouse: An uninvited guest. *Journal of Learning Disabilities* 37 (3): 207–212.

Mastropieri, M. A., and T. E. Scruggs. 1994. Text versus hands-on science curriculum: Implications for students with disabilities. *Remedial and Special Education* 15 (2): 72–85.

National Dissemination Center for Children With Disabilities (NICHCY). 2004. *Learning disabilities.* Fact Sheet 7. *www.nichcy.org/pubs/factshe/fs7txt.htm#top*

North Central Regional Educational Laboratory. 2005. Critical issue: Using technology to improve student achievement. *www.ncrel.org/sdrs/areas/issues/methods/technlgy/te800.htm*

Ormsbee, C. K., and K. D. Finson. 2000. Modifying science activities and materials to enhance instruction for students with learning and behavioral problems. *Intervention in School and Clinic* 36 (1): 10.

Palincsar, A. M., S. J. Magnusson, K. M. Collins, and J. Cutter. 2001. Making science accessible to all: Results of a design experiment in inclusive classroom. *Learning Disability Quarterly* 24 (1): 15–32.

Richardson, M. 1994. We all learned together. *Science Scope* 17 (6): 68–70.

Sandock, B. n.d. Enhancing learning of students with LD without compromising standards: Tips for teaching. *LD Online. www.ldonline.org/ld_indepth/postsecondary/facultytips.html*

Steele, M. M. 2004. Teaching science to students with learning problems in the elementary classroom. *Preventing School Failure* 49 (1): 19–21.

Task Force on Women, Minorities, and the Handicapped in Science and Technology. 1989. *Changing America : The new face of science and engineering, final report.* Washington, DC: National Science Foundation.

TERC. 1990. *The National Geographic Kids Network: Year 4 Final Annual Report.* Cambridge, MA: TERC.

U.S. Department of Education. 1999. Assistance to states for the education of children with disabilities and the early intervention program for infants and toddlers with disabilities: Final regulations. *Federal Register* 64 (48): CFR Parts 300 and 303.

CHAPTER 28

Diversity in the Physical Science Curriculum:
The Intellectual Challenge

Catherine H. Middlecamp

Catherine H. Middlecamp is distinguished faculty associate and director of the Chemistry Learning Center in the Department of Chemistry at the University of Wisconsin–Madison. She earned a PhD in chemistry at the University of Wisconsin–Madison, and her scholarship lies in research on science curriculum development, inclusive teaching, women in science, and writing-across-the-curriculum. She teaches chemistry for nonscience majors and courses in the integrated liberal studies program.

What do race and ethnicity have to do with thermodynamics? A colleague tossed this question in my direction over a decade ago, to both my surprise and dismay. Frankly, it was the first time that I had ever heard the word *thermodynamics* in the same sentence with *race* and *ethnicity*. With his question, our conversation took a turn toward mutual frustration. I was sure that chemistry connected to race and ethnicity, but my colleague failed to see a connection. As it turned out, we both were partly right.

To set this exchange in context, in 1990 I was teaching chemistry to students in an academic support program. The students were African American, Hispanic, first-generation college, and/or low income. Together we worked long hours to solve what seemed an endless string of end-of-chapter problems. We came to know each other not only in the context of chemistry but also as people. We chatted about life, liberty, and the pursuit of a career requiring general chemistry. The students sometimes asked me, "Why do I need to learn this stuff?" or "What is it good for?" In essence, they were questioning what learning chemistry had to do with their lives, their communities, and ultimately their future professions.

Many of the students were not doing well. The reasons underlying their failures were complex and involved their background knowledge, how well the course matched their needs, and the nature of the subject matter itself (Middlecamp and Kean 1983). In contrast, the outcome was simple: the doors to medicine, pharmacy, and engineering were closing in their faces. They were enjoying neither their studies nor the prospect of having their dreams evaporate. Given these realities, the seemingly endless string of H, specific heat, and heat capacity problems just did not appear worth their effort.

In retrospect, my choice of topic for conversation with my colleague probably was not very wise. To do him justice, he was well liked by students for his clarity and sense of humor in the classroom. He also was a good listener. But in hearing me talk about the concerns of my students, he could not see why I thought that issues relating to race and ethnicity should have *anything* to do with teaching general chemistry. Science was objective and value-free. No point of view and no cultural agenda should be permitted to permeate the classroom. Surely I understood this?

Honestly, I did not. Only through an intellectual struggle in the years that followed did I begin to appreciate the complexities of our conversation. As I will describe in this chapter, my first task was to deconstruct his question. I then needed to critically examine my teaching and successively implement a series of changes. And lastly, I needed to find a model that better connected people and science. The intellectual challenge of diversity lies precisely in tasks such as these.

Questions Old and New

What do race and ethnicity have to do with thermodynamics? Scholars from fields such as philosophy, history, and women's studies also tackle this type of question. For example, in her book on gender and Boyle's law of gases, historian Elizabeth Potter writes:

One of the greatest challenges has been to show the influence of gender considerations on the technical content of the physical sciences. To dash cold water on the feminist hunch that no area of science is immune to gender politics, doubters often ask, "What could gender have to do with something like Boyle's Law?"... Work for this book was undertaken following just such a challenge. (Potter 2001, p. ix)

The philosopher Sandra Harding also speaks to gender and the nature of science. She reverses the very question:

We began by asking, "What is to be done about the situation of women in science?"— the "woman question" in science. Now feminists often pose a different question: ... the "science question" in feminism. (Harding 1986, p. 9)

Using insights gained from scholars in other disciplines, I was able to proceed. Instead of asking what race and ethnicity had to do with thermodynamics, I found it more useful to reverse the question, as follows: "What does thermodynamics have to do with race and ethnicity?" I also broadened the inquiry. For example, the terms *class* and *gender* should be included so that the question becomes "What does thermodynamics have to do with race, ethnicity, class, and gender?" Also true to the spirit of the initial question was to view thermodynamics as representative of all topics that we teach in physical science classes. Thus while not quite as catchy, the question might better be phrased as "What does *science* have to do with race, ethnicity, class, and gender?"

My new language was not merely intellectual wordplay. Frankly, as originally posed, the question was unworkable. In contrast, the new question had traction and in essence asked, "What does science have to do with people?" More to the point, what does it have to do with the lives of my students and the world in which they live? As Alan Leshner, chief executive officer of the American Association for the Advancement of Science, remarked at a national meeting, "Ultimately, science is about people and life" (Leshner 2002).

But is it? Therein lies the rub. Certainly one can cite examples of courses in which real-world issues and the people who face them lie at the center of the inquiry. One example is the curriculum for nonscience majors, *Chemistry in Context,* a project of the American Chemical Society that began in 1989 (Eubanks et al. 2006). A more recent project is SENCER (Science Education for New Civic Engagements and Responsibilities; *www.sencer.net/models.cfm*); funded by the National Science Foundation, this project has disseminated dozens of science courses that teach through complex issues to the underlying scientific principles. A third project is ChemConnections (*http://chemlinks.beloit.edu*), again a product of a national dissemination grant that features modules on real-world topics for chemistry majors (Gutwill-Wise 2001). Table 28.1 shows examples of topics for each of these projects.

Table 28.1

Examples of Real-World Science Topics for Nonmajors and Majors

Source	Topics
Chemistry in Context, 5th ed.	The Air We Breathe
	The Chemistry of Global Warming
	The Fires of Nuclear Fission
SENCER models 2000–2005	Coal in the Heart of Appalachian Life
	Mysteries of Migration
	Sustainability and Human Health
ChemConnections modules	Should We Build a Copper Mine?
	Soil Equilibria: What Happens to Acid Rain?
	Would You Like Fries With That? The Fuss
	About Fats in Our Diet

The authors of first-year chemistry textbooks for science majors also make an effort to engage students in wider societal issues. For example, textbooks may contain boxed inserts, margin notes, special end-of-chapter questions, and even interchapter essays devoted to topics such as those listed in Table 28.1. Such features in textbooks, however, have one critical difference from the integrated societal content found in projects such as *Chemistry in Context,* SENCER, and ChemConnections. If these features were deleted, the central chemical story line would remain essentially unchanged.

Inclusive Teaching

What do our first-year chemistry courses have to do with the lives of our students and the world in which they live? Judging by the comments made earlier by my students, the answer was "not much." In this sense, my colleague certainly was right: race and ethnicity had nothing to do with learning thermodynamics or, for that matter, any other general chemistry topic. Notes in the margin about women and people of color truly were just that.

In 1995, for the purposes of a luncheon talk for girls in science, I photographed the illustrations depicting people from the general chemistry textbooks that I had on my shelves. When I projected the images in rapid succession, the message was clear. Men were in the spotlight, not women. And male or female, people of color were virtually absent in textbooks. Even the hands that held the beakers, computer chips, and batteries were usually identifiable as white and male. An earlier paper analyzed textbooks in the life sciences with similar findings (Potter and Rosser 1992).

Thus, as I pursued my question of what science had to do with people, a reasonable point of departure was for me to add men and women of color, and more generally all women. I started searching for cross-cultural examples for my chemistry course. My hope was that the changes I made would help a wider range of students feel included while giving everybody a wider context in which to apply what they were learning.

I incorporated my first examples into my classroom as a result of traveling to Puerto Rico through an interinstitutional linkage program. While in San Juan, I noticed many things, including how my glasses fogged when I went outside from an air-conditioned building to the humid tropical air. In contrast, in Wisconsin my glasses fog when I come inside on a brisk winter day. Similarly, ice forms on the inside of my car windows in winter, whereas moisture condensed on the outside in Puerto Rico. Examples such as these can help students develop a better understanding of why and where water vapor will condense. A colleague in Puerto Rico and I found additional examples, and in using these, we offered instructors two suggestions: (1) examples should be tailored to the students you teach, inclusive of their lives and heritage, and (2) examples should be drawn from a variety of geographic regions and cultures, better both to explain how chemical principles apply and to prepare students for the global marketplace that they will enter once they graduate (Middlecamp and Fernandez 1999, p. 390).

More recently, Project Inclusion (a project of the National Science Foundation) has extensively researched and developed materials on the chemical contributions of women and underrepresented groups (Hayes and Perez 2001).

With the advent of digital cameras and presentation software, my journey to become more culturally inclusive progressed rapidly. I use PowerPoint extensively in the lecture hall, and it was a straightforward process for me to modify the dozens of images that I show each class. For example, Figure 28.1 shows three types of changes that I made for the topic of stratospheric ozone depletion. (It was not possible to reproduce color in this volume. To see Figure 28.1 in color, go to *www.nsta.org/pdfs/Fig28.1.pdf*.) Figure 28.1a, a slide from a lecture on spectrophotometry, is an example of adding a person of color. Previously, a Caucasian person had held the cuvette. Figure 28.1b, the title slide of a later lecture on chlorofluorocarbons (CFCs), is an example showing how I recolored commercial clip art. In the original, the children were shown with pink skin tones. Figure 28.1c, the title slide of a lecture on sunscreens, is a photo that will be recognized either by the students in my class from Hawaii or by others who have traveled there. The photo is of the ahinahina plant (silversword) found at high elevations in Maui and equipped to reflect the high incident solar radiation. Over time, I assembled dozens of slides for my general chemistry course inclusive of a diverse group of people.

Figure 28.1

Examples of More Culturally Inclusive Slides: (a) Cuvette for Spectrophotometer Held by a Person of Color; (b) Title Slide With Clip Art Skin Tones Changed; (c) Title Slide With the Ahinahina From Maui

(To see these slides in color, go to *www.nsta.org/pdfs/ fig28.1.pdf*.)

(a)

(b)

(c)

At the same time that I reworked my visuals, I also reexamined each topic that I taught. With radioactivity, for example, I added the story of the radium dial painters to illustrate both how radium mimics calcium in the body (with deadly consequences) and how women took an activist role for occupational health and safety (Clark 1997; Mullner 1999).

If adding more inclusive content was one side of the coin, then removing biased content was the other. The most glaring examples of bias I found related to sunscreens and tanning. The unspoken assumption was that everyone tanned. For example, a question in the early editions of *Chemistry in Context* read, "Why can't you get a tan by listening to the radio?" The desired response was that you can't tan because radio waves are too low in energy (or even that you could tan if you listened to the radio at the beach). It was as if people with deeply pigmented skin did not exist.

What do race, ethnicity, and gender have to do with the teaching of chemistry? In one sense, a great deal. By including a wider variety of examples and by removing those that implicitly exclude certain groups, an instructor can help students better connect what they are learning to the communities in which they live. Furthermore, inclusive instructional materials better represent the world in which students one day will work.

But in another sense, my inclusive examples were a glorified

Figure 28. 2

Student Changes to General Chemistry Textbook Question

~~L-carvone, a fragrant compound found in the spearmint plant, is used to flavor chewing gum.~~ Its chemical formula is $C_{10}H_{14}O$. What is the formula weight of l-carvone? ~~The isomer d-carvone gives caraway seeds their distinctive smell.~~

Figure 28.3

Teaching Through the Issue of Air Quality to Underlying Concepts

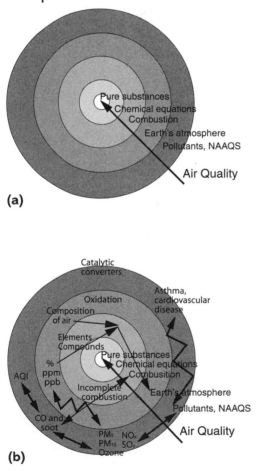

(a)

(b)

Note: AQI = air quality index; NAAQS = National Ambient Air Quality Standards.

version of placing women in the margins of the textbook. My students noticed this as well. For example, I watched a student cross out the words in a textbook problem as she worked it (Figure 28.2). She complained to me, "Why do they put that stuff in there? It just gets in the way." Just like this student, one might remove all the examples that I added to my course, and the story line would have remained essentially unchanged.

What do people, especially people of color, really have to do with the teaching of science? To more fully answer this question, I needed to think in terms of a different model.

A Model That Connects

For over a decade, I have used *Chemistry in Context* with my nonscience majors. As described earlier, each chapter teaches *through* a current complex issue *to* the underlying chemical principles. Concentric circles can be used to represent this process. For example, Figure 28.3a models the air quality chapter, which teaches chemical principles through the National Ambient Air Quality Standards (NAAQS) for pollutants. While useful because of its simplicity, the model does not do justice to the interconnections and multiple instructional pathways. Alternatively, Figure 28.3b emphasizes these complexities.

A key feature of these concentric circles is that they can be extended outward to connect with a community. For example, we could add an outer ring to Figure 28.3a to include the people of Donora, Pennsylvania, who suffered a killer smog in 1948. In fact, we could extend the circles outward to include *any* group of people breathing contaminated air. By so doing, students would learn science through the concerns of real people exposed to air pollutants, one of today's most widespread and pressing public health issues. As epidemiologist Devra Davis graphically points out in her book *When Smoke Ran Like Water*, "Pollution itself never shows up on death certificates" (Davis 2002, p. 56).

Similarly, Figure 28.4a models a chapter of *Chemistry in Context* that teaches atomic structure and radioactivity *through* the topic of nuclear energy. In Figure 28.4b, I have extended the circles further outward so that they connect with a community, namely, the workers who mined the uranium. These wider circles were inspired by *If You Poison Us* (Eichstaedt 1994), a book relating what befell the Diné (Navajo) workers because of the poor conditions in the mines and their families because of the uranium dust carried home.

With nuclear chemistry, I came to more fully understand how compelling the connections were between science and communities of people. For three years, I used *If You Poison Us* as the primary text for Environmental Chemistry and Ethnicity, the first physical science course in the University of Wisconsin System to meet our statewide three-credit ethnic studies requirement (Middlecamp, Bentley, et al., Forthcoming). This course also was selected as one of the SENCER models (*www. sencer.net/models.cfm*).

Currently, I am teaching a physical science course in our Integrated Liberal Studies Program using a model resting on not one but three interlocking content circles. Two of the circles already have been mentioned: the radium dial painters and the Diné uranium miners. The third is the story of the "Firecracker Boys"—the nuclear physicists who proposed using nuclear weapons to blast a harbor in Alaska on the land inhabited for centuries by the Inupiat (Eskimo) (O'Neill 1994). With these three circles, topics such as the properties of radioisotopes, the biological effects of ionizing radiation, the risks and benefits of nuclear fission, and the environmental impacts of our atomic energy policies can be approached from multiple perspectives. Neither the questions nor the answers are straightforward.

The examples presented in this section share an important feature: The cultural content is *integral* to the chemical content and is tightly coupled to the intellectual tasks that the students must accomplish. Unlike my student who crossed out the "extra" words in the end-of-chapter question (Figure 28.2), with these examples no student can cross out the content related to race, ethnicity, or gender and leave the essence of the course intact.

Beyond the Technical Core

To some, teaching through a real-world issue is tantamount to sacrificing the "technical core." Topics such as bonding, equilibrium, thermodynamics, and kinetics usually play on center stage in our first-year chemistry courses. Many contend we *must* cover core topics such as these in our first-year chemistry courses, especially in those for our majors.

Figure 28.4

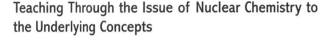

Teaching Through the Issue of Nuclear Chemistry to the Underlying Concepts

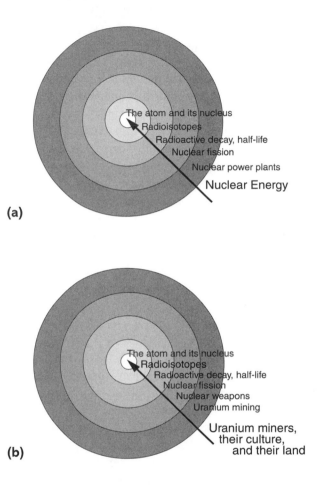

(a)

(b)

Our discussions need to shift from what we are *teaching* to what our students are *learning*. Covering core content is not the issue. An emphasis of the technical core to the exclusion of virtually everything else surely is neither in our students' nor in our profession's best interest. Our science courses need to engage both our future scientists *and* our future citizens. Both deserve meaningful contexts in which to learn. As stated in a recent science publication by the National Academies, "concepts take on meaning in the knowledge-rich contexts in which they are applied" (Donovan and Bransford 2005, p. 6).

In more practical terms, we must articulate course goals beyond covering the content. Tewksbury made this point persuasively in describing the principles of good course design: First specify the desired higher-level outcomes and then select the course content and the learning activities to accompany it. For example, higher-order goals involve tasks such as applying knowledge to new or unfamiliar situations, integrating knowledge from other fields, predicting an outcome, or designing a new model. In contrast, lower-order goals involve reiterative tasks such as listing, identifying, recognizing, explaining, or describing (Tewksbury 2004).

Once the higher-order goals are set, the lower-order ones will follow. For example, in my physical science course I now ask students to apply what they have learned to a new situation—namely, to find another topic that connects chemistry with a cultural issue and report on it. Students get peer review and feedback at every step of the way. This helps students to meet another higher-order goal: to revise work and integrate feedback. One future elementary education teacher in my course commented, "This project was one of my favorites in my college career." In dismay, a chemistry major pointed out to me that without this course, he never would have encountered this type of content. In short, both of these students *engaged* in the issues that bring together people and science and were appreciative of the opportunity to do so.

Concluding Thoughts

In my initial conversation with a colleague about how race, ethnicity, and gender related to teaching science, I knew neither how to frame the questions nor how to frame the answers. But having now pursued this issue for almost two decades, I have come to some conclusions that I will offer to any who would journey along a similar path:

1. Issues involving people (and the problems they face) have a rightful place in the science curriculum. When our students graduate, they will face complex issues embedded in cultural contexts. They will need the intellectual capacity to work within such contexts.
2. Some may fear that highlighting problems will cast science (and scientists) in a bad light. On closer examination, the study of problems has real benefit. The issues involved appeal to a diverse group of students and offer them a means to "make a difference" in the world.
3. Course revision is more than a matter of "add diversity and stir." Although creating a more inclusive learning environment is important, some changes are more cosmetic than substantive, and students will recognize this.
4. A more substantive way to bring people to the curriculum is to widen the circles of content. Teach *through* complex societal issues *to* the underlying science. In the process, you build a case for why it is worth knowing something.
5. Courses are not infinitely elastic. If you add relevant societal content to your curriculum, something else needs to come out.

6. To decide what is important to include (or exclude), articulate learning goals beyond covering topics. In this way, the value of having students wrestle with complex, messy real-world scientific topics becomes readily apparent.

In this chapter I have argued that integrating science with the real and pressing concerns of human beings on this planet is a powerful way to give race, ethnicity, class, and gender a rightful place in our science classrooms. In the process we create a synergism: *We draw our students into the world of science as we in turn are drawn into the world and its communities of people.* As we do this, we will face intellectual challenges. To meet these challenges, we not only must ask new questions but also must keep reexamining what we ask so that we can better meet the needs of our increasingly diverse students and world.

Acknowledgments

Although many deserve recognition, I especially would like to thank two organizations that helped me at critical points along the journey: the Association of American Colleges and Universities for its project Women and Science Literacy, and the University of Wisconsin System Institute on Race and Ethnicity for encouraging and funding course development.

I also extend my gratitude to these colleagues and scholars from many disciplines: Omie Baldwin, David Burns, Fleming Crim, Elizabeth Kean, Emilio Diaz, Heidi Fencl, Angela Ginorio, Paul Kelter, Ingrid Montes, Caryn McTighe Musil, Karen Oates, Ruby Paredes, Sue Rosser, and Banu Subramanium. All of these people asked good questions, gave great answers ... or both.

References

Clark, C. 1997. *Radium girls*. Chapel Hill: University of North Carolina Press.

Davis, D. 2002. *When smoke ran like water: Tales of environmental deception and the battle against pollution*. New York: Basic Books.

Donovan, M. S., and J. D. Bransford, eds. 2005. *How students learn: Science in the classroom*. Washington, DC: National Academies Press.

Eichstaedt, P. 1994. *If you poison us: Uranium and Native Americans*. Santa Fe, NM: Red Crane Books.

Eubanks, L. P., C. Middlecamp, N. Pienta, C. Heltzel, and G. Weaver. 2006. *Chemistry in context: Applying chemistry to society*. 5th ed. Dubuque, IA: McGraw-Hill.

Gutwill-Wise, J. P. 2001. The impact of active and context-based learning in introductory chemistry courses: An early evaluation of the modular approach. *Journal of Chemical Education* 78 (5): 684–690.

Harding, S. 1986. *The science question in feminism*. Ithaca, NY: Cornell University Press.

Hayes, J., and P. Perez. 2001. Project Inclusion: Using the history of diverse cultures to facilitate the teaching of chemistry. In *College pathways to the science education standards,* eds. E. D. Siebert and W. J. McIntosh, 111–114. Arlington, VA: NSTA Press.

Leshner, A. 2002. The global context of 21st century science education. Presentation at the SENCER Summer Institute, Santa Clara University, Santa Clara, CA, August 6.

Middlecamp, C., A. K. Bentley, M. Phillips, and O. Baldwin. Forthcoming. Chemistry, society and civic engagement, part II: Environmental chemistry and ethnicity. *Journal of Chemical Education*.

Middlecamp, C., and M. D. Fernandez. 1999. From Puerto Rico to Wisconsin: Cultural perspectives on teaching general chemistry. *Journal of Chemical Education* 76: 388–391.

Middlecamp, C.. and E. Kean. 1983. Special programs for special students. I. Providing assistance for nontraditional students. *Journal of Chemical Education* 60: 960–962.

Mullner, R. 1999. *Deadly glow*. Washington, DC: American Public Health Association.

O'Neill, D. 1994. *The firecracker boys*. New York: St. Martin's Press.

Potter, E. 2001. *Gender and Boyle's law of gases*. Bloomington: Indiana University Press.

Potter, E. F., and S. V. Rosser. 1992. Factors in life science textbooks that may deter girls' interest in science. *Journal of Research in Science Teaching* 29 (7): 669–686.

Tewksbury, B. J. 2004. Designing a SENCER course: Don't just beat it to fit and paint it to match. Presentation at the SENCER Summer Institute, Santa Clara University, Santa Clara, CA, August 8.

CHAPTER 29

Incorporating Cultural Diversity Into College Science

Michael A. Fidanza

Michael A. Fidanza is associate professor of horticulture at the Berks Campus of Penn State University. He earned a PhD in agronomy (plant and soil science) at the University of Maryland and conducts research on turfgrass ecology, turfgrass pest management methods, and innovative teaching and learning strategies. He teaches botany for nonscience majors, introduction to horticulture, introduction to soil science, and turfgrass science.

Many colleges and universities offer undergraduate courses designed to promote an appreciation and understanding of cultural diversity and to develop and foster international and intercultural competency (Fyte and Figueroa 1993). Because of the globalization of world economies, advances in information technologies, and the complex interconnections of global environmental issues postsecondary institutions recognize the growing importance of offering courses about other cultures and nations (Adams 1992; Fidanza, Sanford, and Shibley 2004). These culture-related courses are often a core curriculum or general education requirement for undergraduate students, and they are also designed to prepare students to work and live in an increasingly diverse and interdependent world (Pascarella and Terenzini, 1991; see also Chapter 28 in this volume).

The guidelines for an intercultural or diversity-focused course are similar among many academic institutions (Bowser, Jones, and Young 1995). At Penn State University, an international cultures course (see *www.psu.edu/bulletins/bluebook/gened/geneduc.html*) must strive to increase student knowledge of the variety of international societies and should

- cultivate student knowledge of the similarities and differences among international cultures;
- convey to students a knowledge of other nations' cultural values, traditions, beliefs, and customs;

- increase students' knowledge of the range of international cultural achievements and human conditions through time;
- increase students' knowledge of nations and cultures in relation to one another; and
- deal to some extent with U.S. culture and its international connections.

At many colleges and universities, most undergraduate courses that address cultural diversity are located in the liberal arts or anthropology-based curriculum (Campbell and Smith 1997; Halpern 1994; McKeachie 2002; Williams 1994). An introductory course in the plant sciences (i.e., agronomy, botany, or horticulture) is ideal for addressing cultural diversity and combining science with the study of issues related to international cultures.

Plants, Places, and People is an undergraduate biology course for nonscience majors offered in-residence at the Berks Campus of Penn State University. The course is worth three credits, is taught during both spring and fall semesters, and is delivered in three 50-minute lectures (Monday, Wednesday, and Friday) over a 15-week academic semester. Typically, the course is offered to 60 students per section, with two sections in the fall semester and one section in the spring semester. The course satisfies core curriculum or general education requirements for three credits each in the natural sciences and international/intercultural competency categories. The specific course focus is plant science and the use of cultivated agricultural crops by humans and society (Levetin and McMahon 2003). For example, a popular lecture is the story of the cacao tree and how its seed pods are harvested and eventually processed into chocolate. Another popular lecture is the biology of the coffee tree and how the coffee bean traveled from its origin in Ethiopia to Europe and eventually to South America. Other biology courses have included student travel to foreign countries to explore and study nature's biodiversity (Zervanos and McLaughlin 2003). A trip to visit an actual coffee production facility in Brazil would be ideal; however, that option is financially and logistically impractical. Therefore, a project was developed in which students assemble information about a foreign country and present that information in the form of a newsletter.

The title of the assignment is "Intercultural and International Team Project: A Culture and Its Economically Important Plants." The primary objective of this assignment is to encourage students to explore the culture and cultural diversity of a foreign country by gathering information on agricultural resources, crops and crop production, and how that society uses plants and plant-derived products. Other minor objectives include working with other students as a team, incorporating and encouraging the development of communication (i.e., writing and speaking) skills, and promoting science to these students who are nonscience majors and who may have a dislike or fear of science.

Materials and Methods

At the start of the semester, students are given specific instructions on how to complete the assignment (Figure 29.1). An entire class lecture period is dedicated to this process, and four students are assigned per team at this time. Students are typically grouped by academic major or common interest. A list is supplied to all students with the team number, name of students on each team, and their e-mail contact information. The expectations of this assignment are discussed, and students are given the opportunity to meet face-to-face with their team members to talk and brainstorm. The teams are encouraged to meet throughout the semester outside of class to work together on the project. Students are required to com-

Figure 29.1

Instructions for the Intercultural and International Team Project Assignment

- Four (4) students will be assigned per team.
- Each team will choose a country for the assignment, however, U.S.A. is not permitted.
- Divide the assignment so that each student will complete one of the four sections listed below.
- Each team will decide which student will complete which section.
- Each student will research and gather information on their section.
- Prepare a neat, type-written, informative newsletter that consists of one page (only one 8½ × 11 inch page). Be creative, but be thorough, clear, and concise. You are encouraged to include a combination of text and graphics.
- Each student will prepare their own newsletter based on their section.
- The instructor will evaluate each student's individual newsletter, and therefore an individual's score for this assignment is not affected by other students on the team.
- Be sure to include your name on the newsletter.
- Include all references used in the production of your newsletter. You can have as many references as you want, and be sure to list all references according to proper format on a separate sheet of paper and not on the actual newsletter.

- The four sections are as follows:
  I. For the country your team has chosen, describe the following agricultural-related items.
     a. Geographic location and natural resources.
     b. Agricultural resources.
     c. Crops and crop production.
  II. For the country your team has chosen, describe an economically important agricultural crop.
     a. Describe the plant/crop and why it is economically important.
     b. How is the plant/crop produced (for example, resources used, land use, farming techniques, etc....)?
     c. What is a by-product (for example, what is produced, how is it used, processed, distributed, etc....)?
  III. For the country your team has chosen, describe another economically important agricultural crop.
     a. Describe the plant/crop and why it is economically important.
     b. How is the plant/crop produced (for example, resources used, land use, farming techniques, etc....)?
     c. What is a by-product (for example, what is produced, how is it used, processed, distributed, etc....)?
  IV. For the country your team has chosen, elaborate on the food and culture.
     a. Describe categories or types of foods and beverages.
     b. If possible, describe the symbolic meaning of food and food products to the culture of the country.
     c. Discuss the importance of food and food products or by-products to the country's economy.

- The written newsletter is due on: *calendar date listed here.*
- The oral presentation is scheduled for: *calendar date listed here.*

plete the assignment by the last week of the semester. During that final week, with three class periods remaining in the semester, each student is asked to give a one-minute oral presentation to the class. These brief presentations serve as a catalyst to stimulate conversation and discussion about the topics presented.

From spring 2003 through spring 2005, during the last scheduled class period in the semester, students were asked to complete a nine-question survey to evaluate the assignment and the instructor. Responses were based on a 7-point, modified Likert-type scale, where lowest rating = 1, average rating = 4, and highest rating = 7.

Results and Discussion

From the spring 2003 through spring 2005 semesters, seven sections of Plants, Places, and People (BIOL 20A) were completed for a total of 425 enrolled students. A total of 39 countries were represented in 110 newsletter teams (each newsletter actually consisted of four individual newsletters from each four-person member of the team). The 39 countries were grouped into six geographic regions (Figure 29.2). The majority of countries chosen for this assignment were located in Europe, followed by South America, Asia and Australia, Central America, Africa, and the Middle East (Figure 29.2). Also, the largest percentage of newsletters submitted were based on European countries and followed in order by the other regions previously listed (Figure 29.3). Among the top five individual countries chosen for the assignment, Italy ranked first, followed by Brazil, Germany, Mexico, and Colombia (Figure 29.4). Italy was a popular culture to explore because of the link between Mediterranean-style cuisine and crops grown (e.g., olives and grapes, and wheat used in the production of pasta). Coffee and sugarcane production made Brazil a popular choice. Germany was investigated mainly because of its barley and wheat fields and how those crops are used in the production of beer. Mexico and Colombia were chosen because of coffee, corn, and a variety of other crops produced in those countries, as well as an abundant amount of information available on plants used by traditional healers (Balick and Cox 1996; Heiser 1990; Hobhouse 1987).

Table 29.1 (p. 295) summarizes the student responses to the end-of-semester survey questions. The overall quality of the assignment was considered favorably by most students, with 69% of responses rated ≥ 6. The following three questions were instructor related, with an average of 80% of responses ≥ 6. The next three questions pertained to the effectiveness of this assignment at helping students to explore and learn about other cultures, with an average of 78% of responses ≥ 6. The next question focused on student opinion about working in groups, and only 48% rated ≥ 6, which indicated a mixed response to the team approach to this assignment. For the final question, the majority of students (86%) rated ≥ 6, which indicated a strong recommendation to include this assignment in future classes.

Student feedback on this assignment was generally positive. Many students liked the fact that they could choose their own country. Other positive comments related to learning about other countries that students hope to visit someday, hearing about the other teams' country through the oral presentations, learning about food and plant-derived products used by other countries and cultures, researching information about other countries that they knew nothing about before completing this assignment, and meeting other students in class. Most students agreed that the "newsletter approach" was a more interesting project that just writing a traditional term paper, and most students favored the idea of an individual grade for their own newsletter even though they were assigned to a team. The newsletter was worth 50 points, and the oral presentation was worth

Figure 29.2

Percent of Countries ($N = 39$) Used to Complete the International and Intercultural Assignment, Grouped by Geographic Region

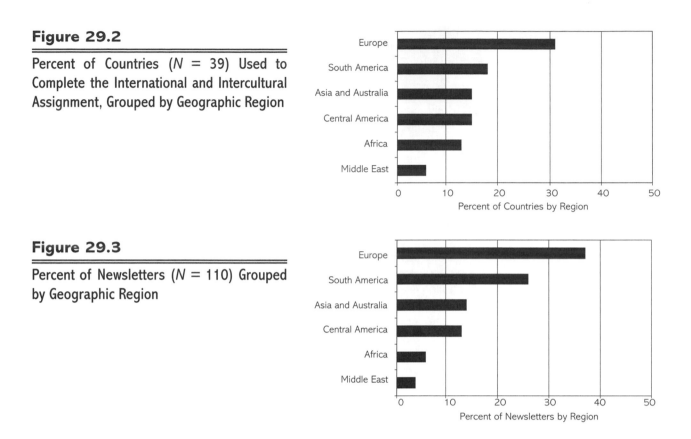

Figure 29.3

Percent of Newsletters ($N = 110$) Grouped by Geographic Region

5 extra-credit points. Since the exams in the course were worth 50 points each, many students liked the fact that the newsletter was worth as much as an exam. Some students did not like to work in teams or speak in front of the class, and a few students did not like to write.

Conclusion

Although most students were enthusiastic about their chosen country and the information about how that culture and society use plants, most students experienced minor difficulty with producing a clear, concise, and well-written newsletter. Future classes could consider mandatory student visits to the campus learning center for help and assistance with the actual writing component of this assignment. The use of a peer-writing program, where students majoring in communications help other students with class writing assignments, could be helpful as well. One or two class lecture periods during the semester could be dedicated to working on the newsletter project, with peer-writing tutors visiting the classroom and working with the teams on first gathering useful information and then assembling that information into a newsletter. Also, future classes could consider stretching the assignment. For example, each week a different team could present its newsletters to generate discussion.

This assignment was considered helpful in reinforcing the process of exploring and gaining a respect and appreciation for other countries and cultures. Although most students did not have a farm background, they did not have difficulty relating their chosen country's crops and crop production systems to food and other useful products. The assignment was useful in integrating science and the science of plants and crop production with an appreciation for how society and other cultures use those plants and plant products.

Figure 29.4

Percent of Newsletters (*N* = 110) Grouped by Individual Country

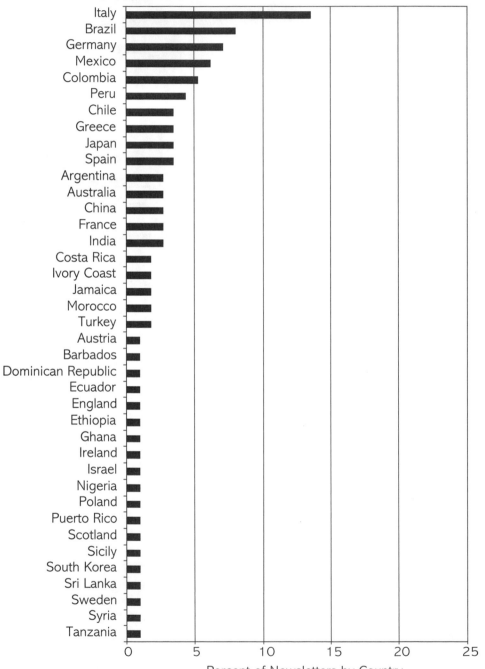

Percent of Newsletters by Country

Table 29.1

Student Responses to the Scaled-Response Survey Questions Regarding the Intercultural and International Assignment

	Student Response Rating (%)*						
	1	2	3	4	5	6	7
Rate the overall quality of the assignment.	0	0	0	4	27	42	27
Rank the effectiveness of the instructions and directions for the assignment as described in the course syllabus.	0	0	0	0	13	33	54
Rate the instructor's interest in whether or not students understood the assignment.	0	0	0	2	17	39	42
Rate the appropriateness of the instructor's encouragement of student participation.	0	0	0	6	21	40	33
Rank the effectiveness of the assignment for its ability to effectively help students explore other cultures.	0	0	0	5	10	43	42
Rank the effectiveness of the assignment for its ability to effectively help students gain an awareness and appreciation for international and intercultural competency.	0	0	0	2	24	38	36
Rank the effectiveness of the assignment to help students gain an appreciation for the diversity that exists among people from other countries and cultures in the world.	0	0	0	4	20	42	34
Rank the effectiveness of the assignment to help students meet other students in class and work in teams.	1	0	8	19	24	19	29
Rate or rank your opinion from the student perspective; would you recommend this assignment to future classes?	0	0	0	1	13	42	44

*Means of student responses were represented as a percentage (N = 348 out of 425, or an 81.8% response rate) and were based on a 7-point, modified Likert-type scale, where lowest rating = 1, average rating = 4, and highest rating = 7.

References

Adams, M. 1992. Cultural inclusion in the American college classroom. *New Directions for Teaching and Learning* 49: 5–7.

Balick, M. J., and P. A. Cox. 1996. *Plants, people, and culture.* New York: Scientific American Library.

Bowser, B. P., T. Jones, and G. A. Young. 1995. *Towards the multicultural university.* Westport, CT: Praeger.

Campbell, W. E., and K. A. Smith. 1997. *New paradigms for college teaching.* Edina, MN: Interlocken Book Company.

Fidanza, M. A., D. L. Sanford, and I. Shibley. 2004. A review of teaching methods and learning styles. In *Annual Meetings Abstracts.* Madison, WI: American Society of Agronomy, Crop Science Society of America, and Soil Science Society of America. Available as a CD-ROM.

Fyte, A., and P. Figueroa. 1993. *Education for cultural diversity.* New York: Routledge.

Halpern, D. F. 1994. *Changing college classrooms: New teaching and learning strategies for an intellectually complex world.* San Francisco: Jossey-Bass.

Heiser, C. B. 1990. *Seed to civilization: The story of food.* Cambridge, MA: Harvard University Press.

Hobhouse, H. 1987. *Seeds of change.* New York: Harper & Row.

Levetin, E., and K. McMahon. 2003. *Plants and society.* New York: McGraw-Hill.

McKeachie, W. J. 2002. *McKeachie's teaching tips: Strategies, research, and theory for college and university teachers.* 11th ed. Boston: Houghton Mifflin.

Pascarella, E. T., and F. Terenzini. 1991. *How college affects students.* San Francisco: Jossey-Bass.

Williams, J. A. 1994. *Classroom in conflict: Teaching controversial subjects in a diverse society.* Albany: SUNY Press.

Zervanos, S. M., and J. S. McLaughlin. 2003. Teaching biodiversity and evolution through travel course experiences. *American Biology Teacher* 65: 658–663.

CHAPTER 30

Alternative Conceptions:
New Directions and Exemplars in College Science Education Research

James H. Wandersee and Jewel J. Reuter

James H. Wandersee is William LeBlanc Alumni Association Professor of Biology Education at Louisiana State University. He earned a PhD in curriculum and instruction (science) at Marquette University and completed postdoctoral work in biology education at Cornell University. He conducts research in biology and geobiology instruction, scientific visualization, and the history of science and teaches courses in science education.

Jewel J. Reuter is a visiting professor of science education at Montana State University and teaches online science and professional development courses at the Louisiana Virtual School. Her research with the 15° Laboratory at Louisiana State University includes the study of how students learn molecular concepts when they integrate animations and digital data collection with their past, present, and future experiences.

The most useful science education research for college science teachers is theory based and includes data collected from studies with college students, along with a discussion of the implications for teaching. Key questions guiding the selection of thought-provoking studies for inclusion in this chapter were (a) Is the research question important both to the science education community and to the advancement of learning theory? (b) Are the methods and participant set adequate and thorough, given the research question being answered? and (c) Are the conclusions appropriate, given the context and limitations of the study?

We were also asked to include some of our own work that fit the chapter's theme. As college biologists and biology educators, most of the examples found in this chapter were derived from biology education research (particularly on photosynthesis and respiration, which is what we know best), but we have not overlooked college chemistry and physics teaching. In

Chapter 17 in this handbook, Wandersee and Clary address college geology teaching.

The chapter by Wandersee, Mintzes, and Novak (1994) on alternative conceptions in science in the *Handbook of Research on Science Teaching and Learning,* edited by Dorothy Gabel, devoted several pages to making the case for using the term *alternative conception* instead of *misconception* in science education research. This stance stemmed from an earlier research paper on biology from the learners' viewpoint (Wandersee, Mintzes, and Arnaudin 1989). Although the term *misconception* may seem more honest and direct to the layperson and to those unfamiliar with the many thousands of such science education research studies in print, we think it also promotes a dualist notion that a student's answer to a given science content question is either completely right (now and forever) and thus maximally useful to the learner or completely wrong and totally useless in the student's everyday life. In such a world, there is no gray. Thus, in this chapter, we use the term *alternative conception* instead of *misconception* and enclose the term *misconception* in quotes whenever it is used by another researcher. We hope that our chapter offers some useful ideas to improve your own teaching and inspires you to delve deeper into the college science teaching research literature related to students' thinking about particular content topic.

Noyd's Theory of Underteaching and Overteaching

It is useful to view college science teaching in the light of Noyd's theory of underteaching and overteaching (Noyd 2005). We think both types of inappropriate instruction can lead to alternative conceptions. We contend that being aware of the two "instructional lenses" identified by Noyd (underteaching and overteaching) can improve college science teaching, as well as help move the alternative conceptions research program in science education forward.

Underteaching is an instructional standpoint that holds the college student almost entirely responsible for understanding the course's content. The instructor's acceptance of responsibility for the student's learning is minimal and the implicit rationale is that the course is a "weed-out" course—the departmental version of the television program *Survivor,* where the mantra is to "outwit, outplay, and outlast" one's classmates. Lectures are crafted for experts, not novices (Hurst 2004). The course is epitomized by the word *challenging.*

In contrast, *overteaching* is an instructional standpoint that supplies what is missing in underteaching—support—but, alas, supplies too much of it. It emphasizes product over process. Often the instructor overly simplifies the process for the student, so the product will look good. Thus, it can foster student dependency on the instructor and yield a gross overestimate of unscaffolded student understanding, while dampening student initiative for meaningful, independent learning. In contrast to underteaching, overteaching targets novices, and it aims to minimize student frustration in understanding all of the course topics. Often the instructor is working harder than the students are—posting all the course notes and lecture slides and offering past test questions, thus unwittingly enabling absence from class.

Noyd (2005) argues that we need to seek a golden mean between underteaching and overteaching—between making a course challenging (but not overly so), and providing learning support (but not so much so that it short-circuits meaningful learning and self-motivation). Noyd reminds his readers that the proper amount of teaching can only be allocated by carefully considering the individual student, the appropriate intervention points in the course, the essential amount of teaching required, the reasons justifying that teaching, and the manner in which it ought to be provided. Pretesting to ascertain each student's prior knowledge before teaching a particular topic is a good first step.

To apply Noyd's theory, we encourage you to visualize three stacked continua with the following poles—challenging-supportive, process-product, and expert-novice—as you weigh the degree of underteaching and overteaching in a specific college science course. We hypothesize that either instructional extreme may enhance the formation of alternative conceptions in science.

College Biology: Using Gaps in Knowledge to Identify and Prevent Alternative Conceptions

Griffard and Wandersee (2001) studied the effectiveness of a two-tier instrument designed by Haslam and Treagust (1987) for revealing alternative conceptions about photosynthesis. They used in-depth clinical interviews with six college biology students to analyze how those students completed the paper-and-pencil tasks on the instrument. The first tier consisted of 13 multiple-choice items, followed by the second tier of multiple-choice items concerning the reasons for their selection, accompanied by blank spaces for their comments about their selection. The interviews revealed shortcomings of the two-tier test method. The first tier often provided clues to the correct choice for justifying their selection and thus prevented participants from activating their own alternative conceptions from their existing knowledge during the second tier. Overall, the method seemed to measure the college students' test-taking ability, rather than their knowledge of photosynthesis.

Griffard and Wandersee (2001) also identified and classified gaps (where links between concepts or mediating concepts have failed to develop) as the primary causes of alternative conceptions because students typically fill such gaps with incorrect information (Griffard and Wandersee 1999). They recommended interviewing students using think-aloud techniques to help them explain their thoughts, while working on a task aimed at helping them to identify gaps. An example of students incorrectly filling a gap is learning or remembering that photosynthesis requires light. Many students incorrectly assume that cellular respiration replaces photosynthesis at night and fill their gap with this alternative conception.

This study is exemplary because it examined the effectiveness of a specific, promising research tool for identifying alternative conceptions. The study is innovative in revealing the benefits of identifying gaps in student learning as a way to prevent or remediate alternative conceptions (Griffard 1999). If researchers identify them, and college science instructors are made aware of these gaps, careful teaching may prevent alternative conceptions from forming. We think more knowledge-gap research findings would be valuable to college science instructors.

College Chemistry: Identifying and Confronting Alternative Conceptions

A study by Mulford and Robinson (2002) focused on the development and use of a set of 22 multiple-choice questions, the Chemical Concepts Inventory (CCI), to reveal various "alternate" conceptions of 14,000 students in first-semester, college-level chemistry—before and after instruction. The area these researchers identified with the most alternative conceptions was the energetics of chemical bonding—with nearly 70% of the students in the study incorrectly thinking that breaking O-O and H-H bonds directly releases energy. The postinstructional results indicated that traditional instruction did not help to remediate the identified alternative conceptions, given that the students, unfortunately, possessed a faulty conceptual framework, to which they attempted to add their newly learned concepts.

In another study, Galley (2004) used preinstructional surveys with 600 biochemistry and physiology students and obtained similar results as the previous researchers, indicating college students incorrectly think that energy is released when a bond is broken. During instruction, Galley successfully helped most students to resolve their misunderstandings by confronting them with the correct answers to his survey questions and using specific visual diagrams. In particular, he used diagrams of the hydrolysis of ATP (ATP + H_2O → ADP + P_i) to show energy is required to break the O-P and O-H bonds of the reactants, but that more energy is released when bonds of the products are formed. The postinstructional survey results not only identified improvement in student understanding but also flagged possible sources of the "misconceptions"—for example, 88% of the students appeared to incorrectly associate diagrams of energy changes with bond-breaking diagrams from their previous chemistry or biology textbooks.

The large Mulford and Robinson study (2002) was exemplary in showing the resistance of alternative conceptions to alteration via traditional instruction. The Galley (2004) study used an exemplary and innovative approach in combining the use of both surveys and diagrams to make students aware of the sources of their bonding "misconceptions" and to help students resolve them successfully.

College Physics: Understanding Archimedes' Principle

In the first part of a two-part study, Loverude, Kautz, and Heron (2003) identified barriers to understanding Archimedes' principle in 2,000 students from mostly first-year introductory college physics and second-year hydrostatics courses. Pre- and postinstructional quiz and examination questions used with the research group were developed from interview results with selected students. The interviews focused on a problem with five blocks of various masses but identical volumes that were submerged in water.

The study revealed that after traditional instruction only 10% of the introductory and 50% of the second-year students correctly explained whether these objects sank or floated in water (if all objects had densities different than water). The most common mistake was to draw the blocks on a descending line according to their relative densities, which was a result of misunderstandings that, surprisingly, included even the most basic concepts of mass, volume, and density.

Using the results of the first study described, Heron, Loverude, Shaffer, and McDermott (2003) created various researched-based versions of hydrostatic instructional materials and evaluated them with the help of college physics students and K–12 practicing teachers. The greatest improvement of understanding for the five-block problem, which increased from 10% to 85%, occurred with the interactive tutorial (version 2) that emphasized *displaced volume* to help students recognize that buoyant force is independent of mass, along with the lab (version 2) that emphasized the nature of *density*.

The preceding two studies are exemplary for their display of the processes of identifying alternative conceptions, developing corrective materials, evaluating the materials, and revising them until there is a significant improvement in understanding. The authors' approaches to improving understanding were also innovative because they included physics students and practicing K–12 teachers, which together promoted both immediate and long-term improvements to physics education.

College Science, Interactive Multimedia Games, and the Value of Guidance to Meaningful Learning

Multimedia games are gaining popularity with educators (National Science Teachers Association 2005), as well as with scientists and Hollywood directors (Ball 2005). Moreno and Mayer (2005) have investigated meaningful learning of college students using the interactive multimedia game Design a Plant, which involves designing and testing plants to withstand weather conditions on alien planets. We reviewed this research specifically for its importance in providing college students with correct solutions (corrective feedback) and explanations about their design selections (explanatory feedback) in order to avoid the formation of alternative conceptions in science.

In one of their experiments, an agent, Herman-the-Bug, served as a guide and provided guidance, in either corrective mode only or corrective mode plus explanatory feedback, at various steps in the game activities (Moreno and Mayer 2005). The results showed that combined use of corrective and explanatory feedback allowed students to achieve higher levels of transfer (e.g., applying information to either a different environment or a different plant design) and greater reduction of alternative conceptions than with corrective feedback alone. Also, in another experiment by the same researchers, inexperienced learners were required to reflect and then explain their own new mental models without feedback during problem solving (Moreno and Mayer 2005). The results showed that the consolidation of an incorrect model for a scientific concept often caused them to develop damaging alternative conceptions. Meaningful learning requires integration of new representations into prior knowledge, a process that tends to be deficient in inexperienced learners. It appears that explanatory feedback is beneficial to them when offered within an interactive multimedia environment.

The Moreno and Mayer study is exemplary in that it evaluated the effect of using an agent as a guide with newly developing multimedia games on meaningful learning. It is innovative in revealing how simple activities such as natural reflection by inexperienced learners without guidance, which typically occurs in association with multimedia learning, can actually consolidate dysfunctional alternative conceptions.

BioDatamation™ Strategy and Theory of Interacting Visual Fields™

Our own research examined how college freshmen at a research university learned photosynthesis and cellular respiration, and we determined the value added to the students' learning with the BioDatamation™ (BDM) Program (Reuter 2005; Reuter and Wandersee 2005). BDM is composed of technology-scaffolded learning strategy components, including animated concept presentations, WebQuest-style activities (Dodge 1997; Watson 1999), data collection, and student-constructed animations. We derived all BDM learning strategies from the human constructivist theory (Mintzes, Wandersee, and Novak 1998), which emphasizes the importance of prior knowledge, hierarchically structured knowledge, conceptual change, and the use of metacognitive tools, such as concept maps, for knowledge construction. Together these constitute the fundamental components of all BDM learning activities.

The BDM strategy uses students' metacognition (i.e., the knowledge, awareness, and control of one's own learning) of (a) prior knowledge of past situations, (b) present knowledge of their current study, and (c) prospective knowledge of future applications to promote cognitive insight and deepen understanding. These strategies help students to learn by using visual fields: (a) what is seen now, (b) what is visualized from the past, or (c) what is visualized in the future (Jones 1995). Also, as we developed BDM learning strategy, it became obvious that principles of excellence in graphic design (Tufte 1990, 1997, 2001) and awareness of variations in students' visual perception (Neisser 1976) were needed to enhance effective graphic design and to establish the visual fields.

From our experiences applying BDM strategies, we formulated a theory that explains the critical components necessary for depicting time-linked, meaningful science knowledge. We called it the Theory of Interacting Visual Fields™ (TIVF) (see Figure 30.1; a color-coded version is at *www.nsta.org/pdfs/Fig30.1.pdf*) (Reuter and Wandersee 2002a, 2002b, 2003a, 2003b), and it states that time-linked meaningful science knowledge is hierarchically constructed using the past, present, and future visual fields constructed with visual metacognitive strategies that are derived from the principles of visual behavior (Jones 1995), human constructivist theory (Mintzes, Wandersee, and Novak 1998), and visual information design (Tufte 1990, 1997, 2001).

Our initial research (Reuter and Wandersee 2005) used our item analysis of 263,267 student exams from the four most recently released Biology Advanced Placement Examinations (College Examination Board 2004; Educational Testing Service 1992, 1994, 1999) to determine

Figure 30.1

Theoretical Basis of BioDatamation™ (BDM) Learning Strategy

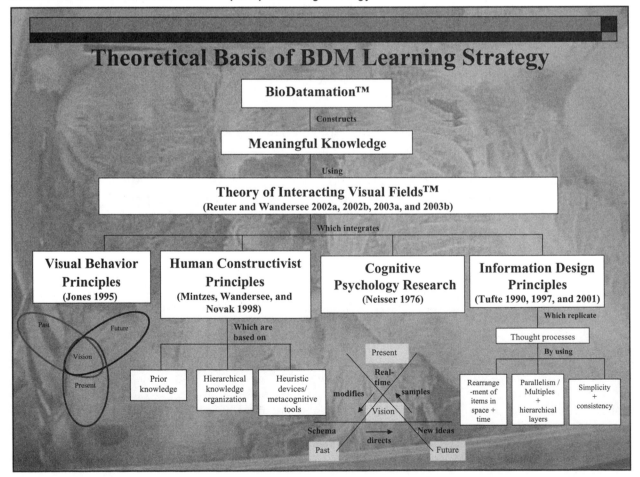

students' alternative conceptions of photosynthesis and cellular respiration. We analyzed the concepts of the multiple-choice items and corresponding statistical data of responses by hierarchically mapping the concepts with propositions (including connecting links) and incorporating the research data with color-coded reference numbers and sublevel letters. The resulting map helped to analyze the items' level of conceptual difficulty. We named this innovative type of map the Concept and Data Analysis Map (CDAM; Reuter and Wandersee 2005). It allowed for the display and analysis of the knowledge representation of more than one student and was feasible to use with a large national group of students. It also allowed for the tracking of various possible thought processes without redrawing the map. A portion of the Krebs Cycle, Chemiosmosis, and Electron Transport CDAM used in our study is shown in Figure 30.2. (Go to *www.nsta.org/pdfs/Fig30.2.pdf* for a color-coded version of this figure.)

The results showed that the most difficult concepts for the students tested were thylakoid structure in prokaryotic cells, the role of light and chlorophyll, carbon fixation, coupling hydrolysis of adenosine triphosphate (ATP) with nonspontaneous reactions, electron transport, and chemiosmosis. This phase of our research not only identified difficult concepts, it offered us possible paths for teaching and assessing those concepts during the next phase.

For example, to address the difficulties and deficiencies with understanding the electron transport chain in relationship to the production of ATP, we developed a layered animation (represented in Figure 30.3) that explained how various poisons, such as rotenone, antimycin A, and cyanide, inhibited electron transport. Our focus was on how cyanide blocks electron transport at cytochrome a_3 at the end of the electron transport chain and, thus, how it prevents the production of ATP and causes death. Also, to arouse student attention and motivate them to think about the concept once again, and to provide application for the concept, we included a brief video clip from the 1979 film *Moonraker* to show how James Bond shot cyanide-laced darts from a wrist dart gun at enemies to kill them quickly.

The next phase of our research involved instructing two groups of college students to supplement traditional lecture presentations, the comparison and BDM groups, with a total of 24 undergraduate students. All participants were enrolled in an introductory-level general biology course at a major research university. The comparison group received the traditional version of instructional and laboratory activities, while the BDM group received innovative BDM instruction and laboratories with the TIVF components (Reuter 2005).

BDM learning strategies developed and organized knowledge by using each visual field. For example, thoughts about prior knowledge for the past visual field and construction of knowledge in the present visual field of cellular respiration were both accomplished by using the following BDM learning activities: viewing a short video clip from a Korean grocery store about the ingredients of kimchee (a spicy Korean fermented Napa cabbage, which is comparable to sauerkraut), participating in WebQuest-style activities about a Korean restaurant chef who was having difficulty making kimchee quickly, doing a data collection and analysis activity using a carbon dioxide sensor with special software to determine the best conditions to ferment Napa cabbage to produce kimchee, and viewing a special instructor-designed animated and layered PowerPoint presentation that explained the concepts of cellular respiration. An example of how we helped students to use prospective knowledge of the future visual field was having the students determine possible solutions to the restaurant problem concerned with making kimchee quickly and prepare a PowerPoint presentation from a toolbox of images and information about their experimental results, which could be presented to the restaurant owner. During this activity

Figure 30.2

Portion of the Concept and Data Analysis Map (CDAM) of Krebs Cycle, Chemiosmosis, and Electron Transport (Reuter and Wandersee 2005)

The CDAM illustrates the hierarchical relationship of concepts. It uses reference numbers with sublevel letters to analyze the conceptual difficulty and to identify possible pathways for learning, assessing, and teaching these concepts.

In this system, a number/letter that appears *in this type* represents a category of greatest item difficulty (***4b, 4c, 4d, 7a, 7b,*** and ***7c***). A category at the next level of difficulty appears as a number/letter **in this type** (**11d, 14a, 14b, 14c, 16a, 18a, 19a, 19b, 25b, 25c,** and **27c**). A category in the next level of difficulty appears as a number/letter **in this type** (**28a, 28b, 32b, 33d, 33e, 35b, 39a, 39b, 40d, 45a,** and **45b**). Finally, a category of least difficulty appears as a number/letter *in this type* (*48b, 50a, 50b,* and *51b*).

An example of an item in the greatest difficulty category was assigned reference numbers ***7a, 7b,*** and ***7c***, which correspond to multiple-choice item 41 of the 1999 Biology Advanced Placement Examination (Educational Testing Service 1999). This item concerns the concepts associated with the production of adenosine triphosphate (ATP) as a result of movement of protons down the concentration gradient, and the reference numbers are printed ***in this type*** because only 33% of the students answered it correctly. The sublevel letters (a–c) track a possible pathway of cognition of the concepts associated with this item.

An example of an item in the least difficult category was assigned reference numbers *50a* and *50b*, which correspond to multiple-choice item 42 of the 2002 Biology Advanced Placement Examination (College Entrance Examination Board 2004). This item concerns the concepts that ATP is a common source of energy and that ATP can be used to do cellular work, and the numbers were printed *in this type* because 84% of the students answered it correctly. (Note that a color-coded type system is used with the numbers/letters when color printing is an option. The color-coded type system version of this diagram is available at *www.nsta.org/pdfs/Figure30.2.pdf*. The use of color-coded reference numbers is a significant feature of a CDAM because it aids the reader in the analysis of the data.)

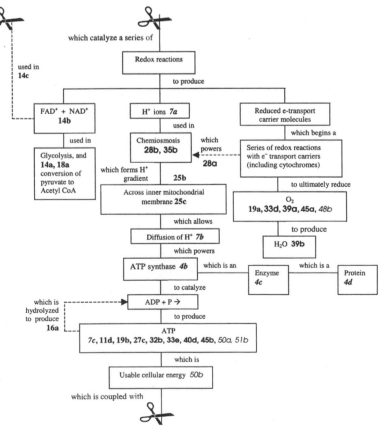

Figure 30.3

Image From Animated PowerPoint Presentation About Poisons That Inhibit Electron Transport

The information was presented in layers beginning with the basic structure of the crista membrane and the sequence of the various cytochromes. Then each poison, in relationship to inhibition of electron transport, was added to the animation to emphasize that oxidative phosphorylation requires electron transport. Analysis of reference items 6a and 6b and 8a, 8b, 8c, and 8d, which correspond respectively to multiple-choice items 78 and 79 of the 2002 Biology Advanced Placement Examination (College Entrance Examination Board 2004), helped to reveal the difficulties with understanding the concepts of the electron transport chain in relationship to the production of adenosine triphosphate (ATP) and the need to strategically introduce these concept relationships with animated instruction.

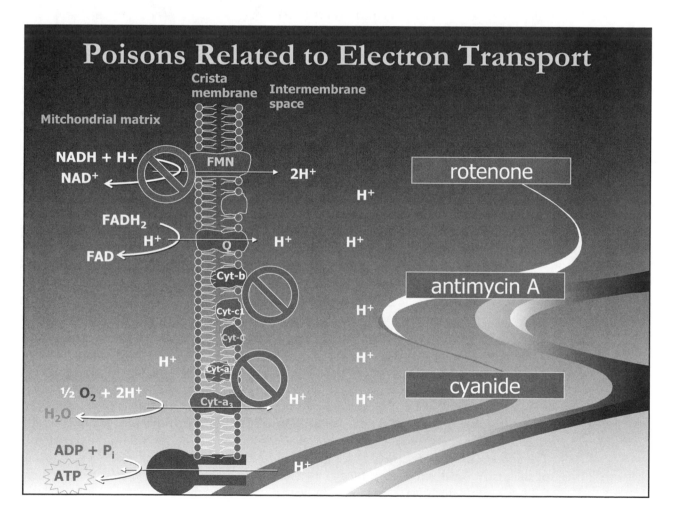

students rearranged words and images to organize knowledge with real-life applications. These examples of BDM learning strategies are summarized in Figure 30.4.

Figure 30.4

Concept Map Showing the Relationship of the BioDatamation (BDM) Learning Strategies to Each Visual Field

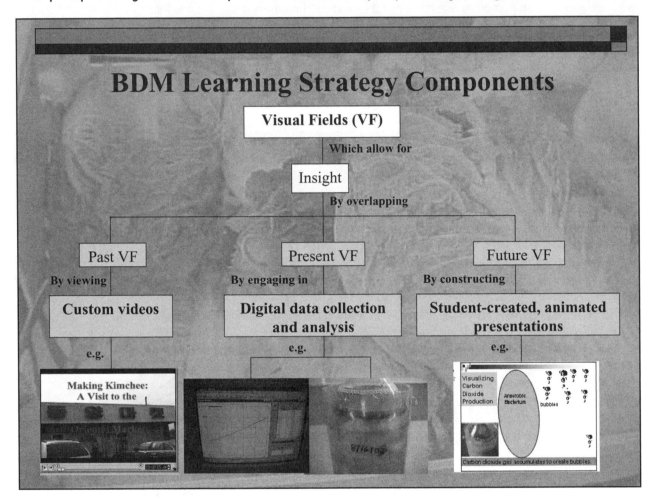

Data collection from this instructional phase of the research included interviews with student's self-constructed concept maps and discussions about the various learning strategies. The concept maps were scored by assigning points to each biochemically correct component of the map (Novak and Gowin 1984). Discussions also included a student-constructed visual field diagram, which was presented as a heuristic in a worksheet format, and it helped students to reflect, organize, and track changes in their past, present, and future visual fields. It also helped the students to explain the interaction of their three fields, which defined their insight. Together these assessment tools helped us to determined the "value added" to learning with BDM learning strategies. The results indicated that the total value added to integrative knowledge associated with BDM instruction with the three visual fields was an average

knowledge increase of 39% for cellular respiration and 43% increase for photosynthesis. There was no decay in memory on the posttest that was administered two weeks after instruction as a conservative measure of knowledge gain. In fact, the delayed-posttest results even indicated improved long-term memory of concepts (perhaps due to integrative reconciliation), in contrast to the posttest results immediately following instruction.

We analyzed the interview transcripts and visual field diagrams with various qualitative methods, such as matrix analysis (Patton 2002) and Lincoln and Guba's (1985) constant comparative method. The following was revealed from our analysis about how BDM strategies affected learning:

- Presentations and activities in the present and future visual fields added to students' long-term memories, due to the application of the concepts.
- Layered animations prevented cognitive overload, facilitated hierarchical organization of concepts, and improved recall.
- Digital data collection and analysis activities allowed for reflection and immediate gratification with diverse experiments that used quick computer graphics of the data.
- Student-constructed animated presentations allowed application of concepts to daily life to rehearse concepts outside formal instruction, which increased long-term memory and understanding.

In contrast to the BDM group results, the comparison group had only a 4% increase in knowledge of cellular respiration and a 9% increase in photosynthesis when taught using traditional methods and equivalent time on task. Additional traditional instruction did not significantly improve learning. There was also decay in long-term memory over the two-week delayed phase. They were not exposed to concept applications during instruction, and they also lacked self-awareness of application, which prevented them from rehearsing concepts—which seems instrumental to long-term memory formation.

BDM is exemplary because it appears to have application to all science education topics. It is innovative in that it uses both the students' prior (past) knowledge and prospective (future) knowledge in association with present learning experiences and selected instructional technology applications to achieve robust meaningful learning. Anticipated future research includes determining the generalization of BDM strategies to other biology topic areas, more specialized life sciences, and the physical science disciplines as well as implementing BDM-based instruction as the sole learning input, including remote delivery and varying levels of technology.

BDM research addresses the National Research Council's concern that "the ways in which most future research biologists are educated are geared to the biology of the past, rather than to the biology of the future" (Committee on Undergraduate Biology Education to Prepare Research Scientists for the 21st Century 2003, p. 1). BDM research also has demonstrated that gaining integrative knowledge through the implementation of the Theory of Interactive Visual Fields with BioDatamation technology-scaffolded instructional components increases the likelihood of meaningful learning, increased long-term retention, and continued concept development. BDM participants see the world through biology concepts they have interconnected as well as arrayed in time.

References

Ball, P. 2005. News@Nature.com. Cartoons and Morphing Software May Help to Convey Scientists' Finds. July 1. *www.nature.com/news/2005/050627/full/050627-16.html* (accessed July 9, 2005).

College Entrance Examination Board (CEEB). 2004. *The 2002 AP biology released exam.* New York: CEEB.

Committee on Undergraduate Biology Education to Prepare Research Scientists for the 21st Century. 2003. *BIO2010: Transforming undergraduate education for future research biologists.* Washington, DC: National Academies Press.

Dodge, B. 1997. FOCUS: Five rules for writing great WebQuest. *Learning and Leading With Technology* 28 (8): 6–9.

Educational Testing Service. 1992. *The 1990 Advanced Placement examination in biology and its grading.* New York: College Entrance Examination Board.

Educational Testing Service. 1994. 1994 *AP biology: Free-response scoring guide with multiple-choice section.* New York: College Entrance Examination Board.

Educational Testing Service. 1999. *1999 AP biology released exam.* New York: College Entrance Examination Board.

Galley, W. 2004. Exothermic bond breaking: Consistent misconception. *Journal of Chemical Education* 81 (4): 523–525.

Griffard, P. 1999. Gaps in college biology students' understanding of photosynthesis: Implications for human constructivist learning theory and college classroom practice. PhD diss., Louisiana State University. UMI Dissertation Services No. 9960057.

Griffard, P., and J. Wandersee. 1999. Exposing gaps in college biochemistry understanding using new cognitive probes. Paper presented at the annual meeting of the National Association for Research in Science Teaching, Boston.

Griffard, P., and J. Wandersee. 2001. The two-tier instrument on photosynthesis: What does it diagnose? *International Journal of Science Education* 23 (10): 1039–1052.

Haslam, F., and D. Treagust. 1987. Diagnosing secondary students' misconceptions about photosynthesis and respiration in plants using a two-tier multiple choice instrument. *Journal of Biological Education* 21 (3): 203–211.

Heron, P., M. Loverude, P. Shaffer, and L. McDermott. 2003. Helping students develop an understanding of Archimedes' principle. II. Development of research-based instructional materials. *American Journal of Physics* 71 (11): 1188–1195.

Hurst, J. 2004. The overlecturing and underteaching of clinical medicine. *Archives of Internal Medicine* 164: 1605–1608.

Jones, B. 1995. *Visual behavior.* Cincinnati, OH: Lockwood Press.

Lincoln, Y. S., and E. G. Guba. 1985. *Naturalistic inquiry.* New York: Sage Publications.

Loverude, M., C. Kautz, and P. Heron. 2003. Helping students develop an understanding of Archimedes' principle. I. Research on student understanding. *American Journal of Physics* 71 (11): 1178–1187.

Mintzes, J. J., J. H. Wandersee, and J. D. Novak. 1998. Epilogue: Meaningful learning, knowledge restructuring, and conceptual change: On ways of teaching science for understanding. In *Teaching science for understanding: A human constructivist view,* eds. J. J. Mintzes, J. H. Wandersee, and J. D. Novak, 327–350. New York: Academic Press.

Moonraker, DVD. Directed by L. Gilbert (1979). Los Angeles: MGM, 2000.

Moreno, R., and R. Mayer. 2005. Role of guidance, reflection, and interactivity in an agent-based multimedia game. *Journal of Educational Psychology* 97 (1): 117–128.

Mulford, D., and W. Robinson. 2002. An inventory for alternative conceptions among first-semester general chemistry students. *Journal of Chemical Education* 79 (6): 739–744.

National Science Teachers Association. 2005. Information technology's role in 21st–century science education. *NSTA Reports* 17 (1): 1.

Neisser, U. 1976. *Cognition and reality.* San Francisco: W. H. Freeman.

Novak, J. D., and D. B. Gowin. 1984. *Learning how to learn.* New York: Cambridge University Press.

Noyd, R. 2005. Applying Aristotle's golden mean to the classroom: Balancing underteaching and overteaching. *The National Teaching and Learning Forum* 14 (3): article 2.

Patton, M. Q. 2002. *Qualitative research and evaluation methods.* 3rd ed. London: Sage Publications.

Reuter, J. J. 2005. Using the BioDatamation™ strategy to learn introductory college biology: Value-added effects on

selected students' conceptual understanding and conceptual integration of the processes of photosynthesis and cellular respiration. PhD diss., Louisiana State University.

Reuter, J., and J. Wandersee. 2002a. Learn about respiration by making kimchee from Chinese cabbage. Paper presented at the state convention of the Louisiana Science Teachers Association, Lafayette, LA, October 2002.

Reuter, J., and J. Wandersee. 2002b. Use BioDatamation™ (data in motion) to teach photosynthesis and respiration visually! Paper presented at the national convention of the National Association of Biology Teachers, Cincinnati, OH, November 2002.

Reuter, J., and J. Wandersee. 2003a. Become a respiration detective. Paper presented at the state convention of the Louisiana Science Teachers Association, New Orleans, LA, December 2003.

Reuter, J., and J. Wandersee. 2003b. Using "speedy kimchee" sensor-based labs and student-made animations to teach 12 difficult ideas about cellular respiration. Paper presented at the national convention of the National Association of Biology Teachers, Portland, OR, October 2003.

Reuter, J., and J. Wandersee. 2005. Understanding photosynthesis and cellular respiration: N = 263,267. (Unpublished manuscript.)

Tufte, E. R. 1990. *Envisioning information.* Cheshire, CT: Graphics Press.

Tufte, E. R. 1997. *Visual explanations.* Cheshire, CT: Graphics Press.

Tufte, E. R. 2001. *The visual display of quantitative information.* Cheshire, CT: Graphics Press.

Wandersee, J., J. Mintzes, and M. Arnaudin. 1989. Biology from the learners' viewpoint: A content analysis of the research literature. *School Science and Mathematics* 89: 654–668.

Wandersee, J. H., J. J. Mintzes, and J. D. Novak. 1994. Research on alternative conceptions in science. In *Handbook of research on science teaching and learning,* ed. D. Gabel, 177–210. New York: Macmillan.

Watson, K. L. 1999. WebQuests in middle school curriculum: Promoting technological literacy in the classroom. *Meridian: A Middle School Computer Technologies Journal* 2 (2): 1–7.

CHAPTER 31

Applying Conceptual Change Strategies to College Science Teaching

Luli Stern, Tamar Yechieli, and Joseph Nussbaum

Luli Stern is a lecturer in the Department of Education in Technology and Science at Technion-Israel Institute of Technology. She earned a PhD in molecular biology at Tel Aviv University and conducts research on conceptual change, formative assessment, and curriculum development.

Tamar Yechieli is a senior lecturer in the Science Department of Michlala Jerusalem College. She earned a PhD in science education at The Hebrew University, Jerusalem, and conducts research on conceptual change and teacher education. She teaches courses for preservice and inservice science teachers.

Joseph Nussbaum is a professor in the Science Department of Michlala Jerusalem College. He earned a PhD in science education at Cornell University and conducts research on conceptual change and teacher education. He teaches courses for preservice and inservice science teachers.

Interviewer (*holding up a seed and a log of wood*):

Imagine that I planted this seed in the ground and that a tree grew from it. Here is a part of that tree. Now, where did all this mass come from?

Student 1: I guess from water that was sucked out from the ground and from minerals that were sucked out from the ground.

Student 2: Water, light, soil.

Student 3: I would guess that most of it is drawn from matter in the soil itself and some of it comes from water.

O n reading the excerpt above, one may think that those interviewed were lower elementary school students. However, this is in fact an excerpt from a videotape made by the Harvard-Smithsonian Center for Astrophysics in which Massachusetts Institute of Technology and Harvard graduates were asked to explain everyday life phenomena on the day of their graduation (Harvard-Smithsonian Center for Astrophysics 1997). Surprisingly, none of those students knew the correct answer, although it was apparent from their answers that they had studied photosynthesis in school.

Why, despite the fact that photosynthesis is one of the most widely taught subjects in school, do so few students hold the scientific conception (i.e., that plants make sugars from carbon dioxide and water) and maintain alternative conceptions instead? And, more importantly, what sort of instruction could have helped students understand the scientifically accepted conceptions and apply their knowledge in a meaningful way?

This chapter will focus on meaningful learning and conceptual change from the perspective of science education. We will describe in detail two case studies of conceptual change–based curricula—one that focuses on the particulate nature of matter and the other on natural selection. Finally, we will propose possible implications for teaching science at the college level.

Barriers to Meaningful Learning

Ideally, students (whether majoring in science or other subjects) develop an appreciation of science and an awareness of scientific issues in their everyday lives. Moreover, they can apply the scientific ideas they were taught and draw on them in a variety of situations. Better yet, rather than knowing fragmented pieces of information or ideas, graduate students possess knowledge that is richly interconnected. What then are the advantages of such meaningful learning for the learners? First and foremost, learners share in the excitement and personal fulfillment that can come from understanding and learning about the natural world (American Association for the Advancement of Science [AAAS] 1989; National Research Council 1996). Second, they can use their knowledge and skills to explain and predict phenomena (including, for example, the explanation for the mass of the log question above), solve practical problems, consider alternative positions on issues that involve science, and make educated choices in their everyday lives.

It is always assumed that students know more than they really do about a particular topic only because they have been taught that topic. High test scores often mislead teachers into thinking that their students understand more than they actually do (and may discourage teachers from seeking better instructional strategies). This may be attributed to current assessment strategies that do not necessarily probe for understanding (Stern and Ahlgren 2002). As research has repeatedly demonstrated, when understanding is probed in effective ways, students do not perform as well as their high school scores suggest they would. Whereas some ideas and intuitions held by students are indeed in accord with scientists' views, others (often labeled "misconceptions" or "alternative conceptions") are in conflict with currently accepted scientific ideas. Since the mid-1970s research studies on student learning have consistently shown that students of all ages—from middle school to college and beyond—have difficulties understanding key ideas in science and hold naive, incorrect ideas instead. Even after instruction, few college students accept the ideas that matter is particulate, that populations change over time by the inadvertent increase in the proportion of individuals that have advantageous characteristics, and that plants make their own food from water and air (Bishop and Anderson 1990; Brumby 1984; Harvard-Smithsonian Center for Astrophysics 1997; Nussbaum 1979, 1981). Moreover, many students are reluctant to accept the scientific ideas when they are explicitly suggested to them (Anderson, Sheldon, and Dubay 1990; Harvard-Smithsonian Center for Astrophysics 1997; Roth and Anderson 1987).

Students' ideas about how the world works have been identified in several content areas. This area of research was established by Driver and Easley (1978), who realized that incorrect answers are systematically repeated by students of all ages and from various countries and cultures. Some of the students' misconceptions work fairly well in familiar contexts and are therefore highly resistant to change. Furthermore, misconceptions are held even by the brightest students and are often similar to ideas supported by scientists in the past that have since been discarded or refined (Wandersee 1985).

Although some educators have suggested that students' difficulties result from their low cognitive level or motivation, we attribute their different understanding of abstract scientific ideas to curriculum and instruction rather than to the students' abilities (Kesidou and Roseman 2002; Stern and Roseman 2004). In fact, as will be shown in the next section, carefully designed instruction can improve student learning of scientific ideas.

Is the Goal of Meaningful Learning Achievable?

Calling attention to misconceptions and suggesting to students that they should be avoided is usually inadequate. Serious difficulties are not successfully addressed by telling students they are wrong and providing them with the "right answer." If students are expected to understand the scientifically accepted concepts, they need to go through a process termed conceptual change. A very powerful model of conceptual change was articulated by a group of science education researchers and science philosophers at Cornell University in the early 1980s. This model is based on Piaget's notions of disequilibration and accommodation (Piaget 1970) as well as on a parallel drawn between Kuhn's well-known description of scientific revolutions (Kuhn 1970) and individual learning. The conceptual change model suggested four conditions that need to occur for learners to replace their intuitive conceptions with scientifically accepted ideas (Posner et al. 1982):

1. *Dissatisfaction with the existing conception:* This may occur when students' predictions about a phenomenon are challenged by an actual experience. For example, to address the commonly held idea that soil is food for plants, students can make predictions regarding the outcome of van Helmont's experiment showing that soil is not the source of the plant's mass. Students can then read the actual experiment and compare their predictions to the actual outcomes.

2. *Intelligibility:* The learner must be able to construct a mental image of the new conception and understand what it means. For example, for a student to meaningfully adopt the idea of vacuum between the particles of matter, he or she needs to understand that the term *vacuum* means "nothing"—that is, no matter whatsoever.

3. *Plausibility:* The learner needs to have a sense of the range of phenomena that the new conception can explain to appreciate the explanatory power of the new conception. Furthermore, a variety of phenomena is often needed for students to find an idea plausible.

4. *Fruitfulness:* The new conception must appear more fruitful than the old one. The stu-

dent should feel that the new conception can be useful in a variety of novel situations.

According to the conceptual change model, when these conditions are met, the new conception seems more plausible and more fruitful to the student than the existing one, and he or she will more likely consider adopting it as a satisfying explanation of a given phenomenon.

The conceptual change model and its later modifications stimulated some curriculum development that highlighted the importance of using students' prior ideas as a foundation for subsequent learning. These curricular efforts emphasized, in addition, the use of relevant phenomena to make the scientific ideas plausible, representations to help students conceptualize ideas, and ample opportunities to apply the ideas. In the following subsections, we will outline two case studies of successful curricular interventions that were based on the conceptual change model.

The Case of the Particulate Nature of Matter

The essential ideas introduced by the kinetic molecular theory are that all matter is made up of tiny particles and that these particles are in perpetual motion, in an absolutely empty space, interacting by collisions and by mutually exerting electrical forces. Although this concept may seem simple, its ramifications are complex (Feynman 1977). It is impossible to understand most of modern science without a good grasp of the kinetic molecular theory. Because of the centrality of this theory throughout the scientific disciplines, it is included in practically all middle school curricula, where it serves as the basis for advanced learning in science. Despite these efforts, many studies in science education indicate that students of all ages have difficulties appreciating the particulate nature of matter (Ben-zvi, Eylon, and Silberstein 1986; Brook, Briggs, and Driver 1984; Johnson 1998a,1998b; Johnston and Driver 1989; Lee et al. 1993; Novick and Nussbaum 1978; Osborne and Cosgrove 1983; Stavy 1990).

It has been shown that middle and high school students have difficulties explaining common phenomena in molecular terms. For example, many secondary school students are strongly committed to the idea that matter is continuous or simply includes particles. Also, students of all ages attribute macroscopic properties to particles and have difficulty accepting the notion of perpetual motion of particles, especially in solids. These intuitive conceptions are particularly resistant to change. Interestingly, college students hold similar ideas (Benson, Wittrock, and Baur 1993).

Since most textbook authors, teachers, and college instructors are not aware of the cognitive difficulties that students have concerning the kinetic molecular theory, they do not recognize that their students need to undergo a process of conceptual change and that it is their responsibility to create the learning conditions that would initiate and promote this process. Our studies, supported by the literature, have shown that three aspects of the particle model are of major importance.

First, each component of the kinetic molecular theory poses a different type and level of cognitive difficulty. While middle and high school teachers readily identify the basic components of the particle theory (invisible tiny particles, empty space [vacuum], variable density of particles, particle motion, and mutual forces of attraction), recognizing those components that require a greater "conceptual change" from the learner compared with others is a much more demanding task (Engels and Driver 1981; Nussbaum 1985). The following anecdote demonstrates the difficulty students have in accepting the notion of absolute vacuum in which particles are continuously moving.

In the course of studying introductory astronomy, a class of college juniors was discussing the structure and size of the solar system. The instructor drew an analogy between the solar system and an individual atom (Bohr's model), emphasizing that both planets and electrons would have fallen toward the center had they not been moving. Judy was among the best students in the class.

Judy:	How can the electron orbit the nucleus forever?
Instructor:	Why shouldn't it do so?
Judy:	Because there's friction!
Instructor:	Friction?… With what?
Judy:	Friction with the air around it.

Second, while moving to the world of particles (the ultra-microscopic world) some of the macroscopic characteristics of matter disappear. Students have difficulty understanding the reasons that characteristics such as mass, kinetics, or electric charges may legitimately be assigned to particles, while other characteristics (such as color, taste, temperature, or malleability) may not (De Voss 1990). Students have difficulty distinguishing between primary characteristics of particles and secondary characteristics that are not applicable to an individual particle. These secondary characteristics represent our subjective psychological impressions of the behavior of a great mass of particles. Our experience shows that many college freshmen, regardless of having taken an introductory course in chemistry, are still confused by questions such as

- Are wax molecules softer than glass molecules?
- Is a copper atom malleable?
- Are the exteriors of glue molecules sticky?
- Are ice molecules colder than boiling water molecules?

Third, adopting the particle model calls for adopting a mechanistic-reductionistic view of all physical phenomena. The mechanistic viewpoint implied by the particle model of the ancient Greeks preceded the mechanistic outlook of Newtonian mechanics by two millennia. Due to the adoption of the particle model in all areas of science, the generally accepted approach is basically a mechanistic one. However, a totally mechanistic view is counterintuitive for children and for adults, and many studies have shown that teleological thinking prevails at all age levels and is applied to explain biological and even physical phenomena (Tamir and Zohar 1991). College students assert, for instance, that physical systems "strive" to reach minimal energy level, that osmosis occurs "in order to" equate concentrations, and that mutations occur "in order to" adapt to environmental changes. Another example is the difficulty in understanding and adopting the ideas of natural selection discussed in the next subsection.

Vacuum and Particles is a curricular unit that was developed to explicitly address students' difficulties as described above (Nussbaum 1996). A longitudinal study conducted on 1,302 middle school students in Israel showed that greater than 80% of the students who studied the Vacuum and Particles unit underwent a conceptual change regarding the particulate nature of matter; far fewer students did so in the control group that studied a different unit (Margel, Eylon, and Scherz 2001). Furthermore, many students who studied Vacuum and Particles demonstrated their understanding as long as a few years after instruction, whereas most students in the control group did not.

The Case of Natural Selection

Evolution of living organisms is a central scientific theory that explains and integrates observations in many different areas of biology. By using ideas related to evolution, and in particular the concept of natural selection, one can explain everyday life phenomena such as the resistance of bacteria to antibiotics, the need to design a new flu vaccine every winter, and the vast diversity of living organisms. For these reasons, many scientists and science educators across the world have advocated the teaching of evolution at the high school level. Research on student learning repeatedly indicates, however, that evolution is one of the most difficult theories to accept (relevant research findings are summarized in AAAS 1993).

Studies conducted since the mid-1970s indicate that high school and college students, even after receiving the relevant instruction, have difficulty understanding the notion of natural selection. This difficulty may be attributed to several causes. First, natural selection appears to contradict intuition and everyday life experiences. For example, in everyday life individuals adapt deliberately to changes in their environment. Consequently, students explain gradual changes that occur in populations in terms of deliberate changes of individuals rather than in terms of inadvertent change in the proportion of individuals expressing advantageous traits in a population. Likewise, students may occasionally observe that traits such as smoking or bodybuilding "run" in some families and intuit incorrectly that acquired traits are inherited. Also, many students believe that environmental conditions induce changes in traits rather than select from existing variants that have advantageous characteristics. Second, understanding evolution relies on understanding additional ideas in biology (e.g., the random nature of mutations) and other scientific disciplines (e.g., the idea that recently deposited rock layers are more likely to contain fossils resembling existing organisms). Finally, understanding evolution requires the integration of two distinct processes, the random occurrence of new traits in a population and the nonrandom process of selection (Bishop and Anderson 1990).

Besides the obvious difficulty in engaging students in direct observations of evolutionary processes, the language used during instruction or in the popular media may be misleading and reinforce misconceptions (Anderson, Fisher, and Norman 2002; Bishop and Anderson 1990). For example, the phrase "the horse" used during instruction or in textbooks may refer to a single horse or to various species of horses. Consequently, the students' commonly perceived idea that natural selection acts on populations, rather than on individuals, is understandable. Explanations such as "the insects are developing resistance" or "the insects are becoming more resistant" instead of "resistance has been evolved" may lead students to believe that the insects intentionally adapt to their environment.

Students' ideas, both ideas that are incorrect and ideas that are partially correct but limited in scope, served as a foundation for planning a nine-week curricular unit on evolution (Stern et al. 2005). *Benchmarks for Science Literacy* (AAAS 1993) and National Science Education Standards (National Research Council 1996) provided further guidance for the development by providing learning goals on which to focus the instruction. Prerequisite ideas were then considered and the learning goals were subsequently mapped. Part of the map is shown in Figure 31.1.

Students' commonly held ideas were explicitly addressed in the unit. For instance, while scientists believe that the experiences an organism has during its lifetime can affect its offspring only if the genes in its own sex cells are changed by the experiences, it was repeatedly found that many secondary school students believe that experiences and traits acquired during an

Figure 31.1

Partial Map of Key Learning Goals Addressed in the First Two Lesson Plans in a Unit on Evolution

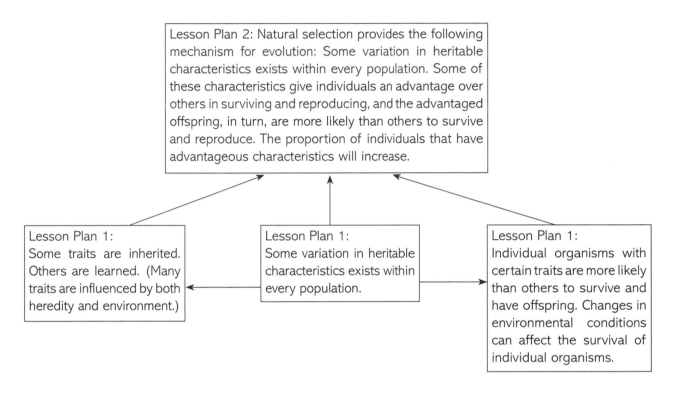

individual's lifetime can be passed on to its offspring (Brumby 1984; Engel-Clough and Wood-Robinson 1985; Jimenez-Aleixandre 1992; Kargbo, Hobbs, and Erickson 1980). This naive idea may hinder understanding of the theory of natural selection, leading to erroneous beliefs concerning the inheritance of environmentally induced characteristics over several generations.

During the course of instruction, students were asked to predict the outcome of an experiment carried out by a scientist at the beginning of the 20th century. The students were then guided through discussions and relevant phenomena toward the current scientific thinking. The episode from the history of science was used not as a means of conveying the entire historical account of the thoughts and experiments that led to the current theory of biological evolution but rather as a pedagogical tool for addressing students' commonly held ideas. Since students' intuitions are often similar to the ideas proposed by scientists in the past (Wandersee 1985), the same observations that persuaded scientists that their initial ideas were incomplete may appeal to students as well. An excerpt from the first lesson plan that attempts to target students' naive ideas about the inheritance of acquired traits is shown in Figure 31.2.

In addition to identifying and addressing students' commonly held ideas, the unit provided students with multiple, varied phenomena to make the scientific ideas plausible for students and various representations to make the abstract ideas intelligible. Students' interpretations and reasoning about their experiences were guided through sequences of questions (Kesidou and Roseman 2002; Stern and Roseman 2004).

Figure 31.2

Lesson 2 (From Lesson Plan 1): Are Acquired Traits Inherited?

August Weissman, a scientist who lived at the end of the 19th century, wanted to study exactly this question: Are traits that organisms acquire during their lifetime inherited? To do so, Weissman cut the tails off mice. He then allowed the tailless mice to reproduce and cut the tails off their offspring, too. He continued to do so for approximately 60 generations.
   Would you expect the tails of the first generation offspring to be:

| Approximately the same length as those of the parents' original tails | A little shorter than the parents' original tails | Much shorter than the parents' original tails | Almost as short as the cut parents' tails |

Explain your answer.

How do you think the tails of the offspring would look after cutting the tails off mice for the next 60 generations? Choose one of the scenarios above and explain your answer.

Weissman cut the tails off mice for 60 generations. How do you think the tails of the offspring would look like if Weissman had continued cutting the tails off the mice for the next 200 generations? Choose one of the scenarios above and explain your answer.

The curricular unit was tried with 53 grade-10 students in two classes in the north of Israel. Our findings (Stern and Hagay, manuscript in preparation) show that more than 60% of the students improved their understanding of natural selection and more than 50% improved their understanding of the idea of common descent following instruction. This was evident in students' responses to familiar and novel questions. Moreover, most students expressed positive sentiments following this learning experience—toward both the instructional strategies and the topic of evolution.

Lessons Learned From Grades 6–12 and Their Implications for the College Level

What Has Been Learned?

Successful curricular interventions that are based on the conceptual change model can be helpful when considering changes needed at the college level. Our cumulative experience suggests that when teaching is structured in a manner that allows students to go through the process of conceptual change, students are indeed successful.

We have also learned that conceptual change is a product of the interplay between cognitive, emotional, and social factors and is by its very nature a long and complex process. Consequently, effective teaching requires more time than is typically allocated. Nonetheless, this type of teaching is extremely rewarding because students learn scientific concepts more thoroughly and meaningfully.

Cognitive Analysis of Content: The First Step Toward Meaningful Teaching

College instructors typically provide their students with a syllabus that includes an outline of the course, its content, requirements, and the relevant bibliography. This syllabus is often compiled based on the course textbook or the instructor's knowledge and experience. This content analysis organizes the topic from a disciplinary perspective (through an expert's eye). We recommend an additional level of analysis, which we term cognitive analysis of content. This analysis examines the product of the content analysis by another criterion, its perception from the student's cognitive perspective (the novice's eye). Cognitive analysis of content seeks to identify the genuine cognitive demands presented to the learner by specific components of the content. It also attempts to characterize the potential sources for cognitive and emotional difficulties presented by the various components.

Many instructors and textbook authors assume erroneously that presenting elementary ideas such as the laws of Newtonian mechanics, inertia, and general gravity is a relatively simple task, and they regard quantitative problems in which one applies those elementary ideas to real phenomena as a more difficult task. Carrying out an algorithmic problem solution, however, does not guarantee the development of a meaningful understanding of the "big ideas." As emphasized by Hawkins (1992), in many science areas the most elementary ideas are not necessarily the simpler ideas, and in many cases they are by far the deeper and more abstract ones. They often are the intellectual product of genius and creative minds of great scientists. Consequently, some of the elementary ideas may be far more difficult to comprehend by students. This implies that in many areas a conceptual change may be required by the student quite early on. Examples of elementary ideas that are counterintuitive and require major conceptual change include the following:

- *Inertia* and *universal gravity,* which explain all forms of motion and provide the most essential definition of *mass* but are contradictory to the intuitive "Aristotelian thinking"
- *Vacuum,* the essential "component" of reality (the universe) and of the structure of all matter, which seems implausible and unbelievable to most people
- The *mechanistic (physico-chemical) approach of modern biology*, which excludes intuitive teleological explanations
- The *mechanistic and statistical approach to explain evolution*, which excludes the notion of "predesign of nature" believed by many people (not necessarily from a religious background)
- *Fields of force in mechanics and in electromagnetism* and the notion of "waves" moving in those fields of force, which are odd concepts both from the naive and the classical mechanics points of view
- The *extraordinarily long geological timescales*, which are far beyond those experienced personally and even beyond the capacity of regular imagination

Implications and Recommendations

To improve learning of abstract scientific ideas, research indicates that critical and thoughtful steps need to be undertaken in planning curriculum and instruction. Sound instruction of scientific ideas at all ages needs to focus on important ideas and to support the learning of these ideas. This support includes the following strategies:

- Taking into account students' prior ideas (both troublesome and helpful) and attempting to address these ideas. Reports on students' misconceptions can be found in numerous journals in science education. A searchable bibliography also appears online at *www.ipn. uni-kiel.de/aktuell/stcse/stcse.html* (this database is periodically updated by Reinders Duit and his colleagues at the University of Kiel).
- Providing appropriate phenomena—either directly through hands-on activities or demonstrations or indirectly through the use of videos or text—that can help students view scientific ideas as plausible (Anderson and Smith 1987; Champagne, Gunstone, and Klopfer 1985; Strike and Posner 1992). A variety of phenomena is often needed for students to accept an idea as plausible.
- Including helpful representations (such as simulations, diagrams, or analogies) to help students conceptualize ideas.
- Providing ample opportunities for students to express, discuss, and apply the ideas that they have learned.

References

American Association for the Advancement of Science (AAAS). 1989. *Science for all Americans.* New York: Oxford University Press.

American Association for the Advancement of Science (AAAS). 1993. *Benchmarks for science literacy.* New York: Oxford University Press.

Anderson, C., T. Sheldon, and J. Dubay. 1990. The effects of instruction on college nonmajors' conceptions of respiration and photosynthesis. *Journal of Research in Science Teaching* 27: 761–776.

Anderson, C. W., and E. Smith. 1987. Teaching science. In *The educator's handbook: A research perspective,* ed. V. Richardson-Koehler, 84–111. New York: Longman.

Benson, D., M. Wittrock, and M. Baur. 1993. Students' preconceptions of the nature of gases. *Journal of Research in*

Science Teaching 30: 587–597.

Ben-Zvi, R., B. S. Eylon, and J. Silberstein. 1986. Is an atom of copper malleable? *Journal of Chemical Education* 63: 64–66.

Bishop, B., and C. Anderson. 1990. Student conceptions of natural selection and its role in evolution. *Journal of Research in Science Teaching* 27: 415–427.

Brook, A., H. Briggs, and R. Driver. 1984. *Aspects of secondary students' understanding of the particulate nature of matter.* Leeds, England: University of Leeds, Centre for Studies in Science and Mathematics Education.

Brumby, M. N. 1984. Misconceptions about the concept of natural selection held by medical biological students. *Science Education* 68 (4): 493–503.

Champagne, A., R. Gunstone, and L. Klopfer. 1985. Instructional consequences of students' knowledge about physical phenomena. In *Cognitive structure and conceptual change,* eds. L. H. West and A. L. Pines, 61–90. Orlando, FL: Academic Press.

De Voss, W. 1990. Seven thoughts on teaching molecules. In *Relating macroscopic phenomena to microscopic particles,* eds. P. L. Lijnse, P. Licht, W. De Vos, and A. J. Waarlo. Utrecht, The Netherlands: University of Utrecht.

Driver, R., and J. Easley. 1978. Pupils and paradigms: A review of literature related to concept development in adolescent science students. *Studies in Science Education* 5: 61–84.

Engel-Clough, E., and C. Wood-Robinson. 1985. How secondary students interpret instances of biological adaptation. *Journal of Biological Education* 19: 125–130.

Engels, E., and R. Driver. 1981. Investigating pupils' understanding of aspects of pressure. In *Proceedings of the International Workshop on Problems Concerning Students' Representation of Physics and Chemistry Knowledge.* Ludwigsburg, Germany: Pedagogische Hochschule.

Feynman, R. 1977. *The Feynman lectures on physics.* Vol. 1. Reading, MA: Addison Wesley.

Gilbert, J. K., and D. J. Swift. 1985. Towards a Lakatosian analysis of the Piagetian and alternative conceptions research programs. *Science Education* 69 (5): 681–696.

Harvard-Smithsonian Center for Astrophysics. 1997. Lessons pulled from thin air. In *Minds of our own* [video documentary]. Program 2. New York: Annenberg/CPB.

Hawkins, D. 1992. Investigative arts: Science and teaching. Opening chairman's address to the Second International Conference on the History and Philosophy of Science and Science Teaching, Kingston, Ontario, Canada.

Jimenez-Aleixandre, M. P. 1992. Thinking about theories or thinking with theories? A classroom study with natural selection. *International Journal of Science Education* 14: 51–61.

Johnson, P. 1998a. Children's understanding of changes of state involving the gas state, part 2: Evaporation and condensation below boiling point. *International Journal of Science Education* 20: 695–709.

Johnson, P. 1998b. Progression in children's understanding of a "basic" particle theory: A longitudinal study. *International Journal of Science Education* 20: 393–412.

Johnston, K., and R. Driver. 1989. *A case study of teaching and learning about particle theory.* Leeds, England: University of Leeds, Centre for Studies in Science and Mathematics Education.

Kargbo D. B., E. D. Hobbs, and G. L. Erickson. 1980. Children's beliefs about inherited characteristics. *Journal of Biological Education* 14: 137–146.

Kesidou, S., and J. Roseman. 2002. How well do middle school science programs measure up? Findings from Project 2061's curriculum review. *Journal of Research in Science Teaching* 39: 522–549.

Kuhn, T. S. 1970. *The structure of scientific revolutions.* 2nd ed. Chicago: University of Chicago Press.

Lee, O., D. C. Eichinger, C. W. Anderson, G. D. Berkheimer, and T. D. Blakeslee. 1993. Changing middle school students' conceptions of matter and molecules. *Journal of Research in Science Teaching* 30: 249–270.

Margel, H., B. Eylon, and Z. Scherz. 2001. A longitudinal study of junior high school students' perceptions of the particulate nature of matter. In *Science and Technology Education: Preparing Future Citizens. 1st IOSTE Symposium in Southern Europe,* ed. N. Valanides. Paralimni, Cyprus: University of Cyprus.

National Research Council. 1996. *National science education standards.* Washington, DC: National Academy Press.

Novick, S., and J. Nussbaum. 1978. Junior high school pupils' understanding of the particulate nature of matter: An interview study. *Science Education* 62: 273–281.

Nussbaum, J. 1979. Children's conceptions of the Earth as a cosmic body: A cross-age study. *Science Education* 63 (1): 83–93.

Nussbaum, J. 1981. Towards the diagnosis by science teachers of pupils' misconceptions: An exercise with student teachers. *European Journal of Science Education* 3 (2): 159–169.

Nussbaum, J. 1985. The particulate nature of matter in the gaseous phase. In *Children's ideas in science,* eds. R. Driver, E. Guesne, and A. Tiberghien, 124–144. Milton Keynes, England: Open University Press.

Nussbaum, J. 1996. *The structure of matter: Vacuum and particles* [in Hebrew]. Rehovot, Israel: Weizmann Institute of Science.

Osborne, R. J., and M. M. Cosgrove. 1983. Children's conceptions of the changes of state of water. *Journal of Research in Science Teaching* 20: 825–838.

Piaget, J. 1970. *Genetic epistemology,* trans. E. Duckworth. New York: Delachaux et Niestlé.

Posner, G. J., K. A. Strike, P. W. Hewson, and W. A. Gertzog. 1982. Accommodation of a scientific conception: Toward a theory of conceptual change. *Science Education* 66 (2): 211–227.

Roth, K., and C. Anderson. 1987. *The power plant: Teacher's guide to photosynthesis.* Occasional Paper No. 112. East Lansing: Michigan State University, Institute for Research on Teaching.

Stavy, R. 1990. Children's conception of changes in the state of matter: From liquid (or solid) to gas. *Journal of Research in Science Teaching* 27: 247–266.

Stern, L., and A. Ahlgren. 2002. Analysis of students' assessments in middle school curriculum materials: Aiming precisely at benchmarks and standards. *Journal of Research in Science Teaching* 39: 889–910.

Stern, L., and G. Hagay. Manuscript in preparation. Teaching evolution through standards-based curriculum materials.

Stern, L., G. Hagay, C. Tsur, and S. Reisfeld. 2005. Evolution: How does it happen? A curricular unit for high school biology students. Department of Education in Technology and Science, Technion-IIT.

Stern, L., and J. Roseman. 2004. Can middle school science textbooks help students learn important ideas? Findings from Project 2061's curriculum evaluation study: Life science. *Journal of Research in Science Teaching* 41: 538–568.

Strike, K. A., and G. J. Posner. 1992. A revisionist theory of conceptual change. In *Philosophy of science, cognitive psychology and educational theory and practice,* eds. R. Duschl and R. Hamilton, 147–176. Albany, NY: SUNY Press.

Tamir, P., and A. Zohar. 1991. Anthropomorphism and teleology in reasoning about biological phenomena. *Science Education* 75: 57–67.

Wandersee, J. H. 1985. Can the history of science help science educators anticipate students' misconceptions? *Journal of Research in Science Teaching* 23: 581–597.

UNIT VII
Pre-College Science Instruction

Although the goals in Science for All Americans are meant to be achieved by high school graduation, few first- or second-year college students are likely to have built this kind of conceptual foundation. As a result, the recommendations in Science for All Americans can also serve as a logical starting place for identifying learning goals for college courses, especially for introductory courses and for students who are not science majors. —Jo Ellen Roseman and Mary Koppal

From the college faculty perspective, the time interval between their experience as first-year students and their students' experiences can be measured in lustra or decades. As a consequence, it is important to remember the variety of competing events and pressures that students face while adjusting to a different life in college. Science faculty need to understand why some students struggle during their first year so that faculty can act empathetically, provide as many opportunities for success as possible, improve faculty and student communication, and modify the science content and teaching methods to make them more relevant and interesting. —Wilson J. González-Espada and Rosita L. Napoleoni-Milán

In this wide-ranging analysis of the connection between high school science experiences and college performance, one common characteristic permeated the findings. Each significant predictor only made a fractional difference in students' college grades.... For college instructors, advisors, and administrators, the message is that high school learning experiences are highly relevant to college science success. However, there is no single indicator that will gauge college science success. —Robert H. Tai, Philip M. Sadler, and John F. Loehr

√II

For most college science teachers, the high school experience is a distant memory, and many of us have only a tenuous relationship with public schools and those who teach there. Yet, the intellectual and emotional foundations and learning habits established in the elementary and secondary grades have a direct and powerful influence on college science success. In this unit several authors discuss the high school science experience, including the implications of pre-college standards, the high-school-to-college transition, and the effect of several classroom teaching practices on achievement in college science courses.

Jo Ellen Roseman and Mary Koppal of the American Association for the Advancement of Science (AAAS) Project 2061 discuss the pre-college *science benchmarks and standards* and their implications for college science teachers. Acknowledging that many (perhaps most) high school graduates lack the level of scientific literacy prescribed in the benchmarks, Jo Ellen and Mary discuss the following steps that college science teachers should take to develop courses based on the K–12 experience of AAAS: identifying learning goals, taking account of students' preconceptions, developing learning activities, sequencing the activities, developing a set of meaningful questions, monitoring student progress, and trying out the activities and course components.

Wilson González-Espada of Arkansas Tech University and Rosita Napoleoni-Milán of the Russellville (Arkansas) Adult Education Center discuss critical issues in the *high-school-to-college transition in science.* Among the factors that affect performance in first-year college science courses, they describe differences between high school and college teaching methods; poor study habits; lack of academic preparation, intellectual ability, and problem-solving skills; the effects of complex social relationships; financial obligations; psychological issues; career decision-making issues; parental support; and the difference between high school culture and college culture. They conclude with a set of concise suggestions for college science teachers who wish to help students make this difficult transition.

Robert Tai of the University of Virginia, Philip Sadler of Harvard University, and John Loehr of the Chicago Public Schools describe a stratified, nationwide study that explored the *effects of high school science instruction on success in first-year college science courses.* Among the factors they explored were content of the high school science courses, instructional practices of high school teachers, the types and frequencies of laboratory experiences, emphasis on memorization versus understanding, degree of lesson structure, use of instructional technology, Advanced Placement course status, and students' mathematics background. The study found that each of these has a variable effect on first-year science achievement.

CHAPTER 32

Ensuring That College Graduates Are Science Literate:
Implications of K–12 Benchmarks and Standards

Jo Ellen Roseman and Mary Koppal

Jo Ellen Roseman is director of Project 2061 of the American Association for the Advancement of Science (AAAS). She earned a PhD in biochemistry at Johns Hopkins University and develops strategies and tools to improve the quality of K–12 science and mathematics teaching and learning. At Johns Hopkins University she designed and developed graduate degree programs for secondary school science teachers.

Mary Koppal is communications director of AAAS Project 2061. She earned a BA in English at the University of Maryland and pursues graduate studies at Johns Hopkins University in communication in contemporary society. At Project 2061, Mary is responsible for publishing and outreach activities.

Are college and university students getting what they need from their science courses? According to a study by Seymour and Hewitt of undergraduate science and engineering education, many students expressed general dissatisfaction with the quality of their course work and instruction. Seniors who were going to graduate with degrees in science or engineering fields reported that their "first two years had given them a shaky foundation for higher level work" and nonmajors felt that their need for basic understanding of science and mathematics had not been met (as cited in Advisory Committee to the National Science Foundation Directorate for Education and Human Resources 1996, p. 38). Findings from this study, along with similar statements from colleges and universities, public and private funding agencies, and scientific societies call attention to the need for reform of undergraduate science courses, particularly those at the introductory level and those intended for nonscience majors. In a 2002 synthesis of 17 years of reports from a range of organizations, Project Kaleidoscope emphasized their shared vision for reform of undergraduate science education:

The vision is of an environment in which all American undergraduates have access to learning experiences that motivate them to persist in their studies and consider careers in these fields; it is of an environment that brings undergraduates to an understanding of science and technology in their world. It is a vision that calls for attention to practices and policies that affect shaping the curriculum and building human and physical infrastructure to sustain strong programs. It is a vision that calls for collective action. (p. 1)

To make this vision a reality requires, among other things, a closer collaboration between higher-education institutions and the K–12 education system. Most educators and policy makers agree that there is a growing recognition of their interdependence. It is also clear that educators at both levels have knowledge and expertise that can be of benefit to the other. In recent years, this has led to the concept of a seamless K–16 continuum in which K–12 and higher-education institutions share common goals and accountability. At least half of all states have initiated some level of K–16 cooperation, particularly in the area of teacher education (Kirst and Usdan 2004).

This chapter draws on some fundamental lessons learned about science teaching and learning at the K–12 level that are likely to be applicable to a higher-education context. Recommendations are made in three areas that seem especially important to improving undergraduate science programs: (1) identifying the goals for learning, (2) designing a curriculum or sequence of learning activities that will enable students to achieve the goals, and (3) fostering a climate that will support continued monitoring, evaluation, and improvement over the long term. The chapter will highlight relevant K–12 tools and strategies that are consistent with a goals-based and learner-based approach to science teaching and learning. Working on their own or collectively, college and university faculty can use these strategies and tools to make progress in improving the content, teaching, and outcomes of undergraduate science education.

Since the mid-1980s, the reform of pre-college science education has focused in large part on science literacy: establishing it as a goal for all citizens, defining what constitutes science literacy for high school graduates and progress toward it for K–12 students, and developing teaching methods and materials that can help all students achieve it. At the same time, a small but growing body of research has enabled K–12 educators to base their reforms on credible findings about how learners develop and apply science knowledge and what that implies for the organization of content and selection of instructional strategies and materials. The American Association for the Advancement of Science (AAAS) with its Project 2061, the National Research Council (NRC), and the National Science Teachers Association (NSTA) have been among the organizations guiding these K–12 reforms. Their efforts have resulted in tools and strategies for specifying the science knowledge and skills that all students need and for promoting a standards-based approach to science teaching and learning. As these reform efforts continue to play out at the K–12 level, they also contribute to an ongoing reevaluation of the nature, purpose, and quality of science education at the undergraduate level.

Developing Goals for Undergraduate Science Learning

The idea of starting out with an end in mind is common in many endeavors, particularly in the design professions such as architecture, engineering, and the graphic arts (AAAS 2001b; Wiggins and McTighe 1998). In education, however, the content of the curriculum and how it is taught are more likely to have their origins in "textbooks, favored lessons, and time-honored activities rather than ... from targeted goals or standards" (Wiggins and McTighe 1998, p. 8). What is needed, say reformers, is precisely the reverse approach. By first establishing the purposes of a curriculum—whether for K–12 or university students—the task of identifying more specific goals for learning can take place within a framework where constraints and trade-offs can be considered carefully.

A K–12 Example

An example of this approach is the process used by AAAS's Project 2061 in its long-term effort to help reform K–12 science education. In the late 1980s, Project 2061 staff convened panels of scientists from across the disciplines to help define the end points—that is, what students should know and be able to do in science, mathematics, and technology after 13 years of schooling. As a first step, the scientific panels formulated a rationale for selecting a credible set of learning goals in the natural and social sciences, mathematics, and technology for all high school graduates (i.e., What would a science-literate adult need to know and be able to do in order to thrive in a world shaped by science and technology?). Next, they considered the degree of specificity that would be required (i.e., How much detail is needed to describe what students are intended to learn?). Finally, they addressed the feasibility of each goal (i.e., What will students actually be able to learn, given the real-world constraints of the classroom?). As will be described below (and in more detail in the works referenced in this section), this process took three years to complete, required substantial funding, and involved hundreds of scientists and educators and multiple levels of review (AAAS 2001b). The product of that effort—one that few college science departments would be willing or able to replicate—was Project 2061's report *Science for All Americans* (AAAS 1990b), which describes the knowledge and skills that science literacy would entail and ends with an agenda for action throughout the education system.

Among the report's recommendations is a call for colleges and universities to establish science literacy as a top priority and to "reshape undergraduate requirements as necessary to ensure that all graduates (from whom, after all, tomorrow's teachers will be drawn) leave with an understanding of science, mathematics, and technology that surpasses" what *Science for All Americans* recommends for high school graduates (1990b, p. 226). Although the goals in *Science for All Americans* are meant to be achieved by high school graduation, few first- or second-year college students are likely to have built this kind of conceptual foundation. As a result, the recommendations in *Science for All Americans* can also serve as a logical starting place for identifying learning goals for college courses, especially for introductory courses and for students who are not science majors.

Science for All Americans describes a coherent body of knowledge that characterizes adult science literacy. It is based on the belief that the science-literate person is one who is aware that science, mathematics, and technology are interdependent human enterprises with strengths and limitations; understands key laws and theories of science; is familiar with the natural world and recognizes both its diversity and unity; and uses scientific knowledge and scientific ways of thinking for individual and social purposes. The recommendations fall into four major categories:

- Chapters 1–3 deal with the nature of science, mathematics, and technology as human enterprises, and Chapter 10 illustrates the evolution and impact of scientific knowledge with examples of some of the great episodes in the history of the scientific endeavor.
- Chapters 4–9 cover basic knowledge about the world as currently seen from the perspective of science and mathematics and as shaped by technology.
- Chapter 11 presents some crosscutting themes that can serve as tools for thinking about how the world works.
- Chapter 12 lays out the habits of mind that are essential for science literacy.

Figure 32.1

Criteria for Selecting Goals for *Science for All Americans*

Utility: Will the proposed content—knowledge or skills—significantly enhance the graduate's long-term employment prospects? Will it be useful in making personal decisions?

Social Responsibility: Is the proposed content likely to help citizens participate intelligently in making social and political decisions on matters involving science and technology?

The Intrinsic Value of Knowledge: Does the proposed content present aspects of science, mathematics, and technology that are so important in human history or so pervasive in our culture that a general education would be incomplete without them?

Philosophical Value: Does the proposed content contribute to the ability of people to ponder the enduring questions of human meaning such as life and death, perception and reality, the individual good versus the collective welfare, certainty and doubt?

Childhood Enrichment: Will the proposed content enhance childhood (a time of life that is important in its own right and not solely for what it may lead to in later life)?

Source: Reprinted from American Association for the Advancement of Science. 1990. *Science for all Americans* (pp. xix–xx.). New York: Oxford University Press. © 1989, 1990 by the American Association for the Advancement of Science.

The recommendations in *Science for All Americans* are intended to apply to everyone, regardless of socioeconomic status or career choice. Selected by disciplinary experts, these science literacy goals represent a consensus of what the scientific community thought was important for all citizens to know. The panels were charged with making recommendations on what content in five domains—biological and health sciences, mathematics, physical and information sciences and engineering, social and behavioral sciences, and technology—is most worth learning by everyone. Panel members proposed the particular knowledge or skills that they believed to be especially important for all students to acquire by the time they graduated from high school. Such arguments as "It's in all the popular textbooks," "I remember learning it when I was in school," or "A Nobel laureate at my university agrees with me" were not adequate endorsements.

Proposals from panel members also had to be clear and unambiguous. For example, "Everyone should understand momentum" would not do; the proponent had to specify what it is about momentum that students would be expected to learn. Is it the general idea of momentum? Its calculation? Its conservation? Its applications? A proposed learning goal was added to the list of possibilities if, in the ensuing discussion, a persuasive case was made for it. Moreover, the case had to take into account the selection criteria that had been agreed to ahead of time (Figure 32.1). The criteria stipulated that learning goals must be important for individuals and important for society, that they must matter in the long run, and that they should define the knowledge and skills students will need for living interesting, socially responsible, and productive lives after leaving school.

In addition to their individual importance, the ideas described in *Science for All Americans* were chosen for their coherence as a set. Ideas that contributed to understanding other ideas were given high priority. But even after applying all of these criteria, the panelists found that there was much more worth knowing than students could be expected to learn in the K–12 years. Having a pre-established set of criteria helped, but that alone did not sufficiently narrow the range of possible content and skills. Curriculum designers at all levels face the same problem: It is simply not feasible to teach everything. Choices must be made and priorities set. How does one decide? Answering that question means choosing the best among many potentially valuable learning goals.

To create an integrated and coherent set of goals from all five of the scientific and technical domains, the panels presented their recommendations to each other and, based on the feedback they received, goals were revised, added, or eliminated. Subsequent drafts were reviewed extensively in an attempt to reduce the goals to a reasonable number. In this phase of the process, panelists asked: What is the relative importance of each idea to be learned in comparison with the other recommended learning goals? Eventually, the five panels issued their reports and then drew on them to create a single unified presentation of the recommendations for science literacy. The question of priority continued to surface both within and across the domains of science, mathematics, and technology. After individuals, scientific societies, educational associations, the National Council for Science and Technology Education, and the board of directors of AAAS had evaluated successive drafts, *Science for All Americans* emerged.

This intensive three-year process led to the formulation of a particular set of learning goals in science, mathematics, and technology, but it is not the only possible formulation. Other groups and other individuals using a similar process would be likely to produce different, but equally valid, sets of learning goals. The point is that the goals derive their validity from a process that generates a broad consensus of expert opinion, provides adequate time for debate and review, and focuses that debate on predefined criteria for selecting appropriate goals.

In 1993, the recommendations for adult science literacy in *Science for All Americans* were elaborated by Project 2061 into a set of specific statements of the ideas and skills that students should learn by the end of grades 2, 5, 8, and 12. Published as *Benchmarks for Science Literacy* (AAAS 1993), these goals provide guidance to educators as they plan and deliver instruction to students, to curriculum developers as they create new instructional materials, and to assessment specialists as they devise ways to evaluate what students know and are able to do. In 1996 the NRC completed a similar multiyear process and published its learning goals as content standards in *National Science Education Standards* (*NSES*; NRC 1996). With considerable overlap between the learning goals in *Benchmarks for Science Literacy* and *NSES*, these two documents represent a strong national consensus on the science that is most important for all students to learn (NRC 2003). From this point on, when we speak of learning goals, we will be referring to the kinds of statements that are found in *Benchmarks for Science Literacy* and *NSES*.

Coherence Is Key

Helping students to develop an interconnected, coherent understanding of science is a central premise of the reform efforts of Project 2061, the NRC, NSTA, and others. To move students toward this level of understanding requires, at the very least, a set of learning goals that are themselves coherent in their logic and structure. Bruner's view on this is apt: "The only possible way in which individual knowledge can keep proportional pace with the surge of available knowledge is through a grasp of the relatedness of knowledge" (1995, p. 333).

Organizing content to emphasize connections both within and across subject areas and grade levels can contribute to the coherence of an entire curriculum and, ultimately, to students' ability to make sense of new ideas and to fit them into their own developing conceptual frameworks. Consider, for example, a central lesson that researchers are drawing from their analyses of data collected for the Third International Mathematics and Science Study (TIMSS). As part of this massive study of K–12 science and mathematics achievement worldwide, researchers considered the coherence of content standards in the top-ranked countries and concluded that coherence in standards is critical:

> *Understanding implies, at least at some level, that the structure of the discipline has become visible to the learner so she or he can move beyond its particulars. We suggest that one way to facilitate such learning is by making the inherent logical structure of the discipline more visible both to teachers and students.* (Schmidt, Wang, and McKnight 2005, p. 554)

This view is also prevalent among those who develop and study K–12 science curriculum materials, and there appears to be a growing consensus that a curriculum or set of goals that attends closely to coherence—in terms of content presentation and learning progressions—is more likely to help students gain deeper and more sophisticated understandings over time (Catley, Lehrer, and Reiser 2004; Commission on Behavioral and Social Sciences and Education 2000; Smith et al. 2004).

The challenge is to make Bruner's "relatedness of knowledge" apparent to educators and to help them appreciate the elegance and simplicity of the fundamental ideas that undergird modern science. In response to this need for coherence, Project 2061 has produced a set of coordinated tools—each with a different purpose and perspective—that is focused on the same coherent set of science learning goals. In *Science for All Americans*, for example, Project 2061 presents more than 60 major topics in science, mathematics, and technology, setting out the central concepts and principles and showing how these threads are woven into the larger story of science literacy. In *Benchmarks for Science Literacy* (and in *NSES* as well), these same topics are unpacked into discrete ideas distributed into sequential K–12 grade bands to show appropriate steps toward science literacy. And in *Atlas of Science Literacy* (AAAS 2001a), these topics are further delineated in "strand maps" that emphasize conceptual developmental connections.

Used during the drafting of *Benchmarks for Science Literacy*, early versions of the strand maps (such as the one in Figure 32.2) helped the development teams think about how students make progress toward the adult literacy goals in *Science for All Americans* and how that progression might take place over the course of grades K–12. These early maps displayed connections among ideas both within a grade band and over time and were intended to facilitate the work of the teachers, researchers, and scientists who were working on *Benchmarks for Science Literacy*. It soon became apparent that the maps were also useful tools for curriculum and textbook adoption committees and for developers of instructional and assessment materials. Project 2061 has now completed a collection of nearly 50 maps and published them in *Atlas of Science Literacy* (AAAS 2001a). Each map focuses on a topic important for science literacy and shows the benchmarks—from primary school to high school—that students need to achieve as they build their understanding of the topic. Maps also depict relationships among benchmarks, us-

Figure 32.2

Example of How Concepts in *Science for All Americans* Related to a Particular Topic (in This Case, the Structure of Matter) Were Backmapped to Develop a Coherent Set of Grade Range Benchmarks

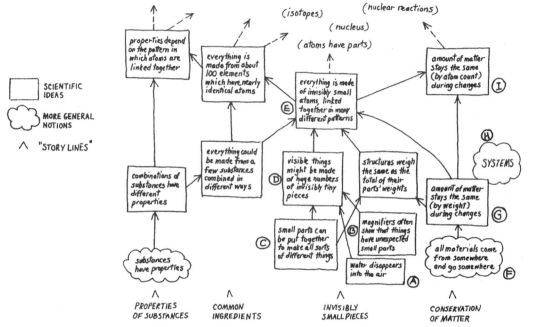

Reprinted from American Association for the Advancement of Science. 1993. *Benchmarks for science literacy* (p. 306). New York: Oxford University Press. © 1993 by the American Association for the Advancement of Science.

ing arrows to suggest how benchmarks in the earlier grades support those that come later (see Figure 32.3 for an example of an *Atlas* strand map).

To illustrate how Project 2061's tools are related and designed to present science concepts as part of a coherent story rather than as isolated bits of information, consider how they deal with the topic of conservation. *Science for All Americans* explicitly introduces this topic in the context of the flow of matter and energy in living systems:

> *However complex the workings of living organisms, they share with all other natural systems the same physical principles of the conservation and transformation of matter and energy. Over long spans of time, matter and energy are transformed among living things, and between them and the physical environment. In these grand-scale cycles, the total amount of matter and energy remains constant, even though their form and location undergo continual change.* (AAAS 1990b, p. 66)

Science for All Americans also presents the topic in a historical context, describing the work of Lavoisier and the law of conservation of mass:

> *He showed that when substances burn, there is no net gain or loss of weight. When wood burns, for example, the carbon and hydrogen in it combine with oxygen from the air to form water vapor and*

carbon dioxide, both invisible gases that escape into the air. The total weight of materials produced by burning (gases and ashes) is the same as the total weight of the reacting materials (wood and oxygen). (AAAS 1990b, p. 154)

Other sections explain the atomic structure of matter, making it clear that high school graduates should understand chemical reactions and the recycling of matter in terms of atoms and molecules. The following sections in *Science for All Americans* address the fundamental concept of conservation:

- 4D. Structure of Matter (pp. 46–47): Matter consists of a small number of "atomic" building blocks that combine and recombine.
- 5E. Flow of Matter and Energy (p. 66): Matter is conserved in living organisms—that is, though its form and location change, elements are recycled.
- 11C. Constancy and Change (pp. 173–174): Conservation is a property of closed systems.
- 10C. Relating Matter and Energy and Time and Space (p. 151): Matter is a form of energy, so mass/energy conservation holds even in nuclear reactions.
- 10F. Understanding Fire (pp. 153–155): Lavoisier's careful measurements demonstrate mass conservation in the burning process.
- 4B. The Earth (p. 44): Some of the earth's resources are nonrenewable.
- 3C. Issues in Technology (p. 33): Nonrenewable resources can be depleted or contaminated.
- 8B. Materials and Manufacturing (p. 112): Matter doesn't "disappear," so waste disposal can be a problem.

The information in these sections reflects Project 2061's vision of the *lasting* knowledge that students should acquire by the time they become adults and can serve as a guide for identifying college-level learning goals related to the concept of conservation.

In *Benchmarks for Science Literacy* and in *NSES*, the idea of mass conservation is listed explicitly as a learning goal for middle school students. *Benchmarks* also expects middle school students to understand conservation in terms of atoms and molecules:

Benchmarks: *No matter how substances within a closed system interact with one another, or how they combine or break apart, the total mass of the system remains the same. The idea of atoms explains the conservation of matter: If the number of atoms stays the same no matter how they are rearranged, then their total mass stays the same.* (AAAS 1993, p. 78)

NSES: *Substances react chemically in characteristic ways with other substances to form new substances (compounds) with different characteristic properties. In chemical reactions, the total mass is conserved.* (NRC 1996, p. 154)

Both the *Benchmarks* and *NSES* versions of the learning goal assume that middle school students will already understand that materials can exist in different states and that water can go back and forth between states (AAAS 1993, pp. 67–68; NRC 1996, p. 127).

Figure 32.3 shows the conservation of matter strand map from *Atlas of Science Literacy*. It

NATIONAL SCIENCE TEACHERS ASSOCIATION

Figure 32.3

Structure of Matter: Conservation of Matter Strand Map

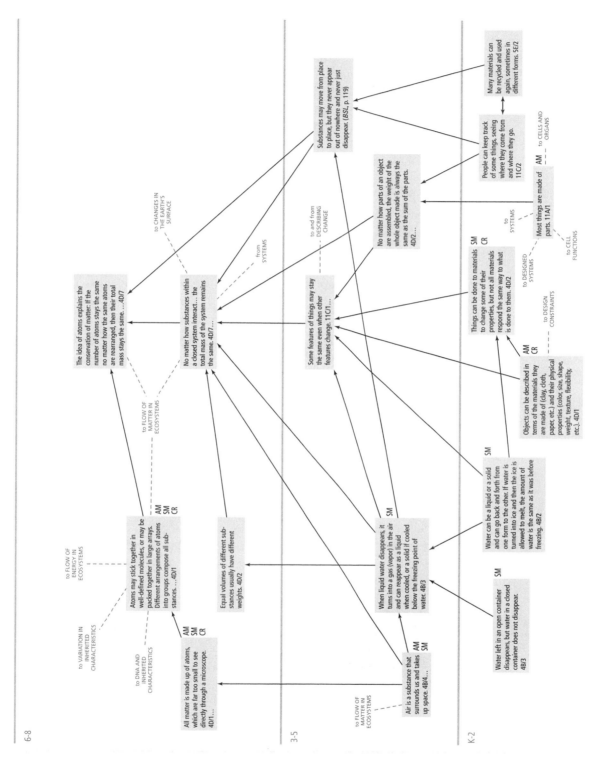

culminates in middle school with the benchmark shown above. The two ideas in the benchmark (mass conservation of substances and its explanation in terms of atoms) are displayed in two separate boxes to distinguish their precursors. This map is unusual because it does not include high school benchmarks. In other *Atlas* maps, however, this middle school benchmark dealing with conservation provides a foundation for high school benchmarks related to the transformation and conservation of matter and energy in ecosystems and the interconversion of matter and energy in nuclear reactions.

With appropriate interest and funding, university faculty could undertake a similar process to articulate a coherent set of learning goals for college programs and courses. Several foundations have supported efforts to rethink and revise undergraduate courses in the past, some of which have resulted in elaborate and interesting course syllabi (e.g., the New Liberal Arts Program funded by the Alfred P. Sloan Foundation in the 1980s, the Project on Liberal Education and the Sciences funded by the Carnegie Corporation of New York [AAAS 1990a], and the National Science Foundation's Collaboratives for Excellence in Teacher Preparation [CETP] program in the 1990s). It was through such funding that Dr. Katherine Denniston of Towson University, along with other science faculty from across the University of Maryland System, developed new science courses such as the biosciences course that is described later in this chapter. The National Science Foundation's Course, Curriculum, and Laboratory Improvement (CCLI) program and the Department of Education's Fund for Improvement of Postsecondary Education (FIPSE) and its Mathematics-Science Partnerships program currently support such efforts. In addition, some universities may offer incentives and support for individuals and department teams engaged in curriculum reform and development projects.

Based on his experience working with Project 2061 to foster closer ties between science faculty and education faculty at Towson University, Laurence Boucher, who was then dean of the College of Science and Mathematics, suggested that a "mini-grant program to provide seed money" for new course development and pilot studies would be "a strong motivating factor for faculty" (Boucher, manuscript in preparation). To help engage Towson faculty in reform efforts, Boucher offered modest stipends to those who were willing to engage in specific tasks such as reviewing new curriculum materials and analyzing courses.

Faculty can work individually or as teams, but there may be more lasting effects if several members of a department are involved. For interdisciplinary courses in particular, it makes sense to involve faculty from all of the relevant departments in designing learning goals for the course. Organizations such as Project Kaleidoscope and scientific societies such as the American Institute of Biological Sciences or the American Association of Physics Teachers often promote and facilitate such collaborations among their members.

Applying a K–12 Process for Undergraduate Course Design

Good designs do not happen by accident. Designing a course, like designing a skyscraper or a highway exit or a garden, needs to be both purposeful and deliberate. Basic design principles drawn from other areas such as engineering or architecture can be helpful. The basic proposition of *Designs for Science Literacy*, Project 2061's guide to curriculum reform, is that "treating curriculum reform as a design problem will contribute significantly to the achievement of the ambitious goals of science literacy" (AAAS 2001b, p. 1). *Designs* points out that course design must be undertaken within a "context of purposes—or goals—and constraints" (AAAS 2001, p. 44). In this section, we describe and illustrate some key steps in any design process that aims to serve the needs of students and the goals of science literacy. Variations of this process are currently being used by several K–12 curriculum developers, and their research is helping to identify its most promising features and applications (Heller 2001; Reiser et al. 2003). Summarized in the following steps, the process can be readily adapted for college course design:

- Identify a coherent set of learning goals as a foundation for your design. Articulate the most important ideas you want your students to remember long after your course has ended.
- Take account of where your students are starting from by becoming familiar with the research base (if one exists) on preconceptions and misconceptions that students commonly have on the topics that your course will address.
- Develop learning activities around phenomena and representations that focus students' attention on the ideas in the learning goals and are likely to help them make progress.
- Sequence the activities carefully, deciding which need to be firsthand or vicarious, how each will be used, and the role each will play in promoting students' understanding.
- Develop meaningful questions to help students relate course activities to the scientific ideas they are expected to learn.
- Monitor students' progress carefully, using assessments that are well aligned to the learning goals of your course and effective in probing precisely what students do and do not know.
- Try out the activities and other course components, assess what students have learned and why, and determine what modifications should be made in the course design.

This basic process is repeated several times, with each round of revision based on feedback from students' assessment responses. More iterative than linear, these cycles of testing and refining all aspects of the course are integrated into the development process itself. Underlying the process is the assumption that students will learn more if their instruction is focused on a coherent set of specific ideas rather than a collection of loosely related ideas that fall into a broad topic area. Clear definition of the most important ideas allows for more precise curriculum design and assessment of student outcomes, which can then lead to more informed revisions.

Faculty can use this basic process for the design of any course—from an integrated science course for nonmajors to an advanced physics course for majors—as long as the learning goals are clearly stated. At The George Washington University, for example, science faculty are working with Project 2061 to develop a set of advanced-level courses for a new master's degree program for professional studies in middle grades science. They are using the process outlined above to design their courses around the 12th-grade learning goals for physical, life, and Earth science topics included in *Benchmarks for Science Literacy*.

Every step in the design process contributes value to the end product. We have already dealt with the first step of identifying an appropriate set of learning goals for a course. In the following subsections, we will consider in more detail three steps that are central to this course design process. We will also point out instances where faculty can take advantage of K–12 tools and resources created by Project 2061 and others to facilitate their course development work.

Take Account of Where Students Are

In an ideal world, students would arrive at colleges and universities with a solid knowledge of the ideas in *Science for All Americans*. University courses could then present students with opportunities to learn more sophisticated ideas that build on their prior knowledge. For ex-

ample, with a solid understanding of matter conservation and its explanation in terms of atoms, college students could apply those ideas to writing balanced chemical equations or to explaining the role of various organisms (including humans) in the cycling of nitrogen in the biosphere. They could be expected to be able to trace various paths of nitrogen from its reservoir in the atmosphere, through its conversion to nitrates and ammonia, their incorporation into proteins and nucleic acids in cells of various living organisms, the production of nitrogen oxides in factories and its contribution to acid rain, and so forth. College students could also apply conservation ideas to understanding the role of bedrock as a reservoir of phosphate in the phosphorus cycle and be expected to be able to describe its course through processes of erosion and deposition, uptake by microorganisms and plant roots, its incorporation into the molecules that make up living things, such as DNA and adenosine triphosphate (ATP), and how it eventually becomes reincorporated into bedrock.

Unfortunately, this scenario is rare. College and university freshmen often arrive with inadequate knowledge and skills and exhibit misconceptions similar to those of middle and high school students. In her work with Project 2061 on a study of undergraduate science education funded by the John D. and Catherine T. MacArthur Foundation, Towson University professor Denniston observed that few students entering her biology classes, including biology majors, had achieved even the eighth-grade benchmarks related to heredity and evolution (Denniston, manuscript in preparation). A number of other university science faculty who have attended Project 2061 workshops have made similar comments about their students. Denniston reported another experience as she began to encounter former students in her more advanced classes:

> *My own introductory biology students came into my medical microbiology class with an appalling lack of understanding of the biological principles that I had taught them. Student evaluations notwithstanding, I had somehow failed to help these students learn.... Why weren't my students learning?* (Denniston, manuscript in preparation)

Of course, Denniston is not alone in her realization that learning is not always the result of teaching and that other factors may be getting in the way of students' understanding. Harvard physics professor Eric Mazur describes his experience in dealing with his students' learning difficulties:

> *Students enter their first physics course possessing strong beliefs and intuitions about common physical phenomena. These notions are derived from personal experiences and color students' interpretations of material presented in the introductory course. Instruction does very little to change these "common-sense" beliefs.... When asked, for instance, to compare the forces in a collision between a heavy truck and a light car, a large fraction of the class firmly believes the heavy truck exerts a larger force on the light car than vice versa. My first reaction was, "Not my students ...!" I was intrigued, however, and [tested my own students]. The results of the test were undeniably eye-opening.* (quoted in Richardson 2005, pp. 19–20)

To find out where students "are" in their understanding of particular concepts, it would make sense to ask them outright. But it is not usually as straightforward as that, particularly where abstract ideas are concerned. What is more, students are rarely expected to reflect on their own learning, so they are often ill equipped to provide useful feedback on where they are in their conceptual development. We can, however, gain helpful insights about starting points for teaching and learning from logical backmapping of learning goals and from research on students' misconceptions about specific science topics. (By "backmapping" we mean a process for working backward from the desired learning goals for high school graduates to identify conceptual steps that students would need to make in the earlier grades to achieve those goals.)

With the likelihood that incoming students may not have achieved even a high school level of science literacy, it makes sense to define appropriate outcomes for courses by first examining the relevant middle and high school benchmarks. Denniston (manuscript in preparation) describes departmental recommendations and her state's core learning goals for high school students as major influences on her choice of topics for her introductory bioscience course. Through her participation in the Project 2061 study, she became acquainted with *Science for All Americans* and *Benchmarks for Science Literacy* and was able to compare her course's content to the learning goals in those documents. She found them to be consistent and found the K–12 benchmarks helpful in elaborating a more detailed set of content objectives. In some cases, the content objectives mirror benchmarks (e.g., "know that mutations of the DNA alter the proteins that are produced; these may alter the phenotype of the organism or cell or kill it"). In other cases, she chose to hold her students to higher expectations (e.g., expecting them to know *how*—rather than just *that*—the structure of DNA encodes genetic information and *how* the genotype of an organism or cell is responsible for the phenotype of the organism or cell). Denniston points out that because college students are likely to have a stronger grasp of chemistry, they may be better able to appreciate the mechanisms of these processes than they are as 9th or 10th graders, when they typically take high school biology. Thus, through this backmapping process, Denniston was able to develop a logical learning trajectory for her students, setting goals that would build on what they were likely to have achieved by the end of high school.

After comparing college-level outcomes with middle and high school benchmarks, a next step is to determine what ideas their own students are likely to have about the topics to be covered in the course. This involves examining relevant learning research, if research has been published on the topic, and probing students' ideas with appropriate assessment tasks. For the topic of conservation of matter, for example, several research studies have shed light on some common student preconceptions and misconceptions. The available research on this topic has been summarized and accompanies the Conservation of Matter strand map in *Atlas of Science Literacy*:

Students cannot understand conservation of matter and weight if they do not understand what matter is, or accept weight as an intrinsic property of matter, or distinguish between weight and density (Lee et al., 1993; Stavy, 1990). By 5th grade, many students can understand qualitatively that matter is conserved in transforming from solid to liquid. They also start to understand that matter is quantitatively conserved in transforming from solid to liquid and qualitatively in transforming from solid or liquid to gas—if the gas is visible (Stavy, 1990). For chemical reactions, especially those that evolve or absorb gas, weight conservation is more difficult for students to grasp (Stavy, 1990). (AAAS 2001a, p. 56)

Other sources of research on middle and high school students on this topic and other topics can be found in *Making Sense of Secondary Science* (Driver et al. 1994), in *Benchmarks for Science Literacy* (AAAS 1993; see Chapter 15, "The Research Base"), and in *Atlas of Science Literacy*, where summaries of the available research accompany each of the conceptual strand maps (AAAS 2001a).

Evidence from research studies indicates that for some topics, at least, many students retain their earlier misconceptions, even at the college level (Berkheimer, Anderson, and Spees 1990). Research on college students' understanding of specific science topics is available in professional journals such as *Journal of College Science Teaching*, *Journal of Chemical Education*, and *Journal of Research in Science Teaching*. In addition to providing research findings that shed light on students' ideas, the research articles are a potential source of assessment tasks that may be useful for probing students' initial ideas about a topic. A typical article, for example, is one from *Journal of Chemical Education* that explores the nature of misconceptions about hydrogen bonding that are common among college-level students (Henderleiter et al. 2001). Although hydrogen bonding is a basic principle with applications in all areas of chemistry, the study finds that even in their second year of college chemistry, some students

> *still possess misconceptions found in younger, less experienced students. They have not abandoned— or have even formed—faulty beliefs, such as hydrogen bonds can be induced, intermolecular forces lead to reactions, or boiling breaks covalent bonds. These misconceptions make it difficult, if not impossible, for students to apply chemical concepts to data interpretation and analysis. Reliance on rote memorization as a means to analyze and interpret data is also problematic.* (Henderleiter et al. 2001, p. 1129)

This article includes the assessment tasks and interview questions the researchers used to probe the students' understanding, along with recommendations for some specific instructional strategies and activities designed to help students overcome their misconceptions and foster their analytical and problem-solving skills.

Even if research provides insights into ideas that students often have about a topic, it is still useful to find out firsthand whether your students have those same ideas. When research is not available, it is especially important to identify appropriate assessments or use other strategies that can effectively probe students' thinking. Interviewing a subset of students on a few questions at the outset can help uncover particularly prevalent or challenging misconceptions. For example, the following questions could be used to probe students' initial ideas about conservation:

Question 1: Jill is investigating the reaction between baking soda and vinegar. She places vinegar in one cup and baking soda in a second cup. Then she places both of the cups on a balance. The balance with the two cups, baking soda, and vinegar reads 120 grams. Then she pours the vinegar into the cup with the baking soda. The baking soda and vinegar react and produce a gas. She places both cups back on the balance. Do you think the balance will read 120 grams after the chemical reaction? Why?

As a follow-up, ask your students how they could modify the procedure so that the reverse of what they said occurred. For those responding that the balance would still read 120 grams, ask, "Is there a way to change Jill's procedure to make the reading change? How?" For those responding that the balance would not read 120 grams, ask, "Is there a way to change Jill's procedure to make the reading stay the same? How?"

Question 2: Which of the following is a possible chemical reaction? Explain your choice(s) and why you think each of the other choices are not possible.
   A. $CuSO_4 \nrightarrow CuSO_4$
   B. $O_2 + CO_2 \nrightarrow CO_2 + O_2$
   C. $NaOH + HCl \nrightarrow NaCl + H_2O$
   D. $O_2 \nrightarrow H_2$

In designing her bioscience courses, Towson University's Denniston built in several strategies for identifying her students' misconceptions. Using questions to accompany reading assignments, classroom exercises in which student groups were asked to explain their understanding of a topic before it has been studied, periodic assignments in which students were asked to write down their current understanding of a targeted concept, and weekly e-mail journals in which students reflected on their learning, Denniston was able to uncover potential problems:

One misconception identified in this way is that students may understand chromosomal events of meiosis (separation of homologous chromosomes into daughter cells) and fertilization (joining new combinations of chromosomes from two parents) and yet have no concept that these random events are the basis for using probability to predict the outcome of genetic crosses. (Denniston, n.d., p. 27)

With those insights, Denniston made changes in the structure of the course and added instructional activities that would address her students' misconceptions head-on. Each year she was able to refine her course further based on the progress her students were making in their understanding.

Develop Activities and Relevant Phenomena

Much of the point of science is explaining real-world phenomena in terms of a small number of ideas. For students to understand and appreciate the explanatory power of scientific ideas, they need to have a sense of the range of phenomena that they can explain and predict. *Benchmarks* and *NSES* present expectations for K–12 students in terms of empirical generalizations and accepted theories. However, neither document presents specific phenomena to illustrate the empirical generalizations or the explanatory power of the theories, leaving decisions about which phenomena are most appropriate to designers of curriculum and instruction. These decisions must take into account the nature of the knowledge or skill to be learned, what is known about difficulties students may have in learning them, and the resources that are likely to be available to students and teachers in the classroom. For example, to enable students to learn the ideas associated with the concept of conservation, a curriculum designer might decide that students should observe a range of phenomena, including phenomena they might encounter in the real world, and that the set of phenomena should include both changes of state and chemical reactions that have gases as reactants or products. Where possible, the reactions should involve simple molecules.

With these kinds of design constraints in mind, the developers of *Chemistry That Applies*, an instructional unit for grades 8–10 produced by the Michigan Science Education Resources Project (1993), focused on matter conservation and included phenomena to illustrate both mass conservation and how the atomic theory accounts for mass conservation. The unit presented students with a range of relevant phenomena: the distillation and decomposition of water; the reaction of calcium chloride with potassium carbonate, of Alka-Seltzer with water, and of baking soda with vinegar; the oxidation of butane; and the rusting of iron. Students first examined reactions involving only solids and liquids and observed that the mass did not change. In examining reactions involving gases, students observed that the mass did not change as long as matter was not allowed to enter or escape from the system.

Students then revisited these same reactions, representing and accounting for their observations using ball-and-stick models of the molecules involved. When considering mass conservation, the developers sequenced the phenomena to postpone consideration of gases until students had observed mass conservation with solids and liquids and to postpone consideration of gaseous reactants until students had experience with gaseous products. In contrast, when considering the atomic explanation for mass conservation, the developers sequenced phenomena to give students experience with simpler molecular recombinations before encountering more complex ones. Additional details about *Chemistry That Applies* and Project 2061's analysis of its content and instructional quality are available at *www.project2061.org/events/meetings/textbook/ literacy/cdrom/CTA/CONTENT/CAcon.htm*; analyses of other middle and high school curriculum materials are available at *www.project2061.org/publications/textbook/default.htm?ql.*

Choosing appropriate phenomena and incorporating them effectively into course work can be as challenging for college faculty as it is for K–12 teachers. Considerations include not only the alignment of phenomena with the ideas that are to be learned but also the use of pedagogical strategies that can help students see the connections between the phenomena and those ideas. For its evaluations of middle and high school textbooks, Project 2061 developed criteria for judging the effectiveness of the phenomena presented in the textbooks in helping students learn specific science concepts and skills. These same criteria can be applied by faculty when making decisions about phenomena and how to use them to further their students' learning. Shaped by both research and teacher craft, the criteria offer faculty a framework for constructing science courses that

- engage students in a variety of vivid firsthand (if possible) experiences with phenomena that are relevant to the ideas that are to be learned,
- link the phenomena (along with related vocabulary and representations) explicitly to the ideas that are to be learned, and
- provide opportunitites and guidance to help students make sense of the phenomena and the ideas.

Even with these criteria as a guide, it may still be difficult to incorporate phenomena into a course design. In the case of middle and high school science textbooks, for example, Project 2061's evaluation studies found that most texts did not do a good job of presenting an adequate variety of appropriate phenomena (particularly in life science) to illustrate the ideas that students were to learn. Consider the following examples of activities designed for middle school students and their alignment (or lack thereof) to the idea that plants use the energy from light to make "energy-rich" sugars from carbon dioxide and water:

An activity in which students separate plant pigments through paper chromatography may fit with the general topic of photosynthesis but does not align with the substance [of this idea about matter and energy transformation].... The pigment chromatography activity could be used to explain the basis for the color change of leaves in the fall because it shows that even green leaves containing the pigments for their fall colors. However, the activity won't be useful for explaining the very important ideas … stated above and, hence, would not be judged to align with them…. Neither [would] an activity in which plants are shown to grow toward the light nor an activity in which students read about and discuss the light-capturing step in photosynthesis address the sophistication of the idea that plants use light…. The former activity addresses the less sophisticated idea that plants need light (grades 3-5), and the latter addresses the more sophisticated idea that a chlorophyll molecule can be excited to a higher-energy configuration by sunlight (grades 9-12). (Roseman and Stern 2003, pp. 271–272; © 2003 by Springer-Verlag, New York, Inc.)

In contrast to these poorly aligned activities, one that is well aligned with the middle school idea about matter transformation might

direct students to use diabetic strips to show that sugar is present in iris leaves grown in the presence of CO_2 but not in its absence. An experiment in which sugar (or starch) is detected on leaves grown in open jars, but is detected only in the first few hours on similar leaves grown in closed jars, would also be aligned. (Stern and Roseman 2001, p. 55)

To help provide educators with a wider variety of resources that can be used with confidence to teach important science ideas, Project 2061 is building an online annotated database of relevant phenomena that are well aligned to national learning goals. The database includes full descriptions of phenomena for more than a dozen important topics, including the solar system, conservation of matter, laws of motion, flow of matter in ecosystems, molecular basis of heredity, and natural selection. These same topics are also central to the science framework being developed for the National Assessment of Educational Progress (NAEP), scheduled to be administered to students beginning in 2009. In some cases, the descriptions in the database include references to detailed activities related to the phenomena or to research studies that shed light on the science itself or on the utility of the phenomena as teaching resources. Although the phenomena are being selected with K–12 teachers and curriculum developers in mind, they are likely to be useful in the design of college-level introductory science courses or courses for nonscience majors. Table 32.1 presents examples of phenomena that could be used to help students in grades 6–16 understand important ideas about matter and energy transformation in living systems ("A Jump-Start" 2004).

Monitor Students' Progress

Finding out what students are learning as a result of instruction is an essential element of any effort to improve curriculum and teaching. Currently, assessment of student learning at the K–12 level plays a much more prominent role as an accountability measure than it does as a diagnostic tool. Nevertheless, research suggests that monitoring students' progress has the potential to promote learning (Stern and Ahlgren 2002) by providing teachers with data that allows them to diagnose problems their students are having and make appropriate adjustments in their instructional strategies. Assessment of student progress is also a powerful tool for curriculum designers, and this application of assessment will be discussed later in this chapter.

At the college level, most institutions focus on students' course evaluations (which may or may not ask students to report on what they have learned) as a primary measure of success for

Table 32.1

Examples of Phenomena Related to Ideas About Matter and Energy Transformations in Living Systems

Idea	Phenomena That Could Be Used to Illustrate This Idea
Plants make sugar molecules from carbon dioxide (in the air) and water, releasing oxygen as a by-product.	• Sugars can be detected in tissues of a variety of plants, such as sugar beets, onion bulbs, and corn. • Sugar levels are reduced or absent in onion bulbs that are sprouted in the absence of carbon dioxide. • Radioautographs of *Chlorella* (a unicellular green algae) grown in the presence of $^{14}CO_2$ show ^{14}carbon in various organic compounds, including sugars.
Plants break down the sugars they have synthesized back into carbon dioxide and water, use them as building materials, or store them for later use.	• Carbon dioxide can be detected in the presence of seeds germinated in the dark but not in the presence of dry seeds. • Geranium leaves kept in the dark for 24 hours have reduced levels of starch, compared with light-grown plants; and corn leaves have reduced levels of sugar. • Chlorella originally grown in the presence of $^{14}CO_2$ release $^{14}CO_2$ and show reduced amounts of ^{14}carbon in various organic compounds, including sugars. • Air, water, and minerals are the only substances given to a hydroponically grown tomato plant, yet it grows and produces structures that look different from these inputs. Furthermore, the plant weighs more than the water and minerals it uses. • If leaves of daffodil bulbs are removed in the spring, the bulbs show less increase in mass by fall than bulbs with leaves left on. The smaller bulbs usually don't produce flowers the next season.

a course or for an instructor's performance. But, as the work of McDermott and the Physics Education Group has shown, "when student learning is used as a criterion,… the outcome is often quite disappointing. Systematic investigations have demonstrated that the gap between what is taught and what is learned is often greater than many instructors realize" (Herron, Shaffer, and McDermott 2005, p. 33). While surveys of students' attitudes about their courses may provide a certain kind of useful feedback, they will not yield the information that is needed to modify instruction to improve students' learning. What is needed are assessments that are carefully linked to the ideas and skills being taught so that judgments about what students do or do not know can be made with a high degree of certainty and specificity. With this learning data in hand, instructors can begin to modify their courses and their teaching to respond to the needs of their students.

For its studies of middle and high school science textbooks, Project 2061 developed criteria for considering how well each book's assessment tasks aligned with the targeted ideas and how well those assessments measured students' understanding of those same ideas (Stern and Ahlgren 2002). Drawing on its textbook evaluations, Project 2061 has now articulated more fully a set of criteria and a procedure for analyzing and profiling assessment items for their alignment with content standards and for other characteristics that affect their usefulness in providing information about what students know about specific ideas. The procedure considers (1) whether the ideas in the content standard are *needed* to complete the assessment task successfully or if the task can be completed without them, and (2) whether those ideas are *enough by themselves* or if other ideas and skills are required. The procedure also involves analyzing assessment items for their comprehensibility; susceptibility to test-wise solution strategies; bias related to gender, class, race, and ethnicity; and appropriateness of the task context.

Project 2061's criteria and procedures are being used to study assessment items of all types—from selected-response items such as multiple-choice questions to more involved performance tasks—and to analyze items for both diagnostic and evaluative purposes. Although Project 2061's approach to assessment analysis does not deal with the psychometric implications of an item, it does help to articulate exactly what is being tested by a particular item, thus improving the validity of interpretations that can be made from performance results.

Using these analytical tools to screen items released from state, national, and international tests and to develop some completely new items, Project 2061 is creating an online bank of more than 300 science and mathematics assessment items for use in grades 6–10. Supported by a grant from the National Science Foundation, the collection will allow users to search for items that are well aligned to learning goals in *Benchmarks for Science Literacy, NSES,* and the content standards of nearly every state. Each item in the collection is also being reviewed for its suitability for use with a wide range of students, including English-language learners (De-Boer 2005).

These high-quality items are likely to be of interest to college faculty who want to determine what their incoming students know prior to instruction. The items can also be used by faculty as models for developing or selecting test items that are aligned to the content they are teaching and responsive to the unique characteristics of their students. In the end, of course, the quality of any test—whether at the K–12 or college level—comes down to the specific tasks that students are asked to perform. We know that not every idea that is taught can be tested and that one item, or even one set of items, can never provide complete confidence that students understand or do not understand an idea. Nonetheless, every item should contribute some knowledge of what students do or do not understand.

To help guide decisions about what and how to test, Project 2061 has found that mapping the ideas and skills that are associated with a particular benchmark or standard can be a powerful tool for assessment design. Assessment maps can provide useful conceptual frameworks for creating single items or multi-item tests. In addition to specifying the ideas and skills targeted by a particular content standard or learning goal, an assessment map also identifies related ideas, common misconceptions, prerequisite ideas, and ideas that come later in the developmental progression. For each of the 16 science and mathematics topic areas covered by its online bank of assessment items, Project 2061 is creating an assessment map to display connections among ideas related to the relevant content standards (see Figure 32.4 for an example). The maps are adapted from those in Project 2061's *Atlas of Science Literacy* (2001a) and are consistent with the work on progress variables in learning by Wilson and Draney (1997).

Assessment maps give test developers a convenient visual boundary around the set of ideas they might want to test and allow them to choose assessment items that can yield diagnostic information about student learning, especially with respect to misconceptions and

Figure 32.4

Example of a Project 2061 Assessment Map

Flow of Matter and Energy in Living Systems Assessment Map

LEGEND:

Key Ideas | Earlier Ideas

Later Idea | strand label

Idea e: Animals and microorganisms use molecules from food to make complex molecules that become part of their body structures.

Animals eat plants and other animals to get building material. 5D/P1 edited

Atoms may stick together in well-defined molecules. 4D/M1

Over a long time, matter is transferred from one organism to another repeatedly and between organisms and their physical environment. As in all material systems, the total amount of matter remains constant, even though its form and location change. 5E/M2

Idea d: Plants use sugar molecules and their breakdown products to make more complex molecules that become part of their body structures.

Idea b: Plants make their own food in the form of sugar molecules from carbon dioxide and water molecules.

As energy is transformed in living systems, some energy is stored in newly made structures but much is dissipated into the environment as heat. Therefore, continual input of energy from sunlight keeps the process going. 5E/H3b

Idea g: If not used immediately as fuel or as building material, sugars and other molecules are stored for later use.

Idea a: Food is a source of molecules that serve as fuel and building material for all organisms.

Some source of "energy" is needed for all organisms to stay alive and grow. 5E/E2

Plants capture energy by absorbing light and using it to form strong (covalent) bonds between the atoms of carbon-containing (organic) molecules. NSES 9-12C4c p.186

Idea f: Organisms get energy to carry out life functions by oxidizing molecules from food, releasing some of their energy as heat.

Idea c: In the process of making sugars, light energy is transformed into chemical energy.

Energy can change from one form to another in living things. 5E/M3a

From food, people obtain energy and materials for body repair and growth. 6C/E1a

Almost all food energy comes originally from sunlight. 5E/M3b

An especially important kind of reaction between substances involves combination of oxygen with something else, as in burning or rusting. 4D/M6b

Heat energy is almost always a product in an energy transformation. 4E/M2b

Animals eat plants and other animals to get energy. 5D/P1 edited

Matter Transformation

Energy Transformation

prerequisite knowledge that pertain to specific ideas on the maps. For college-level courses, instructors can take a similar approach, developing assessment maps for particular units, projects, or an entire course. Tests built around assessment maps can provide important insights into students' thinking. For example, misconceptions shown on an assessment map can be used to develop "distractors" (wrong answer choices) for multiple-choice questions. How students respond to those questions can help instructors determine whether they need to address the misconceptions more directly through readings, discussions, or other classroom activities. Taking a more goals-based and learner-based approach to course design is an ongoing and dynamic process involving several cycles of revising, testing, and refining the key elements of the course.

Fostering a Climate for Reform

So far, this chapter has provided suggestions for reform of the college science curriculum based on K–12 reform efforts that have relied on Project 2061's *Science for All Americans* and *Benchmarks for Science Literacy* and the NRC's *National Science Education Standards*. We have called attention to lessons that can be learned from these efforts, but it is important to note that while curriculum reform is necessary, it is not sufficient to support and sustain improvements in undergraduate science education over the long term. The key is to consider all parts of the education system, knowing that reforms in each depend on and make possible reform in the others. Here we outline the kinds of systemic changes that are required and reflect on the opportunities for and obstacles to those changes.

It may be helpful to first consider how higher education fits into a systemic reform model from the K–12 perspective. In *Blueprints for Reform* (AAAS 1998) Project 2061 examined the role of higher education in the context of designing a K–12 curriculum that would ensure science literacy for all. The report identifies characteristics of higher-education institutions that make them particularly suited as advocates for education reform at the pre-college and college levels. Among the strengths that colleges and universities can build on is their freedom to innovate and an infrastructure for research that can be used to test and refine new approaches in pedagogy, materials development, and instructional technology and to "model the teachers-as-researcher role for their K-12 colleagues" (AAAS 1998, p. 222). *Blueprints* also acknowledges the need to situate reforms within a broader institutional context, beginning with leadership from presidents and provosts, as well as from deans and departments chairs, and extending to collaborations with K–12 educators and relationships with students and their parents.

Each college and university is different, of course, and a "one size fits all" approach to reform is as unlikely to succeed at the undergraduate level as it is at K–12. In its report *Beyond Bio 101*, the Howard Hughes Medical Institute (HHMI, n.d.) takes a far-reaching look at how various institutions are striving to transform their undergraduate biology programs to meet the diverse needs of students, faculty, higher-education institutions, and the increasingly interdisciplinary field of biology itself. Based on its review, HHMI found several factors that were associated with successful reform:

- Teaching that recognizes the personal bond between teacher and student; this is particularly important to the development of young scientists.
- Leadership at the departmental or programmatic level; this is essential in fostering the kinds of changes in attitudes, perceptions, and goals that are needed.

- Commitment to continuous and incremental change, paying attention to what works and building on successful experiences.
- Communities that foster and reward good teaching.

Although the report identifies several promising trends, it warns of the danger of mistaking innovation for lasting change, quoting from education analyst Sheila Tobias's book *Revitalizing Undergraduate Science* (1992):

What hinders students are the pace, the conflicting purposes of the courses (to, variously, provide an introduction or lay a foundation for a research career, or weed out the "unfit"); attitudes of their professors and fellow students; unexplained assumptions and conventions; exam design and grading practices; class size; the exclusive presentation of new material by means of lecture; and the absence of community—a host of variables that are not specifically addressed by most reforms. (p. 18)

The problems identified by Tobias were some of the same problems impeding reform efforts at Towson University, according to Laurence Boucher, who was then dean of the university's College of Science and Mathematics. Reporting on his school's collaboration with Project 2061 to promote a more learner-focused approach to science and mathematics teaching, Boucher noted the change-resistant nature of higher education and the difficulty of institutionalizing reforms. Boucher's aim was to put into place reform strategies that would become part of the institution's culture of best practices. In addition to a variety of workshops and professional development programs for faculty, Boucher also organized a faculty team to analyze one of their introductory physical science courses and a biology course, which he describes as an "archetypal 'bad' course: crammed with material in an attempt at encyclopedic coverage that stresses the superficial learning of facts with cookbook laboratories." By taking a critical look at the courses, it was hoped that faculty would be motivated to make changes and that the improved courses would serve as models for improvement (Boucher, manuscript in preparation). Boucher's colleague Katherine Denniston agrees that university faculty need appropriate kinds of support, resources, and tools to carry out their reform efforts:

The creative effort of curriculum design and implementation requires time and the opportunity to collaborate with colleagues. They need seminars and workshops so they can learn what research shows about best practice in science classrooms. Institutions must consider these seminars and workshops to be an important part of the educators' workload, not events to be crowded into already-overbooked weekends and take time away from family. Finally, for university faculty, the scholarship of teaching must be rewarded at a level commensurate with the scholarship of discovery. When faculty have these kinds of support, standards-based reform efforts such as Project 2061 will have a much greater chance of affecting permanent change in our educational systems…. Until that day, those of us who have had the opportunity to engage in this type of work have the responsibility to share what we have learned with our colleagues. By encouraging university administrators and faculty to consider standards-based course and teaching assessment rather than the typical student and/or peer evaluations, we can facilitate reform while promoting change in the rewards structure at the university. In this way, we can change the system one small step at a time. (Denniston, manuscript in preparation)

Conclusion

This chapter has described ways in which the learning goals established for K–12 students can have useful applications at the college level. It has also explored some of the implications that a goals-based and learner-based approach might have for undergraduate science courses, teaching, and assessment. Although K–12 goals, strategies, and resources can be adapted for use in higher education, it is essential to recognize that colleges and universities have a unique and powerful culture that is likely to overcome even the most vigorous reform efforts. Lasting change will require an equally robust infrastructure to support new ideas and practices.

References

Advisory Committee to the National Science Foundation Directorate for Education and Human Resources. 1996. *Shaping the future: New expectations for undergraduate education in science, mathematics, engineering, and technology.* NSF 96-139. Arlington, VA: National Science Foundation.

American Association for the Advancement of Science (AAAS). 1990a. *The liberal art of science: Agenda for action.* Washington, DC: AAAS.

American Association for the Advancement of Science (AAAS). 1990b. *Science for all Americans.* New York: Oxford University Press.

American Association for the Advancement of Science (AAAS). 1993. *Benchmarks for science literacy.* New York: Oxford University Press.

American Association for the Advancement of Science (AAAS). 1998. *Blueprints for reform: Science, mathematics, and technology education.* New York: Oxford University Press.

American Association for the Advancement of Science (AAAS). 2001a. *Atlas of science literacy.* Washington, DC: AAAS.

American Association for the Advancement of Science (AAAS). 2001b. *Designs for science literacy.* New York: Oxford University Press.

Berkheimer, G. D., C. W. Anderson, and S. T. Spees. 1990. *Using conceptual change research to reason about curriculum.* Research Series Paper No. 195. East Lansing: Michigan State University, Institute for Research on Teaching.

Boucher, L. J. Manuscript in preparation. Working with Project 2061 to change science and mathematics education in the academy. American Association for the Advancement of Science.

Bruner, J. S. 1995. On learning mathematics. *Mathematics Teacher* 88 (4): 330–335. (Reprint of paper presented at the meeting of the National Council of Teachers of Mathematics, Salt Lake City, UT, 1960)

Catley, K., R. Lehrer, and B. Reiser. 2004. *Tracing a prospective learning progression for developing understanding of evolution.* Paper commissioned by the National Academies Committee on Test Design for K-12 Science Achievement, 2005. Washington, DC: National Academy of Sciences. *www7.nationalacademies.org/bota/ Evolution.pdf*

Commission on Behavioral and Social Sciences and Education. 2000. *How people learn: Brain, mind, experience, and school; expanded edition.* Washington, DC: National Academies Press. Also available online at *www.nap.edu*

DeBoer, G. E. 2005. Standard-izing test items. *Science Scope* 28 (4): 10–11.

Denniston, K. J. Manuscript in preparation. Evaluating a college biology course using Project 2061 tools. American Association for the Advancement of Science.

Denniston, K. J. n.d. Elements of course design: Biology 115: Biological Sciences I. (Unpublished manuscript written for American Association for the Advancement of Science Project 2061)

Driver, R., A. Squires, P. Rushworth, and V. Wood-Robinson. 1994. *Making sense of secondary science: Research into children's ideas.* London: Routledge.

Heller, P. 2001. Lessons learned in the CIPS curriculum project. Paper presented at the AAAS Conference on Developing Textbooks That Promote Science Literacy, Washington, DC. *www.project2061.org/events/meetings/textbook/literacy/heller.htm*

Henderleiter, J., R. Smart, J. Anderson, and O. Elian. 2001. How do organic chemistry students understand and apply hydrogen bonding? *Journal of Chemical Education* 78 (8): 1126–1130.

Heron, P. R. L., P. S. Shaffer, and L. C. McDermott. 2005. Research as a guide to improving student learning: An example from introductory physics. In *Invention and impact: Building excellence in undergraduate science, technology, engineering, and mathematics (STEM) education, 33–37.* Washington, DC: American Association for the Advancement of Science.

Howard Hughes Medical Institute (HHMI). n.d. *Beyond Bio 101: The transformation of undergraduate biology education. www.hhmi.org/BeyondBio10*

A jump-start for new science textbook development: Resources for developing curriculum materials that promote science literacy. 2004. *2061 Connections* (May). *www.project2061.org/publications/2061Connections/2004/2004-05a.htm*

Kirst, M. W., and M. Usdan. 2004. Thoughts on improving K–16 governance and policymaking. Paper presented at What Role Does Governance Play in K–16 Reform? symposium conducted at the meeting of the American Educational Research Association, San Diego, CA.

Michigan Science Education Resources Project. 1993. *Chemistry That Applies.* Lansing: Michigan Department of Education.

National Research Council (NRC). 1996. *National science education standards.* Washington, DC: National Academy Press.

National Research Council (NRC). 2003. *What is the influence of the* National Science Education Standards? *Reviewing the evidence, a workshop summary.* Washington, DC: National Academy Press.

Project Kaleidoscope. 2002. *Recommendations for action in support of undergraduate science, technology, engineering, and mathematics.* Washington, DC: Project Kaleidoscope.

Reiser, B., J. Krajcik, E. Moje, and R. Marx. 2003. Design strategies for developing science instructional materials. Paper presented at the annual meeting of the National Association for Research in Science Teaching, Philadelphia, PA. *http://hi-ce.org/iqwst/Papers/reiser_krajcik_NARST03.pdf*

Richardson, J. 2005. Concept inventories: Tools for uncovering STEM students' misconceptions. In *Invention and impact: Building excellence in undergraduate science, technology, engineering, and mathematics (STEM) education, 19–25.* Washington, DC: American Association for the Advancement of Science.

Roseman, J. E., and L. Stern. 2003. Toward ecology literacy: Contributions from Project 2061 science literacy reform tools. In *Understanding urban ecosystems: A new frontier for science and education,* eds. A. R. Berkowitz, C. H. Nilon, and K. S. Hollweg, 261–281. New York: Springer-Verlag.

Schmidt, W. H., H. A. Wang, and C. C. McKnight. 2005. Curriculum coherence: An examination of US mathematics and science content standards from an international perspective. *Journal of Curriculum Studies* 37 (5): 525–559.

Smith, C., M. Wiser, C. W. Anderson, J. Krajcik, and B. Coppola. 2004. *Implications of research on children's learning for assessment: Matter and atomic molecular theory.* Paper commissioned by the Committee on Test Design for K–12 Science Achievement. Washington, DC: National Academy of Sciences.

Stern, L., and A. Ahlgren. 2002. Analysis of students' assessments in middle school curriculum materials: Aiming precisely at benchmarks and standards. *Journal of Research in Science Teaching* 39 (9): 889–910.

Stern, L., and J. E. Roseman. 2001. Textbook alignment. *The Science Teacher* 68 (3): 52–56.

Tobias, S. 1992. *Revitalizing undergraduate science: Why some things work and most don't.* Tucson, AZ : Research Corporation.

Wiggins, G., and J. McTighe. 1998. *Understanding by design*. Alexandria, VA: Association for Supervision and Curriculum Development.

Wilson, M., and K. Draney. 1997. *Developing maps for student progress in the SEPUP assessment system*. BEAR Report Series, SA-97-2. Berkeley: University of California at Berkeley.

CHAPTER 33

The High-School-to-College Transition in Science

Wilson J. González-Espada and Rosita L. Napoleoni-Milán

Wilson J. González-Espada is assistant professor of physical science and science education at Arkansas Tech University. He earned a PhD in science education at the University of Georgia and conducts research on physics education, multicultural science education, science teacher education, and science assessment. He teaches introduction to physical science, general and applied physics, science in elementary and middle school education, and special methods in physical science education.

Rosita L. Napoleoni-Milán is General Education Development (GED) examiner at the Russellville, Arkansas, Adult Education Center. She earned an MA in business education at Interamerican University of Puerto Rico and is working on an MS in college student personnel at Arkansas Tech University. She is interested in student retention and recruitment, academic advising and counseling, and college student development and has taught courses in business education.

General education science courses are required in most U.S. colleges, and many first-year students enroll in such courses. In addition to the inherent difficulty of science courses for most students who are not science majors (Crooks 1980; González-Espada 2004; Hart and Cottle 1993; Hudson and McIntire 1977; Sánchez and Betkouski 1986), students are simultaneously facing a sometimes rocky transition and adjustment to college life. Despite the college science teachers' carefully prepared lectures and instructional activities, a number of science-irrelevant factors might affect student performance in science (Astin 1993, 2002; Barefoot 2002; Keup and Stolzenberg 2004; Noel, Levitz, and Saluri 1985; see also Chapter 34 in this volume).

From the college faculty perspective, the time interval between their experience as first-year students and their students' experiences can be measured in lustra or decades. As a consequence, it is important to remember the variety of competing events and pressures that students face while adjusting to a different life in college. Science faculty need to understand why

some students struggle during their first year so that faculty can act empathetically, provide as many opportunities for success as possible, improve faculty and student communication, and modify the science content and teaching methods to make them more relevant and interesting. The purpose of this chapter is to introduce science faculty to the literature regarding the high-school-to-college transition and to suggest possible ways for them to help first-year students to succeed in their science courses while keeping high academic standards.

Factors That May Affect First-Year Students' Performance in Science

Academics

One important factor that first-year students must cope with is the difference in teaching methods between high school and college. Despite a large body of research that suggests that college science courses should focus on active, more in-depth examination of fewer concepts (Hake 1998; Laws 1997; Thacker, Kim, and Trefz 1994), the reality is that introductory college science courses tend to be comprehensive, quasi-encyclopedic, and fast-paced. Some first-year students will drop out of college if they are not academically and socially prepared for this transition (Tinto 1994). Other students who were originally interested in science will switch from science programs to other majors after their first academic year (Salem et al. 1997; Seymour and Hewitt 1997).

Other reasons for poor science performance among freshmen are inadequate study habits (Hrabowski and Maton 1995). Hansen (1990) found that most first-year students do not have structured study habits. The predominant way of studying reported by freshmen is to read the material several times. Techniques such as creating flash cards, outlining, and highlighting important information from textbooks were seldom reported. Unfortunately, a school culture that assigns excellent grades based on little time and effort is partly responsible for this problem (Schroeder 2003).

Pre-Enrollment Preparation

Not surprisingly, pre-enrollment factors such as prior subject-matter knowledge and previous learning experiences are acknowledged as significant factors affecting student success, especially during the first year (Anthony 2000; Crawford et al. 1998; Mason and Crawley 1993). Other factors such as basic intellectual ability and analytic and problem-solving skills are also related to science success (Hrabowski and Maton 1995).

It is expected that after three or four years of high school courses, students have enough science and mathematics knowledge to tackle an introductory science course. However, the variety of high school curricula, teachers, and grading standards among different counties, regions, and states does not guarantee that this is the case. It is not uncommon to see a 4.0 student struggling with a science class during the first year of college. Other measures of aptitude, such as scores on standardized tests, are not fail proof either. Each semester a proportion of students with high SAT/ACT scores fail science courses, while students with lower scores can succeed in the same courses. Despite their limitations, high school grades and standardized test scores are commonly used to estimate college preparedness or aptitude.

Social Relationships

First-year students express almost as much anxiety about finding and maintaining friendships

as about getting poor grades (Upcraft and Gardner 1989). Once on-campus, many students have a need to develop an identity, and they look for roommates, clubs, student organizations, faith-related activities, and sports. Research suggests that the development of healthy and effective interpersonal relationships is an important element of success during the first year of college (Noel, Levitz, and Saluri 1985).

Leaving the comforts of home and the familiarity of their high school is a stress-inducing process for freshmen (Larose and Boivin 1998). For those who live on-campus, separating from their parents for the first time is an extraordinary situation that brings insecurity and fear. If students do not learn how to overcome these negative feelings during their first semester, they might drop out of school because of their perception of loneliness. These authors also suggest that it is very important that parents communicate with their college students so that they feel secure, encouraged, and motivated. The issue of parental support is discussed in more detail later in this chapter.

Financial Issues

Most studies suggest that receiving financial aid plays a significant, positive role in the students' decision to remain in college (Lichtenstein 2002), although the findings are not conclusive (St. John 2000). In general, the lack of means to finance a college education or the loss of an academic scholarship is a powerful reason why a number of students struggle during their first year. Some students resort to part-time or full-time jobs to maintain themselves, which creates additional tension between two competing priorities: succeeding in school, with limited time for studying outside of regular class hours, and working at jobs that provide enough money to pay for their needs and wants. Students resolve this situation in one of three ways: Some students obtain a scholarship and work less, others take up loans and credit card debt to sustain themselves while in college, and still others leave altogether, thinking that a college education is not worth going into debt for (Hansen 1990).

Psychological Factors

Two important factors that relate to a first-year student's success in science are self-concept and commitment. If students have a realistic and positive attitude toward their ability to succeed in college, the chances of success increase. When students have doubts about their academic ability or when they have an unrealistic perception of academic ability, their chances of success diminish (Anthony 2000; Marsh and Shavelson 1985; Oliver and Simpson 1988). In terms of commitment, when the students have a clear and unambiguous goal of surviving their first year of college, even if difficult times come, their chances of success are higher. Among a number of variables related to college success, Cope and Hannah (1975) identified commitment as the single most important determinant of persistence.

Another important psychological factor is the fact that different students learn differently. For example, the traditional lecture might not be the best way to learn for students with kinesthetic or visual learning styles (Francisco, Nicoll, and Trautman 1998; Lenehan et al. 1994; Willemsen 1995).

The student's cognitive developmental level is another aspect to consider. Although in theory first-year students have accomplished Piaget's formal operations level, the reality is that a number of them might not be developmentally ready for science courses where abstractions and logical thinking are commonplace. A study suggests that about two-thirds of first-year

students are still in the concrete operations levels (White and Sivitanides 2002). The authors cite other studies that show that a majority of adults, including college students and professionals, fail to attain full formal operational thinking.

Career Decision Making

Many first-year students enter college without a clear idea of their future career (Gordon 1995). Others have a good idea but change their minds as they are exposed to a number of possible alternatives. After taking introductory courses in an area of possible career interest, some students realize that it is not what they expected. It is not uncommon for students to change majors more than once during college.

Parental Background and Support

Everybody has the need to feel safe, and that does not change during the high-school-to-college transition. Many college students need to feel security from their parents even when they are away (Sullivan and Sullivan 1980). These authors suggest that adolescents who leave home to board at college exhibit increased security, affection, communication, satisfaction, and independence in relation to their parents, compared with adolescents who remain at home and commute to college.

The socioeconomic status of the student's families is related to the students' persistence (Braunstein, McGrath, and Pescatrice 2000–2001). Students coming from families with few economic resources are more likely to drop out of school to support their family. Many students feel responsible not just for themselves but also for the support of their family. Especially at risk are first-generation college students who might not have siblings who can share their college experience or whose parents are unaware of the challenges of college life.

High School Culture Versus College Culture

There is an obvious difference in expectations between entering freshmen and college faculty. While students tend to place more responsibility for their lack of success on the professor, irrelevant curricula, and boring teaching methods, college faculty tend to place more responsibility for students' lack of success on factors such as poor study techniques, insufficient work and time commitment to the class, inadequate background knowledge, and personal problems (Anthony 2000).

Another aspect of the culture shock is the students' lack of knowledge about university services available to help them cope with their first year of college. Barr and Rasor (1999) found that, regardless of gender, ethnicity, and age, first-year students who consistently received services from student affairs officers performed significantly better than students who received no services from these offices. To be successful, first-year students need strong study habits, time management skills, and a willingness to accept help from academic advisors, faculty, peers, and tutors (Blanc, DeBuhr, and Martin 1983; Hrabowski and Maton 1995).

Suggestions for College Science Faculty

Cultivate more direct interactions between you and your students. College science teachers can help first-year students to avoid common mistakes that might hurt their chances of success, such as enrolling in a course without the prerequisites, enrolling in too many courses, not enrolling in recommended science classes, scheduling too little time for course work, not using university

resources (advising, financial aid, tutoring) until it is too late in the semester, not creating a personal relationship with the faculty, and not striking a balance between academics and extra-curricular/social activities (Hrabowski and Maton 1995). In addition, just the act of listening to students individually can help them articulate problems and challenges. Usually, verbalizing a problem provides the perspective needed to solve it without much help from the instructor (Reinarz 1991).

Genuinely care about your student successes and failures (Salem et al. 1997). If the student is failing the class, help him or her to move beyond excuses and to focus on understanding the circumstances of the semester (Reinarz 1991). Sometimes conversations with students reveal situations such as a student not making the connection between getting poor grades and carrying too many credit hours plus working a full-time job. On other occasions, conversations positively affect talented students who would like to know more about a science topic but who are afraid to express it in front of the group.

Try different teaching methods. Research suggest that the use of lecture as the sole method of teaching is insufficient to meet all the learning needs of students as they attempt to master science content (Birk and Foster 1993). A combination of class discussion, concept mapping, and cooperative learning is suggested (Francisco, Nicoll, and Trautman 1998; see also Chapter 7 in this volume). Other education researchers endorse the use of a combination of remediation (review) sessions, discussion of worked examples, bridging explanations (discussing why the distractors on a multiple-choice item are incorrect), and discussion (Mason and Crawley 1993).

Establish your ground rules, required assessments, and grading procedures early in the semester and avoid changing them midsemester. This way you can alleviate student stress because they can plan their semester better (Reinarz 1991). Also, students have the right to know promptly what their grade in the course is. One of the chapter authors sends weekly updated grades by e-mail. Other faculty post grades on Blackboard (*www.blackboard.com*) for easy student access. On end-of-semester teaching evaluations, students highlight the fact that they are constantly aware of their performance in physical science. Grading quickly and providing feedback will avoid unpleasant surprises and possible course failure.

Determine which students are at risk of failing the class as soon as possible. Some students enroll in courses without being well aware of the prerequisites. Others get frustrated because of a low score on the first assessments. Talk to students individually in private to help them look for additional tutoring, find study groups, or improve their study habits. Several studies have found that students who spend a minimum of one hour per week receiving supplemental instruction led by another student typically do much better than like-qualified students who do not participate in those tutoring opportunities (Schroeder 2003). If a student does not meet the prerequisites for your course, inform him or her so that a decision can be made on whether to stay or leave the course.

Promote, in your science classes, support services that are available to students, especially students who do not live on campus. Research suggests that commuters are much less likely to get involved in college life, to have contact with student affairs officers, and to create identification with the university. These characteristics are related to success in college (Schroeder 2003).

Emphasize class attendance. In general, research suggests that class attendance among first-year students is often low (Romer 1993). Absenteeism is highest in large, first-year courses, especially those in science (Friedman, Rodriguez, and McComb 2001; Moore 2003; Moore et al. 2003). Although an extrinsic motivator, checking attendance regularly could make the dif-

ference between success and failure for some first-year science students.

Make your class personally meaningful to your students. To make a science course a more relevant experience and to create a connection between the students' previous knowledge and the course content, the use of everyday materials is encouraged. For example, Kerber and Akhtar (1996) suggested that it is possible to cover the same topics as a traditional chemistry lab using recognizable, real-world substances as reactants. McHale (1994) proposed the use of current events in students' research projects.

Create a challenging but positive learning environment. The use of humor and the portrayal of the instructor as a human being instead of an all-knowing and inflexible person are two ways to help students feel at ease in the science class. In addition, providing enough opportunities for students to succeed can contribute to a more relaxed classroom atmosphere.

Persuade students to get involved in academic and extracurricular activities, but in moderation. Emphasize among first-year students the concept of balance, that is, that college life includes academic, professional, personal, and social growth. Overemphasizing academics at the expense of other areas is just as counterproductive for many students as overemphasizing the social component of college life.

Pay special attention to the struggles of your female and minority students. It is well documented that females and minorities are underrepresented in science and that the first year is a crucial point in their decision to become scientists or leave science altogether (Seymour and Hewitt 1997). Also, access to financial aid plays an even more important role for underrepresented groups in science compared with other groups (Lichtenstein 2002; St. John, Hu, and Weber 2000).

Get involved in freshman activities (advising, enrollment, welcome programs). A number of faculty members perform service for their institutions by helping during the enrollment and advising of first-year students. This is an excellent way for science faculty to engage in informal conversations with students about their interests, backgrounds, and what students expect from their first year. When students see the instructor in a class, they are probably more likely to ask for help if they have met the instructor outside the classroom.

Motivate your students to move beyond letter grades and into long-term learning. It is important to convince students that the main outcome of a science course is not necessarily obtaining an excellent grade but obtaining the knowledge and skills needed for further science courses or their general science literacy. Science faculty can do this by providing many types of assessments that allow students the maximum chances of success.

Challenge long-held assumptions of the role of science courses. A number of first-year students perceive science courses as hurdles specifically engineered to "weed out" mediocre students from future careers in science (Reinarz 1991; Seymour and Hewitt 1997). This perception exists even if students take general education science courses. These authors suggest that you critically look at your academic department, curriculum, attitude toward students, and teaching methods to "weed out" this unfortunate perception from your students.

References

Anthony, G. 2000. Factors influencing first-year students' success in mathematics. *International Journal of Mathematics Education in Science and Technology* 31 (1): 3–14.

Astin, A. W. 1993. *What matters in college? Four critical years revisited.* San Francisco: Jossey-Bass.

Astin, A. W. 2002. *The American freshman: Thirty-five year trends.* Los Angeles: Higher Education Research Institute.

Barefoot, B. O. 2002. *Second national survey of first-year academic practices.* Brevard, NC: The Policy Center on the First Year of College.

Barr, J. E., and R. Rasor. 1999. Freshman persistence as measured by reaching academic achievement benchmarks. Paper presented at the annual conference of the Research and Planning Group for California Community Colleges, Lake Arrowhead, CA.

Birk, J. P., and J. Foster. 1993. Lecture and learning: Are they compatible? *Journal of Chemical Education* 70 (3): 179–182.

Blanc, R. A., L. E. DeBuhr, and D. C. Martin. 1983. Breaking the attrition cycle: The effects of supplemental instruction on undergraduate performance and attrition. *Journal of Higher Education* 54 (1): 80–90.

Braunstein, A., M. McGrath, and D. Pescatrice. 2000–2001. Measuring the impact of financial factors on college persistence. *Journal of College Student Retention* 2 (3): 191–203.

Cope, R. G., and W. Hannah. 1975. *Revolving college doors: The causes and consequences of dropping out and transferring.* New York: John Wiley.

Crawford, K., S. Gordon, J. Nicholas, and M. Prosser. 1998. Qualitatively different experiences of learning mathematics at university. *Learning and Instruction* 8 (5): 455–468.

Crooks, T. J. 1980. *Grade prediction: The usefulness of context-specific predictors.* (ERIC Document Reproduction Service no. ED194547)

Francisco, J. S., G. Nicoll, and M. Trautman. 1998. Integrating multiple teaching methods into a general chemistry classroom. *Journal of Chemical Education* 75 (2): 210–213.

Friedman, P., F. Rodriguez, and J. McComb. 2001. Why students do and do not attend class. *College Teaching* 49 (4): 124–133.

González-Espada, W. J. 2004. Succeeding in Introduction to Physical Science: Is mathematics background important? *Journal of the Arkansas Academy of Science* 58: 60–64.

Gordon, V. N. 1995. *The undecided college student: An academic and career advising challenge.* 2nd ed. Springfield, IL: Charles C. Thomas.

Hake, R. R. 1998. Interactive engagement versus traditional methods: A six-thousand student survey of mechanics test data for introductory physics courses. *American Journal of Physics* 66: 64–74.

Hansen, S. M. 1990. Reasons for non-persistence of African Americans, Mexican Americans and Hispanic freshmen university students. Doctoral diss., Boston University.

Hart. G. E., and P. D. Cottle. 1993. Academic backgrounds and achievement in college physics. *The Physics Teacher* 31: 470–475.

Hrabowski, F. A., and K. I. Maton. 1995. Enhancing the success of African American students in the sciences: Freshman year outcomes. *School Science and Mathematics* 95 (1): 19–27.

Hudson, H. T., and W. R. McIntire. 1977. Correlation between mathematical skills and success in physics. *American Journal of Physics* 45: 470–471.

Kerber, R. C., and M. J. Akhtar. 1996. Getting real: A general chemistry laboratory program focusing on "real world" substances. *Journal of Chemical Education* 73 (11): 1023–1025.

Keup, J. R., and E. B. Stolzenberg. 2004. *The 2003 Your First College Year (YFCY) survey: Exploring the academic and personal experiences of first-year students.* Columbia, SC: National Resource Center for the First-Year Experience and Students in Transition.

Larose, S., and M. Boivin. 1998. Attachment to parents, social support expectations, and socioemotional adjustment during the high school-college transition. *Journal of Research on Adolescence* 8: 1–27.

Laws, P. W. 1997. Millikan Lecture 1996: Promoting active learning based on physics education research in introductory physics courses. *American Journal of Physics* 65: 4–21.

Lenehan, M. C., R. Dunn, J. Ingham, B. Signer, and J. B. Murray. 1994. Effects of learning-style intervention on college students' achievement, anxiety, anger, and curiosity. *Journal of College Student Development* 35 (6): 461–466.

Lichtenstein, M. 2002. The role of financial aid in Hispanic first-time freshmen persistence. Paper presented at the annual forum for the Association for Institutional Research, Toronto, Canada.

Marsh, H., and R. Shavelson. 1985. Self-concept: Its multifaceted hierarchical structure. *Educational Psychologist* 20: 107–125.

Mason, D., and F. E. Crawley. 1993. Remediation, bridging explanations, worked examples, and discussion: Their effectiveness as teaching strategies in a freshman-level nonscience majors chemistry course. Paper presented at the annual meeting of the National Association for Research in Science Teaching, Atlanta, GA.

McHale, J. L. 1994. Current events as subjects for term papers in an honors freshman chemistry class. *Journal of Chemical Education* 71 (4): 313–314.

Moore, R. 2003. Class attendance and course performance in introductory science classes: How important is it for students to attend class? *Journal of College Science Teaching* 32 (6): 367–371.

Moore, R., M. Jensen, J. Hatch, I. Duranczyk, S. Staats, and L. Koch. 2003. Showing up: The importance of class attendance for academic success in introductory science courses. *American Biology Teacher* 65 (3): 325–329.

Noel, L., R. Levitz, and D. Saluri. 1985. *Increasing student retention*. San Francisco: Jossey-Bass.

Oliver, J. S., and R. D. Simpson. 1988. Influences of attitude toward science, achievement motivation, and science self-concept on achievement in science. A longitudinal study. *Science Education* 72: 143–155.

Reinarz, A. G. 1991. Gatekeepers: Teaching introductory science. *College Teaching* 39 (3): 94–96.

Romer, R. 1993. Do students go to class? Should they? *Journal of Economic Perspectives* 7 (3): 167–174.

Salem, A., J. Dronberger, E. Kos, and R. Wilson. 1997. Freshmen in science program. *Bioscene* 23 (3): 3–8.

Sánchez, K., and M. Betkouski. 1986. A study of factors affecting student performance in community college general chemistry courses. Paper presented at the annual meeting of the National Association for Research in Science Teaching, San Francisco, CA.

Schroeder, C. 2003. The first year and beyond. *About Campus* 8 (4): 9–16.

Seymour, E., and N. M. Hewitt. 1997. *Talking about leaving: Why undergraduates leave the sciences*. Boulder, CO: Westview Press.

St. John, E. P. 2000. The impact of student aid on recruitment and retention: What the research says? *New Directions for Student Services* 89 (1): 61–75.

St John, E. P., S. Hu, and J. Weber. 2000. Keeping public college affordable. A study of persistence in Indiana's public colleges and universities. *Journal of Student Financial Aid* 30 (1): 21–32.

Sullivan, K., and A. Sullivan. 1980. Adolescent-parent separation. *Developmental Psychology* 16: 93–99.

Thacker, B., E. Kim, and K. Trefz. 1994. Comparing problem solving performance of physics students in inquiry-based and traditional introductory physics courses. *American Journal of Physics* 62: 627–633.

Tinto, V. 1994. *Leaving college: Rethinking the causes and cures of student attrition*. Chicago: University of Chicago Press.

Upcraft, M. L., and J. N. Gardner. 1989. *The freshman year experience: Helping students survive and succeed in college*. San Francisco: Jossey Bass.

White, G. L., and M. P. Sivitanides. 2002. A theory of the relationships between cognitive requirements of computer programming languages and programmers' cognitive characteristics. *Journal of Information Systems Education* 13 (1): 59–66.

Willemsen, E. W. 1995. So what is the problem? Difficulties at the gate. In *New directions for teaching and learning: Fostering student success in quantitative gateway courses*, eds. J. Gainen and E. W. Willemsen, 15–21. San Francisco: Jossey-Bass.

CHAPTER 34

Factors Influencing Success in Introductory College Science

Robert H. Tai, Philip M. Sadler, and John F. Loehr

Robert H. Tai is assistant professor in the Curry School of Education, University of Virginia. He earned an EdD in science education at Harvard University and conducts research on the high-school-to-college transition in science, the transition from graduate student to scientist, and eye-gaze tracking in assessment. He teaches courses in elementary science methods, education research projects, and conceptual change research in science education.

Philip M. Sadler is director of the Science Education Department, Harvard-Smithsonian Center for Astrophysics, and is the F.W. Wright Senior Lecturer on Celestial Navigation, Department of Astronomy, Harvard University. He earned an EdD in science education at Harvard University and conducts research on assessment of students' scientific misconceptions, models of enhancing skills of experienced teachers, and effective pre-college teaching strategies.

John F. Loehr is research analyst, Office of Research, Evaluation and Accountability, Chicago Public Schools. He earned a PhD in science education at the University of Virginia and conducts research on the association of high school science pedagogy with student achievement.

Introductory college science courses are widely regarded as gateways to further study, and college instructors view organization and good study habits as keys to these academic gates—more so, even, than a strong high school science background (Hazari, Schwartz, and Sadler 2005; Razali and Yager 1994; Shumba and Glass 1994; Uno 1988). Reflecting on this issue, let us consider as an example two prototypical highly organized and diligent students enrolled in an introductory chemistry course. Suppose these two students work together in the same study group and live across the hall from one another in the same dormitory. Furthermore, suppose they have very similar academic backgrounds (both took Advanced Placement [AP] chemistry, got good grades in high school, and had high SAT scores) and the same aspirations (both want to be pharmacists). Suppose, however, that they experienced very different high school chemistry classes. One student took a class that centered on the critical issue of stoichiometry; the other student took a class that was comprehensive in scope and systematically moved through a variety of topics. Which student would likely do better in introductory college chemistry? We'll get back to this question later in the chapter.

Studies on the influence of pre-college factors on success in college science are well established. Table 34.1 lists a selection of these studies spanning the better part of a century. Most studies have been carried out in single institutions (e.g., Alters 1995; Hart and Cottle 1993), with only a few collecting samples from multiple institutions (e.g., Sadler and Tai 2001; Shumba and Glass 1994). Of the multi-institutional studies, none possessed the capacity to identify cross-disciplinary trends. In 2002, Factors Influencing College Science Success (Project FICSS) sought to remedy this situation. This chapter summarizes findings from this four-year national survey of college science students and offers some suggestions to college instructors.

About Project FICSS

The idea for Project FICSS began in 1992 with Alan Lightman of the Massachusetts Institute of Technology (MIT) and Philip M. Sadler of Harvard University (later joined by Robert Tai), who wondered if high school science lessons had any effect on college science success. Their collaboration developed into a national study of college physics students. Noting the power of public health studies to uncover important associations between personal health and individual habits, Sadler sought to use public health methods to explore relationships between students' college science grades and their educational experiences in high school physics. The first large-scale implementation of these techniques netted over 2,000 surveys from over 20 introductory college physics courses (Sadler and Tai 1997, 2001; Tai and Sadler 2001).

Project FICSS is several times larger, collecting data from students in three disciplines: biology, chemistry, and physics. Survey questionnaires were developed through a series of pilot studies, focus groups, and interviews with college students, high school teachers, and college professors. Questions were written to explore the extent to which respondents were exposed to pedagogical tools and techniques that are widely experienced in high school science classes.

Data were collected from students attending 55 different colleges and universities based on an initial list of 67 colleges and universities selected through a stratified random sampling of more than 1,700 colleges and universities. In all, more than 8,000 surveys were collected from 128 introductory college biology, chemistry, and physics courses.

The surveys were administered and collected by participating college science instructors. Respondents were asked to recall their high school experiences in the corresponding discipline (i.e., college chemistry students were asked about their high school chemistry classes, and so on). The questions focused on eight aspects of the high school science experience: (1) content, (2) instructional practices, (3) laboratories, (4) emphasis on memorization versus understanding, (5) degree of lesson structure, (6) use of instructional technology, (7) AP science status, and (8) students' mathematics background. For purposes of comparability, only college courses using the lecture/recitation/laboratory format were included in the study.

We are aware of studies questioning the validity and reliability of self-reports (Bradburn, Rips, and Shevell 1987); however, more recent studies have shown that self-report surveys, with carefully worded questions addressed to individuals to whom the topics are relevant and

Table 34.1

Selected Studies Linking Pre-College Factors With College Science Performance

Year	Researcher(s)	Schools sampled	Subject	Summary of findings
1925	Everhart & Ebaugh	Single	Chemistry	Prior chemistry experience associated with grade of C or higher; concluded that prior experience does not matter
1931	Herrmann	Single	Chemistry	Prior chemistry experience leads to grade of C or higher; found prior experience matters, but other factors as well
1957	Brasted	Single	Chemistry	Prior chemistry experience associated with grade of A or B; prior experience in math and physics affected grade
1967	Lamb et al.	Single	Chemistry	High school GPA, SAT Math and Verbal, age, number of college math and science courses affected test score
1969	Tamir	Single	Biology	Not having a biology and chemistry background associated with lower final biology grade
1980	Tamir et al.	Single	Biology	Number of inquiry laboratories and degree of biology "specialization" affected biology grade
1988	Yager et al.	Single	Chemistry	Lack of prior chemistry experience increased time studying and support needed
1991	Lord & Rauscher	Single	Biology	Assessment outcome influenced by major and number of previous biology courses
1993	Gibson & Gibson	Single	Biology	More courses led to more confidence in using microscopes and scientific writing
1993	Hart & Cottle	Single	Physics	Prior physics experience led to better grades
1994	Razali & Yager	Multiple	Chemistry	Professors identified personality characteristics and high school teachers identified content knowledge as affecting grades
1994	Shumba & Glass	Multiple	Chemistry	Three years of mathematics, one year each of chemistry and physics, and certain content topics influenced grade
1994	Sundberg et al.	Single	Biology	Biology majors had more knowledge at start of course than nonmajors
1995	Alters	Single	Physics	Prior physics experience led to better grades; corresponds with Hart & Cottle
1995	House	Single	Chemistry	Higher mathematics and academic ability were associated with higher grades
1998	Johnson & Lawson	Single	Biology	Reasoning ability predicted biology grades
2001	Sadler & Tai	Multiple	Physics	Calculus background, coverage of fewer content topics, limiting lab experiences associated with higher college grades
2003	Conley	Multiple	Multiple	List of procedural skills, academic skills, and content knowledge professors believe improved introductory grades
2005	Tai et al.	Multiple	Chemistry	Overstructuring or understructuring high school chemistry instruction is associated with lower college performance

important, can be valid and reasonably accurate (Bradburn 2000; Groves 1989; Kuncel, Credé, and Thomas 2005; Menon and Yorkston 2000; Niemi and Smith 2003). In addition, we carried out a reliability study separate from the overall study that included 113 introductory college chemistry students at a major public university. These students completed the survey on two different occasions, two weeks apart. The results indicated that reliability coefficients ranged from 0.46 to 1.00, which is well within the generally accepted limits (Thorndike 1997).

For the outcome measure of "success," we chose to use final course grades. To account for local differences in grading and student backgrounds, multiple linear regression was selected as the analytical approach. This statistical technique allows student backgrounds and college course–level differences to be held constant, while the significance of the primary research predictors is comparatively analyzed. In addition, this approach was used to account for differences in student academic achievement and student demographic differences.

Findings

The findings presented here summarize the effects of the eight aspects of high school science experience on first-semester college science grades and were extracted from a series of analyses carried out by project researchers, many of which are currently under editorial review. To simplify, we present the results in the form of predicted final course grades of prototypical students. Differences among students are depicted as normalized point values with 10-point ranges among grades (i.e., 90 = A; 80 = B; 70 = C, and so on).

Content

What is the effect of a focus on "critical concepts" in the high school science class on final course grades in first-semester college science? In each of the three surveys, specific content areas that would be familiar to high school biology students were listed, and students were asked to choose the amount of time spent on each of the content topics (i.e., *none*, *a few weeks*, *a month*, *a semester*, and *a recurring topic*). When these responses were analyzed, it became apparent that a particular content area within each discipline was a significant positive predictor of college performance. In biology, this content area was cell biology; in chemistry, it was stoichiometry; in physics, it was mechanics. On average, the difference between two prototypical students who report *none* versus *a recurring topic* was about 2.3 points, a fairly small difference in overall grade. However, in a specific analysis of chemistry the difference was 5.0 points, or half a letter grade. Overall, this result suggests that limited content coverage focused on fundamental content areas ("critical concepts") is generally beneficial for college preparation. The association was larger in chemistry, suggesting that college instructors, especially in chemistry, should pay attention to students with a weak background in these key topics.

Instructional Practices

Significant associations between high school instructional practices and final grade in college science courses were weak. For example, students who reported experiencing lectures every day in high school had higher grades in college than students who reported experiencing lectures very rarely, but the predicted difference in college grade amounted to only a 1.9-point difference. However, four instructional practices were found to be significant, and when taken in combination, a comparison of two prototypical students showed a large predicted difference in final course grade. The prototypical student reporting most of these experiences was

predicted to have a nearly one letter grade advantage (8.4 points) over the prototypical student reporting fewest of these experiences. Greater frequencies of lectures and peer tutoring were positive influences, while greater frequencies of small-group work and standardized examination preparation were both negative. The positive association of lecture-style teaching in high school at first seems contradictory to current conventional wisdom in science learning. However, organized note taking and other skills learned through lecture-style classes in high school may explain some of this positive association.

Another curious result is the positive association for peer tutoring (see Chapter 8 in this volume) versus the negative association for small-group work. However, peer tutoring has clearly defined roles: one student tutors while the other is "tutored." The activity of peer tutoring may only move forward when both are engaged. Small groups often lack this clear structure, leaving some students unengaged with course content throughout the course of an activity. Further, standardized examination preparation was found to be negatively associated with college grades, a result that raises questions about the current national educational policy putting emphasis on high-stakes standardized exit exams.

In summary, it appears that students who have experience with the lecture-based context of college courses and who have engaged in individualized instruction with peers are more prepared for college success than peers who lack these experiences.

Laboratories

Our survey posed a series of questions about high school laboratory experiences, including degree of focus on procedure, degree of lab freedom, repeated use of lab equipment, repeating labs for understanding, connection between student worldviews and lab experiences, conceptual understanding before and after labs, helpfulness of labs, length of class discussions after labs, and amount of time spent writing lab reports.

The analysis produced five significant predictors, three negatively associated with college performance (*number of labs per month*, *read and discuss lab directions in class the day before*, and *degree of student freedom in designing and carrying out labs*) and two positively associated with performance (*frequency of labs directly addressing student beliefs* and *frequency of labs using same equipment*). As with instructional practice, each individual predictor was associated with only small differences in student performance. However, when taken as a group, the predicted difference between two prototypical students, one with highly positive and the other with highly negative experiences, is fairly large at 6.2 points, amounting to slightly more than half of a letter grade. High school courses that used highly structured labs focusing on changing students' beliefs (or addressing misconceptions) and eschewing complex procedures resulted in better college performance. Reusing lab setups benefited students who did not have to become familiar with new techniques but could focus on conceptual understandings. More labs did not predict deeper understandings, nor did open-ended lab experiences.

Memorization Versus Understanding

In a question regarding the type of learning emphasized in their high school science courses, we found that students who reported that their course work required a full understanding of topics outperformed their peers who recalled memorization as an important course work requirement. This contrast in instructional approaches produced a predicted difference in college grades of 3.1 points, amounting to about one-third of a letter grade. Students who recalled memorization as a primary mode of "learning" in their high school science classes may be at a disadvantage in their college courses.

Degree of Lesson Structure

One question we were particularly interested in was the connection between amount of structure (particularly degree of student autonomy) in high school science lessons and college performance. Some teachers offer their students a high degree of autonomy, while others are more rigid in their formats. A common concern among teachers is whether time-consuming, lightly structured learning activities actually place their students at a disadvantage in their college courses.

Our analysis revealed an interaction between students' mathematics backgrounds and degree of lab autonomy, especially in college biology and chemistry performance. High mathematics achievers are not significantly affected by variation in high school laboratory structure. In general, these high mathematics achievers form the main body of students who enter science-related careers.

By contrast, low mathematics achievers who experienced autonomous lab activities in their high school science classes did significantly worse than their peers in biology and chemistry. These results were not replicated in physics. Nonetheless, for low mathematics achievers, lab structure appears to be an important precursor to college science performance. Reasons why this may be the case are outside the scope of our study but certainly represent interesting avenues for further research.

Instructional Technology

Are students who experience modern instructional technology in their high school classes at an advantage over their peers who do not have these experiences? In our study, we considered several different forms and applications of instructional technology. First, we considered the use of computers, the internet, probes, and simulations. Comparing students who reported high levels of use with students who reported no use, we found no difference in their college performance. This result was consistent in college biology and chemistry students. In physics, the result was slightly different; higher-use students actually earned slightly lower grades than non-use students. Overall, the frequency of instructional technology use did not appear to be associated with college science performance.

Next, we analyzed the use of computer graphing tools versus graphing by hand. Students who reported hand graphing were at an advantage over their peers who reported use of computers to graph data. The effect was small but significant.

AP Science

AP science courses, once rare, have grown common in high schools. Though not all students report having taken AP science courses in high schools, significant percentages have. On average, 20 percent of introductory college students have taken an AP science course. Is taking AP science associated with better college science performance? Students who have taken AP science in high school earn grades about 2 points better than their peers who have not. The regression models accounted for students' academic achievement and demographic backgrounds, and, as a result, the difference associated with AP science was small.

Mathematics Background

Mathematics is the "language of science." While this sentiment is certainly true of scientific research, how important is it at the introductory level? The conventional view is that mathematics is critical to learning physics, essential to chemistry, and less important for biology. We decided to analyze this association across these three disciplines, expecting to find some variation.

Three measures of mathematics background and achievement were used in our study: SAT–Quantitative (SAT-Q) scores, last high school mathematics grade, and enrollment in high school calculus (regular, AP A/B, or AP B/C). Students' ACT mathematics scores were converted to SAT mathematics scores using an SAT-ACT concordance table (Dorans et al. 1997). Given the highly sequential nature of mathematics content, if preparation for college science were heavily dependent on students' knowledge of mathematics, one would expect only one of these three variables to be significant in a regression model. On the contrary, our findings reveal that each of the three variables was highly significant in the same regression models in all three disciplines. Suppose we have two prototypical students, one with a strong mathematics background and another with a much weaker mathematics background. The high math achiever earned an A in her last high school mathematics class, had an SAT-Q score of 720, and took AP Calculus B/C in high school. The lower math achiever earned a C in her last high school class, had an SAT-Q score of 520, and did not take calculus in high school. The difference in their predicted college science grades is 11.2 points, or slightly more than one entire letter grade in college science.

Conclusions

In this wide-ranging analysis of the connection between high school science experiences and college performance, one common characteristic permeated the findings. Each significant predictor only made a fractional difference in students' college grades. This analysis offers evidence for thinking about high school science experiences and their association with college performance as a complex, multifaceted process. For college instructors, advisors, and administrators, the message is that high school learning experiences are highly relevant to college science success. However, there is no single indicator that will gauge college science success.

Individually significant predictors, considered collectively, were found to produce large differences in predicted student performance. The results uncovered trends and suggest general high school learning experiences that were more closely associated with higher student performance in college. Less successful students reported less structured science experiences both in class work and in labs as well as broader coverage of science topics. Instructional technology did not appear to play an important role and in some instances was associated with lower college grades. More successful introductory college science students typically had strong mathematics backgrounds (regardless of the science discipline they entered in college), reported concentrating on key topics in high school, focused on understanding rather than on memorization, reported more structured learning experiences such as labs and lectures, and learned through peer tutoring.

Further Research

This research model associating high school science experiences with college science success raises the question: Are introductory college science learning experiences associated with students' subsequent success or persistence in science? Declining numbers of U.S. students entering the sciences have raised questions about the United States' continued leadership in science and technology further into this century. Research to find generalizable trends linking students' experiences with subsequent life choices may provide valuable insight into the development of public policies. Large-scale studies have this potential.

Acknowledgments

This research was supported by funds from the Interagency Educational Research Initiative (IERI) and administered by the National Science Foundation (NSF-REC 0115649). The opinions expressed herein are those of the authors and do not represent either the IERI or the NSF.

References

Alters, B. J. 1995. Counseling physics students: A research basis. *The Physics Teacher* 33: 413–415.

Bradburn, N. M. 2000. Temporal representation and event dating. In *The science of self-report: Implications for research and practice,* eds. A. A. Stone, J. S. Turkkan, C.A. Bachrach, J. B. Jobe, H. S. Kurtzman, and V. S. Cain, 49–61. Mahwah, NJ: Erlbaum.

Bradburn, N. M., L. J. Rips, and S. K. Shevell. 1987. Answering autobiographical questions: The impact of memory and inference on surveys. *Science* 236: 157–161.

Brasted, R. C. 1957. Achievement in first-year college chemistry related to high school preparation. *Journal of Chemical Education* 34 (11): 562–565.

Conley, D. T. 2003. *Understanding university success: A project of the Association of American Universities and the Pew Charitable Trusts.* Eugene, OR: Center for Educational Policy Research.

Dorans, N. J., C. F. Lyu, M. Pommerich, and W. M. Houston. 1997. Concordance between ACT assessment and recentered SAT I sum scores. *College and University* 73 (2): 24–35.

Everhart, W. A., and W. C. Ebaugh. 1925. A comparison of grades in general chemistry earned by students who (a) have had, and (b) have not had high-school chemistry. *Journal of Chemical Education* 2 (9): 770–774.

Gibson, D. J., and L. S. Gibson. 1993. College students' perceptions on adequacy of high school science curriculum as preparation for college level biology. *American Biology Teacher* 55 (1): 8–12.

Groves, R. M. 1989. *Survey errors and survey costs.* New York: John Wiley.

Hart, G. E., and P. D. Cottle. 1993. Academic backgrounds and achievement in college physics. *The Physics Teacher* 31: 470–475.

Hazari, Z., M. S. Schwartz, and P. M. Sadler. 2005. Divergent voices: Views of teachers and professors on pre-college factors that influence college science success. Science Education Department of the Harvard-Smithsonian Center for Astrophysics. (Unpublished manuscript)

Herrmann, G. A. 1931. An analysis of freshman college chemistry grades with reference to previous study in chemistry. *Journal of Chemical Education* 8: 1376–1385.

House, J. D. 1995. Noncognitive predictors of achievement in introductory college chemistry. *Research in Higher Education* 36 (4): 473–490.

Johnson, M. A., and A. E. Lawson. 1998. What are the relative effects of reasoning ability and prior knowledge on biology achievement in expository and inquiry classes? *Journal of Research in Science Teaching* 35 (1): 89–103.

Kuncel, N. R., M. Credé, and L. L. Thomas. 2005. The validity of self-reported grade point averages, class ranks, and test scores: A meta-analysis and review of the literature. *Review of Educational Research* 75 (1): 63–82.

Lamb, D. P., W. H. Waggoner, and W. G. Findley. 1967. Student achievement in high school chemistry. *School Science and Mathematics* 47: 221–227.

Lord, T. R., and C. Rauscher. 1991. A sampling of basic life science literacy in a college population. *American Biology Teacher* 53 (7): 419–424

Menon, G., and E. A. Yorkston. 2000. The use of memory and contextual cues in the formation of behavioral frequency judgments. In *The science of self-report: Implications for research and practice,* eds. A. A. Stone, J. S. Turkkan, C.A. Bachrach, J. B. Jobe, H. S. Kurtzman, and V. S. Cain, 63–79. Mahwah, NJ: Erlbaum.

Niemi, R. G., and J. Smith. 2003. The accuracy of students' reports of course taking in the 1994 National Assess-

ment of Educational Progress. *Educational Measurement: Issues and Practice* 22 (1): 15–21.

Razali, S. N., and R. E. Yager. 1994. What college chemistry instructors and high school chemistry teachers perceive as important for incoming college students. *Journal of Research in Science Teaching* 31 (7): 735–747.

Sadler, P. M., and R. H. Tai. 1997. The role of high school physics in preparing students for college physics. *The Physics Teacher* 35 (5): 282–285.

Sadler, P. M., and R. H. Tai. 2001. Success in introductory college physics: The role of high school preparation. *Science Education* 85: 111–136.

Shumba, O., and L. W. Glass. 1994. Perceptions of coordinators of college freshman chemistry regarding selected goals and outcomes of high school chemistry. *Journal of Research in Science Teaching* 31 (4): 381–392.

Sundberg, M. D., M. L. Dini, and E. Li. 1994. Decreasing course content improves student comprehension of science and attitudes towards science in freshman biology. *Journal of Research in Science Teaching* 31 (6): 679–693.

Tai, R. H., and P. M. Sadler. 2001. Gender differences in introductory undergraduate physics performance: University physics versus college physics in the USA. *International Journal of Science Education* 23 (10): 1017–1037.

Tai, R. H., P. M. Sadler, and J. F. Loehr. 2005. Factors influencing success in introductory college chemistry. *Journal of Research in Science Teaching* 42 (9): 987–1012.

Tamir, P. 1969. High school preparation and college biology. *BioScience* 19 (5): 447–449.

Tamir, P., R. Amir, and R. Nussinovitz. 1980. High school preparation for college biology in Israel. *Higher Education* 9: 399–408.

Thorndike, R. M. 1997. *Measurement and evaluation in psychology and education.* 6th ed. Upper Saddle River, NJ: Merrill.

Uno, G. E. 1988. Teaching college and college-bound biology students. *American Biology Teacher* 5 (4): 213–215.

Yager, R. E., B. Snider, and J. Krajcik. 1988. Relative success in college chemistry for students who experienced a high-school course in chemistry and those who had not. *Journal of Research in Science Teaching* 25 (5): 387–396.

Improving Instruction

In the last few decades, there has been a movement in education toward performance-based or alternative types of assessments. Performance-based assessments have the potential to inform teaching and improve learning, in contrast to traditional assessments that primarily serve as an evaluative tool.... Alternative assessments are said to be more "authentic," engaging students in assignments or projects in a real-world context, similar to tasks of scientists working in the field. —Karleen Goubeaud

If we think about what we really want our teaching to accomplish, we can more easily choose among the teaching strategies available to find those that work best for us individually and for our students.... The take-home message is that no one pedagogical strategy provides the "magic bullet" for student learning, but our choices in the classroom do make a difference. Being intentional in what we want to accomplish in the classroom or lab helps us become more effective teachers. —Linda C. Hodges

Dewey strongly believed that philosophical thinking could reform educational practice, and he campaigned to establish a "laboratory" where these ideas could be implemented and tested. The outcome was the opening in 1896 of the University of Chicago's Laboratory School, which sought to educate its pupils as future members of a democratic society. —Trace Jordan

Conducting research on student learning is part of the scholarship of teaching. Such research can be as useful to the higher-education community as can high-powered scientific research. This is especially true if the investigator conducts studies that are worthy of dissemination in national refereed journals. Research studies that produce new knowledge about the teaching and learning process are candidates for publication in science teaching journals, and these publications are now widely considered to support applications for faculty promotion and tenure. —William H. Leonard

The four chapters in this final unit explore a variety of ways to begin thinking about instructional improvement in college science. Ranging from the philosophical to the practical and empirical, the authors take us from John Dewey to self-reflection, and from testing and assessment methods to research in college science teaching.

Karleen Goubeaud of Long Island University (New York) discusses significant results of the large-scale National Study of Postsecondary Faculty. Specifically, she explores differences in the types of *assessment strategies and grading practices* used by college biology, chemistry, and physics teachers and the importance of performance-based, alternative evaluation techniques as a way to improve college science teaching. Results indicate that important differences exist among disciplines, and comparisons of the 1993 and 1999 study data suggest that the differences are stable. She concludes with some important recommendations on the use of formative, "constructivist" approaches for improving instruction.

Linda Hodges of Princeton University focuses on the *instructional and curricular choices* facing college science instructors and on the kinds of questions we should ask ourselves as we reflect on ways to improve our courses. She suggests that we can become more effective by "being intentional" in our decision making. The most important questions we can ask are related to what we want students to learn, classroom style, coping with students' differing expectations and responses, and assessing student learning.

Trace Jordan of New York University suggests that improvement will require college science instructors to seek out and explore links between their disciplines and the larger society of which we are a part. Drawing on the philosophical foundations of John Dewey and others, Trace suggests that our goals should be broadened to include a greater emphasis on *civic engagement and citizenship in a democratic society* as major goals of college science teaching. He says that we need to include specific instruction on a "deeper understanding of how science is done, how knowledge is tested and advanced, and what science can and cannot offer us" (Ramaley and Haggett 2005, p. 9).

Finally, Bill Leonard of Clemson University discusses research as a practical and useful vehicle for improving college science teaching. He describes the steps involved in doing *qualitative and quantitative classroom research*, provides illustrative examples of research in college science teaching, and discusses the scholarship of teaching as an important contribution to improving teaching effectiveness and as a vehicle for professional advancement.

Reference

Ramaley, J. A., and R. R. Haggett. 2005. Engaged and engaging science: A component of a good liberal education. *Peer Review* 7: 8–12.

CHAPTER 35

Assessment Practices in College Science:
Trends From the National Study of Postsecondary Faculty

Karleen Goubeaud

Karleen Goubeaud is assistant professor of education at the C.W. Post Campus of Long Island University. She earned an EdD in science education at Indiana University of Pennsylvania and conducts research on assessment practices in science education. She teaches science methods and classroom assessment courses at the undergraduate and graduate levels.

Assessment has come to the forefront of educational issues since the mid-1980s as the accountability movement in education continues to grow (Linn, Baker, and Betebenner 2002). This movement extends to higher education, where there is public concern that colleges and universities provide a high-quality education for all students, particularly students entering careers in science and engineering fields as well as science education (Black 2003).

The role of assessment in teaching and learning has also been elevated in importance recently by educators who are responding to the advances of cognitive science that shed light on how students learn. Research indicates that students learn by building their own knowledge structures as they are actively engaged in meaningful learning, in contrast to the transmission model of learning in which students are passive receivers of information (Yager 1991). The recent increased emphasis on inquiry learning in science education should prompt educators to reexamine their science assessment practices, ensuring that not only the products but also the process of scientific knowing are assessed (Duschl 2003). Whereas traditional methods of assessment are consistent with a transmission model of learning, new ideas about instruction based on cognitive science necessitate new assessment techniques (Shepard 2000) that match curricular goals (Atkin and Black 2003).

In the last few decades, there has been a movement in education toward performance-based or alternative types of assessments. Performance-based assessments have the potential to inform teaching and improve learning, in contrast to traditional assessments that primarily serve as an evaluative tool (Bass and Glaser 2004; Wiggins 1998). Alternative assessments are said to be more "authentic," engaging students in assignments or projects in a real-world context, similar to tasks of scientists working in the field (see *www.flaguide.org*). In science teaching, the benefits of using alternative assessments have been recognized by the American Association for the Advancement of Science (1990) and recommended by the National Science Education Standards (National Research Council [NRC] 1996). The Standards recommend using an assortment of assessment types to assess the variety of types of student learning through performance-based or more "authentic" assessment. The Standards document states that "all aspects of science achievement— ability to inquire, scientific understanding of the natural world, understanding of the nature and utility of science—are measured using multiple methods such as performance and portfolios, as well as conventional paper-and-pencil tests" (NRC 1996, p. 76).

Performance-based assessments are more authentic, more complex, and more flexible than traditional assessments (Gronlund 2005). Traditional paper-and-pencil tests often limit the amount of complexity involved in the assessment and decrease the authenticity of the task. For example, multiple-choice assessments use a selected-response format that is considered to be low in complexity because a limited problem is solved with the choice of a correct answer. In addition, the types of questions found on typical multiple-choice or short-answer tests often emphasize recall rather than understanding of science concepts (Stiggins, Griswold, and Wikelund 1989). Performance-based assessments, in contrast, require students to integrate their skills to solve a complex problem through an active learning experience. Performance-based assessments can vary in terms of being more restricted (e.g., essay writing) or open-ended in structure (e.g., student-directed projects), but generally are considered to be more authentic, more consistent with constructivist ideas of student learning, and better suited to inform teaching than paper-and-pencil tests (Stiggins 2002; Wiggins 1998). In the science classroom, performance-based assessments might include learning products such as student essays and other writing activities, portfolios, and science projects that illustrate students' scientific thinking. These types of assessments allow students to demonstrate their understanding, providing faculty with opportunities to monitor students' learning and to individualize student feedback. In addition, assessment strategies in which students critique each other's work offer opportunities for students to revise and polish their performance-based products (Chappuis and Stiggins 2002).

Grading practices are an important part of the assessment process and should be chosen based on the purpose of the assessment and the potential impact on student learning. Criterion-referenced assessments are recommended over traditional norm-referenced assessments, which compare students' scores rather than indicate the degree of competence students have achieved (Gronlund 2005; Sadler 2005). Although grading on a curve or other norm-referenced grading practices may be useful for some evaluation purposes such as school-level comparisons, these practices are not usually recommended for classroom assessment, which should focus on the extent to which learning objectives have been met (Popham 2003).

The trend toward using performance-based or authentic assessment is evident at K–12 levels of schooling (Stiggins 1991) but less evident in college science teaching. Examples of the latter include the use of laboratory practical formats in biology and chemistry (Robyt and White 1990) and portfolios in physics (Slater 1997). Ruiz-Primo and colleagues (2004) success-

fully used student notebooks as an assessment method in science education. However, more information is needed about the types of assessments used by college science faculty and the extent to which science faculty use alternative strategies in their assessment repertoire.

Method

This study used the National Study of Postsecondary Faculty (NSOPF), sponsored by the U.S. Department of Education, as a data source for a large-scale descriptive study examining the assessment practices of science faculty at the college level (see *http://nces.ed.gov/surveys/nsopf*). The types of assessments used by college faculty in various areas of science disciplines are discussed from the perspective of current assessment reform efforts. The purpose of the study is to (a) describe the assessment practices of biology, chemistry, and physics faculty at the college level; (b) compare the assessment practices of faculty from various science disciplines; and (c) examine the recent trends in college faculty assessment practices to determine whether they implement traditional or performance-based assessment strategies. The study uses a nationally representative sample of college science faculty from the NSOPF database, the largest database of higher education faculty in existence.

This study uses two waves of data, NSOPF:93 and NSOPF:99, collected in 1993 and 1999 by the National Center for Education Statistics (U.S. Department of Education 1997, 2002). The 1993 data set provides information about faculty assessment practices from a sample of 31,354 higher-education faculty, including about 2,800 science faculty in the fields of biology, chemistry, and physics. The 1999 data set includes a sample of 28,576 higher-education faculty, including about 2,750 science faculty. The sample drawn from NSOPF includes faculty from all types of institutions, both public and private, and is representative of the composition of science education faculty in the United States in terms of demographics and other characteristics.

In this study, the use of the following assessment strategies by college science faculty are described: multiple-choice exams, essay exams, short-answer exams, term or research papers, peer assessment, and multiple student drafts of written work. Chi-square analysis was used to compare assessment practices of science faculty in the fields of biology, chemistry, and physics to determine differences in their use of alternative or more traditional types of assessment strategies. All analyses were conducted with appropriate weights for the complex survey design of NSOPF:93 and NSOPF:99 to adjust for differential probabilities of selection and nonresponse at the institution and faculty levels (U.S. Department of Education 1997).

Results

Assessment Practices Used by Science Faculty

The results of the study indicated that there were statistically significant differences between the types of assessments and grading practices used by science faculty in the subject areas of biology, chemistry, and physics. There appears to be a slight increase from 1993 to 1999 in the proportion of faculty who used assessment and grading practices that could be considered consistent with constructivist strategies (Table 35.1).

Traditional Types of Assessment

Multiple-choice exams. A greater proportion of biology faculty used multiple-choice exams than chemistry or physics faculty. For example, in 1999, 73.2% of biology faculty used mul-

Table 35.1

Types of Classroom Assessments Used by Science Faculty

Assessment Type	Biology		Chemistry		Physics		χ^2
	N	%	N	%	N	%	
Multiple-choice exams							
1993	1137	77.9	255	55.7	332	37.7	447.94**
1999	1124	73.2	228	56.4	365	44.8	219.94**
Short-answer exams							
1993	741	50.8	310	69.9	465	52.7	56.75**
1999	935	60.9	304	75.3	511	62.7	32.69**
Essay exams							
1993	642	43.9	228	49.7	336	38.1	26.61**
1999	800	52.1	190	47.0	382	46.8	11.19*
Term or research papers							
1993	757	51.9	154	33.6	339	38.4	68.52**
1999	904	58.9	167	41.3	390	47.7	55.63**
Students' evaluation of each others' work (peer assessment)							
1993	451	30.9	71	15.7	168	19.1	68.58**
1999	635	41.4	89	22.0	260	31.8	70.61**
Multiple drafts of written work							
1993	391	26.8	81	17.7	130	14.8	58.02**
1999	398	32.5	83	20.5	220	27.0	30.13**

Note: *$P < 0.05$; **$P < 0.001$.

tiple-choice exams, compared with 56.4% of chemistry faculty and 44.8% of physics faculty. Differences between biology, chemistry, and physics faculty in their use of multiple-choice tests were statistically significant. Similar patterns were found for both 1993 and 1999 data.

Short-answer exams. In 1999 a greater proportion of chemistry faculty (75.3%) used short-answer exams than either biology (60.9%) or physics faculty (62.7%). There was an increase in science faculty's use of short-answer exams between 1993 and 1999 for all three subject areas.

Types of Assessment Consistent With Constructivist Pedagogy

Students' evaluation of each others' work. The practice of using students to critique other students' work (peer assessment) is consistent with a constructivist paradigm in that feedback from peers helps students revise their work and broadens their thinking to understand others' viewpoints. Palomba (1999) recommended that college students be involved in the assessment process and suggested specifically that students assist in grading or critiquing their peers' projects or presentations.

Less than half of science faculty used the practice of students assessing other students' work. The number of faculty using student assessment of their own work increased somewhat between 1993 and 1999 for faculty in biology (30.9% vs. 41.4%), chemistry (15.7% vs. 22.0%), and physics (19.1% vs. 31.8%).

Term or research papers. Using term or research papers as assessments could be considered consistent with a constructivist paradigm because writing activities help students communicate their thinking, facilitating conceptual change (Fellows 1994). Writing assessments also provide an opportunity to assess science inquiry learning (Keys 1999).

A greater proportion of biology faculty used term or research papers than chemistry or physics faculty. In 1993, 51.9% of biology faculty used this type of assessment, compared with only 33.6% of chemistry and 38.4% of physics faculty. Use of term or research papers by faculty across all three science subject areas increased somewhat from 1993 to 1999.

Essay exams. Essay exams involve answering questions that are open-ended; they allow for in-depth student responses and are often considered to be a useful tool for evaluating students' scientific understanding. Essay writing is an assessment strategy consistent with constructivist pedagogy because essays give students an opportunity to articulate their scientific understandings through the writing process. Jacobs (1992) recommended essay writing in higher education because it is suited to assessment of complex learning outcomes better than test items that merely require students to recognize correct responses.

Science faculty's use of essay exams increased slightly from 1993 to 1999 for both biology and physics faculty, but not for chemistry faculty. For example, in 1993 38.1% of physics faculty used essay exams, compared with 46.8% in 1999.

Multiple drafts of written work. In contrast to traditional tests that are administered after a unit of study is complete, alternative assessments are often completed by students as part of the learning process. Students can be given feedback by the teacher or their student peers as the assessment project is being completed. Students are often given opportunities to revise and resubmit their work before a final evaluation takes place.

Science faculty use of multiple drafts of student work in the assessment process increased somewhat from 1993 to 1999. However, fewer than one-third of science faculty in any science subject used this type of assessment strategy. For example, in 1999 32.5% of biology faculty, 20.5% of chemistry faculty, and 27.0% of physics faculty used multiple drafts of written work in their classes.

Summary of Assessment Practices

A comparison of the 1993 and 1999 data indicate that there was a slight increase in the use of several assessment practices that are consistent with constructivist pedagogy. Overall, science faculty's use of essay exams, term or research papers, multiple drafts of written work, and students evaluating each other's work increased slightly during the 1990s. For traditional

assessments such as multiple-choice exams, patterns of changes during the 1990s are less clear. Significantly more biology faculty used multiple-choice exams than chemistry or physics faculty. For short-answer exams, there was a slight increase in use during the 1990s. Because there is no information in the database regarding the types of short-answer questions used in exams, it is difficult to interpret whether the trend is to use more open-ended or unstructured questions, which is more consistent with constructivist practice.

Grading Practices Used by Science Faculty

The practice of grading on a curve is problematic because it forces students to compete for grades without giving them opportunities to improve their performance. Grades should reflect only the achievement of the student (competency-based grading) and should not be affected by other students' performance on an assessment (Sadler 2005). Sadler recommends criterion-referenced types of grading in which students are given the criteria early in the assessment process so that this information can improve students' learning and performance.

Table 35.2 summarizes grading strategies used by science faculty in 1993 and 1999. A greater proportion of physics and chemistry faculty graded on a curve than biology faculty

Table 35.2

Types of Grading Practices Used by Science Faculty

Grading Practice	Biology		Chemistry		Physics		χ2
	N	%	N	%	N	%	
Grading on a curve							
1993	398	27.3	230	50.2	485	55.0	220.56**
1999	421	27.4	185	45.8	430	52.7	186.06**
Competency-based grading							
1993	873	59.8	229	50.0	467	52.9	25.25**
1999	913	59.5	218	53.9	466	57.2	10.04*

Note: *$P < 0.05$; **$P < 0.001$.

(52.7% and 45.8% versus 27.4%, respectively, in 1999). The practice of grading on a curve decreased slightly between 1993 and 1999 for chemistry and physics faculty but remained unchanged for biology faculty.

Slightly more than half of science faculty reported that they use competency-based grading in their classes. In 1999, 59.5% of biology faculty, 53.9% of chemistry faculty, and 57.2% of physics faculty used competency-based grading; similar patterns were seen in 1993.

To summarize the trends in faculty grading practices, there was a slight decrease in the practice of grading on a curve for both chemistry and physics faculty from 1993 to 1999. Note that the proportion of biology faculty grading on a curve did not change during the same time period; it remained at about 27%, less than for chemistry or physics faculty. The opposite

pattern was found for use of competency-based grading in that there was a slight increase in this type of grading for chemistry and physics faculty from 1993 to 1999. About one-half of science faculty reported using competency-based grading.

Summary of Results

This large-scale descriptive study of science faculty assessment practices found that science faculty teaching biology, chemistry, and physics have distinct patterns of assessment and grading practices. Science faculty used both traditional and more constructivist types of assessments. Comparing practices in 1993 with those of 1999, it appears that faculty's use of constructivist-type assessments and grading practices slightly increased during the 1990s (e.g., using multiple drafts of written work, student involvement in the assessment process, and assessment practices that require students' expressing their ideas in writing). Despite this apparent increase, these methods may still be underused.

Note on Study Data

The NSOPF database provides an opportunity to examine the assessment strategies used by college science faculty from a nationally representative sample of science faculty. What remains unclear from the database is how assessment strategies were implemented or administered during instruction. The database does not contain survey items to address how the instructional strategies were executed in the context of the classroom. Further research, particularly qualitative research, is recommended to examine how assessments and grading practices were used by science faculty that might be consistent with a constructivist paradigm.

Recommendations for Using Alternative Assessments in College Science Teaching

Most educators agree on the benefits of formative assessment as a way to enhance learning (Maclellan 2004). More faculty at the college and university levels now view assessment as a way to nurture students' learning as well as an evaluative tool (Heady 2000). Several suggestions are offered to enhance assessment practices in college science teaching.

First, choose an assessment type that matches the type of learning goals in the curriculum. Different types of science learning require different assessment tools. A key consideration in choosing an assessment type is the match between what the program is attempting to achieve (e.g., science inquiry learning) and the culture of learning that is being created in the classroom (Light and Cox 2001).

Second, design assessments with clear guidelines that allow the desired learning outcomes to be assessed. If students' conceptual understanding is being developed through the instruction, then assessments should be used that make students' thinking apparent and measurable.

Third, design rubrics or other evaluative tools to enhance uniformity of the scoring process and increase validity and reliability. Just as objective tests can be unreliable due to inadequate sampling of items or other technical errors (Burton 2001, 2005), care must be taken when evaluating performance-based assessments. It is important to design scoring rubrics or other grading procedures that define the levels of proficiency and provide criteria to guide student performance of the assessment task (Wiggins 1998).

The results of this study suggest that new ideas about instruction based on cognitive science and constructivism necessitate new types of assessment (Shepard 2000). It is hoped that by understanding the assessment practices used by college science faculty, educators can evaluate their own practices and expand their repertoire to include assessment tools that have the potential to inform practice and enhance student learning.

References

American Association for the Advancement of Science. 1990. *Science for all Americans.* New York: Oxford University Press.

Atkin, J. M., and P. Black. 2003. *Inside science education reform: A history of curricular and policy change.* New York: Teachers College Press.

Bass, K. M., and R. Glaser. 2004. *Developing assessments to inform teaching and learning.* CSE Report 628. Los Angeles: University of California, Los Angeles, Graduate School of Education and Information Studies, National Center for Research on Evaluation, Standards, and Student Testing, Center for the Study of Evaluation. Also available online at *www.cse.ucla.edu/reports/R628.pdf.*

Black, P. 2003. The importance of everyday assessment. In *Everyday assessment in the science classroom*, eds. J. M. Atkin and J. Coffey, 1–11. Washington, DC: NSTA Press.

Burton, R. F. 2001. Quantifying the effects of chance in multiple choice and true/false tests: Question selection and guessing of answers. *Assessment & Evaluation in Higher Education* 26: 41–50.

Burton, R. F. 2005. Multiple-choice and true/false tests: Myths and misapprehensions. *Assessment & Evaluation in Higher Education* 30: 65–72.

Chappuis, S., and R. J. Stiggins. 2002. Classroom assessment for learning. *Educational Leadership* 60: 40–43.

Duschl, R. A. 2003. Assessment of inquiry. In *Everyday assessment in the science classroom*, eds. J. M. Atkin and J. Coffey, 41–59. Washington, DC: NSTA Press.

Fellows, N. J. 1994. A window into thinking: Using student writing to understand conceptual change in science learning. *Journal of Research in Science Teaching* 31: 985–1001.

Gronlund, N. E. 2005. *Assessment of student achievement.* 8th ed. Boston: Allyn & Bacon.

Heady, J. E. 2000. Assessment—a way of thinking about learning—now and in the future: The dynamic and ongoing nature of measuring and improving student learning. *Journal of College Science Teaching* 29: 415–421.

Jacobs, L. C. 1992. *Developing and using tests effectively: A guide for faculty.* San Francisco: Jossey-Bass.

Keys, C. W. 1999. Language as an indicator of meaning generation: An analysis of middle school students' written discourse about scientific investigations. *Journal of Research in Science Teaching* 36: 1044–1061.

Light, G., and P. Cox. 2001. *Learning and teaching in higher education: The reflective professional.* London: Paul Chapman.

Linn, R. L., E. L. Baker, and D. W. Betebenner. 2002. Accountability systems: Implication of requirements of the No Child Left Behind Act of 2001. *Educational Researcher* 31: 3–16.

Maclellan, E. 2004. How convincing is alternative assessment for use in higher education? *Assessment & Evaluation in Higher Education* 29: 311–321.

National Research Council (NRC). 1996. *National science education standards.* Washington, DC: National Academy Press.

Palomba, C. A. 1999. *Assessment essentials: Planning, implementing, and improving assessment in higher education.* San Francisco: Jossey-Bass.

Popham, J. 2003. The seductive allure of data. *Educational Leadership* 60: 48–51.

Robyt, J. F., and B. J. White. 1990. Laboratory practical exams in the biochemistry lab course. *Journal of Chemical Education* 67: 600–601.

Ruiz-Primo, M. A., M. Li, C. Ayala, R. Park, and R. J. Shavelson. 2004. Evaluating students' science notebooks as an assessment tool. *International Journal of Science Education* 26: 1477–1506.

Sadler, D. R. 2005. Interpretations of criteria-based assessment and grading in higher education. *Assessment & Evaluation in Higher Education* 30: 175–194.

Shepard, L. A. 2000. The role of assessment in a learning culture. *Educational Researcher* 29: 4–14.

Slater, T. F. 1997. The effectiveness of portfolio assessments in science: Integrating an alternative, holistic approach to learning into the classroom. *Journal of College Science Teaching* 26: 315–318.

Stiggins, R. J. 1991. Facing the challenges of a new era of educational assessment. *Applied Measurement in Education* 4: 263–273.

Stiggins, R. J. 2002. Assessment crisis: The absence of assessment FOR learning. *Phi Delta Kappan* 83: 758–765. Also available online at *www.pdkintl.org/kappan/k0206sti.htm*.

Stiggins, R. J., M. M. Griswold, and K. R. Wikelund. 1989. Measuring thinking skills through classroom assessment. *Journal of Educational Measurement* 26: 233–246.

U.S. Department of Education. National Center for Education Statistics (NCES). 1997. *1993 National Study of Postsecondary Faculty (NSOPF-93): Methodology Report*. NCES 97467. Written by L. A. Selfa, N. Suter, S. Myers, S. Kock, R. A. Johnson, D. A. Zahs, B. D. Kuhr, and S. Y. Abraham; Project Officer L. J. Zimbler. Washington, DC: NCES.

U.S. Department of Education, National Center for Education Statistics (NCES). 1999. *National Study of Postsecondary Faculty (NSOPF:99) Methodology Report*. NCES 2002154. Written by S. Y. Abraham, D. M. Steiger, M. Montgomery, B. D. Kuhr, R. Tourangeau, B. Montgomery, and M. Chattopadhyay; Project Officer L. J. Zimbler. Washington, DC: NCES.

Wiggins, G. 1998. *Educative assessment: Designing assessment to inform and improve student performance*. San Francisco: Jossey-Bass.

Yager, R. E. 1991. The constructivist learning model: Towards real reform in science education. *The Science Teacher* 58: 52–57.

CHAPTER 36

Making Choices About Teaching and Learning in Science

Linda C. Hodges

Linda C. Hodges is director of the McGraw Center for Teaching and Learning at Princeton University. She earned a PhD in biochemistry at the University of Kentucky and conducts research on teaching approaches that promote deep learning and on professors' beliefs. She has taught courses in biochemistry, organic chemistry, general chemistry, and pharmacology.

A number of groups, from college professors to policy makers, are talking about changing the way undergraduate science is traditionally taught. The National Science Foundation (among others) has provided extensive funds and resources for this effort. Part of the reasoning behind this push is that the methods advocated, such as various forms of group work, cooperative or collaborative learning, and case-based teaching, seem to engage the modern student better, promoting student learning and student retention to a greater extent than the traditional mode of lecture alone. A growing number of studies strongly suggest that these approaches develop students' critical-thinking and problem-solving abilities and increase students' engagement in their learning. Many of these methods seem to fit within the idea of best practices from constructivist theory—that is, the view that knowledge cannot be transferred intact from lecturer to listener but must be actively constructed by the learner in part through interactions with others. Research in cognitive science seems to validate some of these approaches in that they often involve students in processing information in multiple ways that activate parts of the brain used for long-term memory (see Chapters 11 and 12 in this volume).

As we think about the various modes of teaching now under discussion, the choices facing us as instructors can seem to be overwhelming, confusing, and onerous, adding even more demands to our busy schedules. How do we know which, if any, of these teaching approaches may be helpful for us in our classes? What do we stand to gain by trying something new? Or worse, what might we lose? Is there one approach that holds the key to student learning?

Suffice it to say that one size does not fit all when it comes to how teaching promotes learning. For one thing, what we mean by learning varies from discipline to discipline, instructor to instructor, and even course to course. In science classes we certainly wish to convey certain facts, principles, and concepts to students, but in many classes we also hope to cultivate students' abilities to understand the processes of science, think critically about evidence, and conduct scientific work. We may also hope to change the way students view the natural world and the place of humans in it, and perhaps to inspire students with a passion for the field.

Most of us who are practicing scientists probably experienced lecture as the predominant mode of teaching in our science classes, and perhaps we benefited richly from that kind of teaching. But the vast majority of students in our science classes today do not gain as much from lecture alone. For most of these students, we need to intentionally design our teaching approaches to foster the specific aims we have for our courses; we need to move beyond just teaching as we were taught. Fortunately, if we think about what we really want our teaching to accomplish, we can more easily choose among the teaching strategies available to find those that work best for us individually and for our students. In this chapter I draw from my perspective as director of a teaching and learning center and a veteran science professor and provide questions to help you think through your options. I have found these questions very useful in guiding my own teaching choices. I also provide a brief overview of some of the research showing the connections between teaching and learning and the range of pedagogical practices that can support student learning. The take-home message is that no one pedagogical strategy provides the "magic bullet" for student learning, but our choices in the classroom do make a difference. Being intentional in what we want to accomplish in the classroom or lab helps us become more effective teachers.

What Do You Want Students to Learn?

We all want students to learn certain content in our classes, but to what end? What do you want them to do with that content? Do you expect them to weigh evidence and make decisions based on data and logic? Do you want them to think like scientists in solving problems? Do you want them to apply content from your course in a subsequent science course?

Thinking about what you hope to accomplish in your teaching, that is, what you hope students will learn, can be illuminated by research on how people learn. Many of us agree that we want students to remember certain ideas from our courses after the final examination, and we'd like our students to use what they've learned in future classes or in making decisions as a concerned citizen. Research in cognitive science has uncovered a number of key ideas related to humans' ability to retain information and "transfer" what is learned in one context to another area, problem, course, or subject (Halpern and Hakel 2003). By keeping these key ideas in mind as we design our classes, we increase the chances that our students' learning will extend beyond the boundaries of our classroom and the time frame of our exams.

- *Assessing and building on prior knowledge:* The most important factor affecting students' learning is prior knowledge. What students think they know often impedes their learning more than what they know nothing about, and, conversely, adding new knowledge to existing frameworks is easier than constructing knowledge from scratch. Finding out what students already know about a topic and building on it is fundamental to generating meaningful and lasting knowledge (see Chapter 12 in this volume).

- *Varying the learning conditions; providing practice at retrieval:* Using different class formats that require students to pull information from memory and use it in slightly different ways helps them generate a more diverse set of "cues" for accessing this information in the future (see Chapter 5 in this volume).
- *Re-representing information:* Providing some time in class when students re-represent information (e.g., moving from words to graphs, from symbols to words) increases their ability to use knowledge in different ways and recognize information in different formats (see Chapter 7 in this volume).
- *Interpreting information and thinking about thinking:* Providing opportunities for students to do interpretative work helps them process information more deeply, as does guiding students in thinking about how they know what they know (metacognition).
- *Remembering helps remembering:* Finally, asking students to call up certain information, as in a testing situation, actually "hardwires" that information, often at the expense of something else. Thus, designing assessments that test what we most want students to know is crucial to what students actually remember.

How can we incorporate these ideas into our teaching? Some instructors probe students' background knowledge at the beginning of the class through quizzes. Another option is to use ConcepTests during class. These are conceptually challenging questions that you pose to students and ask them to answer from a list of options. You can ask students to answer either just by themselves, or preferably both alone and then again after discussion with a partner, an approach called Peer Instruction (Mazur 1997; see Chapter 8 in this volume). Students' responses are tallied, often using some kind of technological aid such as classroom response systems or "clickers." In this case, responses are displayed in graphical form to the class. Then, before disclosing the best answer, you ask students to turn to a student, or a few students, next to them and share their answer and reasoning, trying to convince the others. After this brief discussion, students are polled again, and the new set of answers displayed. The increase in the number of correct answers in the second case is often quite dramatic. Not only does this kind of activity uncover students' naive preconceptions, but also it helps them see differences in ways to reason through a problem and requires them to retrieve information from memory. Other ways to get students to call up information from memory include the age-old practice of Socratic questioning and interrupting class with group problem-solving sessions. Mixing up class activities and asking students to produce evidence of what they've learned improves their knowledge retention and transfer and also energizes students and extends their attention span, so that any lecturing you do choose to do can be better received.

Interpreting and re-representing concepts involves students in reformulating ideas, enhancing their ability to apply this information in other settings. Giving students practice in interpretative work can be accomplished by a bit of a shift in what we may perceive as our role in the class. For example, rather than telling students the meaning of a graph in lecture, you can take a few minutes in class and have students work in pairs or groups to decode information presented in this way. You then have a number of options for publicizing the results. You can ask for the "right" or best answer and end the discussion as soon as it's given. Another option is to ask some groups to share their conclusions without your comments, compile their answers on the board, and have the rest of the class decide on the best interpretation. An advantage to these extra steps is that students see the range of responses, thus dispelling their naive notion of one easy answer. You are also giving students practice in thinking through and critiquing alternative explanations. This process helps them deepen their understanding of concepts. Asking students to defend their choice and explain it helps them be explicit with themselves on how they think through an issue—how they know what they know (metacognition).

Many of us hesitate to try these strategies because they appear to cost us in terms of content coverage. As instructors, we often comfort ourselves by assuming that if we cover content, students can or should be able to learn it. The research on learning is quite clear on this point: What students do in class is much more important than what we do in class. Although lecture is a reasonable way to convey information or motivate interest, lecture alone does not promote retention of information or the ability of students to be able to apply this information. Lecture preparation is hard work on our part, and we learn a lot as we grapple with the information, organize it, reframe it, anticipate questions, and look for weaknesses in our arguments; our thinking often clears and gels as we write. Is it realistic to think that students can derive the same benefits by just listening? Given the many other sources of information available to students, we professors may more productively spend our class time engaging students in the intellectual processes involved in learning in our discipline.

What's Your Classroom Style?

If lecture is your usual mode of teaching, then thinking about more student-active approaches can be a bit daunting. The continuum of student-active strategies (many are dealt with in other chapters in this volume) includes those that may be considered lower risk and less time-intensive: interactive lectures, one-minute papers, student writing exercises, paired activities, and use of case studies. Strategies that are often considered higher risk and more time intensive include extensive use of case studies, student projects, role-playing, small-group work, cooperative or collaborative learning, and problem-based learning. The various models of group work, cooperative learning, and case study teaching all involve instructors relinquishing some control of the classroom dynamic to students. In these approaches, the faculty member's role focuses more on facilitating process and less on disseminating content. Likewise, the instructor's class preparation consists more in generating or finding meaningful exercises to push students beyond rote learning or challenge students working in groups. Materials are available from book suppliers, at conferences, or on the internet, or instructors may choose to create their own materials. How much time are you willing to invest in and out of class in generating and testing new materials? How willing are you to invest time in monitoring group function rather than preparing lectures?

Many of these methods involve students talking about ideas with other students. This conversation helps them uncover prior knowledge and integrate new ideas into their previous understanding, promoting retention and transfer as mentioned earlier. In addition, having students make "products" of their learning through talking and writing seems to promote long-term memory better than solitary musing on ideas in their heads, during lecture, for example (Zull 2002). The real concern of students' perpetuating misconceptions in these activities may be counterbalanced by the increased student engagement resulting from these formats.

That said, if we're most used to lecturing, then approaches involving extensive use of student groups require us to make a rather dramatic change in our classroom style. Some faculty find this transition ultimately highly rewarding. Many good resources exist for getting started in working with student groups, but if this intense interpersonal involvement isn't your cup of tea, other options for student interactions exist, for example, brief intervals of paired work during lecture. The success of strategies such as peer instruction seems to affirm the power of even short intervals of productive student conversation in class.

Our pedagogical choices need to fit not only our goals for student learning but also our personality and comfort level. New strategies that stretch us a bit beyond our comfort zone are certainly worth trying, and we all improve with practice. But there is the reality that some of us just do not have the time or personality to try the more intensive methods. There is no shame in this. We must be genuine in our teaching if we hope to engender authentic learning in our students.

How Will You Cope With Students' Differing Expectations and Responses?

As we think about the kinds of learning we hope to encourage in our students, the kinds of teaching methods we think best match these goals, and our comfort level with different kinds of teaching, we need to realize that students have expectations of the class and of us that may be different from ours. Not only are many students taking science classes for a college requirement, but also they have their own prior experiences of what science classes are. If our approach differs significantly from what they've come to expect, they may feel disoriented and fearful and may take their stress out on us.

Students' intellectual development may also affect their response to a particular teaching strategy. Work by William Perry (1999, originally published in 1968) and Belenky and colleagues (1986), for example, showed that more novice learners often expect classes to provide right/wrong answers to questions. If our teaching strategy asks students to deal with questions for which the answers are ambiguous (often an important prerequisite to developing critical-thinking skills), they may think that we are deliberately withholding information or playing games with them. Conversely, for more experienced learners, courses that seem very fact-driven may be unchallenging. Novice learners may need support as you ask them to struggle with ways of knowing in the discipline. You may need to explicitly talk about and provide exercises to demonstrate how models in science develop and evolve as new information is discovered. More senior students, on the other hand, may welcome the chance to explore more controversial ideas on their own. Thinking about who your students are as learners and sharing your thoughts with them about the kind of learning you hope to cultivate are important elements of any pedagogical choice.

How Will You Assess Student Learning?

How we assess student learning is a critical part of our overall teaching approach. Not only do our assessment methods help foster (or impede) the kind of learning that we hope to achieve, but also students see what we value in learning by what we assess (see "Field-Tested Learning Assessment Guide" at *www.flaguide.org* and Chapter 35 in this volume). Do our tests, exams, papers, and grading allocations match our professed goals for student learning? This volume includes ideas and examples for various options to assess student learning. Once we decide what kind of learning we most want students to gain from our teaching approach, then we can design our assessment measures appropriately. Keep in mind that students' real intellectual development is often incremental. Students learn best when given opportunities to take intellectual risks with subsequent feedback and without facing dire penalties. Thus designing some exercises that give students practice, so-called formative assessments, allows you both to monitor their progress and provide guidance to help them develop as learners, before the final, summative, assessment.

The research observation mentioned earlier, that remembering promotes remembering, provides a cautionary note for those of us who often like to use exams to test the exception rather than the rule. This practice arises when we assume that most students are familiar with the rule and that we will be sorting the wheat from the chaff through this assessment approach. In actuality, for students who have a tenuous grasp of both rule and exception, we may be reinforcing the exception and driving the rule from their memories. Thus, our assessment of student learning plays a pivotal role in deciding what students will actually remember from our classes.

Finally, although helping students understand content is often a major goal of our teaching, we usually want students to benefit in other ways as well. We may want them to be able to use evidence to support a claim, design a scientific experiment, or work productively with others on a project. These types of learning goals may not lend themselves to assessment via a traditional exam. How will activities that you have students do to achieve these ends factor into their grade? Time is a precious commodity for faculty and students alike, and students often prioritize their work in a class around those activities that are reflected in our grading of the course. Likewise we instructors indicate what we truly value in student learning through our grading practices. Deciding what kind of learning you most want students to gain allows you to design assessments that gauge that learning.

Conclusions

Just as in our research fields we recognize that our goals and methods affect our outcomes, so too, being intentional in our teaching helps our teaching effectiveness. There is now a substantial amount of evidence that suggests that different teaching methods promote different kinds of learning. That said, however, we as well as our students have prior experiences that can make it challenging to accept different approaches than those with which we are familiar. Communicating our teaching goals to our students helps them "buy in" to our methods. Recognizing that they, like us, differ in their comfort level with various strategies and factoring that into our course planning is prerequisite to course success, especially in terms of their and our satisfaction. We show students what we value in learning through what we assess, so we need to design our assignments and tests so that they align with our self-professed goals for student learning. And, finally, no single pedagogical strategy provides the key to student learning, so we may feel free to experiment with options and adapt methods that fit most closely with what we hope to achieve.

References

Belenky, M. F., B. M. Clinchy, N. R. Goldberger, and J. R. Tarule. 1986. *Women's ways of knowing*. New York: Basic Books.

Halpern, D., and M. Hakel. 2003. Applying the science of learning to the university and beyond. *Change* 35: 2–13.

Mazur, E. 1997. *Peer instruction: A user's manual*. Upper Saddle River, NJ: Prentice Hall.

Perry, W. G., Jr. 1999. *Forms of intellectual development in the college years: A scheme*. San Francisco: Jossey-Bass (originally published in 1968 by Holt, Rinehart and Winston).

Zull, J. 2002. *The art of changing the brain*. Sterling, VA: Stylus.

CHAPTER 37

Science and Civic Engagement:
Changing Perspectives From Dewey to DotNets

Trace Jordan

Trace Jordan is associate director of the Morse Academic Plan at New York University. He earned a PhD in chemistry at Princeton University and conducts research on science education for nonmajors and on science and civic engagement. He teaches courses about human genetics, energy and the environment, and molecules of life.

A prominent theme in current discourse about U.S. higher education is the goal of "civic" education. In its "Statement on Liberal Learning," the American Association of Colleges and Universities (1998) advocates that "we explore connections among formal learning, citizenship, and service to our communities." In a monograph entitled *Educating Citizens*, Colby and coauthors (2003) encourage institutional learning goals that enable students to "see the moral and civic dimensions of issues, to make and justify informed moral and civic judgements, and to take action where appropriate" (p. 17).

But what exactly do we mean by civic engagement? Does it imply a way of thinking about knowledge in a democratic society? Or does it require personal action in a civic context? For the readers of this handbook, what relevance does civic education have for our role as science teachers?

This chapter will explore three related perspectives. First, I will examine how John Dewey viewed the relationship between the educated individual and democratic society. Next, I will highlight ways in which contemporary authors are exploring the connection between science and civic engagement, both in broad terms and in specific applications. Finally, I will summarize the results of a recent survey that examined the civic viewpoints of high school and college students.

John Dewey on Education, Democracy, and Science

The relationship between education and civic ideals is not a new idea. Over a century ago, John Dewey expounded on this theme in an influential article entitled "My Pedagogic Creed" (Dewey 1897/1998).

> *I believe that the only true education comes through the stimulation of the child's powers by the demands of the social situations in which he finds himself. Through these demands he is stimulated to act as a member of a unity, to emerge from his original narrowness of action and feeling, and to conceive of himself from the standpoint of the welfare of the group to which he belongs.* (p. 229)

When he wrote these words in 1897, Dewey was entering an exciting new phase in his personal and professional life. Three years earlier, he had arrived at the University of Chicago as a newly appointed professor of philosophy. He was also beginning to abandon his earlier, European-influenced views and embrace a new philosophical perspective that would later be called pragmatism. Dewey strongly believed that philosophical thinking could reform educational practice, and he campaigned to establish a "laboratory" where these ideas could be implemented and tested. The outcome was the opening in 1896 of the University of Chicago's Laboratory School, which sought to educate its pupils as future members of a democratic society.

In his extensive repertoire of later writings, Dewey expanded on this core educational idea of the relationship between the individual and society. He criticized the "limited" and "rigid" focus on "training for citizenship," where "citizenship is then interpreted in a narrow sense as meaning capacity to vote intelligently, disposition to obey laws, etc." Dewey saw "citizenship" as a far more capacious commitment that extended beyond voting and incorporated the student's current and future roles as a family member, parent, worker, and "member of some particular neighborhood and community" (Dewey 1909/1998, p. 246). This perspective exemplified Dewey's concept of democracy, which extended beyond political institutions and encompassed all aspects of society.

Dewey also wrote thoughtfully about the profound impact of science and technology on contemporary life. Although these articles were written decades ago, some themes sound familiar to our modern ears as we face the rapid expansion of scientific knowledge in the 21st century. Dewey (1931/1998, p. 364) began one essay by asserting that "science is by far the most potent social factor in the modern world." In the next breath he sounds overwhelmed by its far-reaching effects, in which "domestic life, political institutions, international relations and personal contacts are changing with kaleidoscopic rapidity before our eyes. We cannot appreciate and weigh the changes; they occur too quickly." Despite this bewilderment, Dewey realized what was at stake with respect to scientific knowledge.

> *The problem involved is the greatest which civilization has ever had to face. It is, without exaggeration, the most serious issue of contemporary life. Here is the instrumentality, the most powerful force for good and evil, the world has ever known. What are we going to do with it?* (p. 364)

Dewey wrote these urgent words in 1931, before the development of atomic weapons, the invention of recombinant DNA techniques, the creation of nanoscale devices, and the ability to manipulate human embryos. His quote concludes with a profound question about scientific knowledge, which has become even more pressing in modern times: What are we going to do with it? In the type of democracy that Dewey envisioned, this is a question that must be grappled with by all members of society, not just those with specialized scientific knowledge. Robert Westbrook summarizes this view in his book *John Dewey and American Democracy*: "Learning to think scientifically was important not just for future scientists but for all members of a democratic society because scientific intelligence was a resource essential to effective freedom. In a democratic society, every man had to be his own scientist" (Westbrook 1991, p. 169).

Science and Civic Education in the 21st Century

Over a century has passed since Dewey wrote "My Pedagogic Creed," and there is now a resurgence of interest in "civic" and "citizenship" education. Some of the contemporary literature on this subject does not have much room for science. In fact, it sometimes exhibits a wistful nostalgia for an earlier time when the liberal arts did not have to compete with the surging research agenda of the modern university. But other scholars and educators are using this expansion of knowledge as an engaging framework to explore the intersection of science and society. This goal has been embodied in the National Research Council's science education standards; Standard F for grades 9–12 is "science in personal and societal perspectives" (National Research Council 1996, pp. 193–199). The reason for this standard was explained in *College Pathways to the Science Education Standards*: "An understanding of science adds to the ability of citizens to make good decisions at the personal and societal (and political) level" (Siebert and McIntosh 2001, p. 107). Drawing on their experiences at the National Science Foundation and National Academy of Science, Ramaley and Haggett (2005, p. 9) argue that "fostering a deeper understanding of how science is done, how knowledge is tested and advanced, and what science can and cannot offer us must be critical goals of a quality education in the twenty-first century."

To illustrate the possibilities of teaching science in a civic context, I have selected several articles that have appeared in the *Journal for College Science Teaching* during the past five years. To focus the presentation, I have grouped them under two scientific themes—genetics and the environment.

It is truly stunning how much has been learned about genes and genomes since the mid-1990s. Terms like *human genome project* and *stem cells* have passed beyond their original confines of scientific specialization into the vocabulary of everyday discourse. Moreover, the social and ethical dilemmas raised by the new research are becoming increasingly urgent, ranging from genetic tests to embryo research. Julie Omarzu (2002) explored these issues in a case study, "Selecting the Perfect Baby." Some of the details were fictional, but the case was based on events from the late 1990s when a couple had a daughter, Molly, with a rare form of genetic disorder called Fanconi's anemia. Desperate to treat her, Molly's parents arranged to have a second child using in vitro fertilization and preimplantation genetic diagnosis. Each of the potential embryos was screened, and the only ones selected were those that could provide Molly with a sibling who was a compatible bone marrow match. In the context of the case, students examine the principles of recessive inheritance, the techniques of in vitro fertilization, and the difficult ethical choices faced by real families.

Katayoun Chamany (2001) designed a case study that examines the links between genetics and human rights. It is based on the children who "disappeared" during the Argentine civil war of the 1970s, taken from their homes and given for adoption to other families who were often members of the ruling military junta. Many years later, a group of courageous grandmothers formed an organization to locate these children and reunite them with their original families.

This case entices students to learn about techniques used for genetic identification and the variation of these markers within a population. In her teaching notes, Chamany explains how she has "specifically chosen material that would reach underrepresented minority students who often fail to see the connection between science and its application to their world" (p. 63). The case study also features women as the primary agents of social and scientific change.

The science of genetics can also be used as a framework for discussing complex civic questions of race and identity that lie at the core of our pluralistic and multicultural society. Today's students are members of a college population whose demographics are changing to include more underrepresented minorities (*Chronicle of Higher Education* 2005, p. 15). In *Educating Citizens in a Multicultural Society*, James A. Banks argues that "students must develop multicultural literacy and cross-cultural competency if they are to become knowledgeable, reflective, and caring citizens in the twenty-first century" (Banks 1997, p. 13). Alan McGowan's course on genes and race begins with the historical development of racial categories and how modern studies of human genetic variation have confounded these simplistic and socially motivated divisions (McGowan 2005). The course also addresses the ongoing debate among physicians about whether to use "race" as a criterion in medical diagnosis. A different approach to this theme is taken by Patricia Schneider (2004), who uses a short story as an entryway into the complex genetics of skin color.

To switch topics, environmental issues provide an excellent opportunity for engaging students with the civic dimensions of science that span the local, national, and global scale. On a local level, Walsh and colleagues (2005) used a campus lake as the focal point for a learning community that joined students who were studying environmental science, environmental engineering, English composition, and landscape architecture. Multiple teams with diverse members were given the assignment of examining current problems facing the lake and presenting solutions to campus and community leaders. Two tangible outcomes from the projects were an increase in students' understanding of water issues and a gain in students' confidence in being an effective member of a team.

McDonald and Dominguez (2005) explore the meaning of "scientific literacy" and how this goal can be achieved through personal engagement with environmental issues in the context of service-learning projects. The authors point out that the National Science Education Standards make "an explicit link between science literacy and stewardship of natural resources" (p. 19).

A different set of challenges is described by Pratte and Laposata (2005), who offer a large-enrollment environmental course as part of a general education curriculum. They and their colleagues developed a set of "activity modules" that emphasize each student's impact on the environment (or vice versa). Each module has a custom-designed website providing interactive exercises, which are used in combination with field and laboratory exercises.

It is worth noting that involving students in activities outside the classroom can raise a complex set of educational and administrative challenges. Grossman and Cooper (2004) provide an honest appraisal of a service-learning course in which students studying environmental science were placed with community-based partners to develop "civic skills" in the context of environmental problem solving. Despite general enthusiasm for the concept of service learning, students expressed disappointment with the learning outcomes from their weekly three-hour investment. The authors conclude the article with a series of recommendations for organizing community partnerships in ways that ameliorate the frustrations experienced by their students. There are also some excellent published resources on service learning, ranging from detailed research studies (Eyler and Giles 1999) to practical handbooks for faculty instructors (Oates and Leavitt 2003).

During the past five years, the role of science as an educational framework for civic engagement has been developed and expanded by a national dissemination project called SENCER (Science Education for New Civic Engagements and Responsibilities); see *www.sencer.net*. Some of the "SENCER ideals" are as follows (see *www.sencer.net/pdfs/SENCER/SENCERIdeals.pdf* for the complete list):

- *SENCER robustly connects science and civic engagement by teaching "through" complex, capacious, current, and unresolved issues "to" basic science.*
- *SENCER invites students to put scientific knowledge and scientific method to immediate use on matters of immediate interest to students.*
- *SENCER shows the power of science by identifying the dimensions of a public issue that can be better understood with certain mathematical and scientific ways of knowing.*
- *SENCER locates the responsibility (the burdens and pleasures) of discovery as the work of the student.*

With funding from the National Science Foundation, the SENCER project has published model courses, developed "backgrounder" papers on topics at the interface of science and civic engagement, and offered an annual faculty development workshop called the SENCER Summer Institute. The themes embraced by SENCER span the scientific disciplines (and mathematics), with a particular emphasis on using authentic, complex issues as a context for stimulating students to explore both the scientific and civic dimensions of each topic.

Civic Views of the DotNet Generation

We have seen how many educators value the goal of civic engagement. But how does this goal align with the current viewpoints and actions of students? A team of researchers (Keeter et al. 2002) conducted a study entitled *The Civic and Political Health of the Nation: A Generational Portrait* (see *www.civicyouth.org/research/products/youth_index.htm* for more information about the study). They used a carefully designed survey instrument that contained 19 "core indicators" of engagement, ranging from participation in the electoral process to volunteering in the local community (Andolina et al. 2003). The survey also probed attitudes on civic issues, such as the role of the government in addressing society's problems. The authors were particularly interested in responses from 15- to 25-year-olds, whom they dubbed the "DotNet" generation because of the pervasive influence of the internet on their lives.

An overview of engagement among this population is provided in Figure 37.1. According to the researchers, "more than half of the DotNets (57%) are completely disengaged from civic life according to the study's criteria." Among the remaining 43% of young people who are engaged, there is a noticeable divide between two types of activities. One group of DotNets (17%)—called *civic specialists* by the researchers—perform regular volunteer work and participate in community groups. Yet these students and recent graduates have little involvement in political processes such as campaigning for an electoral candidate or even voting. A slightly smaller proportion of DotNets (15%) exhibit mirror image characteristics and are classified as *electoral specialists*. These young people are politically active but not engaged with their local communities. Only 11% of the 15–25 age group are so-called dual activists who are engaged in both electoral politics and civic activities in their local communities. In summing up their findings, the researchers note that "the survey reveals two distinct modes of engagement: the civic and the political." By their behavior, students are exposing the ambiguity of meaning inherent in the word *civic*. According to the *Oxford English Dictionary*, one meaning of the word is "pertaining to citizens," which includes voting and political action. But a second meaning is "pertaining to a city, borough, or municipality," which suggests a different type of commitment.

Figure 37.1

Civic Engagement Among the DotNet Generation (Ages 15–25)

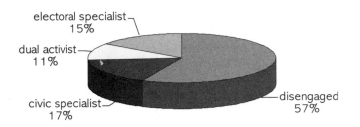

Source: Data from S. Keeter, C. Zukin, M. Andolina, and K. Jenkins. 2002. *The civic and political health of the nation: A generational portrait.* www.civicyouth.org/research/products/Civic_Political_Health.pdf

By using follow-up questions, the survey revealed interesting perspectives among the DotNet generation. A large proportion (40%) had participated in some volunteer activity during the past year. When the numbers are subdivided by age, they reveal that volunteer activity is highest during high school and drops off during the college years. It is not clear whether this is a consequence of "compulsory volunteerism" in some high schools or simply a reflection of different time pressures (school and work) during college. A significant number of DotNets (38%) express their displeasure with a company by boycotting its products, and many (35%) show their support by expressly buying something from a company they favor ("buycotting"). This type of activism surprised the survey researchers, although it is certainly consistent with the increased buying power of 15- to 25-year-olds. In an apparent contradiction, few DotNets are actively involved in national politics yet over half believe that "government should do more to solve problems." Only slightly over a third (38%) believe that "citizenship entails certain obligations," which has important implications for current discussions of citizenship education.

Some interesting findings on civic perspectives of the DotNet generation can be summarized as follows:

- 24% follow government and public affairs "very often."
- Approximately one-third regularly follow the news using newspapers, radio, television, or the internet.
- 70% agree that "most people look out for themselves."
- 64% agree that "government should do more to solve problems."
- 38% agree that "citizenship entails special obligations," while 58% agree that simply "being a good person is enough."

Conclusion

Within this chapter I have explored several themes that link science education with civic engagement. John Dewey set the stage for these discussions several decades ago, and contemporary educators have written eloquently on the vital need for scientific literacy as a foundation for 21st-century society. The pages of the *Journal of College Science Teaching* show that faculty members have created a variety of frameworks for stimulating students' scientific curiosity within a civic context.

Yet in reviewing the current state of affairs, the various perspectives on this issue seem like a scattering of points that have not yet been connected. For example, can we still use Dewey's philosophy of pedagogy as a useful articulation of science and civic engagement, or do we need a different model for what has sometimes been called *social epistemology*? How can science be effectively integrated into the mainstream discourse on "civic education"? How can civic issues be integrated into a more diverse range of science courses? Should surveys of student engagement—like the one discussed in the previous section—influence the design and implementation of our science courses? There is still much to explore and learn. To use the words of SENCER, science and civic education remains a complex, capacious, and unresolved issue.

References

American Association of Colleges and Universities. 1998. Statement on liberal learning. *www.aacu.org/About/statements/liberal_learning.cfm*

Andolina, M., S. Keeter, C. Zukin, and K. Jenkins. 2003. *A guide to the index of civic and political engagement. www.civicyouth.org/PopUps/IndexGuide.pdf*

Banks, J. A. 1997. *Educating citizens in a multicultural society.* New York: Teachers College Press.

Chamany, K. 2001. Niños desaparecidos. *Journal of College Science Teaching* 31: 61–65.

Chronicle of Higher Education. 2005. Vol. 52 (Almanac issue).

Colby, A., T. Erlich, E. Beaumont, and J. Stephens. 2003. *Educating citizens: Preparing America's undergraduates for lives of moral and civic responsibility.* San Francisco: Jossey Bass.

Dewey, J. 1897/1998. My pedagogic creed. In *The essential Dewey.* Volume I, *Pragmatism, education, democracy*, eds. L. A. Hickman and T. M. Alexander, 229–235. Bloomington: Indiana University Press.

Dewey, J. 1909/1998. Moral principles in education. In *The essential Dewey.* Volume I, *Pragmatism, education, democracy*, eds. L. A. Hickman and T. M. Alexander, 246–249. Bloomington: Indiana University Press.

Dewey, J. 1931/1998. Philosophy and civilization. In *The essential Dewey.* Volume I, *Pragmatism, education, democracy*, eds. L. A. Hickman and T. M. Alexander, 363–368. Bloomington: Indiana University Press.

Eyler, J., and G. E. Giles. 1999. *Where's the learning in service-learning?* San Francisco: Jossey-Bass.

Grossman, J., and T. Cooper. 2004. Linking environmental science students to external community partners: A critical assessment of a service learning course. *Journal of College Science Teaching* 33: 32–35.

Keeter, S., C. Zukin, M. Andolina, and K. Jenkins. 2002. *The civic and political health of the nation: A generational portrait. www.civicyouth.org/research/products/Civic_Political_Health.pdf*

McDonald, J., and L. Dominguez. 2005. Moving from content knowledge to engagement. *Journal of College Science Teaching* 35: 18–22.

McGowan, A.H. 2005. Genes and race in the classroom: Science in a social context. *Journal of College Science Teaching* 34: 30–33.

National Research Council. 1996. *National science education standards.* Washington, DC: National Academy Press.

Oates, K. K., and L. H. Leavitt. 2003. *Service-learning and learning communities: Tools for integration and assessment.* Washington, DC: Association of American Colleges and Universities.

Omarzu, J. 2002. Selecting the perfect baby. *Journal of College Science Teaching* 34: 30–33.

Oxford English Dictionary. http://dictionary.oed.com (accessed September 10, 2005).

Pratte, J., and M. Laposata. 2005. The ESA21 project: A model for civic engagement. *Journal of College Science Teaching* 35: 39–43.

Ramaley, J. A., and R. R. Haggett. 2005. Engaged and engaging science: A component of a good liberal education. *Peer Review* 7: 8–12.

Schneider, P. 2004. The genetics and evolution of human skin color: The case of Desiree's baby. *Journal of College Science Teaching* 34: 20–22.

Siebert, E. D., and W. J. McIntosh. 2001. *College pathways to the science education standards*. Arlington, VA: NSTA Press.

Walsh, M., D. Jenkins, K. Powell, and K. Rusch. 2005. The campus lake learning community: Promoting a multidisciplinary approach to problem solving. *Journal of College Science Teaching* 34: 24–27.

Westbrook, R. B. 1991. *John Dewey and American democracy*. Ithaca, NY: Cornell University Press.

CHAPTER 38

Using Research on Teaching to Improve Student Learning

William H. Leonard

William H. Leonard is professor of science education emeritus at Clemson University. He earned a PhD in biology education at the University of California at Berkeley and conducts research on science teaching and learning at the secondary and college levels. He teaches courses in general biology, evolutionary biology, conceptual themes in biology, science teaching methods, and research in science teaching.

Research on teaching contains a broad range of investigation on teaching methodologies, curricula, and other general approaches to helping students learn science. Such inquiries can be quantitative or qualitative in nature or contain a combination of quantitative and qualitative research methods. Research often gives instructors many insights into the effectiveness of the teaching approaches or curricula they employ; it may also serve as a tool for using classroom data to learn about one's own instruction. Finally, publication of instructional research in scholarly journals may inform other teachers of college science courses about productive new ways for students to learn, and it may help faculty progress in their career advancement.

This chapter will describe general procedures for research on college and university science teaching, examples and benefits of several very different research models that can be used, examples of published studies, and suggestions on how to get your research on student learning published so that other instructors of science may benefit from your findings. Another goal of this chapter is to invite and encourage science instructors in higher education to use research on their teaching on a regular basis to continuously improve their teaching effectiveness.

General Procedures for Research on Teaching

Most productive research follows a common general research procedure that exists in all of the natural sciences and, for that matter, nearly all other disciplines. Although these steps do

not always follow a linear sequence, each of the following is still a component of solid research on any question.

1. Making Observations That Lead to Questions

When we reflect on our teaching, we often wonder if the particular approach, method, or sequence is effective. Or we wonder which approaches, methods, or sequences are most effective in promoting student learning. We all have found times when our students seem to respond enthusiastically, learn easily the concepts and principles of our courses, or tell us that they "liked that lecture or experiment." We have also had instances where we feel our students could be more successful learners or where our students do not seem satisfied with our courses. Still, we have little more than a feeling to lead us to believe that these thoughts or comments are true. Such observations are viable sources for researchable questions.

2. Formulating a Researchable Question

Among the many questions we may ponder about the effectiveness of our teaching, only some can be productively researched. Only some are probably important enough to invest our time in, resulting in insight that may improve our teaching. The selection and formulation of a research question needs to apply to most students and needs to be specific enough to test. Research questions such as "Am I a good lecturer?" or "Do my students learn the material in my syllabus?" are probably not very productive because they are not specific enough to either do a search in the literature or provide an answer that will improve instruction. Some better questions that can be researched would be "What aspects of my lectures receive positive, neutral, or negative reactions by my students?" or "What specific learning approaches helped my students to better learn a specific set of concepts and principles of my course?" Other interesting and promising questions may be

- Do my students learn about osmosis and diffusion better through lecture or lecture with demonstration?
- Do my students understand the characteristics of science better through directed laboratory investigations or inquiry laboratory investigations?
- Will my students better learn the effects of temperature on the rate of respiration by doing experiments alone or in small groups?

3. Searching the Literature for Possible Answers to the Research Question

There are two productive approaches here. The first is to hand search article titles in selected journals that appear to be in the area of the question being asked. Science education journals such as *Journal of College Science Teaching* and *Journal of Research in Science Teaching* and general education journals such as *American Educational Research Journal* and *Review of Educational Research* are available in most university libraries and address all areas of the natural sciences. The content-specific science education journals such as *American Biology Teacher, Journal of Chemical Education,* and *The Physics Teacher* may have reports of specific instructional studies in one area of the sciences. Finally, both *Science* and *Nature* sometimes address educational issues and give summaries of research studies on teaching and learning.

A second recommended method of searching the literature is to conduct keyword searches through online databases such as ERIC, BIOSIS, GeoRef, and SciFinder. Finally, one can

simply do a Google search online, keeping in mind that the authenticity and accuracy of the search results may be questionable. As an example of using an online database to research the question on osmosis and diffusion given above, the following descriptors may be entered: "learning and osmosis AND lecture and laboratory." A second descriptor can then be entered using "diffusion" instead of "osmosis." Searching online databases will usually result in abstracts and citations from which more information is available, and one can then consult the original articles. The difficult and often frustrating part of using online databases to find answers to questions is that most of the results will not be relevant because of the nature of the search process being used. However, one can quickly discard or neglect irrelevant results and keep trying combinations of variable descriptors that seem appropriate.

Conducting a search of the current literature will assist in both refining the question asked and formulating a testable hypothesis. Results of a literature search may even answer the question, although this would be rare. Nevertheless, a brief review of the literature should be done before studying the question further.

4. IRB Requirements

All educational and research institutions now have Institutional Research Board (IRB) requirements that protect the anonymity, confidentiality, and privacy of research subjects. All potential adult subjects need to give their informed consent to participate in a research study. If minor subjects may be involved, both their informed consent and their parent's or guardian's written assent is required. These procedures are now very specific, and, although they may vary somewhat across colleges and universities, researchers must adhere to them. It is recommended that the investigator attend the short classes on IRB requirements that are widely available and obtain institutional certification before making observations or collecting data of any kind. The consequences of not complying with IRB requirements can be lawsuits by subjects or parents of subjects and academic disciplinary action against the investigator. Given how easy it usually is to gain consent and/or assent, there is no excuse for investigators not to comply with institutional IRB requirements.

These four procedures are recommended for almost any research study on a question about instructional methods, curriculum, facilities, instructors, or any other variable that may influence how or how effectively students learn. Additional research procedures will likely depend on the research methods being used. For example, an experimental study that attempts to control for variables other than the one being tested will likely lend itself to the collection of quantitative data from sources such as student test or report scores that can be treated statistically. On the other hand, a more qualitative study, such as many action research studies, may lend itself to the collection of narrative data from sources such as observations and interviews that may allow the researcher to better see a larger picture of the question being asked. Further procedures for each of these general research models will now be discussed separately below for experimental methods and qualitative methods, with the procedures for the former designated "a" and the procedures for the latter designated "b."

Experimental or Quasi-Experimental Research Studies

Experimental or quasi-experimental studies on teaching use research methods similar to those used in the natural sciences, psychology, and the social sciences. The questions that are asked

address the causes of specific classroom or learning events, and the researchers attempt to generalize the findings to other students. For example, during the 1980s, audio-tutorial learning approaches were quite popular and one obvious question was, "Do students learn more from audio-tutorial settings, where students work individually, or do they learn more from group-lecture settings?" To control for other possible influencing variables, many other conditions such as the instructor, the laboratory sessions, curriculum sequence, and textbook were kept the same. The assumption was that any measured differences in student learning would be due to whether students attended lecture or audio-tutorial sessions. Such a study could never become a true experimental study, however, because there would be other variables that the investigator could not control, such as the time of day and/or days of the week the student would attend the class or which students self-elected to go to lecture or audio-tutorial sessions.

To avoid the problem that some students may elect to go to lecture during part of the semester and to audio-tutorial sessions at other times, the experimenter would need to randomly select the students who went to each environment and ask the students to attend only that environment. Still, the study may become a quasi-experiment because, although attending lecture or audio-tutorial sessions may be the variable that most influences the degree of learning, the other variables mentioned above are still not fully controlled. Such studies were still conducted and published as legitimate ways to learn about new instructional approaches, with the caution that the research question was not completely answered. Replicating the same study with different students would be one way to make the results more valid and generalizable.

5a. Crafting a Research Hypothesis

Most research hypotheses are stated in the null form, such as "There will not be a difference in student learning between instructional method X versus method Y." Sometimes multiple hypotheses are tested simultaneously if there are more than two instructional methods. A research hypothesis will frequently be in the form of an "if ..., then ..." statement, the "if" being the independent variable (the method) and the "then" being the dependent variable (measures of student learning). If there is a significant difference in student learning, then the null hypothesis is rejected and the inference is that one method produces greater learning than the other.

6a. Designing an Experiment to Test the Research Hypothesis

There are entire books on experimental designs for education research. A popular reference is *Experimental and Quasi-Experimental Designs for Generalized Causal Inference* by Shadish, Cook, and Campbell (2002). Typically one group of students is the experimental group, using a new instructional method, and another group is the control group, using the existing or old instructional approach. Since most educational studies are not true experiments that closely control for all variables other than the one being tested, the groups using old and new methods simply become comparison groups. In either case, both the older method and newer method (the independent variables) need to be described thoroughly and used instructionally as described without deviation. All dependent variables need to be described thoroughly as well. It is helpful to give examples of test items or lab report requirements in any publications resulting from the study.

It is important to try to control for instructional variables other than the one being studied, especially student academic ability. Other variables to consider keeping the same are the number of students in each group, time and day of class meetings, and the instructor in both

lab and lecture if both lab and lecture are part of the study. (For example, it has been shown that better-performing students elect to attend class earlier in the day.) If there is evidence that there are differences in variables such as SAT scores, prior course test scores, or student attendance between control and experimental groups, then analysis of covariance on the data may be necessary, with the covariate being those variables that seem to be unequal.

7a. Collecting and Analyzing the Data

The experiment is conducted as planned and data for dependent variables are collected. To demonstrate that there are real and meaningful differences between student performance measures of the methods being studied, statistical tests on means of data such as t-tests or analysis of variance are needed. Even though differences in means may be statistically different (which they often can be due simply to large group sizes), they need to be large enough for the experimenter to conclude that one instructional approach is superior to the other. Measures of explained variance or large differences in standard deviations between samples can be reported to support the argument for cause and effect.

8a. Drawing Conclusions and Asking Additional Questions

In experimental or quasi-experimental studies with quantitative data, the conclusions follow naturally from the data analysis. If group performance means differ statistically and the means differ by as much as half a standard deviation, the experimenter can be fairly confident that the approach with the higher mean scores is superior. Of course, the argument for cause and effect is much stronger if the experiment is replicated, and it is even stronger if it is replicated at another institution. If the study is replicated with similar results, the experimenter can then generalize these results to other similar populations such as the same course at other comparable institutions. When this happens, new knowledge is added to the theory base on the instructional approaches used. Such studies need to be disseminated in the appropriate publications so that the entire university science community can benefit from these studies. This has actually happened with well-tested learning approaches such as cooperative learning, using concept maps, and learning through inquiry.

Conducting experiments on science learning approaches often raises other questions of interest. For example, what kinds of students benefit most from a new instructional approach? A question such as this could be investigated from the original data collected if there are data available on differences among students such as level of performance in the course, gender, ethnicity, academic major, or age. Results from additional data analyses can help the instructor provide variations in the instructional process that may be of specific benefit to specific groups of students.

Action Research and More Qualitative Research Studies

Action research is a very flexible and increasingly popular approach to answering many questions about classroom instruction without the need for exacting experimental procedures. Action research is often used to explore questions but not necessarily to provide definitive answers. In fact, many instructional questions cannot be well answered through experiments. Action research data are mostly (but not exclusively) qualitative and include rich narrative descriptions of what is found through observations, questionnaires, and interviews. The following are some examples of instructional questions that lend themselves to more qualitative

studies: "What are student reactions to different learning methods?" "What level of student-instructor or student-student interaction is encouraged by the instructor?" "How can the instructional process be differentiated to benefit students with different learning styles?" "Do high levels of instructor enthusiasm result in more student learning?" Results from exploring answers to these questions through more qualitative means can lead to more specific questions that can be tested experimentally at a later time.

Action research procedures are not well-known in higher education, particularly within academic science departments, yet this form of research can inform instructors of how best to stage student learning in their classes.

5b. Refining the Research Question

"What are the effects of ...?" are typical questions, similar to those of an experimental study, except that most of the data will be narrative. Others may be "How do I best begin a laboratory lesson?" or "How long do students take to ...?" All of these are intentionally open-ended to accommodate a wide range of possible answers, perhaps depending on groups of different students.

6b. Designing the Study

Procedures for action research and other qualitative research are often very flexible so that they can be modified during the early phases of data collection. Systematic and representative observations of what is happening in the classroom during an intervention are important, so a sampling of times at which observations will be made is necessary. The goal is to be able to make inferences on what happens as the students learn, even though there may be many different student responses. The sample population needs to be defined carefully, whether it is one student, a few selected and representative students, or an entire class. The role of the investigator also needs to be defined. Will the investigator be only an unobtrusive observer or will the investigator interact with the students, and if so, to what extent? Even though the design is a plan, changes in the plan are common; any changes need to be carefully described in the data. If the design involves any questionnaires or survey instruments, they need to be developed, reviewed by others who are knowledgeable and who can provide input, and trial tested and revised as needed to collect the most informative data.

7b. Conducting the Study and Collecting Data

As the intervention is implemented, new questions arise and the intervention may even be modified so long as narrative descriptions in the changes are carefully made. One of the biggest challenges with action and interpretative research is keeping and organizing the data, so creating data categories is necessary. Laptop computers are frequently used because keystroking observations is quicker than handwriting. The data in a word processor file can also be searched and organized more quickly than handwritten notes. Attempts to find out what students are thinking during instruction is very useful, so causal or interview questions are common. Getting perspectives from different points of view is useful, so multiple data sources are needed. Examples and specific procedures can be found in Johnson (2005), Mills (2003), and Stringer (2004).

8b. Analyzing the Data and Making Inferences

Analyzing volumes of narrative data, even if they are organized into categories, is much more difficult than calculating means and doing statistical analyses in experimental studies. Since making sense of volumes of narrative data is always open to the interpretation of the investigator, qualitative research is under constant question by persons trained in the natural sciences. Nevertheless, these interpretations can often give significant insights into the learning process that would not be possible through numerical data. The process is time-consuming and requires that the investigator carefully read and categorize the data, reflect, and make initial assumptions and inferences over different periods of time. After several rounds of the latter, the investigator can begin looking for patterns and generalizations in the data. These need to be recorded and verified or revised through additional review of the data until the investigator is confident that the inferences are consistent, valid, and evidence based. Again, examples and specific procedures can be found in Johnson (2005), Mills (2003), and Stringer (2004). Inferences from action and other qualitative research are always viewed as tentative and subject to change with additional data or analyses. The generalizations are viewed as the best understandings of the question at that time.

Examples of Published Studies

Three published examples of experimental, qualitative, and hybrid instructional studies, respectively, in college science reported in the "Research and Teaching" column of *Journal of College Science Teaching* are abstracted below. Additional examples can be found in other "Research and Teaching" articles and in the general articles in *Journal of College Science Teaching,* as well as in the subject-specific science teaching journals mentioned earlier.

- Moore, R. 2003. Attendance and performance: How important is it for students to attend class? *Journal of College Science Teaching* 32 (6): 367–371. This is a experimental study with statistical analysis that demonstrated positive effects of attending lecture on student achievement in general biology. The study was very clean experimentally, with most other variables controlled, and it was clearly written.
- Raubenheimer, D., and J. Myka. 2005. Using action research to improve teaching and student learning in college. *Journal of College Science Teaching* 34 (6): 12–16. This action research study examined revisions made to the design and delivery of a freshman zoology laboratory section that involved iterative cycles of planning, acting, observing, and reflection, resulting in evidence that increased levels of student investigation were possible and productive.
- Fencl, H., and Scheel, K. 2005. Engaging students: An examination of the effects of teaching strategies on self-efficacy and course climate in a nonmajors physics course. *Journal of College Science Teaching* 35 (1): 20–24. This study used a mix of quantitative and qualitative research methods to support using increased levels of questions and answers, collaborative learning, conceptual problems, electronic applications, and inquiry labs.

The Scholarship of Teaching

Conducting research on student learning is part of the scholarship of teaching. Such research can be as useful to the higher-education community as can high-powered scientific research. This is especially true if the investigator conducts studies that are worthy of dissemination in

national refereed journals. Research studies that produce new knowledge about the teaching and learning process are candidates for publication in science teaching journals, and these publications are now widely considered to support applications for faculty promotion and tenure. For a manuscript to be accepted in a science teaching journal, it usually must describe a study using a novel instructional intervention that contains data to support the notion that improved learning is a result. The manuscript should be clearly written, be devoid of content jargon, specify the research question, and contain a review of the literature, a summary of research procedures, original data, and an appropriate data analysis. It should further make data-based recommendations for improved student learning.

It is hoped that this chapter convinces college science teachers that classroom research on learning is relatively easy to implement with the procedures and considerations described here.

References

Johnson, A. P. 2005. *A short guide to action research*. 2nd ed. Boston: Pearson.

Mills, G. E. 2003. *Action research: A guide for the teacher researcher*. 2nd ed. Upper Saddle River, NJ: Merrill/Prentice Hall.

Shadish, W. R., T. D. Cook, and D. T. Campbell. 2002. *Experimental and quasi-experimental designs for generalized causal inference*. Boston: Houghton Mifflin.

Stringer, E. 2004. *Action research in education*. Upper Saddle River, NJ: Pearson/Prentice Hall.

Final Thoughts

Many instructors don't have any idea of what research findings bear on an activity that consumes a significant amount of their working effort. It would be one thing if instructors knew about relevant work but found it inapplicable … but many have no idea that there is a body of knowledge bearing on what they are doing…. As a result, much teaching is idiosyncratic, rarely building on research findings or even others' experiences…. We cannot conceive of doing science this way, but much science instruction proceeds as if it had no history and is not guided by any discipline. (Paldy 2003, p. 422)

Work on this handbook began several years ago and was stimulated by Lester Paldy's editorial in the *Journal of College Science Teaching*, which suggested that, even though much theoretical and empirical work exists on the subject, the practice of college science teaching has largely evolved in a conceptual and empirical vacuum. He decried the fact that we scientists, who pride ourselves on our "objectivity" and adherence to principles emerging from disciplinary knowledge, have generally ignored research on a subject that bears directly on so much of our daily efforts. Instead we teach pretty much as our predecessors did, and we are guided heavily by tradition, consensus, intuition, and the expectations of our colleagues and peers. In some ways we practice and propagate a kind of "folklore" of teaching. This handbook is an attempt to begin addressing this problem. In our limited space, however, we have merely scratched the surface of topics that every college science teacher should understand.

Accordingly, we invite readers to write us with your suggestions as we contemplate a potential second volume of this work. Specifically we solicit your opinions in several areas: Which chapters of the current volume did you find most interesting or most helpful in your work? Which were least interesting or least helpful? What general topics did we overlook? Which topics were addressed too heavily? Should the next volume emphasize theory, research, or practical applications? Are you interested in contributing to a second volume? If so, please consider writing a brief (one-page) proposal outlining your areas of interest and expertise. Please write to the editors of this handbook directly at *mintzes@uncw.edu* and *leonard@clemson.edu*.

Reference

Paldy, L. G. 2003. Editorial: Forgotten history, ignored research, little progress. *Journal of College Science Teaching* 32 (7): 422.

Index

*Page numbers in **boldface** type indicate figures or tables.*

NATIONAL SCIENCE TEACHERS ASSOCIATION